# SuperCourse™
## FOR THE
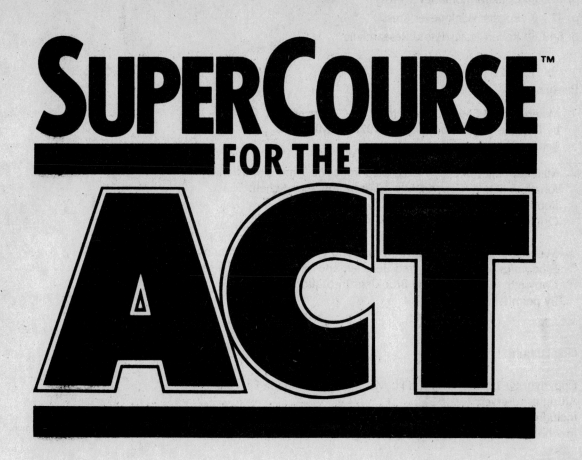

**Thomas H. Martinson**  **Juliana Fazzone**

**Robert S. Haynes**  **Richard A. Haynes**

*Contributing Editors*
**Barbara Branca**
**Peter I. Zahler**

## ARCO
## NEW YORK

Photo Credits

p. 1    © Conklin/Monkmeyer Press

p. 41   © Rogers/Monkmeyer Press

p. 549 © Robert Issacs/Photo Researchers


Permissions

1. Material page 569 excerpted from *The Ungovernable City*
   by Douglas Yates. Copyright © 1978 by MIT Press.
   Reprinted by permission.

2. Material pages 570–571 excerpted from *The Time of Illusion* by
   Jonathan Schell. Copyright © 1975 by Jonathan Schell.
   Reprinted by permission of Alfred A. Knopf, Inc.
   Originally appeared in *The New Yorker*.

3. Material page 620 excerpted from *World Politics and International
   Economics,* edited by C. Fred Bergsten and Lawrence B. Krause.
   Copyright © 1975 by The Brookings Institution. Reprinted
   by permission.


First Edition

 **ARCO**

Simon & Schuster, Inc.
Gulf+Western Building
One Gulf+Western Plaza
New York, NY 10023

DISTRIBUTED BY PRENTICE HALL TRADE

Manufactured in the United States of America

1  2  3  4  5  6  7  8  9  10


**Library of Congress Cataloging-in-Publication Data**

Supercourse for the ACT.

  1. ACT Assessment—Study guides.  I. Martinson,
Thomas H.  II. Branca, Barbara.  III. Zahler, Peter I.
LB2353.48.S87  1988        378'.1664        88-7400
ISBN 0-13-003170-4

# CONTENTS

# Part Three    Practice Tests

# A Letter to the Reader

Dear Reader,

The book you have just purchased is worth hundreds of dollars. Never before has a total—and academically respected—ACT preparation course been available in book form.

This year thousands of students will spend $300 to $600 (and even more) for expensive test preparation courses. Yet, this book can provide you with the benefits of an expensive course. You get:

- hundreds of proven strategies that take you inside the ACT
- advice that helps you think like the testmakers
- thousands of practice questions with complete explanations
- an English grammar diagnostic test plus comprehensive grammar review
- a diagnostic math test
- a comprehensive review of social studies
- a comprehensive review of natural sciences
- successful methods to control test anxiety

I know for a fact that this book offers the same kinds of strategies taught in expensive preparation courses because I personally developed several courses for nationally known test preparation schools.

In other words, this book contains everything you need to make sure you get your top score on the ACT. In my professional opinion, there is little offered by most commercial test preparation courses that you can't get for yourself by conscientious study of this book.


Thomas H. Martinson

# PART ONE

# The Anatomy of a Test

# Getting Started

✔ **Objective**

To learn the meanings of certain key terms.

1. What is the ACT?
2. How to Register

# SYMBOLS

 strategy

 eliminating suspects

 fact

 estimating

 common error

 inquiry/ guessing

 measuring

 pattern

 calculating

 unlocking the mystery

 Dr. Watson

 Sherlock Holmes

 smoking gun

 ladder of difficulty

# What Is the ACT?

The letters A-C-T stand for American College Testing. Technically speaking, American College Testing is not the real name of any organization or test. The letters ACT are used loosely to refer to American College Testing Program and to the ACT Assessment Program.

The American College Testing Program is a nonprofit corporation with headquarters in Iowa City, Iowa. The ACT Assessment Program, part of which is a battery of tests, is one of the most important services provided by the American College Testing Program. So if someone asks you if you plan to take the ACT, they are asking whether you plan to register for the ACT Assessment Program. And if someone asks you if you know the address for ACT, they are asking whether you know the address for the American College Testing Program, the company. Incidentally, the address for ACT (the company) is:

ACT Registration
P.O. Box 414
Iowa City, Iowa 52243

Telephone: (319) 337—1270

The ACT Assessment Program consists of several elements. Part of the ACT Assessment Program is a complex informational service that provides you with information about the colleges you are considering; provides information about you to the colleges; and provides information about you and the colleges to your guidance counselor. Other parts of the ACT Assessment Program are the Student Profile Section and ACT Interest Inventory. You complete the forms for these parts when you register for the various ACT services, and later you will receive an analysis of your responses that is designed to help you evaluate your abilities and career options.

For our purposes, however, the most important component of the ACT Assessment Program is the battery of four tests that you will take on a certain date. This battery will include tests on English, mathematics, social studies, and natural sciences. The scores you receive on these tests will be reported to the colleges you are applying to, and those colleges will probably use them in making their decisions on your applications for admission. In addition, college financial aid offices may use the scores to determine your eligibility for certain scholarships and other financial aid.

This book is designed to help you get your top score on the test portion of the ACT Assessment. To keep things simple, from here on, we will use the term ACT to refer to the four test batteries. But you should keep in mind that ACT refers to many other things.

# Let's Look at the ACT

## ✔ Objectives

To learn the names and forms of the different types of questions used on the ACT.

To learn how the test is scored and the difference between raw scores and scaled scores.

1. The Four Sections
   - English
   - Mathematics
   - Social Studies
   - Natural Sciences
2. English Usage Test
3. Mathematics Usage Test
4. Social Studies Reading Test
5. Natural Sciences Reading Test
6. Scoring the ACT

## The Four Sections

The ACT test consists of four sections:

| Subject | Number of Questions | Time Limit |
|---|---|---|
| English | 75 | 40 minutes |
| Mathematics | 40 | 50 minutes |
| Social Studies | 52 | 35 minutes |
| Natural Sciences | 52 | 35 minutes |
| TOTALS | 219 | 2 hours 40 minutes |

On certain test dates, the ACT may consist of five rather than four sections, but on these dates the fifth section is not scored. Rather, the extra section contains new questions that are being tried out for possible use on future ACTs.

# English Usage Test

The English section tests your ability to recognize standard written English. Items in this section test grammar, sentence structure, and punctuation, among other things. The section includes several prose passages, parts of which have been underlined. You must determine whether the underlined portions contain an error (some don't) and if they do, how to correct it. Next to each underlined part you will find four answer choices. The first indicates that there is no error, and the other three choices present various ways of rewriting the underlined part.

**EXAMPLE:**

Wood decay is caused by minute plants called fungi. These plants consist of microscopic threads <u>that's</u> visible to the naked eye only when many of them occur together. But it is easy to see the flowering bodies of fungi, from which spores are distributed. Some fungi merely discolor wood, but decay fungi destroy the fiber. Decayed wood <u>drying often</u> in the final stages but not while the decay is taking place (because fungi cannot work in dry wood). That is why there is no such thing as "dry rot" <u>and why</u> decay is a minor problem in the driest parts of the country.

1. **A.** NO CHANGE
   **B.** that are
   **C.** which is
   **D.** which were

2. **F.** NO CHANGE
   **G.** drying—often
   **H.** often drying
   **J.** often dries

3. **A.** NO CHANGE
   **B.** and being why
   **C.** and that's being why
   **D.** because

1. (B) *That's* is a contraction for *that is,* but in this sentence *that* refers to *threads,* a plural noun. Therefore, you must use a plural verb: *are.* Although choice D also uses a plural verb, the use of the past tense is inconsistent with the choice of tenses for the other verbs in the paragraph.

2. (J) This sentence is only a sentence fragment because it lacks a main verb. You can correct this error by changing *drying* to *dries*—as J does. Additionally, J corrects the placement of *often* to create a more idiomatic expression.

3. (A) The sentence is correct as written. B and C contain phrasings that are not acceptable in standard written English, and D distorts the intended meaning of the sentence.

## Mathematics Usage Test

The Mathematics Usage part of the ACT tests your mastery of arithmetic, algebra, and geometry. The problems in this section are ordinary multiple-choice problems with five answer choices. (The math section is the only section of the ACT that uses five instead of four choices.) Some of the problems ask for nothing more than arithmetic calculation or algebraic operation. Some problems ask for you to apply your knowledge of arithmetic and algebra to practical situations to set up a formula or an equation or to find a value for a quantity. Geometry questions usually ask you to use your knowledge of geometric principles to determine the measure of some angle, line, or area. Only a few problems in the section test advanced topics.

**EXAMPLES:**

1. When $x = 2$, what is the value of $2x(3x - 2)$?
   A. $-6$
   B. 0
   C. 8
   D. 12
   E. 16

2. Elizabeth reads at a constant rate of 45 pages per hour. If she reads without being interrupted, how many hours will it take her to read a book 360 pages long?
   F. 4
   G. 6
   H. 8
   J. 9
   K. 10

3. In the figure below, $x$, $y$, and $z$ are the measures, in degrees, of the angles indicated. If $x + y = 100$, then what is the measure of $z$?
   A. 40
   B. 50
   C. 60
   D. 80
   E. 90

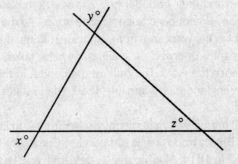

1. (E) This problem is a simple algebraic manipulation. Just substitute 2 for $x$ in the expression:

$$2(2)[3(2) - 2] = 4[6 - 2] = 4(4) = 16$$

**2.** (H)  This problem asks you to apply your knowledge of arithmetic to a practical situation.  To find the length of time, divide the total number of pages to be read by the rate at which Elizabeth reads:

360 pages ÷ 45 pages per hour = 8 hours

**3.** (D)  Since opposite angles are equal, the three angles inside the triangle have degree measures of $x$, $y$, and $z$.  Since the sum of the degree measure of the interior angles of a triangle is 180:

$x + y + z = 180$

And since $x + y = 100$:

$100 + z = 180$
$z = 180 - 100$
$z = 80$

# Social Studies Reading Test

The Social Studies section of the ACT contains two different types of questions. Thirty-seven questions are based on reading passages taken from the fields of history, government, economics, and sociology, psychology, or anthropology.  Generally, the test will use one selection each from history, government, and economics and one selection from one of the remaining areas.  The questions are distributed approximately evenly over the four selections (e.g., 9, 9, 9, and 10).  The remaining fifteen questions are free-standing questions; that is, they are not based on a reading selection.  Instead, you must answer them based on your background knowledge.

Here is a portion of a social studies reading selection with questions plus typical free-standing questions:

At the beginning of the War of 1812, the United States army had only 6,744 regular soldiers, and they were inadequately equipped and poorly trained.  In addition, the morale of the troops was very low.  Congress had authorized an increase in the number of troops to 25,000, but the number of regular soldiers never reached 10,000 during the war.  Members of the state militias volunteered to serve, but then only for very short terms and usually only in their own home states.  In fact, the governments of New England states prohibited their militia from traveling beyond their boundaries.  The southern states were too far removed from the fighting to feel any urgent need to contribute troops, so most of the soldiers, regular and irregular, who fought in the war came from Tennessee, Kentucky, and the old northwest.

Congress was adamantly opposed to levying any new taxes, so the government was forced to borrow to finance the war.  The bulk of the capital in the country, however, was concentrated in the New England states, and the New England states were, in general, bitterly opposed to the war.

Fortunately, England herself was fighting on another front—in Europe against Napoleon. As a result, only 7,000 British troops were stationed in Canada to protect a line of defense nearly 1,000 miles long.  In 1814, Napoleon was defeated, and England sent veteran troops to Canada.  But by that time, Americans were accustomed to the war and there was in the country more general support of the war.  The campaign in Canada closed with neither side having won a definite victory.

1. Which of the following factors inhibited the United States from winning a decisive victory against England in Canada?
   - **I.** Poorly equipped troops.
   - **II.** Inadequate numbers of troops.
   - **III.** Lack of funding for the war.
   - **IV.** Lack of geographical knowledge of the fighting area.
   - **A.** I and II only
   - **B.** II and III only
   - **C.** I, II, and III only
   - **D.** I, II, III, and IV

2. If England had not been fighting Napoleon, then probably:
   - **F.** England would have won a decisive victory in Canada.
   - **G.** England would have withdrawn her 7,000 troops from Canada.
   - **H.** the South would have contributed its militia.
   - **J.** New England would have contributed more money to the war effort.

1. **(C)** In the first paragraph, the author specifically states that the United States had very few troops and that these were inadequately equipped and poorly trained. The author also mentions that the government had difficulty in raising the money to finance the war. So, I, II, and III are each part of the correct choice. IV, however, is not part of the correct choice. The author does not say that the soldiers fighting for the United States did not know the terrain.

2. **(F)** The passage states that the United States was extremely weak and that it was fortunate that England had so few troops stationed in Canada. According to the selection, the war against Napoleon was the reason England had not committed more troops to Canada. As a result, neither side won a decisive victory in Canada. We can infer, therefore, that had England not been engaged against Napoleon, she would have sent more troops to Canada and that with more troops England could have defeated the weak U.S. forces.

Here are some examples of free-standing items that are not based on a reading selection:

1. The Gross National Product is defined as:
   - **A.** the total value of all final goods and services produced in a given year.
   - **B.** the total value of all consumer goods produced in a given year.
   - **C.** total government spending plus total income earned by all individuals.
   - **D.** total income earned by individuals and corporations adjusted for inflation.

2. The Supreme Court decision in *Marbury v. Madison* established the authority of the Supreme Court to:
   - **F.** advise the President on foreign affairs.
   - **G.** set ethical standards for practicing attorneys.
   - **H.** review the constitutionality of legislation.
   - **J.** hear cases between state governments.

1. **(A)** The Gross National Production (GNP) is defined as the total value of all final goods and services produced in a given year.

2. **(H)** In *Marbury v. Madison*, the Supreme Court struck down a law as unconstitutional, thereby establishing the principle of judicial review.

# Natural Sciences Reading Test

Like the Social Studies test, the Natural Sciences test contains two types of questions. Thirty-seven questions are based on four reading selections taken from the fields of biology, chemistry, physics, and physical sciences, and 15 questions are free-standing. Each test contains one selection from each field, and the questions are distributed as evenly as possible over the four sections.

Here is a portion of a a sample natural sciences reading selection:

About once every 50 years, one of the massive stars in our galaxy blows itself apart in a supernova explosion. The force of the explosion hurls vast quantities of radiation and matter into space and generates shock waves that sweep through the arms of the galaxy. The shock waves heat the interstellar gas, evaporate small clouds, and compress larger ones to the point at which they collapse under their own gravity to form new stars.

Recent discoveries of meteorites with anomalous concentrations of certain isotopes indicate that a supernova might have precipitated the birth of our solar system more than four and a half billion years ago. The cloud that collapsed to form the Sun and the planets contained an important legacy of stars that exploded even longer ago. Although composed mostly of hydrogen and helium, the cloud was enriched with carbon, nitrogen, and oxygen, elements that are essential for life as we know it. All the elements heavier than helium are manufactured deep in the interior of stars and would for the most part remain there if it were not for the cataclysmic supernova explosions.

1. A supernova can be expected to occur in our galaxy about:
   A. twice a century.
   B. once every 200 years.
   C. once every 500 years.
   D. once every 10,000 years.

2. Without supernova explosions, it is probable that:
   I. life as we know it would not exist.
   II. no stars would ever have been formed.
   III. our Sun would never have been formed.
   F. I only
   G. II only
   H. I and III only
   J. I, II, and III

1. (A) The first sentence of the passage states that a supernova occurs in our galaxy about once every 50 years, which is about twice a century.

2. (H) The passage states that the elements necessary for life are created in the interior of stars and released by a supernova explosion. So we can infer that without such explosions the elements needed for life would not be available. So I is part of the correct choice. As for II, since supernovas are exploding stars, this choice must be wrong. As for III, the author states that a supernova probably precipitated the birth of our Sun. So the correct choice consists of I and III only.

Here are some examples of free-standing natural sciences questions:

1. Different isotopes of the same element have:
   A. the same number of protons but a different number of neutrons.
   B. the same number of neutrons but a different number of protons.
   C. the same number of neutrons but a different number of electrons.
   D. the same number of electrons but a different number of protons.

2. A moraine is a geological feature created by the action of:
   F. the wind.
   G. a stream.
   H. a glacier.
   J. man.

1. (A) The identity of an element is determined by the number of protons in the nucleus, so different isotopes of the same element must all have the same number of protons. The difference in atomic weight is attributable to the different number of neutrons.

2. (G) A moraine is a ridge of dirt and debris created by a glacier.

# Scoring the ACT

Your ACT reports will show five different ACT scores, one for each of the four tests and a composite score (which is the average of the four test scores). The scores reported on ACT score reports do not include the actual number of questions answered correctly. Instead, the reported scores are called standard scores. They are reported on a scale ranging from 1 (the bottom) to 36 (the top), although the top score attainable varies from test to test. The maximum possible score for English Usage is 33; for Mathematics Usage, 40; for Social Studies Reading, 34; and for Natural Sciences Reading, 35.

The scoring system for the ACT is fairly simple. First, a raw score is calculated for each of the four tests. The raw score is simply the total number of items you answered correctly—no deduction is made for wrong answers. Second, raw scores are converted to standard scores using a table devised by the test-writers.

The following table shows some typical standard score–raw score equivalents:

| English Raw Score | English Standard Score | Mathematics Usage Raw Score | Mathematics Usage Standard Score |
|---|---|---|---|
| 75 | 33 | 40 | 36 |
| 70 | 29 | 38 | 32 |
| 65 | 25 | 36 | 29 |
| 60 | 23 | 34 | 27 |
| 55 | 22 | 32 | 26 |
| 50 | 20 | 30 | 25 |
| 45 | 19 | 28 | 24 |
| 40 | 17 | 26 | 23 |
| 35 | 14 | 24 | 22 |
| 30 | 12 | 22 | 20 |
| 25 | 10 | 20 | 18 |
| 20 | 7 | 18 | 16 |
| 15 | 5 | 16 | 14 |
| 10 | 3 | 14 | 12 |
|  |  | 12 | 10 |
|  |  | 10 | 7 |
|  |  | 8 | 4 |

| Social Studies Raw Score | Social Studies Standard Score | Natural Sciences Raw Score | Natural Sciences Standard Score |
|---|---|---|---|
| 52 | 34 | 52 | 35 |
| 48 | 32 | 48 | 34 |
| 44 | 28 | 44 | 32 |
| 40 | 25 | 40 | 31 |
| 36 | 22 | 36 | 29 |
| 32 | 19 | 32 | 26 |
| 28 | 16 | 28 | 24 |
| 24 | 12 | 24 | 21 |
| 20 | 10 | 20 | 17 |
| 16 | 7 | 16 | 14 |
| 12 | 5 | 12 | 10 |
| 8 | 2 | 8 | 6 |

**Important Note:** The scoring tables above are not derived from any particular ACT. The raw score–standard score equivalents are unique to each form of the ACT. For this reason, the table should not be used to score the tests in this book.

2

In addition to your standard scores on each of the four tests, your ACT score report will include a composite score. The composite score is just an average of your standard scores in each of the four subject areas.

In addition to your ACT scores, your score report will include percentile rankings for your scores to help you understand how your ACT scores compare with those of other students who took the ACT.

## Summary

1. The ACT consists of four separately timed sections:
   English Usage: 40 minutes—75 Questions
   Mathematical Usage: 50 minutes—40 Questions
   Social Studies Reading: 35 minutes—52 Questions
   Natural Sciences Reading: 35 minutes—52 Questions

2. The ACT generates five scores plus percentile rankings. The raw score for each part of the test is just the number of questions you answer correctly. The standard score for each part is determined by a table. And the composite score is an average of the standard scores on the four parts.

3

# Nuts and Bolts

✔ **Objectives**

To learn how to maximize your performance within the time limit.

To learn how to handle the special time pressure.

To learn how to manage the test booklet and answer sheet so that you get full credit for your performance.

To learn how to respond to the special pressures of the ACT by adjusting your outlook.

1. **The Guessing Gold Mine**
2. **As Time Goes By . . .**
3. **Pace Makes the Race**
   - **Don't Stop to Read Directions**
   - **The Tradeoff**
   - **Leapfrogging**
   - **Throwing in the Towel**
4. **The Test Booklet and the Answer Sheet**
5. **Special Pressures**

## The Guessing Gold Mine

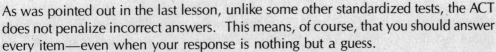

As was pointed out in the last lesson, unlike some other standardized tests, the ACT does not penalize incorrect answers. This means, of course, that you should answer every item—even when your response is nothing but a guess.

As obvious as this is, I think that students sometimes don't understand what a gold mine guessing is because they think in terms of an individual item and not in terms of a test as a whole. Suppose, for example, that by guessing you pick up exactly two more questions in the math section than you otherwise would have gotten. That could raise your standard score for the math test by two points. Is that important? Well, supposing your raw score on the math was 24 instead of 22, your standard score for the math test would be 22 instead of 20, and you would be in the 69th percentile instead of the 60th percentile. And since almost 800,000 students take the ACT each year, this would catapult you over nearly 80,000 students.

And imagine that this pattern held true for all four of the tests. If your composite score was 22 rather than 20, your percentile ranking would be 70 instead of 59. And that is a difference of nearly 90,000 students.

On any question that you cannot answer confidently, eliminate as many wrong choices as you can, and then make a guess anyway. (Pick a letter, any letter!) And even if you run out of time, fill in the rest of the answer spaces. (Pick letters!) You have nothing to lose and everything to gain.

## As Time Goes By . . .

Your ACT will consist of four *separately* timed tests. The test supervisors will tell you when you can begin working on a test and when your time is up. Once a test is over, you cannot go back to it, so you must answer everything you can in a test during the time given.

In order to do this, you have to keep track of the passing time.

### Be in Control

Bring your own watch to the exam. If you have one with a stop-watch function, then use it. A word of warning! Do not use an alarm. The constant "beep beep" will unfairly distract other test-takers, and the proctors might confiscate your watch for the duration of the exam. Also, don't bring a watch with a calculator function—you won't be allowed to use the watch at all.

In some ways, a simple watch with a minute hand is the best watch to use because you can set it for "test time." To set a watch for test time, subtract the number of minutes in the time limit for the test from 60. Then set the minute hand for that many minutes past the hour. (The hour hand is irrelevant for test time.) Here are the appropriate test times for the various tests:

| Test | Set Minute Hand On |
|------|:---:|
| English Usage | 4 |
| Math Usage | 2 |
| Social Studies | 5 |
| Natural Sciences | 5 |

When the minute hand reaches 12, the time for the test will be over. The nice thing about test time is that you can tell at a glance, within a minute or so, just how much time remains—without having to do a calculation.

# Pace Makes the Race

Keeping track of time, however, is not your end goal. The real goal is to *use* the time—and to use it effectively. You must pace yourself, working as rapidly as possible without working so quickly that you sacrifice accuracy to speed. Here are some suggestions to help you get the most out of your time.

### 1. Don't Stop to Read Directions

No extra time is given for reading the instructions for a section. If you have to read the directions, you are using time that could be better spent answering questions.

There is no reason to read the instructions included in the test booklet. You can review the exact directions that will appear on the exam when you get your registration materials. In any event, after you have done the practice materials in this book, you'll know what to do—even without reading directions.

### 2. The Tradeoff

The time limit places you in a dilemma. On the one hand, you cannot afford to work so slowly and carefully that you do not try as many questions as you otherwise could. On the other hand, you cannot afford to work so quickly that you make foolish errors. Somewhere between the two extremes is the answer.

You will develop your own sense of pacing and find the answer by doing this book's practice exercises. If you find that you are not finishing most of the questions in a practice exercise, then on the next exercise you should speed up. If you find that you are answering most questions but are making a lot of silly mistakes, then slow down.

Finding the best tradeoff is not a science. It is a practical art. Only practice will help you find the answer to the problem.

### 3. Leapfrogging

A third important technique of pacing is leapfrogging, that is, jumping over difficult questions. A question may seem to you to be difficult either because it really is one of the hard ones or because you just happen to have a blind spot for that particular item. Whatever the reason, you cannot afford to spend a lot of time working on a single question.

Remember that each correct answer counts exactly one point toward the raw score—not more, not less. The easiest question on the test adds one to the raw score; the most difficult question on the test adds one to the raw score. Why spend five minutes on a difficult item when there are easy questions later in the section just waiting to be picked?

### 4. Throwing in the Towel

The final key to effective pacing is knowing when to give up. You cannot afford to keep working on a question after you have invested a reasonable amount of time with no reward. If you spend three minutes worrying about a question, just waiting for the lightning to strike, so to speak, when you could have used that time to answer four or five other questions, then you are squandering your time.

Once you reach a dead end (you know you do not know what to do or you know it will take too long), throw in the towel. Make your guess and move on to the next question.

## The Test Booklet and the Answer Sheet

Your answers to questions must be entered on a separate answer sheet by darkening spaces on a grid. This grid is then read by a machine. The ACT is absolutely unforgiving of mistakes in this respect. If you know the answer to a question but forget to mark your answer sheet, you get no credit. If you mark the wrong space on the answer sheet, you get no credit. If you do not mark your answer sheet clearly, the result is the same: no credit.

It is important to enter your answer choices clearly and correctly. Take a look at a portion of a sample answer sheet:

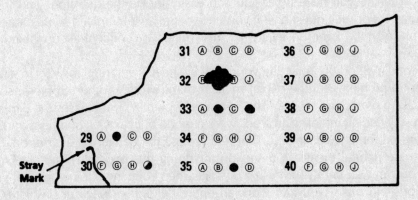

The marks for questions 29 and 35 are made correctly. They are neat and dark, and they completely fill the spaces. The mark for question 30 does not completely fill the space, so the machine might miss it, giving no credit for the question. The mark for question 31 is not dark enough; and again, the machine might miss it, giving no credit. The mark for question 32 is messy; the machine could read F, or G, or H as the intended response.

Question 33 will be graded as an omitted question, since there are two answers entered. (No penalty, but no credit either.)

Question 34 is blank—no credit at all. (A mistake, since there is no penalty for guessing.)

### Entering Your Answers

The very worst mistake that you can make with your answer sheet is to enter your responses in the wrong place. You could skip a question in your test booklet and fail to skip the corresponding answer space on your answer sheet. As a result, a whole series of responses is displaced by one question. The correct pattern is there, but it is in the wrong place. The grading machine doesn't grade your intentions, so it reads the marks just as they stand.

You can avoid this error. Aside from taking care in coding answers, check every now and then to make sure that your problem numbers and answer space numbers match up. The answer choices for the odd-numbered questions are lettered A through D (for math, A through E), and the answer choices for the even-numbered questions are lettered F, G, H, and J (for math, F, G, H, J and K). There are two further safeguards you should use.

First, keep a separate record of your answer choices in your test booklet. Simply draw a circle around your correct answer choice. If you should make an error in coding responses, this safeguard allows you to retrieve the information without having to rework every question.

Circle the number of any question that you leapfrog over. This will enable you to locate the questions when you have finished your work and have time to go back and study them. If you do go back and arrive at an answer, then blacken in the circle around the number. This lets you know that you have already taken care of the question.

For questions that you answer but are not sure about, place a "?" beside the number. Then, if you have time, you can easily locate the questions and review your solution. For such questions, if you have definitely eliminated some choices as correct, place an "x" over those letters. This will let you concentrate on the remaining choices.

A second method of protecting your answer sheet is entering answers in groups. Why work a problem, shuffle paper, make a mark, work another problem, shuffle paper, make a mark, and so on? This is not only clumsy; it increases the danger of making a silly coding mistake. Instead, work a group of five or six questions and then mark them on the answer sheet. That will reduce the danger of such errors.

There are natural breaks in a section for doing this coding chore. In English Usage, you can wait until you finish a passage, then code the choices for that group of questions. In math, you can work an entire column or page of problems and then code responses. In Social Studies and Natural Sciences, you can work the problems associated with a reading passage and then make the marks.

**Warning:** As time for a test draws to a close (five minutes left), begin coding your answers one by one. The reason for this is that the test rules state that once time is called, you must put your pencil down. You are not allowed any extra time to complete the answer sheet. Also, if you can see that you are going to run out of time before you get to some questions, make your guesses before the supervisor calls time.

Additionally, you should feel free to make any other marks in your test booklet that you might find helpful. You can underline phrases, circle words, draw connecting arrows, write notes to yourself, or make any other marks. Do not be afraid to write in the test booklet. You paid for it and the test booklets are not reused. They are eventually destroyed.

## Special Pressures

The ACT, as you know by now, is different in some very important respects from the teacher-prepared tests you usually get in school. These differences can put special pressures on you.

In the first place, you may experience some time pressure. You may feel that you are running out of time and that if you only had more time, you could definitely answer most if not all of the questions. And this happens not just once, but four times during the test. Just because you feel time pressure does not mean that you are not doing well. The objective is to do as many questions as you can within the time limit allowed.

Additionally, you may get the idea that you are not doing very well because you are not answering with confidence. At the back of your mind is the gnawing thought "I like answer C, but it could be B, or even E." Everyone feels this way. Use your best judgment, enter your choice, and do not second-guess yourself.

## Summary

1. **Learn to pace yourself.** (1) Don't stop for directions; (2) learn by practice the optimal tradeoff for you between speed and accuracy; (3) know when to leapfrog over a question; and (4) learn when to throw in the towel.

2. Mark your answer sheet carefully, coding in groups. Develop your own record system to keep track of your progress in your test booklet.

3. Understand the special pressures that are created by the ACT and learn to ignore them.

# Test Anxiety

## ✔ Objective

**To learn to control the fear of the ACT with knowledge.**

1. **The ACT and the Fear of Final Judgment**
   - **ACT's Authority**
   - **Superpeople?**
   - **The Test Is Not that Precise**
   - **Power to the Test-taker**
   - **The Score Isn't Everything**
2. **Exploding the Myth of Final Judgment**

# The ACT and the Fear of Final Judgment

Many, even most, students experience a sense of dread or foreboding about the ACT. For some, the feeling is no more than an uncomfortable and vague sense of uneasiness. For others, the dread can become unmanageable, leading to what is called test anxiety. In extreme cases, test anxiety can be crippling and can seriously interfere with a person's ability to take a test. This extreme anxiety, the fear of the ACT as a final judgment, is created by a group of mistaken beliefs or impressions that work together to create the greater anxiety. You do not have to experience all of the impressions to feel the strong sense of anxiety. What are these mistaken beliefs and impressions?

## ACT's Authority

Most people regard the ACT as having a kind of natural authority over them, something like the physical laws that govern the universe. Why is there an ACT? Well, that's like asking why there is gravity. It's just there, a fact of the world—and at some point in your life you have to take it (or some similar test). This impression is mistaken.

To see that this impression of natural authority is an error, you need only think about the nature of your relationship to the ACT. When you register to take the ACT, you are entering into a legal contract with ACT Testing Program (the nonprofit corporation that owns the ACT). You are paying them a fee, and they agree in turn to provide you with certain services. One of those services is to administer to you a test and to report your scores to the schools you designate. Because you pay the fee, ACT has a legal obligation to you.

The registration form you sign and the information booklet you receive from ACT set forth in detail the specific provisions of your agreement with them. Don't worry that all of this is not one single typed document (like a deed). It's still a legal contract. (In fact, most contracts are just verbal agreements, and they are still legally binding.) So you and the ACT are parties to a business contract.

Two factors, however, tend to obscure the fact that the relationship between you and ACT is a business contract. First, ACT is a nonprofit organization. People reason "since they are not in business to make a profit, they must administer the ACT for altruistic reasons." This reasoning is mistaken. Though ACT is a nonprofit organization, the people who work there are motivated by many of the same concerns that motivate the people who run General Motors or IBM. They are concerned about income, expenses, the quality of their product, customer relations, and so on.

This doesn't mean that the people who work at ACT don't believe in what they do. They believe that they produce a good product and they are proud of it, but the fact that a business does not make a profit does not necessarily make it morally better than any other business—and it doesn't give ACT any additional authority over you.

The second factor that helps to create the impression of natural authority is the size of ACT. It may seem to you that you have no alternative to taking the ACT. (In fact, the ACT is not the only admission test in the country. More people take the Scholastic Aptitude Test, or SAT, each year than the ACT.)

In any event, your relationship to ACT is that of a contract—and it takes two parties to make a contract. You are an equal partner to the contract, and you have certain legal rights under it.

## Superpeople?

The testing process also creates another impression. You sit down in a classroom at the testing center. You are given the test booklet and told to answer 219 questions in just a little more than two and a half hours. You begin to think that the person who wrote these questions must really be superhuman, because you are expected to answer them (and many of them are very difficult) in so short a time. This impression that a genius is behind the test is an error.

This test is not written by a single person, nor by two, nor even three people. Rather, the test is the product of a large group of people including teachers, reviewers, experts in the various fields, and statisticians. Each question is a group effort.

In fact, you may be involved in the process of creating ACT questions. As a final check, questions are included in nonscoring sections of the ACT that are administered on certain test dates. Then computers are used to check for patterns. Do the questions work in the way they are supposed to? Student responses on the pre-test sections of ACTs are essential to the development of new versions of the exam.

## The Test Is Not that Precise

The ACT also seems to be a very precise measuring device. After all, virtually everything is done by computers, and we all know that computers are usually very precise (except when human beings give them the wrong information). And your score report will be covered with numbers: standard scores, percentile equivalents, and so on. Because of this impression of precision, you may be tempted to think that score differences of two or three points are very important. In fact, they are not. The ACT is not that precise.

Built into the scoring mechanism for each test is a four-point range of error! The technical term for this is the standard error of measurement. The standard error of measurement for each test is about two points. This means that two-thirds of all scores are within about two points above or below the so-called true score.

Thus, in a group of three students who each received 18 on the math test, the true scores for two of those students are anywhere from 16 to 22 (and their true percentile rankings are anywhere from 42 to 57). And for the other student, the score is even less precise. (Imagine putting $1 bills into three stacks of 50 with only this much precision: "Well, I'm pretty sure that in two of the stacks I have somewhere between $42 and $57, though which two stacks I'm not sure. And as for the other stack—who knows?") This does not mean there is anything wrong with the ACT; it's just that tests like the ACT can't be made any more precise.

It is an error, therefore, to treat an ACT score as though it measures anything with decimal-point precision. In fact, ACT Testing Program is aware of the limitations of the ACT and specifically cautions against attributing too much precision to the scores.

On your student score report, you will find that your percentile rankings are given only in very broad ranges.

## Power to the Test-taker

The testing process can also create a mistaken impression that ACT is all-powerful and that you are powerless. ACT sets the testing dates, the fees, the locations, and the conditions under which you will take the exam. It is true that you have very little say in these matters. Just remember, this is the result of ACT's quasi-monopoly in this area.

You have to do business with ACT. That is an economic fact of life, like public utilities. But ACT is no more omnipotent than your local electric, gas, or phone company.

This impression of omnipotence can also haunt you as you take the test. You are told where to sit; what you may and may not have with you; when you can use the restroom. And when the proctor reads the rules governing the testing procedure, it may sound as though you are hearing sentence passed. It may be difficult; but try to ignore this feeling. The supervisors and proctors maintain an air of authority to make sure that they can keep control of the situation.

Finally, you may also find yourself thinking that ACT is a kind of priesthood that guards the mysteries of the ACT, and to a certain extent this impression is correct. After all, ACT is not going to give away any secrets of the ACT if it can avoid doing so. Times have changed, however, in one important respect. Several years ago, the State of New York enacted legislation that is popularly called the "Truth-in-Testing" law. Under this law, businesses that administer standardized tests in New York are required to release copies of the exams and other information to persons who have taken the exam. Although this law technically applies only in New York, it has caused nationwide changes in testing procedures.

Prior to this law, most businesses that engaged in testing released very little information about their exams—at most a handful of sample questions and a few paragraphs of descriptive material. And test-takers were not allowed to review the exams they took. You will be given the opportunity to obtain a copy of the questions that were used to create your ACT score.

Of course, the test-development process must always, to a certain extent, be shrouded in mystery. After all, if the ACT is to serve any function at all, each new test form must remain a secret until the day that form is actually administered.

## The Score Isn't Everything

One of the most important aspects of the fear of final judgment is the impression of finality created by the testing process. In fact, you may retake the examination. You would want to consider retaking the exam under the following circumstances:

Something occurred during the test that interfered with your ability to do your best, e.g., you became physically ill, you were extremely nervous, or you made a mistake in coding answers.

Your academic situation has changed, e.g., you have completed more coursework relevant to the ACT or are otherwise better prepared to take the test.

Your score reports seem out of line, e.g., you have very high grades but got low ACT scores, or one or two of your ACT scores were (for no good reason) very low compared to the other ACT scores.

You absolutely must have a higher score in order to be competitive for a school you have chosen.

The decision to retake the test is not an easy one and depends on a number of factors. I suggest that before deciding to retake the ACT you discuss the matter with a guidance counselor.

Beyond the question of retaking the ACT, many people have the mistaken impression that bad (or good) things are automatically going to happen as a result of a test such as this. In fact, the ACT is a lot less important than you might think.

First, while it cannot be denied that ACT may be an important part of the admissions process, very few schools—if indeed any at all—regard ACT scores as either passing or failing. The score is just one more factor used in making a decision, like grades, activities, motivation, and so on. So a "poor" mark will not necessarily keep you out of a school, and a "good" mark will not guarantee you will get in.

Second, a year after you take the test, no one else will care what your score was. Your professors will grade you on the basis of your course work. New acquaintances will accept you on the basis of your personality. Student associations will want you as a member for your motivation, energy, and ability.

## Exploding the Myth of Final Judgment

I have examined several different impressions about the ACT that I believe are mistaken. No one individual impression would be a very serious cause for concern. But when the individual impressions are taken as a group, they add up to create the fear of final judgment. And it is understandable. You think you are about to be judged by some supreme authority who is both omniscient and omnipotent and that this judgment will be final.

In discussing the "myth" of final judgment, I do not mean to imply that anyone or any group set out to perpetrate a hoax. In fact, the information bulletins distributed by ACT to students, parents, and guidance counselors say many of the same things I have just said.

I suppose that this mistaken impression of final judgment could be just an accident of history, but you do not have to live with it. (After all, at the time of Columbus, almost everyone believed the world was flat.) If you take care to avoid falling under the spell of any one of the individual misconceptions, you should be able to keep any fears you might have about the ACT under control.

# Unlocking the Mystery

## ✔ Objective

**To learn, through the device of the "Sherlock Holmes ACT Casebook," how to solve the mysteries of the ACT.**

1. **Advance Warning**
2. **Multiple-Choice**
3. **Adventures of the ACT**
   * **The Case of the Missing Reading Passage**
   * **The Case of the Missing Numbers**
   * **The Case of the Hidden Clues**

5

Wouldn't it be great to take a test where you have all of the questions in advance and the answers right there on the test paper? Well, the ACT comes close. First, in the English Usage and Mathematics Usage tests, it is almost possible to know in advance what questions will be asked. Second, in all four tests, the answers are actually given to you in the test booklet. These two features of the test form the basis for our system.

## Advance Warning

Year after year the ACT is given to hundreds of thousands of students, and scores are supposed to be comparable—not just from administration to administration within a given year, but even from year to year. But how is that possible since different test forms with completely different questions are used? The answer is found in the design specifications for the test. Each form of the exam, indeed each question, is written according to special criteria. A question is not acceptable for use on an ACT unless it fits a particular pattern. These patterns are there for you to learn, and that is like having the questions before the test. Of course, you cannot literally have the exact questions that will appear on your particular ACT, but certain patterns are so clearly identifiable that it almost amounts to the same thing.

## Multiple-Choice

Additionally, you are actually given the answer to every question on your ACT. Since every question on the exam is a multiple-choice question, the right answer is there on the page. Of course, the correct answer is camouflaged in a group of wrong answers; but even though it is partially hidden, it's there for the taking. To demonstrate how important this is, we interrupt this discussion for a:

### Social Studies Pop Quiz

Who was the fourth Chief Justice of the United States Supreme Court?

Time's up! I am not going to give you the correct answer just yet. (If you do know the answer, that's good, and I would want you as my partner in a game of trivia. But for right now, let's assume that you do not know the answer.) It is not the answer to the question that is important to us, but the form of the question.

With a question in this form, you have to come up with an answer from scratch. Either you know the name of the fourth Chief Justice of the Supreme Court or you do not. And if not, you must either leave the question blank or make a wild guess. Either way, your chance of getting credit for the question is very small.

Things change, however, if the question is converted to a multiple-choice format:

### Social Studies Pop Quiz

Who was the fourth Chief Justice of the United States Supreme Court?
**A.**   xxxxx xxxxxx
**B.**   xxxxx xxxxxx
**C.**   xxxxx xxxxxx
**D.**   xxxxx xxxxxx

Notice that the choices have been covered. Still, even though you cannot read the choices, you are in a much better position than you were before. Given the form of the earlier question, without the knowledge needed to answer the question, you had literally no chance of getting credit for it. Now, even though you may not have knowledge that will allow you to answer with confidence, you at least have a fighting chance: pick any letter, and you have a one-out-of-four chance of getting credit for the question.

With real answer choices, you can tip the odds even more in your favor.

### Social Studies Pop Quiz

Who was the fourth Chief Justice of the United States Supreme Court?
**A.**   Julius Caesar
**B.**   Mickey Mouse
**C.**   Roger Taney
**D.**   Madonna
Enter the letter of your choice here: _____

The correct answer is C, and almost everyone can answer correctly even though they may have never before seen the name Roger Taney. (Incidentally, this question would never appear on an ACT Social Studies test. The fact is too obscure. So you don't have to run out and memorize a list of all the Chief Justices.)

How is it possible to answer correctly and even confidently when you don't have the historical fact needed to answer the question? "Easy," you say. "Just eliminate the three choices that could not possibly be correct and select the one that remains."

This method of reasoning is called the Process of Elimination, and it takes advantage of an inherent weakness in the multiple-choice format. One—and only one—of the choices is correct. If you keep eliminating wrong choices, eventually only the correct choice will remain. Granted, eliminating wrong choices on the ACT will not usually be this easy, but the principle is the same.

Patterns and answers are inherent in the ACT. Get rid of either one, and the ACT is no longer the ACT. Therefore, so long as there is an ACT there will be patterns that can be learned and there will be a multiple-choice format that can be taken advantage of.

You are surely familiar with Sherlock Holmes, the fictional detective created by the British writer Sir Arthur Conan Doyle. Using clues and logic, Holmes is able to solve case after case, even though to everyone else the situations seem to present insoluble mysteries. Most people are also familiar with the character of Dr. Watson, Holmes' good-natured friend and sometimes bachelor roommate. Watson, a medical doctor, is clearly a bright person; but his powers of investigation and logical reasoning do not quite equal those of his friend Holmes.

What would happen if these characters took the ACT? I imagine that Watson would do fairly well. He would be able to answer a good many of the questions, but he would likely miss a lot of the more difficult ones. On the other hand, Holmes would surely do very well, getting answers to difficult questions by methods that seem almost magical.

In solving cases, Holmes relies heavily on two techniques: looking for established patterns and the process of elimination. First, in case after case, Holmes refers to his studies of patterns—footprints, cigar ashes, chemicals, and so on. Having foreknowledge of what to look for is often the key to Holmes' solution of a mystery.

Second, Holmes also uses logical reasoning, in particular the process of elimination. In the "Adventure of the Bruce-Partington Plans," Holmes explains to Watson, "When all other contingencies fail, whatever remains, however improbable, must be the truth." That is the process of elimination.

Thus, Holmes succeeded where others failed because he was able to identify patterns and because he reasoned logically. You will notice that these two techniques are the same ones we talked about above.

If Watson and Holmes were to encounter the ACT, here is what I think would happen.

## ADVENTURES OF THE ACT

### The Case of the Missing Reading Passage

One day Watson came to his friend Sherlock Holmes with a problem. "Holmes," said Watson, "I have a Social Studies Reading Test question that I must answer, but I seem to have lost the reading selection on which the question is based. Now I'll never be able to answer the question."

"Show me the question," insisted Holmes, taking the page offered by Watson. On the page was written:

> 5. Assume a chapter in a history book quotes extensively from the speeches of a president. The author of the book probably holds which theory of history?
>
> A. The economic forces theory
> B. The class struggle theory
> C. The great men theory
> D. The impersonal forces theory

"Why, Watson," exclaimed Holmes, "this is a multiple-choice question. My methods are perfectly suited to it. If we can eliminate three of the four choices by any means whatsoever, then the one choice that remains must be the correct one."

Holmes studied the question for a moment before he spoke further. "We can infer from the question and the answer choices," he began, "that the missing reading selection discusses several different theories of history. The choices contain phrases that are descriptive of the different theories. From these phrases we can infer that one theory emphasizes economic forces, another class conflicts, another the actions of important people, and another impersonal forces."

"In the first place, Watson, choice A does not seem to be a possible answer. While the speeches of a president might mention economic conditions, it doesn't seem that someone interested primarily in economic conditions would rely heavily on quotations from such speeches. Instead, a person with such a theory would rely on economic statistics. Choice B doesn't seem any better. While a speech by an important person might cast some light on conflicts between different groups, an historian of the type suggested by B would be interested in both sides. Of course, the question stem doesn't say whether or not the chapter also includes quotations from other sources. But, on balance, if B were going to be the correct answer, the question-writer would probably have said something indicating the chapter includes quotations from leaders on both sides of a conflict. Finally, choice D cannot possibly be right. Someone who holds that history is the result of impersonal forces would not be likely to give prominence to the views of a person. We can infer, therefore, that C is the correct choice."

"By Jove, Holmes, that's ingenious!" exclaimed Watson. "Now, I can guess that the answer is C."

"Not guess," insisted Holmes, "answer with confidence. We have eliminated all possibilities but C. To be sure, perhaps we made an error in eliminating one of the other choices; but so long as we have confidence in our eliminations, we are not guessing."

### The Case of the Missing Numbers

Watson approached Holmes with the following math problem:

> During a sale, the price of a book is reduced by 20 percent. If the price of the book after the reduction is D dollars, what was the original price of the book?
> A. 2D
> B. 1.25D
> C. 1.20D
> D. 0.80D
> E. 0.75D

"I was able to answer this question," announced Watson, "but the algebra took considerable time."

Holmes, smiling, said "Good, Watson! Though I think you might have saved yourself considerable trouble by employing my methods. In the first place, I immediately eliminated choices D and E. They are both *less* that the final reduced price of D dollars, and I know that the original price must be *greater* than D dollars.

"Next, I eliminated A. If a price is reduced from 2D dollars to D dollars, it is cut in half. Cutting a price in half reduces it by 50 percent—not 20 percent."

At this point Watson interjected, "But now you are forced to guess. You do have a fifty–fifty chance, but with my approach I can answer with complete certainty."

"Not too quickly," Holmes said. "With one very simple calculation, I can easily arrive at the same position. Since no numbers are provided in the question, I will just supply some of my own. Let us assume that D, the new price, is $1, a very convenient assumption.

"Now let's test choice B. If D, as we assume, is $1, then 1.25D is $1.25. Is that consistent with what are told in the question? Yes. We are told the original price was reduced by 20 percent, or $\frac{1}{5}$. One fifth of $1.25 is $0.25, and if you reduce $1.25 by $0.25, the result is $1. This simple calculation proves that the original price was 1.25D. So B is correct."

"But, Holmes," objected Watson, "you were merely lucky. Had you selected choice C instead of choice B for your experiment, you would then have had to do two calculations, not just one. And such calculations are time-consuming."

"No so," countered Holmes. "Even had I selected choice C rather than choice B for my test, I still would have needed only one calculation. When a calculation showed choice C to be incorrect, that, in and of itself, would establish by the process of elimination that the one remaining choice, B, was correct."

### The Case of the Hidden Clues

One wintery afternoon, Holmes and Watson were riding in the compartment of a train on their way back to London. Watson, looking up from the book he was reading, blurted out, "Blast these social studies questions, Holmes! I can't remember the answer to this one, so I'll have to look it up in my history book when we get back to the flat." And he read to Holmes the following:

30. Which of the following concepts were stressed by Enlightenment thinkers?
    I. Reason
    II. Progress
    III. Natural Law
    F. I only
    G. I and III only
    H. II and III only
    J. I, II, and III

Holmes furrowed his brow and read the problem. After a brief pause, he said, "There's no need to wait until we arrive home, Watson. The correct choice is J."

"Well, it's nice that you remember so much history," Watson responded, "but I still want to look up the answer."

"Actually," Holmes said, "I did not answer on the basis of my knowledge of history. Instead, I used clues I found in the question itself. You see, I know that the word *enlighten* means 'to help someone understand something' or 'to eliminate ignorance.' So an historical period that is called the Enlightenment must have stressed knowledge—and reason is a form of knowledge."

"But," objected Watson, "that's not enough to get the right answer. How did you know that Enlightenment thinkers also emphasized progress?"

"Because, Watson, the word *enlighten* has very positive overtones, so I inferred that progress was an aspect of the Enlightenment as well."

"Well," responded Watson, "how did you know that the Enlightenment also stressed natural law—whatever that is?"

"Elementary, Watson; only one of the answer choices includes both 'I' and 'II' —choice J. Therefore J has to be the correct choice, and from that I inferred that the Enlightenment also emphasized natural law."

Most people who take the ACT are in the position of Dr. Watson. They are able to answer most of the easy questions; they answer many of the questions of medium difficulty; but they are forced to guess on many of the very difficult items. Additionally, they take longer than necessary to solve a problem. Holmes, on the other hand, with his knowledge of patterns and power of logical thinking, would fare better. The more you are able to think like Holmes, the better you will do on the ACT.

# PART TWO

# The Coaching Program

# English Usage: Part I

## ✔ Objectives

To learn what is tested by the English Usage Test.

To become familiar with the format used by the English Usage Test.

To review important principles of grammar, sentence construction, and idiomatic expression tested by the English Usage Test.

To learn strategies useful for the English Usage Test format.

To practice the principles and strategies learned in this chapter.

1.  English Diagnostic Test
2.  Avoiding Common Problems with Sentence Structure
    - Faulty Parallelism
    - Incomplete Split Constructions
    - Verb Tense
    - Logical Errors
    - Sentence Fragments
    - Excessive Wordiness
    - Misplaced Modifiers

The first of the four tests on your ACT will be the English Usage test. The English Usage test consists of several reading passages, parts of which have been underlined. To the right of the underlined parts will be four answer choices. The first choice is always "NO CHANGE," which you select if you believe the underlined portion is correct as written. Otherwise, select the choice that you think is most appropriate. The English Usage test contains 75 questions, and the time limit for the test is 40 minutes.

## English Diagnostic Test

On the following pages you will find a diagnostic test that will help you determine whether you need to do additional work on the basics of English grammar and punctuation. If you do reasonably well on the test, missing only a few items, and if after reading the explanations for those items you understand why you missed them, you probably do not need to do an extensive review of the basics of grammar. If you miss more than a few items—and certainly if the explanations for the items are not clear to you—you may need to dig out a grammar book and brush up on those points on which you are not clear.

## ENGLISH DIAGNOSTIC TEST
### 35 Questions
### No Time Limit

> Directions: Each of the following sentences contains an error of grammar, sentence structure, usage, or punctuation. Circle the letter of the underlined part of the sentence containing the error. Although there is no time limit, you should work as quickly as possible. After you have finished, review your work using the explanations that follow.

**6**

1. Her and the other members of the team spoke to the press after their final victory.
   A                                    B        C              D

2. In early America, there has been very little to read except for the books sent from
                     A              B            C                              D
   Europe.

3. Still remaining in the ancient castle are the Duke's collection of early Dutch
   A                                      B
   paintings, which will be donated to a museum.
            C            D

4. After having took the entrance examination, she was absolutely sure that she
   A                                                    B                  C
   would be admitted to the college.
   D

5. Most students preferred courses in the liberal arts to courses in science—unless
                 A                                    B                        C
   they are science majors.
   D

6. The point of the coach's remarks were obviously to encourage the team and
                                A       B
   to restore its competitive spirit.
   C        D

7. When Mozart wrote *The Marriage of Figaro*, the Emperor was shocked at him using
               A                                          B              C
   mere servants as main characters.
                  D

8. Since he was called back for a third reading, the actor expected being chosen for the
   A                    B                                  C            D
   part.

9. For a young woman who is ready to join the work force, there now exists many more
                    A                                               B         C
   opportunities than existed for her mother.
                   D

10. Movie fans claim there is no greater director than him, although most critics
                 A           B                    C
    would mention the names of Bergman or Kurosawa.
    D

11. When the Senate meeting was televised, the first issue to be discussed were Federal
        A            B        C                                        D
    grants and loans for higher education.

12. Although the average person watches a news program every day, they do not always
    A                          B                                 C
    understand the issues discussed.
               D

13. It was said of the noted author Marcel Proust that he goes out only at night.
                                                 A  B      C    D

14. Most people do not realize that white wines, including champagne, are often made
                A                 B             C
    of red grapes.
    D

15. The earliest architecture in the New World resembled neither that of the European
                                                    **A**               **B**
    Renaissance or that of the early Baroque period, but rather the medieval architecture
            **C**                                **D**
    of European towns.

16. Like many composers of the period, Debussy was familiar and admired contemporary
    **A**                                        **B**    **C**
    poetry and used it as the inspiration for his music.
               **D**

17. Americans used to go to the movies as often as they watched television; but now that
                                     **A**
    they can watch movies in their homes, they are doing more of it.
    **B**                 **C**                **D**

18. After hearing Joan Sutherland perform live at the Metropolitan Opera on
    **A**                          **B**
    December 1, 1984, I am convinced that she is greater than any prima donna
                                           **C**
    of this century.
        **D**

19. Like Andy Warhol, the "pop art" of Roy Lichtenstein is filled with familiar images
    **A**                                      **B**     **C**
    such as cartoon characters.
    **D**

20. Because the project had been a team effort, we had divided the bonus equally among
    **A**                                 **B**             **C**
    the five of us.
      **D**

21. Postponing marriage and having little or no children are not revolutionary choices for
              **A**                 **B**       **C**
    women; they were choices made by the grandmothers of many postwar women.
           **D**

22. Being that black bears are large and powerful, most people fear them even though the
    **A**           **B**                            **C**
    bears are really quite shy.
        **D**

23. Because consumers believe there to be a correlation between price and quality, the cost
    **A**           **B**         **C**
    of computer software is steadily raising.
              **D**

24. Travel to countries with less than ideal sanitary conditions increases the amount of
    **A**           **B**                           **C**      **D**
    victims of hepatitis.

25. The fuel truck overturned on the highway, stopped traffic for over four hours during
                **A**              **B**                        **C**
    the busiest part of the day.
       **D**

26. Primarily found in the remote mountainous regions of the southeastern states, very few
                                       **A**
    people die of the bite of the copperhead or highland moccasin because very few
          **B**                                     **C**
    people come into contact with them.
                          **D**

27. When Peter started the business in 1982, it was hardly nothing more than a one-room operation
                **A**                              **B**
    with a single telephone line, but today Peter has offices in six different states.
                       **C**             **D**

28. Unlike the 1960s, when drugs were used primarily by "hippies," cocaine is used today
                                  **A**                        **B**
    by people in all walks of life, including lawyers.
    **C**                     **D**

29. While the Reagan–Gorbachev summit cannot be described as a complete waste of
                                        **A**           **B**
    time, nothing particular significant was accomplished during the ten-day meeting.
         **C**          **D**

30. There are some people <u>who are unusually sensitive</u> to bee stings and who
               A                B
    may experience allergic reactions <u>including</u> swelling, chills, nausea, fever, and
                                  C
    <u>they may even become delirious.</u>
               D

31. When Robert introduced the guest <u>speaker he</u> described <u>his</u> accomplishments in great
                            B           C
    detail but then forgot <u>to mention</u> the speaker's name.
    A                        D

32. The fog <u>was very dense, they</u> were unable <u>to make out</u> the beacon light
          A            B                 C
    on <u>the opposite shore.</u>
           D

33. Gordon told the clerk <u>that he wanted</u> to order three bottles of <u>Beaujolais two</u> bottles
              A                B                        C
    <u>of port, and</u> one bottle of claret.
         D

34. "Guernica," one of Picasso's many <u>masterpieces was exhibited</u> in the New York
                                      A          B
    Museum of Modern Art <u>until,</u> as specified in Picasso's will, it <u>was returned</u> to Spain
                              C                                        D
    once democracy was reinstated.

35. Mary Alice who is the dean's choice has indicated <u>that she</u> would be willing to serve
                              A                        B
    as chairperson *pro tem* only on the condition that a search committee <u>be formed</u> within
          C                                                      D
    the next three weeks.

6

# Explanatory Answers

1. (A) *Her* is an object pronoun and cannot be used as a subject.

2. (A) The verb tense is incorrect. The past tense, *was*, is needed here.

3. (B) The subject here is the collection of paintings, which is singular; therefore the verb should be singular.

4. (A) The past participle for *to take* is *taken*, not *took*.

5. (A) The sentence suffers from an illogical combination of verb tenses, a problem that can be corrected by changing *preferred* to *prefer*.

6. (A) The subject here is *point*, which is singular; therefore, the plural verb *were* is incorrect.

7. (C) The modifier is intended to modify the gerund; *him* should be *his*.

8. (D) The infinitive is required here; *he expected to be chosen*.

9. (B) The subject is *many opportunities*, which is plural. The verb should be *exist*.

10. (C) The subject pronoun is required for the predicate nominative; *him* should be *he*.

11. (D) The subject here is *issue*, which is singular, so the verb should also be singular—*was*.

12. (C) *They* represents a shift in subject from *the average person*. The correct pronoun would be *he or she*.

13. (C) Since the first verb is in the past tense, the second verb cannot be in the present tense.

14. (D) This is an error of idiomatic expression. The wines are made *from* red grapes, not *of* red grapes.

15. (C) The correct expression in English is *neither/nor*; here, *or* is incorrect.

16. (C) This is an incomplete construction. The sentence should say that Debussy was familiar *with* and admired.

17. (D) Here, the pronoun *it* has no specific referent.

18. (C) This is not a logical statement. The sentence says that Joan Sutherland is greater than herself. It should say that she is greater than any other prima donna.

19. (A) This is an illogical comparison; the sentence compares the art of Lichtenstein to Andy Warhol, not to his art.

20. (B) The use of the past perfect tense here is unnecessary. The simple past is required.

21. (B) This is a mistake of expression. The correct expression is *few*, not *little*.

22. (A) *Being that* is colloquial usage for *since* or *because* and should not be used.

23. (D) This is an error in diction. The correct word here is *rising*.

**24.** (D) The sentence contains an error in diction. The correct word is *number*, not *amount*.

**25.** (B) *Stopping* should be used instead of *stopped* to indicate simultaneous action and to avoid a run-on sentence.

**26.** (A) The sentence contains a dangling modifier. The writer does not mean to say that people are found in the remote mountainous regions but that the snakes are found in those regions.

**27.** (B) The sentence contains a double negative: *hardly nothing*.

**28.** (A) The sentence contains a dangling modifier. The phrase *the 1960s* cannot modify *cocaine*.

**29.** (D) *Particular* is an adjective and cannot be used to modify another adjective. The correct word would be *particularly*.

**30.** (D) The sentence suffers from faulty parallelism.

**31.** (B) A long introductory phrase or dependent clause must be separated from the main clause by a comma: "When Robert introduced the guest speaker, he . . . ."

**32.** (B) This sentence contains a comma splice. You cannot join two independent clauses (independent thoughts) with a comma. You must either use a semicolon instead of a comma or include a conjunction: "The fog was very dense; they were . . . ."

**33.** (C) You must set off a series of three or more similar elements with commas. Although a comma is not required between the final two elements, commas are required between the other elements. Thus, the comma following *port* is optional, but you do need a comma following *Beaujolais*.

**34.** (A) An appositive should be set off by commas: "'Guernica,' one of Picasso's many masterpieces, was . . . ." The other two commas are correct. They set off a parenthetical expression.

**35.** (A) A nonrestrictive clause must be set off by commas: "Mary, who is the dean's choice, . . . ."

6

# Common Grammatical Errors to Avoid

## 1. Subject–Verb Agreement

As you know, a subject must agree with its verb.

> **EXAMPLE:**
>
> The professor were traveling in Europe when she received notice of her promotion.

The construction *were traveling* is an error. The subject is *professor*, a singular noun. The verb *were traveling* should be *was traveling*. The sentence should read: "The professor was traveling in Europe." This example is very simple; the error is easy to spot because the subject and verb are next to each other. Most errors occur when the subject and the verb are separated, when the sentence structure is inverted, or when you cannot recognize whether the subject is singular or plural.

**First, the connection between the subject and the verb may be obscured because the subject and the verb are separated.**

> **EXAMPLES:**
>
> The professor voted Teacher of the Year by the students were traveling in Europe when she received notice of her promotion.

*Professor* is singular, yet the verb *were traveling* is plural. This is more difficult to spot in this version of the sentence because of the proximity of the noun *students*, which might be mistaken for the subject of the verb. The sentence sounds correct to the ear: "... students were ...." The sentence should read: "The professor voted Teacher of the Year by the students was traveling in Europe when she received notice of her promotion."

> Most teachers, unless they have an appointment to a prestigious university, earns relatively less as a teacher than they might in business.

The subject of *earns* is *teachers*. *Teachers earns* is incorrect. The correct construction is *teachers earn*. But it's easy to mistake *university* for the true subject of the sentence. The sentence should read: "Most teachers, unless they have an appointment to a prestigious university, earn relatively less as a teacher than they might in business."

> Many nutritionists now believe that a balanced diet and not large doses of vitamins are the best guarantee of health.

The true subject of the verb *are* is *diet*. The phrase *not large doses* is not part of the subject. The correct construction is: "diet ... is." The corrected sentence should read: "Many nutritionists now believe that a balanced diet and not large doses of vitamins is the best guarantee of health."

> Television comedies in which there is at least one really detestable character captures the interest of viewers.

The true subject of the verb *captures* is *comedies*. The correct construction is "comedies ... capture." The correct sentence is: "Television comedies in which there is at least one really detestable character capture the interest of the viewers."

**Second, the connection between the subject and verb may be obscured by an inverted structure.** An inverted sentence is one in which the verb comes before the subject.

**EXAMPLES:**

Although this is the wealthiest country in the world, within a few blocks of the White House there is scores of homeless people who live on the streets.

The subject of the verb *is* is not *there* but *scores*, which is plural. The correct construction is: "there are scores." The sentence should read: "Although this is the wealthiest country in the world, within a few blocks of the White House there are scores of homeless people who live on the streets."

Just a few miles from the factories and skyscrapers stand a medieval castle that looks exactly as it did in the 12th century.

The subject of the verb *stand* is *castle*. The correct construction is: "stands a medieval castle." The sentence should read: "Just a few miles from the factories and skyscrapers stands a medieval castle that looks exactly as it did in the 12th century."

**Third, there are some subjects that are a bit tricky.**

**EXAMPLES:**

Either the governor or one of his close aides prefer not to have the senator at the head table.

When a subject consists of two or more parts joined by *or*, the verb must agree with the element that follows the *or*. So for the purpose of agreement, the subject of the sentence is *one*. The correct construction is: "one . . . prefers." The sentence should read: "Either the governor or one of his close aides prefers not to have the senator at the head table."

Surrounded by layers of excelsior, none of the crystal goblets were broken when the workers dropped the crate.

The subject of the verb *were broken* is *none*, and *none* is singular. The correct construction is: "none . . . was broken." The corrected sentence is: "Surrounded by layers of excelsior, none of the crystal goblets was broken when the workers dropped the crate."

John, his wife, and the rest of his family plans to attend the awards dinner to be given by the company for the employees with the most seniority.

A subject consisting of two or more elements joined by *and* is plural. The correct construction is: "John, his wife, and the rest of his family plan to attend the awards dinner to be given by the company for the employees with the most seniority."

## 2. Pronoun Usage

There are three areas of pronoun usage that frequently cause problems and should be reviewed: whether a pronoun has a proper antecedent, agreement between pronoun and antecedent, and choice of pronoun case.

**1. A pronoun is a word that takes the place of a noun, so a properly used pronoun will have an antecedent (also called a referent).** This is the word the pronoun substitutes for. Setting aside certain idioms— such as *It's raining*, in which the *it* does not have an identifiable antecedent—a pronoun that lacks a clear antecedent is used incorrectly.

**EXAMPLES:**

During her rise to fame, she betrayed many of her friends; and because of it, very few people trust her.

A pronoun must have an antecedent, but *it* doesn't refer to anything. It "wants" to refer to the woman's *behavior*, but that word doesn't appear in the original sentence. Corrected, the sentence reads "During her rise to fame, she betrayed many of her friends; and because of her behavior, very few people trust her."

In New York City, they are brusque and even rude but quick to come to one another's assistance in a time of crisis.

This construction might be called the "ubiquitous they." "They" are everywhere: In New York, *they* are rude; in Chicago, *they* like the Cubs; in Atlanta, *they* speak with a southern accent; in California, *they* like parties. "They" do get around! The trouble with this use of "they" is that "they" has no antecedent.

In conversation, the "ubiquitous they" may be acceptable, but not in standard written English. The sentence above is corrected by using the word *people* in place of *they*. So the sentence should read: "In New York City, the people are brusque and even rude but quick to come to one another's assistance in a time of crisis."

Ten years ago, the United States imported ten times as much French wine as Italian wine, but today Americans are drinking more of it.

Here, the antecedent of *it* is unclear. Does the sentence mean to state that Americans are drinking more French wine or more Italian wine? It could be either. The sentence is corrected by specifying which. Corrected, the sentence reads: "Ten years ago, the United States imported ten times as much French wine as Italian wine, but today Americans are drinking more Italian wine."

## 2. A pronoun must agree with its antecedent, both in number and person.

**EXAMPLES:**

Although a police officer used to be a symbol of authority, today they receive little respect from most people.

In this sentence the pronoun *they* refers to *police officer*, which is singular. The best way to correct it is to say "he or she is." So, the sentence should read: "Although a police officer used to be a symbol of authority, today he or she receives little respect from most people."

The Abbot was an effective administrator who attempted to assign each monk a task particularly suited to their talents and training.

In this sentence, *their* refers to *each monk*. But *their* is plural and *each monk* is singular. The sentence is corrected by changing *their* to *his*: "The Abbot was an effective administrator who attempted to assign each monk a task particularly suited to his talents and training."

After three years of college education, a person should be allowed to apply to graduate school, because by that time you are ready to choose a profession.

In the third sentence, *you* refers to *person*. But *you* is a second person pronoun and *person* requires a third person pronoun. This is called the error of shifting subject. The sentence could be corrected by changing *you are* to *one is* or vice versa: "After three years of college education, a person should be allowed to apply to graduate school, because by that time one is ready to choose a profession."

> If one wishes to apply for a scholarship, you must submit a completed application
> by March 1.

The error can be corrected by eliminating the incorrect pronoun altogether: "If one wishes to apply for a scholarship, a completed application must be submitted by March 1."

**3. Pronouns have case, and a pronoun's function in a sentence determines which case should be used.** Subjective case (also called nominative case) pronouns are used as subjects of sentences; objective case pronouns are used as objects (direct objects, indirect objects, and objects of prepositions); and possessive case pronouns are used to show possession.

**EXAMPLES:**

> The judges were unable to make a final decision on a single winner, so they
> divided first prize between John and he.

In this sentence, *he* cannot serve as the object of a preposition since it is a subject pronoun. The correct pronoun here is the object pronoun *him*. Corrected, the sentence reads: "The judges were unable to make a final decision on a single winner, so they divided first prize between John and him."

> Although Peter had been looking forward to the debate for weeks, a sore throat
> prevented him taking part.

In this sentence, *him* modifies *taking*, but the correct choice of pronoun is *his*. (When a pronoun modifies a gerund, the *-ing* form of a verb, you must use the possessive case.) The sentence should read: "Although Peter had been looking forward to the debate for weeks, a sore throat prevented his taking part."

### 3. Adjective versus Adverb

Adjectives are used to modify nouns. Adverbs are used to modify verbs and to modify adjectives.

**EXAMPLES:**

> Some psychologists maintain that a child who has seen violence on television is
> more likely to react violent in situations of stress.

*Violent* is intended to modify *to react*, a verb form. So the adverb *violently* is required. The sentence should read: "Some psychologists maintain that a child who has seen violence on television is more likely to react violently in situations of stress."

> The recent created commission has done nothing to address the problem except
> to approve the color of its stationery.

In this sentence, *recent* is intended to modify *created*, which is itself an adjective form modifying *commission*. So *recent* should be *recently*. The corrected sentence reads: "The recently created commission has done nothing to address the problem except to approve the color of its stationery."

### 4. Double Negatives

Double negatives are not acceptable usage in standard written English.

> **EXAMPLES:**
>
> Not hardly a sound could be heard in the auditorium when the speaker approached the dais to announce the result of the contest.

In this sentence, *not hardly* is a double negative. The sentence must read: "Hardly a sound could be heard in the auditorium when the speaker approached the dais to announce the result of the contest."

> Although she had been hired by the magazine to write book reviews, she knew scarcely nothing about current fiction.

*Scarcely nothing* is a double negative. The sentence must read: "Although she had been hired by the magazine to write book reviews, she knew scarcely anything about current fiction."

(Answers, page 64)

**6**

**Directions:** The following exercise contains 25 sentences. Each sentence makes a grammatical error of the sort just reviewed. Circle the letter of the underlined part of the sentence containing the error.

1. The professor deals harsh with students who are not prepared and he is even
                  A                           B          C
   more severe with those who plagiarize.
       D

2. A recent study indicates that the average person ignores most commercial advertising
                  A                          B
   and does not buy products because of them.
      C             D

3. Despite the fact that New York City is one of the most densely populated areas in the
        A                      B
   world, there are many parks where one can sit on a bench under the trees and you can
        C                                                    D
   read a book.

4. Charles Dickens wrote about the horrifying conditions in the English boarding
                A        B
   schools which he learned about on one of his trips to Yorkshire.
     C                          D

5. André Breton initiated the Surrealist movement with the publication of a manifesto, and
             A                            B
   it incorporated the theories of Freud as well as his own.
    C                        D

6. The review of the concert published in the morning's paper mentioned that the soloist is
                     A                                          B
   a very promising talent and that the orchestra played capable.
                  C           D

7. During the war, there were many people in the Polish countryside that sheltered those
       A                                       B         C
   who had escaped from concentration camps.
      D

8. The dean lectured to we students on the privilege and responsibility of attending the
         A      B        C                       D
   university.

9. You taking the initiative in the negotiations will profit the company to a great degree.
           A               B         C              D

10. The members of the club insisted that I be the representative of the organization at the
                       A    B
    conference which was something I had hoped to avoid.
           C              D

11. No one knows for sure whether there was a real person about which Michelangelo
     A                    B               C
    wrote his sonnets.
      D

12. Although the director of the zoo takes great pains to recreate the natural habitats of the
        A                   B          C
    animals, none of the exhibits are completely accurate in every detail.
                      D

13. Climatic differences between the north and south of some countries helps to account
                                          A           B
    for the differences in temperament of the inhabitants of the two regions.
       C                                 D

**14.** The month of August <u>was particularly cold</u>; <u>hardly no</u> daily temperatures <u>were recorded</u>
                         **A**                     **B**                  **C**
above 80 degrees, and <u>none was</u> recorded above 90 degrees.
                                     **D**

**15.** The diaries of Stendhal, <u>which make entertaining reading</u>, <u>also provides</u> a great wealth of
                                                            **A**                 **B**
information <u>about musical taste</u> and performance practice <u>in the last century</u>.
                            **C**                           **D**

**16.** <u>Given the evidence</u> of the existence of a complicated system of communication
              **A**
<u>used by whales</u>, <u>it is necessary</u> to acknowledge <u>its</u> intelligence.
     **B**        **C**             **D**

**17.** <u>Him being</u> at the rally does not necessarily mean <u>that</u> the Congressman <u>agrees</u> with the
    **A**                 **B**        **C**           **D**
President's entire platform.

**18.** Although there is no perfect form of government, representative democracy,
<u>as it is practiced in America</u>, <u>is a system</u> that is <u>working well</u> and <u>more than satisfactorily</u>.
        **A**                **B**           **C**          **D**

**19.** Alfred Stieglitz <u>launched</u> the career of Georgia O'Keeffe, <u>who</u> <u>he</u> later <u>married</u>, by
                                    **A**                       **B** **C**    **D**
exhibiting her paintings in his gallery.

**20.** After driving <u>past Trinity Church</u>, the bus <u>stopped at the recent constructed</u> World Trade
                              **A**                         **B**
Tower, the <u>tallest</u> building in the world, <u>to allow the passengers to take</u> the special
      **C**                              **D**
elevators to the observation tower.

**21.** The student senate <u>passed</u> the resolution <u>banning smoking in the cafeteria</u>
                                  **A**                  **B**
<u>with scarcely any</u> dissenting <u>votes which angered</u> many members of the faculty.
      **C**               **D**

**22.** Most employers <u>assume</u> that one's professional personality and work habits <u>are formed</u>
                            **A**                                **B**
<u>as a result of</u> <u>your</u> early work experience.
     **C**     **D**

**23.** <u>Only a small number</u> of taxi drivers <u>fail to insure</u> their vehicles, but usually
      **A**                 **B**
<u>these are the ones</u> who need <u>it</u> most.
      **C**        **D**

**24.** <u>Angered</u> by the double standard society <u>imposed</u> on women, Edna St. Vincent Millay
    **A**                      **B**
<u>wrote candid about</u> her opinions and <u>her</u> personal life.
      **C**        **D**

**25.** Unless <u>they</u> hire players <u>who</u> <u>are</u> better hitters, the fans <u>will gradually lose</u> interest in the
             **A**         **B**  **C**                **D**
team despite the fine efforts of the pitching staff.

# Avoiding Common Problems with
## Sentence Structure

6

### 1. Faulty Parallelism

In a correctly written sentence, similar elements must have a similar form.

> **EXAMPLES:**
>
> To abandon their homes, leave behind their families, and traveling across the ocean required great courage on the part of the immigrants who moved to America.

In this, the three verb forms *abandon*, *leave*, and *traveling* should be parallel. The sentence is corrected by changing *traveling* to *travel* so that the sentence reads: "To abandon their homes, leave behind their families, and travel across the ocean required great courage on the part of the immigrants who moved to America."

> The review praised the wit, charm, and interpreting of the recitalist but never once mentioned her voice.

In this sentence, *wit* and *charm* are nouns, so *interpreting*, too, should be a noun. The sentence is corrected by changing *interpreting* to *interpretation*. So, the corrected sentence reads: "The review praised the wit, charm, and interpretation of the recitalist, but never once mentioned her voice."

> To acknowledge that one has something to learn is taking the first step on the road to true wisdom.

This sentence has a structure similar to a mathematical equation: *This* is the same as *that*. Both parts of the "equation" must have the same form. The sentence is corrected by changing *taking* to *to take*. Corrected, the sentence reads: "To acknowledge that one has something to learn is to take the first step on the road to true wisdom."

### 2. Incomplete Split Constructions

A split construction is a sentence structure in which two otherwise separate ideas are joined together by a later element. For example, "The Mayor knew or should have known about the corruption." This is a perfectly acceptable split construction in which the ideas *knew* and *should have known* are joined together by the single object *corruption*. In some split constructions, one half or the other never gets completed.

> **EXAMPLES:**
>
> The students are critical of the dean because he is either unfamiliar or doesn't care about the urgent need for new student housing on campus.

The split construction, *is either unfamiliar or doesn't care*, never gets completed. Leave out the idea following the *or* and the sentence reads: "is unfamiliar the urgent need." Nonsense! The sentence should read: "The students are critical of the dean because he is either unfamiliar with or doesn't care about the urgent need for new student housing on campus."

> Baseball has and probably always will be the sport that symbolizes for people in other countries the American way of life.

The first half of the split verb construction is never completed. Leave out the second idea and the sentence reads "Baseball has the sport." The sentence should read "Baseball has been and probably always will be the sport that symbolizes for people in other countries the American way of life."

### 3. Verb Tense

The choice of verb tenses in a correctly written sentence reflects the sequence of events described.

> **EXAMPLES:**
>
> The teacher began to discuss the homework assignment when he will be interrupted by the sound of the fire alarm.

The sentence reads "The teacher began . . .and will be interrupted." One or the other verb tense is wrong. The sentence can be corrected by changing *will be interrupted* to *was interrupted*. Corrected, the sentence reads: "The teacher began to discuss the homework assignment when he was interrupted by the sound of the fire alarm."

> The conductor announced that the concert would resume as soon as the soloist replaces the broken string on her violin.

There is a mismatch between the verbs *would resume* and *replaces* in the second sentence. The sentence reads: *the concert would resume as soon as the soloist replaces*. Corrected, the sentence might read: "The conductor announced that the concert would resume as soon as the soloist replaced the broken string on her violin."

> Many patients begin to show symptoms again after they stopped taking the drug.

This sentence reads: *patients show symptoms after they stopped*. The sentence can be corrected by changing *stopped* to *stop*. The sentence would read: "Many patients begin to show symptoms again after they stop taking the drug."

### 4. Logical Errors

Sometimes a sentence will "want" to say one thing but end up saying something completely illogical.

> **EXAMPLES:**
>
> The great pianist Vladimir Horowitz played the music of the romantic era better than any pianist in history.

As written, the first sentence asserts that Vladimir Horowitz was better than anyone —including himself. But that is a logical impossibility. The sentence should read: "The great pianist Vladimir Horowitz played the music of the romantic era better than any other pianist in history."

> Educators are now expressing their concern that American schoolchildren prefer watching television to books.

The sentence makes an illogical comparison between *watching television* and *books*. Watching television is an activity; the books are objects. The sentence should read: "Educators are now expressing their concern that American schoolchildren prefer watching television to reading books."

> The novels of Nathaniel Hawthorne contain characters that are every bit as sinister and frightening as the master of cinematic suspense, Alfred Hitchcock.

This sentence, too, commits the error just discussed. The sentence literally compares the characters in the novels of Nathaniel Hawthorne to Alfred Hitchcock, the person. The sentence should read: "The novels of Nathaniel Hawthorne contain characters that are every bit as sinister and frightening as those of the master of cinematic suspense, Alfred Hitchcock."

> A Japanese firm has developed a computer so small that users can carry it in their briefcase.

As written, the sentence asserts that all of the users have but a single, jointly owned briefcase. What the sentence means to say is that users can carry the new computer in their briefcases (plural). It should read: "A Japanese firm has developed a computer so small that users can carry it in their briefcases."

Another type of logical error tested is illogical transitions. Words like *therefore*, *consequently*, and *so* signal logical transitions.

> **EXAMPLE:**
>
> Carlos has a very pleasant personality and he is a talented musician; therefore, he gets good grades in school.

*Therefore* seems to signal a logical transition from the first two ideas to the third, but there is no logical connection between having a good personality and being a talented musician, on the one hand, and getting good grades, on the other. So the *therefore* is out of place. Substitute *and* for *therefore*. Here is an example of the correct use of *therefore*:

I see the newspaper is not on the front porch; therefore, my brother must already be home.

Words such as *moreover*, *further*, and *furthermore* signal the continuation of an idea.

> **EXAMPLE:**
>
> John had already been granted three extensions of the deadline; moreover, the dean refused to grant him another.

The two ideas in this sentence create a contrast, so the *moreover* is out of place. You could correct the sentence by substituting *so* for *moreover*.

*However*, *in spite of*, and *instead* are used to contrast ideas.

> **EXAMPLE:**
>
> A poll of students shows that Helen is the top choice for student body president. Helen, however, is likely to win the election.

The *however* seems to signal a contrasting idea, but the logic of the second sentence continues the idea of the first. You can correct the problem by eliminating the *however*:

A poll of students shows that Helen is the top choice for student body president. Consequently, Helen is likely to win the election.

## 5. Sentence Fragments

A sentence must have a main verb.

> **EXAMPLE:**
>
> Post-modern art, with its vibrant colors and bold shapes, taking its inspiration from artists such as Cézanne but reacting against the pastel indistinctness of the Impressionist canvases.

The original sentence lacks a main verb. This is corrected by changing *taking* and *reacting* (which function as adjectives modifying *art*) to *took* and *reacted*. So, the corrected sentence reads:

Post-modern art, with its vibrant colors and bold shapes, took its inspiration from artists such as Cézanne but reacted against the pastel indistinctness of the Impressionist canvases.

## 6. Excessive Wordiness

Watch out for excessive wordiness.

> **EXAMPLES:**
>
> After months of separation, Gauguin finally joined Van Gogh in Arles in October of 1888, although Gauguin left a few weeks later.

This sentence is awkward and needlessly wordy. It would be more concise to say: "After months of separation, Gauguin finally joined Van Gogh in Arles but left a few weeks later."

> The nineteenth-century composers Wagner and Mahler did more than just write music; as composers they did their own works.

This sentence is also awkward and needlessly wordy. The very same idea can be expressed more directly:

The nineteenth-century composers Wagner and Mahler did more than just write music; they conducted their own works.

Some underlined expressions are needlessly repetitious.

> **EXAMPLES:**
>
> Since only the ruling party is allowed to vote, its members are able to maintain the existing status quo.
>
> Each year, the geese make their annual migration from Northern Canada to their winter habitats in the United States.
>
> Although the committee met for over two weeks and issued a 50 page report, its findings were of little importance or consequence.

Each of these sentences contains needless repetition. The first can be corrected by eliminating *existing*. The second can be corrected by eliminating either *each year* or *annual*. The third can be corrected be eliminating either *importance* or *consequence*.

## 7. Misplaced Modifiers

Another error that is frequently made by writers is the problem of the misplaced modifier.

> **EXAMPLES:**
>
> Wrapped in several thicknesses of newspaper, packed carefully in a strong cardboard carton, and bound securely with tape, the worker made sure that the fragile figurines would not be broken.

The sentence as originally written suggests that it was the worker who was wrapped, packed, and bound. In general, a modifier should be placed as closely as possible to the part of the sentence it is to modify. The corrected version of this sentence reads: "To make sure that the figurines would not be broken, the worker wrapped them in several thicknesses of newspaper, packed them carefully in a strong cardboard carton, and securely bound the carton with tape."

> Riding in a coach and wearing the crown jewels, the crowd cheered the royal couple.

The sentence as originally written suggests that the crowd is wearing the crown jewels and riding in the carriage. This sentence can be made clear by changing it to: "Riding in a coach and wearing the crown jewels, the royal couple was cheered by the crowd."

6

(Answers, page 65)

**Directions:** The following exercise contains 25 sentences. Each sentence makes a grammatical error of the sort just reviewed. Circle the letter of the underlined part of the sentence containing the error.

1. The owner of the collection <u>requested that</u> the museum <u>require</u> all people <u>with a camera</u>
   <sub>A</sub>     <sub>B</sub>     <sub>C</sub>
   <u>to leave</u> them at the door.
   <sub>D</sub>

2. The young comic <u>found</u> that capturing the audience's attention was easy, <u>but to maintain</u>
   <sub>A</sub>     <sub>B</sub>
   <u>their</u> interest <u>was</u> difficult.
   <sub>C</sub>     <sub>D</sub>

3. <u>Written in almost total isolation from the world</u>, Emily Dickinson <u>spoke of</u> love <u>and</u>
   <sub>A</sub>     <sub>B</sub>     <sub>C</sub>
   death in <u>her</u> poems.
   <sub>D</sub>

4. <u>Early in his career</u>, the pianist entertained thoughts <u>of becoming</u> a composer; but after
   <sub>A</sub>     <sub>B</sub>
   receiving bad reviews for his own work, <u>he</u> <u>had given it up</u>.
   <sub>C</sub>     <sub>D</sub>

5. The praying mantis <u>is welcomed by</u> homeowners for its ability <u>to control</u> destructive
   <sub>A</sub>     <sub>C</sub>
   garden pests, <u>unlike the cockroach which serves no useful function</u>.
   <sub>D</sub>

6. The fact that she is bright, articulate, and <u>has charisma</u> will <u>serve</u> her well in her
   <sub>A</sub>     <sub>B</sub>
   campaign for governor, <u>particularly</u> since her opponent <u>has none</u> of those qualities.
   <sub>C</sub>     <sub>D</sub>

7. Puritans such as William Bradford <u>displaying</u> the courage and piety <u>needed to survive</u>
   <sub>A</sub>     <sub>B</sub>
   in the New World, a world <u>both</u> promising and threatening <u>which</u> offered unique
   <sub>C</sub>     <sub>D</sub>
   challenges to their faith.

8. The baseball game was halted due to rain and <u>rescheduled</u> for the following day,
   <sub>A</sub>
   <u>even though</u> the fans <u>would not leave</u> the stadium.
   <sub>B</sub>     <sub>C</sub>     <sub>D</sub>

9. Unfortunately, <u>before</u> cures are found for diseases such as cancer, many lives
   <sub>A</sub>
   <u>would have been</u> lost and millions of dollars in medical services <u>spent to treat symptoms</u>
   <sub>B</sub>     <sub>C</sub>
   <u>rather than</u> provide a cure.
   <sub>D</sub>

10. <u>Being highly qualified for the position</u>, the bank president <u>will conduct</u> a final interview
    <sub>A</sub>     <sub>B</sub>
    of the new candidate tomorrow, <u>after which</u> <u>he will make</u> her a job offer.
    <sub>C</sub>     <sub>D</sub>

11. For many people it is difficult <u>to accept</u> compliments graciously and <u>even more difficult</u>
    <sub>A</sub>     <sub>B</sub>
    <u>taking</u> criticism <u>graciously</u>.
    <sub>C</sub>     <sub>D</sub>

12. The literature of Native Americans <u>has been overlooked</u> by <u>most</u> scholars, and the
    <sub>A</sub>     <sub>B</sub>
    reason is <u>because</u> most university courses in literature <u>are taught</u> in departments that
    <sub>C</sub>     <sub>D</sub>
    also teach a language, such as French.

13. The French poet Artaud <u>believed</u> <u>that</u>, <u>following</u> the climax of a drama, the audience
                                **A**    **B**    **C**
    <u>experienced</u> a violent catharsis and is thereby "reborn."
      **D**

14. <u>In broken English</u>, the police officer patiently listened to the tourist ask for directions to
    **A**
    Radio City Music Hall, <u>after which</u> she <u>motioned</u> the tourist and his family into the
                       **B**       **C**
    squad car and drove <u>them</u> to their destination.
                 **D**

15. Bullfighting <u>remains</u> a controversial sport and <u>many</u> are repulsed by it, <u>since</u> Hemingway
             **A**                    **B**       **C**
    was an aficionado of the sport and glorified <u>it</u> in his writing.
                                 **D**

16. <u>Wagering</u> on the Kentucky Derby favorite is a bad <u>betting</u> <u>proposition</u>, for in the last
    **A**                            **B**    **C**
    fifteen years, the horse that was the crowd favorite at post time of the Kentucky Derby
    <u>loses</u> the race.
    **D**

17. <u>Following the recent crash of the stock market</u>, Peter <u>bought</u> a book on portfolio
                      **A**                 **B**
    management <u>in order to learn</u> methods to protect his investments
                 **C**
    <u>from a well-known investment banker</u>.
              **D**

18. During the years she spent <u>searching for a cure</u> for the disease, Dr. Thompson
               **A**         **B**
    interviewed hundreds of patients, ran thousands of tests, and <u>cross-checking</u> millions
                                              **C**
    of bits of data.
        **D**

19. <u>Since</u> we have a <u>broader</u> technological base, American scientists believe that our space
    **A**         **B**
    program <u>will ultimately prove</u> superior <u>to the Soviet Union</u>.
                 **C**               **D**

20. Although a person may always represent <u>himself</u> in a judicial proceeding, licensed
                                     **A**
    lawyers <u>only</u> may represent <u>others</u> in <u>such</u> proceedings for a fee.
         **B**                **C**     **D**

21. <u>Unlike the pale and delicately built ballerinas of romantic ballet</u>, Judith Jamison's
                         **A**
    movement <u>seems</u> <u>more African than</u> European-American, and her physical appearance
             **B**       **C**
    <u>reinforces</u> the contrast.
    **D**

22. Market experts <u>predict</u> that in ten years, when the harmful effects of caffeine become
                 **A**
    <u>more generally known</u>, the number of tons of decaffeinated coffee <u>consumed by</u>
    **B**                                               **C**
    Americans each year will exceed <u>coffee containing caffeine</u>.
                                **D**

23. Illiteracy, <u>a widespread problem in the United States</u>, <u>undermines</u> productivity because
                       **A**             **B**
    many mistakes are made by workers who do not know how to read <u>on the job</u>.
             **C**                                   **D**

24. Because sailors are often <u>assigned</u> to ships <u>that remain</u> at sea for months at a time, men
                      **A**           **B**
    in the Navy <u>spend</u> more time away from home <u>than any branch of the service</u>.
           **C**                         **D**

25. <u>Like A.J. Ayer</u>, much of Gilbert Ryle's philosophical argumentation <u>relies</u> on an analysis
    **A**                                         **B**
    of the way <u>people</u> <u>ordinarily</u> use language.
             **C**      **D**

6

# Explanatory Answers

### EXERCISE 1

1. (A) *Harsh* is intended to modify *deals*, a verb. The adverb *harshly* is needed here.

2. (D) *Them* is intended to be a pronoun substitute for *advertising*, but *advertising* is singular, not plural. *It* should replace *them*.

3. (D) *You* is intended to refer to *one*, but *one* is in the third person while *you* is in the second person. The sentence could be corrected simply by omitting the second pronoun altogether.

4. (C) *Which* has no clear referent. *Which* might refer either to *horrifying conditions* or to *English boarding schools*. The ambiguity could be avoided by rewording the sentence: "... about the horrifying conditions in the English boarding schools, conditions which he learned about...."

5. (C) *It* has no clear referent. *It* might refer either to the movement or to the manifesto. The sentence can be corrected by including an appropriate noun to clarify the speaker's meaning, e.g., "... of a manifesto, a work that incorporated...."

6. (D) *Capable* is intended to modify *played*, a verb. So the adverb form must be used: "... played capably."

7. (B) *Who* and *whom* are the correct pronouns to use for people: "... countryside who sheltered ...."

8. (B) *We* cannot be used as the object of *to*. The correct choice of pronoun is *us*.

9. (A) When a pronoun is used to modify a gerund, the pronoun must be in the possessive case: "Your taking the initiative...."

10. (C) *Which* has no clear antecedent. Had the speaker hoped to avoid the conference or just being selected to be the representative of the group at the conference? To avoid the ambiguity, the sentence will have to be substantially revised: "... at the conference, and I had hoped to avoid the conference altogether."

11. (C) *Whom* should be used here instead of *which*, since the pronoun refers to *person*.

12. (D) The subject of the main clause is *none*, a singular pronoun, so the verb should be *is* rather than *are*.

13. (B) The subject of the sentence is *differences*, a plural noun, so the verb should be *help* rather than *helps*.

14. (B) *Hardly no* is a double negative. The sentence should read *hardly any*.

15. (B) The subject of the sentence is *diaries*, a plural noun. So the verb should be *provide* rather than *provides*.

16. (D) *Its* intends to refer to *whales*, so the sentence should use the plural pronoun *their*.

17. (A) A pronoun used to modify a gerund must be in the possessive case: "His being at the rally...."

**18.** (D) *Satisfactory* is either intended to modify *working* or *system*. If it modifies *working*, then the adverb should be used: "...and more than satisfactorily." If the word modifies *system*, then another verb is required: "...and is more than satisfactory."

**19.** (B) *Who* is intended to be the object of the verb *married*, so the objective case pronoun *whom* is required.

**20.** (B) *Recent* is intended to modify *constructed*, an adjective. But an adjective cannot be used to modify another adjective. Here the adverb *recently* should be used.

**21.** (D) *Which* has no clear referent. Were the faculty angry because the resolution passed or because it passed with few dissenting votes? The sentence must be rewritten to clarify the speaker's intention.

**22.** (D) *Your* is intended to refer *one's*, so you need some kind of third person pronoun, for example, *his or her*.

**23.** (D) *It* lacks a referent. *It* seems to refer to something like *insurance*, but there is no such noun in the sentence. The sentence could be corrected by using the noun *insurance* in place of the pronoun *it*.

**24.** (C) *Candid* is intended to modify *wrote*, so the sentence must use the adverb *candidly*.

**25.** (A) The sentence commits the error of the "ubiquitous they." The sentence can be corrected by using a noun in place of the *they*.

## EXERCISE 2

**1.** (C) The sentence commits an error of logical expression, because it implies that all the people coming into the museum have but a single camera. It could be corrected by changing *camera* to *cameras*.

**2.** (B) The sentence is flawed by faulty parallelism. It could be corrected by changing *to maintain* to *maintaining*.

**3.** (A) The sentence is afflicted with a dangling modifier. As written, the sentence implies that Emily Dickinson herself was written. To correct this error, it would have to be rewritten to bring the introductory modifier closer to the noun it modifies (*poems*): "The poems by Emily Dickinson, written in almost total isolation from the world, spoke of love and death."

**4.** (D) The use of the perfect tense *had given up* is not consistent with the use of the past tense *entertained*, for the use of the perfect tense implies that the pianist gave up his attempt to become a composer before he even entertained the idea of becoming one. The sentence can be corrected by substituting *gave up* for *had given up*.

**5.** (D) The final phrase is out of place. As written, the sentence implies that the cockroach is unlike destructive garden pests, but the speaker means to say that the cockroach is not like the praying mantis. The sentence can be corrected by relocating the offending phrase closer to the noun it modifies: "The praying mantis, unlike the cockroach, which serves no useful function, is welcomed by homeowners...."

**6.** (A) The sentence is flawed by a lack of parallelism, an error that can be corrected by substituting the adjective *charismatic* for the phrase *has charisma*.

**7.** (A) This item is a sentence fragment that lacks a conjugated verb. The fragment can be changed into a complete sentence by substituting *displayed* for *displaying*.

**8.** (B) The sentence commits an error of illogical expression, for, as written, it implies that the fans' leaving the stadium would ordinarily be sufficient to halt a game and reschedule it for later. The problem of illogical expression can be corrected by substituting the conjunction *but* for *even though*. (This particular error of logical expression is called illogical subordination.)

**9.** (B) The use of the subjunctive *would have been* is illogical. The use of the subjunctive incorrectly implies that the loss of lives and money is contingent upon some event, but no such event is mentioned in the sentence. The sentence can be corrected by substituting *will have been*.

**10.** (A) The sentence is afflicted with a dangling modifier. As written, it implies that the bank president is highly qualified for the position. The sentence needs substantial revision: "The bank president will conduct a final interview of the new candidate tomorrow. Since the candidate is highly qualified for the position, the president will make her a job offer after the interview."

**11.** (C) The sentence suffers from a lack of parallelism. This deficiency can be corrected by changing *taking* to *to take*. (In any event, the use of the gerund, *taking*, instead of the infinitive, *to take*, is not idiomatic, a point taken up in the next part of this lesson.)

**12.** (C) The sentence commits an error of logical expression by implying that the *reason* is an effect of some other cause, when the speaker really means to say that the *reason* and the *cause* are the same thing, the explanation for the phenomenon. The error can be corrected by substituting *that* for *because*. (**Note:** This use of *because* to introduce a noun clause can also be considered an example of an expression that is not acceptable in English usage, a point taken up in the next part of this lesson.)

**13.** (D) The tense of the first verb is not consistent with the tense of the second verb. The sentence can be corrected by substituting *experiences* for *experienced*.

**14.** (A) The sentence contains a dangling modifier. As written, it implies that the police officer is listening *in* broken English (not listening *to* broken English). The sentence can be corrected by relocating the modifier: "The police officer patiently listened to the tourist ask in broken English for directions to Radio City Music Hall, . . . ."

**15.** (C) The choice of *since* is illogical, because *since* implies that there is a causal or explanatory connection between Hemingway's view of bullfighting and the fact that bullfighting is a controversial sport that repulses some people. The problem of illogical subordination can be corrected by substituting *but* for *since*.

**16.** (D) The use of the present tense *loses* is illogical and inconsistent with the use of the past tense *was* earlier in the sentence. The error can be corrected by substituting *lost* for *loses*.

**17.** (D) The sentence contains a misplaced modifier. As written, it implies that Peter hopes to learn how to protect his investments from the threat posed by a well-known investment banker. The sentence must be rewritten: ". . . in order to learn from a well-known investment banker methods to protect his investments."

**18.** (C) The elements of the sentence are not parallel. The sentence would be correct if *cross-checked* were substituted for *cross-checking*.

**19.** (D) The sentence makes an error of logical expression, for it seems to compare our space program to the Soviet Union. The error can be eliminated by using the phrase *to that of* instead of *to* immediately after *superior*.

**20.** (B) The sentence contains a misplaced modifier. The placement of *only* seems to imply a restriction on the verb rather than on the subject. The sentence can be easily corrected by moving *only* and placing it just before *licensed lawyers.*

**21.** (A) The sentence contains a dangling modifier and seems to compare ballerinas of the romantic ballet with the movement of Judith Jamison. To correct this error, the sentence would have to be substantially rewritten: "Judith Jamison's movement seems more African than European-American, and her physical appearance, which is unlike the pale and delicately built ballerinas of romantic ballet, reinforces the contrast."

**22.** (D) The sentence contains an error of logical expression. It attempts to compare an amount of decaffeinated coffee with coffee containing caffeine. The sentence can be corrected by inserting clarifying phrases: ". . . the number of tons of coffee containing caffeine consumed by Americans."

**23.** (D) The sentence contains a misplaced modifier. As written, it implies that the workers are illiterate because they don't know how to read on the job. The sentence can be corrected by relocating the offending phrase so that it is closer to the noun it modifies: ". . . many mistakes are made on the job by workers . . . ."

**24.** (D) The sentence makes an illogical statement. It attempts to compare *time* and *branch of the service*. The sentence can be corrected by inserting a clarifying phrase: ". . . than do men in any other branch . . . ."

**25.** (A) The sentence contains a dangling modifier. As written, it implies a comparison between A.J. Ayer, the person, and the philosophical writings of Gilbert Ryle. The error can be corrected in the following way: "Like the writing of A.J. Ayer, much of . . . ."

6

# English Usage: Part II

# Nonidiomatic Expressions

Often, sentences are not correct because they are not "idiomatic." An expression that is not idiomatic is one that is not acceptable English for any of several reasons.

## 1. Wrong Prepositions

In English, as in other languages, only certain prepositions can be used with certain verbs.

> **EXAMPLES:**
>
> In contrast of the prevailing opinion, the editorial places the blame for the strike on the workers and their representatives.

In this sentence, the expression *in contrast of* is not idiomatic. The expression should be *in contrast to*. So the sentence would read: "In contrast to the prevailing opinion, the editorial places the blame for the strike on the workers and their representatives."

> Although ballet and modern dance are both concerned in movement in space to musical accompaniment, the training for ballet is more rigorous than that for modern dance.

The expression *concerned in* is not idiomatic. The sentence should read: "Although ballet and modern dance are both concerned with movement in space to musical accompaniment, the training for ballet is more rigorous than that for modern dance."

## 2. Right Idea, Wrong Word

Make sure the you use words that mean what you intend to say. Be careful not to use an incorrect word that sounds like the word you really mean to use.

> **EXAMPLES:**
>
> By midnight the guests still had not been served anything to eat and they were ravishing.

The first sentence intends to state that the guests were very hungry, but that is not the meaning of the word *ravishing*. The sentence can be corrected by changing *ravishing* to *ravenous*. Corrected, the sentence reads: "By midnight the guests still had not been served anything to eat and they were ravenous."

> The raise in the number of accidents attributable to drunk drivers has prompted a call for stiffer penalties for driving while intoxicated.

This sentence can be corrected by changing *raise* to *rise*. The correct sentence reads: "The rise in the number of accidents attributable to drunk drivers has prompted a call for stiffer penalties for driving while intoxicated."

### 3. Gerund versus Infinitive

The infinitive is the "to" form of a verb, and the gerund is one of the "-ing" forms of a verb. Both are used as nouns. In some circumstances you can use either: "Adding an extra room to the house is the next project", or "To add an extra room to the house is the next project." In some circumstances, however, gerund and infinitive are not interchangeable.

**EXAMPLES:**

> The idea of trying completing the term paper by Friday caused Ken to cancel his plans for the weekend.

Although *completing* can be a noun, here you need the infinitive. The first sentence should read: "The idea of trying to complete the term paper by Friday caused Ken to cancel his plans for the weekend."

> Psychologists think that many people eat satisfying a need for affection that is not otherwise fulfilled.

Again you need the infinitive, not the gerund. The sentence should read: "Psychologists think that many people eat to satisfy a need for affection that is not otherwise fulfilled."

### 4. Unacceptable Expressions

There are a few expressions that are heard frequently in conversation that are regarded as low-level usage and unacceptable in standard written English.

**EXAMPLES:**

> Being that the hour was late, we agreed to adjourn the meeting and reconvene at nine o'clock the following morning.

*Being that* is not acceptable in standard written English. The sentence is corrected by changing the phrase to *Since*. The sentence should read: "Since the hour was late, we agreed to adjourn the meeting and reconvene at nine o'clock the following morning."

> Why some whales beach themselves in what seems to be a kind of suicide remains a mystery to marine biologists.

*Why* cannot be the subject of a sentence. The sentence is corrected by changing *Why* to *That*. So, the sentence now reads: "That some whales beach themselves in what seems to be a kind of suicide remains a mystery to marine biologists."

> The reason Harriet fired her secretary is because he was frequently late and spent too much time on personal phone calls.

*Because* cannot introduce a noun clause. The sentence is corrected by changing *because* to *that*. The corrected sentence reads: "The reason Harriet fired her secretary is that he was frequently late and spent too much time on personal phone calls."

> I read in a magazine where scientists believe that they have discovered a new subatomic particle.

*Where* cannot introduce a noun clause. The sentence is corrected by changing *where* to *that*. So the corrected sentence reads: "I read in a magazine that scientists believe that they have discovered a new subatomic particle."

(Answers, page 84)

**Directions:** The following exercise contains 15 sentences. Each sentence makes a grammatical error of the sort just reviewed. Circle the letter of the underlined part of the sentence containing the error.

1. Economists <u>have established</u> that there is a <u>relation</u>—albeit an indirect one—between
   A ........................ B
   the <u>amount</u> of oil imported into this country and the <u>number</u> of traffic accidents.
   C ........................................................ D

2. Ironically, Elizabeth I and <u>her</u> rival for the English throne, Mary Stuart, <u>whom</u> <u>she</u> had
   A ........................................................ B .. C
   executed, <u>lay</u> side by side in Westminster Abbey.
   D

3. Although the script is interesting and well-written, it is not clear <u>whether</u> it can be
   A
   <u>adopted</u> for television since the original story contains scenes that <u>could not be broadcast</u>
   B ........................................................ C
   <u>over</u> the public airwaves.
   D

4. If he <u>had known</u> how difficult law school would be, he <u>would of chosen</u> a different
   A ........................................ B
   profession or perhaps even <u>have followed</u> the <u>tradition</u> of going into the family business.
   C ........................ D

5. When shopping malls and business complexes <u>get built</u>, quite often the needs of the
   A
   handicapped <u>are</u> not considered; as a result, it later becomes necessary to make <u>costly</u>
   B ........................................................ C
   modifications to structures to make them <u>accessible</u> to persons of impaired mobility.
   D

6. Researchers <u>have found</u> that children <u>experience</u> twice as much deep sleep <u>than</u>
   A ........................ B ........................................ C
   adults, a fact <u>which may</u> teach us something about the connection between age and
   D
   learning ability.

7. <u>Despite</u> the ample evidence that smoking <u>is hazardous</u> to one's health, <u>many</u> people
   A ........................................ B ........................ C
   seem to find the warnings neither frightening <u>or</u> convincing.
   D

8. No matter how <u>many</u> encores the audience demands, Helen Walker <u>is always willing</u>
   A ........................................................ B
   to sing <u>yet</u> another song <u>which pleases</u> the audience.
   C ........................ D

9. In light of <u>recent</u> translations of stone carvings <u>describing</u> scenes of carnage, scholars
   A ........................................ B
   are now questioning <u>as to whether</u> the Incas were <u>really</u> a peace-loving civilization.
   C ........................ D

10. In galleries containing works of both Gauguin and Cézanne, you will find an equal
    number of admirers <u>in front of</u> the works of <u>each</u>, but most art critics agree that
    A ........................ B ........................ C
    Gauguin is not of the same artistic stature <u>with</u> Cézanne.
    D

11. The Board of Education <u>will never be</u> <u>fully</u> <u>responsive</u> to the needs of Hispanic children
    A ........ B ........ C
    in the school system so long <u>that</u> the Mayor refuses to appoint a Hispanic educator to
    D
    the Board.

12. The judge <u>sentenced</u> the president of the corporation to ten years in prison for
                 A
   <u>embezzling</u> corporate funds but <u>gave</u> his partner in crime <u>less of a sentence.</u>
      B                  C             D

13. Scientists <u>have recently discovered</u> that mussels <u>secrete</u> a powerful adhesive that
                 A                    B
   allows them <u>attaching</u> themselves to rocks, concrete pilings, and <u>other</u> stone or masonry
              C                             D
   structures.

14. Wall paintings found recently in the caves of Brazil are <u>convincing</u> evidence that cave art
                                                   A
   <u>developed</u> in the Americas at an earlier time <u>as</u> <u>it</u> did on other continents.
     B                                  C D

15. The <u>drop</u> in oil prices and the slump in the computer industry <u>account for</u> the recent
      A                                           B
   <u>raise</u> in unemployment in Texas and the <u>associated</u> decline in the value of real
    C                            D
   estate in the region.

# Punctuation Errors

## 1. Commas

Use a comma before *and*, *but*, *so*, *yet*, *or*, and *nor* when those words are used to join two main clauses.

**EXAMPLES:**

I think that Doré's illustrations of Dante's *Divine Comedy* are excellent, but my favorite drawing is "Don Quixote in His Library."

Practically all nitrates are crystalline and readily soluble, and they are characterized by marked decrepitation when heated on charcoal by a blowpipe.

The general rule stated above should be qualified in two respects. First, when the two clauses joined by the conjunction are very short, the comma is optional.

**EXAMPLE:**

The door was ajar and the house had been ransacked.
The door was ajar, and the house had been ransacked.

Each of the sentences is correct.

For clarity, if either clause itself contains commas, you may need to use a semicolon before the conjunction.

**EXAMPLE:**

Because many diseases and insects cause serious damage to crops, special national legislation has been passed to provide for the quarantine of imported plants; and under provisions of various acts, inspectors are placed at ports of entry to prevent smugglers from bringing in plants that might be dangerous.

Given the length of the two clauses and the fact that each clause contains a comma, you should use a semicolon following *plants*, rather than a comma.

Use commas to separate the elements of a series.

**EXAMPLES:**

A full train crew consists of a motorman, a brakeman, a conductor, and two ticket takers.

The procedure requires that you open the outer cover plate, remove the thermostat, replace the broken switch, and then replace the thermostat.

Use a comma to separate a subordinate clause at the beginning of a sentence from the main clause.

**EXAMPLES:**

After Peter finished painting the bird feeder, he and Jack hung it from a limb of the oak tree.

When Pat explained to his mother that ten was the highest mark given on the entrance test, she breathed a sigh of relief.

If the subordinate clause follows the main clause, you do not need to set it off with a comma.

**EXAMPLE:**

Tim hopes to score well on the exam because he plans to go to an Ivy League school.

Use a comma after a long introductory phrase.

**EXAMPLES:**

In this impoverished region with its arid soil, a typical diet may contain only 800 calories per day.

At the height of the moral war against sensational journalism, Horace Greeley moved into the forefront of the journalistic picture.

Regardless of their length, use a comma after introductory gerunds, participles, and infinitives.

**EXAMPLES:**

Begun in 1981 and completed in 1985, the bridge provided the first link between the island and the mainland.

To slow the bleeding, Van tied a tourniquet around the lower portion of the leg.

Use commas to set off nonrestrictive clauses and phrases and other parenthetical elements.

**EXAMPLES:**

Niagara Falls, which forms part of the border between the United States and Canada, was the site of a saw mill built by the French in 1725.

The second Nicene Council, the seventh ecumenical council of the Church, was summoned by the Empress Irene and her son Constantine.

The last hope of the French expired when Metz, along with 180,000 soldiers, was surrendered by Bazaine.

Secretary of State Acheson, however, made a reasoned defense of the treaty.

(Nonrestrictive clauses and phrases are ones not essential to the meaning of the main clause. In general, if you can omit the material without changing the meaning of the main clause, then the material is nonrestrictive and should be set off by commas.)

These rules summarize the most important uses of commas. If you use them in just these situations, then you won't make a mistake in their use. In particular, do **NOT** use commas in the following situations.

Do not use a comma to separate a subject from its verb.

**EXAMPLE:**

Until the end of the 18th century, the only musicians in Norway, were simple unsophisticated peasants who traveled about.

(The underlined comma is incorrect.)

Do not use commas to set off restrictive or necessary clauses or phrases.

**EXAMPLES:**

Prizes will be awarded in each event, and the participant, who compiles the greatest overall total, will receive a special prize.

Since learning of the dangers of caffeine, neither my wife nor I have consumed any beverage, containing caffeine.

(The underlined commas are incorrect.)

Do not use a comma in place of a conjunction.

**EXAMPLE:**

After months of separation, Gauguin finally joined Van Gogh in Arles in October of 1888, Gauguin left a few weeks later.

The sentence is incorrect because clauses cannot be spliced together using only a comma. If you want to join two main clauses, you can use a conjunction (such as *and*) plus a comma or semicolon or even just a semicolon. The sentence above could have been written: "After months of separation, Gauguin finally joined Van Gogh in Arles in October of 1888, but Gauguin left a few weeks later."

## 2. Semicolons

One use of the semicolon has already been mentioned: use a semicolon between main clauses linked by a coordinate conjunction (*and, but, etc.*) when the main clauses are complex, e.g., when they themselves contain commas. (See above.) Another use of semicolons is to separate two main clauses that are not linked by a coordinate conjunction.

**EXAMPLES:**

He grew up on a farm in Nebraska; he is now the captain of a navy ship.

The Smithtown players cheered the referee's decision; the Stonybrook players booed it.

Notice that in these examples, each clause separated by the semicolon could stand alone as an independent sentence.

He grew up on a farm in Nebraska. He is now the captain of a navy ship.

The Smithtown players cheered the referee's decision. The Stonybrook players booed it.

Unless each clause can function as an independent sentence, it probably is wrong to use a semicolon.

When John entered the room; everyone stood up.

Clem announced that the prize would be donated to Harbus House; a well-known charity.

The semicolons in the examples above are used incorrectly. Notice that the elements separated by the semicolons cannot stand as independent sentences.

When John entered the room.  Everyone stood up.

Clem announced that the prize would be donated to Harbus House.  A well known charity.

The sentences can be corrected by using commas in place of the semicolons.

## 3. Colons

A colon may be used to introduce or to call attention to elaboration or explanation.

### EXAMPLES:

The teacher announced that the course would require three papers: one on Shakespeare, one on Dickens, and one on a contemporary writer.

Will's suggestion was truly democratic: let everyone serve as chair for one meeting.

Be careful not to use a colon to introduce or call attention to material that is already signalled by some other element of the sentence.

### EXAMPLES:

The seemingly tranquil lane has been the scene of many crimes including: two assaults, three robberies, and one murder.

In addition to test scores, college admissions officers take into consideration many other factors such as: grades, extracurricular activities, and letters of recommendation.

In each example, the colon is used incorrectly because the special material is already signalled by some other element in the sentence:

The seeming tranquil lane has been the scene of many crimes including two assaults, three robberies, and one murder.

In addition to test scores, college admissions officers take into consideration many other factors such as grades, extracurricular activities, and letters of recommendation.

This shows that the colons in the original examples were superfluous and wrong.

## 4. Periods

The only use you should have for a period on the test is to mark the end of a sentence.  Make sure, however, that any underlined material that includes a period does not create a sentence fragment.

### EXAMPLE:

Peter notified <u>Elaine.  The</u> guidance counselor, that he had been accepted.

The first period creates a sentence fragment out of what follows.  The sentence can be corrected as follows:

Peter notified Elaine, the guidance counselor, that he had been accepted.

## 5. *Dashes*

Dashes can be used to set off for emphasis or clarity an explanatory, illustrative, or parenthetical remark.

> **EXAMPLES:**
>
> Careful attention to the details of one's personal appearance—neatly pressed clothing, shined shoes, and a neat haircut—is an important part of preparing for a job interview.
>
> Many colleges—including the nation's top schools—set aside a certain number of freshman seats for students who show academic promise in spite of low test scores.
>
> Peanuts—blanched or lightly roasted—add an interesting texture and taste to garden salads.

The dashes in the sentences above have a function similar to commas when they are used to set off parenthetical remarks. The difference between the two is a matter of emphasis. The dashes mark a more dramatic shift or interruption of thought. Do not, however, mix dashes and commas:

> Peanuts—blanched or lightly roasted, add an interesting texture and taste to garden salads.

The example above is incorrect. You must use either two dashes or two commas.

# Punctuating for Clarity

Punctuation is a part of written English because punctuation helps to make ideas clearer. (Imagine reading an entire book that consisted of one sentence several hundred pages long containing absolutely no punctuation.) The items on the English Usage part that test punctuation generally test punctuation as it pertains to clarity. Therefore, a good Holmesian strategy is this: when in doubt, read the sentence silently to yourself as though you were reading to an audience. Where you would pause reading aloud, you probably need some sort of punctuation.

The length of the pause is a pretty good measure of what kind of mark you need. For full stops, you need a period. For slight pauses, you need a comma. For intermediate-length pauses in between slight pauses, use a semicolon. And for special situations, use colons and dashes.

### EXAMPLE:

On Monday (slight pause) Mark received a letter of acceptance from State College (full stop) He immediately called his mother (pause) herself a graduate of State College (pause) to tell her about his acceptance (full stop) When he told her he had also been awarded a scholarship (slight pause) she was very excited (full stop) After hanging up (slight pause) Mark's mother decided to throw a surprise party for Mark (full stop) She telephoned his brother (slight pause) his sister (slight pause) and several of his friends (full stop) Because the party was supposed to be a surprise (pause) she made them all promise not to say anything to Mark (full stop) Mark (slight pause) however (slight pause) had a similar idea (pause) a party for his mother to celebrate his acceptance at her alma mater (full pause) He telephoned his brother (slight pause) his sister (slight pause) and several of his parents' friends to invite them to a party at his house on Saturday night (pause) and he made them all promise to say nothing to his mother (full stop) On Saturday night (slight pause) both Mark and his mother were surprised (full stop)

That is how you might read the paragraph above, and here is how you might punctuate it:

On Monday, Mark received a letter of acceptance from State College. He immediately called his mother—herself a graduate of State College—to tell her about his acceptance. When he told her he had also been awarded a scholarship, she was very excited. After hanging up, Mark's mother decided to throw a surprise party for Mark. She telephoned his brother, his sister, and several of his friends. Because the party was supposed to be a surprise, she made them all promise not to say anything to Mark. Mark, however, had a similar idea: a party for his mother to celebrate his acceptance at her alma mater. He telephoned his brother, his sister, and several of his parents' friends to invite them to a party on Saturday night, and he made them all promise to say nothing to his mother. On Saturday night, both Mark and his mother were surprised.

(Answers, page 84)

**Directions:** Punctuate the following sentences using commas, semicolons, and periods.

1. Neurology is the science that deals with the anatomy physiology and pathology of the nervous system

2. Nursery lore like everything human has been subject to many changes over long periods of time

3. In order to provide more living space we converted an attached garage into a den

4. Begun while Dickens was still at work on *Pickwick Papers Oliver Twist* was published in 1837 and is now one of the author's most widely read works

5. Given the great difficulties of making soundings in very deep water it is not surprising that few such soundings were made until the middle of this century

6. The root of modern Dutch was once supposed to be Old Frisian but the general view now is that the characteristic forms of Dutch are at least as old as those of Old Frisian

7. Moose once scarce because of indiscriminate hunting are protected by law and the number of moose is once again increasing

8. Perhaps the most interesting section of New Orleans is the French Quarter which extends from North Rampart Street to the Mississippi River

9. Writing for a skeptical and rationalizing age Shaftesbury was primarily concerned with showing that goodness and beauty are not determined by revelation authority opinion or fashion

10. A great deal of information regarding the nutritional requirements of farm animals has been accumulated over countless generations by trial and error but most recent advances have come as the result of systematic studies at schools of animal husbandry

11. *Omoo* Melville's sequel to *Typee* appeared in 1847 and went through five printings in that year alone.

12. Although the first school for Blacks was a public school established in Virginia in 1620 most educational opportunities for Blacks prior to the Civil War were provided by private agencies

13. As the climate of Europe changed the population became too dense for the supply of food obtained by hunting and other means of securing food such as the domestication of animals were necessary

14. In Faulkner's poetic realism the grotesque is somber violent and often inexplicable in Caldwell's writing it is lightened by a balladlike humorous sophisticated detachment

15. The valley of the Loir a northern tributary of the Loire at Angers abounds in rock villages and they occur in many other places in France Spain and northern Italy

# Organizing Your Attack on English Usage

The first thing to think about as we design an overall strategy for this test is how many questions you must answer and how much time you have to answer them. With 75 questions and only 40 minutes to answer them, you'll have to answer—on the average—one question every 32 seconds. Of course, some questions will take longer than others, so half a minute per question is just an approximation.

The reading selections in the English Usage Test are organized into paragraphs, and a couple of questions in the test may ask about the correct assignment of sentences to paragraphs. These "global" questions do require an understanding of the overall structure of the selection. Most questions, however, are "local" questions that can be answered using just one or two sentences. I recommend, therefore, that you NOT read through the entire selection before answering any questions. Instead, read one paragraph and answer the questions based on that paragraph, read the next paragraph and answer questions, and so on. Skip over any questions that ask about the "global" or overall organization of the selection. Then, after you have worked through the entire passage, go back and answer those.

When you answer a question that asks about the correct assignment of a sentence to a paragraph, keep in mind that a good paragraph is unified by a topic sentence. Locate the topic sentence and ask yourself whether the sentence in question belongs to that topic. Also, study the passage to determine whether there is an overall organizational theme, e.g., the author makes three points and clearly signals them by transitional phrases such as:

In the first place, . . . .
Moreover, . . . .
Finally, . . . .

Such transitional phrases clearly mark the divisions into paragraphs.

As you attack each individual item, use the technique of Anticipate and Test. First, try to determine what, if anything, is wrong with the underlined part and ANTICIPATE how it might be corrected. Then examine the choices. If a choice corresponds to your anticipated correction, then select that choice. If no choice corresponds exactly to your anticipated correction, then study the choices to find one that most closely matches your anticipated correction.

After you have identified a choice that you consider correct, TEST it. Substitute the choice for the underlined portion and read the sentence silently to yourself. If the sentence seems to read correctly, treat that choice as the correct choice.

If you still have not arrived at a final choice, study each answer choice. Many choices are incorrect because they make changes that introduce new errors. Substitute each choice for the original underlined part and consciously ask yourself whether the resulting sentence is incorrect. If the sentence that results from substituting an answer choice for the underlined part is incorrect, then the answer choice is definitely wrong—eliminate it.

Eliminate as many choices as you can. If more than one choice remains, then select one as your guess and move along to the next item.

Finally, do not be afraid to answer "NO CHANGE." For about one-fifth of the questions, "NO CHANGE" will be the correct response.

# English Usage Summary

1. Be alert for the following types of errors:

   —Subject–verb agreement
   —Pronoun usage (antecedents, ambiguity, case)
   —Adjectives and adverbs (correct modification)
   —Double negatives (incorrect)
   —Parallelism (similar elements in similar form)
   —Split constructions properly completed
   —Logical choice of verb tense
   —Logical expression
   —Sentence fragments
   —Excessive wordiness
   —Misplaced modifiers
   —Wrong prepositions
   —Right idea, wrong word
   —Gerund versus infinitive
   —Unacceptable expressions
   —Punctuation errors

2. Use the attack strategy of ANTICIPATE and TEST. Save "global" questions about the overall organization of the selection until last. Eliminate any choice that introduces a new mistake. And whenever you are unable to settle on one correct choice: GUESS!

7

# Explanatory Answers

## EXERCISE 1

1. (B) Substitute *relationship*.
2. (D) Substitute *lie*.
3. (B) Substitute *adapted*.
4. (B) Substitute *would have chosen*.
5. (A) Substitute *are built*.
6. (C) Substitute *as*.
7. (D) Substitute *nor*.
8. (D) Substitute *to please*.
9. (C) Substitute *whether*.
10. (D) Substitute *as*.
11. (D) Substitute *as*.
12. (D) Substitute *a shorter sentence*.
13. (C) Substitute *to attach*.
14. (C) Substitute *than*.
15. (C) Substitute *rise*.

## EXERCISE 2

1. Neurology is the science that deals with the anatomy, physiology, and pathology of the nervous system.
2. Nursery lore, like everything human, has been subject to many changes over long periods of time.
3. In order to provide more living space, we converted an attached garage into a den.
4. Begun while Dickens was still at work on *Pickwick Papers*, *Oliver Twist* was published in 1837 and is now one of the author's most widely read works.
5. Given the great difficulties of making soundings in very deep water, it is not surprising that few such soundings were made until the middle of this century.
6. The root of modern Dutch was once supposed to be Old Frisian, but the general view now is that the characteristic forms of Dutch are at least as old as those of Old Frisian.
7. Moose, once scarce because of indiscriminate hunting, are protected by law; and the number of moose is once again increasing. (You could use a comma in place of the semicolon.)
8. Perhaps the most interesting section of New Orleans is the French Quarter, which extends from North Rampart Street to the Mississippi River.

9. Writing for a skeptical and rationalizing age, Shaftesbury was primarily concerned with showing that goodness and beauty are not determined by revelation, authority, opinion, or fashion. (The final comma is optional.)

10. A great deal of information regarding the nutritional requirements of farm animals has been accumulated over countless generations by trial and error, but most recent advances have come as the result of systematic studies at schools of animal husbandry.

11. *Omoo*, Melville's sequel to *Typee*, appeared in 1847 and went through five printings in that year alone.

12. Although the first school for Blacks was a public school established in Virginia in 1620, most educational opportunities for Blacks prior to the Civil War were provided by private agencies.

13. As the climate of Europe changed, the population became too dense for the supply of food obtained by hunting; and other means of securing food, such as the domestication of animals, were necessary. (Here, given the complexity of the independent clauses, you should use a semicolon and not a comma.)

14. In Faulkner's poetic realism, the grotesque is somber, violent, and often inexplicable; in Caldwell's writing, it is lightened by a balladlike, humorous, sophisticated detachment. (The comma following *violent* is optional, but the comma following *humorous* is required—because there is no conjunction between *humorous* and *sophisticated*. The semicolon is required here. A comma would create a comma splice, because there is no conjunction to join the two clauses.)

15. The valley of the Loir, a northern tributary of the Loire at Angers, abounds in rock villages; and they occur in many other places in France, Spain, and northern Italy.

7

# English Usage Test

# Lesson 8

In this lesson you will find an English Usage Test.  There is no time limit for the test. Following the test, you will find explanations for the questions. Use this test as practice before trying the two timed tests that follow.

# English Usage Test

## Passage 1

In 1964, the U.S. Surgeon General issued his Report on Smoking and Health documenting the health hazards of smoking. During that time, the
<u>1</u>
incidence of smoking among adults has declined; but there is discouraging evidence that smoking among teenage boys has remained <u>constant virtually</u> and that
<u>2</u>

among teenage girls <u>is actually increasing.</u>
<u>3</u>

Prevention programs directed at children and adolescents have generally <u>focused to teach</u> children
<u>4</u>
and adolescents about the dangers of smoking—on the assumption that once they are aware of the dangers, children and adolescents will simply refuse to begin to smoke. <u>Moreover, it is evident</u> that fear of
<u>5</u>

the consequences of smoking may not <u>by themselves</u>
<u>6</u>
be sufficient to discourage most children from smoking as they approach adolescence.

Some investigators in this field have contended that at an earlier level of development, children

1.  A.  NO CHANGE
    B.  By that
    C.  Since that
    D.  That

2.  F.  NO CHANGE
    G.  virtually constant
    H.  virtual constant
    J.  constantly

3.  A.  NO CHANGE
    B.  is increasing actually.
    C.  actually increasing.
    D.  has actually increased.

4.  F.  NO CHANGE
    G.  focusing to teach
    H.  focus on teaching
    J.  focused on teaching

5.  A.  NO CHANGE
    B.  It is evident, moreover,
    C.  It is evident, however,
    D.  In spite of it, it is evident

6.  F.  NO CHANGE
    G.  in themselves
    H.  by itself
    J.  for itself

quite literally took the dangers of smoking.  In fact,
                    7

it is often observed at this level of development

that children may be especially worried if they

observe a parent or an older sibling smoking.

Yet, they will begin smoking.
        8


It is evident, therefore, that more knowledge is
                    9


needed about ways discouraging teenager smoking.
                    10

### Passage 2

The first Europeans who adapted Appalachia as

home, followed the trails pounded out by those earli-
    11

est mountain engineers: the buffalo, elk, deer, and
                    12

other wild game.  Later they found the great traces

forged by the Indian tribes on their trading and

fighting forays.  Gradually, these first Europeans hewed

out passages that become part of America's history
                    13

and portions of which may still be discovered along

today's interstates and backroads.  Their very names

connect us to the past in the region: The Great
    14

Warrior's Trail, Boone's Trace (which became the

Wilderness Road), and the Cumberland Gap.

Geographic isolation greatly influenced the re-
        15

gion's culture.  From the beginning, numerous ethnic

groups contributed to Appalachian settlement.  Dur-

ing the late 1600s and into the next century, Germans

7.  A.  NO CHANGE
    B.  took the dangers quite literally
    C.  quite literally has taken the dangers
    D.  take quite literally

8.  F.  NO CHANGE
    G.  Yet, they later begin
    H.  Further but later, they do begin
    J.  Beginning, however, later

9.  A.  NO CHANGE
    B.  so,
    C.  anyway,
    D.  nevertheless

10.  F.  NO CHANGE
    G.  to discourage teenager smoking
    H.  to discourage teenagers' smoking
    J.  to discourage teenagers from smoking

11.  A.  NO CHANGE
    B.  home followed
    C.  home, following
    D.  have followed

12.  F.  NO CHANGE
    G.  engineers, being
    H.  engineers, those being
    J.  engineers including:

13.  A.  NO CHANGE
    B.  became parts of
    C.  became part of
    D.  became part

14.  F.  NO CHANGE
    G.  connecting us to
    H.  connected us to
    J.  connect us for

15.  A.  NO CHANGE
    B.  Geographically isolated
    C.  Isolated geographically
    D.  Isolated geography

from the Rhineland settled in the Great Appalachian Valley.  Building fat barns and tight houses on the fertile fields of Pennsylvania, Maryland, Virginia, and North Carolina.  They were called "Pennsylvania Dutch."

One of the important contributions by the German settlers for frontier life was the Pennsylvania rifle—also called the Kentucky rifle and the Long rifle.  A weapon born of necessity and economy, its extended barrel assured greater accuracy and precision than could be achieved with the old muskets, and its smaller bore required less powder and lead for each shot (precious commodities).  Such rifles were highly prized possessions, and their manufacture was one of the central industries of pioneer Appalachia.

## Passage 3

Art of the Middle Ages is first, and foremost, a sacred script, the symbols and meanings of which are well settled. A circular halo placed vertically behind the head of a figure signifies sainthood, meanwhile the halo impressed with a cross signifies divinity.

A tower with a window indicates a village; and should an angel be watching from the battlements, that city would thereby be identified as Jerusalem.

16. F. NO CHANGE
    G. Valley, building
    H. Valley: building
    J. Valley, built

17. A. NO CHANGE
    B. by the German settlers with
    C. by the German settlers to
    D. made by the German settlers'

18. F. NO CHANGE
    G. accuracy as well as precision
    H. accuracy plus precision
    J. accuracy

19. A. NO CHANGE
    B. (place immediately after *powder*)
    C. (place immediately after *lead*)
    D. (place immediately after *shot*)

20. F. NO CHANGE
    G. is well settled
    H. are settled well
    J. would be well settled

21. A. NO CHANGE
    B. sainthood, because
    C. sainthood because
    D. sainthood, while

22. F. NO CHANGE
    G. (Do NOT begin a new paragraph) A tower
    H. Towers
    J. Having a tower

Mathematics, too, is an important element of this iconography. " The Divine Wisdom," wrote Saint Augustine, "reveals itself everywhere in numbers." A doctrine derived from the neo-platonists who revived the teachings of Pythagoras. And numbers require symmetry. At Chartres, a stained-glass window shows the four prophets Isaac, Ezekiel, Daniel, and Jeremiah carrying on their shoulders the four evangelists Matthew, Mark, Luke, and John.

Every painting is also an allegory, showing us one thing and invites us to see another. In this respect, the artist was asked to imitate God, who had hidden a profound meaning behind the literal and who wished nature to be a moral lesson to man. In a painting of the final judgment, the foolish virgins can be seen by us at the left hand of Jesus and the wise on the right, and we understand that this symbolizes those who are lost and those that have been saved.

Within such a system even the most mediocre talent was elevated by the genius of the centuries, and the first artists of the Renaissance broke with tradition at great risk. Even when they are great, they are no more than the equals of the old masters who

23. A. NO CHANGE
    B. numbers," which
    C. numbers," a doctrine
    D. numbers" which

24. F. NO CHANGE
    G. (Do NOT begin a new paragraph) Every painting
    H. (Begin a new paragraph) However, every painting
    J. (Do NOT begin a new paragraph) However, every painting

25. A. NO CHANGE
    B. inviting
    C. invited
    D. would invite

26. F. NO CHANGE
    G. one behind
    H. meaning being behind
    J. meaning behind and in back of

27. A. NO CHANGE
    B. OMIT
    C. by each of us
    D. by all of us

28. F. NO CHANGE
    G. those who have been saved
    H. those who are saved
    J. the saved

29. A. NO CHANGE
    B. (Do NOT begin a new paragraph) Within such a system
    C. (Do NOT begin a new paragraph) Inside of such a system
    D. (Do NOT begin a new paragraph) To be inside such a system

passively following the sacred rules; and when they are
___
30

not outstanding, they scarcely avoid banality and

insignificance in their religious works.

**30.** F. NO CHANGE
     G. passively followed
     H. following passively
     J. were following passively

## Passage 4

A persistent and universal symbol in the mythol-

ogy of virtually every culture, is that of a bottomless
___
31

pit or an engulfing whirlpool. It was the maw of the

abyss: and those venturing too close were dragged
___
32

inward toward Chaos by an irresistible force. Socrates

(a Greek philosopher who committed suicide)
___
33

talked of a chasm that pierced the world straight

through from side to side. Ulysses also encountering it
___
34

as did a mythical Cherokee who escaped, but not

before he was drawn down to the narrowest circle of

the maelstrom where he could peer in the nether
___
35

world of the dead.

On the other hand, the search for a solution to
___
36

one of astronomys' most persistent and perplexing
___
37

riddles, black holes, could be viewed by one as a
___
38

continuation of the search for the whirlpool that is the

maw of the abyss, a depth our telescopes cannot reach

**31.** A. NO CHANGE
     B. culture is
     C. culture are
     D. cultures are

**32.** F. NO CHANGE
     G. abyss, and those
     H. abyss, those
     J. abyss, while

**33.** A. NO CHANGE
     B. OMIT
     C. (a Greek philosopher who had committed suicide)
     D. (a philosopher from Greece who committed suicide)

**34.** F. NO CHANGE
     G. also encountered it
     H. also encountered them
     J. encountered them also

**35.** A. NO CHANGE
     B. could peer into
     C. can peer in
     D. can peer into

**36.** F. NO CHANGE
     G. (Do NOT begin a new paragraph.) The search
     H. (Begin a new paragraph.) The search
     J. (Begin a new paragraph.) Also, the search

**37.** A. NO CHANGE
     B. astronomy's
     C. astronomy
     D. astronomys

**38.** F. NO CHANGE
     G. OMIT
     H. by those
     J. by one astronomer

and from which nothing will have returned. What is
39

incredible to contemplate, and what sets us apart from
40

the ancients, is that not only do we think we have a

fair idea as to how they are formed, but how large they
41

are and so forth.  A combination of theory and

observation have led to the growing suspicion among
42

astrophysicists that the nucleus of virtually every gal-

axy harbors a massive black hole.

## Passage 5

Instead of casting aside traditional values during

the Meji Restoration of 1888, those who strove to

dismantle feudalism and to modernize the country

chose to preserve three traditions as the foundations

on which they could build a modern Japan upon.
43

The older tradition and basis of the entire Japan-
44

ese value system was respect for and even worshipping
45

the Emperor.  During the early centuries of Japanese

history, the Shinto cult, in which the imperial family

traced its ancestry to the Sun Goddess, became the

people's sustaining faith.  Being later subordinated to
46

imported Buddhism and Confucianism, Shintoism

was perpetuated in Ise and Izumo, the great shrines of

**39.** A. NO CHANGE
B. will return
C. returns
D. returning

**40.** F. NO CHANGE
G. setting us
H. and that sets us
J. and we are set

**41.** A. NO CHANGE
B. as
C. to
D. whereas to

**42.** F. NO CHANGE
G. has led to
H. has led
J. led

**43.** A. NO CHANGE
B. on which they were building a modern
Japan upon
C. on which they could build a modern Japan
D. upon which they will build a modern Japan

**44.** F. NO CHANGE
G. oldest
H. old
J. OMIT

**45.** A. NO CHANGE
B. respecting and even worshipping
C. respect for and even worship of
D. respect of and even worship

**46.** F. NO CHANGE
G. Later subordinated
H. Later subordinated,
J. Subordinated later,

the Imperial family, until the Meji modernizers estab-

lished it as a quasi state religion to unify the people

and restore the Emperor as the symbol of national

unity and the object of loyalty to the Japanese.
                                        47

   Another tradition that was enduring was the
                    48
hierarchical system of social relations based on feudal-

ism.  Confucianism prescribed a pattern by ethical
                              49
conduct between groups of people within a fixed

hierarchy.  Four of five Confucian relationships (those

between ruler and subject, husband and wife, father

and son, and elder brother and younger brother) were
                                                50

vertical since they required loyalty and obedience
              51
from the inferior toward the superior and benevolence

and protection from the superior to the inferior.  Only

the fifth relationship, that between friend and friend
                    52

—was horizontal.  A third tradition was respect for
                53

learning, another basic idea of Confucius's. In tradi-
                              54
tional Japan, study was the absolute duty of man.  It

was a religious mandate as well as a social duty and
                    55
was a means of promoting a harmonious and stable

47.  A.  NO CHANGE
     B.  the Japanese had
     C.  by the Japanese
     D.  for the Japanese

48.  F.  NO CHANGE
     G.  (Do NOT begin a new paragraph) Another
         tradition that was enduring
     H.  (Begin a new paragraph) Another tradition
     J.  (Begin a new paragraph) The other tradition

49.  A.  NO CHANGE
     B.  patterns by
     C.  a pattern of
     D.  patterns with

50.  F.  NO CHANGE
     G.  was
     H.  are
     J.  could be

51.  A.  NO CHANGE
     B.  vertical, they
     C.  vertical since it
     D.  vertical, being they

52.  F.  NO CHANGE
     G.  relationship that
     H.  relationship—that
     J.  relationship

53.  A.  NO CHANGE
     B.  (Begin a new paragraph) A
     C.  (Do NOT begin a new paragraph) Further,
         a
     D.  (Begin a new paragraph) Also a

54.  F.  NO CHANGE
     G.  Confucius idea
     H.  idea of Confucianism
     J.  Confucianism idea

55.  A.  NO CHANGE
     B.  mandate as well as being
     C.  mandate as well,
     D.  mandate,

society.  The individual's behavior was strictly prescribed by law and custom.  Only the Samurai had the

right to retaliate with force if they were displeased.

But his primary duty was to the lord.

## Passage 6

Georgia O'Keeffe, who's death at age ninety-
eight closed one of the most fertile chapters of Ameri-

can creativity and flourished as a maverick in her life

and work.  Since other painters spent a season or two

in the country trying to come to terms with the scenes

and settings of the Southwest—O'Keeffe stayed a

lifetime.  When the canvases of other artists, working

in the region faded from view and then were neglected

in the chronicle of American visual history, her styl-

ized images made an indelible and permanent impres-

sion on countless eyes.

Between 1900 and 1945, the region now called

New Mexico both fascinated and also it perplexed two

generations of American artists.  Despite successes,

many of those artists wearied of the industrial world

of the east.  The vast expanse of the American west

offered a promise for inspiration.  For these artists,

life and art, so separate in New York and Paris, seemed

56. F. NO CHANGE
G. An individual behavior
H. Behavior by individuals
J. Behavior patterns of an individual

57. A. NO CHANGE
B. But their
C. Being that their
D. Because their

58. F. NO CHANGE
G. which
H. that
J. whose

59. A. NO CHANGE
B. creativity, and flourished
C. creativity—flourished
D. creativity, flourished

60. F. NO CHANGE
G. Because other
H. In that other
J. Other

61. A. NO CHANGE
B. artists working in the region,
C. artists working in the region
D. artists, who worked in the region,

62. F. NO CHANGE
G. indelible
H. indelible—and permanent—
J. indelible but permanent

63. A. NO CHANGE
B. and perplexed
C. while perplexing
D. but perplexed

64. F. NO CHANGE
G. Despite successes many
H. Inspite of their successes
J. Ensuring successes,

<u>inextricably bounded</u> in Southwestern cultures.  Paint-
<sub>65</sub>

ers of every persuasion were convinced that sampling

this mysterious phenomenon <u>will strengthen</u> and en-
<sub>66</sub>

rich their own work.  Most were touched by what

D.H. Lawrence called the "spirit of the place."

Beside the scenic beauty bathed in clear golden

<u>light.  The</u> rich traditions of New Mexico's Indian and
<sub>67</sub>

Hispanic people became frequent subjects of the

artists who traveled to Taos and Santa Fe.

## Passage 7

Acupuncture, the inserting of needles at various

points of the body to block pain and cure <u>ailments, is</u>
<sub>68</sub>

several thousand years old.  As early as 2,000

years ago, the classic works of Chinese medicine

reported the treatment of headaches, lumbago, and

abdominal pain.  Today, acupuncture is used as anes-

thesia, allowing patients to undergo major surgery

<u>consciously.</u>
<sub>69</sub>

In 1958 a mass movement began in China to unite

traditional medicine with Western medicine, and West-

ern physicians <u>had begun to learn</u> traditional medi-
<sub>70</sub>

cine.  Before then, acupuncture was limited to a few

large cities and hospitals.  Afterward, many regions

organized medical personnel into medical and surgical

teams to travel up mountains and in the countryside

<u>to developing</u> acupuncture anesthesia.  A training
<sub>71</sub>

65. A. NO CHANGE
B. inextricably bound
C. inextricable bounding
D. inextricably bounding

66. F. NO CHANGE
G. would strengthen
H. strengthens
J. strengthening

67. A. NO CHANGE
B. light, the
C. light the
D. light: the

68. F. NO CHANGE
G. ailments is
H. ailments are
J. ailments—is

69. A. NO CHANGE
B. conscious
C. while conscious
D. and yet be still conscious

70. F. NO CHANGE
G. had begun learning
H. began the learning of
J. began to learn

71. A. NO CHANGE
B. developing
C. for the purposes of developing
D. to develop

program was started and new applications discovered,
72
including the use of acupuncture in many common

types of surgery.

The new technique was used to serve the masses

of poor and middle-class farmers. A large amount of
73
barefoot doctors and rural educated youths had tre-

mendous success treating common ailments.

In May 1970, the Ministry of Public Health

arranged national training classes to promote

the use of acupuncture during the eight years before,
74
fewer than 10,000 operations were performed under

this type of anesthesia. Since then, it has exceeded
75
40,000.

72. **F.** NO CHANGE
    **G.** newly discovered applications
    **H.** new applications had been discovered
    **J.** new applications were discovered

73. **A.** NO CHANGE
    **B.** Large amounts
    **C.** A large number
    **D.** Numerous

74. **F.** NO CHANGE
    **G.** the use of acupuncture. In
    **H.** using acupuncture. During
    **J.** the use of acupuncture, during

75. **A.** NO CHANGE
    **B.** Since then, the number
    **C.** Then, since the number
    **D.** Since, then,

# Explanatory Answers

**1.** (C) The underlined part commits a diction error (wrong word). *During* is used to refer to an ongoing period, but *that time* refers to a specific date, 1964. C correctly renders the thought: "Since that time, . . . ."

B is incorrect because B implies that the phenomenon described (the changes in behavior) occurred before 1964. And D is wrong because it seems to refer to one of a series of occurrences, e.g., that time we were successful.

**2.** (G) The underlined portion is not idiomatic. The correct expression is *virtually constant,* choice G.

H is incorrect because *virtually* modifies *constant,* and you must use an adverb to modify an adjective. As for J, as an adverb, *constantly* would have to modify a verb such as "has remained," but "smoking has remained constantly" is not the intended meaning of the sentence.

**3.** (D) The underlined portion contains an error of parallelism. The two verb elements *has remained* and *is actually increasing* refer to the same time period, so they should have similar forms. D supplies the correct form: "has remained . . . and has actually increased."

B fails to correct the original error because the tenses are still not coordinated. And C is wrong because *increasing* seems to become an adjective to modify *girls,* but that is not the intended meaning of the sentence.

**4.** (J) The underlined portion is not idiomatic English. Here you need to use *on teaching,* choice J.

G fails to correct the error in the original. As for H, although this choice corrects the error of the original, it introduces a new error of verb tense. "Have . . . focus" is not acceptable English.

**5.** (C) The original sentence contains an illogical transition. The second sentence of that paragraph is supposed to offer an idea that contrasts with the idea contained in the first sentence. The transitional word, *moreover,* is used to indicate a continuation of an idea. C corrects the error by providing the correct transitional word.

As for B, merely changing the location of *moreover* doesn't correct the original error. As for D, though this choice does provide an appropriate transitional phrase (the phrase "in spite of" is used to show contrast), it introduces a new error: the first *it* is a pronoun with no referent (antecedent). You can prove this to yourself by trying to find a referent for the pronoun. And when you think you've found one, substitute the referent for the first *it* in choice D. If you have found the referent, then the resulting substitution will make sense. But you won't find one that does make sense.

**6.** (H) The underlined portion contains an error of pronoun usage. *Themselves,* which is plural, is intended to refer to *fear,* which is singular. H corrects the error by using a singular pronoun.

G fails to correct the pronoun error, and J creates a phrase that is not idiomatic English.

**7.** (D) The underlined part contains an error of verb tense. The second sentence of the third paragraph is written using verbs in the present tense to refer to an ongoing condition. Thus, the underlined portion here should also use a verb that refers to an existing state of affairs. D does this.

B and C fail to correct the original error.

**8.** (G) Again, we have an error of verb tense. The underlined portion should be in the present tense, not the future tense. G makes the correction. Further, the *later* used in G indicates the correct sequence of events: children generally are afraid of smoking but lose their fear as they become adolescents.

The phrases suggested by H and J are needlessly wordy and awkward.

**9.** (A) The underlined portion is correct. The *therefore* is a good choice as a logical transition here, since the author intends to draw a further conclusion from the evidence presented.

As for B, *so* can sometimes take the place of *therefore*, but usage would require that it be the first word of the sentence: "So it is evident. . . ." As for C and D, these expressions have meanings that are not appropriate here since they do not show a logical transition.

**10.** (J) The underlined portion is not idiomatic. Here you need the infinitive (*to discourage*) and not the gerund. In addition, the relationship between the other two elements, *teenager* and *smoking*, is not clear in the original. Is *teenager* intended to be the object, of the verb or is smoking the object? *Teenager* should be the object, but as written the original seems to suggest that *smoking* is the object of the *discouraging*. J corrects both of these problems.

G and H correct the first error but not the second. In G and H, the relationship between *teenager* and *smoking* is still not clear. On balance, J expresses that relationship more clearly and more idiomatically than either G or H.

**11.** (B) The original contains an error of punctuation. The clause "who . . . home" is essential to the sentence because it serves to identify the *Europeans* being spoken of. So the clause should not be set off by commas. Additionally, notice that the beginning of the clause is not set of by commas, so you do not need a second comma to complete the enclosure of the thought. B makes the correction by eliminating the offending mark.

C fails to correct the punctuation error and introduces a new error by eliminating the only conjugated verb in the sentence. As a result, you are left with a sentence fragment. As for D, the verb tense here suggests a past action that continues into the present. But the verb in the next sentence clearly refers to completed past events. So the verb tense in D is not appropriate in this context.

**12.** (F) A colon can be used to introduce a list of examples. So the colon here is used correctly.

As for G and H, *being* is here both unneeded and low-level usage. And as for J, do not use a colon when the list is already introduced by some other element in the sentence, e.g., *including* or *such as*.

**13.** (C) Again, we have a problem of verb tense. The verb in the second sentence clearly refers to a completed past act, so the present tense *become* is out of place. C makes the needed correction.

B and D both make the needed correction but introduce new errors. As for B, *parts* is not idiomatic. As for D, the missing preposition results in a phrase that is not idiomatic.

**14.** (F) The verb tense here is correct. The present tense is appropriate because the author is describing the effects of the names on us today. And *us* is correct because the pronoun is the object of the verb. Finally, *to* is the idiomatic preposition.

G eliminates the one conjugated verb in the sentence, so the result is a sentence fragment rather than a sentence. As for H, the use of the past tense *connected* is wrong since the author is referring to the present effects of the names. Finally, as for J, *for* is not the correct preposition to use with *correct*.

**15.** (A) The original is correct. Each of the other choices introduces an error. As for B and C, these choices consist of past participles used as adjectives, and since they are adjectives, they must modify something. But there is nothing for them to modify. As for D, the result here is to make *geography* the subject of the sentence, but the result is a highly awkward sentence which at best renders the thought of the original only ambiguously.

**16.** (G) The original contains an error of grammar: what follows the period is a fragment with no main verb. G solves this problem by making that element a part of the first sentence, which does contain a main verb.

As for H, the use of the colon still results in a sentence fragment. (The colon would not be used here to highlight a list of examples or to provide explanatory material. Instead, a colon here would seem to separate two independent clauses, but the second element is not a clause at all because it lacks a conjugated verb.) As for J, the use of the past participle is not idiomatic. *Built* would be used to modify a structure, e.g., "the bridge, built in 1987." Here, the intent of the author is to use *building* to modify *Germans*. (It describes the Germans as people who built things.)

**17.** (C) The underlined portion contains a nonidiomatic preposition: *for.* The use of *for* in the expression *contribution for* suggests that a contribution has been made on someone else's behalf, e.g., "John made a contribution for Mary, who had forgotten her wallet." But that is not the meaning of the sentence here. The correct preposition is *to.*

B just substitutes one wrong preposition for another, and D changes the intended meaning of the original. D implies that the frontier life, rather than the German settlers, was responsible for introducing the Pennsylvania rifle.

**18.** (J) The original sentence contains needless repetition, since *accuracy* and *precision* are synonyms. J correctly eliminates one of the two words.

**19.** (C) The sentence contains an error of logical expression. The phrase *precious commodities* refers to *powder* and *lead,* so it should be placed immediately after the second of those. If placed anywhere else, the phrase does not clearly refer to *powder* and *lead.*

**20.** (F) The underlined portion is correct as written. The subject of *are* is *symbols and meaning,* and a plural subject requires a plural verb. Therefore, G is incorrect. On first reading, you may wonder whether the use of the present tense is correct, but once you've read the next couple of sentences, you know that the author intends to write in the present tense, so the original is correct. J, therefore, is incorrect. Finally, H is less idiomatic than the original because of the placement of *well.*

**21.** (D) The original suffers from an illogical transition. *Meanwhile* is used to imply events that occur simultaneously. ("Meanwhile, back at the ranchhouse, the cook was making dinner, unaware that the bandits were ready to strike.") *While* can be used to create a contrast: "John is tall, while his brother is short."

As for B and C, *because* is incorrect here because the author does not intend to imply a causal connection between the two ideas.

**22.** (G) This question is a "global" question about the overall structure of the passage. The first three ideas are: (1) this art is a sacred script; (2) mathematics is important in this art; and (3) this art also is allegorical. The sentence begun by this underlined portion belongs to the first idea, so it should be part of the first paragraph.

H and J fail to correct the error of the original. Additionally, H introduces a problem of logical expression: several towers would not have a single window. As for J, the expression *having a tower* seems to be an adjective phrase, but there is nothing for it to modify.

**23.** (C) The words following the period are a sentence fragment. C corrects this error of grammar by incorporating those words into the preceding sentence. B and D attempt this correction but fail because they use a pronoun (*which*) with no referent. (Try to find the noun that *which* substitutes for.)

**24.** (F) As noted above (number 22), this paragraph develops one of the main ideas of the selection. Thus, the original is correct. Since you do need a new paragraph here, G and J must be wrong. As for H, the *however* signals a contrast between two ideas. But the second main idea of the selection (mathematics is important) and the third main idea (every painting is also an allegory) are not contrasting ideas. (It would be permissible to use a *moreover* or a *furthermore* in place of the *however,* though it is not necessary to do so.)

**25.** (B) The sentence as written suffers from faulty parallelism. The paintings do two things: show and invite. So *invites* must be parallel in form to *showing*: *inviting.* Only B provides the proper parallelism.

**26.** (F) The underlined portion is correct as written. G is incorrect because there is no referent for *one* (once the *meaning* is eliminated). As for H, *being* is not needed and is low-level usage. And J is needlessly repetitious.

**27.** (B) The thought is rendered clearly and most concisely just by dropping out the phrase altogether, and you don't need to replace it with the suggestions of C and D.

**28.** (H) The underlined portion commits an error of parallelism. The last part of the sentence now reads: those who are lost and those that have been saved. But the two elements joined by *and* should have similar forms. Only H provides the needed parallelism.

**29.** (A) In discussing number 22, above, I highlighted three of the main ideas of the selection. This final paragraph introduces yet another idea or a conclusion. Since the idea discussed in the final paragraph is not part of the idea of painting as an allegory, it must be set off in a separate paragraph.

**30.** (G) The tense of the verb in the underlined part is not consistent with the tense of the other verbs in the sentence. The other verbs (both *are*) are in the historical present tense, meaning the present tense is used to describe a historical event. But the painting of the old masters came before that time, so it must be described in the past tense.

**31.** (B) The underlined portion contains a punctuation mistake. Do not use a comma to separate the subject of the sentence (*symbol*) and the verb (*is*). B corrects the error.

C also corrects the error but introduces a new mistake. The subject of the sentence is singular (*symbol*), so you must use a singular verb. As for D, the plural noun (*cultures*) cannot be modified by the singular *every*.

**32.** (G) The use of the colon here is incorrect. Although you might occasionally use a colon to join two independent clauses, you would not also use a coordinate conjunction (*and*). G makes the correction by deleting the colon and using just the conjunction.

As for H, substituting a comma for the colon and deleting the conjunction results in a comma splice (running two ideas together by joining them with a comma). As for J, this results in illogical subordination. The two ideas in the original sentence should have equal weight. The use of the subordinate conjunction (*while*) suggests that the second idea is somehow dependent upon the first idea.

**33.** (B) The parenthetical comment has nothing to do with the logical development of the passage, so it should simply be deleted.

**34.** (G) The sentence suffers from faulty parallelism. The first clause contains two verbs that describe similar actions. So they should both have the same form: "Ulysses encountered it as did a mythical Cherokee." G makes the needed correction.

H and J make the correction also but introduce a new error. *It* refers to *chasm*, which is singular. *Them* is plural.

**35.** (B) The underlined part contains a wrong preposition. In English, we would use "peer into"—not "peer in."

C fails to correct the error and also introduces an error of verb tense. D corrects the area of idiomatic expression but also introduces an error of verb tense.

**36.** (H) The underlined part contains an illogical transitional phrase. "On the other hand" is used to signal an idea that contrasts with what has gone before, but the idea of the first paragraph and the idea of the second paragraph do not contrast. Rather, the second paragraph is further development of an idea contained in the first paragraph. You do, however, need to begin another paragraph at this point, for the second paragraph develops a new idea. H correctly eliminates the illogical phrase while starting a new paragraph.

G is wrong because a new paragraph is required. As for J, the *also* is used incorrectly because two similar ideas are not being connected.

**37.** (B) The original contains an error of punctuation. The apostrophe following the *s* is used to show plural possession—an impossibility since there is only one study of astronomy. You do, however, need a possessive form because *astronomy's* modifies *riddles*. B makes the needed correction. The *'s* correctly shows possession.

**38.** (G) The *by one* is superfluous and makes the sentence needlessly wordy. The best course of action is simply to omit it.

The phrases suggested by H and J are also unneeded. Additionally, the phrase suggested by J changes the intended meaning of the original sentence.

**39.** (C) The verb tense here is incorrect. The other verb (*cannot reach*) is in the present tense, so this verb, too, should be present tense. C makes the needed change.

B is in the future tense and therefore is incorrect. And D is not a conjugated verb at all. B is the participle, and use of a participle would destroy the parallelism between *cannot reach* and *returns*.

**40.** (F) The underlined part is correct as written.

G is incorrect because the use of the participle (*setting*) destroys the parallelism of the sentence: "What is incredible . . . and setting us . . . ." H is incorrect because *that* seems to be a pronoun, but there is nothing for *that* to refer to. Finally, J, too, destroys the parallelism of the sentence, for now one element of the subject is a noun clause in the active voice while the other element is a noun clause in the passive voice.

**41.** (A) The phrase *as to* is an acceptable English idiom in this context. The other choices are not acceptable.

**42.** (G) Here there is a failure of agreement between subject and verb. The subject is *combination,* a singular noun, so the verb should be the singular *has led to.*

H and J make the needed correction, but the result of using either of them is not idiomatic.

**43.** (C) The verb tense of the underlined part is consistent with the other verb in the sentence (*chose*), but there is in the underlined part a redundant *upon.* You don't need both *on* and *upon.* C eliminates the extra preposition while using the correct verb tense.

B gratuitously changes the verb tense, thereby introducing a new error —without eliminating the original error. D eliminates the original error but introduces a wrong verb tense.

**44.** (G) The first paragraph mentions three traditions. This sentence, therefore, should refer to the *oldest* of them, not to the *older* of them. H and J change the intended meaning of the original, as indicated by the discussion that is contained in the second paragraph. (Shintoism was the oldest of the three traditions.)

**45.** (C) The underlined portion suffers from faulty parallelism. The two elements (*respect and worshipping*) should have similar forms. C makes the needed correction and correctly adds the *of* that is necessary to make a correct, idiomatic English expression.

B attempts to correct the problem of parallelism, but the result is awkward and not truly idiomatic. D also attempts to correct the problem of parallelism, but again the result is not idiomatic English.

**46.** (G) The *being* of the underlined part is not only superfluous, it is low-level usage not acceptable in standard written English. Simply eliminate the offending word.

H attempts the needed correction, but the comma is incorrect. You can prove this to yourself by reading the sentence silently: "Later subordinated [pause] to imported Buddhism and Confucianism . . . ." A pause there makes no sense. Finally, J contains the same error.

**47.** (D) "Object of something to someone" is not idiomatic English. The correct idiom would be "object of something for someone." D makes the needed correction; the other choices do not.

**48.** (H) The third paragraph starts the discussion of a second tradition, so you must start a new paragraph at this point. The original underlined portion, however, is needlessly wordy. The phrase *that was enduring* is superfluous. H corrects this error while still calling for a new paragraph.

G is wrong because it doesn't call for a new paragraph. As for J, the phrase *the other* is inconsistent with the "global" development of the selection. The author discusses three, not two, traditions.

**49.** (C) The phrase *pattern by something* (meaning that the pattern governs behavior) is not idiomatic. The correct expression is *pattern for something* or *pattern of something*. C makes the needed correction, while B does not. D is incorrect because *with* cannot be used in place of *for*.

**50.** (F) The verb *were* is correct and agrees with the plural subject *relationships*. G, therefore, is incorrect. And H and J make changes in verb tense that make them incorrect.

**51.** (A) The sentence is correct as written. Although you use a comma when a dependent clause precedes an independent clause, you don't need a comma when a dependent clause follows an independent clause.

B creates a comma splice (two independent clauses run together and joined by a comma with no coordinate conjunction). C makes an error of pronoun usage. The antecedent of *they* is *relationships,* which is plural. Therefore, it is incorrect to use the singular *it*. Finally, *being* is low-level usage.

**52.** (H) The underlined part contains an error of punctuation. The parenthetical expression can be set off using either two commas or two dashes but not one of each. H corrects the problem by using two dashes. G and J are incorrect since the second dash requires the use of the first dash.

**53.** (B) This sentence introduces the third tradition and fourth major point discussed in the selection, so you should begin a new paragraph here. For this reason, C is incorrect. As for D, the *also* is superfluous and illogically implies a connection between the third and fourth paragraphs that does not exist (such as the enumeration of a series).

**54.** (H) This question just tests idiomatic usage. The most idiomatic way of rendering this thought (that is, the phrasing that most fluent speakers of English would use) is provided by H.

**55.** (A) The use of *as well as* correctly shows the relationship between the elements *mandate* and *social duty*. B is wrong because the *being* is not needed. C is incorrect because the comma illogically separates two ideas that are to be joined by the phrase *as well as*. (You can hear this clearly if you read the sentence to yourself, pausing at the place indicated for a comma: "a religious mandate as well [pause] as a social duty.") Finally, omitting the joining phrase creates a series of elements that should not be in a series together: *religious mandate, a social duty,* and *was a means of promoting*. The result is logically flawed and lacks parallelism.

**56.** (F) The underlined part is correct. In English, we can use the definite article in this way to refer generally to individuals: the seal (meaning not one particular animal but all seals) is a penniped.

G is incorrect because it changes the intended meaning of the original sentence. The sentence is about the behavior of an individual, not an individual instance of behavior. As for H, the indirect phrasing here is not as concise as that offered by the original. (And in general, conciseness in writing is a virtue.) Finally, J is also needlessly wordy and also introduces an error of subject–verb agreement.

**57.** (B) The underlined original contains an error of pronoun usage. *His* is intended to refer to *they* (and *Samurai*), which is plural. So *his* should be *their*.

C and D make the needed correction but introduce new errors. As for C, this phrasing is not only low-level usage; it also turns a sentence into a sentence fragment (because the main verb *was* becomes the verb in a noun clause which is intended to be the object of *being*.) As for D, the use of *because* also creates a single dependent clause with no main clause—a sentence fragment.

**58.** (J) *Who's* is a contraction of "who is." The possessive of *who* is *whose*. G and H are wrong, because in English we use the *who* pronouns to refer to people.

**59.** (D) The clause "whose death . . . creativity" is a nonessential clause modifying Georgia O'Keefe and should be set off by commas. The first comma is already in place, and D supplies the second comma.

B also provides the second comma, but the *and* is superfluous and creates an illogical structure. As for C, since the first comma is already in place, you cannot use a dash to finish setting off the clause.

**60.** (J) The use of the conjunction *since* turns the sentence into a dependent clause, but it is not connected to an independent clause. The result is a sentence fragment. J solves the problem by turning the dependent clause into an independent clause and, therefore, a complete sentence.

G substitutes one subordinate conjunction for another and so fails to solve the problem of the sentence fragment. As for H, the result is still a sentence fragment.

**61.** (C) The underlined part contains an error of punctuation. The placement of the comma divides the dependent clause into two parts, thus separating the subject of the clause from the verb. There should, however, be a comma following *history* to set off the entire dependent clause from the independent clause.

C makes one change but not the other. And D makes the mistake of using commas to set off an essential clause.

**62.** (G) *Permanent* is needlessly repetitious of *indelible*, so one or the other must go. Only G does this.

**63.** (B) The *it* destroys the parallelism of the phrase "both something and something else." The error can be corrected simply by omitting *it*. Additionally, the *also* is superfluous. B correctly omits both words.

C and D create illogical phrases by substituting different conjunctions for *and*.

**64.** (F) The original is correct as written. G is incorrect because you need a comma to set off the introductory phrase from the rest of the sentence. (Read the sentence through without pausing between *successes* and *many*.) H is wrong for the same reason and for the further reason that, compared to the original, it is needlessly wordy. Finally, J is wrong because *ensuring* changes the intended meaning of the original.

**65.** (B) The original contains an error of diction. *Bounded* means "limited." The sentence should use *bound,* meaning "tied together." B makes the needed change.

As for C and D, *bounding* is the present participle of *to bound* (meaning "to leap"), not of *to bind.* Also, C incorrectly uses an adjective to modify a verb form.

**66.** (G) The underlined part contains a wrong verb tense. Following verbs in the past tense that indicate belief or conviction, you must use the "would" form (the subjunctive), e.g., "He hoped it would rain." G uses the correct verb form; H and J do not.

**67.** (B) The period in the underlined part creates a sentence fragment of what comes before the period. B corrects this problem by joining what comes before the comma to what follows the comma. B also correctly punctuates the resulting sentence by setting off with a comma the lengthy introductory phrase begun with *beside.* C solves the problem of the sentence fragment but fails to include the correct punctuation. As for D, the use of the colon fails to correct the problem of the sentence fragment.

**68.** (F) The sentence is correct as written. The comma there is the second of a set used to set off the parenthetical expression that begins just after *acupuncture.* G is incorrect because the second comma has been omitted. H is incorrect because the subject of the sentence is *acupuncture,* a singular noun. So a singular verb is needed. Finally, as for J, you cannot use a dash in place of the second comma.

**69.** (C) The underlined part contains a problem of word choice. To do something *consciously* means to do it knowingly, but that is not what the sentence intends to say. It means to say it is possible to undergo surgery while conscious—which is choice C. Choice B is incorrect because the adjective *conscious* has no connection to any other element in the sentence. Finally, D is needlessly wordy in comparison to C.

**70.** (J) The verb tense here is incorrect. The "had done something" structure is used to indicate that whatever is mentioned occurred before some other event. But the sentence means to say here that the two events mentioned ("mass movement began" and "western physicians began to learn") occurred in the same time frame. So the correct choice of verb tenses is just the past tense. G, therefore, is incorrect. As for H, while it employs the past tense, it is not idiomatic.

**71.** (D) The original sentence is incorrect because you cannot combine the gerund and the infinitive forms. The infinitive is the best choice here because it conveys the idea of "for the purpose of." B is incorrect because it creates an ambiguity. Is it the countryside that is developing acupuncture? C conveys the correct idea but it is wordy and awkward.

**72.** (J) The original is a split construction. The auxiliary verb *was* cannot function as an auxiliary for *discovered* because the new subject, *applications,* is plural.

G changes the meaning of the sentence and creates a fragment since there is no main verb. H is incorrect because there is no need to use the past perfect tense here. J is correct because the auxiliary verb *were* is plural and agrees with the subject.

73. (C) The original contains an error of word choice. *Amount* is used to refer to quantities that cannot be counted out individually, such as air, water, sand. *Number* is used to refer to quantities that can be counted out individually, such as cubic feet of air, buckets of water, and grains of sand. So here you must use *number*.

74. (G) The original is a run-on sentence. G correctly separates the ideas into separate sentences, while J does not. Although H creates two sentences, the use of *in* is not idiomatic.

75. (B) The *it* in the underlined part of the original has no antecedent. The problem can be corrected by substituting a noun. Although B, C, and D do this, C and D both use *since* as a conjunction, which results in a sentence fragment rather than a sentence.

8

# English Usage Warm-Up Test 1

**DIRECTIONS:** In the passages below, certain parts are underlined and numbered. In the right-hand column are alternative ways of rendering each underlined part. The first alternative is always "NO CHANGE." Choose "NO CHANGE" if you believe that the original underlined part is correct. Otherwise, choose the best alternative. In making your selection, choose the lettered choice that best expresses the thought and observes the requirements of standard written English. Some questions ask you to determine what is required by the interrelationship between two or more parts of the passage.

*Passage 1*

**(1)**

In the course of billions of years, millions of stars may sometimes occasionally be concentrated into a region only a few light years across, and in these crowded conditions colliding with one another. Some of these collisions would occur at high speeds, in which case the stars are partially or completely torn apart. Other collisions are gentle bumps, but the stars coalesce. The bigger the star becomes, the more likely it is to be hit again and the faster it grows until it reaches instability, collapses on itself, and forms a black hole.

1.  A. NO CHANGE
    B. sometimes, occasionally
    C. occasionally
    D. off and on

2.  F. NO CHANGE
    G. colliding
    H. and in these crowded conditions they collide
    J. which then causes them to collide

3.  A. NO CHANGE
    B. will occur
    C. to occur
    D. occur

4.  F. NO CHANGE
    G. bumps with the coalescence of the stars
    H. bumps, and the stars coalesce
    J. bumps, the stars coalesce

5.  A. NO CHANGE
    B. becomes the more
    C. becomes the more,
    D. becomes; the more

6.  F. NO CHANGE
    G. and a black hole is formed
    H. forms a black hole
    J. and thus a black hole is formed

(2)

When most of the stars and gas in the core of a

galaxy <u>has been</u> swallowed up by the black hole, the
     <sub>7</sub>


nucleus of the galaxy settles down <u>to a relative</u> quiet
                                    <sub>8</sub>

existence.  This is probably the state of the nucleus of

our own galaxy, but every hundred million years or so it

may flare <u>upto</u> a brightness 100 times its present level
          <sub>9</sub>

when a globular cluster or especially large gas cloud


<u>spirals</u> into the nucleus.
<sub>10</sub>


(3)

Once formed, a central "seed" black hole grows

mainly through the accretion of gas accumulated in the

<u>nucleus;</u> gas obtained from other disrupted stars, from
<sub>11</sub>

supernova explosions, or from stars torn apart by the

gravitational field of the black hole.  Perhaps an entire

galaxy can collide with another <u>galaxy, and the result</u>
                                <sub>12</sub>

<u>would be</u> the transfer of large amounts of gas from one


galaxy <u>to each other.</u>
       <sub>13</sub>

7.  A.  NO CHANGE
    B.  have been
    C.  will have been
    D.  would have been

8.  F.  NO CHANGE
    G.  to a relatively
    H.  for a relative and
    J.  for a relative

9.  A.  NO CHANGE
    B.  up
    C.  up to
    D.  OMIT

10. F.  NO CHANGE
    G.  will spiral
    H.  spiral
    J.  spiraled

11. A.  NO CHANGE
    B.  nucleus, gas
    C.  nucleus.  Gas
    D.  nucleus gas

12. F.  NO CHANGE
    G.  galaxy to result in
    H.  galaxy.  Such a collision could result in
    J.  galaxy with the results that

13. A.  NO CHANGE
    B.  to the other
    C.  and other
    D.  and another

14. Which of the following represents the most logical
    sequence for the paragraphs?
    F.  1, 2, 3
    G.  1, 3, 2
    H.  2, 3, 1
    J.  3, 1, 2

## Passage 2

No writer can please many readers and please them

for a long time <u>excepting by</u> the accurate representation
<sub>15</sub>

of human nature. Shakespeare is, above all writers, the

poet of human nature, the writer who holds up to his

readers a <u>faithful and true</u> mirror of manners and life.
<sub>16</sub>

Shakespeare's characters are not modified by the

customs of particular places unknown to the rest of the

world, by peculiarities of study or professions known

<u>to just a few, or</u> by the latest fashions of popular opinions.
<sub>17</sub>

Shakespeare's characters are <u>each</u> genuine representa-
<sub>18</sub>

tions of common humanity. His characters <u>act and speak</u>
<sub>19</sub>

according to the general passions and principles that

affect all of us. In the writings of other poets, a character

is too often an individual; in <u>that of Shakespeare</u> it is
<sub>20</sub>

commonly a species.

Other dramatists can gain attention only by using

exaggerated characters. Shakespeare <u>has no heroes; his</u>
<sub>21</sub>

scenes <u>only</u> are occupied by persons who act and speak
<sub>22</sub>

as the reader thinks he <u>would of spoken</u> or acted on the
<sub>23</sub>

same occasion. This, therefore, is the praise of

<u>Shakespeare that his drama is the mirror of life.</u>
<sub>24</sub>

15. A. NO CHANGE
    B. except by
    C. except for
    D. excepting

16. F. NO CHANGE
    G. faithful
    H. faithfully true
    J. true and real

17. A. NO CHANGE
    B. about by only a few and
    C. to just a few but
    D. to only a few since

18. F. NO CHANGE
    G. every
    H. all
    J. each one a

19. A. NO CHANGE
    B. acting and speaking
    C. acted and spoke
    D. acted and spoken

20. F. NO CHANGE
    G. the one of Shakespeare
    H. those of Shakespeare's
    J. those of Shakespeare

21. A. NO CHANGE
    B. has no heroes; their
    C. had no heroes; the
    D. having no heroes, his

22. F. NO CHANGE
    G. place after *act*
    H. place before *act*
    J. place after *occupied*

23. A. NO CHANGE
    B. would have speaked
    C. would have spoken
    D. would speak

24. F. NO CHANGE
    G. Shakespeare, that
    H. Shakespeare. That
    J. Shakespeare: that

*Passage 3*

Most people have a certain crime <u>that one believes</u>
                                    25
should be ranked as the worst of all crimes.  For some

<u>its'</u> murder; for others it may be selling drugs to chil-
 26
dren.  I believe, <u>moreover,</u> that the worst of all crimes
                   27
may be the confidence scheme.

The confidence scheme may seem an odd choice

for the worst crime, since con games are usually

<u>nonviolent.  Although,</u> it is a crime that ranks in heart-
 28
lessness.  Con artists are the most devious, the most

harmful, and the most disruptive of society because

<u>they break</u> down the most important bonds of the social
 29

<u>order, honesty and trust.</u>
 30

The con games themselves are <u>simplistic almost</u>
                                    31

infantile.  They work <u>on account of a con artist can win</u>
                        32
complete confidence, talk fast enough to keep the victim

slightly confused, <u>and dangling</u> enough temptation to
                    33
suppress any suspicion or skepticism.  The primary tar-

gets of these criminals <u>will be</u> the elderly and women,
                         34
and they prefer to work where there are large crowds.

25. **A.** NO CHANGE
    **B.** that they believe
    **C.** which one believes
    **D.** that you believe

26. **F.** NO CHANGE
    **G.** they are
    **H.** it's
    **J.** its

27. **A.** NO CHANGE
    **B.** however
    **C.** further
    **D.** therefore

28. **F.** NO CHANGE
    **G.** nonviolent; though
    **H.** nonviolent; but
    **J.** nonviolent; and

29. **A.** NO CHANGE
    **B.** it breaks
    **C.** of its breaking
    **D.** of them breaking

30. **F.** NO CHANGE
    **G.** order, honesty, and trust
    **H.** order: honesty and trust
    **J.** order: honest, and trust

31. **A.** NO CHANGE
    **B.** simplistic; almost infantile
    **C.** simplistic, almost infantile
    **D.** simplistic, yet almost infantile

32. **F.** NO CHANGE
    **G.** on account of a con artist's ability to
    **H.** owing to a con artist's ability to
    **J.** because a con artist can

33. **A.** NO CHANGE
    **B.** dangles
    **C.** has dangled
    **D.** dangle

34. **F.** NO CHANGE
    **G.** to be
    **H.** are
    **J.** is

## Passage 4

In the 1950s, the development of antipsychotic drugs called neuroleptics radically changed the clinical outlook for patients in mental institutions (that had previously been considered hopelessly psychotic.) Daily medication
<u>35</u>

controlling delusions and made psychotherapy possible.
<u>36</u>

Many who otherwise might never have left institutions
<u>37</u>
returned to society.

Recently, physicians had learned that there is a price
<u>38</u>
to be paid for these benefits.  Approximately 10 to 15 percent of patients who undergo long-term treatment with antipsychotic drugs develop a cluster of symptoms called tardive dyskinesia, the most common symptoms of that are involuntary repetitive movement of the tongue,
<u>39</u>
mouth, and face.

The risk of developing tardive dyskinesia
<u>40</u>

is not so great that doctors have considered
<u>41</u>

abandoning using antipsychotic drugs.  Patients generally
<u>42</u>

are bothered only slightly by the physical side effects,
<u>43</u>
though the abnormal movements are troubling and may

**35.** **A.** NO CHANGE
**B.** who had previously been considered hopelessly psychotic.
**C.** that had previous to this, been considered hopelessly psychotic.
**D.** OMIT

**36.** **F.** NO CHANGE
**G.** controls delusions but
**H.** controlled delusions, yet
**J.** controlled delusions and

**37.** **A.** NO CHANGE
**B.** never might have left
**C.** might never had left
**D.** might never be leaving

**38.** **F.** NO CHANGE
**G.** have learned
**H.** were learning
**J.** learned

**39.** **A.** NO CHANGE
**B.** them
**C.** which
**D.** these

**40.** **F.** NO CHANGE
**G.** The risk for developing
**H.** The risk developing
**J.** Developing

**41.** **A.** NO CHANGE
**B.** as great that
**C.** as great as
**D.** as great such that

**42.** **F.** NO CHANGE
**G.** abandoning the use of
**H.** to abandon the use of
**J.** abandoning to use

**43.** **A.** NO CHANGE
**B.** Place before *Patients*
**C.** Place after *effects*
**D.** Place before *physical*

hinder social adjustment.  Additionally early diagnosis
                           ‾‾‾‾‾‾‾‾‾‾‾‾‾‾‾‾‾‾‾‾‾‾‾
                                    44

and prompt discontinuation of the neuroleptics might

decrease the incident of the movement disorders.  Un-
              ‾‾‾‾‾‾‾
                45

fortunately, without neuroleptic drugs, psychotic behav-

ior returns because researchers have tried to achieve a
    ‾‾‾‾‾‾‾‾‾‾‾‾‾‾
          46

satisfactory balance between the two effects, by lowering

the dosage to a level that minimizes movement disorders

controlling psychosis.
‾‾‾‾‾‾‾‾‾‾‾‾‾‾‾‾‾‾‾‾
        47

**Passage 5**

Elizabeth I had a sensuous and indulgent nature that

she inherited from her mother, Ann Boleyn.  Splendor

and pleaure is the very air she breathed.  She loved
          ‾‾
          48

gaiety, laughter, and wit.  Her vanity remained even, to
                                    ‾‾‾‾‾‾‾‾‾‾‾‾‾‾‾
                                          49

old age.  The vanity of a coquette.
‾‾‾‾‾‾‾

The statesmen who she outwitted believed, almost to
              ‾‾‾‾‾‾‾‾‾‾‾‾‾
                   50

the end, that Elizabeth I was little more than a frivolous

woman.  But the Elizabeth whom they saw was far from

being all of Elizabeth.  The wilfullness of Henry and the
‾‾‾‾‾
  51

triviality of Ann played over the surface of a nature

as hard as steel—a purely intellectual temperament.
‾‾‾‾‾‾‾‾‾‾‾‾
     52

Her vanity and caprice carried no weight whatever in
                                        ‾‾‾‾‾‾‾‾
                                           53

state affairs.  The coquette of the presence-chamber

---

**44.**  **F.**  NO CHANGE
         **G.**  Additionally with early
         **H.**  Additionally, early
         **J.**  In addition to this, with early

**45.**  **A.**  NO CHANGE
         **B.**  incidence
         **C.**  incidents
         **D.**  incidences

**46.**  **F.**  NO CHANGE
         **G.**  returns.  Because
         **H.**  returns.  So
         **J.**  return, so

**47.**  **A.**  NO CHANGE
         **B.**  since they control psychosis
         **C.**  yet control psychosis
         **D.**  yet controls psychosis

**48.**  **F.**  NO CHANGE
         **G.**  is,
         **H.**  was
         **J.**  was,

**49.**  **A.**  NO CHANGE
         **B.**  remains, even to old age, the
         **C.**  remains, even to old age the
         **D.**  remained, even to old age, the

**50.**  **F.**  NO CHANGE
         **G.**  that she outwitted
         **H.**  whom she outwitted
         **J.**  who she was outwitting

**51.**  **A.**  NO CHANGE
         **B.**  to be
         **C.**  having been
         **D.**  OMIT

**52.**  **F.**  NO CHANGE
         **G.**  as hard than
         **H.**  so hard as
         **J.**  as hard like

**53.**  **A.**  NO CHANGE
         **B.**  whomsoever
         **C.**  whatsoever
         **D.**  whomever

had became the coolest and hardest of politicians at
__54__

the council-board.

It was this part which gave her her marked

superiority over the statesmen of her time.  No
__55__

more nobler a group of ministers ever gathered round the
__56__

council-board than those of Elizabeth, but she was the

instrument of none.  She listened and she weighed, but

her policy, as a whole, was her own.  It was the policy of

good sense, not genius, she endeavored to keep her
__57__

throne, to keep England out of war, and she wanted to
__58__

restore civil and religious order.

### *Passage 6*

Early in November 1850, the work of a logging detail

from Fort Gaines in the Minnesota Territory was inter-

rupted by a party of Chippewa warriors who demanded

payment for the timber.  The loggers refusing, the Indi-
__59__

ans, acting at the direction of Chief Hole-in-the-Day
__60__

confiscated the government's oxen.  The loggers had

established their camp on Chippewa lands without his
__61__

authorizing it.  Therefore, in a move designed to

force reimbursement for the timber, Hole-in-the-Day

was ordering his braves to seize the oxen.
__62__

54.  F. NO CHANGE
     G. became
     H. used to become
     J. becomes

55.  A. NO CHANGE
     B. superiority in regard to
     C. superiority about
     D. superior quality to

56.  F. NO CHANGE
     G. nobler a group,
     H. nobler group
     J. more nobler of a group,

57.  A. NO CHANGE
     B. not genius because she
     C. not genius.  She
     D. but not genius, she

58.  F. NO CHANGE
     G. wanting
     H. and wanting
     J. and

59.  A. NO CHANGE
     B. With the refusal of the loggers;
     C. When the loggers refused,
     D. When the loggers had refused—

60.  F. NO CHANGE
     G. that acted at the direction of Hole-in-the-Day,
     H. acting at the direction of Hole-in-the-Day,
     J. (acting at the direction of Hole-in-the-Day),

61.  A. NO CHANGE
     B. without his authorization
     C. without their authorizing it
     D. without his authorization of it

62.  F. NO CHANGE
     G. gave orders that
     H. orders
     J. ordered

Captain John Todd, the commanding officer at Fort Gaines, demanded that the cattle had to be returned to them.
63

The chief's reply was firm, and at the same time, it was friendly.
64

In his message to Captain Todd, Hole-in-the-Day explained that he delayed to seize the cattle until
65

he could meet Todd in council and had sent a messenger to the officer requesting a conference at Crow Wing. When Todd had not come, he acted, additionally he later
66

decided that since the army had not paid for timber cut the previous winter, he intended to keep the oxen until the tribe was reimbursed by all the timber taken for the
67

fort. Hole-in-the-Day concluded by saying: "Do not think hard of me, but I do as others would—the Timber is mine."

## Passage 7

As befits a nation made up of immigrants from all
68

over the Christian world, Americans have no distinctive Christmas symbols. Instead, we have taken the symbols
69

of all nations and made them our own. The Christmas tree, the holly and the ivy, and the mistletoe are all elements in the American Christmas of the mid-twentieth century, though we have no Christmas symbols of our
70

own, the American Christmas still has a distinctive aura on account of two characteristic elements.
71

63. **A.** NO CHANGE
　　**B.** the return of the cattle
　　**C.** the cattle's returning
　　**D.** that they return the cattle

64. **F.** NO CHANGE
　　**G.** but, at the same time, it was friendly
　　**H.** yet friendly
　　**J.** at the same time—friendly

65. **A.** NO CHANGE
　　**B.** delayed to have seized
　　**C.** had delayed to seized
　　**D.** delayed seizing

66. **F.** NO CHANGE
　　**G.** acted but additionally
　　**H.** acted. Additionally,
　　**J.** acted additionally,

67. **A.** NO CHANGE
　　**B.** reimbursed for
　　**C.** reimbursed
　　**D.** was reimbursed for

68. **F.** NO CHANGE
　　**G.** made up from
　　**H.** made of
　　**J.** which made of

69. **A.** NO CHANGE
　　**B.** symbols, and
　　**C.** symbols, but
　　**D.** symbols. Furthermore,

70. **F.** NO CHANGE
　　**G.** century. Though
　　**H.** century. Because
　　**J.** though. (begin new sentence with *We*)

71. **A.** NO CHANGE
　　**B.** (because of)
　　**C.** by virtue of
　　**D.** including

First, as might be expected in a nation dedicated to

business, Christmas has became to serve as a stimulus to
                     _____
                          72

retail business.   Second, the Christmas season of festivi-

ties have been gradually combined with the New Year's
_____
              73

celebration into one lengthened period of Saturnalia,

which starts with "office Christmas parties" and contin-
_____
   74

ues as far as New Year's Eve.
_____
   75

72. **F.** NO CHANGE
    **G.** has come
    **H.** has become
    **J.** have come

73. **A.** NO CHANGE
    **B.** has gradually combined with
    **C.** have gradually combined to
    **D.** has combined to gradually

74. **F.** NO CHANGE
    **G.** that starts
    **H.** that start
    **K.** which start

75. **A.** NO CHANGE
    **B.** so far as
    **C.** through
    **D.** for

# Explanatory Answers

1. (C) This original is incorrect because it is needlessly wordy: *sometimes* and *occasionally* mean the same thing. B fails for the same reason. D is incorrect because *off and on* does not have a meaning that is appropriate here.

2. (H) The original is incorrect because the material following the comma lacks a conjugated verb. Why does it need a conjugated verb? Because it has no logical connection to anything that comes before the comma and so must stand on its own as an independent clause. H solves the problem by providing a subject and verb, thereby creating an independent clause. G is incorrect because the material following the comma still has no logical relationship to the rest of the sentence. *Colliding* is the participle of *to collide* and seems to be an adjective. But there is no noun in the first part of the sentence for *colliding* to modify. J suffers from a similar problem. *Which* is a relative pronoun, and as a pronoun it needs an antecedent. But there is no noun to which *which* refers.

3. (D) The original sentence is incorrect because the use of the subjunctive is incorrect. The use of the subjunctive, *would occur,* suggests that the event is contingent upon some other event, but that is not the intended meaning of the original. B is wrong because the use of the future tense here is inconsistent with the use of the present tense in the rest of the paragraph. C is wrong because the use of the infinitive creates a meaningless sentence. D is the correct choice because the present tense is consistent with the rest of the paragraph.

4. (H) The original sentence is incorrect because the *but* signals an opposition that is not meant here. The coalescing is the result of the bump, so the best choice is H. G is incorrect because it changes the meaning of the sentence. As written, G says that the stars bump with the coalescence. Finally, J is a run-on sentence because a comma is not adequate to separate two independent clauses.

5. (A) The original is correct as written. A comma is needed following *becomes* to make the comparison clear. The best way to prove this to yourself is to read the sentence without the comma: *The bigger the star becomes the more....* (Compare this structure with the old saying "The bigger they are, the harder they fall.") B is incorrect because without the comma, the sentence is subject to misreading. Finally, the comma in C and the semicolon in D would actually encourage a misreading of the sentence.

6. (F) The original is correct because the present tense is consistent with the other tenses in the sentence and the verb form maintains a parallel structure (*grows, collapses,* and *forms*). G and J are wrong because a shift to the passive voice disrupts the parallelism of the sentence. H is incorrect because, without the conjunction *and,* a run-on sentence is created.

7. (B) This is simply a question of subject–verb agreement. Since the subject is *most of the stars* (which is plural), the verb must be plural. But the verb *has been* is singular. B is the correct answer because the plural verb *have been* agrees with the subject. C is incorrect because the future tense is inconsistent with the other verb tenses in the paragraph. (The other verbs are in the present tense, e.g., *settles* and *is*.) D is wrong because the use of the subjunctive implies that the event referred to is contingent upon some other event, but the sense of the sentence is that the "swallowing" does occur—not that it might occur if something else happens.

8. (G) The original is incorrect because an adverb is required to modify the adjective *quiet*. G is correct because the adverb *relatively* modifies *quiet*. H is wrong because it is not idiomatic—the correct expression is *settle down to*, not *settle down for*. Additionally, the sentence would say that the nucleus settles down to a *relative* existence, a phrase that is meaningless. Finally, J fails because it is not idiomatic (it makes the same mistake as H) and because, as in the original, the adjective instead of the adverb is used to modify the adjective *quiet*.

9. (C) The original is incorrect because this expression must be rendered in two words, i.e., *up to*. So C is the correct choice. B is incorrect because it is not idiomatic. Finally, D is incorrect because the omission of the phrase creates a meaningless sentence.

10. (F) The original is correct because the present tense is required here to keep the verbs consistent and because the verb must be singular to agree with the subject *gas cloud*. (When a subject consists of two or more elements joined by *or*, the verb agrees with the element closest to it.) G is incorrect because the future tense is incorrect. H is wrong because the verb *spiral* is plural. Finally, J is wrong because using the past tense would create a conflict of tenses.

11. (B) The material that follows the semicolon is not an independent clause because it lacks a conjugated verb. So the semicolon is incorrect. The material following the semicolon must be incorporated into the main body of the sentence. How to accomplish this is the question. Begin by asking yourself what logical function is served by the material. It is an appositive that expands upon the word *gas* in the main part of the sentence, and as an appositive it should be set off by a comma. Thus, B is the correct choice. C is incorrect because everything following the period would be a sentence fragment. And as for D, with no punctuation at all to signal the status of the material following the semicolon, the result is a run-on sentence.

12. (H) The original is incorrect because it is awkward and ambiguous. It is not clear whether the *perhaps* is intended to govern both clauses of the sentence. H solves the problem by starting a new sentence. The period clearly limits the scope of the *perhaps*. G is incorrect because it, too, is ambiguous. The sentence resulting from the substitution of G seems to imply that the galaxies collide for the purpose of transferring gas, but that is not the intended meaning of the original. As for J, the *that* seems to introduce a clause, but there is no verb in the remaining part of the sentence.

13. (B) The original commits an error of logical expression. The sentence means to say that one galaxy transfers its gas to the other galaxy involved in the collision. For this you need the expression in B.

9

**14.** (G) The question tests your understanding of the overall logic and organization of the selection. The selection is organized chronologically. (1) describes the formation of a black hole. (3) describes its growth. (2) describes its mature stage. So the best order for the paragraphs is (1), (3), and (2).

**15.** (B) The original contains an error of diction. The preposition *excepting* means *excluding,* but that is a meaning not appropriate here. B provides the correct preposition. C is incorrect because *for* has a meaning that is not appropriate here. The *by* in B correctly indicates that the accurate representation of human nature is the means by which the writer accomplishes his task. Finally, D makes the same mistake as the original.

**16.** (G) The original is incorrect because *faithful* and *true* mean more or less the same thing, so the sentence is needlessly wordy. G corrects the error. H and J are, like the original, needlessly wordy.

**17.** (A) The original is correct. B is incorrect because it is wordy. C is wrong because *but* creates an opposition not intended. Finally, D creates a meaningless sentence.

**18.** (H) The referent of *each* is *characters,* but *each* is singular while *characters* is plural. G and J are also incorrect for this reason. H corrects the problem by using a plural pronoun.

**19.** (A) The underlined original is correct. B reduces the sentence to a sentence fragment by eliminating the only conjugated verbs. C and D both create conflicts of verb tenses between this sentence and the other sentences of the paragraph (which use present tense verbs).

**20.** (J) The original is incorrect because the pronoun *that* does not agree with its plural antecedent, *writings.* G fails for the same reason. H uses the correct prououn, but the use of the *'s* is incorrect. Possession is already indicated by the *of.* J is correct because the pronoun *those* agrees with *writings,* and the possessive is correctly formed.

**21.** (A) The original is correct because the semicolon correctly separates two independent clauses, and the pronoun *his* agrees with its antecedent, *Shakespeare.* B is wrong because the possessive pronoun *their* does not agree with its antecedent, *Shakespeare.* C is wrong because the switch to the past tense creates a conflict of tenses. (The rest of the verbs are all in the present tense, e.g., *can, gain,* and *has.*) D is wrong because it is awkward.

**22.** (J) The placement of *only* in the original is incorrect. The original intends to say that all of Shakespeare's characters act and speak as ordinary people would. J places *only* in the best place to make this clear.

**23.** (C) The original commits an error of diction. *Would of* does not exist in English. The correct expression is *would have.* C is correct because *would have spoken* is the correct form of the verb. B is wrong because *speaked* is not the past particple of *to speak.* The correct form is *spoken.* Finally, D is wrong because it creates an incorrect complete construction. *Acted* is dependent upon *would have,* so eliminating the *have* leaves you with a split construction that is not properly completed.

**24.** (J) The original is incorrect because it is a run-on sentence. J corrects this. The colon serves to introduce an explanation or a restatement. G results in a comma splice (two independent clauses joined by a comma with no conjunction). H creates a sentence fragment of everything following the period.

25. (B) The original is incorrect because the pronoun *one* does not agree with its antecedent, *most people*. B corrects the problem. C is wrong because it, too, uses a singular rather than a plural pronoun. Additionally, *that* should be used instead of *which* since the material introduced serves to define the type of crime referred to. Finally, though D uses a plural pronoun, it creates a problem of shifting point of view.

26. (H) The contraction of *it is* is written *it's*. *Its* is a possessive pronoun, and *its'* doesn't exist in English. G is incorrect because *they* is intended to refer to *certain crime*, which is singular.

27. (B) *Moreover* is not a logical choice of transitional words. *Moreover* signals a continuation of a thought, but the author here clearly implies a contrast. *However* is an appropriate word to signal a contrast. C is wrong for the same reason that the original is wrong. Finally, *therefore* is used to signal a logical transition, so D, too, is incorrect.

28. (H) The underlined portion of the original begins a sentence fragment. *Although* is a subordinate conjunction that is used to introduce a dependent clause, and a dependent clause cannot stand alone as a sentence by itself. H corrects this problem by replacing *although* with the coordinate conjunction *but* and creating a correctly punctuated compound sentence. G eliminates the sentence fragment problem but makes the mistake of illogical subordination. The intended meaning of the original requires that the second idea (that the crime is heartless) have the same emphasis as the first idea (the crime is nonviolent). But *though* is used to introduce a subordinate idea. J eliminates the fragment problem and creates a proper compound sentence in which the two ideas are given equal importance, but *and* signals a similarity of ideas. What is required here is a conjunction that signals a contrast.

29. (A) The original is correct. B is wrong because *it* does not agree with its antecedent, *con artists*. C and D are both awkward. Additionally, C is incorrect because *its* has no antecedent. Finally, D is also wrong because the possessive pronoun *their* and not the objective pronoun *them* must modify the gerund.

30. (H) The original is incorrect because the punctuation makes it seem as though honesty and trust are something other than important social bonds. J clarifies the meaning of the sentence. Honesty and trust are the most important social bonds. G fails to eliminate the ambiguity of the original. As for J, the comma is unnecessary and serves only to disrupt the logical relationship created by the conjunction *and*.

31. (C) The original runs together two ideas (*simplistic* and *almost infantile*). C correctly separates them with a comma. B is incorrect because a semicolon would isolate *almost infantile* from the rest of the sentence, and the phrase cannot stand alone. As for D, the *yet* signals a contrast of ideas but the two ideas here are similar, not contrasting.

32. (J) The use of *on account* to indicate a causal relationship is low-level usage and is not acceptable in standard written English. G fails to correct this error and compounds the problem by creating a very awkward sentence. H, too, is awkward and merely substitutes another unacceptable phrase (*owing to*) for the one used in the original.

33. (D) The original is incorrect because it does not maintain the parallel structure of the sentence. The auxiliary verb *can* governs the other verbs in the sentence, so the verb must be parallel to *win* and *talk*. Only D provides this form.

34. (H) The use of the future tense in the original conflicts with the other verbs in the paragraph (which are in the present tense). G is wrong because the use of the infinitive eliminates the only conjugated verb in the clause, thus reducing the clause to a fragment. And J is wrong because *is* is singular and does not agree in number with the plural noun *targets*.

35. (B) The original is wrong because the parentheses are incorrect. The material enclosed in parentheses is essential to the sentence because it defines or specifies the kind of patients discussed. Additionally, the pronoun *that* cannot be used to refer to people. B is correct because the parentheses are omitted, and the correct pronoun, *who,* is used to refer to the patients. C is incorrect because it uses an incorrect pronoun and because it is wordy. Finally, D is wrong because the fact that these patients were previously considered to be hopelessly psychotic is important to the general development of the passage and should not be omitted.

36. (J) The original underlined portion is guilty of faulty parallelism. *Controlling* should be a conjugated verb and should have the same form as *made*. J corrects this problem. G is incorrect because the use of the present tense creates a conflict with the rest of the paragraph, which is in the past tense. Additionally, G is wrong because *but* suggests a contrast between ideas that is not intended. H is also incorrect for this reason. *Yet* implies a contrast of ideas where no contrast is intended.

37. (A) The original is correct as written. *Might* is a modal auxiliary (it indicates the "mode" of possibility). *Might* does not have the full range of verb forms that most English verbs have. For example, *might* doesn't have an infinitive (*to might?*). Additionally, *might* cannot be conjugated in the future tense. (Future possibilities would be indicated by an adverb, e.g., "It might rain tomorrow.") *Might,* however, can be conjugated with *have* to indicate a possibility that existed in the past but no longer exists. This is why the original is correct. The *might never have* construction indicates that there was a possibility (they might not have left) that existed before but came to an end with some event (they left). B is awkward compared to the original and therefore wrong. And C and D are not possible conjugated verbs using *might*.

38. (G) The original is incorrect because the passage intends to switch from a discussion about the past in the first paragraph to a discussion of the present. This shift is signalled by *recently*. Therefore, the use of the past perfect tense is wrong here. G is correct because the use of the present perfect to indicate an action in the past that continues to the present is logical here. H and J are incorrect because they are past tenses as well. (*Were learning* is the past progressive tense, and *learned* is the simple past tense.)

39. (C) The original sentence is ambiguous. *That* can be either a relative pronoun or a demonstrative pronoun. Here, *that* sounds too much like a demonstrative pronoun when what is required is a relative pronoun. Since *which* can only be a relative pronoun, C eliminates the ambiguity. B is incorrect because *them* is not a relative pronoun. *Them* cannot join the subordinate clause to the independent clause, so the resulting construction sounds like a run-on sentence. D suffers from the same problem. Since *these* is a demonstrative pronoun, the sentence seems to combine two independent clauses with a comma.

**40.** (F) The original is correct. As for G, *for* is not idiomatic in this context. The correct preposition is *of*. As for H, elimination of the preposition makes *developing* seem like an adjective modifying *risk,* but then the phrase *tardive diskinesia* has no logical relationship to the rest of the sentence. Finally, J distorts the intended meaning of the sentence. It is the risk of developing the symptoms that doctors worry about.

**41.** (A) The original is idiomatic and correct. B and D are simply not English idioms. As for C, while *as great as* is an acceptable idiom, it doesn't have the meaning required by the sentence.

**42.** (G) The original is incorrect because it is not idiomatic to use two gerunds together. G is the correct answer because *considered abandoning the use of* is an idiomatic phrase. H is incorrect because *considered to abandon* is not idiomatic. J fails for the same reason—*abandoning to use* is not idiomatic English.

**43.** (A) The original is correct. It is logical that *only* come before *slightly* since the adverb should be close to the adverb it modifies. This creates a sentence that fits the context of the passage since the extent of the side effects of the drugs is obviously an issue. B is wrong because *only* should not modify *patients*—this changes the meaning of the sentence. C is not idiomatic English. D changes the intended meaning of the original by implying that the symptoms mentioned are the only physical symptoms that occur.

**44.** (H) The original is incorrect because a comma is required after *additionally.* (Read the sentence to yourself, and you will see that you must pause after *additionally.*) G is wrong because it leaves the sentence with no clear subject, thus creating confusion. Finally, J fails for the same reason as G and is wordy as well.

**45.** (B) The original is incorrect because it commits an error of diction. The correct word here is not *incident* or *incidents,* which mean "occurrence" or "occurences," but *incidence,* which refers to the rate or range of occurrence. Therefore, B is the correct choice.

**46.** (H) The original is incorrect because it uses an illogical transition word. *Because* suggests that psychotic behavior returns because of what the researchers have attempted to do. H corrects this problem by making it clear that the problem has prompted researchers to look for a solution—not that the search for a solution has caused a problem. G is incorrect because it fails to correct the error of the original (*because* is the offending word). And G results in a sentence fragment. (*Because* introduces a dependent clause, and dependent clauses are not, by themselves, complete sentences.) J is incorrect because the verb *return* is plural, but the subject of the verb is *behavior,* a singular noun.

**47.** (D) The original is incorrect because it suggests that the disorders are controlling the psychosis. B incorrectly suggests that the disorders control psychosis. C is wrong because the verb *control* does not agree with its subject, *that,* a pronoun that is singular since it refers to *level.* D is correct because the subject and verb agree and the sentence is logical—the level minimizes movement disorders yet controls psychosis.

48. (H) The original is incorrect because the verb *is* is singular and should be plural to agree with *splendor and pleasure*. (A compound subject requires a plural verb.) Also, the past tense should be used here to agree with the other past tense verbs used in the passage. H and J both provide the correct verb, but the comma in J incorrectly separates the subject from its verb.

49. (D) The original is incorrect because the period after *age* creates a fragment. Also, the comma after *even* is incorrect because *even* is intended to be a part of the parenthetical phrase *even to old age*. B is wrong because the use of the present tense creates a conflict of tenses, since the rest of the paragraph is in the past tense. C fails because it, too, is in the present tense and because a second comma is required after *age* to complete the parenthetical expression. D is the correct answer because its verb is in the past tense and because the parenthetical expression is correctly set off by two commas.

50. (H) The original is incorrect because the object pronoun *whom*, not *who*, is required here. (She outwitted them.) G is incorrect because the pronoun *that* should not be used to refer to people. Finally, J is incorrect because the *who* is incorrect, and the past progressive tense is awkward here.

51. (A) The original is correct. B is wrong because it is not idiomatic. C is incorrect because the tense is incorrect—it suggests that Elizabeth was *being* before and up to the time the statesmen saw her. The original indicates that she was *being* Elizabeth at the same time that they saw her. Finally, omitting the gerund changes the meaning of sentence. D suggests *far* in the sense of distance, which makes little sense in this context.

52. (F) The idiomatic form of comparison in English is "as . . . as." So, F is the only possible choice.

53. (C) The original commits an error of diction. Only C creates an idiomatic expression.

54. (G) The original is incorrect because the past perfect tense is wrong here and because the past participle should be *become*, not *became*. H is incorrect because it suggests an ongoing state of affairs, but the sense of the sentence is that the transformation occurred and was completed at a certain point in time. J is incorrect because the switch to the present tense creates a conflict of tenses. So, G is correct because the simple past tense is correct.

55. (A) The original is correct. B is incorrect because it is not idiomatic. In English we say that someone has *superiority over* someone or that someone is *superior to* someone. Both C and D are unidiomatic as well.

56. (H) The original is incorrect because *more nobler* is not idiomatic, since *nobler* is already the comparative form of the adjective. G is incorrect for two reasons. First, *a* is superfluous and not idiomatic. Second, the comma illogically separates the subject from its verb. J fails to correct the error of the original and is needlessly wordy as well.

57. (C) The original is incorrect because it is a run-on sentence. The comma after *genius* is not enough to separate the two independent clauses. As for B, the *because* establishes a causal connection not intended by the original. C is correct because here the period separates the two sentences. D fails for the same reason as the original and for the additional reason that *but not* is a double negative.

**58.** (J) The original is incorrect because it fails to preserve the parallel structure of the sentence. G is wrong because it changes the meaning of the sentence. It implies that Elizabeth endeavored to keep her throne and keep England out of war because she wanted to restore civil and religious order. H is incorrect because it does not maintain the parallelism of the sentence. J is correct because it does preserve the parallel construction.

**59.** (C) The original is wrong because it is a run-on sentence. The comma is not sufficient to separate the two independent clauses, and what results is a comma splice. B is wrong because the semicolon after *loggers* creates a fragment of what comes before. D is wrong because the dependent clause should not be separated from the rest of the sentence by a dash and because the past perfect tense creates a conflict of tenses. C eliminates the problem of the run-on sentence by subordinating one idea (the loggers refused) to another (Hole-in-the-Day acted).

**60.** (H) The original is wrong because there should be another comma after *Hole-in-the-Day*. G is incorrect because the pronoun *that* should not be used to refer to people. Finally, the parentheses in J are incorrect since they do the same job as the commas. H is correct because it is correctly punctuated—there is another comma after *Hole-in-the-Day*.

**61.** (B) The original is incorrect because the pronoun *it* has no antecedent. B eliminates the problem by getting rid of the pronoun altogether. C and D fail to correct the error of the original. Additionally, in C the pronoun *their* doesn't seem to have a referent. Finally, D is awkward.

**62.** (J) The original is wrong because the past progressive tense conflicts with the simple past tense used throughout the story. G is wrong because it creates an unidiomatic sentence. H is incorrect because the present tense also creates a conflict of tense. J is correct because it uses the simple past tense, which is appropriate here.

**63.** (B) The original is wrong because it is awkwardly worded and because *them* has no referent. C is incorrect because it is not idiomatic. Finally, D is incorrect because *they* has no clear referent. B eliminates the pronoun problem by simply deleting the pronoun altogether (the pronoun isn't necessary) and is direct in its wording.

**64.** (H) The original is needlessly wordy, as you can see by comparing it to H. Additionally, it would be better to replace *and* with a conjunction that signals a contrast of ideas, since the sentence intends to contrast the ideas of *firm* and *friendly*. Although G uses a better conjunction, G, like the original, is needlessly wordy. J is incorrectly punctuated.

**65.** (D) The original is not idiomatic. The sentence requires a gerund rather than an infinitive. B and C are incorrect because they use some form of the infinitive. (In any event, *to seized* doesn't exist in English.) D correctly supplies the gerund form. (The use of *in* is optional here.)

**66.** (H) The underlined original is the location of a comma splice, which creates a run-on sentence. H eliminates the problem by creating a new sentence. G and J fail to solve the problem of the run-on sentence.

**67.** (D) The original is not idiomatic. The phrase *reimbursed by* refers to the source doing the repayment, but the sense of the sentence is that the timber is the cause for reimbursement. For this, you need *reimbursed for*. As for B, the structure of the sentence requires the passive voice. And C changes the meaning of the sentence by implying that the tribe will reimburse the timber.

**68.** (F) The original uses idiomatic English and is otherwise correct. G uses nonidiomatic English. (The correct idiom is *made up of,* not *made up from.*) H uses an English idiom that is not appropriate here. *Made from* implies that something has been constructed or fabricated from something else, but the sentence does not mean to say that the nation has been constructed out of immigrants in the same way that a coat is made out of wool. J suffers from a similar problem. The phrase *which made of* would be found only in older forms of English (e.g., "an experience which made of him a man") and would not, in any event, have the meaning intended here.

**69.** (A) The original is correct as written. B is incorrect for two reasons. First, the intended meaning of the original is to signal a contrast between two ideas, but *and* cannot do that job. Second, you need a semicolon here because the two independent clauses joined at this point are fairly complex. (In general, when joining two independent clauses one or both of which also includes a dependent clause, you should employ a semicolon rather than a comma.) C is wrong for this second reason as well. Finally, as for D, *furthermore* does not have a meaning that is appropriate here.

**70.** (G) The original underlined portion contains a comma splice. Two main clauses are joined with a comma but no conjunction. G is one way of correcting the problem: Just start a new sentence. Further, *though* correctly introduces the dependent clause that follows and also correctly signals the contrast of ideas intended by the original. H and J correctly start new sentences. H fails, however, since *because* does not have the meaning of *though.* (*Because* suggests a causal explanation: "It is because Americans have no symbols of their own that they have a distinctive aura." But that makes no sense.) J fails because the lack of an introductory subordinate conjunction such as *though* makes everything down to the comma an independent clause, and the comma then fuses two independent thoughts (a comma splice).

**71.** (C) *On account of* should not be used to mean "because." ("On account of having a lot of homework to do, John could not go to the game" is not acceptable in standard written English.) As for B, it is incorrect to put the subordinate conjunction, a vital part of the sentence, in parentheses. D is just not idiomatic. The correct choice, C, uses a correct idiom to show that something is what it is "by virtue of" certain characteristics.

**72.** (G) The original is wrong for two reasons. First, the intended meaning of the sentence requires the verb *come,* not *become.* Second, the verb tense of the original is incorrect. The author here wants to indicate a development that was begun in the past but continues to affect the future. G provides the correct word in the correct tense. H uses the correct tense—but the wrong word. J uses the right word in the correct tense, but *have come* is plural. The subject of the underlined verb is *Christmas*—a singular noun.

**73.** (B)  The original is incorrect because "have . . . combined" is plural but the subject (*season*) is singular.  B correctly changes the verb to the singular form: "has . . . combined."  C fails to correct the error of the original and introduces a new error.  The correct idiom is *combined with*, not *combined to*.  As for D, the placement of *gradually* destroys the sense of the sentence.

**74.** (A)  The original is correct.  B is incorrect because *that* is used to introduce material that is essential to the sentence.  Here the clause introduced by *which* could be left out without materially altering the sense of the sentence (even though some information would be omitted).  C and D both use a verb that will not agree in number with its subject, since *that* refers to *period* and must be singular.

**75.** (H)  The underlined original is not idiomatic.  The correct word for the sense of the sentence is *through*.  G and J are wrong for the same reason.

9

# English Usage Warm-Up Test 2

**DIRECTIONS:** In the passages below, certain parts are underlined and numbered. In the right-hand column are alternative ways of rendering each underlined part. The first alternative is always "NO CHANGE." Choose "NO CHANGE" if you believe that the original underlined part is correct. Otherwise, choose the best alternative. In making your selection, choose the lettered choice that best expresses the thought and observes the requirements of standard written English. Some questions ask you to determine what is required by the interrelationship between two or more parts of the passage.

### Passage 1

No matter how important we may think school life is, there is no denying the fact that children spend more time at home than in the classroom. Therefore, the great influence of parents should not be ignored by administrators and teachers. Parents are becoming strong allies of school personnel, or they can consciously or unconsciously thwart the achievement of curricular objectives.

Administrators have long been aware of the need to keep parents appraised of new methods used in the school; and many principals have conducted workshops explaining such matters like reading readiness, writing, and developmental mathematics programs. Provided that, classroom teachers can also play an important role in enlightening parents. In addition to traditional ways of reporting student progress (such as report cards), personal

1. **A.** NO CHANGE
   **B.** can become
   **C.** became
   **D.** have become

2. **F.** NO CHANGE
   **G.** apprised with
   **H.** in appraisal of
   **J.** apprised of

3. **A.** NO CHANGE
   **B.** matters, such like
   **C.** matters: such as
   **D.** such matters as

4. **F.** NO CHANGE
   **G.** Moreover,
   **H.** Instead,
   **J.** On the contrary,

5. **A.** NO CHANGE
   **B.** progress, (such as report cards),
   **C.** progress, such as report cards
   **D.** progress: report cards and

interviews can aid in achieving <u>significantly</u> a harmonious
<sub>6</sub>

interplay between school and home. Consider an

example:

<u>Suppose that</u> a father has been drilling Junior in arith-
<sub>7</sub>

metic processes night after night. In a friendly interivew,

the teacher can help the parent sublimate his natural

paternal interest into productive <u>channels. You might be</u>
<sub>8</sub>

persuaded <u>that letting</u> Junior discuss the family budget,
<sub>9</sub>

go to the store, and engage in other activities that require

the use of mathematics. If the father <u>followed</u> the ad-
<sub>10</sub>

vice, he will soon see that his son's work in mathematics

is improving and that the son is enjoying the learning

process.

Too often, however, <u>teachers conferencing</u> with par-
<sub>11</sub>

ents are devoted to petty accounts of children's misde-

meanors, complaints about laziness and poor work habits,

and <u>suggestions about</u> penalties and rewards at home.
<sub>12</sub>

**6.** **F.** NO CHANGE
**G.** place before *can*
**H.** place before *aid*
**J.** place before *achieving*

**7.** **A.** NO CHANGE
**B.** supposing that
**C.** suppose that;
**D.** it is supposed that

**8.** **F.** NO CHANGE
**G.** channels. He
**H.** channels, you
**J.** channels. One

**9.** **A.** NO CHANGE
**B.** letting
**C.** of letting
**D.** to let

**10.** **F.** NO CHANGE
**G.** had followed
**H.** follows
**J.** will follow

**11.** **A.** NO CHANGE
**B.** teacher's conferences
**C.** teachers' conferences
**D.** the conferences of teachers

**12.** **F.** NO CHANGE
**G.** suggestions for
**H.** suggestions as regards
**J.** to suggest

## *Passage 2*

### (1)

In the seventeenth century, people believed that

maggots came from decaying things. But Francesco

<u>Redi a scientist</u> could not accept this conclusion. Redi
<sub>13</sub>

<u>begun to suspect</u> that the worms found in meat were
<sub>14</sub>

**13.** **A.** NO CHANGE
**B.** Redi—a scientist,
**C.** Redi, a scientist,
**D.** Redi, a scientist

**14.** **F.** NO CHANGE
**G.** had begun to suspect
**H.** had began to suspect
**J.** had begun suspecting

derived from the droppings of <u>flies and not from</u> decaying
<sub>15</sub>

meat.  This, of course, was a guess and not a conclusion.

(Scientists call a good guess like this a "working

<u>hypothesis."  Because</u> it gives them an idea of how and
<sub>16</sub>

where <u>to start their</u> work.)
<sub>17</sub>

(2)

Redi observed <u>the flies flying</u> to the open jar and laid
<sub>18</sub>

their eggs on the meat.  These eggs hatched into mag-

gots.  Flies also flew to the jar covered with cheesecloth,

although they could not get into the jar to lay their eggs

on the meat.  Flies rarely flew to the airtight jar.

(3)

Then Redi designed an experiment to determine

whether his hypothesis was correct.  He prepared three

<u>jars and a piece of meat was placed in each.</u>  One was
<sub>19</sub>

left <u>open another one</u> was covered with cheesecloth;
<sub>20</sub>
and the third was made airtight.

(4)

Redi was not <u>satisified from doing</u> the experiment
<sub>21</sub>

just once.  <u>Rather,</u> he performed this experiment many
<sub>22</sub>

15. A. NO CHANGE
    B. flies however not from
    C. flies, but not by
    D. flies, and not from,

16. F. NO CHANGE
    G. hypothesis." Due to the fact that
    H. hypothesis." As
    J. hypothesis" because

17. A. NO CHANGE
    B. to start one's
    C. starting their
    D. to be starting one's

18. F. NO CHANGE  .
    G. that the flies flying
    H. that the flies flew
    J. that the flies would fly

19. A. NO CHANGE
    B. jars, and a piece of meat was placed in each
    C. jars in which he placed a piece of meat
    D. jars and placed a piece of meat in each

20. F. NO CHANGE
    G. open, another
    H. open, another being
    J. open; another was

21. A. NO CHANGE
    B. satisfied with doing
    C. satisfied about doing
    D. satisfying to do

22. F. NO CHANGE
    G. But,
    H. Since,
    J. Nevertheless,

times before to arrive at his conclusion.  In this manner
_____23_____

he eliminated the possiblity that his results were due to

chance (luck).  From observations derived from many rep-
_____24_____

etitions of the experiment—Redi concluded that mag-
_____25_____

gots came from flies' eggs and not from the meat.
_____26_____

## Passage 3

"La Bohème" is a grand opera in four acts

and it was written by Giacomo Puccini.  The plot
_____28_____

consisting in four loosely connected scenes, each com-
____29____

plete by themselves, and is set in the Latin Quarter of
____30____

Paris around 1830.  The cast includes four friends, Rodolfo,

Marcello, Schaunard, and Colline are respectfully— a
_____31_____

poet, a painter, a musician, and a philosopher; the

consumptive Mimi; and the frivolous but kind-hearted

Musetta.

The music of the opera is typical Italian.  It is melo-
_____32_____        ____33____

dious but sincere; and even when the characters are at

their gayest, Puccini's melodies are particularly well-suited

23.  A.  NO CHANGE
     B.  he had arrived at
     C.  arriving at
     D.  OMIT

24.  F.  NO CHANGE
     G.  (luck)
     H.  (being lucky)
     J.  OMIT

25.  A.  NO CHANGE
     B.  experiment Redi
     C.  experiment, Redi
     D.  experiment: Redi

26.  F.  NO CHANGE
     G.  of flies
     H.  about from flies'
     J.  from fly's

27.  Choose the sequence of paragraph numbers that
     will make the essay's structure most logical.
     A.  NO CHANGE
     B.  1, 2, 4, 3
     C.  1, 4, 3, 2
     D.  1, 3, 2, 4

28.  F.  NO CHANGE
     G.  written
     H.  that were written
     J.  and it had been written

29.  A.  NO CHANGE
     B.  consists in
     C.  consists of
     D.  consisted of

30.  F.  NO CHANGE
     G.  as itself
     H.  in themselves
     J.  in itself

31.  A.  NO CHANGE
     B.  who are, respectfully
     C.  who are, respectively
     D.  who are, respectively,

32.  F.  NO CHANGE
     G.  (Do NOT begin a new paragraph.) The music
         of the opera
     H.  (Begin a new paragraph.) However, the opera's
         music
     J.  (Do NOT begin a new paragraph.) Since the
         music of the opera

33.  A.  NO CHANGE
     B.  typically Italian
     C.  Italian typically
     D.  Italian typical

to the mood, in this respect, the scene at the Cafe Momus
<u>34</u>

in the second act is particularly noteworthy. The scene,

with its rapid and colorful motion, has an almost kaleido-
<u>35</u>

scopic effect. Occasionally, there are outbursts of crude

and uncontrolled passion, typical of the *verismo* school;

since, generally Puccini's music exhibits the softened and
<u>36</u>

refined sentiments of the later Verdi.

### Passage 4

There is extraordinary exposure in the United States

of the risks of harmful injury and death from motor
<u>37</u>      <u>38</u>

vehicle accidents. More than 80 percent of all

households own passenger cars, and each of these

are driven an average of more than 11,000 miles each year.
<u>39</u>

Amost one-half of fatally injured drivers have a blood

alcohol concentration of 0.1 percent or higher. The aver-

age adult would have to consume over five ounces of 80-

proof spirits in a short period of time to attain these lev-

els. A third of drivers who have been drinking, but fewer

than 4 percent of all drivers, demonstrate these levels.

There are several different approaches with reducing in-
<u>40</u>                                      <u>41</u>

juries in which intoxication plays a role. Based on the

observation that excessive consumption correlates with

the total alcohol consumption of a country's population,

it has been suggested that higher taxes on alcohol would
<u>42</u>

---

**34.** **F.** NO CHANGE
   **G.** mood in
   **H.** mood, with
   **J.** mood. In

**35.** **A.** NO CHANGE
   **B.** having its
   **C.** because its
   **D.** with it's

**36.** **F.** NO CHANGE
   **G.** but, in general,
   **H.** since, in a general way
   **J.** therefore, in general,

**37.** **A.** NO CHANGE
   **B.** risking
   **C.** of risking
   **D.** to the risk

**38.** **F.** NO CHANGE
   **G.** injurious harm
   **H.** harm and injury
   **J.** injury

**39.** **A.** NO CHANGE
   **B.** is driven
   **C.** get driven
   **D.** drives

**40.** **F.** NO CHANGE
   **G.** (Begin a new paragraph.) There is several
   **H.** (Begin a new paragraph.) There are several
   **J.** (Do NOT begin a new paragraph.) There being several

**41.** **A.** NO CHANGE
   **B.** to reducing
   **C.** to reduce
   **D.** of reducing

**42.** **F.** NO CHANGE
   **G.** they suggest
   **H.** it had been suggested
   **J.** they suggested

reduce both. While the heaviest drinkers would be taxed
                                                      43
mostly, anyone who drinks at all would be penalized by

this approach.

    To make drinking and driving a criminal offense is an
            44
approach directed only at intoxicated drivers. In some

states, the law empowers police to request breath tests of

drivers cited for any traffic offense, and elevated blood-

alcohol concentration can be the basis for arrest. The

National Highway Traffic Safety Administration estimates,

however, that even with increased arrests, there are about

700 violations for every arrest. At this level there is little

evidence that laws serving as deterrents to driving while
                     45
intoxicated.

## *Passage 5*

    Why should there be more crime in urban areas than

in rural areas? For one thing, the forces that generate

conditions conducive to crime and riots are more stronger
                                          46
in urban communities as in rural areas. Urban living is
                                47
more anonymous living; and anonymity releases the indi-

vidual of community restraints more commonly in tradition-
       48                    49

oriented societies. Instead, more freedom from constraints
                          50
offers greater opportunity for deviation from accepted

standards of behavior.

43. A.  NO CHANGE
    B.  mostly, would be taxed,
    C.  would mostly be taxed,
    D.  would be taxed the most,

44. F.  NO CHANGE
    G.  The making of drinking and driving
    H.  Drinking and driving being made
    J.  To drink and to drive being made

45. A.  NO CHANGE
    B.  served as deterrents to
    C.  serve as deterrents to
    D.  serve as deterrents of

46. F.  NO CHANGE
    G.  are stronger
    H.  is stronger
    J.  to be stronger

47. A.  NO CHANGE
    B.  then
    C.  than
    D.  as they are

48. F.  NO CHANGE
    G.  from restraints of the community
    H.  of community restraining
    J.  from community restraints

49. A.  NO CHANGE
    B.  common, as
    C.  common
    D.  common like

50. F.  NO CHANGE
    G.  Since more freedom from constraints
    H.  But less contraints
    J.  More freedom from constraints, however,

140

Moreover, in a more impersonalized, formally controlled urban society, regulatory orders of conduct is often directed by distant bureaucrats.  The police are strangers executing these prescriptions on—at worst, an alien subcommunity, and, at best, an anonymous set of subjects.  In a small town or village, minor offenses are often handled without resort to official police action.  This policy results in fewer recorded violations of the law compared to the city.

Finally, urban areas—with mass populations, greater wealth, more commerical establishments, and more products of our technology—also provides more frequently

opportunities for thieving.

## Passage 6

Vacations, once the prerogative of the privileged few —even as late as the nineteenth century.  Now, except for such unfortunate masses as (for example), the bulk

of Chinas and Indias populations, for whom life,

save for sleep and brief periods of rest, are uninterrupted toil, workers consider vacations a right.

51. A. NO CHANGE
    B. are often
    C. is frequently
    D. often get

52. F. NO CHANGE
    G. on, at worst,
    H. on—at the worse—
    J. on at worst

53. A. NO CHANGE
    B. compared with
    C. than
    D. than in

54. F. NO CHANGE
    G. provide more frequently
    H. provide frequenter
    J. provide more

55. A. NO CHANGE
    B. for theft
    C. to thieve
    D. as thieves

56. F. NO CHANGE
    G. Vacations were once
    H. Vacations, once was
    J. Vacations once having been

57. A. NO CHANGE
    B. (for example)
    C. as,
    D. as

58. F. NO CHANGE
    G. Chinese and Indian populations
    H. China and India's population
    J. China's and India's populations

59. A. NO CHANGE
    B. save of sleep
    C. but of sleep
    D. OMIT

60. F. NO CHANGE
    G. are endless
    H. is
    J. seem an

The idea of vacations, as we conceive them would be
<sub>61</sub>
incomprehensible to primitive peoples.  Of course, rest

of some kind has always been a part of the rhythm of
<sub>62</sub>

human life.  For earlier ages did not find it necessary to
<sub>63</sub>
organize it in the way that modern man has done.  Holi-

days and feast days were sufficient.

    Vacations being more important today, because the
<sub>64</sub>
life of the average person is less well-rounded and

had become more compartmentalized.  With the tension
<sub>65</sub>
created by modern life and the stultifying quality of so

much of today's work, this break in the year's routine has
<sub>66</sub>
become increasily important.  Vacations are now con-

sidered essentially for the purpose of renewal and repair.
<sub>67</sub>
And so, in the United States, the most tense and yet the

most self-indulgent of nations, vacations have come to

occupy a dominant place in domestic conversation.


## Passage 7

Man, said Aristotle, is a social animal.  This sociabil-
<sub>68</sub>
ity requires peaceful congregation, and the history of man-

kind is mainly primarily a movement through time of
<sub>69</sub>

human collectivities that range of migrant tribes and large
<sub>70</sub>
and complex civilizations.  Survival depends on the abil-

ity to create the means by which people in groups retain

**61.** A. NO CHANGE
    B. as we conceive them,
    C. in accordance with our conception of it,
    D. as we conceive it,

**62.** F. NO CHANGE
    G. Place after *been*
    H. Place before *Rest*
    J. Place after *part*

**63.** A. NO CHANGE
    B. life, but
    C. life, and
    D. life: however,

**64.** F. NO CHANGE
    G. (Begin a new paragraph.) Vacations are more important
    H. (Begin a new paragraph.) Vacation's being more important
    J. (Do NOT begin a new paragraph.) It is important for you to take a vacation

**65.** A. NO CHANGE
    B. would become
    C. will have become
    D. has become

**66.** F. NO CHANGE
    G. years
    H. year—
    J. year:

**67.** A. NO CHANGE
    B. essential for
    C. for essentially
    D. essentially

**68.** F. NO CHANGE
    G. Man said Aristotle,
    H. Man said Aristotle
    J. Man, said Aristotle

**69.** A. NO CHANGE
    B. mainly
    C. mainly and primarily
    D. on the main

**70.** F. NO CHANGE
    G. ranges from migrant tribes to
    H. range from migrant tribes to
    J. ranging from migrant tribes to

their unity and allegiance to one another.
$$\underline{\hspace{2cm}}$$
71

 Order was created by the need and desire

of surviving the challenge of the environment.  This
72

orderly condition came to be called the "state," and the

rules that maintain it, we call the "law."  In time the
73

partner to this tranquility, man marched across the cen-

turies of his evolution to the brink of exploring the

boundaries of his own galaxy.  Of all living organisms,

only man has the capacity to interpret his own evolution

as progress.  As social life has changed, the worth and
74

rights of each member in the larger group, of which he

was a part, increased.  As the groups grew from clans to
75

civilizations, the value of the individual did not diminish,

but became instead a guide to the rules that govern all men.

71. A. NO CHANGE
    B. them
    C. themselves
    D. each another

72. F. NO CHANGE
    G. for surviving
    H. to survive
    J. of having survived

73. A. NO CHANGE
    B. it, the
    C. its
    D. them,

74. F. NO CHANGE
    G. had changed
    H. is changing
    J. changed

75. A. NO CHANGE
    B. The group's growing
    C. The groups' growing
    D. The groups having grown

# Explanatory Answers

1. (B) The choice of verbs in the original underlined part is inconsistent with the meaning of the second clause of the sentence. The author intends to say that either of two states of affairs could occur: parents can be this or they can do that. B provides the right verb. C and D, both of which describe events of the past, are inconsistent with the intended meaning of the sentence.

2. (J) This is a diction question. To appraise means to evaluate, so F and H are not possible choices. J is correct because the idiomatic expression in English for keeping someone informed is to keep him or her *apprised of* a situation, not *apprised with*.

3. (D) The original is incorrect because the correct idiom here is *such . . . as,* not *such . . . like.* B is simply not standard English. As for C, you should not use a colon to introduce a listing when the listing is also introduced by a phrase in the sentence, e.g., *such as.*

4. (G) The original sentence is incorrect for two reasons. First, *provided* indicates that one idea depends upon another, but the idea that comes before *provided* does not depend on the idea introduced by *provided.* Second, the construction introduced by *provided* lacks a main verb. *Moreover,* which signals a continuation of a thought, is the best choice. (The sense of the paragraph is that administrators can help in this area and so can teachers.) H is incorrect because efforts on the part of teachers are not advocated as substitutes for the efforts of administrators. Yet, *instead* indicates that one thing is substituted for another. As for J, *on the contrary* is used to introduced a contrast, but the author intends a continuation of the first thought.

5. (A) The original is correct. The example of report cards is an aside and can be placed in parentheses. Further, the comma is needed after the second parenthesis to set off the long introductory phrase that begins the sentence. As for B, the comma following *progress* is unnecessary and disrupts the logical flow of the sentence by creating a double pause before the parenthetical expression. As for C, although you might elect to set off *such as report cards* by commas, you would need two of them. The lack of a comma following *cards* creates an ambiguous sentence because *personal interviews,* the subject of the sentence, seems to be a part of the parenthetical expression signalled by the first comma. Finally, the colon in D is wrong because it doesn't serve an appropriate colon function and because what comes before the colon lacks a main verb.

6. (H) In general, a modifier should be placed as close as possible to that which it modifies. Here, *significantly* is an adverb intended to modify *aid,* but its proximity to the gerund of the verb *to achieve* makes it seem as though *significantly* is intended to modify *achieving*—even though *achieving* in this sentence is not a verb. The placement of *significantly* provided by H makes it clear that the adverb modifies *aid.* G is less idiomatic than H because of the proximity of *significantly* to *can.* And J is less idiomatic than H because of the proximity of *significantly* to *achieving.*

7. (A) The original is correct. *Suppose* is the imperative that instructs you, the reader, to make an assumption. B would turn the sentence into a fragment by eliminating the only conjugated verb. C would also create a fragment because of the faulty punctuation. Finally, D is needlessly wordy and changes the meaning of the sentence. The phrase *it is supposed* means *it is believed*—a statement of fact, not a command.

8. (G) The original is incorrect because *you* is intended to refer to *father,* but *you* is a second person pronoun. G supplies the correct pronoun. Further, G correctly begins a new sentence where a new idea is introduced. H, which fails to create a new sentence, results in a comma splice. J is incorrect because *one* is used in English to refer generally to any person, but in this sentence a particular person—the father—is referred to.

9. (D) The original is incorrect because *that* seems to introduce a noun clause but no conjugated verb follows. D avoids this problem by using an infinitive (which is a noun form of a verb) in place of a noun clause. As for B, while the gerund is also a noun form, the use of the gerund here is just not idiomatic. Finally, C, too, is not idiomatic English.

10. (H) The use of the past tense *followed* is inconsistent with the rest of the paragraph. Father's following the teacher's advice is something that might or might not occur in the future. The use of the present tense coupled with the conditional *if* makes it clear that this event might or might not occur. G, like the original, uses a verb that describes past action, so G is also incorrect. As for J, the use of the future tense plus *if* is not idiomatic.

11. (C) The original is ambiguous because it is not clear whether the subject is *conferencing* (a noun modified by *teachers*) or *teachers* (which is modified by *conferencing*). If *teachers* is read as the subject, the sentence lacks meaning. (The sentence would read, "Teachers are devoted to petty accounts. . . .") *Conferencing* is the true subject, but the phrasing is not idiomatic. Moreover, if *conferencing* is read as a noun, then *teachers* should be *teachers'*. C eliminates the ambiguity by making it clear that the subject of the sentence is *conferences,* a noun which is modified by *teachers'* to indicate what kind of conferences are referred to. B is wrong because the noun *teachers* is plural, so the singular possessive (*teacher's*) is incorrect. (If the noun were intended to be singular, it would be preceded by *a.*) The apostrophe must come after the *s* as it does in C. Finally, D is not idiomatic. We use the phrase *teachers' conferences.*

12. (G) The idiomatic expression here is *suggestions for.* H is also unidiomatic. Finally, J destroys the parallelism of the sentence.

13. (C) Although *a scientist* is more or less parenthetical here, it is best to set it off with commas since it is an essential fact. B and D are incorrectly punctuated. A parenthetical remark or aside can be set off with two commas or two dashes, but not a combination of a comma and a dash. Also, the aside requires both an opening and a closing punctuation mark.

14. (G) The original is incorrect because it uses the past participle instead of some conjugated verb. (*Begun* is by itself not a complete verb.) By providing the auxiliary or helping verb *had,* G creates a complete, conjugated verb. H is incorrect because *had* must be followed by the past participle of the verb, but *begun,* and not *began,* is the past participle of *to begin.* Finally, though J also provides a complete verb, the use of the gerund *suspecting* is less idiomatic than the use of the infinitive *to suspect.*

10

15. (A) The original is correct. As for B and C, *however* and *but* are words that signal contrasts, but the *not* in those choices also does this job. Thus, B and C contain constructions that are like double negatives. Additionally, C is incorrect because the preposition must be *from* to go with *derived*. Finally, D is incorrect because the use of commas in D disrupts the logic of the sentence. (Substitute D for the original and read the sentence aloud to yourself, pausing at the commas.)

16. (J) The original is incorrect because the period between *hypothesis* and *because* creates a sentence fragment of everything following the period. G and H are wrong for the same reason. J eliminates the problem of the original by joining the fragment to its main clause.

17. (A) The original is correct. B is incorrect because the pronoun *one's* does not agree in number with its antecedent, *scientists*. C is wrong because the gerund cannot be used in place of the infinitive here. Finally, D is incorrect because the *to be* construction is low-level usage and because D incorrectly uses a singular pronoun instead of a plural one.

18. (H) The original sentence is ambiguous. As written, it seems to say that Redi saw the flies flying. (Here *flies* is the direct object of *saw* and *flying* an adjective modifying *flies*.) But when read in this way, the entire sentence seems to say that Redi saw the flies and laid their eggs. That is obviously not what is intended! The alternatives all avoid this problem. The use of *that* makes it clear that a noun clause, and not *flies*, is supposed to be the object of *saw* (telling what Redi observed). But then *flies* becomes a subject of the noun clause and requires a conjugated verb. Thus, H is correct. *Flew* is a conjugated verb, the subject of which is *flies*. And *flew* is parallel in its tense to the other verb of the noun clause, *laid*.

19. (D) The original sentence shifts illogically from the active voice (*prepared*) to the passive voice (*was placed*). The two verbs should be parallel to each other. D corrects this problem by using the active voice (*placed*). B is wrong because the problem of faulty parallelism is not solved by a comma. C is ambiguous. C seems to suggest that the same piece of meat was placed in all three jars.

20. (J) The original is incorrect because it is a run-on sentence. (There is no punctuation to separate the first two in a series of three complete thoughts.) G does not correct the error because a comma is not sufficient to separate the two thoughts. This just creates a type of run-on sentence called a "comma splice." H fails for the same reason and for the further reason that *being* is not idiomatic here. J is correct because the semicolon separates the two thoughts.

21. (B) The original is incorrect because *satisfied from* is not idiomatic. The correct expression is *satisfied with*. C and D are not idiomatic.

22. (F) The original is correct. *Rather* correctly signals a contrast between the idea of doing the experiment just once and the idea of doing it many times. As for G, although *but* can be used to signal a contrast, *but* doesn't have exactly the meaning required here. Additionally, *but* is a conjunction—not an adverb—so it should not be followed by a comma. H is incorrect for this second reason and for the further reason that *since* does not signal a contrast. Finally, J is wrong because *nevertheless* conveys the meaning "in spite of," not "instead."

23. (C) The original is incorrect because the gerund (*arriving*), not the infinitive (*to arrive*), is required here. B is wrong because there is no need for the past perfect

tense here. (The past perfect tense is used to show that some past event oc-curred before some other past event.) Finally, as for D, the resulting construction (*he performed this experiment many times before his conclusion*) is not meaningful.

24. (J) The best thing to do here is to omit the word in any form because it is redundant. *Luck* means "due to chance," and that has already been stated.

25. (C) The original is incorrectly punctuated. Some punctuation is required to separate the long introductory phrase (*From . . . experiment*), but the correct mark is a comma, not a dash or a colon.

26. (F) The original is correct. G and H are incorrect because the correct expres-sion is *came from*, not *came of* or *came about*. Finally, J incorrectly uses the singular possessive rather than the plural, but the sense of the sentence is that the eggs come from flies in general, not a particular fly.

27. (D) Several clues help you find the correct order of the paragraphs. First, (1) must come first. The first sentences of the other paragraphs refer either explic-itly or implicitly to something that has been mentioned earlier. Paragraph (2), however, cannot be second. Paragraph (2) illogically describes the result of the experiment before the reader is even told about the structure of the experiment. Paragraph (3), which describes the structure of the experiment, must come be-fore (2). Finally, (4) is an appropriate final paragraph because it sets forth the conclusion Redi drew from the result of his experiment.

28. (G) The original is needlessly wordy, as you can see by comparing the original to choice G. G accomplishes in a single word what it takes the original four words to accomplish. Since G is more concise, it is a better rendering. As for H, *were* fails to agree in number with the noun to which *that* refers (*opera*). J is needlessly wordy and uses an incorrect verb tense.

29. (C) The original contains two errors. First, the underlined part should contain a conjugated (main) verb that is parallel to *is*. Second, the correct idiom is *consists of*, not *consists in*. C makes both corrections. B makes the first correc-tion and not the second. D makes both corrections but uses an incorrect verb tense. The author is using the present tense to describe the opera: "It consists of four acts and is set . . . ." So the underlined verb should be in the present, not the past, tense.

30. (J) The original is wrong in two respects. First, the pronoun *themselves* refers to *each*, a singular pronoun. Second, the correct idiom to state that something is self-contained is *in itself*. G is not idiomatic, and H uses the wrong pronoun. Only J corrects both errors.

31. (D) The original is incorrect for two reasons. One, it contains a diction error. The word *respectively*, and not *respectfully*, is used to describe two lists, the elements of which are parallel. Two, the original is ambiguous. As written, it seems as though *Rodolfo, Marcello, Schaunard, and Colline* might be the sub-ject of *are*. Both C and D correct the problem of diction and eliminate the ambiguity, but only D is correctly punctuated. The parenthetical *respectively* must be set off by commas, one before and one after the word.

32. (F) It is correct to begin a new paragraph here because the emphasis of the discussion shifts from a general description of the structure of the opera to a critical commentary on its musical virtues. Since it is appropriate to begin a new paragraph at this point, both G and J are wrong. Additionally, J would

10

create a sentence fragment of the sentence. As for H, *however* is used to signal a contrast of ideas, but the idea contained in the first sentence does not contrast with the ideas presented in the first paragraph.

33. (B) In this sentence, *typical* is intended to modify *Italian;* but since *Italian* is an adjective, it can be modified only by an adverb. B makes the needed correction. As for C, the placement of *typically* behind *Italian* is not idiomatic.

34. (J) The original is a run-on sentence. J corrects the problem by simply creating two separate sentences. G just makes the original worse. With G, there is not even an attempt to keep the different ideas from running together. Finally, H is not idiomatic.

35. (A) The original underlined portion is correct as written. B is awkward and not really idiomatic. C is incorrect because the *because* seems to introduce a clause, but there is no verb in that part of the sentence. Finally, D is wrong because *it's* is the contraction for *it is,* but a verb has no logical function in a prepositional phrase.

36. (G) The original is incorrect because *since* creates an illogical transition from the idea contained in the first clause to the idea contained in the second clause. The author intends to say that there are occasional outbursts and that these are the exceptions rather than the rule. So you need a word to signal a contrast, and *but* serves very well. H and J suffer from the same problem as the original.

37. (D) The original is incorrect because *exposure of risks* is not idiomatic English. B and C are also unidiomatic. Only D is idiomatic English.

38. (J) The original is correct. G and H are all redundant, since *harm* and *injury* mean virtually the same thing. J is the best choice because it eliminates the needless repetition.

39. (B) The original is incorrect because *each* is singular and requires a singular verb. B is correct because the verb is singular and in the correct form. C is incorrect because the use of *get* to suggest the passive voice is low-level usage. Finally, D is wrong because the active voice suggests that the car does the driving.

40. (H) A new paragraph is appropriate here since a new idea is being introduced: from the problem of drunk driving to some suggestions for eliminating the problem. Because a new paragraph is needed, both the original and J are wrong. G is incorrect because the the verb must be plural to agree with *approaches.* This leaves H, which is the correct choice. H correctly begins a new paragraph, and the verb *are* agrees with *approaches.*

41. (B) The original underlined part is not idiomatic. The correct idiom is *approaches to reducing* (or perhaps *for reducing*). The original and the other two choices are simply not idiomatic English.

42. (F) The original is correct. The use of the present perfect tense (*has been*) indicates that the suggestion was made sometime in the past and further implies that the force of the suggestion continues even into the present. G is wrong because *they* has no referent. H is incorrect because there is no need to use the past perfect tense here. (The past perfect is used to refer to a past event that occurred before another past event.) Finally, J is wrong because, again, there is no referent for the subject pronoun *they* and no reason for the switch in tense.

**43.** (D) The original contains an error of diction. *Mostly* means "for the most part," but the sense that is needed here is "to the greatest extent." So *most* should be substituted for *mostly*. B fails to correct the error of the original and makes an error of punctuation. (Substitute B for the original and read the resulting sentence, pausing at the commas.) C fails to eliminate the error of the original. Additionally, C is wrong because it omits a needed comma. (Use a comma to separate an introductory subordinate clause from the main clause of the sentence: "While . . . , anyone . . . .")

**44.** (F) The original is correct. G is incorrect because it is awkward. G would have been more nearly correct had it read *Making drinking and driving,* but even that is a bit awkward. H is wrong because it is low-level usage. Finally, J is incorrect because here, too, the use of *being* represents low-level usage.

**45.** (C) The original is incorrect because there is no conjugated verb. The result is a fragment rather than a paragraph. While B provides a conjugated verb, the past tense (*served*) conflicts with the tenses of the other verbs in the sentence (e.g., *estimates*, which is present). C provides a conjugated verb in the correct tense. D is incorrect because *deterrents of* is not idiomatic.

**46.** (G) The original is incorrect because *more stronger* is not idiomatic English. The *-er* itself indicates a comparison, so G is correct. H is wrong because the subject *forces* is plural and cannot take the singular verb *is*. J is incorrect because the resulting construction would be a sentence fragment with no conjugated main verb.

**47.** (C) The correct construction to make a comparison is *stronger than,* not *stronger as*. C corrects the error of the original. B makes an error of diction, confusing *then* with *than*. Finally, D results in an illogical statement: forces are stronger in urban areas as they are (stronger) in rural areas.

**48.** (J) In English the correct idiom is *released from*. Therefore the original sentence and choice H are incorrect. J is a better choice than G because it is more concise and more idiomatic.

**49.** (C) The original is incorrect because *commonly* is an adverb, but what verb (or adjective or other adverb) does *commonly* modify? The sentence intends for *commonly* to modify *restraints,* but an adjective is required for that job. C corrects this problem by using the adjective *common*. B is incorrect because the comparison (*more common*) never gets completed. As a result, the two elements *more common* and *as in . . .* have no logical relationship to the rest of the sentence. D would create a phrase that is not idiomatic English.

**50.** (J) The *instead* in the original is not an appropriate transition word because the idea it introduces is not intended to replace the idea expressed in the preceding sentence. Rather, the idea expressed by the sentence introduced by *instead* is intended to contrast with the idea expressed in the preceding sentence: Urban life offers freedom *but* this is not always good. G is incorrect because *since* does not create the sense of contrast required here and for the further reason that the use of a subordinate conjunction would reduce the sentence to a dependent clause with no supporting independent clause. H contains a diction error. *Fewer* should be used rather than *less*. Additionally, *constraints* is plural but the verb in the sentence is singular.

10

**51.** (B) The original is incorrect because the verb *is* does not agree with its plural subject, *orders*. This reasoning also eliminates choice C. In D, the verb *get* is plural, but the use of *get* to suggest the passive voice is low-level and therefore unacceptable. B correctly supplies the plural verb.

**52.** (G) The original is incorrect because although the *at worst* should be set off from the rest of the sentence, it cannot be set off by a combination of dashes and commas. H sets the phrase off correctly, but the phrase itself is not idiomatic. J is not correctly punctuated. G is the correct answer because it is idiomatic and because the parenthetical remark is correctly set off by commas.

**53.** (D) The original sentence makes an illogical comparison. It attempts to compare violations with a city. B doesn't address this error. C makes a change in the offending structure, but the result is still an illogical comparison between violations and the city. D makes the needed correction: "fewer violations than (there are) in the city."

**54.** (J) The original is incorrect for two reasons. First, the verb *provides* is singular but the subject of the sentence, *areas*, is plural. Second, the placement of *more frequently* creates ambiguity. Given its placement, *more frequently* seems to modify *opportunities*, but *frequently* is an adverb, not an adjective. G eliminates the first error but not the second. H eliminates both errors of the original but introduces a new error: *frequenter opportunities* is not idiomatic. J corrects both errors of the original.

**55.** (B) The original and the other answer choices are simply not idiomatic English. Only B is idiomatic.

**56.** (G) The original is incorrect because there is no main verb. The construction is therefore a fragment. Choice G provides a conjugated verb in the appropriate past tense. H is incorrect because there is no need for a comma after *vacations* and because the verb *was* does not agree with its subject, *vacations*. J is wrong for the same reason as the original—it fails to supply a conjugated main verb.

**57.** (D) In the original the *(for example)* is redundant. The examples have already been introduced by the phrase *such . . . as*. While B attempts to eliminate the redundancy by eliminating *as*, the result is an incomplete construction: *except for such unfortunate masses (for example)*. As for C, the comma following *as* incorrectly separates what is introduced from the introductory *such as*.

**58.** (J) The original is incorrect because although the intention is to show possession, the nouns *China* and *India* do not show possession. Only J correctly puts these nouns in the possessive case. (Both nouns must be possessive since each nation has its own population, as indicated by the plural noun, *populations*. If only the second word were followed by the apostrophe, this would indicate joint possession, e.g., *Tom and Julie's house*—Tom and Julie possess the same house). G is not idiomatic, and H illogically suggests that China and India have a single population.

**59.** (A) The original is correct. *Save for* is an English idiom that means "except for." B and C are not idiomatic phrases. Finally, D is wrong because the resulting sentence would read "for whom life, and brief periods of rest, are uninterrupted." This suggests illogically that the brief periods of rest are uninterrupted.

**60.** (H) The original is incorrect because the verb *are* is plural and does not agree with its subject, *life*. G fails to correct the error of the original and is verbose. J is wrong because *seem*, like *are*, is plural. H provides the singular verb needed here.

**61.** (D) The original is incorrect because *them* is intended to refer to *idea*. (*Them* must refer to *idea* because you can conceive an idea, but you can't conceive a vacation.) Since *idea* is singular, a singular pronoun is required. The original is also incorrect because a comma must follow the pronoun to mark the end of the parenthetical remark. D makes both corrections. B makes the second correction but not the first. C makes both corrections but is extremely wordy and awkward in comparison to the correct choice.

**62.** (F) The placement of *always* in the original is correct. The placements suggested by H and J are less desirable because *always* is too far from the verb it modifies. (Distance creates ambiguity.) Finally, the placement suggested by G is less idiomatic than that of the original.

**63.** (B) The original contains two errors. First, the period following *life* makes a sentence fragment of everything that follows. Second, the *for* is an illogical choice of conjunctions. *For* suggests a continuation of ideas, but the sentence means to contrast what was the case in the past with what is presently the case. B solves both problems. *But* creates a logical transition and makes of the fragment a second independent clause that is then properly married to the first independent clause. C solves the fragment problem but not the transition problem. D attempts to solve both problems of the original but fails because it is incorrectly punctuated. (There is no colon-type role for the colon to play.)

**64.** (G) The original is incorrect because the intended main clause of the sentence (*Vacations . . . today*) lacks a conjugated verb. G corrects this problem. H fails to supply a main verb. As for J, the switch from the third-person, narrative point of view (to *you*) disrupts the logic of the selection. Additionally, a paragraph is required here to mark the transition from the discussion of the past to the discussion of the present.

**65.** (D) The use of the past perfect (*had become*) in the original is inconsistent with the other verbs in the sentence (e.g., *is*). The sense of the sentence is that the life of the average person became less well-rounded at some time in the past and that this condition still continues today. For this, you should use the present perfect—as D does. The *has become* shows that the action began in the past and culminates in the present. B and C are wrong because they use incorrect tenses.

**66.** (F) The original is correct as written. *Year* is a noun, so if it is to be used to modify *routine*, it must be possessive. The *year's routine* means "routine of the year." G is incorrect because *years* is simply a plural noun that cannot modify *routine*. H and J are incorrect because breaking the sentence at this point leaves everything that has become before with no main verb, so it cannot stand by itself.

**67.** (B) The adverb *essentially* seems to modify the verb *considered*, but it is really intended as a predicate adjective modifying *vacations*. Thus, the adjective form should be used—as in B.

10

**68.** (F)  The original is correct because the *said Aristotle* should be set off from the rest of the sentence.  Since the other choices do not correctly set this phrase off, they cause confusion.  (Substitute each into the sentence and read it to yourself, pausing at the commas.)

**69.** (B)  The original and C are redundant, since *mainly* and *primarily* mean just about the same thing.  B solves this problem by eliminating one of the two words.  D is wrong because it is not idiomatic.  The correct idiom is *in the main*. (*On the main* would mean "at sea.")

**70.** (H)  The correct expression in English is *range from . . . to . . . .* The original does not have this form.  G is incorrect because the verb *ranges* is singular but should be plural to agree with *collectivities*.  J is wrong because it fails to supply a conjugated verb.  Thus, the adjective clause introduced by *that* is left with no verb.  H supplies the correct idiom with an appropriate verb form.

**71.** (A)  The original is correct as written.  The phrase *to one another* correctly shows that each individual has a relationship to every other person in the group.  B and C fail to make this clear.  B and C imply that the group has a relationship to itself, and that implies that each person has a relationship to every person in the group—which would mean that a person has a relationship to himself or herself as well.  Finally, D is not idiomatic (though it would be possible to use *each other*).

**72.** (H)  The correct idiom in English is "desire to do something."  H supplies the correct idiom.  The other choices are simply not idiomatic English.

**73.** (B)  The original is incorrect because the sentence lacks parallelism. *The condition came to be called* is in the passive voice, but the underlined part uses the active voice.  B corrects the problem.  In the construction created by B, the verb is understood: the *rules* (came to be called) the *law*.  C destroys the logical structure of the sentence.  The most logical antecedent for *its* is *state*.  But on this reading, C implies that the rules mentioned maintain the *state's* law.  D suffers from a similar problem.  Since *them* is plural, it seems to refer to *rules*.  But then D asserts that the rules maintain themselves.

**74.** (J)  The verb tense of the underlined part is incorrect.  The use of the present perfect (*has changed*) suggests that the change in question continues into the present, but the other verb in the sentence, *increased,* indicates that the process belongs entirely to the past.  As for G, the use of the past perfect (*had changed*) illogically suggests that the change belongs to a period prior to the increase, but the change was manifested as an increase.  So the two, change and increase, belong to the same time frame.  Finally, for this reason, H, too, is wrong, since it implies that the change belongs to the present while the increase belongs to the past.

**75.** (A)  The original is correct as written.  The *as* introduces an adverbial clause that modifies the main verb of the sentence (*did not diminish*).  The other choices all suggest participial phrases, but a participial phrase can be used only as an adjective to modify a noun.  What noun would *growing* or *having grown* modify?  Its proximity to *value* suggests that *value* is the noun modified; but on that reading, the sentence makes no sense.

# Math Diagnostic Test

The ACT tests arithmetic, basic algebra, and elementary geometry. To help you decide what you must study, here is a diagnostic test.

## MATH DIAGNOSTIC TEST
### 40 Questions
### No Time Limit

*Directions:* Enter your answers to the following questions in the blanks provided. Use the available space for scratch work. Although there is no time limit for the exercise, you should work as quickly as possible. After you have finished, review your work using the explanations that follow.

1. To increase the number 12,345,678 by exactly 10,000, it is necessary to increase which digit by one? _____

2. $\dfrac{(7 + 2)(16 \div 4)}{(2 \times 3)(6 \div 2)} =$ _____

3. List all of the factors of 36: _____

4. List all of the prime numbers greater than 10 but less than 30: _____
_____

### Questions 5–7

Indicate whether or not the following *must always* be an even number. Enter *yes* or *no*.

5. Even Number × Odd Number _____

6. Odd Number + Odd Number _____

7. Even Number ÷ Even Number _____

8. In a string of consecutive odd numbers, what is the fifth number following the number 13? _____

**9.** $\dfrac{\left(\dfrac{5}{6}+\dfrac{1}{2}\right)\times\left(\dfrac{4}{3}\times\dfrac{1}{4}\right)}{\left(\dfrac{3}{2}-\dfrac{1}{3}\right)\times\left(\dfrac{2}{3}\div\dfrac{8}{2}\right)}=$ _____

**10.** Convert $2\dfrac{2}{5}$ to a decimal: _____

**11.** Convert 1.125 to a fraction: _____

**12.** $0.001 + 0.01 + 0.227 - 0.027 =$ _____

**13.** $0.1 \times 0.01 =$ _____

**14.** $1.5 \div 0.75 =$ _____

**15.** Convert $2\dfrac{3}{4}$ to a percent: _____

**16.** 2 is what percent of 10? _____

**17.** The price of a certain item increased from $2.00 to $2.50. What was the percent increase in the price? _____

**18.** $\dfrac{(3 - 6) \times (12 \div -2)}{(6 - 8)} =$ _____

**19.** Bob's average score on five tests was 85. If he received scores of 90, 80, 78, and 82 on four of the five tests, what was his score on the remaining test? _____

**20.** In a certain class, a student's final grade is a function of the grades she receives on a midterm exam, a final exam, and a term paper. The term paper counts twice as much as the final exam, and the final exam counts twice as much as the midterm exam. If a student receives a midterm score of 75, a final exam score of 80, and a grade of 90 on the term paper, what is the student's final grade for the course? _____

**21.** A jar contains black and white marbles in the ratio 2:3. If the jar contains a total of 30 marbles, how many of the marbles are black? _____

**22.** In a certain game, if 2 wixsomes are worth 3 chags, and 4 chags are worth 1 plut, then 6 pluts are worth how many wixsomes? _____

**23.** In the proportion $\dfrac{x}{6} = \dfrac{12}{24}$, $x =$ _____

**24.** What is the value of 3 raised to the third power? _____

**25.** $\sqrt{4} + \sqrt{9} =$ _____

**26.** $y - x + 3x - 4y + 3y =$ _____

**27.** $\dfrac{(x^3y^4)^2}{(x^2y^2)(x^4y^6)} =$ _____

**28.** $(a + b)(a + b) =$ _____

**29.** Factor the expression $12x^3 + 3x^2 + 18x$: _____

**30.** Factor the expression $x^2 + 2xy + y^2$: _____

**31.** If $2x + y = 12$ and $y - x = 3$, then $x =$ _____

**32.** If $x^2 + x = 2$, and $x > 0$, then $x =$ _____

**33.** If $x + y \leqq 5$ and $y \geqq 2$, then what is the maximum possible value of $x$?
_____

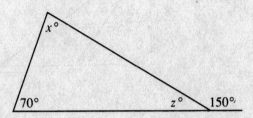

**34.** In the figure above, what is the value of $x$? _____

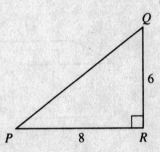

**35.** In the figure above, what is the length of side $PQ$? _____

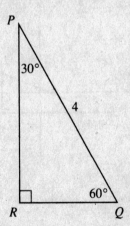

**36.** In the figure above, what is the length of sides $PR$ and $RQ$?

PR: _____ RQ: _____

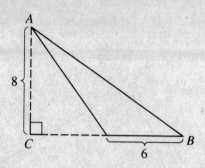

**37.** In the figure above, what is the area of triangle *ABC*? _____

**38.** A circle has a diameter of 4.  What is the area of the circle? _____

What is the circumference of the circle? _____

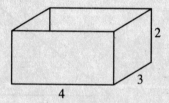

**39.** What is the volume of the rectangular box shown above? _____

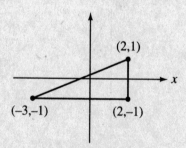

**40.** In the figure above, what is the area of the triangle? _____

# Explanatory Answers

1. Changing the digit 4 to 5 will increase the number by 10,000 to 12,355,678.

2. 2

   $$\frac{(7 + 2)(16 \div 4)}{(2 \times 3)(6 \div 2)} = \frac{(9)(4)}{(6)(3)} = \frac{36}{18} = 2$$

3. 1 and 36; 2 and 18; 3 and 12; 4 and 9; and 6 and 6

4. 11, 13, 17, 19, 23, and 29

5. Yes. For example, $2 \times 3$ is 6, which is even.

6. Yes. For example, $3 + 5$ is 8, which is even.

7. No. For example, $2 \div 4$ is a fraction and therefore not an even number.

8. 23

| | First | Second | Third | Fourth | Fifth |
|---|---|---|---|---|---|
| 13 | 15 | 17 | 19 | 21 | 23 |

9. $\dfrac{4}{9}$

   $$\frac{\left(\frac{5}{6}+\frac{1}{2}\right)\times\left(\frac{4}{3}\times\frac{1}{4}\right)}{\left(\frac{3}{2}-\frac{1}{3}\right)-\left(\frac{2}{3}\div\frac{8}{2}\right)} = \frac{\left(\frac{8}{6}\right)\left(\frac{4}{12}\right)}{\left(\frac{7}{6}\right)-\left(\frac{1}{6}\right)} = \frac{\frac{4}{9}}{1} = \frac{4}{9}$$

10. 2.4

    $$2\frac{2}{5} = \frac{12}{5} = 2.4$$

11. $1\dfrac{1}{8}$

    $$1.125 = 1 + 0.125 = 1 + \frac{125}{1,000} = 1 + \frac{1}{8} = 1\frac{1}{8}$$

**12.**

$$\begin{array}{r} 0.001 \\ 0.010 \\ +\ 0.227 \\ \hline 0.238 \\ -\ 0.027 \\ \hline 0.211 \end{array}$$

**13.** 0.001

$$\begin{array}{r} 0.01 \\ \times\quad .1 \\ \hline 0.\overline{001} \end{array}$$

**14.** 2

$$0.75\,\overline{)1.50}\quad \overset{2}{\phantom{)}}$$

**15.** 275%

$$2\frac{3}{4} = \frac{11}{4} = 2.75 = 275\%$$

**16.** 20%

$$\frac{2}{10} = 0.20 = 20\%$$

**17.** 25%

$$\frac{\text{Increase}}{\text{Original Price}} = \frac{\$0.50}{\$2.00} = \frac{1}{4} = 25\%$$

**18.** −9

$$\frac{(3-6) \times (12 \div -2)}{(6-8)} = \frac{-3 \times -6}{-2} = \frac{18}{-2} = -9$$

**19.** 95

$$\frac{90 + 80 + 78 + 82 + x}{5} = 85$$

$$\frac{330 + x}{5} = 85$$

$$330 + x = 85(5)$$
$$x = 425 - 330$$
$$x = 95$$

**20.** 85

$$\frac{75 + 2(80) + 4(90)}{7} = \frac{595}{7} = 85$$

**21.** 12

There are $2 + 3 = 5$ ratio parts. So each part has the value $30 \div 5 = 6$. Two of the parts are black marbles, and $2 \times 6 = 12$.

**22.** 16

Since 2 wixsomes equal 3 chags, 8 wixsomes equal 12 chags. Since 4 chags equal 1 plut, 12 chags equal 3 pluts. Therefore, 8 wixsomes equal 3 pluts, and 16 wixsomes equal 6 pluts.

**23.** $x = 3$

Cross-multiply: $24x = 72$
Divide by 24: $x = 3$

**24.** 27

$3 \times 3 \times 3 = 27$

**25.** 5

$\sqrt{4} = 2$ and $\sqrt{9} = 3$, and $2 + 3 = 5$

**26.** $2x$

$y - x + 3x - 4y + 3y = 3x - x + y - 4y + 3y = 2x$

**27.** 1

$$\frac{(x^3 y^4)^2}{(x^2 y^2)(x^4 y^6)} = \frac{x^6 y^8}{x^6 y^8} = 1$$

**28.** $a^2 + 2ab + b^2$

**29.** $3x(4x^2 + x + 6)$

**30.** $(x + y)(x + y)$

**31.** $x = 3$

Since $y - x = 3$, $y = 3 + x$. Therefore,
$2x + (3 + x) = 12$
$3x + 3 = 12$
$3x = 9$
$x = 3$

11

**32.** $x = 1$

Rewrite the original equation: $x^2 + x - 2 = 0$.
Factor: $(x + 2)(x - 1) = 0$.
So the two solutions are $x = -2$ or $x = +1$.

**33.** 3

$x$ will be the greatest when $y$ is the least. So let's use the minimum possible value for $y$: $x + 2 \leqq 5$, so $x \leqq 3$. The maximum value for $x$ is 3.

**34.** $80°$

The unlabeled angle with the $150°$ angle form a straight line, for a total of $180°$. Therefore the unlabeled angle is $180°$ less $150°$, or $30°$. Then, the interior angles of the triangle total $180°$. So:
$70° + 30° + x° = 180°$
$x + 100 = 180$
$x = 80$

**35.** 10

This is a right triangle, so you can use the Pythagorean Theorem to find the length of the hypotenuse:
$PR^2 + QR^2 = PQ^2$
$(8)^2 + (6)^2 = PQ^2$
$64 + 36 = PQ^2$
$PQ^2 = 100$
$PQ = 10$

**36.** $PR = 2\sqrt{3}$ and $RQ = 2$

In a triangle with angles of $30°$, $60°$, and $90°$, the side opposite the $30°$ angle is one-half the length of the hypotenuse, while the side opposite the $60°$ angle is one-half the length of the hypotenuse times the square root of 3.

**37.** 24

The area of a triangle is equal to $\frac{1}{2} \times$ altitude $\times$ base. So $\frac{1}{2} \times 8 \times 6 = 24$.

**38.** The radius of a circle is one-half the diameter, so the radius of this circle is 2.

Area $= \pi r^2 = \pi(2)^2 = 4\pi$

Circumference $= 2\pi r = 2\pi(2) = 4\pi$

**39.** 24

To find the volume of a rectangular solid, multiply the length by the width by the depth: $2 \times 3 \times 4 = 24$.

**40.** 5

The length of the altitude is 2; the length of the base is 5; so the area is $\frac{1}{2}(2)(5) = 5$.

11

# Introduction to Math Usage

## ✔ Objectives

To learn the general rules that govern math usage items.

To learn about figures that may not be drawn to scale.

To learn what is tested in the math usage sections.

To learn to avoid attractive but wrong choices.

To learn to use the ladder of difficulty to eliminate wrong choices.

1. **Two Important Facts about Math Usage**
   - Scale of Figures
   - Areas Tested

2. **The Six Problem Types**
   - Arithmetic Manipulation
   - Arithmetic Application
   - Algebra Manipulation
   - Algebra Application
   - Geometry Manipulation
   - Geometry Application

3. **Don't Be Misled by Sloppy Detective Work!**

Math Usage questions are standard multiple-choice items with five answer choices. A Math Usage Test should contain 40 items, and the time limit should be 50 minutes.

## Two Important Facts about Math Usage

**1. The figures that accompany the problems in the Math Usage Test may or may not be drawn to scale.**

**EXAMPLE:**

In the figure below, $x = ?$

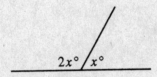

A. 15
B. 30
C. 45
D. 60
E. 120

Since the sum of the measures in degrees of the angles of a straight line is 180, $2x° + x° = 180°$. So $3x° = 180°$, and $x = 60°$. If you measure angle $x$ with a protractor, you will find it is indeed 60°.

Sometimes, however, a figure will not be drawn to scale.

**EXAMPLE:**

In the figure below, AB = ?

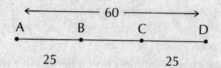

F.  5
G.  10
H.  15
J.  20
K.  25

The answer to this question is G.  Although the three segments are drawn so that they appear to be equal, the accompanying labels make it clear that the segments are not equal.  The correct answer, therefore, is not 25.

$$AB + BC + CD = 60$$
$$AB + 25 + 25 = 60$$
$$AB = 60 - 50$$
$$AB = 10$$

Although the distances are not drawn to scale, you are entitled to assume that points ABCD are on line AD in the order shown.  Therefore, regardless of the accuracy of the drawing, you can deduce mathematically that AB is equal to 10.

Here are other examples to illustrate the difference between valid and invalid conclusions based on figures that are not drawn to scale.

**EXAMPLES:**

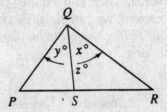

Which of the following must be true?
 I.  PS < SR
 II. z = 90
 III. x > y
 A.  I only
 B.  I and II only
 C.  I and III only
 D.  I, II, and III
 E.  Neither I, II, nor III

Which of the following must be true?
 I.  PR > PS
 II. z > x
 III. x + y = z
 F.  I only
 G.  I and II only
 H.  II and III only
 J.  I, II, and III
 K.  Neither I, II, nor III

The answer to the first question is E.  Although all three statements look like they are true the way the figure is drawn, the figure might also be drawn as follows:

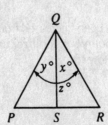

Notice the lines and points in this redrawn figure are in the same position relative to each other as they are above.  However, in this figure it appears that all three statements are false.  Therefore, none of the three statements is necessarily true.

The answer to the second question, however, is J. No matter how the figure is drawn, all three of these statements must be true. Statement I must be true, since PS is only a part of PR. For the same reason, II must be true: Angle x is only a part of angle z. And III must be true since x and y are the only two parts of z.

**2. Math Usage tests arithmetic, algebra, and geometry.** Some of the questions will look just like math drill items; others will require you to apply your knowledge of math to new situations. Therefore, we can classify math usage questions according to whether they just test your ability to do mathematical manipulations or require you to do some original thinking:

|              | Arithmetic | Algebra | Geometry |
|--------------|:----------:|:-------:|:--------:|
| Manipulation | 1          | 3       | 5        |
| Application  | 2          | 4       | 6        |

Your methods for attacking a particular problem will depend on what type of problem you have. The following problems illustrate the six categories.

### 1. Arithmetic Manipulation

What is the average of 8.5, 7.8, and 7.7?
A. 8.3
B. 8.2
C. 8.1
D. 8.0
E. 7.9

No original thinking is needed to solve this question. To find the average of the three numbers, you simply total them and divide the sum by 3:

$$\frac{8.5 + 7.8 + 7.7}{3} = \frac{24.0}{3} = 8.0$$

So the answer is D.

### 2. Arithmetic Application

If the price of fertilizer has been decreased from three pounds for $2 to five pounds for $2, how many more pounds of fertilizer can be purchased for $10 than could have been purchased before?
F. 2
G. 8
H. 10
J. 12
K. 15

The operations required here are the basic ones of arithmetic, but applying them to this new situation requires some original thinking.

To solve the question, you have to determine how many pounds of fertilizer could have been purchased at the old price and how many can be purchased at the new price. With $10, it's possible to buy five $2 measures of fertilizer ($10 \div 2 = 5$). At the old price, this would mean $5 \times 3 = 15$ pounds. At the new price, this would be $5 \times 5 = 25$ pounds. Therefore, it's possible to buy $25 - 15 = 10$ more pounds at the new price than at the old price. So the answer is H.

### 3. Algebra Manipulation

If $x - 5 = 3 - x$, then $x = $ ?
A. $-8$
B. $-2$
C. $2$
D. $4$
E. $8$

To answer this question, you need only to solve for $x$—one of the basic manipulations of algebra:

$$x - 5 = 3 - x$$

Add $x$ to both sides:

$$x - 5 + x = 3 - x + x$$
$$2x - 5 = 3$$

Add 5 to both sides:

$$2x - 5 + 5 = 3 + 5$$
$$2x = 3 + 5$$
$$2x = 8$$

Divide both sides by 2:

$$2x \div 2 = 8 \div 2$$
$$x = 4$$

So the answer is D.

### 4. Algebra Application

A vending machine dispenses $k$ cups of coffee, each at a cost of $c$ cents, every day. If $M$ is the total amount of money in *dollars* taken in by the vending machine during a period $d$ days long, which of the following equations can be used to find $M$?

**F.** $M = \dfrac{100kc}{d}$

**G.** $M = kcd$

**H.** $M = \dfrac{dk}{c}$

**J.** $M = \dfrac{kcd}{100}$

**K.** $M = \dfrac{kc}{100d}$

This question requires more than just basic manipulation. You must apply your knowledge of algebra to a new situation. Let's first find the total amount of money received by the vending machine in cents. It sells $k$ cups each day at $c$ cents per cup, so it takes in $k$ times $c$, or $kc$, cents every day. And it does this for $d$ days, so the total taken in (in cents) is $kc$ times $d$, or $kcd$. But $M$ is the total amount in dollars. Since there are 100 cents in every dollar, we need to divide $kcd$ by 100. So $M$ is equal to $\frac{kcd}{100}$—choice J.

### 5. Geometry Manipulation

If a circle has a radius of 1, what is its area?

**A.** $\dfrac{\pi}{2}$

**B.** $\pi$

**C.** $2\pi$

**D.** $4\pi$

**E.** $\pi^2$

This very easy question just requires that you substitute 1 into the formula $\pi r^2$: $\pi(1)^2 = \pi(1 \times 1) = \pi(1) = \pi^2$.

Very few ACT geometry questions are as easy as this. Virtually all require that you apply your knowledge of formulas to a new situation.

### 6. *Geometry Application*

In the figure below, a triangle is inscribed in a circle with center O. What is the area of the circle?

F. $\dfrac{\pi}{2}$

G. $\dfrac{\pi}{\sqrt{2}}$

H. $\pi$

J. $\pi\sqrt{2}$

K. $2\pi$

To answer this question, we will have to find the radius of the circle. Since the hypotenuse of the triangle is also the diameter of the circle, we can find the radius of the circle by calculating the length of the hypotenuse of the triangle. First we use the Pythagorean Theorem:

$PR^2 = PQ^2 + QR^2$

$PR^2 = (\sqrt{2})^2 + (\sqrt{2})^2$

$PR^2 = 2 + 2 = 4$

$PR = \sqrt{4} = 2$

So the diameter of the circle is 2, which means the radius of the circle is 1. Now we use the formula for calculating the area of a circle, just as we did above: $\pi r^2 = \pi(1)^2 = \pi$. So the answer is H.

## Don't be misled by sloppy detective work!

Although this part of the ACT is a "math" test, you must also read carefully in this section. While this is always important, there are three special cases where it becomes even more important.

**First, pay very careful attention to any words in the question stem that are emphasized.** When a question stem contains a thought-reverser, it is usually capitalized. Why? To catch your attention. A thought-reverser is a negative word that turns a question around.

> **EXAMPLE:**
>
> A jar contains black and white marbles. If there are ten marbles in the jar, which of the following could NOT be the ratio of black to white marbles?
>
> **A.** 9:1
>
> **B.** 7:3
>
> **C.** 1:1
>
> **D.** 1:4
>
> **E.** 1:10

Ordinarily, questions are phrased in the affirmative, such as "Which of the following is . . .?" or "Which of the following could be . . .?" This question, however, contains the thought-reverser *NOT*. So a wrong answer here would ordinarily be a right answer, and vice versa.

The answer is E. Since there are ten marbles, the number of ratio parts in the ratio must be a factor of 10. E is not possible since $1 + 10 = 11$, and 10 is not evenly divisible by 11.

**Second, pay careful attention to words like "least" and "smallest."**

> **EXAMPLE:**
>
> If $n$ is a negative number, which of the following is the least?
>
> **F.** $-n$
>
> **G.** $n - n$
>
> **H.** $n + n$
>
> **J.** $n^2$
>
> **K.** $n^4$

Make sure that you don't do what you would ordinarily do and look for the largest value. The correct answer is H. Since $n$ is a negative number, F, J, and K are all positive. Then G is just zero since it is one number subtracted from itself. H is the smallest since a negative added to a negative yields a negative number, which is even less than zero.

**Third, pay careful attention to the units used in asking the question.**

> **EXAMPLE:**
>
> If a machine produces 240 thingamabobs per hour, how many minutes are needed for the machine to produce 30 thingamabobs?
>
> **(A)** 6    **(B)** 7.5    **(C)** 8    **(D)** 12    **(E)** 12.5

The answer is B. A machine that produces 240 units per hour produces 240 units/60 minutes = 4 units/minute. To produce 30 units will take $30 \div 4 = 7.5$ *minutes*.

When you encounter questions of the sort just discussed, draw a circle around the key words (e.g., *NOT* or *smallest* or the units). Then, after you have found your solution, stop and ask yourself, "Did I solve for the right thing?" The circles around the key words will catch your eye and remind you of the significance of the emphasized word, and the last step of asking yourself whether you got the right solution will help you avoid making a silly mistake.

# It's One of the Five Suspects

The Math Usage Test affords you an excellent opportunity to apply Holmesian thinking to the ACT.  One of the most important principles to keep in mind is that the correct answer choice is one of the five "suspects" you are given.  Since the suspects are right there in front of you, you may be able to solve the problem just by "cross-examining" them.

**EXAMPLE:**

Which of the following is the prime factorization of 120?
A.   (2)(2)(15)
B.   (2)(3)(4)(5)
C.   (2)(2)(3)(10)
D.   (2)(2)(2)(3)(5)
E.   (2)(2)(3)(3)(5)

This question asks that you find all of the prime factors of 120, and one way of attacking the question is to try to factor 120 into its prime components.  Alternatively, you could use the Holmesian strategy of "cross-examining" the five suspects, that is, testing each choice.

A.   (2)(2)(15) = 60
B.   (2)(3)(4)(5) = 120
C.   (2)(2)(3)(10) = 120
D.   (2)(2)(2)(3)(5) = 120
E.   (2)(2)(3)(3)(5) = 180

Immediately you can see that A and E must be wrong, because the product of those numbers is not 120.  Now examine the remaining choices.  Which of the remaining choices consists solely of prime numbers?  Not B, which includes 4 (not a prime because $2 \times 2 = 4$).  Not C, which includes 10 (not a prime because $2 \times 5 = 10$).  The answer is D.  The product of those numbers is 120, and each of those numbers is a prime.

Which of the following is the factorization of $x^2 + 4x - 2$?

F.   $(6x + 1)(x - 3)$
G.   $(6x + 3)(x - 1)$
H.   $(3x - 1)(2x - 2)$
J.   $(2x + 2)(3x - 1)$
K.   $(2x + 4)(3x - 2)$

12

This question is similar to the one above. Instead of trying to factor the expression $6x^2 + 4x - 2$, just test each answer choice. Multiply the expression in each of the answer choices until you find the one that is equal to $6x^2 + 4x - 2$:

**F.** $(6x + 1)(x - 3) = 6x^2 - 17x - 3$  (Wrong.)

**G.** $(6x + 3)(x - 1) = 6x^2 - 3x - 3$  (Wrong.)

**H.** $(3x - 1)(2x - 2) = 6x^2 - 8x + 2$  (Wrong.)

**J.** $(2x + 2)(3x - 1) = 6x^2 + 4x - 2$  (Right!)

**K.** $(2x + 4)(3x - 2) = 6x^2 + 8x - 8$  (Wrong.)

Which of the following is the complete solution set to the equation $2x^2 - 3x = 2$?

**A.** $\{\frac{1}{2}, 2\}$

**B.** $\{-\frac{1}{2}, 2\}$

**C.** $\{-\frac{1}{2}, -2\}$

**D.** $\{2, -2\}$

**E.** $\{2, 4\}$

One way of attacking this question is to find the roots of the quadratic equation. Of course, to do this, you'll have to put the equation in standard form, factor, and then solve for $x$. An alternative strategy is just to "cross-examine" the five suspects. Test the values given in the equation to find which values work. Start with A:

$$2\left(\frac{1}{2}\right)^2 - 3\left(\frac{1}{2}\right) = 2$$

$$2\left(\frac{1}{4}\right) - \frac{3}{2} = 2$$

$$\frac{1}{2} - \frac{3}{2} = 2$$

$$-1 = 2$$

Wrong. So $\frac{1}{2}$ is not a solution to the equation, and A is not the correct choice. Now try B:

$$2\left(-\frac{1}{2}\right)^2 - 3\left(-\frac{1}{2}\right) = 2$$

$$2\left(\frac{1}{4}\right) - \left(-\frac{3}{2}\right) = 2$$

$$\frac{1}{2} + \frac{3}{2} = 2$$

Correct. So $-\frac{1}{2}$ is one of the solutions to the equation. Now try the other part of B:

$$2(2)^2 - 3(2) = 2$$

$$2(4) - 6 = 2$$

$$8 - 6 = 2$$

$$2 = 2$$

Correct. So 2 is also a solution to the equation. This proves that the solution set for the equation is $\{-\frac{1}{2}, 2\}$ and that B is the correct answer.

Which of the following equations correctly describes the relationship between the values $x$ and $y$ in the table below?

| $x$ | $-2$ | $-1$ | 0 | 1 | 2 |
|-----|------|------|---|---|---|
| $y$ | $\dfrac{10}{3}$ | $\dfrac{8}{3}$ | 2 | $\dfrac{4}{3}$ | $\dfrac{2}{3}$ |

   **A.**  $3x + 2y = 6$
   **B.**  $3x - 2y = 3$
   **C.**  $3x + 3y = -6$
   **D.**  $6x + 4y = 7$
   **E.**  $2x + 3y = 6$

Instead of trying to devise an equation that fits the values in the table, just plug the pairs of values into each equation until you find the equation that works. Make things easy on yourself and start with the integral values:

   **A.**  $3x + 2y = 6$
       $3(0) + 2(2) = 6$   (Wrong.)
   **B.**  $3x - 2y = 3$
       $3(0) - 2(2) = 3$   (Wrong.)
   **C.**  $3x + 3y = -6$
       $3(0) + 3(2) = -6$   (Wrong.)
   **D.**  $6x + 4y = 7$
       $6(0) + 4(2) = 7$   (Wrong.)
   **E.**  $2x + 3y = 6$
       $2(0) + 3(2) = 6$   (Right!)

12

# Summary

1. The Math Usage Test should contain 40 items, and the time limit should be 50 minutes.

2. Geometry figures are not necessarily drawn to scale. You CANNOT rely on the apparent magnitudes of lines, angles, or areas; but you can trust that lines drawn as straight are straight and that points are in the order shown.

3. Math Usage items test both basic manipulations and further applications of arithmetic, algebra, and geometry.

4. Read the questions carefully. Circle any capitalized words such as SMALLEST and LEAST. Pay careful attention to the units in which your answer must be given. After working a problem, consciously ask yourself whether you have answered the question that is asked.

5. The correct answer choice must be one of the five choices given. Look for opportunities to use the principle of the "five suspects" to get answers by testing the choices themselves.

# Math Usage: Arithmetic

✔ **Objectives**

To learn basic attack strategies for arithmetic items.

To learn advanced Holmesian strategies to simplify or avoid arithmetic manipulations.

To learn to handle complicated application problems.

To learn specific strategies for the five most important areas of arithmetic.

To learn to use the answer choices themselves to generate solutions.

1. **Arithmetic Manipulations**
   - **Divisibility**
   - **The Flying-X**
   - **Decimal–Fraction Equivalents**
   - **Approximation**
2. **Arithmetic Applications**
3. **Some Common Types of Problems**
   - **Properties of Numbers**
   - **Percents**
   - **Ratios**
   - **Averages**
   - **Proportions**
4. **It's One of the Five Suspects**

13

In this chapter, we discuss three topics: techniques for handling pure arithmetic manipulations; strategies for dealing with problems that require some original thinking; and hints for dealing with some frequently used question types.

# Arithmetic Manipulations

### 1. Watson's Favorites

Some easy problem-solving questions ask for nothing more than simple addition, subtraction, multiplication, or division. These are Watson's favorites, since the obvious and correct strategy is to perform the indicated operation.

FOR ARITHMETIC MANIPULATIONS, JUST DO THE OPERATIONS.

**EXAMPLES:**

$\dfrac{8}{9} - \dfrac{7}{8} = ?$

A. $\dfrac{1}{72}$

B. $\dfrac{15}{72}$

C. $\dfrac{1}{7}$

D. $\dfrac{1}{8}$

E. $\dfrac{15}{7}$

The answer is A, and the arithmetic is so simple that you should not hesitate to perform the subtraction indicated:

$$\frac{8}{9} - \frac{7}{8} = \frac{64 - 63}{72} = \frac{1}{72}$$

$$\sqrt{1 - \left(\frac{1}{9} + \frac{1}{6} + \frac{1}{36}\right)} = \ ?$$

F. $\dfrac{1}{5}$

G. $\sqrt{\dfrac{2}{3}}$

H. $\dfrac{5}{6}$

J. $1$

K. $\sqrt{3}$

Again, you should perform the indicated operations:

$$\sqrt{1 - \left(\frac{1}{9} + \frac{1}{6} + \frac{1}{36}\right)} =$$

$$\sqrt{1 - \left(\frac{4}{36} + \frac{6}{36} + \frac{1}{36}\right)} =$$

$$\sqrt{1 - \frac{11}{36}} = \sqrt{\frac{36}{36} - \frac{11}{36}} = \sqrt{\frac{25}{36}} = \frac{5}{6}$$

## 2. Holmes Helps

Here are some hints to help you do calculations more quickly.

### Divisibility

If a number is even, then it is divisible by two; for example, 9,999,992 is divisible by two.

If a number ends in zero or five, it is divisible by five; for example, 1,005 and 1,230 are divisible by five.

If the sum of the digits of a number is divisible by three, then the number is divisible by three; for example, 12,327. Since $1 + 2 + 3 + 2 + 7 = 15$ and 15 is divisible by three, 12,327 is divisible by three.

### The Flying-X

Ordinarily when we add or subtract fractions, we look for a lowest common denominator. But that's only because we want the result in lowest terms for reasons of convenience. So long as you are prepared to reduce your final result, you don't really need to use a lowest common denominator. Instead, you can add or subtract any two fractions in the following way:

THE FLYING-X METHOD OF ADDING AND SUBTRACTING FRACTIONS

$$\frac{a}{b} + \frac{c}{d} = \frac{a}{b} \diagdown + \diagup \frac{c}{d} = \frac{ad + bc}{bd}$$

$$\frac{a}{b} - \frac{c}{d} = \frac{a}{b} \diagdown - \diagup \frac{c}{d} = \frac{ad - bc}{bd}$$

The method is called the "flying-x" because of the picture it creates—an x flying above the ground.  (Also, it helps you fly through the calculation).  The steps are:

1. Find the new denominator by multiplying the old denominators.
2. Multiply the numerator of the first fraction by the denominator of the second fraction.
3. Multiply the denominator of the first fraction by the numerator of the second fraction.
4. Add (or subtract) the results of steps (2) and (3).

**EXAMPLES:**

$$\frac{4}{5} + \frac{3}{4} \overset{\longleftarrow}{\underset{\longleftrightarrow}{+}} \frac{3}{4} = \frac{16 + 15}{20} = \frac{31}{20}$$

$$\frac{4}{5} - \frac{3}{4} \overset{\longleftarrow}{\underset{\longleftrightarrow}{-}} \frac{3}{4} = \frac{16 - 15}{20} = \frac{1}{20}$$

Of course, this method does not guarantee your results will be in lowest terms, but you can correct that by reducing.

**Decimal/Fraction Equivalents**

You should memorize the following decimal/fraction equivalents:

$$\frac{1}{2} = 0.50$$

$$\frac{1}{3} = 0.33\frac{1}{3} = 0.333\ldots$$

$$\frac{1}{4} = 0.25$$

$$\frac{1}{5} = 0.20$$

$$\frac{1}{6} = 0.16\frac{2}{3} = 0.1666\ldots$$

$$\frac{1}{7} = 0.14\frac{2}{7} = 0.1428\ldots$$

$$\frac{1}{8} = 0.125$$

$$\frac{1}{9} = 0.11\frac{1}{9} = 0.1111\ldots$$

What about fractions like $\frac{4}{9}$ or $\frac{5}{8}$?  No need to memorize more equivalents; just multiply.  Since $\frac{1}{9}$ is approximately 0.111, $\frac{4}{9}$ is approximately 4 × 0.111 or 0.444; and since $\frac{1}{8}$ is 0.125, $\frac{5}{8}$ is 5 × 0.125, or 0.625.

Sometimes it is easier to use fractions than decimals in a calculation.

**EXAMPLES:**

0.125 × 0.125 × 64 = ?

A.  0.625
B.  0.125
C.  0.5
D.  1
E.  8

The answer is D. The problem can be solved quickly if you convert 0.125 to its fraction equivalent, $\frac{1}{8}$:

$$\frac{1}{8} \times \frac{1}{8} \times 64 = \frac{1}{64} \times 64 = 1$$

$\dfrac{0.111 \times 0.666}{0.166 \times 0.125}$ is approximately

**F.** 6.8

**G.** 4.3

**H.** 3.6

**J.** 1.6

**K.** 0.9

Convert the decimals to their fractional approximations.

$$\frac{\frac{1}{9} \times \frac{2}{3}}{\frac{1}{6} \times \frac{1}{8}} = \frac{2}{27} \div \frac{1}{48} = \frac{2}{27} \times 48 =$$

$$\frac{96}{27} = 3\frac{5}{9} \cong 3.555$$

The final conversion can even be done in your head. Since $\frac{1}{9} \cong .111$, $\frac{5}{9} \cong 5 \times .111 = .555$.

### Approximation

The answer choices in the Math Usage Test are always arranged in numerical order, and they are sometimes far enough apart to permit approximation.

**EXAMPLE:**

$-4.01(3.2) + 0.2(0.4) = ?$

**A.** $-12.752$

**B.** $-4.536$

**C.** $0.432$

**D.** $1.251$

**E.** $12.783$

$-4.01$ times $3.2$ is about $-12$, and $0.2$ times $0.4$ is a small number. Therefore, the correct answer choice must be approximately $-12$—clearly choice A.

### Arithmetic Applications (Alas, poor Watson!)

On each ACT, there are arithmetic questions that require some original thinking, and Watson often has difficulty with these items. Why should Watson have trouble with arithmetic questions? Because he fails to attack them in a systematic fashion. When Watson can't envision the needed sequence of operations all at once, he goes off in just any direction, adding and subtracting, multiplying and dividing, until he finally gets a wrong answer or gets so discouraged he abandons the problem as too difficult.

Holmes, on the other hand, thrives on such items because he analyzes them step by step. He knows that the question stem gives him all the clues needed to solve the mystery, if he can only put them together in the right order.

HOLMES' METHOD FOR SOLVING COMPLICATED PROBLEMS:
1. What is the question to be answered?
2. What information have I been given?
3. How can I bridge the gap between (1) and (2)?
4. Execute the needed operations.

Notice that Holmes doesn't start doing arithmetic (step 4) until he has formulated his solution to the problem.

Here is how the method works:

### EXAMPLE:

If the senior class has 360 students, of whom $\frac{5}{12}$ are women, and the junior class has 350 students, of whom $\frac{4}{7}$ are women, how many more women are there in the junior class than in the senior class?

**A.** $(350 - 360)\left(\frac{4}{7} - \frac{5}{12}\right)$

**B.** $\dfrac{(350 - 360)\left(\frac{4}{7} - \frac{5}{12}\right)}{2}$

**C.** $\left(\frac{4}{7} \times \frac{5}{12}\right)(360 - 350)$

**D.** $\left(\frac{4}{7} \times 350\right) - \left(\frac{5}{12} \times 360\right)$

**E.** $\left(\frac{5}{12} \times 350\right) - \left(\frac{4}{7} \times 350\right)$

This is a good question to illustrate logical thinking, because you don't even have to do the arithmetic. All you need to do is set up the problem.

STEP 1: What is the question to be answered?
If the senior class has 360 students, of whom $\frac{5}{12}$ are women, and the junior class has 350 students, of whom $\frac{4}{7}$ are women, how many more women are there in the junior class than in the senior class?

Depending on how complex the problem is, Holmes might make a note of what is required:

Women Juniors − Women Seniors

STEP 2: What information am I given? The question states the total number of students in each class and the fraction who are women.

STEP 3: How can I bridge the gap? Multiplying the total number by the fraction who are women will fill in the blanks in the statement in Step 1.

STEP 4: Execute. The solution is $(\frac{4}{7} \times 350)$ minus $(\frac{5}{12} \times 360)$, which is choice D.

13

Here is another question to illustrate how Holmes breaks a solution down into several steps.

**EXAMPLE:**

If the price of candy increases from five pounds for $7 to three pounds for $7, how much less candy (in pounds) can be purchased for $3.50 at the new price than at the old price?

F.  $\frac{2}{7}$

G.  $1\frac{7}{35}$

H.  $3\frac{4}{35}$

J.  1

K.  2

STEP 1: What is the question to be answered?
If the price of candy increases from five pounds for $7 to three pounds for $7, how much less candy (in pounds) can be purchased for $3.50 at the new price than at the old price (the amount $3.50 used to buy minus the amount $3.50 now buys)? Because the question is fairly complex, Holmes might write this down:

$$\text{amt. } \$3.50 \text{ old} - \text{amt. } \$3.50 \text{ new}$$

STEP 2: What information am I given? The question gives pounds and dollars for two different prices.

STEP 3: How can I bridge the gap? Find the cost per pound and divide the amount you have to spend by the cost per pound. The result is the quantity you can buy.

STEP 4: Execute. If $7 buys five pounds, the cost is $7 \div 5 = \frac{7}{5}$ dollars per pound. $3.50 = \frac{7}{2}$ dollars, and $\frac{7}{2} \div \frac{7}{5} = \frac{7}{2} \times \frac{5}{7} = \frac{5}{2}$. If $7 buys three pounds, the cost is $7 \div 3 = \frac{7}{3}$ dollars per pound, and $\frac{7}{2} \div \frac{7}{3} = \frac{7}{2} \times \frac{3}{7} = \frac{3}{2}$. Finally, $\frac{5}{2} - \frac{3}{2} = 1$. So the answer is J. (As was suggested above, we used fractions rather than decimals. This made the arithmetic in Step 4 easier.)

Learning to think in a systematic way is not easy, and it is not a skill that can be acquired just by reading about it. In this respect, systematic thinking is like playing a sport or a musical instrument. You can't just read a book about basketball or the violin and expect to become a star player or virtuoso performer overnight. Still, the more you practice logical thinking, the better you'll become at it. So as you do practice problems later in this book, try to break down your solutions to difficult questions into steps.

# Some Common Types of Problems

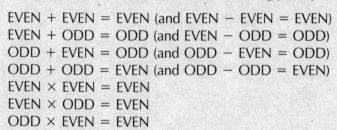

### Properties of Numbers

You should be familiar with the following principles of odd and even numbers:

EVEN + EVEN = EVEN (and EVEN − EVEN = EVEN)
EVEN + ODD = ODD (and EVEN − ODD = ODD)
ODD + EVEN = ODD (and ODD − EVEN = ODD)
ODD + ODD = EVEN (and ODD − ODD = EVEN)
EVEN × EVEN = EVEN
EVEN × ODD = EVEN
ODD × EVEN = EVEN
ODD × ODD = ODD

**Note:** The multiplication properties do <u>not</u> hold for division. This is because division may not result in a whole number; for example, $2 \div 4 = \frac{1}{2}$, a fraction. Odd and even are properties of integers, not fractions.

Questions based on these principles usually ask that you make a judgment about the "structure" of a number.

> **EXAMPLE:**
>
> If $n$ is an odd integer, which of the following must also be odd?
>  I. $n + n$
>  II. $n + n + n$
>  III. $n \times n \times n$
>  **A.** I only
>  **B.** II only
>  **C.** III only
>  **D.** II and III only
>  **E.** I, II, and III

The answer is D. As for I, since $n$ is odd, $n + n$ must be even—not odd. As for II, since $n + n$ is even, $n + (n + n)$ must be odd. And as for III, since $n$ is odd, $n \times n$ is odd and so, too, $n \times (n \times n)$ is odd.

In the example just studied, the question specifies that $n$ is an odd number. You get a different answer if the question is changed to specify that $n$ is an even number:

> **EXAMPLE:**
>
> If $n$ is an even integer, which of the following must also be even?
>  I. $n + n$
>  II. $n + n + n$
>  III. $n \times n \times n$
>  **F.** I only
>  **G.** II only
>  **H.** III only
>  **J.** II and III only
>  **K.** I, II, and III

13

Now the answer is K.

Some structures are odd or even no matter what the value of $n$.

> **EXAMPLE:**
>
> If $n$ is an integer, which of the following must be even?
> I. $2n$
> II. $2n + n$
> III. $2n \times n$
> A. I only
> B. II only
> C. III only
> D. I and II only
> E. I and III only

The answer is E. As for I, $2n$ has the structure "2 times $n$", so no matter what the value of $n$, $2n$ must be even. As for III, since $2n$ is even, $2n \times n$ must be even (an even number times any other number always yields an even number). II, however, may or may not be even. Although we know that $2n$ is even, $2n + n$ will be even only if $n$ is even (even plus even); if $n$ is odd, $2n + n$ will be odd (even plus odd).

A variation on this type of question uses the phrase *consecutive integers*.

CONSECUTIVE INTEGERS ARE INTEGERS IN A ROW: 3, 4, 5, AND 6 ARE CONSECUTIVE INTEGERS, AS ARE $-2$, $-1$, 0, 1, AND 2.

Since a number in a series of consecutive integers is just one more than its predecessor and one less than its successor, consecutive integers can be represented as: $n$, $n + 1$, $n + 2$, $n + 3$, and so on.

> **EXAMPLE:**
>
> Which of the following represents the product of two consecutive integers?
> F. $2n + 1$
> G. $2n + n$
> H. $2n^2$
> J. $n^2 + 1$
> K. $n^2 + n$

The answer is K. If $n$ is an integer, the next larger consecutive integer is just one more: $n + 1$. And the product of $n$ and $n + 1$ is $n(n + 1) = n^2 + n$.

Sometimes a question will ask about consecutive even numbers or consecutive odd numbers.

> **EXAMPLE:**
>
> If $n$ is an odd number, which of the following represents the third odd number following $n$?
> A. $n + 3$
> B. $n + 4$
> C. $n + 6$
> D. $3n + 3$
> E. $4n + 4$

The answer is C. If $n$ is an odd number, the next odd number is $n + 2$, then $n + 4$, then $n + 6$.

**EXAMPLE:**

If $n$ is the first number in a series of three consecutive even numbers, which of the following represents the sum of the three numbers?

F.  $n + 2$

G.  $n + 4$

H.  $n + 6$

J.  $3n + 6$

K.  $6(3n)$

The answer is J. Since $n$ is even, the next even number is $n + 2$ and the one following that is $n + 4$. The sum of $n$, $n + 2$, and $n + 4$ is $n + n + 2 + n + 4 = 3n + 6$.

Notice that in the two previous examples it was stipulated that $n$ was either odd or even. This is important, because $n + 2$ can be either odd or even, depending on whether $n$ is odd or even.

**EXAMPLE:**

If $n$ is any integer, which of the following is always an odd integer?

A.  $n - 1$

B.  $n + 1$

C.  $n + 2$

D.  $2n + 1$

E.  $2n + 2$

The answer is D. Since $n$ can be either even or odd, $n - 1$, $n + 1$, and $n + 2$ can be either even or odd. $2n + 1$, however, must always be odd. No matter what $n$ is, $2n$ is even, and $2n + 1$ must be odd. By the same reasoning, E must always be even.

The behavior of positive and negative numbers is also a basis for questions. You should know the following principles:

POSITIVE × POSITIVE = POSITIVE (and POSITIVE ÷ POSITIVE = POSITIVE)
POSITIVE × NEGATIVE = NEGATIVE (and POSITIVE ÷ NEGATIVE = NEGATIVE)
NEGATIVE × POSITIVE = NEGATIVE (and NEGATIVE ÷ POSITIVE = NEGATIVE)
NEGATIVE × NEGATIVE = POSITIVE (and NEGATIVE ÷ NEGATIVE = POSITIVE)

**EXAMPLE:**

If $n$ is a negative number, which of the following must be positive?

I.  $2n$

II.  $n^2$

III.  $n^5$

F.  I only

G.  II only

H.  III only

J.  I and II only

K.  II and III only

The correct answer is G. Since $n$ is negative, $2n$ must also be negative. As for III, since $n$ is negative, $(n \times n) \times (n \times n) \times n$ is a positive times a positive, which is a positive, multiplied by a negative. So the final result is negative. II, however, must be positive since $n^2$ is just $n \times n$, and a negative times a negative yields a positive.

Finally, fractions have a peculiar characteristic that might be the basis for a question.

THE RESULT OBTAINED FROM MULTIPLYING A FRACTION BY ITSELF IS SMALLER THAN THE ORIGINAL FRACTION; FOR EXAMPLE, $\frac{1}{2} \times \frac{1}{2} \times \frac{1}{2} = \frac{1}{8}$ AND $\frac{1}{8} < \frac{1}{2}$.

**EXAMPLE:**

If $0 < x < 1$, which of the following is the largest?
A. $x$
B. $2x$
C. $x^2$
D. $x^3$
E. $x + 1$

The answer is E. When a fraction is raised to a power, the result is smaller than the original fraction, so C and D are smaller than A. B, however, is double A, so B is larger. But finally, E is larger than B. $2x$ is equal to $x + x$, and since $1 > x$, E must be larger than B.

AS A LAST RESORT, TRY SUBSTITUTING NUMBERS.

Just pick some values and test them in the choices.

**EXAMPLE:**

If $-1 < x < 0$, which of the following is the largest?
F. $-1$
G. $x$
H. $2x$
J. $x^3$
K. $x - 1$

The answer is J, but the problem is a little tricky. You might want to test a value, for example, $-\frac{1}{2}$. On the assumption that $x = -\frac{1}{2}$, the choices have the values:

F. $-1$

G. $-\dfrac{1}{2}$

H. $-1$

J. $-\dfrac{1}{8}$

K. $-1\dfrac{1}{2}$

The largest of these is $-\frac{1}{8}$.

Some questions require that you use the concept of absolute value. Absolute value just means the magnitude of the number without regard to its sign, and it is indicated in this way: $|x|$. Thus:

$$|-2| = 2 \quad |2| = 2 \quad |-0.1| = 0.1 \quad |0.1| = 0.1$$

In other words, whatever is inside the absolute value brackets must be taken to be positive. (This is somewhat like talking about distance without regard to direction. Twenty miles to the east and 20 miles to the west are both distances of 20 miles—in opposite directions. Likewise, $-20$ and $+20$ are distances of 20 units on a number line, but one is positive and the other negative.)

**EXAMPLE:**

What is $|5| - |-5| + |-3|$?
A. $-8$
B. $-3$
C. 3
D. 8
E. 13

The answer is C: $|5| = 5$, $|-5| = 5$, and $|-3| = 3$. And $5 - 5 + 3 = 3$.

13

# Properties of Numbers (Answers, page 213)

1. If $n$ is an even number, all of the following must also be even EXCEPT:
   A. $n^3$.
   B. $n^2$.
   C. $2n$.
   D. $2n + n$.
   E. $2n + 5$.

2. If $3n$ is an even number, which of the following must be an odd number?
   F. $n$
   G. $2n$
   H. $n + 1$
   J. $n + 2$
   K. $n^2$

3. If $n$ is an integer, which of the following *must* be an odd number?
   A. $n + 1$
   B. $2n$
   C. $2n + 1$
   D. $2(n + 1)$
   E. $n^2$

4. If $m$, $n$, $o$, $p$, and $q$ are integers, then $m(n + o)(p - q)$ must be even when which of the following is even?
   F. $m + n$
   G. $n + p$
   H. $m$
   J. $o$
   K. $p$

5. If $n$ is an integer, which of the following *must* be even?
   A. $n - 1$
   B. $n + 1$
   C. $3n + 1$
   D. $2n + 2$
   E. $2n + n$

6. If $p$ is the smallest of three consecutive integers, $p$, $q$, and $r$, then what is the sum of $q$ and $r$ expressed in terms of $p$?
   F. $3p + 3$
   G. $3p + 1$
   H. $2p + 3$
   J. $2p + 1$
   K. $2p$

7. If the fifth number in a series of five consecutive integers has the value $n + 3$, then what is the first number in the series expressed in terms of $n$?
   A. $0$
   B. $1$
   C. $n - 1$
   D. $n - 3$
   E. $-4n$

8. If $n$ is negative, then all BUT which of the following must also be negative?
   F. $n^5$
   G. $n^3$
   H. $\dfrac{1}{n}$
   J. $\dfrac{1}{n^2}$
   K. $\dfrac{2}{n^3}$

9. If $x = -1$, then which of the following is the largest?
   A. $2x$
   B. $x$
   C. $\dfrac{x}{2}$
   D. $x^2$
   E. $x^3$

10. If $x$ is greater than zero but less than 1, which of the following is the largest?
    F. $\dfrac{1}{x^2}$
    G. $\dfrac{1}{x}$
    H. $x$
    J. $x^2$
    K. $x^3$

11. $|-2| + |3| - |4| = ?$
    A. $-1$
    B. $1$
    C. $2$
    D. $6$
    E. $9$

12. $|-3| - |-2| + |10| = ?$
    F. $-4$
    G. $-1$
    H. $3$
    J. $5$
    K. $11$

13. $-301 + |-301| + -114 + |-114| = ?$
    A. $-830$
    B. $-423$
    C. $0$
    D. $611$
    E. $830$

14. $|-3| \times |-4| = ?$
    F. $-12$
    G. $-1$
    H. $1$
    J. $6$
    K. $12$

13

**15.** $|-12| \div |-3| = ?$
   A.   $-4$
   B.   $-3$
   C.   3
   D.   4
   E.   6

## Percents

Aside from the very basic operation of taking a percent of some number (for example, 25% of 60 = 15), there are really only two different kinds of percent questions. One question asks for the ratio of two numbers expressed as a percent (for example, 4 is what percent of 20?); the other asks about percent change in a quantity.

All percent questions in the first category can be solved by a simple little Holmesian device called the "this-of-that" strategy. Compare the following questions:

What percent is 4 of 20?
4 is what percent of 20?
Of 20, what percent is 4?

The questions are equivalent, for they all ask for the same thing: express $\frac{4}{20}$ as a percent. Notice also that in each there is the phrase "of 20" and the other number, 4.
   Generally, then, these questions all have the form:

What percent is this of that?
This is what percent of that?
Of that, what percent is this?

You can solve any question of this type using the "this-of-that" strategy.

THIS-OF-THAT: CREATE A FRACTION IN WHICH THE NUMBER IN THE PHRASE "OF THAT" IS THE DENOMINATOR AND THE OTHER NUMBER IN THE QUESTION (THE "THIS") IS THE NUMERATOR. CONVERT THE FRACTION TO A PERCENT.

### EXAMPLES:

If a jar contains 24 white marbles and 48 black marbles, then what percent of all the marbles in the jar are black?
   A.   10%
   B.   25%
   C.   $33\frac{1}{3}\%$
   D.   60%
   E.   $66\frac{2}{3}\%$

Using the "this-of-that" strategy, we create a fraction:

$$\frac{\text{black marbles}}{\text{of all marbles}} = \frac{48}{(24 + 48)} = \frac{48}{72} = \frac{2}{3} = 66\frac{2}{3}\%$$

Three friends shared the cost of a tape recorder. If Andy, Barbara, and Donna each paid $12, $30, and $18, respectively, then Donna paid what percent of the cost of the tape recorder?

**F.** 10%

**G.** 20%

**H.** $33\frac{1}{3}$%

**J.** 50%

**K.** $66\frac{2}{3}$%

In this question the phrase *of the cost* establishes the denominator. The cost is 12 + 30 + 18 = 60. The numerator is the other item in the question, Donna's contribution:

$$\frac{\text{Donna's}}{\text{Total}} = \frac{18}{60} = \frac{3}{10} = 30\%$$

The other type of percent question asks about the percent change in a quantity. The Holmesian strategy for such questions is the "change-over" formula.

**EXAMPLE:**

If the price of an item increased from $5.00 to $5.25, what was the percent increase in the price?

**A.** 50%

**B.** 25%

**C.** 20%

**D.** 5%

**E.** 4%

The answer is D.

CHANGE-OVER STRATEGY: TO FIND PERCENT CHANGE, CREATE A FRACTION. PUT THE CHANGE IN THE QUANTITY OVER THE ORIGINAL AMOUNT. CONVERT THE FRACTION TO A PERCENT.

13

$$\frac{\text{Change}}{\text{Original Amount}} = \frac{(5.25 - 5.00)}{5.00} = \frac{0.25}{5.00} = 0.05 = 5\%$$

The "change-over" strategy works for decreases as well.

**EXAMPLE:**

If the population of a town was 20,000 in 1970 and 16,000 in 1980, what was the percent decline in the town's population?

**F.** 50%

**G.** 25%

**H.** 20%

**J.** 10%

**K.** 5%

$$\frac{\text{Change}}{\text{Original Amount}} = \frac{(20,000 - 16,000)}{20,000} = \frac{4,000}{20,000} = \frac{1}{5} = 20\%$$

So there was a 20-percent decline in the town's population.

Be careful that you don't confuse the two strategies. Compare the following three questions:

If 20 people attended Professor Rodriguez's class on Monday and 25 attended on Tuesday, then the number of people who attended on Monday was what percent of the number who attended on Tuesday?

A. 5%

B. 20%

C. 25%

D. 80%

E. 125%

If 20 people attended Professor Rodriguez's class on Monday and 25 attended on Tuesday, then the number of people who attended on Tuesday was what percent of the number who attended on Monday?

F. 5%

G. 20%

H. 25%

J. 80%

K. 125%

If 20 people attended Professor Rodriguez's class on Monday and 25 attended on Tuesday, then what was the percent increase in attendance from Monday to Tuesday?

A. 5%

B. 20%

C. 25%

D. 80%

E. 125%

Only the third question asks about percent *change*; the first two questions are of the form "this-of-that." So the answer to the first question is $\frac{20}{25} = \frac{4}{5} = 80\%$, or D. The answer to the second question is $\frac{25}{20} = \frac{5}{4} = 125\%$, or K. And the answer to the third question, using the "change-over" strategy, is $\frac{(25 - 20)}{20} = \frac{5}{20} = \frac{1}{4} = 25\%$.

# Percents (Answers, page 214)

1. A certain company has 120 employees. If 24 of the employees are in the union, what percent of the employees are NOT in the union?
   A. 12%
   B. 24%
   C. 48%
   D. 80%
   E. 96%

2. In 1960, a certain tree was 12 meters tall. If the tree measured 15 meters in 1985, by what percent did its height increase?
   F. 3%
   G. 25%
   H. 40%
   J. 80%
   K. 125%

3. At 9:00 a.m. on Monday the price of gold was $450 per ounce. If the price of gold at 3:00 that same day was $441 per ounce, what was the percent decease in the price of gold during the day?
   A. 98%
   B. 9.8%
   C. 9%
   D. 2%
   E. 0.2%

4. In 1940, the price of a certain item was $0.20. If the same item cost $1.00 in 1987, what was the percent increase in the price of the item?
   F. 20%
   G. 80%
   H. 120%
   J. 400%
   K. 500%

5. In a certain school, 40 percent of the students are boys. If there are 80 boys in the school, what is the total number of students in the school?
   A. 32
   B. 50
   C. 120
   D. 200
   E. 320

6. The price of an item increased by 25 percent. If the new price of the item after the increase is $2.00, what was the *original* price?
   F. $1.50
   G. $1.60
   H. $1.75
   J. $2.50
   K. $3.20

13

| Average Price of Metal X (per ounce) | |
|---|---|
| 1981 | $10 |
| 1982 | $11 |
| 1983 | $12 |
| 1984 | $15 |
| 1985 | $18 |
| 1986 | $21 |

**7.** The greatest percent increase in the average per-ounce price of metal x occurred during which period?
A.  1981–1982
B.  1982–1983
C.  1983–1984
D.  1984–1985
E.  1985–1986

## Questions 8–10

| Number of Fires in City Y | |
|---|---|
| 1982 | 100 |
| 1983 | 125 |
| 1984 | 140 |
| 1985 | 150 |
| 1986 | 135 |

**8.** The number of fires in 1982 was what percent of the number of fires in 1983?
F.  25%
G.  $66\frac{2}{3}$%
H.  80%
J.  100%
K.  125%

**9.** The number of fires in 1986 was what percent of the number of fires in 1985?
A.  90%
B.  82%
C.  50%
D.  25%
E.  10%

**10.** What was the percent decrease in the number of fires from 1985 to 1986?
F.  10%
G.  25%
H.  50%
J.  82%
K.  90%

## Ratios

In addition to the basic idea of a ratio, you may be asked to divide a quantity according to ratio parts or to work with a three-part ratio.

First, you may be asked to divide a quantity according to a ratio.

TO DISTRIBUTE A QUANTITY ACCORDING TO A RATIO, DIVIDE THE QUANTITY BY THE TOTAL NUMBER OF RATIO PARTS. THEN MULTIPLY THAT RESULT BY THE NUMBER OF PARTS TO BE DISTRIBUTED.

**EXAMPLE:**

A groom must divide 12 quarts of oats between two horses. If Dobbin is to receive twice as much as Pegasus, how many quarts of oats should the groom give to Dobbin?

A. 4

B. 6

C. 8

D. 9

E. 10

The answer is C. The oats must be divided according to the ratio 2:1. There are 2 + 1 = 3 ratio parts, so each part is 12 ÷ 3 = 4 quarts. Dobbin gets 2 parts, or 2 × 4 = 8 quarts.

The other type of ratio question involves three parts.

**EXAMPLE:**

If the ratio of John's allowance to Lucy's allowance is 3:2, and the ratio of Lucy's allowance to Bob's allowance is 3:4, what is the ratio of John's allowance to Bob's allowance?

F. 1:6

G. 2:5

H. 1:2

J. 3:4

K. 9:8

The answer is K. In a problem like this, the middle term (the one that appears in both ratios) joins the other two terms like a common denominator. Here the common term is Lucy's allowance. Adjust the ratios so that the "Lucy" term has the same value in both ratios. The ratio of John's allowance to Lucy's is 3:2, and that is equivalent to 9:6. The ratio of Lucy's allowance to Bob's is 3:4, and that is equivalent to 6:8. So the ratio John:Lucy:Bob is 9:6:8, and the ratio John:Bob is 9:8.

13

# Ratios (Answers, page 215)

1. In a certain box of candy, the ratio of light chocolates to dark chocolates is 4:5. If the box contains 36 candies, how many of the candies are dark chocolates?
   A. 9
   B. 18
   C. 20
   D. 24
   E. 27

2. In a certain school, the ratio of Seniors to Juniors is 5:4, and the ratio of Seniors to Sophomores is 6:5. What is the ratio of Sophomores to Juniors?
   F. 2:3
   G. 24:25
   H. 1
   J. 25:24
   K. 3:2

3. In a certain library, the ratio of fiction to nonfiction books is 3:5. If the library contains a total of 8,000 books, how many of the books are nonfiction?
   A. 2,400
   B. 3,000
   C. 3,600
   D. 4,800
   E. 5,000

4. In a certain game, three nurbs are equal to two zimps, and six clabs are equal to one zimp. Four clabs are equal to how many nurbs?
   F. 1
   G. 2
   H. 3
   J. 4
   K. 5

5. A $1,000 bonus is to be divided among three people so that Jane receives twice as much as Robert, who receives one-fifth as much as Wendy. How much money should Wendy receive?
   A. $100
   B. $125
   C. $250
   D. $375
   E. $625

### Averages

Aside from the very simple questions that ask you to calculate the average of several numbers, there are two questions about averages that you should know about.

The first kind asks about a missing element.

**EXAMPLE:**

If the average of 35, 38, 41, 43, and x is 37, what is x?

**A.** 28
**B.** 30
**C.** 31
**D.** 34
**E.** 36

The answer is A.  Using the general idea of average:

$$\frac{35 + 38 + 41 + 43 + x}{5} = 37$$

So: $35 + 38 + 41 + 43 + x = 5(37)$

$$157 + x = 185$$

$$x = 28$$

THE DIFFERENCE OF THE SUMS METHOD FOR FINDING THE MISSING QUANTITY (OR QUANTITIES) OF AN AVERAGE:

(1) FIND THE SUM OF ALL THE QUANTITIES BY MULTIPLYING THE AVERAGE BY THE TOTAL NUMBER OF QUANTITIES.
(2) ADD UP THE KNOWN QUANTITIES.
(3) SUBTRACT THE RESULT OF (2) FROM THE RESULT OF (1).  THE DIFFERENCE IS THE MISSING QUANTITY (OR THE SUM OF THE MISSING QUANTITIES).

In the question above, the total of all five elements in the average had to be 185.  But the total of the four we were given was only 157.  So the missing element had to be 185 − 157 = 28.

There is a Holmesian shortcut you can use with this type of problem.

THE AVERAGE IS THE "MIDPOINT" OF THE NUMBERS AVERAGED.

So if the average of 35, 38, 41, 43, and x is 37, the values in excess of 37 must equal the values below 37.  Instead of doing an "official" calculation, you can reason that 35 is 2 below the average, or −2; 38 is one over, or +1; 41 is 4 over, or +4; 43 is 6 over, or +6.  Now you add up those numbers: −2 + 1 + 4 + 6 = +9.  To offset this overage and bring the average down to 37, the missing number must be nine less than 37, or 28.  You can check this result by calculating the average using 28.

As you might have already guessed, there are some variations on this theme, but all can be solved in essentially the same way.

**EXAMPLE:**

For a certain student, the average of ten test scores is 80. If the high and low scores are dropped, the average is 81. What is the average of the high and low scores?

F.  76
G.  78
H.  80
J.  81
K.  82

The answer is F. The sum of the ten test scores is $80 \times 10 = 800$. The sum of the eight scores after the two scores have been dropped is $8 \times 81 = 648$. So the two scores that were dropped total $800 - 648 = 152$. And since there are two of them, their average is $152 \div 2 = 76$.

**EXAMPLE:**

In a certain shipment, the average weight of six packages is 50 pounds. If another package is added to the shipment, the average weight of the seven packages is 52 pounds. What is the weight (in pounds) of the additional package?

A.  2
B.  7
C.  52
D.  62
E.  64

The answer is E. The total weight of the original six packages is $6 \times 50 = 300$ pounds. The total weight of the seven packages is $7 \times 52 = 364$ pounds. So the weight of the final package is $364 - 300 = 64$ pounds.

The other unusual average question that you might encounter is a weighted average.

**EXAMPLE:**

In a certain course, a student's final exam grade is weighted twice as heavily as his midterm grade. If a student receives a score of 84 on his final exam and 90 on his midterm, what is his average for the course?

F.  88
G.  87.5
H.  86.5
J.  86
K.  85

The answer is J. You have to be sure you weight the final exam grade twice as much as the midterm grade:

$$\frac{90 + 2(84)}{3} = \frac{258}{3} = 86$$

In calculating a weighted average, there are two things to watch out for. First, make sure you have the average weighted properly. Second, make sure you divide by the correct number of quantities.

**EXAMPLE:**

In a certain group of children, three children are ten years old and two are five years old. What is the average age in years of the children in the group?

A. 6

B. 6.5

C. 7

D. 7.5

E. 8

The answer is E:

$$\frac{3(10) + 2(5)}{5} = \frac{40}{5} = 8$$

Notice that we weight the ages according to the number of children in the group, and then we divide by five (the number of children in the group).

13

# Averages (Answers, page 215)

1. If the average of six numbers, 12, 15, 18, 14, 13, and $x$, is 14, what is $x$?
   A. 10
   B. 11
   C. 12
   D. 13
   E. 14

2. The average weight of four packages on a scale is 16 pounds. When one of those packages is removed, the average of the remaining three packages is 14 pounds. What is the weight in pounds of the package that was removed?
   F. 16
   G. 18
   H. 21
   J. 22
   K. 24

3. Herman purchased three books that cost $2, five books that cost $3, and one book that cost $6. What was the average cost of the books?
   A. $3
   B. $4
   C. $5
   D. $6
   E. $7

4. On a certain toll road, the toll charge is 10 cents per mile for the first 50 miles, 20 cents per mile for the next 20 miles, and 30 cents per mile for the last 10 miles. What is the average cost per mile (in cents) for the entire trip?
   F. 10.5
   G. 12
   H. 12.5
   J. 15
   K. 18

5. The average weight of ten people sitting in a boat is 145 pounds. If one person gets out of the boat, the average weight of the remaining people is 150 pounds. What is the weight in pounds of the person who got out of the boat?
   A. 90
   B. 100
   C. 120
   D. 150
   E. 175

## Proportions

The simplest of all problems with a proportion asks that you solve for an unknown quantity.

> **EXAMPLE:**
>
> If $\frac{2}{3} = \frac{x}{12}$, $x = ?$
>
> **A.** 3
> **B.** 4
> **C.** 6
> **D.** 8
> **E.** 9

To solve, you cross-multiply:

$$\frac{2}{3} = \frac{x}{12}$$

$$2(12) = 3x$$

$$3x = 24$$

Then you divide both sides by 3:

$$3x \div 3 = 24 \div 3$$

$$x = 8$$

Proportions also provide you with a powerful Holmesian strategy for solving word problems that ask about things like cost, output, distance, and so on.

IF A QUESTION INVOLVES QUANTITIES THAT CHANGE IN THE SAME DIRECTION WITH ONE ANOTHER, USE A PROPORTION TO SOLVE FOR UNKNOWN QUANTITIES.

> **EXAMPLE:**
>
> If 4.5 pounds of chocolate cost $10, how many pounds of chocolate can be purchased for $12?
>
> **F.** $4\frac{3}{4}$
>
> **G.** $5\frac{2}{5}$
>
> **H.** $5\frac{1}{2}$
>
> **J.** $5\frac{3}{4}$
>
> **K.** 6

This is not a difficult question, and Watson will probably get it right. He reasons that $10 buys $4\frac{1}{2}$ pounds of chocolate, so the cost per pound is $10 $\div$ $4\frac{1}{2}$ = $2\frac{2}{9}$. (We use a fraction to avoid the repeating decimal 2.222 . . . .) Next Watson divides: $12 \div 2\frac{2}{9} = 5\frac{2}{5}$. So (B) is the correct answer.

There is nothing conceptually wrong with what Watson has done, but the same result can be achieved more easily by using a proportion:

$$\frac{\text{Amount } X}{\text{Amount } Y} = \frac{\text{Cost } X}{\text{Cost } Y}$$

$$\frac{4\frac{1}{2}}{x} = \frac{10}{12}$$

Cross-multiply:

$$4\frac{1}{2}(12) = 10x$$

$$54 = 10x$$

Solve for $x$: $x = 5\frac{2}{5}$.

> **EXAMPLE:**
>
> At a certain school, 45 percent of the students purchased a yearbook. If 540 students purchased yearbooks, how many students did NOT buy a yearbook?
> **A.** 243
> **B.** 540
> **C.** 575
> **D.** 660
> **E.** 957

Set up a proportion. Since 45 percent bought a yearbook, 55 percent did not:

$$\frac{45\%}{55\%} = \frac{540}{x}$$

First, you can cancel the percent signs:

$$\frac{45}{55} = \frac{540}{x}$$

Cross-multiply:

$$45x = 55(540)$$

Solve for $x$:

$$x = \frac{55(540)}{45} = \frac{11(540)}{9} = 660$$

This method will work in all of the following situations and more:

The greater (or less) the quantity, the greater (or less) the cost. (And vice versa)

The greater (or less) the quantity, the greater (or less) the weight. (And vice versa)

The greater (or less) the number, the greater (or less) the percent of the whole. (And vice versa)

The longer (or shorter) the working time, the greater (or less) the output (assuming constant rate of operation). (And vice versa)

The longer (or shorter) the travel time, the greater (or less) the distance traveled (assuming constant speed). (And vice versa)

The only things to watch for are those situations in which the quantities vary indirectly.

**EXAMPLE:**

Walking at a constant rate of four miles per hour, it takes Jill exactly one hour to walk home from school. If she walks at a constant rate of five miles per hour, how many *minutes* will the trip take?

F.   48

G.   54

H.   56

J.   72

K.   112

In this case, the faster the speed, the shorter the time. So we use an indirect proportion. Set up the proportion as usual (being sure to group like terms):

$$\frac{60}{x} = \frac{4}{5}$$

Then invert the right side of the proportion:

$$\frac{60}{x} = \frac{5}{4}$$

And solve for $x$:

$$5x = 4(60)$$

$$x = \frac{4(60)}{5} = 48 \text{ minutes}$$

13

# Proportions (Answers, page 216)

1. A roll of metal ribbon that weighs 12 pounds is cut into two pieces. One piece is 75 feet long and weighs nine pounds. What was the length, in feet, of the original roll?
   A. 60
   B. 90
   C. 100
   D. 120
   E. 150

2. A car traveling at a constant 50 miles per hour covers the same distance in one hour as a car traveling at a constant 25 miles per hour for how many hours?
   F. $\frac{1}{3}$
   G. $\frac{1}{2}$
   H. 1
   J. 2
   K. 3

3. A recipe calls for three eggs and two cups of milk. If a quantity of the recipe is prepared using eight eggs, how many cups of milk should be used?
   A. 4
   B. $4\frac{2}{3}$
   C. $5\frac{1}{3}$
   D. $5\frac{1}{2}$
   E. $5\frac{2}{3}$

4. If eight pounds of coffee costs $50, how much does 12 pounds of coffee cost?
   F. $25.00
   G. $62.50
   H. $75.00
   J. $80.00
   K. $84.00

5. Three printing presses can finish a certain job in 60 minutes. How many minutes will it take five such printing presses to do the same job?
   A. 15
   B. 20
   C. 30
   D. 36
   E. 100

6. If four gallons of water occupy 30 cubic feet of space, how many gallons of water are needed to completely fill a tank with a capacity of 360 cubic feet?
   F. 12
   G. 24
   H. 30
   J. 36
   K. 48

7. A repair shop can paint three cars every four hours. At that rate, how many hours will it take the shop to paint five cars?
   A. $6\frac{1}{3}$
   B. $6\frac{2}{3}$
   C. $7\frac{1}{3}$
   D. $7\frac{1}{2}$
   E. $7\frac{3}{4}$

8. A machine seals cans at the rate of $4\frac{1}{2}$ cans every three seconds. How many *minutes* will it take the machine to seal 720 cans?
   F. 6
   G. 8
   H. 18
   J. 36
   K. 48

9. At a certain factory, it takes five metal fasteners to attach a muffler to a car. If a box containing 500 fasteners costs $42, how much will it cost to buy the exact number of fasteners needed to attach 300 mufflers?
   A. $14
   B. $36
   C. $56
   D. $126
   E. $4,200

10. In a certain population, only 0.03 percent of the people have physical trait X. On the average, it will be necessary to screen how many people to find six with trait X?
    F. 180
    G. 200
    H. 1,800
    J. 2,000
    K. 20,000

13

# It's One of the Five Suspects

It cannot be said often enough that the correct answer to every single math problem is right there on the page. This sets up a Holmesian strategy that can be applied to many different kinds of problems:

TEST THE TEST.

Instead of trying to devise a mathematical solution to a problem, just test the available choices until you find one that works.

> **EXAMPLE:**
>
> Which of the following is the larger of two numbers the product of which is 600 and the sum of which is five times the difference between the two?
> A.  10
> B.  15
> C.  20
> D.  30
> E.  50

It would be foolish to try to devise some mathematical approach to this question. All you need to do is test answers until you find one that works. First, we can eliminate A, B, and C. Though those are factors of 600, they are not the *larger* of their respective pairs, as required by the question.

Next we test D. $30 \times 20 = 600$, and $30 + 20 = 50$, which is five times $30 - 20 = 10$. Since 30 meets the requirements, it must be the correct choice.

# Testing the Test (Answers, page 219)

**Directions:** Solve each of the following questions by testing answer choices.

1. If $\frac{1}{3}$ of a number is three more than $\frac{1}{4}$ of the number, then what is the number?
   A. 18
   B. 24
   C. 30
   D. 36
   E. 48

2. If $\frac{3}{5}$ of a number is four more than $\frac{1}{2}$ of the number, then what is the number?
   F. 20
   G. 28
   H. 35
   J. 40
   K. 56

3. When both 16 and 9 are divided by $n$, the remainder is 2. What is $n$?
   A. 3
   B. 4
   C. 5
   D. 6
   E. 7

4. The sum of the digits of a three-digit number is 16. If the tens digit of the number is three times the units digit, and the units digit is $\frac{1}{4}$ of the hundreds digit, then what is the number?
   F. 446
   G. 561
   H. 682
   J. 862
   K. 914

5. If the sum of five consecutive integers is 40, what is the smallest of the five integers?
   A. 4
   B. 5
   C. 6
   D. 7
   E. 8

# Summary

**1.** If a problem presents an arithmetic manipulation, just do the indicated operations.

**2.** If a problem is very complicated, break your solution of the problem down into steps:
(1) What is the question to be answered?
(2) What information have I been given?
(3) How can I bridge the gap between (1) and (2)?
(4) Execute the needed operations.

**3.** The following principles are often tested:
(a) properties of numbers
(b) percents
(c) ratios
(d) averages
(e) proportions

**4.** Since the correct answer is one of the "five suspects," sometimes the best attack strategy is just to test answer choices until you find the correct one.

# Explanatory Answers

## EXERCISE 1

1. (E) $2n$ must be even, so $2n + 5$, which is an even number plus an odd, must be odd. Or, you could substitute a number such as 2 into each choice. (E) turns out to be $2(2) + 5 = 9$, an odd number.

2. (H) The only way 3 times $n$ can be even is if $n$ is even. Since $n$ is even, $n + 1$ is odd.

3. (C) Since $2n$ will be even no matter what the value of $n$, $2n + 1$ must be odd. Again, you can substitute numbers to prove to yourself that the other choices do not guarantee an odd number.

4. (H) Regardless of whether $n + o$ or $p - q$ is even, so long as $m$ is even the entire number is even.

5. (D) Regardless of whether $n$ is itself odd or even, $2n$ must be even, and $2n + 2$ must be even as well.

6. (H) Since $p$ is the smallest of the three, the next number is $p + 1$ and the next is $p + 2$. So the sum of the next two consecutive integers is $p + 1 + p + 2 = 2p + 3$.

7. (C) Since these are consecutive integers, each number in the series is one less than the number that follows it. So the number before $n + 3$ is $n + 2$, and the number before that is $n + 1$, and the one before that is just $n$, and the one before that is $n - 1$. So the first of the five numbers is $n - 1$.

8. (J) A negative times a negative is a positive, so $n^2$ must be positive. So $\frac{1}{n^2}$ is positive.

9. (D) Just substitute $-1$ for $x$ in each choice:

   A. $2x = 2(-1) = -2$
   B. $x = -1$
   C. $\frac{x}{2} = -\frac{1}{2} = -\frac{1}{2}$
   D. $x^2 = (-1)(-1) = 1$
   E. $x^3 = (-1)(-1)(-1) = -1$

10. (F) When a fraction is raised to a power, the result is smaller than the original fraction. Therefore, J and K are both smaller than H. On the other hand, when you divide by a fraction, the result is larger than the number divided, so both F and G are larger than one and so larger than H. Between F and G, since $x^2$ is smaller than x, $\frac{1}{x^2}$ will be larger than $\frac{1}{x}$. You can arrive at the same conclusion by testing a number such as $\frac{1}{2}$.

11. (B) $|-2| = 2$, $|3| = 3$, and $|4| = 4$. And $2 + 3 - 4 = 1$.

12. (K) $|-3| = 3$, $|-2| = 2$, and $|10| = 10$. And $3 - 2 + 10 = 11$.

13. (C) $|-301| = 301$ and $|-114| = 114$. And $-301 + 301 - 114 + 114 = 0$.

14. (K) $|-3| = 3$ and $|-4| = 4$. And $3 \times 4 = 12$.

15. (D) $|-12| = 12$ and $|-3| = 3$. And $12 \div 3 = 4$.

13

## EXERCISE 2

1. (D)  $120 - 24 = 96$ are not in the union.  Next, use the "this-of-that" strategy:

$$\frac{\text{nonmembers}}{\text{total number of employees}} = \frac{96}{120} = 0.8 = 80\%$$

2. (G)  This is a percent increase question.  Use the "change-over" strategy.  Change $= 15 - 12 = 3$.  Original amount $= 12$.  $\frac{3}{12} = \frac{1}{4} = 25\%$.

3. (D)  Though this question involves a percent decrease, you still use the "change-over" strategy.  Change $= 450 - 441 = 9$.  Original amount $= 450$.  $\frac{9}{450} = 0.02 = 2\%$.

4. (J)  This question asks about percent change, so you use the "change-over" strategy.  Change $= 1.00 - 0.20 = 0.80$.  Original amount $= 0.20$.  $\frac{0.80}{0.20} = 4 = 400\%$.

5. (D)  This question can be answered using the "this-of-that" strategy.  $\frac{80}{\text{Total}} = 40\%$.  $80 = 40\%$ of Total, so Total $= \frac{80}{0.4} = 200$.

6. (G)  This question can be answered with the "change-over" strategy even though you don't know the change or the original price.  The key is to see that the original price is equal to $2.00 minus the change.

$$\frac{\text{Change}}{\$2.00 - \text{Change}} = 25\%$$

Let C stand for Change:

$$\frac{C}{2 - C} = 0.25$$

$$C = 0.25 \,(2 - C)$$

$$C = 0.5 - 0.25C$$

$$C + 0.25C = 0.5 - 0.25C + 0.25C$$

$$1.25C = 0.5$$

$$C = 0.5 \div 1.25$$

$$C = 0.4$$

So the change was $0.40, which means the original price was $2.00 − $0.40 = $1.60.  You can check this result by using the "change-over" formula to calculate the percent increase from 1.60 to 2.00.

7. (C)  This question calls for the "change-over" strategy.  Since you are only interested in finding the largest percent growth, there you can compare your fractions and skip the step of converting them to percents:

A. $\frac{1}{10}$   B. $\frac{1}{11}$   C. $\frac{3}{12}$ or $\frac{1}{4}$

D. $\frac{3}{15}$ or $\frac{1}{5}$   E. $\frac{3}{18}$ or $\frac{1}{6}$

8. (H)  Use the "this-of-that" strategy.  $\frac{100}{125} = \frac{4}{5} = 80\%$.

9. (A)  Use the "this-of-that" strategy.  $\frac{135}{150} = \frac{9}{10} = 90\%$.

10. (F)  Use the "change-over" strategy.  Change $= 150 - 135 = 15$.  $\frac{15}{150} = \frac{1}{10} = 10\%$.

## EXERCISE 3

**1.** (C)  Add the ratio parts: $4 + 5 = 9$.  Divide the total quantity by that result: $36 \div 9 = 4$.  So each ratio part is worth four.  Since five of the ratio parts are dark chocolates, the number of dark chocolates is $5 \times 4 = 20$.

**2.** (J)  "Seniors" must function as a common term.  Change 5:4 to 30:24 and 6:5 to 30:25.  The ratio of Seniors to Juniors is 30:24, and the ratio of Seniors to Sophomores is 30:25.  So the ratio of Sophomores to Juniors is 25:24.

**3.** (E)  Find the total number of ratio parts: $3 + 5 = 8$.  Divide: $8,000 \div 8 = 1,000$.  Then multiply by the number of parts that are nonfiction: $5 \times 1,000 = 5,000$.

**4.** (F)  *Zimp* is the common term.  Since six clabs equal one zimp, 12 clabs equal two zimps.  Therefore, three nurbs equal 12 clabs, and four clabs are worth one nurb.

**5.** (E)  The tricky thing here is setting up the ratio.  The ratio of Robert's share to Wendy's share is 1:5, and the ratio of Robert's share to Jane's share is 1:2.  So the ratio of the shares of Wendy:Jane:Robert is 5:2:1.  Now add the ratio parts: $5 + 2 + 1 = 8$.  Divide: $\$1,000 \div 8 = \$125$.  And finally, multiply by the number of parts Wendy is to receive: $5 \times \$125 = \$625$.

## EXERCISE 4

**1.** (C)  The total of all the numbers must be $14 \times 6 = 84$.  The total of the known quantities is only 72.  So the missing number is $84 - 72 = 12$.

Or, you might have used the "midpoint" method.  12 is two below 14, for $-2$.  15 is one above 14, and (keeping a running total) $-2 + 1 = -1$.  Then 18 is four above 14, and $4 - 1 = +3$.  14 is equal to 14, so our running total is still $+3$.  Finally, 13 is one less than 14, which brings our running total to $+3 - 1 = +2$.  This means that the missing number must offset this $+2$ by being two less than 14, or 12.

**2.** (J)  The total weight of the four packages is $16 \times 4 = 64$.  The weight of the remaining three is $3 \times 14 = 42$.  The difference is $64 - 42 = 22$.  So the package that was removed weighed 22 pounds.

**3.** (A)  Here you must use a weighted average:

$$\frac{3(\$2) + 5(\$3) + 1(\$6)}{9} = \frac{\$6 + \$15 + \$6}{9} = \frac{\$27}{9} = \$3$$

**4.** (J)  Again, you can use a weighted average:

$$\frac{50(.10) + 20(.20) + 10(.30)}{80} = \frac{5 + 4 + 3}{80} = \frac{12}{80} = 0.15$$

**5.** (B)  The weight of the ten people is $145 \times 10 = 1,450$.  The weight of the remaining nine is $9 \times 150 = 1,350$.  So the person who got out of the boat weighed $1,450 - 1,350 = 100$ pounds.

13

## EXERCISE 5

**1.** (C) The longer the piece, the greater the weight. So you can use a direct proportion:

$$\frac{\text{Length } X}{\text{Length } Y} = \frac{\text{Weight } X}{\text{Weight } Y}$$

$$\frac{75}{x} = \frac{9}{12}$$

Simplify: $\frac{75}{x} = \frac{3}{4}$.

Cross-multiply: $4(75) = 3x$.

Solve for $x$: $x = \frac{4(75)}{3} = 100$.

**2.** (J) The faster the speed, the shorter the time (and vice versa). So here you must use an indirect proportion. Set up a normal proportion, being sure to group like terms:

$$\frac{\text{Speed } X}{\text{Speed } Y} = \frac{\text{Time } X}{\text{Time } Y}$$

$$\frac{50}{25} = \frac{1}{x}$$

Invert the right side: $\frac{50}{25} = \frac{x}{1}$.

Cross-multiply: $50(1) = 25x$.

Solve for $x$: $x = \frac{50}{25} = 2$.

**3.** (C) The more eggs, the more milk, so you should use a direct proportion:

$$\frac{\text{Eggs } X}{\text{Eggs } Y} = \frac{\text{Milk } X}{\text{Milk } Y}$$

$$\frac{3}{8} = \frac{2}{x}$$

Cross-multiply: $3x = 16$.

Solve for $x$: $x = \frac{16}{3} = 5\frac{1}{3}$.

**4. (H)** The more of a thing purchased, the greater the cost. Use a direct proportion:

$$\frac{\text{Quantity } X}{\text{Quantity } Y} = \frac{\text{Cost } X}{\text{Cost } Y}$$

$$\frac{8}{12} = \frac{50}{x}$$

Cross-multiply: $8x = 50(12)$.

Solve for $x$: $x = \frac{50(12)}{8} = 75$.

**5. (D)** The more machines working, the shorter the time needed to do a job. Here you need an indirect proportion. Set up a proportion being sure to group like terms:

$$\frac{\text{Number of Machines } X}{\text{Number of Machines } Y} = \frac{\text{Time } X}{\text{Time } Y}$$

$$\frac{3}{5} = \frac{60}{x}$$

Invert the right side:

$$\frac{3}{5} = \frac{x}{60}$$

Cross-multiply: $5x = 3(60)$.

Solve for $x$: $x = \frac{3(60)}{5} = 36$.

**6. (K)** The more water, the greater the space occupied. So you can use a direct proportion.

$$\frac{\text{Water } X}{\text{Water } Y} = \frac{\text{Space } X}{\text{Space } Y}$$

$$\frac{4}{x} = \frac{30}{360}$$

Cross-multiply: $30x = 4(360)$.

Solve for $x$: $x = \frac{4(360)}{30} = 48$.

**7. (B)** The greater the number of cars, the longer the time needed for the job. So use a direct proportion.

$$\frac{\text{Cars } X}{\text{Cars } Y} = \frac{\text{Time } X}{\text{Time } Y}$$

$$\frac{3}{5} = \frac{4}{x}$$

Cross-multiply: $3x = 4(5)$.

Solve for $x$: $x = \frac{4(5)}{3} = 6\frac{2}{3}$.

13

**8.** (G)  The more cans, the longer the time.  So we can use a direct proportion, but we must take care that our final result is expressed in minutes and not seconds.  First, set up a proportion to find how many seconds will be needed:

$$\frac{\text{Cans } X}{\text{Cans } Y} = \frac{\text{Time in Seconds } X}{\text{Time in Seconds } Y}$$

$$\frac{4\frac{1}{2}}{3} = \frac{720}{x}$$

Cross-multiply: $4\frac{1}{2}x = 3(720)$.

Solve for $x$: $x = 3(720) \div 4\frac{1}{2} = 480$ seconds.

To convert that number of seconds to minutes, divide by 60:

$480 \div 60 = 8$ minutes

**9.** (D)  This problem is a bit complex, but we will take it step by step.  To find the total cost of the fasteners, we must first find how many we need.  Since more mufflers means more fasteners, use a direct proportion:

$$\frac{\text{Mufflers } X}{\text{Mufflers } Y} = \frac{\text{Fasteners } X}{\text{Fasteners } Y}$$

$$\frac{1}{300} = \frac{5}{x}$$

Cross-multiply: $x = 1,500$.

Now to figure cost, you set up another direct proportion:

$$\frac{\text{Cost } X}{\text{Cost } Y} = \frac{\text{Number } X}{\text{Number } Y}$$

$$\frac{42}{x} = \frac{500}{1,500}$$

Cross-multiply: $500x = 42(1,500)$.

Solve for $x$: $x = \frac{42(1,500)}{500} = 126$.

**10.** (K)  Here too you can use a direct proportion.

$$\frac{\text{Percent } X}{\text{Percent } Y} = \frac{\text{Number } X}{\text{Number } Y}$$

$$\frac{0.03\%}{100\%} = \frac{6}{x}$$

Clear the percents: $\frac{0.03}{100} = \frac{6}{x}$.

Cross-multiply: $0.03x = 6(100)$.

Solve for $x$: $x = \frac{600}{0.03} = 20,000$.

## EXERCISE 6

**1.** (D) 36
$\frac{1}{3}$ of 36 = 12. $\frac{1}{4}$ of 36 = 9. And 12 is three more than 9. So (D) fits the requirements.

**2.** (J) 40
$\frac{3}{5}$ of 40 = 24. $\frac{1}{2}$ of 40 = 20. And 24 is four more than 20. So (J) fits the requirements.

**3.** (E) 7
16 ÷ 7 = 2 plus remainder 2. 9 ÷ 7 = 1 plus remainder 2. So (E) fits the requirements.

**4.** (J) 862
The sum of the three digits of 862 is 8 + 6 + 2 = 16. The tens digit is 6, which is three times the units digit, which is 2. Finally, 2, the units digit, is $\frac{1}{4}$ of 8, the hundreds digit.

**5.** (C) 6
If the smallest integer is 6, then the sum is 6 + 7 + 8 + 9 + 10 = 40.

13

# Math Usage: Algebra

✔ **Objectives**

To learn to use the answer choices to generate solutions to algebra problems.

To review key concepts needed to solve the most common types of algebra problems.

1. One of the Five Suspects
2. Algebra Manipulations
   • Rewriting Expressions
   • Solving Equations
3. Algebra Applications

14

Some ACT problems test algebra.

> **EXAMPLE:**
>
> If $a^3 + b = 3 + a^3$, then $b = ?$
> **A.** $3^3$
> **B.** $3\sqrt{3}$
> **C.** $3$
> **D.** $\sqrt[3]{3}$
> **E.** $-\sqrt{3}$

The problem is solved by a simple manipulation. Subtract $a^3$ from both sides of the equation:

$$a^3 + b - (a^3) = 3 + a^3 - (a^3)$$
$$a^3 - a^3 + b = 3 + a^3 - a^3$$
$$b = 3$$

So the answer is C.

Of course, not all algebra problems are so simple. Here is one of moderate difficulty.

> **EXAMPLE:**
>
> Diana spent one-half of her allowance on a book and another three dollars on lunch. If she still had one-sixth of her original allowance, how much is Diana's allowance?
> **F.** $24
> **G.** $18
> **H.** $15
> **J.** $12
> **K.** $9

You can solve the problem by setting up an equation. In words, the problem states:

Diana's allowance minus one-half her allowance minus another three dollars is equal to one-sixth of Diana's allowance.

If we use $x$ for Diana's allowance, our equation is:

$$x - \frac{1}{2}x - 3 = \frac{1}{6}x$$

And now we solve for x. First, combine like terms:

$$\left(x - \frac{1}{2}x\right) - 3 = \frac{1}{6}x$$

$$\frac{1}{2}x - 3 = \frac{1}{6}x$$

Next we get all of the x terms on one side (by subtracting $\frac{1}{6}x$ from both sides of the equation):

$$\left(\frac{1}{2}x - \frac{1}{6}x\right) - 3 = \frac{1}{6}x - \frac{1}{6}x$$

$$\left(\frac{3}{6}x - \frac{1}{6}x\right) - 3 = 0$$

$$\frac{2}{6}x - 3 = 0$$

$$\frac{1}{3}x - 3 = 0$$

Next, isolate the x term by adding 3 to both sides of the equation:

$$\frac{1}{3}x - 3 + 3 = 0 + 3$$

$$\frac{1}{3}x = 3$$

Finally, we solve for x by multiplying both sides by 3:

$$(3)\frac{1}{3}x = 3(3)$$

$$x = 9$$

The solution was described in excruciating detail. The problem can actually be solved in fewer steps, but even so, wouldn't it be nice if there were a way to avoid the algebra altogether? Well, there is an alternative.

If Holmes were studying the problem above, he would begin by thinking "The guilty party is one of the five suspects. I only need to prove which one." This sets up two Holmesian strategies that we will discuss before we talk any further about algebra.

## One of the Five Suspects

We concluded our discussion of arithmetic problems with the topic "Testing the Test." You learned that it is sometimes possible to get a right answer just by testing choices. That principle can be extended to cover algebra questions.

Let's apply the principle to the problem of Diana's allowance. Start by testing F. If Diana's allowance is $24, then after she spends $\frac{1}{2}$ on a book, she has $12.

Subtract the $3 for lunch, and she has $9.  But $\frac{9}{24}$ is not equal to $\frac{1}{6}$—so F cannot be correct.

Next, try G.  If her allowance is $18, then she has $9 after she buys the book and $6 after she pays for lunch.  But $\frac{6}{18}$ is not $\frac{1}{6}$, so G, too, is incorrect.

Next, try H, $15.  Half of that is $7.50, which, less the $3 for lunch, leaves Diana with $4.50.  But $\frac{4.5}{15}$, which is $\frac{\frac{9}{2}}{15} = \frac{9}{30}$, is not $\frac{1}{6}$.  So you would try J, $12.  Half of $12—$6—less $3 more for lunch is $3; but $\frac{3}{12}$ is not $\frac{1}{6}$.

By this point you *know* that the correct answer must be K.  But we will check it anyway.  Half of $9—$4.50—less $3 is $1.50.  And $\frac{1.5}{9} = \frac{\frac{3}{2}}{9}$ $= \frac{3}{18} = \frac{1}{6}$.

But, you object, that is too many calculations!  Yes and no.  Yes, but the algebra itself required several steps.  And with the "five suspects" strategy, at least you may be able to do something if the algebra proves impossible.  And no, because the process really doesn't require all of those calculations.

Answer choices to questions like this one are arranged in order, from largest to smallest or vice versa.  This cuts the calculations to a maximum of two.  Start by testing choice H.  Your result is $\frac{3}{12}$, which is $\frac{1}{4}$ (which proves H is wrong).  So ask yourself, is H incorrect because $15 is too much money or too little?  Since $\frac{1}{4}$ is more than $\frac{1}{6}$, $15 must be too much money.  So you should test the next smaller number.

You test J.  It doesn't work.  By the process of elimination, K must be correct—and you don't need to do that calculation (unless you are ahead of schedule and can afford the time for a failsafe check).

We will apply this "five suspects" strategy to another problem.

**EXAMPLE:**

In a certain game, a player had five successful turns in a row, and after each one the number of points added to his total score was double what was added the preceding turn.  If the player scored a total of 465 five points, how many points did he score on the first play?

A.  15
B.  31
C.  93
D.  155
E.  270

Start with C.  If the player scored 93 points on the first turn, he scored $2 \times 93 = 186$ on the second, for a total of $93 + 186 = 279$.  Then on the third turn, he scored $2 \times 279 = 558$.  But wait!  This cannot possibly be the correct answer.  We have already exceeded the total number of points scored.

Which suspect should we grill next?  If 93 generated a result that was too large, logically, we should try the next smaller number.  Assuming the player won 31 points on the first turn, he won $2 \times 31 = 62$ on the second, for a total of $31 + 62 = 93$.  On the third he won, $2 \times 62 = 124$, for a total of $93 + 124 = 217$.  On the fourth he won, $2 \times 124 = 248$, for a total of $217 + 248 = 465$, with still another round to go.  B must be wrong.

By the process of elimination, therefore, A is correct.  And if you care, you can prove it by doing the calculation.

Notice that in both of our examples, the correct answer was located at the extreme —either E or A.  This was to demonstrate that even with the worst luck, only two calculations are required.  Sometimes you will be lucky and hit upon the correct choice on the first try.

The principle of the five suspects gives rise to another strategy called "If you don't see what you want, ask for it." This "ask for it" strategy is useful when the problem asks you to invent a formula.

**EXAMPLES:**

At a certain firm, $d$ gallons of fuel are needed per day for each truck. At this rate, $g$ gallons of fuel will supply $t$ trucks for how many days?

**F.** $\dfrac{dt}{g}$

**G.** $\dfrac{gt}{d}$

**H.** $dgt$

**J.** $\dfrac{t}{dg}$

**K.** $\dfrac{g}{dt}$

This is a fairly difficult question, and what makes it difficult is the use of unknowns. If the question had read:

At a certain firm, 20 gallons of fuel are needed per day for each truck. At this rate, 1,000 gallons of fuel will supply five trucks for how many days?

Then the question wouldn't be difficult. You would reason that five trucks using 20 gallons of fuel per day would consume $5 \times 20 = 100$ gallons per day. So 1,000 gallons would be used up in $1,000 \div 100 = 10$ days.

Numbers are what you want. You don't see them. So ask for them. Or rather, you make them up as we just did. On the assumption that there are five trucks ($t = 5$), that each truck consumes 20 gallons per day ($d = 20$), and that we have 1,000 gallons of fuel ($g = 1,000$), the correct formula should generate the number 10.

**F.** $\dfrac{dt}{g} = \dfrac{20(5)}{1,000} = \dfrac{100}{1,000} = \dfrac{1}{10}$   (Wrong.)

**G.** $\dfrac{gt}{d} = \dfrac{1,000(5)}{20} = \dfrac{5,000}{20} = 250$   (Wrong.)

**H.** $dgt = (20)(1,000)(5) = 100(1,000)$   (Wrong.)

**J.** $\dfrac{t}{dg} = \dfrac{5}{(20)(1,000)} = \dfrac{5}{20,000}$   (Wrong.)

**K.** $\dfrac{g}{dt} = \dfrac{1,000}{20(5)} = \dfrac{1,000}{100} = 10$   (Right!)

Here is another problem.

$Y$ years ago, Paul was twice as old as Bob. If Bob is now 18 years old, how old is Paul now in terms of $Y$?

**A.** $36 + Y$

**B.** $18 + Y$

**C.** $18 - Y$

**D.** $36 - Y$

**E.** $36 - 2Y$

In our first example, we used realistic numbers. A truck might use 20 gallons of fuel per day, and a firm might have five trucks and a 1,000-gallon tank. But an unknown can stand for any number at all (so long as you don't divide by zero). So pick numbers that are easy to work with.

For starters, why not assume that $Y = 0$, which is to say right now Paul is twice as old as Bob. Since Bob is now 18, Paul is 36. So with $Y = 0$, the correct formula should generate the value 36.

A. $36 + Y = 36 + 0 = 36$
B. $18 + Y = 18 + 0 = 18$
C. $18 - Y = 18 - 0 = 18$
D. $36 - Y = 36 - 0 = 36$
E. $36 - 2Y = 36 - 0 = 36$

What happened? Our strategy yielded three choices, not one. There's nothing wrong with the strategy. The problem is with the value we used. A, D, and E all yielded 36 because $-0$, $+0$, and $-2(0)$ are all zero. To eliminate the two incorrect choices, just pick another easy number.

Assume that $Y = 1$. On that assumption, a year ago Bob was 17 years old and Paul was 34 years old. And today, one year later, he is $34 + 1 = 35$. So if $Y = 1$, the correct choice should yield 35:

A. $36 + Y = 36 + 1 = 37$    (Wrong.)
D. $36 - Y = 36 - 1 = 35$    (Right!)
E. $36 - 2Y = 36 - 2 = 34$    (Wrong.)

You may also encounter a problem if you use the value 1 because $1 \times 1 = 1 \div 1$. For example, if you assume that $x = 1$, the formula $xy$ will give you the same result as the formula $\frac{y}{x}$. This doesn't mean you should never use 1. You can and should use 1 as an assumption; but if you get more than one seemingly correct formula, try another set of numbers.

What are the solutions for the equation $2x^2 - 2x = 12$?
F.   $-3$ and $-2$
G.   $-2$ and $3$
H.   $\frac{2}{3}$ and $3$
J.   $\frac{3}{2}$ and $2$
K.   $2$ and $3$

This is a difficult quadratic equation. Instead of trying to factor and solve for $x$, just test the test: substitute the values given in each answer choice back into the original equation until you find the pair that works. The correct choice is G:

$$2(-2)^2 - 2(-2) = 12$$

And:

$$2(3)^2 - 2(3) = 12$$

So the solutions to the equation are $-2$ and $3$.

# Algebra Manipulations

On each exam, a few of the math problems require algebraic manipulation. And sometimes there is no better way to attack the problem than to do the operations indicated. We will divide our discussion of algebraic manipulations into two parts: (1) rewriting expressions and (2) solving equations.

## 1. Rewriting Expressions

### Evaluating Expressions

The easiest rewriting problems ask you to change an algebraic expression into a number by having you substitute values. This is called evaluating an expression.

> **EXAMPLE:**
>
> If $x = 2$, what is the value of $x^2 + 2x - 2$?
> A. $-2$
> B. 0
> C. 2
> D. 4
> E. 6

We use the same strategy here that we would employ for an analogous arithmetic problem: if the operations are manageable, just do them. Here you substitute 2 for $x$ and do the easy arithmetic:

$$x^2 + 2x - 2 = 2^2 + 2(2) - 2 = 4 + 4 - 2 = 8 - 2 = 6$$

A testwriter might try to make a problem like this more difficult by using fractions.

> **EXAMPLE:**
>
> If $x = 2$, then $\frac{1}{x^2} + \frac{1}{x} - \frac{x}{2} = ?$
> F. $-\frac{3}{4}$
> G. $-\frac{1}{4}$
> H. 0
> J. $\frac{1}{4}$
> K. $\frac{1}{2}$

The answer is G. Just substitute 2 for each occurrence of $x$:

$$\frac{1}{x^2} + \frac{1}{x} - \frac{x}{2} = \frac{1}{2^2} + \frac{1}{2} - \frac{2}{2} =$$

$$\frac{1}{4} + \frac{1}{2} - 1 = \frac{3}{4} - 1 = -\frac{1}{4}$$

Just as was the case with arithmetic manipulations, there is a limit to the complexity of manipulations. You might find something like this.

> **EXAMPLE:**
>
> If $p = 1$, $q = 2$, and $r = 3$, then $\dfrac{(q \times r)(r - q)}{(q - p)(p \times q)} = ?$
>
> A. $-3$
> B. $-1$
> C. $0$
> D. $3$
> E. $6$

Just substitute for the different letters and execute:

$$\frac{(q \times r)(r - q)}{(q - p)(p \times q)} = \frac{(2 \times 3)(3 - 2)}{(2 - 1)(1 \times 2)} = \frac{(6)(1)}{(1)(2)} = \frac{6}{2} = 3$$

## Exponents

A knowledge of the rules for manipulating exponents is essential for many algebraic manipulations:

1. $(x^m)(x^n) = x^{(m+n)}$

2. $\left(\dfrac{x^m}{x^n}\right) = x^{(m-n)}$

3. $(x^m)^n = x^{m \cdot n}$
4. $(x^m \times y^m)^n = x^{mn} \times y^{mn}$

5. $\left(\dfrac{x^m}{y^m}\right)^n = \dfrac{x^{mn}}{y^{mn}}$

Occasionally, you may be asked to demonstrate your knowledge of these rules.

> **EXAMPLE:**
>
> $\dfrac{9(x^2\,y^3)^6}{(3x^6y^9)^2} = ?$
>
> F. $1$
> G. $3$
> H. $x^2y^3$
> J. $3x^2y^3$
> K. $x^{12}y^{12}$

The answer is F.

$$\frac{9(x^2y^3)^6}{(3x^6y^9)^2} = \frac{9(x^{2\cdot6}y^{3\cdot6})}{3^2x^{6\cdot2}y^{9\cdot2}} = \frac{9x^{12}y^{18}}{9x^{12}y^{18}} = 1$$

14

### Factoring

You might be asked to do simple factoring.

**EXAMPLES:**

$2x^3 + 4x^2 + 6x = ?$

**A.** $2x(2x^2 + 2x + 6)$

**B.** $2x(x^2 + 2x + 3)$

**C.** $2x(x + 5)$

**D.** $3x(x + 2x + 2)$

**E.** $6x(x + 2x + 1)$

The answer is B, as you can prove to yourself by multiplying:

$$2x(x^2 + 2x + 3) = 2x^3 + 4x^2 + 6x$$

You should memorize the following patterns:

$x^2 - y^2 = (x + y)(x - y)$  (Called the difference of two squares)

$x^2 + 2xy + y^2 = (x + y)(x + y)$  (Also written $(x + y)^2$)

$x^2 - 2xy - y^2 = (x + y)(x - y)$  (Not used that often, but easy to recognize)

Whenever you see one of these three expressions, you should have an irresistible urge to factor.

$$\frac{x^2 - y^2}{x + y} = ?$$

**F.** $x^2 - y^2$

**G.** $x^2 + y^2$

**H.** $x^2 + y$

**J.** $x + y^2$

**K.** $x - y$

The answer is K. Just factor the numerator, using the method for the difference of two squares:

$$\frac{x^2 - y^2}{x + y} = \frac{(x + y)(x - y)}{x + y} = x - y$$

You could also be asked to factor a quadratic expression that is not one of the three shown above.

**EXAMPLE:**

$$\frac{x^2 - x - 6}{x + 2} = ?$$

**A.** $x^2 - \dfrac{1}{2x} - 3$

**B.** $x^2 - 2$

**C.** $x - 2$

**D.** $x - 3$

**E.** $x$

The answer is D. And the trick is to see that $x + 2$ must be a factor of $x^2 - x - 6$. Now you can figure out what the other factor is:

$$(x + 2)(?\ ?) = x^2 - x - 6$$

The first question mark must be filled in by an $x$. That's the only way to get $x^2$ in the final result:

$$(x + 2)(x\ ?) = x^2 - x - 6$$

The second question mark must be 3:

$$(x + 2)(x\ 3) = x^2 - x - 6$$

Finally, to get $-6$ in the final result, the sign must be $-$:

$$(x + 2)(x - 3) = x^2 - 3x + 2x - 6 = x^2 - x - 6$$

Once you know this, you rewrite the original expression:

$$\frac{x^2 - x - 6}{x + 2} = \frac{(x + 2)(x - 3)}{x + 2} = x - 3$$

And what happens if you fail to see the trick? You can use one of the other techniques we have already used to good advantage. Try numbers. Assume that $x = 1$:

$$\frac{x^2 - x - 6}{x + 2} = \frac{1^2 - 1 - 6}{1 + 2} = \frac{1 - 1 - 6}{3} = \frac{-6}{3} = -2$$

So substituting 1 for $x$ into the correct choice will yield $-2$:

A. $x^2 - \dfrac{1}{2x} - 3 = 1^2 - \dfrac{1}{2(1)} - 3 = -3\dfrac{1}{2}$   (Wrong.)

B. $x^2 - 2 = 1^2 - 2 = 1 - 2 = -1$   (Wrong.)

C. $x - 2 = 1 - 2 = -1$   (Wrong.)

D. $x - 3 = 1 - 3 = -2$   (Right!)

E. $x = 1$   (Wrong.)

## Functions

In algebra, you learned about the expression $f(\ )$, which signals a function. $f(x)$ tells you to do something to the term inside the parentheses. Algebraic functions are tested by the ACT.

**EXAMPLES:**

If $f(x) = x^2 - x$ for all whole numbers, then $f(-2) = ?$

F.   $-6$

G.   $-2$

H.   0

J.   4

K.   6

The answer is K. "$f(-2)$" tells you to substitute $-2$ for each occurrence of $x$ in the expression $x^2 - x$. So $f(-2)$ is equal to $(-2^2) - (-2) = 4 + 2 = 6$.

If $f(x) = x^2 - x$, then $f(f(3)) = ?$
A. 27
B. 30
C. 58
D. 72
E. 123

The answer is B. You must first find the value of $f(3)$. Then you substitute that result for $x$ back into the expression $x^2 - x$. So the first step is:

$$f(3) = (3)^2 - 3 = 9 - 3 = 6$$

And the second step is:

$$f(6) = (6)^2 - 6 = 36 - 6 = 30$$

So $f(f(3)) = 30$.

If $f(x) = x + 3$ and $g(x) = 2x - 5$, what is $f(g(2))$?
F. −2
G. 0
H. 2
J. 4
K. 10

The answer is H. Take the problem one step at a time. First find $g(2)$:

$$g(2) = 2(2) - 5 = 4 - 5 = -1$$

Then substitute −1 for $x$ in the other function:

$$f(-1) = (-1) + 3 = 2$$

## 2. Solving Equations

### One Equation with One Simple Variable

Some equations are very simple.

**EXAMPLE:**

If $(2 + 3)(1 + x) = 25$, then $x = ?$

A. $\dfrac{1}{5}$

B. $\dfrac{1}{4}$

C. 1

D. 4

E. 5

The answer is D.  Solve for $x$:

$$(2 + 3)(1 + x) = 25$$

$$5(1 + x) = 25$$

Divide both sides by 5:

$$\frac{5(1 + x)}{5} = \frac{25}{5}$$

$$1 + x = 5$$

Subtract 1:

$$1 + x - 1 = 5 - 1$$

$$x = 4$$

It is possible to employ our "test the test" technique by substituting the choices back into the equation.  But given that the equation is so simple, it's probably easier to solve for $x$ directly.  You may, however, use the testing technique to check your solution.  Substitute 4 back into the original equation:

$$(2 + 3)(1 + 4) = (5)(5) = 25$$

This proves our solution is correct.

Sometimes the testwriters will attempt to jazz up their simple equations a bit by using decimals or fractions, but this really doesn't change things much.

> **EXAMPLE:**
> If $T \times \frac{3}{7} = \frac{3}{7} \times 9$, then $T = ?$
>
> F. $\frac{1}{9}$
>
> G. $\frac{1}{7}$
>
> H. 1
>
> J. 7
>
> K. 9

The answer is K.  Once you divide both sides by $\frac{3}{7}$ to eliminate the fractions, the equation becomes $T = 9$.  So there's no need for a strategy other than just doing the simple algebra.

There is one variation on this theme for which you might look for something different.

**EXAMPLE:**

If $2x + 3 = 7$, then $2x = ?$

A.  4
B.  6
C.  8
D.  14
E.  21

The answer is A, and it would not be wrong to solve for $x$. $2x = 4$, so $x = 2$. Therefore, $2x = 2(2) = 4$. However, you don't really need to do the last two steps. Once you have $2x = 4$, you have your solution.

**EXAMPLE:**

If $\frac{1}{3}x = 10$, then $\frac{1}{6}x = ?$

F.  $\frac{1}{15}$

G.  $\frac{2}{3}$

H.  2

J.  5

K.  30

The answer is J. Again, it would not be wrong to solve for $x$ and then substitute your solution for $x$ in $\frac{1}{6}x$. But you can save a few seconds if you can see that $\frac{1}{6}$ is one-half of $\frac{1}{3}$, so $\frac{1}{6}x$ is half of $\frac{1}{3}x$. Therefore, half of 10 is 5.

In general, then, if the problem is an equation with one simple variable, you are safe solving for the variable. But if the question asks for a multiple or a fraction of the variable, you can save a little time if you can compare things directly without solving for the variable itself.

### One Equation with Two Variables

With one equation and one variable, you can solve for the variable. But with two variables and only one equation, you won't be able to get a solution for either variable alone.

**EXAMPLE:**

If $x + y = 3$, then $2x + 2y = ?$

A.  $\frac{2}{3}$

B.  $\frac{1}{2}$

C.  3

D.  6

E.  8

The answer is D. Although it is not possible to find values for $x$ and $y$ individually, $2x + 2y = 2(x + y)$, so $2x + 2y$ is double 3, which is 6.

For questions with two variables and only one equation, look for a way of transforming the first expression into the second. The transformation will give you a solution.

## Two Equations with Two Variables

With two equations and two variables, you solve using the technique of simultaneous equations. Given two equations with two variables, $x$ and $y$, to solve for $x$:

STEP 1: In one of the equations, define $y$ in terms of $x$ ($y$ = some form of $x$).

STEP 2: Substitute the value of $y$ (from step 1) for every occurrence of $y$ in the other equation. (This will eliminate the $y$s, leaving only $x$s.)

STEP 3: Solve for $x$. (And if necessary, substitute the value of $x$ for $x$ into either equation to get the value of $y$.)

In simplest form, such problems look like this:

**EXAMPLE:**

If $2x + y = 8$ and $x - y = 1$, then $x = ?$

F.   $-1$

G.   1

H.   2

J.   3

K.   5

The answer is J.

First, use one of the equations to define $y$ in terms of $x$. Since the second equation is simpler, use it:

$$x - y = 1$$

$$x = 1 + y$$

$$x - 1 = y, \text{ so } y = x - 1$$

Second, substitute $x - 1$ into the other equation for every occurrence of $y$. (There is only one occurrence of $y$ in the other equation.)

$$2x + y = 8$$

$$2x + (x - 1) = 8$$

Third, solve for $x$:

$$2x + (x - 1) = 8$$

$$3x - 1 = 8$$

$$3x = 9$$

$$x = 3$$

14

Sometimes it may be necessary to continue the process to solve for the second variable.

> **EXAMPLE:**
>
> If $2x + y = 8$ and $x - y = 1$, then $x + y = $?
> A.   $-1$
> B.   1
> C.   2
> D.   3
> E.   5

The answer is E, and this is the question we just answered except that we are looking for $x + y$, not just $x$. You follow the same procedure, and once you know $x = 3$, substitute 3 for $x$ into either equation. Since the second is simpler, we will use it:

$$x - y = 1$$

$$3 - y = 1$$

$$y = 2$$

$$\text{So } x + y = 5.$$

If you keep your eyes open, you might find a chance to make a direct substitution, thereby avoiding some algebra.

> **EXAMPLE:**
>
> If $7x = 2$ and $3y - 7x = 10$, then $y = $?
> F.   2
> G.   3
> H.   4
> J.   5
> K.   6

The answer is H. The problem can be solved using the procedure outlined above; but in solving for $x$, you get a fraction. And fractions are a pain in the neck. You can avoid the problem, however, if you see not only that $7x = 2$ but that $7x$ is one of the terms of the second equation. Just substitute 2 for $7x$ in the second equation:

$$3y - 2 = 10$$

$$3y = 12$$

$$y = 4$$

And such shortcuts become absolutely necessary with more difficult problems.

> **EXAMPLE:**
>
> If $4x + 5y = 12$ and $3x + 4y = 5$, then $7(x + y) = ?$
> A.  7
> B.  14
> C.  49
> D.  77
> E.  91

The answer is C. You could, if you had to, solve for both $x$ and $y$, but it would be a tedious process. The best attack on this question is to see that the final answer requires the *sum* of $x$ and $y$ $(x + y)$, not the individual values of $x$ and $y$.

We can simply rewrite our equations so that we get a value for $x + y$:

$$
\begin{array}{r}
4x + 5y = 12 \\
- \underline{[3x + 4y = \phantom{0}5]} \\
x + y = \phantom{0}7
\end{array}
$$

Since $x + y = 7$, $7(x + y) = 7(7) = 49$.

In general, then, "two equation/two variable" questions should be attacked as simultaneous equations, unless that process would be too complicated. Then look for an alternative.

### Quadratic Equations (Equations with a Squared Variable)

Quadratic equations are equations with squared variables.

> **EXAMPLE:**
>
> If $x^2 - 3x = 4$, then which of the following shows all possible values of $x$?
> F.  4,1
> G.  4,−1
> H.  −4,1
> J.  −4,−1
> K.  −4, 1, 4

The answer is G.

To solve a quadratic equation:

STEP 1: Set all the terms equal to zero.
STEP 2: Factor.
STEP 3: Set each of the factors equal to zero.
STEP 4: Solve each equation.

First, set all the terms equal to zero:

$$x^2 - 3x = 4$$

$$x^2 - 3x - 4 = 0$$

Next, factor:

$$(x - 4)(x + 1) = 0$$

14

Now create equations with each of the factors equal to zero:

$x - 4 = 0$ or $x + 1 = 0$

Finally, solve each equation:

$x - 4 = 0$ or $x + 1 = 0$

$x = 4 \qquad x = -1$

And if you need to, you can check these solutions by substituting 4 and $-1$ back into the original equation.

You should also remember to use the three patterns you memorized in the previous chapter:

$x^2 - y^2 = (x + y)(x - y)$   (The difference of two squares)

$x^2 + 2xy + y^2 = (x + y)(x + y) = (x + y)^2$

$x^2 - 2xy + y^2 = (x - y)(x - y)$

**EXAMPLE:**

If $x^2 - y^2 = 0$ and $x + y = 1$, then $x - y = ?$
A.  $-1$
B.  0
C.  1
D.  2
E.  4

The answer is B.  Factor:

$x^2 - y^2 = 0$

$(x + y)(x - y) = 0$

Either $x + y = 0$ or $x - y = 0$.

The question stipulates that $x + y = 1$ and not zero, so $x - y$ must be zero.

Finally, keep in mind that you can always attack a question that asks for the solutions to a quadratic equation by testing the answer choices.

**EXAMPLE:**

What is the solution set for the equation $3x^2 + 3x = 6$?
F.  [1, $-2$]
G.  [1,2]
H.  [1/2,1]
J.  [1/2, 1/3]
K.  [$-1,-2$]

You can answer this question just by testing the answer choices, starting with F:

$$3(1)^2 + 3(1) = 6$$
$$3 + 3 = 6$$
$$6 = 6$$

So 1 is one of the solutions.   Next:

$$3(-2)^2 + 3(-2) = 6$$
$$12 - 6 = 6$$
$$6 = 6$$

So $-2$ is the other solution.   And the answer is F.

14

# Algebra Manipulations (Answers, page 246)

1. Which of the following is equal to $3x^3 + 3x^2 + 3x$?
   - **A.** $9x^6$
   - **B.** $3x^6$
   - **C.** $3x(x^3 + x^2 + x)$
   - **D.** $3x(3x^2 + 3x + 3)$
   - **E.** $3x(x^2 + x + 1)$

2. $\dfrac{x^2 + 2xy + y^2}{x + y} = ?$
   - **F.** $x + y$
   - **G.** $x - y$
   - **H.** $x^2 + y$
   - **J.** $x + y^2$
   - **J.** $x^2 + y^2$

3. If $x - y = 3$, then $\dfrac{x^2 - y^2}{x + y} = ?$
   - **A.** 0
   - **B.** 1
   - **C.** 3
   - **D.** 9
   - **E.** 12

4. $(x + y)^2 - (x - y)^2 = ?$
   - **F.** $4xy$
   - **G.** $x^2$
   - **H.** $x + y$
   - **J.** $x - y$
   - **K.** $x^2 + y^2$

5. $\dfrac{x^2 + 2x + 1}{x + 1} = ?$
   - **A.** $x$
   - **B.** $x + 1$
   - **C.** $x - 1$
   - **D.** $x^2$
   - **E.** $x^3$

6. If $f(x) = 2x + 4$, then $f(2) = ?$
   - **F.** 12
   - **G.** 8
   - **H.** 6
   - **J.** 2
   - **K.** $\dfrac{1}{2}$

7. If $f(x) = x^2 - 2x + 3$, then $f(3) = ?$
   A. $-3$
   B. 2
   C. 3
   D. 6
   E. 9

8. If $f(x) = 2x + x$, then $f(f(2)) = ?$
   F. 12
   G. 18
   H. 21
   J. 24
   K. 27

9. If $f(x) = 3x + 3$ and $g(x) = 2x + 2$, what is $f(g(2))$?
   A. 15
   B. 21
   C. 24
   D. 36
   E. 48

10. If $n + n + 1 + n + 2 = 12$, then $n = ?$
    F. 0
    G. 1
    H. 2
    J. 3
    K. 4

11. $\frac{1}{x} + \frac{1}{x} = 4$, then $x = ?$
    A. $\frac{1}{4}$
    B. $\frac{1}{2}$
    C. 1
    D. 2
    E. 4

12. If $x + y = 9$, then $\frac{1}{3}x + \frac{1}{3}y = ?$
    F. 1
    G. 3
    H. 18
    J. 27
    K. 54

13. If $2x + y = 5$ and $x + y = 3$, then $x = ?$
    A. 0
    B. 1
    C. 2
    D. 4
    E. 5

14

**14.** If $3m = 5$ and $4n - 3m = 3$, then $n = ?$
    **F.**   0
    **G.**   1
    **H.**   2
    **J.**   3
    **K.**   4

**15.** If $7m - 2 = 3k$, then $\dfrac{7m - 2}{3} = ?$
    **A.**   $\dfrac{k}{3}$
    **B.**   $k$
    **C.**   $3k$
    **D.**   $9k$
    **E.**   $27k$

**16.** If $x = 4y$, then $12y - 3x = ?$
    **F.**   0
    **G.**   1
    **H.**   7
    **J.**   15
    **K.**   20

**17.** If $x + \dfrac{1}{3} = \dfrac{x + 2}{3}$, then $x = ?$
    **A.**   $\dfrac{1}{2}$
    **B.**   1
    **C.**   $\dfrac{3}{2}$
    **D.**   2
    **E.**   3

**18.** If $(x + y)^2 = x^2 + y^2$, then $xy = ?$
    **F.**   0
    **G.**   1
    **H.**   2
    **J.**   5
    **K.**   12

**19.** If $(x + y)^2 - (x - y)^2 = 20$, then $xy = ?$
    **A.**   0
    **B.**   1
    **C.**   2
    **D.**   5
    **E.**   10

**20.** What is the complete solution set for the equation $x^2 + 3x + 2 = 0$?
    **F.**   $[-2, -3]$
    **G.**   $[-2, 3]$
    **H.**   $[-1, -2]$
    **J.**   $[-1, 2]$
    **H.**   $[1, 2]$

**21.** What is the complete solution set for the equation $x^2 + 2x - 8 = 0$?
    **A.** $[-4,-2]$
    **B.** $[-4,2]$
    **C.** $[-2,-1]$
    **D.** $[-1,2]$
    **E.** $[2,-4]$

**22.** What is the complete solution set for the equation $x^2 + 5x = -6$?
    **F.** $[-3,-4]$
    **G.** $[-3,-2]$
    **H.** $[-2,-1]$
    **J.** $[0,-2]$
    **K.** $[1,2]$

**23.** Which of the following choices provides all of the solutions for the equation $x^2 + 4x = -4$?
    **A.** $-2$
    **B.** $-2, 0$
    **C.** $-2, 2$
    **D.** $2, 4$
    **E.** $4, 6$

**24.** Which of the following choices provides all of the solutions for the equation $3x^2 - 3x - 6 = 0$?
    **F.** $[-2, -1]$
    **G.** $[-2, 1]$
    **H.** $[-1, 2]$
    **J.** $[-1, 3]$
    **K.** $[2, 3]$

**25.** Which of the following is the complete solution set for the equation $4x^2 = 2 - 2x$?
    **A.** $\left[-1, -\dfrac{1}{2}\right]$
    **B.** $\left[-1, \dfrac{1}{2}\right]$
    **C.** $\left[-\dfrac{1}{2}, 1\right]$
    **D.** $\left[\dfrac{1}{2}, -1\right]$
    **E.** $\left[\dfrac{1}{2}, 1\right]$

14

# Algebra Applications (Answers, page 250)

Some questions ask for you to apply your algebra skills to practical situations. You can brush up on your algebra by doing some problems.

1. On a shopping trip, Peter spent one-third of his money for a jacket and another five dollars for a hat. If Peter still had one-half of his money left, how much money did he have originally?

2. After filling the car's fuel tank, a driver drove from P to Q and then to R. She used two-fifths of the fuel driving from P to Q. If she used another seven gallons to drive from Q to R and still had one-quarter of a tank left, how many gallons does the tank hold?

3. A school meeting was attended only by sophomores, juniors, and seniors. Five-twelfths of those who attended were juniors, and one-third were seniors. If 36 sophomores attended, what was the total number of students who attended the meeting?

4. If $p$ pounds of coffee costs $d$ dollars, how many pounds of coffee can be purchased for $x$ dollars?

5. If $p$ pounds of coffee costs $d$ dollars, how many pounds of coffee can be purchased for $x + 10$ dollars?

6. If pencils costs $x$ cents per pencil, how many pencils can be purchased for $y$ dollars?

7. If the profit on an item is two dollars and the sum of the cost and the profit is ten dollars, what is the cost of the item?

8. A candy bar weighing four ounces costs $c$ cents. If the size of the candy bar is reduced to 3.6 ounces while the price remains the same, then the old price per ounce is what fraction of the new price per ounce?

9. A merchant increased the original price of an item by 10 percent. If she then reduces the new price by 10 percent, what is the final price in terms of the original price?

10. Harold is twice as old as Jack, who is three years older than Dan. If Harold's age is five times Dan's age, how old in years is Jack?

11. A tank with capacity $T$ gallons is empty. If water flows into the tank from Pipe X at the rate of $X$ gallons per minute, and water is pumped out by Pipe Y at the rate of $Y$ gallons per minute, and $X$ is greater than $Y$, in how many minutes will the tank be filled?

12. If 144 pencils cost $d$ dollars, how many pencils can be purchased for 50 cents?

13. Machine X produces $w$ widgets in five minutes. Machine X and Machine Y working at the same time produce $w$ widgets in two minutes. How long will it take Machine Y working alone to produce $w$ widgets?

14. If a train travels $m$ miles in $h$ hours and 45 minutes, expressed in terms of $m$ and $h$, what is its average speed in miles per hour?

15. In a playground, there are $x$ seesaws. If 50 children are all riding on seesaws, two to a seesaw, and five seesaws are not in use, what is $x$?

# Summary

1. Some problems require simple algebraic manipulations such as evaluating an expression, working with exponents, or factoring. Do the operations.

2. If the question stem is an equation (or equations), solve for an unknown or find a way of directly transforming one expression into another.

3. The Holmesian principle "one of the five suspects" is the basis for two powerful strategies:
   A. Test answer choices.
   B. Assume actual numbers for unknowns.

14

# Answers

### EXERCISE 1

**1.** (E) Factor by removing the common factor of $3x$ from each of the terms:
$3x^3 + 3x^2 + 3x = 3x(x^2 + x + 1)$

**2.** (F) The numerator fits the second of the three factoring patterns you learned:
$(x + y)(x + y)$. Then simplify by cancelling the $(x + y)$. The final result is $x + y$.

**3.** (C) Again, you should have an irresistible urge to factor. The numerator of the expression is the difference of two squares, the first of the three factoring patterns you learned. So the numerator is equal to $(x + y)(x - y)$. Next, cancel the $(x + y)$ terms. The result is $x - y$, which is said to be equal to 3.

**4.** (F) Do the indicated operations, and subtract:

$$(x + y)^2 = (x + y)(x + y) = x^2 + 2xy + y^2$$
$$(x - y)^2 = (x - y)(x - y) = \frac{x^2 - 2xy + y^2}{0 + 4xy + 0}$$

**5.** (B) $x^2 + 2x + 1$ fits the pattern $x^2 + 2xy + y^2$, where $y = 1$. But even if you didn't recognize that, you should think that $(x + 1)$ is one of the factors of the numerator and work backwards to find the other factor, which is also $(x + 1)$. Then cancel, and the final result is $x + 1$.

**6.** (G) Just substitute 2 for $x$:

$2(2) + 4 = 8$

**7.** (D) Just substitute 3 for $x$:

$(3)^2 - 2(3) + 3 = 9 - 6 + 3 = 6$

**8.** (G) First, substitute 2 for $x$:

$2(2) + 2 = 6$

And now substitute 6 for $x$:

$2(6) + 6 = 18$

**9.** (B) First, substitute 2 for $x$ in $g(x)$:

$2(2) + 2 = 6$

And substitute 6 for $x$ in $f(x)$:

$3(6) + 3 = 21$

**10.** (J) Solve for $n$:

$n + n + 1 + n + 2 = 12$

$3n + 3 = 12$

$3n = 9$

$n = 3$

**11.** (B) Solve for $x$:

$$\frac{1}{x} + \frac{1}{x} = 4$$

$$\frac{2}{x} = 4$$

$$2 = 4x$$

$$x = \frac{2}{4} = \frac{1}{2}$$

**12.** (G) Before you start solving for $x$, look for a way of converting $x + y$ to $\frac{1}{3}x + \frac{1}{3}y$. You can do that by multiplying $x + y$ by $\frac{1}{3}$: $\frac{1}{3}(x + y) = \frac{1}{3}x + \frac{1}{3}y$. So $\frac{1}{3}x + \frac{1}{3}y$ must be equal to $\frac{1}{3}(9)$, or 3.

**13.** (C) Two variables and two equations call for the simultaneous equations technique. To solve for $x$, first isolate $y$ in one of the equations. We will use the second since it is simpler:

$$x + y = 3$$

$$y = 3 - x$$

Now substitute $3 - x$ for $y$ in the first equation:

$$2x + (3 - x) = 5$$

And solve for $x$:

$$2x + 3 - x = 5$$

$$2x - x + 3 = 5$$

$$x + 3 = 5$$

$$x = 2$$

**14.** (H) Simultaneous equations again, so to solve for $n$, you isolate $m$: $3m = 5$, so $m = \frac{5}{3}$. Now substitute $\frac{5}{3}$ for $m$ in the second equation:

$$4n - 3\left(\frac{5}{3}\right) = 3$$

$$4n - 5 = 3$$

$$4n = 8$$

$$n = 2$$

Or you might have recognized that since $3m = 5$, you can substitute 5 for $3m$ in the second equation without solving for $m$.

**15.** (B) You could solve for $m$ in the first equation, getting $m$ in terms of $k$:

$$7m = 3k + 2$$

$$m = \frac{3k + 2}{7}$$

14

Then substitute this into $\frac{7m-2}{3}$:

$$\frac{7\left(\dfrac{3k+2}{7}\right)-2}{3} = \frac{3k+2-2}{3} = \frac{3k}{3} = k$$

That's conceptually correct, but it's too much work. Instead, you should see that you can turn $7m - 2$ into $\frac{(7m-2)}{3}$ by dividing by 3. So $\frac{(7m-2)}{3} = \frac{3k}{3} = k$.

16. (F) Notice that $12y$ is 3 times $4y$ and that $3x$ is 3 times $x$. Start by multiplying $x = 4y$ by 3:

$3(x) = 4y(3)$

$3x = 12y$

Now to turn $3x = 12y$ into $12y - 3x$, subtract $3x$ from both sides of the equation:

$3x = 12y$

$3x - 3x = 12y - 3x$

$0 = 12y - 3x$

So $12y - 3x$ is equal to zero.

17. (A) You can solve for $x$. First, multiply both sides of the equation by 3:

$3\left(x + \dfrac{1}{3}\right) = x + 2$

$3x + 1 = x + 2$

$2x = 1$

$x = \dfrac{1}{2}$

Or, if you need to, you can use the technique of substituting numbers.

18. (F) The natural starting point is to do the indicated multiplication. (It's one of the patterns you memorized.)

$(x + y)^2 = (x + y)(x + y) = x^2 + 2xy + y^2$

So:

$x^2 + 2xy + y^2 = x^2 + y^2$

Subtract $x^2$ and $y^2$ from both sides. The result is:

$2xy = 0$

So $xy = 0$

19. (D) First do the multiplication. You should be able to do this by memory.

$(x + y)^2 = x^2 + 2xy + y^2$

$(x - y)^2 = x^2 - 2xy + y^2$

So:

$$x^2 + 2xy + y^2 - (x^2 - 2xy + y^2) = 20$$
$$x^2 + 2xy + y^2 - x^2 + 2xy - y^2 = 20$$
$$x^2 - x^2 + 2xy + 2xy + y^2 - y^2 = 20$$
$$4xy = 20$$
$$xy = 5$$

**20.** (H)

$$x^2 + 3x + 2 = 0$$
$$(x + 2)(x + 1) = 0$$

So either $x + 2 = 0$ and $x = -2$ or $x + 1 = 0$ and $x = -1$.

**21.** (B)

$$x^2 + 2x - 8 = 0$$
$$(x + 4)(x - 2) = 0$$

So either $x + 4 = 0$ and $x = -4$ or $x - 2 = 0$ and $x = 2$.

**22.** (G)

$$x^2 + 5x = -6$$
$$x^2 + 5x + 6 = 0$$
$$(x + 3)(x + 2)$$

So either $x + 3 = 0$ and $x = -3$ or $x + 2 = 0$ and $x = -2$.

**23.** (A)

$$x^2 + 4x = -4$$
$$x^2 + 4x + 4 = 0$$
$$(x + 2)(x + 2) = 0$$

So $x + 2 = 0$ and $x = -2$.

**24.** (H)

$$3x^2 - 3x - 6 = 0$$
$$(3x + 3)(x - 2) = 0$$

So either $3x + 3 = 0$ and $x = -1$ or $x - 2 = 0$ and $x = 2$.

14

**25.** (D)

$$4x^2 = 2 - 2x$$

$$4x^2 + 2x - 2 = 0$$

$$(4x - 2)(x + 1) = 0$$

So either $4x - 2 = 0$ and $x = \frac{1}{2}$ or $x + 1 = 0$ and $x = -1$.

**Note:** For items like this that involve difficult factoring problems, you might choose to use the alternative Holmesian strategy of eliminating suspects by testing the test.

## EXERCISE 2

1. (30) In English: The original amount minus one-third of the original amount minus another five dollars is equal to one-half of the original amount.
   With $x$ designating the original amount, in algebra:

   $$x - \frac{1}{3}x - 5 = \frac{1}{2}x$$

   $$\frac{2}{3}x - 5 = \frac{1}{2}x$$

   $$\frac{2}{3}x - \frac{1}{2}x = 5$$

   $$\frac{1}{6}x = 5$$

   $$x = 30$$

2. (20) In English: A full tank minus two-fifths of a tank minus another seven gallons is equal to one-quarter of a tank. Let $x$ be the number of gallons the tank holds:

   $$x - \frac{2}{5}x - 7 = \frac{1}{4}x$$

   $$\frac{3}{5}x - 7 = \frac{1}{4}x$$

   $$\frac{3}{5}x - \frac{1}{4}x = 7$$

   $$\frac{7}{20}x = 7$$

   $$x = 7\left(\frac{20}{7}\right) = 20$$

3. (144) In English: Five-twelfths of the total number who attended plus one-third of the total number who attended plus 36 students is equal to the total number who attended.  Let $T$ represent the total number who attended:

$$\frac{5}{12}T + \frac{1}{3}T + 36 = T$$

$$\frac{9}{12}T + 36 = T$$

$$36 = T - \frac{3}{4}T$$

$$36 = \frac{1}{4}T$$

$$T = 36 \times 4 = 144$$

4. $\left(\frac{xp}{d}\right)$ To find how much of something can be purchased for a certain amount, you divide the amount of money by the cost.  The cost of coffee is $d$ dollars per $p$ pounds, or $\frac{d}{p}$.  Then divide $x$ dollars by $\frac{d}{p}$: $x \div \frac{d}{p} = x\left(\frac{p}{d}\right) = \frac{xp}{d}$.

5. $\left(\frac{p(x+10)}{d}\right)$ Follow the same procedure.  The cost of coffee is $\frac{d}{p}$.  Next, divide $x + 10$ by $\frac{d}{p}$: $(x+10) \div \frac{d}{p} = (x+10)\left(\frac{p}{d}\right) = \frac{p(x+10)}{d}$.

6. $\left(\frac{100y}{x}\right)$ Again, divide the amount available by the cost.  The cost of a pencil is $\frac{x}{1}$.  The available amount is $y$ dollars, which is $100y$ cents.  $100y \div x = \frac{100y}{x}$.

7. (8) In English: Cost plus two dollars equals ten dollars.  Let C be cost:

$$C + 2 = 10$$

$$C = 8$$

8. $\left(\frac{9}{10}\right)$ The old price was $\frac{c}{4}$ ounces, and the new price is $\frac{c}{3.6}$ ounce.  Using the "this-of-that" strategy:

$$\frac{\text{old price per ounce}}{\text{new price per ounce}} = \frac{\frac{c}{4}}{\frac{c}{3.6}} = \frac{c}{4} \times \frac{3.6}{c} = \frac{3.6}{4} = \frac{9}{10}$$

9. (1%) Let $P$ be the original price.  The price increases by 10 percent, or $\frac{1}{10}$: $P + 0.1P = 1.1P$.  Then that price decreases by 10 percent: $1.1P - 0.11P = 0.99P$.  So the net decrease was $0.01P$, and the percent decrease was $\frac{0.01P}{P} = 0.01 = 1\%$.

10. (5) In English: Harold's age is twice Jack's age; Jack's age is three more than Dan's; and Harold's age is five times Dan's age.  Let $H$, $J$, and $D$ stand for the ages of Harold, Jack, and Dan:

$$H = 2J \text{ and } J = D + 3 \text{ and } H = 5D$$

Since $H = 2J$, substitute $2J$ for $H$ in the third equation:

$$H = 5D \text{ so } 2J = 5D$$

Solve for $D$:

$$2J = 5D$$

$$D = \frac{2}{5}J$$

14

Now substitute $\frac{2}{5}J$ for $D$ in the equation $J = D + 3$:

$$J = \frac{2}{5}J + 3$$

$$J - \frac{2}{5}J = 3$$

$$\frac{3}{5}J = 3$$

$$J = 3\left(\frac{5}{3}\right) = 5$$

**11.** $\left(\frac{T}{X-Y}\right)$ Since water comes in at $X$ gallons per minute and goes out at $Y$ gallons per minute, the net gain is $X - Y$. To find how long it will take to fill the tank, divide the capacity of the tank by the net rate at which the tank is being filled: $T \div (X - Y)$, which is $\frac{T}{X-Y}$.

**12.** $\left(\frac{72}{d}\right)$ Divide the available amount by the cost of each pencil. The available amount is 50 cents. Pencils cost $d$ dollars or $100d$ cents per 144. $50 \div \left(\frac{100d}{144}\right) = 50\left(\frac{144}{100d}\right) = \frac{144}{2d} = \frac{72}{d}$.

**13.** (3 minutes, 20 seconds) In English: Machine X operates at the rate of $w$ widgets per five minutes. Machines X and Y together operate at the rate of $w$ widgets per two minutes. Take away Machine X's contribution, and you will have the rate at which Machine Y operates.

Rate of X and Y together $-$ Rate of X = Rate of Y

$$\frac{w \text{ widgets}}{2 \text{ minutes}} - \frac{w \text{ widgets}}{5 \text{ minutes}} = \frac{w \text{ widgets}}{x \text{ minutes}}$$

$$\frac{w}{2} - \frac{w}{5} = \frac{w}{x}$$

$$\frac{5w - 2w}{10} = \frac{w}{x}$$

$$\frac{3w}{10} = \frac{w}{x}$$

$$x = w\left(\frac{10}{3w}\right) = \frac{10}{3}, \text{ which is 3 minutes and 20 seconds.}$$

**14.** $\left(\frac{m}{h + \frac{3}{4}}\right)$ The speed is to be expressed in miles. Miles traveled is $m$, and time traveled is $h$ hours plus another three-quarters of an hour, or $h + \frac{3}{4}$. So the speed was $\frac{m}{h + \frac{3}{4}}$.

**15.** (30) In English, the total number of seesaws less five seesaws is equal to enough seesaws for 50 children.

$$x - 5 = \frac{50}{2}$$

$$x - 5 = 25$$

$$x = 30$$

# Math Usage: Geometry

## ✔ Objectives

To review the key principles of geometry frequently tested.

To learn strategies for handling problems involving composite and shaded-area figures.

To learn strategies for solving unusual items.

To learn strategies that avoid the use of geometry formulas altogether.

1. Angles
2. Triangles
3. Rectangles and Squares
4. Circles
5. Solids
6. Coordinate Geometry
7. Complex Figures
8. Nonformulaic Techniques
   - "Guestimating"
   - Measuring
   - "Meastimating"

15

Several problems in the Math Usage Test will test your knowledge of geometry. You won't be asked to give formal proofs of theorems, but you will need to use logic and your knowledge of basic formulas to do things like finding the size of an angle, the length of a line, or the area of a figure.

### Holmes' Attic

In the Holmes stories, Dr. Watson occasionally remarks on the curious imbalance in the detective's learning. Holmes had remarkably detailed knowledge of some areas, such as the geography of London and the effects of exotic poisons, but no knowledge at all of other areas that most people would think important, like literature or politics. To explain this seeming shortcoming, Holmes draws an analogy between the mind and an attic. The mind, like an attic, is a storage facility—with limited space. To make effective use of the space, you have to be sure you don't clutter it up with things you don't need.

Although the term *geometry* covers a lot of knowledge, relatively few principles are tested by the ACT. These are the ones to keep in your "attic."

---

## Angles

THE NUMBER OF DEGREES OF ARC IN A CIRCLE IS 360.

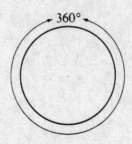

360°

**EXAMPLE:**

In the figure below, x = ?

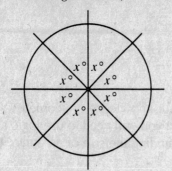

A.  15
B.  30
C.  45
D.  60
E.  75

The answer is C.

$$x + x + x + x + x + x + x + x = 360$$

$$8x = 360$$

$$x = 45$$

**THE MEASURE IN DEGREES OF A STRAIGHT ANGLE IS 180.**

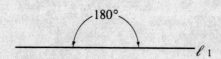

**EXAMPLE:**

In the figure below, x = ?

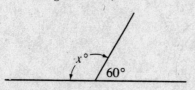

F.  45
G.  60
H.  75
J.  90
K.  120

The answer is K.

$$x + 60 = 180$$

$$x = 120$$

THE NUMBER OF DEGREES IN A RIGHT ANGLE IS 90.

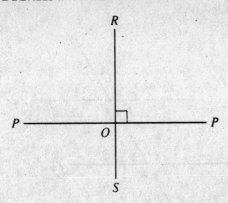

In the figure above, *POR* and angle *ROQ* are both right angles, so each measures 90°. And *RS* is perpendicular to *PQ*.

### EXAMPLE:

In the figure below, x = ?

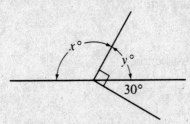

A. 45
B. 60
C. 90
D. 105
E. 120

The answer is E.

$$y + 30 = 90$$

$$y = 60$$

$$x + y = 180$$

$$x + 60 = 180$$

$$x = 120$$

15

WHEN PARALLEL LINES ARE CUT BY A THIRD LINE, THE RESULTING ANGLES ARE RELATED AS FOLLOWS:

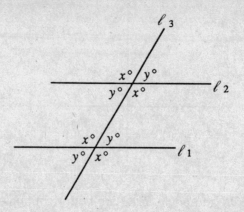

$x = x = x = x$; $y = y = y = y$; and $x + y = 180$. This is the "big angle/little angle" theorem. All the big angles are equal; all the little angles are equal; and any big angle plus any little angle equals 180. (In the event the third line intersects the parallel lines on the perpendicular, then all angles equal 90°.)

**EXAMPLE:**

In the figure below, which of the following must be true?
  I. $w = a$
 II. $y + b = 180°$
III. $x + d = 180°$
 F.  I only
 G.  II only
 H.  I and II only
 J.  II and III only
 K.  I, II, and III

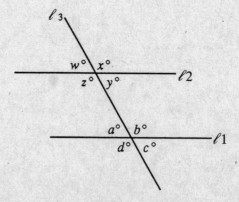

The answer is H. $w$ and $a$ are "small" angles, so they are equal, and statement I is true. $y$ is a "small" angle and $b$ is a "large" angle, so their sum is 180°, and II is true. III, however, is not true. $x$ and $d$ are both "large" angles. They would total 180° only in the special case where both are 90°.

THE SUM OF THE MEASURES IN DEGREES OF THE INTERIOR ANGLES OF A
TRIANGLE IS 180°.

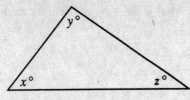

In the figure above, $x + y + z = 180$.

> **EXAMPLE:**
>
> In the figure below, $x = ?$
> A.   30
> B.   45
> C.   60
> D.   75
> E.   90

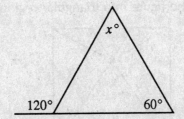

The answer is C. Let $y$ be the measure of the third and unlabeled angle inside the
triangle:

$$120 + y = 180$$

$$y = 60$$

$$x + y + 60 = 180$$

$$x + 60 + 60 = 180$$

$$x + 120 = 180$$

$$x = 60$$

THE SUM IN DEGREES OF THE INTERIOR ANGLES OF A POLYGON OF $N$
SIDES IS $180(N - 2)$.

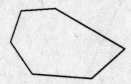 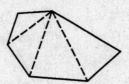

The figure above has six sides, so the sum of the six angles is $180(6 - 2) = 180(4)$
$= 720°$. Instead of memorizing the formula just given, you can reason that the
figure is composed of four triangles, each with angles totaling 180°.

15

**EXAMPLE:**

In the figure below, what is the sum of the indicated angles?

F.  540

G.  720

H.  900

J.  1,080

K.  1,260

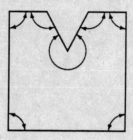

The answer is H.  Divide the figure into triangular regions:

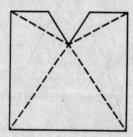

There are five triangles, so the sum of the angles is 5(180) = 900°.

   **Note:** This principle gives you the sum of the interior angles of the polygon.  You might be asked about the average size of the angles.  In that case, divide the sum of the angles by the total number of angles inside the figure.

**Triangles**

WITHIN A TRIANGLE, IF TWO ANGLES ARE EQUAL, THE LENGTHS OF THEIR OPPOSITE SIDES ARE EQUAL, AND VICE VERSA.

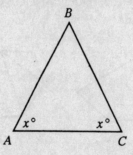

In the figure above, $AB = BC$.

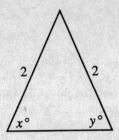

In the figure above, $x = y$.

THE PYTHAGOREAN THEOREM: IN A RIGHT TRIANGLE, THE SQUARE OF
THE LONGEST SIDE (THE HYPOTENUSE) IS EQUAL TO THE SUM OF THE
SQUARES OF THE OTHER TWO SIDES.

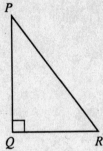

In the figure above, $PR^2 = PQ^2 + QR^2$.

> **EXAMPLE:**
>
> In the figure below, $AB = ?$
> **A.** 2
> **B.** $2\sqrt{3}$
> **C.** 4
> **D.** $4\sqrt{2}$
> **E.** 8

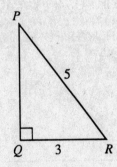

The answer is C.

$$BC^2 = AB^2 + AC^2$$
$$5^2 = AB^2 + 3^2$$
$$25 = AB^2 + 9$$
$$AB^2 = 16$$
$$AB = \sqrt{16} = 4$$

15

ANY TRIANGLE WITH SIDES OF 3, 4, AND 5 (OR MULTIPLES THEREOF) IS A RIGHT TRIANGLE.

This is a two-edged sword. First, any triangle having sides that fit the Pythagorean Theorem is a right triangle. Since $3^2 + 4^2 = 5^2$, a triangle with those sides must be a right triangle. Additionally, any triangle with sides that are multiples of 3, 4, and 5 is a right triangle. For example, since $6^2 + 8^2 = 10^2$, a triangle with sides of 6, 8, and 10 is a right triangle (as are triangles with sides of 18, 24, and 30; 30, 40, and 50; and so on).

The other edge of the sword gives you an easy method for finding the length of a side in such triangles.

**EXAMPLE:**

In the figure below, what is the length of *AC*?

**F.** 5
**G.** 10
**H.** 12
**J.** 16
**K.** 20

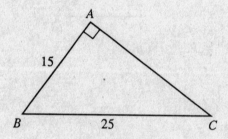

The answer is E. Since *ABC* is a right triangle, you can use the Pythagorean Theorem. Or, you can save time by reasoning that one side is $3 \times 5$ and the hypotenuse is $5 \times 5$, so the missing length must be $4 \times 5 = 20$.

IN A TRIANGLE WITH ANGLES OF 45°, 45°, AND 90°, THE LENGTH OF THE HYPOTENUSE IS EQUAL TO THE LENGTH OF EITHER SIDE MULTIPLIED BY $\sqrt{2}$, AND EACH OF THE SHORTER SIDES IS EQUAL TO $\frac{1}{2}$ TIMES THE LENGTH OF THE HYPOTENUSE TIMES $\sqrt{2}$.

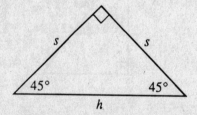

Both of these conclusions follow from the Pythagorean Theorem (coupled with the rule that sides opposite equal angles are equal in length).

$$h^2 = s^2 + s^2$$
$$h^2 = 2s^2$$
$$h = s\sqrt{2}$$

Which is to say, the hypotenuse of the $45-45-90$ triangle is equal to either side times $\sqrt{2}$. Conversely,

$$s^2 + s^2 = h^2$$

$$2s^2 = h^2$$

$$s^2 = \frac{h^2}{2}$$

$$s = \frac{h}{\sqrt{2}} = (\tfrac{1}{2})(h\sqrt{2})$$

Which is to say, either side of the $45-45-90$ triangle is equal to $\frac{1}{2}$ times the hypotenuse times $\sqrt{2}$.

These conversions can save you time.

**EXAMPLE:**

In the figure below, $PQ = ?$

A.  1
B.  $\sqrt{2}$
C.  $2\sqrt{2}$
D.  4
E.  5

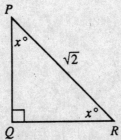

The answer is A. Since the triangle contains a right angle and two equal angles, it must be a $45-45-90$ triangle. Rather than use the general form of the Pythagorean Theorem, just reason that $PQ$, one of the sides, is equal to $\frac{1}{2}$ times the length of the hypotenuse times $\sqrt{2}$: $\frac{1}{2}(\sqrt{2} \times \sqrt{2}) = \frac{1}{2}(2) = 1$.

IN A TRIANGLE WITH ANGLES OF 30°, 60°, AND 90°, THE LENGTH OF THE SIDE OPPOSITE THE 30° ANGLE IS $\frac{1}{2}$ TIMES THE LENGTH OF THE HYPOTENUSE, AND THE LENGTH OF THE SIDE OPPOSITE THE 60° ANGLE IS $\frac{1}{2}$ TIMES THE LENGTH OF THE HYPOTENUSE TIMES $\sqrt{3}$.

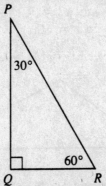

In the figure above, $PR = \frac{1}{2} QR$, and $PQ = \frac{1}{2} QR\sqrt{3}$.

**EXAMPLE:**

In the triangle below, what is the length of *AC*?

F.  2

G.  √3

H.  2√3

J.  3√3

K.  6

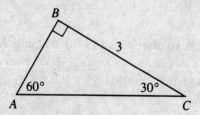

The answer is H.  Since two of the angles of the triangle are 30° and 60°, the remaining angle must be 90°.  So we have a 30–60–90 triangle, in which the side opposite the 60° angle is equal to $\frac{1}{2}$ times the length of the hypotenuse times √3:

$$BC = \frac{1}{2} AC\sqrt{3}$$

$$3 = \frac{1}{2} AC\sqrt{3}$$

$$6 = AC\sqrt{3}$$

$$AC = \frac{6}{\sqrt{3}} = \frac{6\sqrt{3}}{3} = 2\sqrt{3}$$

AN EQUILATERAL TRIANGLE (3 EQUAL SIDES) HAS THREE 60° ANGLES. CONVERSELY, A TRIANGLE WITH THREE EQUAL ANGLES IS EQUILATERAL.

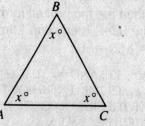
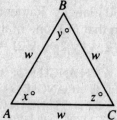

In the figure on the left, $x = 60$, and $AB = BC = AC$.  In the figure on the right, since all three sides are equal, $x = y = z = 60$.

THE PERIMETER OF A TRIANGLE IS THE SUM OF THE LENGTHS OF ITS SIDES.

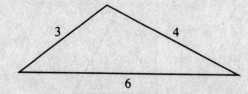

In the figure above, the perimeter is $3 + 4 + 6 = 13$.

**EXAMPLE:**

In the figure below, the perimeter of triangle $PQR$ = ?

**A.**  $12 + \sqrt{3}$

**B.**  $12 + 2\sqrt{3}$

**C.**  $12 + 4\sqrt{3}$

**D.**  28

**E.**  56

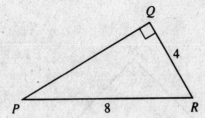

The answer is C.  To find the perimeter of the triangle, you must first find the length of $PQ$.

$$PR^2 = PQ^2 + QR^2$$
$$8^2 = PQ^2 + 4^2$$
$$64 = PQ^2 + 16$$
$$PQ^2 = 64 - 16 = 48$$
$$PQ = \sqrt{48} = \sqrt{16 \times 3} = 4\sqrt{3}$$

So the perimeter is $4 + 8 + 4\sqrt{3} = 12 + 4\sqrt{3}$.

You can skip over a large number of the steps we just did if you remember the facts about a 30−60−90 triangle.  $PQR$ is a right triangle in which one of the sides is half the hypotenuse.  So $PQR$ must be a 30−60−90 triangle and $QR$ is opposite the 30° angle.  This means that $PQ = 4\sqrt{3}$.

THE AREA OF A TRIANGLE IS EQUAL TO $\frac{1}{2}$ TIMES THE ALTITUDE TIMES THE BASE.

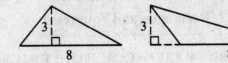

The area of the triangle on the left is $\frac{1}{2} \times 3 \times 8 = 12$.  And the area of the triangle on the right is also $\frac{1}{2} \times 3 \times 8 = 12$.

15

**EXAMPLE:**

What is the area of triangle *MNO*?

F.  $\dfrac{1}{2}$

G.  $\dfrac{\sqrt{2}}{2}$

H.  1

J.  $\sqrt{2}$

K.  2

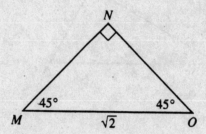

The answer is F. This is a 45−45−90 triangle, so each of the two shorter sides is $\frac{1}{2} \times \sqrt{2} \times MO = \frac{1}{2} \times \sqrt{2} \times \sqrt{2} = \frac{1}{2} \times 2 = 1$. Since *MN* and *NO* form a right angle, we can use them as altitude and base:

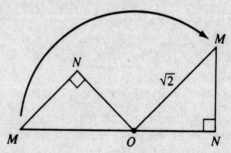

$\frac{1}{2} \times 1 \times 1 = \frac{1}{2} \times 1 = \frac{1}{2}$

## Rectangles and Squares

THE PERIMETER OF A RECTANGLE IS EQUAL TO THE SUM OF THE LENGTHS OF THE FOUR SIDES. THE AREA OF A RECTANGLE IS EQUAL TO THE WIDTH MULTIPLIED BY THE LENGTH.

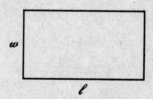

The perimeter of the rectangle above is $w + \ell + w + \ell = 2w + 2\ell$. The area is equal to $w$ times $\ell = w\ell$.

**EXAMPLE:**

If the area of the rectangle below is 18, what is the perimeter?

A.  9
B.  12
C.  18
D.  24
E.  30

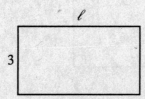

The answer is C. The area of a rectangle is $w \times \ell$.

$3 \times \ell = 18$

$\ell = 18 \div 3 = 6$

So the perimeter is $3 + 6 + 3 + 6 = 18$.

THE DIAGONAL OF A RECTANGLE IS THE HYPOTENUSE OF A RIGHT TRIANGLE WITH SIDES THAT ARE THE LENGTH AND WIDTH OF THE RECTANGLE.

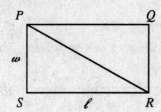

In the figure above, *PQRS* is a rectangle. *PSR* and *PQR* are right triangles, so $PR^2 = w^2 + \ell^2$.

**EXAMPLE:**

In the figure below, *PQRS* is a rectangle. If *PR* = 5, then what is the area of the rectangle?

F.  2
G.  3
H.  4
J.  8
K.  12

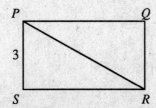

15

The answer is K.  *PSR* is a right triangle with hypotenuse of 5 and one side of 3, so the missing side must be 4.  The area of the rectangle is 3 × 4 = 12.

A SQUARE IS A RECTANGLE WITH FOUR EQUAL SIDES.  SO THE PERIMETER OF A SQUARE IS 4 TIMES THE LENGTH OF A SIDE, AND THE AREA IS SIDE TIMES SIDE.

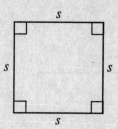

The perimeter of the square is $s + s + s + s = 4s$, and the area of the square is $s \times s = s^2$.

THE DIAGONAL OF A SQUARE IS EQUAL TO $\frac{1}{2}$ TIMES ITS SIDE TIMES $\sqrt{2}$, AND THE SIDE OF A SQUARE IS EQUAL TO ITS DIAGONAL TIMES $\sqrt{2}$.

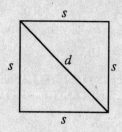

In the square above, $d = s\sqrt{2}$, and $d = \frac{1}{2} \times s\sqrt{2}$.  This is just a variation on the Pythagorean Theorem.  The two sides of the square and the diagonal create a 45−45−90 triangle.

GIVEN (1) THE SIDE, (2) THE DIAGONAL, OR (3) THE AREA OF A SQUARE, YOU CAN DEDUCE THE OTHER TWO QUANTITIES.
(1)  Given that the side has a length of $s$, the area is $s \times s = s^2$, and the diagonal $= s\sqrt{2}$.
(2)  Given that the diagonal has a length of $d$, the side is $\frac{1}{2} \times d\sqrt{2}$, and the area is
$$(\tfrac{1}{2} \times d\sqrt{2}) \times (\tfrac{1}{2} \times d\sqrt{2}) = \frac{d^2}{2}.$$
(3)  Given that the area is $s^2$, the side is $s$, and the diagonal is $s\sqrt{2}$.

## Circles

THE RADIUS OF A CIRCLE IS $\frac{1}{2}$ OF THE DIAMETER, AND THE
DIAMETER OF A CIRCLE IS 2 TIMES THE RADIUS.

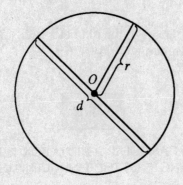

If a circle has a radius of 1, its diameter is 2. Conversely, if a circle has a diameter of 2, its radius is 1.

CIRCUMFERENCE = $2\pi r$

AREA = $\pi r^2$

If a circle has a radius of 3:

CIRCUMFERENCE = $2\pi(3) = 6\pi$

AREA = $\pi(3^2) = 9\pi$

GIVEN (1) THE RADIUS, (2) THE DIAMETER, (3) THE CIRCUMFERENCE, OR (4) THE
AREA OF A CIRCLE, YOU CAN DEDUCE THE OTHER THREE.

(1)  Given a radius of $r$, the diameter is $2r$, the circumference is $2\pi r$, and the area is $\pi r^2$.

(2)  Given a diameter of $d$, the radius is $\frac{1}{2}d$, the circumference is $2\pi\left(\dfrac{d}{2}\right) = \pi d$ and the area is $\pi\left(\dfrac{d}{2}\right)^2 = \dfrac{\pi d^2}{4}$.

(3)  Given a circumference of $2\pi r$, the radius is $r$, the diameter is $2r$, and the area is $\pi r^2$.

(4)  Given an area of $\pi r^2$, the radius is $r$, the diameter is $2r$, and the circumference is $2\pi r$.

### EXAMPLE:

If the area of a circle is $9\pi$, which of the following is (are) true?

I.   The radius is 3.
II.  The diameter is 6.
III. The circumference is $6\pi$.

A.  I only
B.  II only
C.  III only
D.  I and II only
E.  I, II, and III

15

The answer is E.  If the area of the circle is $9\pi$, then

$$\pi r^2 = 9\pi$$
$$r^2 = 9$$
$$r = \sqrt{9} = 3$$

So statement I is true.  Then if $r = 3$, the diameter is $2 \times 3$, so II is also true.  Finally, if $r = 3$, then the circumference is $2\pi(3) = 6\pi$.

**Solids**

THE VOLUME OF A RECTANGULAR SOLID (A BOX) IS THE WIDTH OF THE BASE MULTIPLIED BY THE LENGTH OF THE BASE MULTIPLIED BY THE HEIGHT OF THE SOLID.

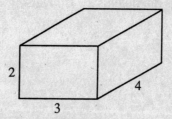

The volume of the rectangular solid above is $2 \times 3 \times 4 = 24$.

THE AREA OF THE FACE OF A RECTANGULAR SOLID (SIDE OF A BOX) IS THE PRODUCT OF THE LENGTH OF ONE EDGE OF THE FACE AND THE LENGTH OF AN ADJACENT EDGE.

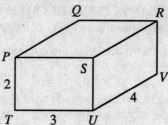

The area of $PTUS = 2 \times 3 = 6$.
The area of $SRVU = 2 \times 4 = 8$.
The area of $PQRS = 3 \times 4 = 12$.

THE TOTAL SURFACE AREA OF A RECTANGULAR SOLID (THE OUTSIDE OF A BOX) IS THE SUM OF THE AREAS OF THE SIX FACES.

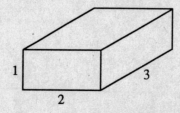

The front has an area of $1 \times 2 = 2$.
The side has an area of $1 \times 3 = 3$.
The bottom has an area of $2 \times 3 = 6$.
Since there are two of each (front = back, side = side, bottom = top), the total surface area is $(2 + 2) + (3 + 3) + (6 + 6) = 22$.

A CUBE IS A RECTANGULAR SOLID WITH THREE EQUAL DIMENSIONS.  GIVEN (1) THE LENGTH OF AN EDGE, (2) THE AREA OF A FACE, (3) THE TOTAL SURFACE AREA OF THE CUBE, OR (4) THE VOLUME OF THE CUBE, YOU CAN DEDUCE THE OTHER THREE QUANTITIES.

(1)  If the edge is $s$, then the area of each face is $s^2$, the total surface area is $6s^2$, and the volume is $s^3$.

(2)  If the area of a face is $s^2$, then the length of each edge is $s$, the total surface area is $6s^2$, and the volume is $s^3$.

(3)  If the total surface area is $6s^2$, then the area of each face is $s^2$, the length of each edge is $s$, and the volume is $s^3$.

(4)  If the volume is $s^3$, then the length of each edge is $s$, the surface area of each face is $s^2$, and the total surface area is $6s^2$.

## Coordinate Geometry

A COORDINATE PLANE IS DESCRIBED WITH REFERENCE TO AN X-AXIS (HORIZONTAL AXIS) AND A Y-AXIS (VERTICAL AXIS) WHICH ARE PERPENDICULAR TO EACH OTHER.  THEIR INTERSECTION IS CALLED THE ORIGIN.

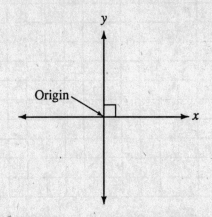

COORDINATE PAIRS ARE USED TO LOCATE POINTS ON THE PLANE.  THE GENERAL FORM IS $(x,y)$.  THE FIRST ELEMENT GIVES LOCATION WITH REFERENCE TO THE X-AXIS, THE SECOND WITH REFERENCE TO THE Y-AXIS.

15

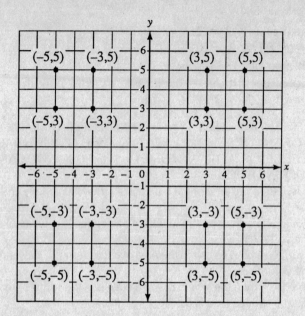

THE LENGTH OF A LINE PARALLEL TO AN AXIS IS THE DIFFERENCE BETWEEN THE
END-POINT COORDINATES FOR THAT AXIS.

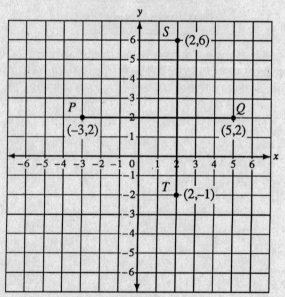

Line *PQ* runs from (−3,2) to (5,2), parallel to the *x*-axis.  So the distance is just the
difference between the *x* coordinates, 5 and −3: 5 − (−3) = 5 + 3 = 8.  Line *ST*
runs from (2,6) to (2,−1), so the length is the difference between the *y* coordinates:
6 − (−1) = 6 + 1 = 7.

THE LENGTH OF LINES NOT PARALLEL TO EITHER AXIS CAN BE DETERMINED BY
THE PYTHAGOREAN THEOREM.

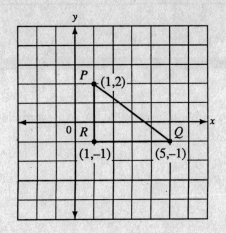

*PQR* is a right triangle.  *PR* = 3, and *RQ* = 4.  So *PQ* = 5.

15

# Holmes' Attic (Answers, page 290)

**Directions:** The following problems require the use of the formulas discussed in the preceding section.

1. In the figure below, x = ?
    A. 10
    B. 15
    C. 18
    D. 24
    E. 25

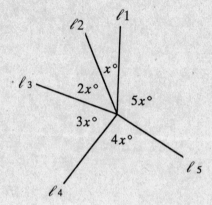

2. In the figure below, what is the measure of the angle formed by the intersection of $\ell 1$ and $\ell 3$?
    F. 30°
    G. 45°
    H. 60°
    J. 90°
    K. 120

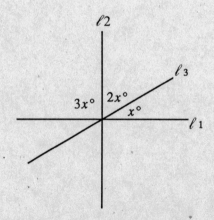

**3.** In the figure below, x = ?

  **A.** 30
  **B.** 45
  **C.** 55
  **D.** 60
  **E.** 75

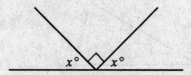

**4.** In the figure below, y = ?

  **F.** 15
  **G.** 30
  **H.** 45
  **J.** 60
  **K.** 90

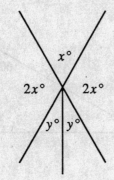

**5.** In the figure below, x − y = ?

  **A.** 0
  **B.** 45
  **C.** 60
  **D.** 90
  **E.** 135

**15**

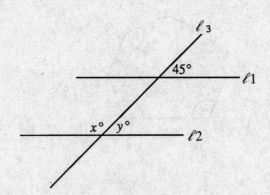

**6.** In the figure below, x = ?

   **F.**   25

   **G.**   35

   **H.**   45

   **J.**   55

   **K.**   75

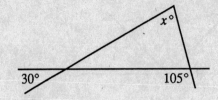

**7.** In the figure below, x = ?

   **A.**   15

   **B.**   30

   **C.**   45

   **D.**   60

   **E.**   90

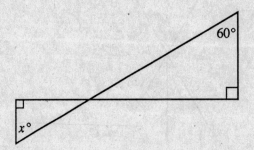

**8.** In the figure below, what is the sum of the indicated angles?

   **F.**   360

   **G.**   540

   **H.**   720

   **J.**   900

   **K.**   1,020

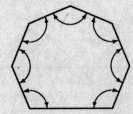

**9.** In the figure below, $PQ = ?$

   **A.** 1
   **B.** 3
   **C.** $3\sqrt{2}$
   **D.** $\sqrt{41}$
   **E.** $\sqrt{47}$

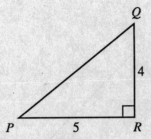

**10.** In the figure below, $AB = ?$

   **F.** 1
   **G.** 5
   **H.** $5\sqrt{2}$
   **J.** $5\sqrt{3}$
   **K.** 11

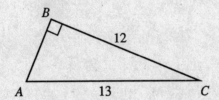

**11.** Triangles with sides in which of the following ratios must be right triangles?

   I. $2:1:\sqrt{3}$
   II. $1:1:\sqrt{2}$
   III. $\sqrt{2}:\sqrt{2}:2$

   **A.** I only
   **B.** II only
   **C.** III only
   **D.** I and III only
   **E.** I, II, and III

15

**12.** In the figure below, $AB = ?$

    **F.**  3
    **G.**  $3\sqrt{2}$
    **H.**  $3\sqrt{3}$
    **J.**  9
    **K.**  $\dfrac{9\sqrt{3}}{2}$

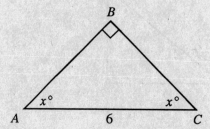

**13.** In the figure below, $NM = ?$

    **A.**  $x$
    **B.**  $\sqrt{3}$
    **C.**  $3x$
    **D.**  $2x\sqrt{3}$
    **E.**  $3x\sqrt{3}$

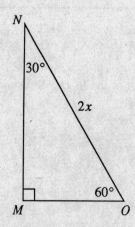

**14.** What is the area of triangle *PQR*?

    **F.** $2\sqrt{3}$

    **G.** 9

    **H.** $9\sqrt{3}$

    **J.** 18

    **K.** $18\sqrt{3}$

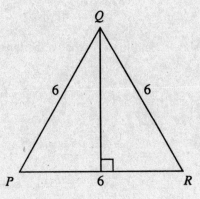

**15.** What is the area of the rectangle shown below?

    **A.** 8

    **B.** 12

    **C.** 15

    **D.** 18

    **E.** 30

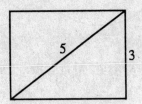

**16.** What is the area of the square shown below?

    **F.** 1

    **G.** $\sqrt{2}$

    **H.** 2

    **J.** $2\sqrt{2}$

    **K.** $4\sqrt{2}$

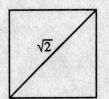

15

**17.** If the number of units in the circumference of a circle is equal to the number of square units in the area of the circle, what is the length of the radius of the circle?

- **A.** 1
- **B.** $\sqrt{2}$
- **C.** 2
- **D.** $\pi$
- **E.** $2\pi$

**18.** If the radius of Circle O, shown below, is 3, what is the length of arc *AXB*?

- **F.** $\frac{1}{6}\pi$
- **G.** $\frac{1}{3}\pi$
- **H.** $\pi$
- **J.** $3\pi$
- **K.** $6\pi$

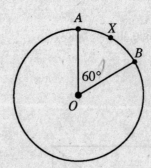

**19.** If a cube has a total surface area of 54, what is the length of the edge of the cube?

- **A.** 3
- **B.** $2\sqrt{2}$
- **C.** $3\sqrt{2}$
- **D.** 6
- **E.** 9

**20.** In the figure below, what is the length of *PQ*?

    **F.**   1

    **G.**  $3\sqrt{2}$

    **H.**  4

    **J.**   5

    **K.**  7

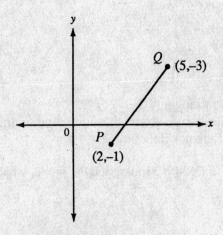

---

## Complex Figures

Thus far we have discussed the most commonly used principles of geometry as they apply to simple figures such as intersecting lines, triangles, squares, and circles. Many of the drawings used on the ACT, however, are made up of more than one figure.

### EXAMPLES:

If *BCDE* is a square with an area of 4, what is the perimeter of triangle *ABE*?

    **A.**  3

    **B.**  4

    **C.**  6

    **D.**  8

    **E.**  12

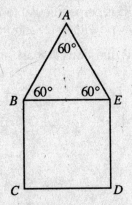

15

The answer is C. *ABE* has three 60° angles, so it is equilateral. To find the perimeter, you need to find the length of one of the sides. The only information given in the question is the area of the square. To bridge the gap, you must see that one side of the square is also a side of the triangle. If you can find the side of the square, you have everything you need to know.

Since the area of the square is 4, the side of the square is 2:

$$\text{side} \times \text{side} = \text{area}$$
$$s^2 = 4$$
$$s = \sqrt{4} = 2$$

So the perimeter of the triangle is $2 + 2 + 2$.

The key to such questions is to see that some line or angle serves two functions. Here is an example of greater difficulty:

In the figure below, if *QRST* is a square and $PQ = \sqrt{2}$, what is the length of *RU*?

F.   $\sqrt{2}$
G.   $\sqrt{6}$
H.   $2\sqrt{2}$
J.   4
K.   $4\sqrt{3}$

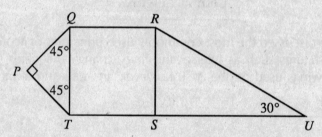

The question doesn't supply a lot of information—at least not explicitly. So it must be possible to deduce some further conclusions from what is given.

The hypotenuse of *PQT* is also a side of square *QRST*. And *RS* is not only a side of the square, it is a side of triangle *RSU*. If we can find the length of *QT*, we can deduce the length of *RU*. Since *PQT* is a 45−45−90 triangle and $PQ = \sqrt{2}$, $QT = \sqrt{2} \times \sqrt{2} = 2$. All four sides of a square are equal, so $RS = QT = 2$. *RS* is also a side in a 30−60−90 triangle (*RS* is perpendicular to *TU*). Since *RS* is opposite the 30° angle, it is $\frac{1}{2}$ the length of *RU*. So $\frac{1}{2}RU = 2$, and $RU = 4$.

A variation on this theme is questions that ask about shaded portions of a figure.

**EXAMPLE:**

In the figure below, *PQRS* is a square, and *PS* is the diameter of a semicircle. If
*PQ* = 2, what is the area of the shaded portion of the diagram?

A.  $4 - 2\pi$

B.  $4 - \pi$

C.  $4 - \dfrac{\pi}{2}$

D.  $8 - \pi$

E.  $8 - \dfrac{\pi}{2}$

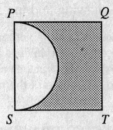

The answer is C. What makes the problem a little tricky is that you are asked to find
the area of a figure that looks like this:

And that is not a figure for which you have a ready-at-hand formula. The key to the
solution is to see that the irregular shaded part of the figure is what's left over after
you take away the semicircle from the square:

Square *PQRS* minus Semicircle = Shaded Area

So if you can find the area of the square and the area of the semicircle, you can
answer the question.

Now we proceed as we did above. *PS* is not only a side of the square, it is the
diameter of the semicircle. Since the side of the square is 2, the square has an area
of 4. And since *PS* = 2, the semicircle has a radius of 1. The area of an entire circle
with radius 1 is $\pi r^2 = \pi(1^2) = \pi$. And since this is half a circle, the semicircle has an
area of $\frac{\pi}{2}$. So the area of the shaded portion of the figure is $4 - \frac{\pi}{2}$.

15

# Monster Figures (Answers, page 293)

Take a quick glance at the three figures below.  They are more complex than anything you should expect to see on your ACT, but they make excellent practice.  The interesting thing about the drawings is that if you know the length of any line or the area of any part of the figure (no matter how weird its shape) you can find the length of every other line in the drawing and the area of every other shape.

*Directions:* Below each drawing is a table you are to fill in.  You are asked to assume values for various aspects of the drawings and to deduce values for other parts of the drawings.  In the explanations at the end of the chapter you will find a correctly completed table and an outline of the procedures to follow.

## MONSTER DRAWING 1

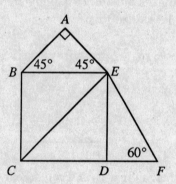

**Note:** *BCDE* is a square.

|  | AB | BC | CE | DF | EF | Area △ABE | Area BCDE | Area △EDF |
|---|---|---|---|---|---|---|---|---|
| AB = 1 | 1 |  |  |  |  |  |  |  |
| BC = 1 |  | 1 |  |  |  |  |  |  |
| CE = 1 |  |  | 1 |  |  |  |  |  |
| DF = 1 |  |  |  | 1 |  |  |  |  |
| EF = 1 |  |  |  |  | 1 |  |  |  |

## MONSTER DRAWING 2

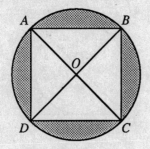

| | $AB$ | Radius | Area $ABCD$ | Circum-ference of Circle | Area of Circle | Shaded Area |
|---|---|---|---|---|---|---|
| $AB = 1$ | 1 | | | | | |
| Radius = 1 | | 1 | | | | |
| Area of $ABCD$ = 4 | | | 4 | | | |
| Circumference of Circle = $2\pi$ | | | | $2\pi$ | | |
| Area of Circle = $4\pi$ | | | | | $4\pi$ | |

15

# MONSTER DRAWING 3

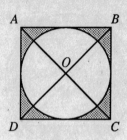

|  | AB | AO | Radius | Area ABCD | Circum-ference of Circle | Area of Circle | Shaded Area |
|---|---|---|---|---|---|---|---|
| AB = 1 | 1 |  |  |  |  |  |  |
| AO = 1 |  | 1 |  |  |  |  |  |
| Radius = 1 |  |  | 1 |  |  |  |  |
| Area ABCD = 16 |  |  |  | 16 |  |  |  |
| Circumference = 8π |  |  |  |  | 8π |  |  |
| Area Circle = 9π |  |  |  |  |  | 9π |  |

IF YOU DON'T SEE WHAT YOU WANT, ASK FOR IT.

This is a strategy we developed for algebra problems, but it applies to some geometry questions as well.

> **EXAMPLE:**
>
> If the width of a rectangle is increased by 10 percent and the length of the rectangle is increased by 20 percent, the area of the rectangle increases by what percent?
>
> A.  2%
> B.  10%
> C.  15%
> D.  32%
> E.  36%

The answer is D. Assume that the original width of the rectangle is 10 and the original length is 10. (Yes, the width is equal to the length, but a square is a rectangle too, and 10 is a convenient number.)

On the assumption that $w = 10$ and $\ell = 10$, the original area is 100. Now increase the width by 10 percent from 10 to 11 and the length by 20 percent from 10 to 12. The new area is $11 \times 12 = 132$. Using the "change-over" formula, the change is $132 - 100 = 32$ and the original amount is 100, so the percent change is $\frac{32}{100} = 32\%$.

ONE PICTURE IS WORTH A THOUSAND WORDS.

Some ACT geometry questions do not come equipped with a figure, and this makes them more difficult. When no sketch is provided, make one yourself.

> **EXAMPLE:**
>
> If a circle of radius 1 is inscribed in a square, what is the area of the square?
> F.  1
> G.  $\frac{\sqrt{2}}{2}$
> H.  $\sqrt{2}$
> J.  2
> K.  4

The answer is K. This can be seen more easily if you draw the figure:

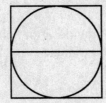

Now you can see that the diameter of the circle is equal to the side of the square. Since the radius of the circle is 1, the diameter is 2. So the side of the square is 2, and the area of the square is $2 \times 2 = 4$.

Sometimes you may be given a figure that is in some respect incomplete. To see the solution, you may need to add one or more lines to the drawing.

15

**EXAMPLE:**

What is the area of the quadrilateral below?

A.   6
B.   6 + √3
C.   12
D.   18
E.   24

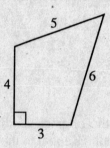

The correct choice is D, and the numbers 3, 4, and 5 are highly suggestive of one of those famous triangles. Divide the quadrilateral into two triangles:

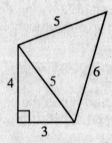

Now the problem turns into a composite figure problem. You have one triangle with an altitude and a base of 3 and 4. So it has an area of $\frac{1}{2}$ x 3 x 4 = 6. As for the other triangle, it has a base of 6, but you need an altitude. So sketch it in:

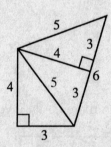

Since the altitude bisects the base (divides it in half), you have created two 3–4–5 triangles. So the area of the second triangle is $\frac{1}{2}$ x 4 x 6 = 12. And the area of the entire quadrilateral is 6 + 12 = 18.

**EXAMPLE:**

An isosceles right triangle is inscribed in a semicircle with radius 1. What is the area of the triangle?

F. $\dfrac{1}{2}$

G. $\dfrac{\sqrt{2}}{2}$

H. 1

J. $\sqrt{2}$

K. $2\sqrt{2}$

The correct choice is H, which is more easily seen if you draw the figure:

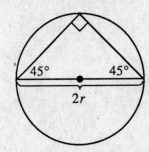

Now you can see that the diameter of the circle is the base of the triangle. But what about an altitude? Sketch that also:

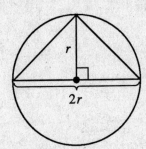

So the altitude is equal to the radius of the circle. And the area of the triangle is $\frac{1}{2} \times 2 \times 1 = 1$.

15

# Explanatory Answers

### EXERCISE 1

**1.** (D)

$$x + 2x + 3x + 4x + 5x = 360$$
$$15x = 360$$
$$x = 24$$

**2.** (F)

$$x + 2x + 3x = 180$$
$$6x = 180$$
$$x = 30$$

**3.** (B)

$$x + x + 90 = 180$$
$$2x + 90 = 180$$
$$2x = 90$$
$$x = 45$$

**4.** (G)

$$2x + x = 180$$
$$3x = 180$$
$$x = 60$$
$$y + y = x$$
$$y + y = 60$$
$$2y = 60$$
$$y = 30$$

**5.** (D) Since $\ell 1$ // $\ell 2$, you can use the "big angle/little angle" theorem.

$$y = 45$$
$$x + y = 180$$
$$x + 45 = 180$$
$$x = 135$$
$$x - y = 135 - 45 = 90$$

**6. (K)** The angle inside the triangle and opposite the 30° angle is also 30°. The angle inside the triangle and next to the 105° angle is $180 - 105 = 75°$.

$$30 + 75 + x = 180$$
$$105 + x = 180$$
$$x = 75$$

**7. (D)** The third angle of the larger triangle is 30°. The angle directly opposite it (in the smaller triangle) is also 30°. So:

$$90 + 30 + x = 180$$
$$x = 60$$

**8. (J)** The figure has seven sides, so the sum of the degree measures of its interior angles is $180(7 - 2) = 900$. (Or, you can divide the polygon into five triangular regions.)

**9. (D)**

$$PQ^2 = PR^2 + RQ^2$$
$$PQ^2 = 5^2 + 4^2$$
$$PQ^2 = 25 + 16$$
$$PQ^2 = 41$$
$$PQ = \sqrt{41}$$

**10. (G)**

$$AB^2 + BC^2 = AC^2$$
$$AB^2 = AC^2 - BC^2$$
$$AB^2 = 13^2 - 12^2$$
$$AB^2 = 169 - 144$$
$$AB^2 = 25$$
$$AB = \sqrt{25} = 5$$

**11. (E)** A 30–60–90 triangle has sides in the ratio $2:1:\sqrt{3}$. A 45–45–90 triangle has sides in the ratio $1:1:\sqrt{2}$. And a triangle with sides of $\sqrt{2}:\sqrt{2}:2$ fits the Pythagorean Theorem:

$$(\sqrt{2})^2 + (\sqrt{2})^2 = 2^2$$

(Also, a triangle with sides in the ratio of $\sqrt{2}:\sqrt{2}:2$ is a 45–45–90 triangle.)

**12. (G)** $AC$ is the hypotenuse of a 45–45–90 triangle, so $AB$ is equal to $\frac{1}{2}$ times 6 times $\sqrt{2}$:

$$AB = \frac{1}{2}(6)(\sqrt{2}) = 3\sqrt{2}$$

15

**13.** (B) *MNO* is a 30–60–90 triangle. *NM* is equal to $\frac{1}{2}$ times *NO* times $\sqrt{3}$:

$$NM = \frac{1}{2}(2x)(\sqrt{3})$$

$$NM = x\sqrt{3}$$

**14.** (H) Since *PQR* is equilateral, the altitude creates two 30–60–90 triangles. The altitude is the side opposite the 60° angle, so it is equal to $\frac{1}{2}$ times 6 times $\sqrt{3}$:

Altitude $= \frac{1}{2}(6)(\sqrt{3}) = 3\sqrt{3}$

Area $PQR = \frac{1}{2}$ (alt.)(base) $= \frac{1}{2}(3\sqrt{3})(6) = 9\sqrt{3}$

**15.** (B) The diagonal creates a right triangle with a hypotenuse of 5 and side of 3. The remaining side, which is the length of the rectangle, is 4.

Area = length × width

Area = 4 × 3 = 12

**16.** (F) The diagonal of the square creates two 45–45–90 triangles. So the side of the square is equal to $\frac{1}{2}$ times the diagonal times $\sqrt{2}$:

side $= \frac{1}{2}(\sqrt{2})(\sqrt{2}) = \frac{1}{2}(2) = 1$

Area of square = side × side = 1 × 1 = 1

**17.** (C)

Area = Circumference

$\pi r^2 = 2\pi r$

$r^2 = 2r$

$r = 2$

(**Note:** In algebra, $r = +2$ or 0. But *r* here indicates a distance that can only be positive.)

**18.** (H) The circumference of Circle *0* is $2\pi r = 2\pi(3) = 6\pi$. Since the entire circle measures 360°, $AXB = \frac{60}{360} = \frac{1}{6}$ of the circle. And $\frac{1}{6}$ of $6\pi = \pi$.

**19.** (A) Since a cube has six faces, each face has an area of $54 \div 6 = 9$. The area of a face is a function of the length of the edge or side: side × side = 9, $s^2 = 9$, $s = 3$.

**20.** (J) Drop a line from *Q* parallel to the *Y*-axis. Draw a line through *P* parallel to the *X*-axis. The point where the two intersect (call it *R*) is $(5, -1)$: *PQ* is the hypotenuse of the right triangle you have created. The triangle has sides with lengths of 3 and 4, so the length of *PQ* is 5.

## EXERCISE 2

| | AB | $BE = AB \times \sqrt{2}$ | $CE = BE \times \sqrt{2}$ | $DF = BE + \sqrt{3}$ | $EF = 2DF$ | $\frac{1}{2}(AB)(AE)$ | $BE^2$ | $\frac{1}{2}(ED \times DF)$ |
|---|---|---|---|---|---|---|---|---|
| | AB | BE | CE | DF | EF | Area ABE | Area BCDE | Area EDF |
| AB = 1 | 1 | $\sqrt{2}$ | 2 | $\frac{\sqrt{2}}{\sqrt{3}} = \frac{\sqrt{6}}{\sqrt{3}}$ | $\frac{2}{3}\sqrt{6}$ | $\frac{1}{2}$ | 2 | $\frac{\sqrt{3}}{3}$ |
| BE = 1 | $\frac{\sqrt{2}}{2}$ | 1 | $\sqrt{2}$ | $\frac{1}{\sqrt{3}} = \frac{\sqrt{3}}{3}$ | $\frac{2}{3}\sqrt{3}$ | $\frac{1}{4}$ | 1 | $\frac{\sqrt{3}}{6}$ |
| CE = 1 | $\frac{1}{2}$ | $\frac{\sqrt{2}}{2}$ | 1 | $\frac{\sqrt{2}}{\sqrt{3}} = \frac{\sqrt{6}}{\sqrt{6}}$ | $\frac{\sqrt{6}}{3}$ | $\frac{1}{8}$ | $\frac{1}{2}$ | $\frac{\sqrt{3}}{12}$ |
| DF = 1 | $\frac{\sqrt{6}}{2}$ | $\sqrt{3}$ | $\sqrt{6}$ | 1 | 2 | $\frac{3}{4}$ | 3 | $\frac{\sqrt{3}}{2}$ |
| EF = 1 | $\frac{\sqrt{6}}{4}$ | $\frac{\sqrt{3}}{2}$ | $\frac{\sqrt{6}}{2}$ | $\frac{1}{2}$ | 1 | $\frac{3}{16}$ | $\frac{3}{4}$ | $\frac{\sqrt{3}}{8}$ |

| | AB | $r = \frac{1}{2} \times AB \times \sqrt{2}$ | $AB^2$ | $2\pi r$ | $\pi r^2$ | $\pi r^2 - AB^2$ |
|---|---|---|---|---|---|---|
| | AB | Radius | Area ABCD | Circumference of Circle | Area of Circle | Shaded Area |
| AB = 1 | 1 | $\frac{\sqrt{2}}{2}$ | 1 | $\sqrt{2}\,\pi$ | $\frac{\pi}{2}$ | $\frac{\pi}{2} - 1$ |
| Radius = 1 | $\sqrt{2}$ | 1 | 2 | $2\pi$ | $\pi$ | $\pi - 2$ |
| Area of ABCD = 4 | 2 | $\sqrt{2}$ | 4 | $2\sqrt{2}\,\pi$ | $2\pi$ | $2\pi - 4$ |
| Circumference of Circle = $2\pi$ | $\sqrt{2}$ | 1 | 2 | $2\pi$ | $\pi$ | $\pi - 2$ |
| Area of Circle = $4\pi$ | $2\sqrt{2}$ | 2 | 8 | $4\pi$ | $4\pi$ | $4\pi - 8$ |

15

|  | AB | AO | Radius | Area ABCD | Circum-ference of Circle | Area of Circle | Shaded Area |
|---|---|---|---|---|---|---|---|
| AB = 1 | 1 | $\frac{\sqrt{2}}{2}$ | $\frac{1}{2}$ | 1 | $\pi$ | $\frac{\pi}{4}$ | $1 - \frac{\pi}{4}$ |
| AO = 1 | $\sqrt{2}$ | 1 | $\frac{\sqrt{2}}{2}$ | 2 | $\sqrt{2}\,\pi$ | $\frac{\pi}{2}$ | $2 - \frac{\pi}{2}$ |
| Radius = 1 | 2 | $\sqrt{2}$ | 1 | 4 | $2\pi$ | $\pi$ | $4 - \pi$ |
| Area ABCD = 16 | 4 | $2\sqrt{2}$ | 2 | 16 | $4\pi$ | $4\pi$ | $16 - 4\pi$ |
| Circumference = $8\pi$ | 8 | $4\sqrt{2}$ | 4 | 64 | $8\pi$ | $16\pi$ | $64 - 16\pi$ |
| Area Circle = $9\pi$ | 6 | $3\sqrt{2}$ | 3 | 36 | $6\pi$ | $9\pi$ | $36 - 9\pi$ |

# Math Usage Test

This lesson contains a Math Usage Test with no time limit. Instead, in the right-hand column, alongside the problems, you will find answers and explanations so that you can "walk through" the test.

16

# Walk-Through

1. A certain number increased by 6 equals three times itself. Which of the following equations could be used to find the value of the number?

   A. $x + 6 = 3x$
   B. $x + 3 = 6x$
   C. $6x = x + 3$
   D. $6x = 3x$
   E. $x = 3x + 6$

2. If $2x = 5y$, then $10y - 4x = $ ?

   F. 0
   G. 1
   H. 2
   J. 5
   K. 7

3. In the figure below, what is the value of $x$?

   A. 30
   B. 60
   C. 75
   D. 90
   E. 105

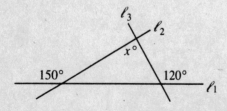

1. (A)
   A number plus 6 is equal to 3 times the number.

   $x + 6 = 3$ times $x$

   $x + 6 = 3x$

2. (F) Here you have one equation with two variables. It isn't possible to solve for either variable individually, and that's not what is required. The question asks for the value of $10y - 4x$.
   Multiply both sides of $2x = 5y$ by 2:

   $(2)2x = (2)5y$

   $4x = 10y$

   And you need $10y - 4x$:

   $0 = 10y - 4x.$

   The answer is F.

3. (D) The task here is to deduce the value of $x$ from the information already given, and there is really only one route to take. Assign the letter $y$ to the angle inside the lower left vertex of the triangle and $z$ to the angle inside the lower right vertex:

   $150 + y = 180$ and $120 + z = 180$

   $y = 30 \qquad z = 60$

   $30 + 60 + x = 180$

   $x = 90$

**4.** A machine operating at a constant rate without interruption produced 1,200 square yards of fabric in six hours. If the machine continues to operate at the same rate without interruption, how much fabric (in square yards) will it produce in the next four hours?

F. 800
G. 900
H. 1,400
J. 1,800
K. 2,000

**5.** A student must see her dean, her physics professor, and her adviser. If she must visit each person exactly once, in how many different orders can she arrange her appointments?

A. 3
B. 4
C. 6
D. 9
E. 12

**6.** The figure below is a rectangle. If the width is increased by 20 percent and the length is decreased by 10 percent, expressed in terms of $w$ and $\ell$, what is the new area of the rectangle?

F. $0.09\, w\ell$
G. $0.92\, w\ell$
H. $1.1\, w\ell$
J. $1.08\, w\ell$
K. $1.3\, w\ell$

**4.** (F) The longer the machine operates, the more fabric it produces. A direct proportion makes this an easy question:

$$\frac{\text{Time } X}{\text{Time } Y} = \frac{\text{Cloth } X}{\text{Cloth } Y}$$

$$\frac{6}{4} = \frac{1,200}{x}$$

Cross-multiply:

$$6x = 4(1200)$$

$$x = \frac{4(1200)}{6} = 4(200) = 800$$

**5.** (C) You don't need a formula to solve the problem; just count the number of possibilities (D is for dean; P is for professor; and A is for advisor): DPA, DAP, PDA, PAD, ADP, and APD, or 6.

If this doesn't occur to you, it's better to skip the problem, hoping to come back to it.

**6.** (J) The width of the rectangle increases by 20 percent from $w$ to $1.2\,w$, and the length decreases by 10 percent from 1 to $0.9\,\ell$. The area of a rectangle is width times length. So the old area was $w\ell$, and the new area is $1.2\,w \times 0.9\,\ell = 1.08\, w\ell$.

If working with unknowns is not your cup of tea, then assume some numbers, for example, $w = 1$ and $\ell = 2$. The new dimensions are 1.2 and 1.8, and the new area is 2.16 $w\ell$. Now substitute 1 for $w$ and 2 for $\ell$ into each answer choice. The correct one will generate the number 2.16:

F. $0.09(1)(2) = 1.8$ (Wrong.)
G. $0.92(1)(2) = 1.84$ (Wrong.)
H. $1.1(1)(2) = 2.2$ (Wrong.)
J. $1.08(1)(2) = 2.16$ (Right!)
K. $1.3(1)(2) = 2.6$ (Wrong.)

**7.** If *n* is an odd integer, all of the following are odd EXCEPT:

  **A.** $n - 2$.
  **B.** $2n + n$.
  **C.** $n^2$.
  **D.** $(n + 2)^2$.
  **E.** $n^2 + n$.

**7.** **(E)** This question tests properties of numbers. One way of attacking the problem is to reason about each choice in the following way. Since *n* is odd:

  **A.** This is an odd minus 2, so the result is still odd.

  **B.** $2n$ is even, plus *n*, which is odd; so $2n + n$ is odd.

  **C.** An odd number times itself is odd.

  **D.** *n* plus 2 is still odd; so this is an odd times an odd and therefore odd.

  **E.** $n^2$ is odd; *n* itself is odd; so this is an odd plus an odd, and that's an even number.

Or you could have substituted a number, say 1. If $n = 1$, then

  **A.** $n - 2 = 1 - 2 = -1$.
  (An odd number.)

  **B.** $2n + n = 2(1) + 1 = 2 + 1 = 3$.
  (An odd number.)

  **C.** $n^2 = (1)^2 = 1 \times 1 = 1$.
  (An odd number.)

  **D.** $(n + 2)^2 = (1 + 2)^2 = 3^2 = 9$.
  (An odd number.)

  **E.** $n^2 + n = (1)^2 + 1 = 1 + 1 = 2$.
  (An even number!)

**8.** The figure below shows three rectangular garden plots that lie side by side. If *AE*, not shown, is equal to 100 feet, what is the area, in square feet, of plot *BCFG*?

  **F.** 240
  **G.** 300
  **H.** 360
  **J.** 480
  **K.** 600

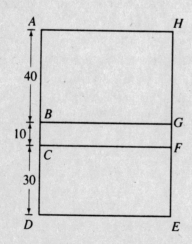

**8.** **(K)** The area of a rectangle is equal to its width times its length. The diagram already provides the width, so you'll have to find the length.

An important piece of information, $AE = 100$, is not entered on the diagram. The first thing you should do is draw *AE*. This creates a right triangle with sides *AD* and *DE* and hypotenuse *AE*. And *DE* is not only a side of triangle *ADE*, it is the length of the rectangles. You know the length of *AD* and *AE*, so you can find *DE* with the Pythagorean Theorem:

$$AD^2 + DE^2 = AE^2$$

$$DE^2 = AE^2 - AD^2$$

$$DE^2 = 100^2 - 80^2$$

$$DE^2 = 10,000 - 6,400$$

$$DE^2 = 3,600$$

$$DE = \sqrt{3,600} = 60$$

The area of rectangle *BCFG* is $10 \times 60 = 600$.

You can save yourself the calculation if you notice that 80 and 100 are multiples of 8 and

**9.** If $x = 2k - 2$ and $y = 4k^2$, what is $y$ in terms of $x$?

A. $x + 2$

B. $(x + 2)^2$

C. $\dfrac{(x + 2)^2}{2}$

D. $\dfrac{(x + 2)^2}{4}$

E. $x^2 + 4$

10, which are in turn multiples of 4 and 5. This triangle must have sides of 60, 80, and 100.

**9.** (B) Here you are asked to express one variable in terms of another. You have $x$ in terms of $k$ and $y$ in terms of $k^2$; so there must be a way of rewriting one equation to correspond to the other. Since it's usually easier to square something than to take the square root of something, work from $k$ towards $k^2$.

To rewrite the first equation so that $x$ is expressed in terms of $k^2$, you'll first need to get rid of the $-2$ on the right side:

$$x = 2k - 2$$

$$x + 2 = 2k$$

$$(x + 2)^2 = 4k^2$$

$$y = (x + 2)^2$$

You can also attack the question by assuming numbers. Assume a value for $k$, say 1. If $k = 1$, then $x = 2(1) - 2 = 0$ and $y = 4(1^2) = 4$. When you substitute zero for $x$ into the formulas in the choices, the correct choice will yield the value 4 (which is $y$).

A. $0 + 2 = 2$    (Wrong.)

B. $(0 + 2)^2 = 4$

C. $\dfrac{(0 + 2)^2}{2} = \dfrac{4}{2} = 2$    (Wrong.)

D. $\dfrac{(0 + 2)^2}{4} = \dfrac{4}{4} = 1$    (Wrong.)

E. $0^2 + 4 = 4$

This first substitution eliminated all but B and E.

Try another number, say, $k = 2$. If $k = 2$, then $y = 4(2^2) = 16$, and $x = (2)2 - 2 = 2$. So when $x = 2$, the correct formula should generate 16:

B. $(2 + 2)^2 = 16$    (Right!)

E. $2^2 + 4 = 8$    (Wrong.)

10. What is the area of the square in the figure below?

F. 4
G. $2\sqrt{2}$
H. 8
J. $8\sqrt{2}$
K. 16

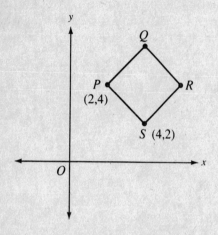

10. **(H)** To find the area of the square, you need only to know the length of its side. And you can find the length of the side with the Pythagorean Theorem. Draw a line from the point (2,4) straight down the page parallel to the y axis. Draw another line from point (4,2) across the page parallel to the x axis. The lines intersect at the point (2,2) and form a right angle. The length of each line is 2.

Now you can use the Pythagorean Theorem to find the length of the hypotenuse, which is also the length of the side of the square. Let s be the hypotenuse:

$$s^2 = 2^2 + 2^2$$
$$s^2 = 8$$
$$s = \sqrt{8}$$

So the area of the square is $\sqrt{8} \times \sqrt{8} = 8$.

11. The cost of x meters of wire is d dollars. If k is the cost of y meters, which of the following equations correctly expresses k in terms of x, d, and y?

A. $k = xyd$
B. $k = \dfrac{yd}{x}$
C. $k = \dfrac{xd}{y}$
D. $k = \dfrac{x - d}{y}$
E. $k = \dfrac{xy}{d}$

11. **(B)** This question asks you to devise a formula. The easiest approach is to set up a direct proportion, using k as our unknown:

$$\frac{\text{Length } X}{\text{Length } Y} = \frac{\text{Cost } X}{\text{Cost } Y}$$
$$\frac{x}{y} = \frac{d}{k}$$
$$xk = yd$$
$$k = \frac{yd}{x}$$

You can also assume some values for the unknowns. Assume that two meters of wire costs $4, so five meters costs $10. On the assumption that x = 2, d = 4, and y = 5, then k = 10:

A. $10 = (2)(4)(5)$ (Wrong.)

B. $10 = \dfrac{20}{2}$ (Right!)

C. $10 = \dfrac{2(4)}{5}$ (Wrong.)

D. $10 = \dfrac{(2 - 4)}{5}$ (Wrong.)

E. $10 = \dfrac{2(5)}{4}$ (Wrong.)

**12.** $\frac{5}{3} + \frac{x}{3} = 2$, then $x = ?$

    **F.** $\frac{5}{9}$

    **G.** $\frac{3}{5}$

    **H.** $\frac{5}{9}$

    **J.** $\frac{5}{6}$

    **K.** 1

**12.** (K) Solve for $x$:

$$\frac{5}{3} + \frac{x}{3} = 2$$

$$\frac{5 + x}{3} = 2$$

$$5 + x = 2(3)$$

$$x = 6 - 5 = 1$$

If you look closely at the equation, you might be able to avoid doing all those steps. What number when added to $\frac{5}{3}$ makes 2, which is $\frac{6}{3}$? The answer is $\frac{1}{3}$. So $x$ must be 1.

You might test the choices. If you do, start with the easiest value to work with, 1.

**13.** What was the average number of units sold by the sales representatives shown below?

| Sales Representative | Sales for May (Units Sold) |
|---|---|
| Victor | 6 |
| Mary | 9 |
| Randy | 8 |
| Sue | 4 |
| Carla | 3 |

    **A.** 4
    **B.** 5
    **C.** 6
    **D.** 9
    **E.** 30

**13.** (C) Just calculate the average:

$$\frac{6 + 9 + 8 + 4 + 3}{5} = 6$$

**14.** If a machine can produce 50 meters of steel cable every 30 seconds, how many meters of steel cable can the machine produce in an hour?

    **F.** 100
    **G.** 250
    **H.** 600
    **J.** 2,500
    **K.** 6,000

**14.** (K) If the machine produces 50 meters of cable every 30 seconds, it produces 100 meters every minute. Since one hour = 60 minutes, the machine produces $100 \times 60 = 6,000$ meters of cable in an hour.

**15.** In the figure below, what is the value of $x + y$?

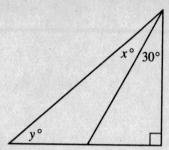

A. 15
B. 30
C. 60
D. 90
E. 120

**15.** (C) Label the other two angles:

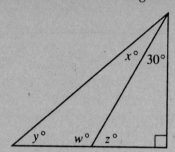

$z + 30 + 90 = 180$

$z = 180 - 120 = 60$

$w + z = 180$

$w + 60 = 180$

$w = 120$

$x + y + w = 180$

$x + y + 120 = 180$

$x + y = 180 - 120 = 60$

**16.** If the sum of the three terms arranged vertically in the figure below is equal to the sum of the three terms arranged horizontally, then what is the value of $x$?

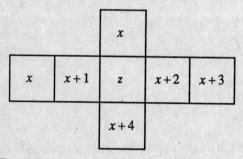

F. $-2$
G. $-1$
H. 0
J. 1
K. 2

**16.** (G) Set up an equation:

$(x) + (x + 1) + (z) + (x + 2) + (x + 3) = (x) + (z) + (x + 4)$

$4x + 6 + z = 2x + 4 + z$

$4x + 6 = 2x + 4$

$2x = -2$

$x = -1$

You can also get the correct answer by assuming a value for $z$, say $z = 0$, and testing the choices.

**17.** Carl has only $5 bills and $10 bills in his wallet. If he has $x$ $5 bills and ten more $10 bills than $5 bills, in terms of $x$, how much money, in dollars, does Carl have in his wallet?

A. $15x$
B. $15x + 10$
C. $15x + 15$
D. $15x + 100$
E. $50x + 100$

**17.** (D) You can set up the formula. Carl has $x$ $5 bills, or $5x$ dollars in $5 bills. And he has (10 + $x$) $10 bills, or $10(x + 10) = 10x + 100$ dollars in $10 bills. Combine them: $5x + 10x + 100 = 15x + 100$.

You can assume some numbers. To make it easy, assume Carl has one $5 bill; in other words, $x = 1$. Then he would have 11 $10 bills. The total amount would be $5 + 11(10) =$ 115. So when $x = 1$, the correct formula will generate the value 115:

**A.** $15(1) = 15$     (Wrong.)
**B.** $15(1) + 10 = 25$     (Wrong.)
**C.** $15(1) + 15 = 30$     (Wrong.)
**D.** $15(1) + 100 = 115$     (Right!)
**E.** $50(1) + 100 = 150$     (Wrong.)

**18.** If $x$ and $y$ are positive integers and $\frac{x}{y} < 1$, which of the following is greater than 1?

**F.** $\dfrac{x}{2y}$

**G.** $\dfrac{\sqrt{x}}{y}$

**H.** $\left(\dfrac{x}{y}\right)^2$

**J.** $x - y$

**K.** $\dfrac{y}{x}$

**18.** **(K)** This question tests properties of numbers. Since $x$ and $y$ are positive integers such that $\frac{x}{y} > 1$, $x$ must be less than $y$. Given that $x$ is less than $y$:

**F.** $\dfrac{x}{2y}$ is also less than 1, since $2y$ is a larger denominator than $y$;

**G.** $\dfrac{\sqrt{x}}{y}$ is less than 1, since $\sqrt{x}$ is less than $x$ (or equal to $x$ if $x = 1$)

**H.** $\left(\dfrac{x}{y}\right)^2$ is less than 1, since the square of a fraction is smaller than the original fraction;

**J.** $x - y$ is less than 1, since $y$ is larger than $x$; but

**K.** $\dfrac{y}{x}$ is greater than 1, since $y$ is larger than $x$.

You can also use the technique of assuming some numbers. Assume that $x = 1$ and $y = 2$. Then,

**F.** $\dfrac{1}{2(2)} = \dfrac{1}{4}$;

**G.** $\dfrac{\sqrt{1}}{2} = \dfrac{1}{2}$;

**H.** $\left(\dfrac{1}{2}\right)^2 = \dfrac{1}{4}$;

**J.** $1 - 2 = -1$; and

**K.** $\dfrac{2}{1} = 2$, which is greater than 1.

**19.** If $p = q + 2$ and $r = 2q^2$, then $r = ?$

    **A.**  $(p - 2)^2$

    **B.**  $2(p - 2)^2$

    **C.**  $\dfrac{p - 2}{2}$

    **D.**  $\dfrac{p - 2}{4}$

    **E.**  $\dfrac{p - 2^2}{4}$

**19.** **(B)** Rewrite one equation so that its form corresponds to the other. If we are to have $r$ expressed in terms of $p$, we need to express $p$ in terms of $2q^2$:

$$p = q + 2$$

$$p - 2 = q$$

$$(p - 2)^2 = q^2$$

$$2(p - 2)^2 = 2q^2$$

So $r = 2(p - 2)^2$.

    You can also assume some values. Assume that $q = 1$. On that assumption, $p = (1) + 2 = 3$ and $r = 2(1)^2 = 2$. Using the value 3 for $p$ in the correct answer choice will generate the number 2:

    **A.**  $(3 - 2)^2 = 1^2 = 1$   (Wrong.)

    **B.**  $2(3 - 2)^2 = 2(1^2) = 2(1) = 2$   (Right!)

    **C.**  $\dfrac{2 - 2}{2} = \dfrac{0}{2} = 0$   (Wrong.)

    **D.**  $\dfrac{2 - 2}{4} = \dfrac{0}{4} = 0$   (Wrong.)

    **E.**  $\dfrac{(2 - 2)^2}{4} = \dfrac{0}{4} = 0$   (Wrong.)

**20.** In the figure below, $PQ$ is a diameter of the circle and $PR = 2$. What is the area of the circle?

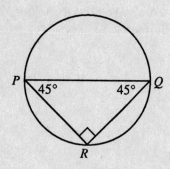

    **F.**  $\dfrac{\pi}{2}$

    **G.**  $\pi$

    **H.**  $2\pi$

    **J.**  $2\sqrt{2}\pi$

    **K.**  $4\pi$

**20.** **(H)** $PQR$ is an isosceles right triangle. Since $PR = 2$, $PQ = 2\sqrt{2}$. Since the diameter of the circle is $2\sqrt{2}$, the radius is $\sqrt{2}$. And the area of the circle is $\pi r^2 = \pi(\sqrt{2})^2 = 2\pi$.

**21.** A marksman in a shooting contest hit the bull's eye on 85 percent of his shots. He scored 112 bull's eyes. Which of the following equations determines the correct value of $x$, the total number of shots fired by the marksman?

A.  $x = 0.85(112)$
B.  $85x = 112$
C.  $112x = 0.85$
D.  $\dfrac{x}{85} = 112$
E.  $0.85x = 112$

**21.** (E)  Set up a direct proportion:

$$\frac{\text{Number of Bull's Eyes}}{\text{Number of Tries}} = \frac{\text{Percent of Bull's Eyes}}{\text{Percent of Tries}}$$

Since all tries is equal to 100%:

$$\frac{112}{x} = \frac{85\%}{100\%}$$

Cross-multiply:

85% of $x$ = 100% of 112

$0.85x = 112$

**22.** If $\dfrac{3}{4}x = 1$, then $\dfrac{2}{3}x = ?$

F.  $\dfrac{1}{3}$
G.  $\dfrac{1}{2}$
H.  $\dfrac{2}{3}$
J.  $\dfrac{8}{9}$
K.  2

**22.** (J)  Solve for $x$. $\frac{3}{4}x = 1$, so $x = \frac{4}{3}$. Then substitute this for $x$ in the expression $\frac{2}{3}x$. $(\frac{2}{3})(\frac{4}{3}) = \frac{8}{9}$.

**23.** In the figure below, what is the value of $x$?

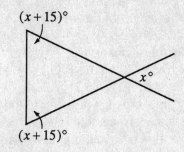

$(x+15)°$

$x°$

$(x+15)°$

A.  20
B.  35
C.  50
D.  65
E.  90

**23.** (C)  Since the unlabeled angle inside the triangle is equal to $x$:

$(x + 15) + (x + 15) + x = 180$

$3x + 30 = 180$

$3x = 150$

$x = 50$

**24.** If $x = \dfrac{y}{7}$ and $7x = 12$, then $y = ?$

F.  3
G.  5
H.  7
J.  12
K.  72

**24.** (J)  Treat the two equations as simultaneous equations. You can substitute $\frac{y}{7}$ for $x$ in the second equation. $7(\frac{y}{7}) = 12$, so $y = 12$.

**25.** A rectangular box with a top is created by folding the figure below along the dotted lines. What is the volume of the box in cubic feet?

A. 6
B. 9
C. 12
D. 18
E. 24

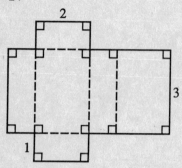

**25. (A)** The box when assembled looks like this:

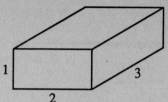

Its volume is $1 \times 2 \times 3 = 6$.

**26.** What is the difference of the areas of two squares with sides of 5 and 4, respectively?

F. 3
G. 4
H. 9
J. 16
K. 41

**26. (H)** Area of square with side 5 minus area of square with side 4 = $(5 \times 5) - (4 \times 4) = 25 - 16 = 9$.

**27.** If the spaces between the lettered points in the figure below are all equal, then $\dfrac{PT}{2} - \dfrac{QS}{2}$ is equal to which of the following?

A. $PS - QR$
B. $QR - QS$
C. $PR$
D. $QT$
E. $ST$

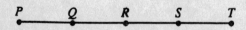

**27. (E)** $\frac{PT}{2}$ is $\frac{1}{2}$ of the length of the entire segment. $QS$ is $\frac{1}{2}$ the length of the segment, and $\frac{QS}{2}$ is $\frac{1}{4}$ of the segment. So $\frac{PT}{2} - \frac{QS}{2}$ is $\frac{1}{2}$ of the segment minus $\frac{1}{4}$ of the segment, which is $\frac{1}{4}$ of the length of the segment. Only (E) is $\frac{1}{4}$ the length of the segment.

You can also assign numbers to the lengths. Assume that each segment is equal to 1. Then $PT$ is 4, and $\frac{PT}{2} = 2$. And $QS$ is 2, and $\frac{QS}{2} = 1$. Finally, $2 - 1 = 1$. So the correct answer choice should have a length of 1:

A. $3 - 1 = 2$ (Wrong.)
B. $1 - 2 = -1$ (Wrong.)
C. 2 (Wrong.)
D. 3 (Wrong.)
E. 1 (Right.)

**28.** Exactly three years before the year in which Anna was born, the year was $1980 - x$. In 1995, Anna will be 20 years old. Which of the following equations can be used to determine the value of $x$?

**F.** $x + 3 + 20 - 1,995 = 1,980$
**G.** $1,980 - x + 3 = 1,995 - 20$
**H.** $1,980 - x - 3 = 1,995 - 20$
**J.** $1,995 - 1,980 = x + 3 + 20$
**K.** $1,995 - 1,980 = x + 3 - 20$

**29.** If $x = k + \dfrac{1}{2} = \dfrac{k + 3}{2}$, then $x = ?$

**A.** $\dfrac{1}{3}$

**B.** $\dfrac{1}{3}$

**C.** $1$
**D.** $2$
**E.** $\dfrac{5}{2}$

**28.** (G) Set up an equation. Since $1980 - x$ was three years before Anna was born, Anna was born in $(1980 - x) + 3$. That number plus 20 is equal to 1995 (the year of her 20th birthday):

$$1,980 - x + 3 + 20 = 1,995$$

Subtract 20 from both sides, and $1,980 - x + 3 = 1,995 - 20$.

You could also "test the test." Since Anna will be 20 in 1995, she was born in 1975. Three years before that was 1972. Since 1972 is eight years before 180, $x = 8$. Now substitute the value 8 for $x$ into each equation to find the one that preserves the quality. Only G works:

$$1980 - 8 + 3 = 1,995 - 20$$
$$1975 = 1975 \quad \text{(Right!)}$$

**29.** (E) You really have two equations:

$$x = k + \frac{1}{2} \text{ and } k + \frac{1}{2} = \frac{k + 3}{2}$$

Solve for $k$:

$$k + \frac{1}{2} = \frac{k + 3}{2}$$

$$2\left(k + \frac{1}{2}\right) = k + 3$$

$$2k + 1 = k + 3$$

$$k = 2$$

Now substitute 2 for $k$:

$$x = k + \frac{1}{2} = 2 + \frac{1}{2} = \frac{5}{2}$$

You can also try testing the choices, but the process is tedious. For example, assume that $x = 1$. On that assumption, the first equation gives the value of $k$ as $\frac{1}{2}$; but when $\frac{1}{2}$ is substituted for $k$ into the second equation, the second equation is false. So C is incorrect. E, however, does work. If $x = \frac{5}{2}$, then the value of $k$ in the first equation is 2. And substituting 2 for both $k$s in the second equation produces a true statement.

**30.** In the figure below, if the radius of the circles is 1, then what is the perimeter of the shaded part of the figure?

   **F.** $\dfrac{\pi}{6}$

   **G.** $\dfrac{2\pi}{3}$

   **H.** $\dfrac{4\pi}{3}$

   **J.** $3\pi$

   **K.** $\pi$

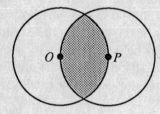

**31.** If $7 - x = 0$, then $10 - x = ?$

   **A.** $-3$

   **B.** $0$

   **C.** $3$

   **D.** $7$

   **E.** $10$

**32.** A triangle with sides of 3, 6, and 9 has the same perimeter as an equilateral triangle with side of length

   **F.** $2$.

   **G.** $\dfrac{3}{2}$.

   **H.** $3$.

   **J.** $6$.

   **K.** $8$.

**33.** In the figure below, what is the value of $x$?

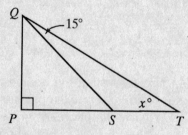

$PQ = PS$

   **A.** $15$

   **B.** $30$

   **C.** $40$

   **D.** $60$

   **E.** $75$

**30.** (H) The solution to this item depends on seeing the following:

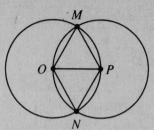

The triangles are equilateral ($OM$, $ON$, $PM$, $PN$, and $OP$ are all radii), and angles $MON$ and $MPN$ are both 120°. So each arc is 120°, or $\frac{1}{3}$ of the circle. Since the radius of the circle is 1, the circumference of each circle is $2\pi(1)$ $= 2\pi$. Therefore each arc is $\frac{1}{3}$ of $2\pi$, or $\frac{2\pi}{3}$. Together, the arcs total $\frac{2\pi}{3} + \frac{2\pi}{3} = \frac{4\pi}{3}$.

**31.** (C) Solve for $x$: $7 - x = 0$, so $7 = x$. Then substitute 7 for $x$ in the expression $10 - x$: $10 - 7 = 3$.

**32.** (J) A triangle with sides 3, 6, and 9, has a perimeter of $3 + 6 + 9 = 18$. An equilateral triangle with the same perimeter would have a side of $18 \div 3 = 6$.

**33.** (B) Since $PQ = PS$, $PQS$ is a $45-45-90$ triangle. Angle $PQR$ is $45° + 25° = 60°$. And $x = 180° - 90° - 60° = 30°$.

**34.** If $x$ and $y$ are negative numbers, which of the following is negative?

   **F.**   $xy$

   **G.**  $(xy)^2$

   **H.**  $(x - y)^2$

   **J.**   $x + y$

   **K.**  $\dfrac{x}{y}$

**34.** (J) Since $x$ and $y$ are negative, both A and E must be positive. As for B and C, so long as neither $x$ nor $y$ is zero, those expressions must be positive. (Any number other than zero squared gives a positive result.) D, however, is negative since it represents the sum of two negative numbers. And you can also test the choices with numbers.

**35.** If the area of the rectangle shown below is equal to one, then what is the value of $\ell$?

   **A.**  $\dfrac{4}{9}$

   **B.**  $1$

   **C.**  $\dfrac{4}{3}$

   **D.**  $\dfrac{9}{4}$

   **E.**  $3$

**35.** (C) Just use the formula for the area of a rectangle. $\ell \times \frac{3}{4} = 1$, so $\ell = \frac{4}{3}$. You can also test choices until you find one that works in the area formula, but you should be able to solve a simple equation like that without needing to substitute.

**36.** In the figure below, if $\ell_1$ is parallel to the Y axis, which of the following points falls within the shaded area?

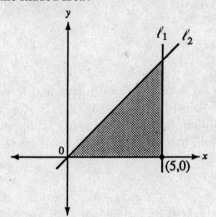

   **F.**  $(1,2)$

   **G.**  $(2,3)$

   **H.**  $(3,4)$

   **J.**  $(4,5)$

   **K.**  $(4,3)$

**36.** (K) $\ell_2$ contains all the points for which $x = y$, such as $(1,1)$ and $(2,2)$. Since $\ell_1$ is parallel to the y axis, $\ell_1$ and $\ell_2$ intersect at $(5,5)$. Once you know this, you just plot points until you find one that falls within the shaded area.

**37.** If $\dfrac{x}{z} = c$ and $\dfrac{y}{z} = c - 1$, then $x$ and $y$ are related in which of the following ways?

  **A.** $x = y - 1$
  **B.** $x = y + 1$
  **C.** $x = z + y$
  **D.** $x = z - y$
  **E.** $x = \dfrac{y}{1}$

**37.** (C) To relate $x$ and $y$, you must use the term $c$. Since $\dfrac{y}{z} = c - 1$, $\dfrac{y}{z} + 1 = c$. Next:

$$\dfrac{x}{z} = \dfrac{y}{z} + 1$$

$$x = \left(\dfrac{y}{z} + 1\right)z$$

$$x = y + z = z + y$$

You can save some steps if you recognize that $\dfrac{x}{z}$ can be substituted directly for $c$ in the second equation. You can also avoid the algebra entirely by assuming some numbers. Suppose that $z = 2$ and $c = 3$. Then $x = 6$ and $y = 4$. Plug these numbers into the equations in the answer choices:

  **A.** $6 = 4 - 1$   (False, so [A] is wrong.)
  **B.** $6 = 4 + 1$   (False, so [B] is wrong.)
  **C.** $6 = 4 + 2$   (True, so [C] is correct.)
  **D.** $6 = 2 - 4$   (False, so [D] is wrong.)
  **E.** $6 = \dfrac{4}{1}$   (False, so [E] is wrong.)

**38.** A dean must select three students to serve on a committee. If she is considering five students, from how many different possible threesomes must she choose?

  **F.** 2
  **G.** 3
  **H.** 10
  **J.** 15
  **K.** 18

**38.** (H) You can solve the problem by counting the possibilities. Let A, B, C, D, and E be the individuals. The possible committees are: ABC, ABD, ABE, ACD, ACE, ADE, BCD, BCE, BDE, and CDE.

**39.** Which of the following can be divided by both 2 and 3 with no remainder?

  **A.** 46
  **B.** 54
  **C.** 64
  **D.** 75
  **E.** 98

**39.** (B) To be divisible by both two and three, a number must be divisible by $2 \times 3 = 6$. B is the only choice divisible by 6. Additionally, you could try dividing both 2 and 3 into each choice.

**40.** If $2x = 3$ and $3y + 2x = 6$, then $y = ?$

  **F.** 1
  **G.** 2
  **H.** 3
  **J.** 4
  **K.** 5

**40.** (F) Two equations and two variables. Approach the problem as an exercise in solving simultaneous equations. You can substitute 3 directly for $2x$ in the second equation:

$$3y + 3 = 6$$

$$3y = 3$$

$$y = 1$$

# Math Usage
# Warm-Up
# Test 1

In this lesson you will find a Math Usage Test to be done within the 50-minute time limit. Set aside an hour during which you won't be interrupted. Using a watch or clock, do the test under timed conditions.

After your time is up but *before* you use the answer key to check your work, finish any problems you did not finish before time ran out. Then check your work against the answers and explanations on page 321.

# Math Usage

1. If $x$ and $y$ are positive numbers, $xy = 96$, and $\dfrac{x}{y} = \dfrac{3}{2}$, what is the value of $x$?

   A. 6
   B. 9
   C. 12
   D. 15
   E. 18

2. If $y = 5x$, then the average (arithmetic mean) of $x$ and $y$, in terms of $x$, is equal to:

   F. $x$.
   G. $2x$.
   H. $3x$.
   J. $4x$.
   K. $5x$.

3. In the figure below, if the measure of angle $POR$ is 144° and the measure of angle $QOS$ is 120°, what is the measure in degrees of angle $QOR$?

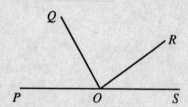

   A. 24
   B. 36
   C. 48
   D. 72
   E. 156

4. In the figure below, if the edge of each small cube has a length of 1, what is the surface area of the entire rectangular solid?

   F. 84
   G. 62
   H. 42
   J. 31
   K. 18

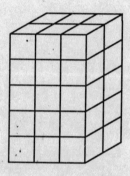

5. In the figure below, what is the sum in degrees of the indicated angles?

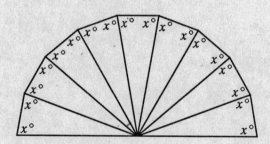

   A. 105
   B. 90
   C. 80
   D. 60
   E. 40

**6.** If one star equals four circles and three circles equals four diamonds, then what is the ratio star:diamond?

F. $\dfrac{3}{16}$

G. $\dfrac{1}{3}$

H. $\dfrac{3}{4}$

J. $\dfrac{3}{1}$

K. $\dfrac{16}{3}$

**7.** In the figure below, $O$ is the center of the large circle. If the radius of Circle $O$ is $r$, what is the area of the shaded region in terms of $r$?

A. $\pi$

B. $3\pi$

C. $\pi r^2$

D. $\dfrac{\pi r^2}{2}$

E. $\dfrac{3\pi r^2}{2}$

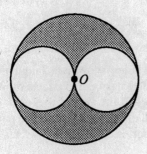

**8.** If $y + x^3 = 7 + x^3$, then $y = ?$

F. $7^3$

G. $7$

H. $3\sqrt{7}$

J. $-3^7$

K. $-7$

**9.** In the figure below, what is the value of $x$?

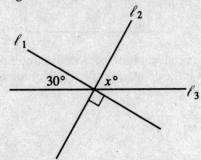

A. 180

B. 120

C. 90

D. 60

E. 30

**10.** If $x = -2$ and $y = -1$ then $x^3 - y = ?$

F. $-9$

G. $-8$

H. $-7$

J. $0$

K. $8$

**11.** If $n > 1$ and the remainder when 12 and 17 are divided by $n$ is 2, then $n = ?$

A. 3

B. 4

C. 5

D. 6

E. 7

**12.** If the product of the digits of a two-digit number is odd, then the sum of those two digits must be:

F. even.

G. odd.

H. greater than or equal to 3.

J. less than or equal to 17.

K. equal to 18.

**13.** $4^2 \times 4^3 = ?$

A. $\dfrac{1}{4}$

B. $4$

C. $4^5$

D. $4^6$

E. $8^6$

**14.** If the perimeter of a triangle $PQR$ is 30 units and if side $PQ$ is 5 units longer than side $QR$, then what is the length of side $PR$?

F. 5

G. 10

H. 15

J. 20

K. Cannot be determined.

**15.** In the figure below, what is the value of $x$?

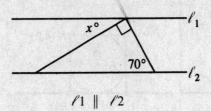

$\ell 1 \parallel \ell 2$

A. 70

B. 55

C. 40

D. 30

E. 20

16. If $\sqrt{n}$ is a whole number, then which of the following is NOT necessarily a whole number?

F. $\dfrac{n}{2}$

G. $n$

H. $\sqrt{4n}$

J. $4\sqrt{n}$

K. $n^3$

17. The table below shows the number of students in a senior class with last names beginning with the letters indicated. If a total of 300 students are in the class, what is the maximum number of students whose names could begin with the letters P through T?

| Names | Number of students |
| --- | --- |
| A through F | 65 |
| G through L | 43 |
| K through O | 69 |
| P through T | x |
| U through Z | y |

A. 60
B. 128
C. 177
D. 223
E. 300

18. In the figure below, point $O$ is the center of the circle. If $JKLM$ is a square, what are the coordinates of point $O$?

F. (2,1)
G. (2,2)
H. (3,0)
J. (3,1)
K. (3,2)

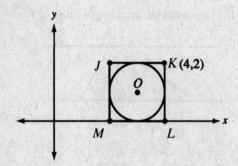

19. Which of the following fractions is the least?

A. $\dfrac{12}{13}$

B. $\dfrac{4}{5}$

C. $\dfrac{7}{8}$

D. $\dfrac{19}{20}$

E. $\dfrac{14}{15}$

20. If $30 \times 2{,}000 = 6 \times 10^x$, then $x = $ ?

F. 2
G. 3
H. 4
J. 5
K. 6

21. If $n = \dfrac{x}{15} + \dfrac{x}{15} + \dfrac{x}{15} + \dfrac{x}{15} + \dfrac{x}{15}$, then what is the least positive integer $x$ for which $n$ is an integer?

A. 3
B. 5
C. 12
D. 15
E. 20

22. The figure below shows a rectangular parcel of land divided into lots of equal size as shown by the dotted lines. If the area of the lots is equal to one-fourth of the total area in the parcel, then how wide, in feet, is each lot?

F. 30
G. 40
H. 60
J. 90
K. 120

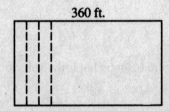

360 ft.

23. If the product of five consecutive integers is zero, what is the greatest possible sum of these integers?

A. $-2$
B. $-1$
C. 0
D. 4
E. 10

**24.** On a certain production line, the ratio of parts produced that are inspected to those that are not inspected is 1:3. What fraction of the parts that are produced are inspected?

F. $\dfrac{2}{3}$

G. $\dfrac{1}{2}$

H. $\dfrac{1}{3}$

J. $\dfrac{1}{4}$

K. $\dfrac{1}{5}$

**25.** If 50 equally priced tickets cost a total of $d$ dollars, then, in terms of $d$, ten of those tickets cost how much?

A. $5d$

B. $10d$

C. $\dfrac{5}{d}$

D. $\dfrac{10}{d}$

E. $\dfrac{d}{5}$

**26.** Bob and Mary together have $8.00. If the amount that Mary has is one-third of the amount that Bob has, how much money does Mary have?

F. $2.00

G. $3.60

H. $4.80

J. $5.60

K. $6.00

**27.** If $\dfrac{x}{y} - 1 = 0$, then $\dfrac{x}{y} - \dfrac{y}{x} = $ ?

A. $-2$

B. $-1$

C. $0$

D. $2$

E. $4$

**28.** If $n$ is an integer, which of the following represents the product of $2n + 1$ and the next greater integer?

F. $4n + 2$

G. $4n^2 + 2$

H. $4n^2 + 2n + 1$

J. $4n^2 + 2n + 2$

K. $4n^2 + 6n + 2$

**29.** If $\dfrac{x}{y} = \dfrac{4}{5}$ and $\dfrac{z}{y} = \dfrac{2}{5}$, then $\dfrac{x}{z} = $ ?

A. $\dfrac{2}{5}$

B. $\dfrac{1}{2}$

C. $\dfrac{8}{25}$

D. $2$

E. $\dfrac{5}{2}$

**30.** If $4 < x < 8$ and $0 < y < \dfrac{3}{2}$, which of the following gives all possible values of $xy$?

F. $0 < xy < 6$

G. $0 < xy < 12$

H. $\dfrac{3}{2} < xy < 4$

J. $\dfrac{3}{2} < xy < 8$

K. $4 < xy < 8$

**31.** In the figure below, if the $x$ coordinate of Point $P$ is 4 and the length of $OP$ is 5, what is the $y$ coordinate of Point $P$?

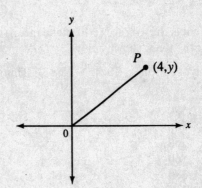

A. $4$

B. $3\sqrt{3}$

C. $3$

D. $\sqrt{3}$

E. $\sqrt{2}$

**32.** If the figure below is composed of a semicircle and a right triangle, what is the area of the shaded region?

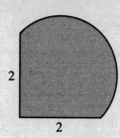

2

2

F. $\pi + \sqrt{2}$
G. $\pi + 2$
H. $2\pi + 1$
J. $\pi\sqrt{2} + 1$
K. $\pi\sqrt{2} + \sqrt{2}$

**33.** If $x = \frac{1}{4}$, which of the following is the greatest?

A. $x^3$
B. $x^2$
C. $x$
D. $2x$
E. $\frac{1}{x}$

**34.** What is the average (arithmetic mean) daily sales for the week shown below?

| Day | Mon. | Tues. | Wed. | Thurs. | Fri. |
|-----|------|-------|------|--------|------|
| Sales | $40 | $60 | $80 | $20 | $50 |

F. $20
G. $40
H. $50
J. $60
K. $80

**35.** In the figure below, what is the value of $x$?

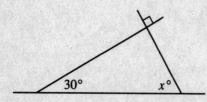

30°    $x°$

A. 20
B. 30
C. 60
D. 75
E. 90

**36.** For all $k \neq 0$, $k \times \frac{1}{k} = ?$

F. $k^2$
G. $k$
H. $\frac{(k+1)}{k}$
J. 1
K. 0

**37.** If the sum of two consecutive integers is 29, what is the least of these integers?

A. 10
B. 11
C. 12
D. 13
E. 14

**38.** In $ABC$ below, if $AB \parallel ED$, what is the value of $x$?

F. 20°
G. 30°
H. 40°
J. 50°
K. 60°

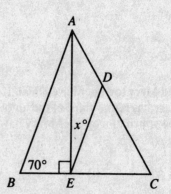

**39.** In a certain game, players win or lose points that are added to a running total after each round of play. In four consecutive rounds, Robin increases his total by five, doubles his total score, loses three points from his total score, and triples his total score. If Robin started with $x$ points, how many points does he have following the four rounds of play?

A. $4x + 2$
B. $4x + 3$
C. $5x + 3$
D. $6x + 3$
E. $6x + 21$

**40.** If $f(x) = 2x^3 - 3x^2 + 4x + 8$, then $f(-2) = ?$

F. $-28$
G. $-16$
H. $-4$
J. 0
K. 6

# Answer Key

| | | | |
|---|---|---|---|
| 1. C | 11. C | 21. C | 31. C |
| 2. H | 12. F | 22. F | 32. G |
| 3. A | 13. C | 23. E | 33. E |
| 4. G | 14. K | 24. J | 34. H |
| 5. C | 15. E | 25. E | 35. C |
| 6. K | 16. F | 26. F | 36. J |
| 7. D | 17. B | 27. C | 37. E |
| 8. G | 18. J | 28. K | 38. F |
| 9. D | 19. B | 29. D | 39. E |
| 10. H | 20. H | 30. G | 40. F |

# Explanatory Answers

1. **(C)** You can treat this as a problem involving simultaneous equations.

$$\frac{x}{y} = \frac{3}{2}$$

$$x = \frac{3y}{2}$$

$$2x = 3y$$

$$y = \frac{2x}{3}$$

$$x\left(\frac{2x}{3}\right) = 96$$

$$\frac{2x^2}{3} = 96$$

$$2x^2 = 288$$

$$x^2 = 144$$

$$x = +\sqrt{144} = 12 \text{ or } -\sqrt{144} = -12$$

Since the problem stipulates that $x$ and $y$ are positive, $x = 12$.

That's a long process. You can also try substituting numbers. Start with C. If $x = 12$ and $xy = 96$, then $y = 8$, and $\frac{12}{8}$ is $\frac{3}{2}$. So C is correct.

2. **(H)** Just use the method for finding an average:

$$\text{Average} = \frac{x + y}{2}$$

Substitute into that equation $5x$ for $y$:

$$\text{Average} = \frac{x + (5x)}{2} = \frac{6x}{2} = 3x$$

Or, you can assume some values for $x$ and $y$. Assume that $x = 1$. Then $y = 5$. And the average of 5 and 1 is 3. If $x = 1$, the correct formula generates the value 3. Only H works.

3. **(A)** One way of handling the question is to reason that angle $QOR$ is the overlap between $POR$ and $QOS$. So the measure of $QOR$ must be the difference between $POR$ and $QOS$: $144 - 120 = 24$.

You can reach the same conclusion, though via a more circuitous route, by setting up equations.

4. **(G)** Find the area of each face. The "front" of the solid has an area of $3 \times 5 = 15$. The "side" has an area of $2 \times 5 = 10$. And the "top" has an area of $2 \times 3 = 6$. Remember, however, that there are two of each face, a "front" and a "back," two "sides," and a "top" and a "bottom." So the entire surface area is $15 + 15 + 10 + 10 + 6 + 6 = 62$.

5. (C) The sum of all the angles marked as $x$ plus the unmarked angles is the sum of the angles contained in nine triangles: $9(180) = 1620$. The unmarked angles form a straight line, so their sum is 180. The sum of the remaining angles is $1,620 - 180 = 1,440$. Since there are 18 angles marked $x$, $x$ is $1,440 \div 18 = 80$.

    Or, you might have reasoned that the unmarked angles are equal. Since nine of them form a straight line, each is $180 \div 9 = 20$. In each triangle, you have $x + x + 20 = 180$, so $2x = 160$ and $x = 160 \div 2 = 80$.

6. (K) Using the letters $s$ for star, $c$ for circle, and $d$ for diamond, we do the following:

$1s = 4c$ and $3c = 4d$

$3s = 12c$ and $12c = 16d$

So $3s = 12c = 16d$, and $3s = 16d$.

$3s = 16d$

$$\frac{3s}{d} = \frac{16}{1}$$

$$\frac{s}{d} = \frac{16}{3}$$

So the ratio of star:diamond is 16:3.

7. (D) This is a shaded area problem. The shaded area is the area of the larger circle minus the sum of the areas of the two smaller circles.

    The radius of the large circle is also the diameter of each of the smaller circles, so the radius of the two smaller circles is $\frac{r}{2}$. The large circle has an area of $\pi r^2$. Each of the smaller circles has an area of $\pi \left(\frac{r}{2}\right)^2 = \frac{\pi r^2}{4}$. So the shaded area is equal to $\pi r^2 - \left(\frac{\pi r^2}{4} + \frac{\pi r^2}{4}\right) = \pi r^2 - \frac{\pi r^2}{2} = \frac{\pi r^2}{2}$.

8. (G) Once you eliminate the $x^3$ terms from both sides of the equation, you have $y = 7$.

9. (D) You can use the principles of geometry to deduce the value of $x$. The angle vertically opposite the right angle is also a 90° angle. So:

$30 + 90 + x = 180$

$120 + x = 180$

$x = 60$

10. (H) This question asks you to evaluate an expression. Just substitute the given values into the expression:

$(-2)^3 - (-1) =$

$-8 + 1 = -7$

11. (C) One of the five suspects is guilty. Just test answer choices. Divide 12 and 17 by each until you find the one that leaves a remainder of 2 in both cases. $12 \div 5 = 2$ with a remainder of 2, and $17 \div 5 = 3$ with a remainder of 2.

12. (F) This question tests properties of numbers. You can get the correct answer by reasoning as follows: If the product of the two digits is odd, then both of the digits themselves must be odd. (If one or more of the digits of the number are even, then the product of the digits is even.) Since both digits are odd, the sum of the digits must be even.

17

**13.** (C)  This question tests your knowledge of the rules of exponents, and no tricks will get you around the need for that information.  You have to know that when you multiply powers of like bases, you add exponents:

$$4^2 \times 4^3 = 4^{(2+3)} = 4^5$$

**14.** (K)  Start by sketching a figure:

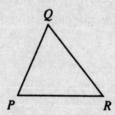

You can prove that the answer is K algebraically.  The perimeter of the triangle is the sum of the lengths of the three sides:

$$PQ + QR + PR = 30$$

And:

$$PQ = QR + 5$$

There are three variables with only two equations, so it's not possible to find the lengths of any one side.

You can also reach this conclusion by trying different values for the sides. $PQ$ might be 10, in which case $QR$ is 5 and $PR$ is 15.  Or $PQ$ might be 15, in which case $QR$ is 10 and $PR$ is 5.

**15.** (E)  Since $\ell 1$ is parallel to $\ell 2$, the "big angle/little angle" theorem establishes that $x$ is equal to the third and unlabeled angle of the triangle.  Find the size of that angle and you have the size of $x$.  Let the unlabeled angle be $y°$:

$$y + 90 + 70 = 180$$

$$y + 160 = 180$$

$$y = 20$$

So, $x = 20$ as well.

**16.** (F)  This question tests properties of numbers.  You might reason as follows: If $\sqrt{n}$ is a whole number, then

**F.** $\frac{n}{2}$ might or might not be a whole number.  The square root of a whole number might be odd, for example, $\sqrt{9}$, in which case $\frac{n}{2}$ is not a whole number;

**G.** $n$ must be a whole number; for $n$ is the product of $\sqrt{n} \times \sqrt{n}$, and a whole number times a whole number generates a whole number;

**H.** $\sqrt{4n}$ must be a whole number; for $\sqrt{4n} = \sqrt{4} \times \sqrt{n} = 2\sqrt{n}$;

**J.** $4\sqrt{n}$ must be a whole number; it's just a whole number, 4, times another whole number; and

**K.** $n^3$ must be a whole number, since $n$ is a whole number (see G above).

**17.** (B) First, find the total number of students whose last names begin with the letters A through O:

$$65 + 43 + 69 = 177$$

Assume for the purpose of argument that $y = 0$, that is, that no students have names beginning with letters U through Z. The maximum number of studemts whose names could begin with the letters P through T is:

$$300 - 177 = 123$$

**18.** (J) This question tests your knowledge of coordinate geometry. To deduce the coordinates of point O, you need to know the length of the side of the square. Given that K has coordinates of (4,2), L has coordinates of (4,0). (Since *JKLM* is a square, *KL* is parallel to the y-axis.) The length of *KL* is 2. (The difference of the y-coordinates of K and L is 2.)

Since the circle is inscribed in a square with side 2, the radius of the circle is 1. Point O, therefore, is located one more unit above the x-axis than K and L. (So its x coordinate is 3.) Therefore, the coordinates of point O are (3,1).

**19.** (B) You know that it would take too long to convert each of these fractions to a decimal for purposes of comparing them. So you look for a benchmark. There is a pattern to the choices. The numerator of each is one less than its denominator. At this point, you should conclude that the correct choice must either be B or D—those are the choices with the smallest and the largest numbers.

The answer is B, and you can reach that conclusion in several ways. First, you might convert both B and D to decimals. B is $\frac{4}{5}$ and $\frac{4}{5} = 0.8$; D is $\frac{19}{20}$ and $\frac{19}{20} = 0.95$. Or, you might conclude that $\frac{4}{5} = \frac{16}{20}$, so B is smaller than D.

**20.** (H) Perform the indicated operation. $30 \times 2{,}000 = 60{,}000$. And $60{,}000 = 6 \times 10^4$. (One power of ten for each of the zeros.)

**21.** (C) There is no reason to try to devise a mathematical approach to this question. Just test the answer choices:

**A.** $\frac{3}{15} + \frac{3}{15} + \frac{3}{15} + \frac{3}{15} + \frac{3}{15} = \frac{1}{5} + \frac{1}{5} + \frac{1}{5} + \frac{1}{5} + \frac{1}{5} = 1$

At this point, stop. The choices are arranged in order.

**22.** (F) The question stem doesn't give you the depth of each lot, but you don't need it. It's the same for all the lots.

Since the area of the three lots is $\frac{1}{4}$ the area of the entire rectangle, three lots must together have a width of 90. And since they are all equal, each has a width of 30.

**23.** (E) This question asks about properties of numbers. If the product of five consecutive integers is zero, then one of the integers must be zero. The greatest possible sum for five consecutive integers, one of which is zero, occurs when the least of the integers is zero: 0, 1, 2, 3, and 4. $0 + 1 + 2 + 3 + 4 = 10$.

**24.** (J) The total number of ratio parts is $3 + 1 = 4$, of which one part is "inspected parts." So the fraction of the parts produced that are inspected is $\frac{1}{4}$.

17

**25.** (E) You can solve the problem in one of three ways. First, you can reason that ten tickets equals $\frac{1}{5}$ of 50 tickets, so the cost should be $\frac{1}{5}$ of the cost of 50 tickets. And $\frac{1}{5}$ of $d$ is $\frac{d}{5}$. If you are a little squeamish about working things out in your head, you can create a formula by using a direct proportion. The more tickets, the greater the cost:

$$\frac{\text{Tickets X}}{\text{Tickets Y}} = \frac{\text{Cost X}}{\text{Cost Y}}$$

$$\frac{50}{10} = \frac{d}{x}$$

Cross-Multiply:

$$50x = 10d$$

$$x = \frac{10d}{50} = \frac{d}{5}$$

Finally, you can assume some numbers. Assume tickets cost $1 each. The cost of 50 tickets is $50 ($d = 50$). The cost of ten tickets is $10. So when $d = 50$, the correct formula will yield 10. Only E works.

**26.** (F) You might attack this problem with simultaneous equations. Let $B$ stand for the amount Bob has and $M$ for the amount Mary has. Then:

$$B + M = 8$$

$$M = \frac{1}{3} B$$

Substitute $\frac{1}{3} B$ for $M$ into the first equation:

$$B + \frac{1}{3} B = 8$$

$$\frac{4}{3} B = 8$$

$$B = 8\left(\frac{3}{4}\right) = 6$$

So Mary has $2.

Or, you can test answer choices, starting with H. Assume that Mary has $4.80. Then Bob has three times that much, which is much more than $8 (the sum they have together). So H is wrong and too large. Try the next smaller number, G. Again, $3.60 × 3 is too large. So the correct choice must be $2.00. And $2.00 × 3 = $6.00, and $6.00 + $2.00 = $8.00.

**27.** (C) Use the equation to find what $x$ is in terms of $y$:

$$\frac{x}{y} - 1 = 0$$

$$\frac{x}{y} = 1$$

$$x = y$$

Since $x = y$, $\frac{x}{y}$ and $\frac{y}{x}$ are equal and $\frac{x}{y}$ minus $\frac{y}{x}$ is equal to zero.

Or, you can assume numbers. Let $x = 1$. Then to ensure that $\frac{x}{y} - 1 = 0$, $y$ must also be equal to 1. On that assumption, $\frac{x}{y} - \frac{y}{x} = \frac{1}{1} - \frac{1}{1} = 0$.

28. (K) You can attack by using the expression $2n + 1$. The next integer larger than $2n + 1$ is 1 larger, or $2n + 2$, and their product is:

$$(2n + 1)(2n + 2) = 4n^2 + 6n + 2$$

29. (D) There are at least three ways to attack this problem. One, you can see that the first equation has $x$ and $y$ in it and that the second equation has $z$ and $y$ in it. If you rewrite the first equation so that $y$ is defined in terms of $x$ and rewrite the second equation so that $y$ is defined in terms if $z$, then you can create an equation between $x$ and $z$:

$$\frac{x}{y} = \frac{4}{5} \qquad x = \frac{4y}{5} \qquad 5x = 4y \qquad y = \frac{5x}{4}$$

$$\frac{z}{y} = \frac{2}{5} \qquad z = \frac{2y}{5} \qquad 5z = 2y \qquad y = \frac{5z}{2}$$

So $\frac{5x}{4} = \frac{5z}{2}$:

And:

$$\frac{x}{4} = \frac{C}{2}$$

$$\frac{x}{2} = z$$

$$\frac{x}{z} = 2$$

This solution is lengthy and tedious, but it is effective.

There is a simpler solution, and you should be looking for it. $\frac{z}{y}$ is exactly half of $\frac{x}{z}$ ($\frac{2}{5}$ is half of $\frac{4}{5}$), so $x$ must be twice $z$, and $\frac{x}{z}$ must be 2.

Finally, it is also possible to substitute numbers. Assume that $y = 5$. On that assumption $x = 4$ and $z = 2$, so $\frac{x}{z} = \frac{4}{2} = 2$.

30. (G) Work through the problem step by step. First, if $x$ could be 4 and $y$ could be zero, then $xy$ would be zero. $x$ and $y$ cannot be zero (they are greater than zero), but zero marks the lower limit of their product. This eliminates choices H, J, and K.

Next, if $x$ and $y$ could be 8 and $\frac{3}{2}$, their product would be $8 \times \frac{3}{2} = 12$. So 12 marks the upper limit of their product. And the correct choice is G.

31. (C) Draw a line from point P down the page parallel to the $y$-axis.

This creates a right triangle, the hypotenuse of which is OP. And the newly drawn line intersects the $x$-axis at 4. This means that the side of the triangle that lies on the $x$-axis has a length of 4.

So you have a right triangle with sides of 5 and 4; the remaining side is 3. This means that the $y$-coordinate of point P is 3.

17

**32.** (G) This is a composite figure: a 45°−45°−90° triangle plus a semicircle. The shaded area is the sum of the area of the triangle and the semicircle.

First, calculate the area of the triangle. Since this is a right triangle, you can use the two sides forming the right angle as altitude and base:

$$\text{Area of triangle} = \frac{1}{2} \times 2 \times 2 = \frac{1}{2} \times 4 = 2$$

The diameter of the circle is the hypotenuse of that triangle, and the hypotenuse of a 45°−45°−90° triangle is equal to the length of the side times $\sqrt{2}$. So the hypotenuse is equal to $2 \times \sqrt{2} = 2\sqrt{2}$. The diameter of the semicircle is $2\sqrt{2}$, so the radius is $\sqrt{2}$. The area of an entire circle with that radius is $\pi(\sqrt{2})^2 = 2\pi$. But the figure is a semicircle with an area only half that of a full circle: $2\pi \div 2 = \pi$. So the area of the composite figure is $\pi + 2$.

**33.** (E) Just substitute $\frac{1}{4}$ for $x$ in each of the choices:

**A.** $(\frac{1}{4})^3 = \frac{1}{64}$
**B.** $(\frac{1}{4})^2 = \frac{1}{16}$
**C.** $\frac{1}{4}$
**D.** $2(\frac{1}{4}) = \frac{1}{2}$
**E.** $\frac{1}{\frac{1}{4}} = 4$

**34.** (H) The direct and best line of attack is to do the simple calculation to find the average:

$$\frac{40 + 60 + 80 + 20 + 50\ 250}{5} = \frac{250}{5} = 50$$

**35.** (C) You can deduce the value of $x$. The angle vertically opposite the right angle is also 90°. Then $30 + 90 + x = 180$, so $x = 60$.

**36.** (J) Just do the indicated operation: $k \times \frac{1}{k} = \frac{k}{k} = 1$.

**37.** (E) You can attack this question by setting up an equation. Let $x$ be the smaller of the two numbers. The other number is $x + 1$. And:

$x + (x + 1) = 29$

$2x + 1 = 29$

$2x = 28$

$x = 14$

Or you can just test the test. Start with choice C. 12 plus the next larger integer is $12 + 13 = 25$. That's not enough, so try the next larger choice, D. 13 plus the next larger choice is $13 + 14 = 27$. So E must be correct.

**38.** (F) First, label one of the unlabeled angles:

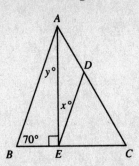

Since *AB* is parallel to *DE*, the "big angle/little angle" theorem establishes that $x$ = $y$. So we find the size of $y$:

$y + 70 + 90 = 180$

$y + 160 = 180$

$y = 20$

So $x = 20$.

**39.** (E) You can devise a formula to show Robin's score. He starts with $x$ and then wins 5 points:

$x + 5$

Then his score doubles:

$2(x + 5) = 2x + 10$

Then he loses 3 points:

$2x + 10 - 3 = 2x + 7$

Finally, his score triples:

$3(2x + 7) = 6x + 21$

**40.** (F) Just substitute $-2$ for $x$:

$f(-2) = 2(-2)^3 - 3(-2)^2 + 4 (-2) + 8$

$f(-2) = -16 - 12 - 8 + 8$

$f(-2) = -28$

17

# Math Usage Warm-Up Test 2

In this lesson you will find another Math Usage Test to be done within the 50-minute time limit. Again, set aside an hour during which you won't be interrupted. Using a watch or a clock, do the test under timed conditions.

After your time is up but *before* you use the answer key to check your work, finish any problems you did not finish before time ran out. Then check your work against the answers and explanations that begin on page 338.

1. If $\frac{1}{2}N + \frac{1}{2}N = 4$, then $N = $ ?

   A. 4
   B. 2
   C. 1
   D. $\frac{1}{2}$
   E. $\frac{1}{4}$

2. In the figure below, $x = $ ?

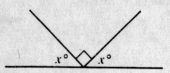

   F. 30
   G. 45
   H. 60
   J. 75
   K. 90

3. In a certain game, a person's age is multiplied by 2 and then the product is divided by three. If the result of performing the operations on John's age is 12, what is John's age?

   A. 2
   B. 8
   C. 12
   D. 18
   E. 36

4. For all positive $x$ and $y$, $\sqrt{24x^7y^5} = $ ?

   F. $3x^2y^2$
   G. $4x^3y^2$
   H. $2x^3y^2\sqrt{6xy}$
   J. $4x^4y^3\sqrt{2xy^2}$
   K. $6x^4y^3\sqrt{2xy^2}$

5. What is the sum of the solutions of the equation $x^2 - 5x + 6 = 0$?

   A. $-2\frac{1}{2}$
   B. $-1\frac{1}{4}$
   C. 0
   D. $\frac{1}{2}$
   E. 5

6. For all numbers, $(a-b)(b-c)-(b-a)(c-b) = $ ?

   F. $-2$
   G. $-1$
   H. 0
   J. $ab - ac - bc$
   K. $2ab - 2ac - 2bc$

7. $n$ is a positive integer. If $n$ is a multiple of 6 and a multiple of 9, what is the least possible value of $n$?

   A. 12
   B. 18
   C. 27
   D. 36
   E. 54

8. If $f(x) = x^2 - x$, what is $f(2)$?

   F. 0
   G. 1
   H. 2
   J. 4
   K. 8

9. The figure below shows a square piece of land that is divided into nine smaller square lots. The shaded portion is a railroad right-of-way. If the area of the shaded portion of the figure is five square miles, what is the area, in square miles, of the entire piece of land?

   A. 9
   B. 10
   C. 13
   D. 18
   E. 36

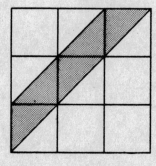

10. For how many different ordered pairs $(x, y)$, where $x$ is a number selected from List $X$ and $y$ is a number selected from list $Y$, is $x - y > 0$?

| List $X$ | List $Y$ |
|---|---|
| 1 | 1 |
| 2 | 2 |
| 3 | 3 |
| 4 | 4 |

   F.  24
   G.  18
   H.  15
   J.  12
   K.  6

11. If $x$ and $y$ are negative integers and $x > y$, which of the following is the greatest?

   A.  $-(xy)^2$
   B.  $x^2 y$
   C.  $xy$
   D.  $x + y$
   E.  $y - x$

12. A student receives an average of 75 on three exams that are scored on a scale of zero to 100. If one of her test scores was 75, what is the lowest possible score she could have received on any of the three tests?

   F.  0
   G.  1
   H.  25
   J.  40
   K.  50

13. In $ABC$ below, what is the length of side $AC$?

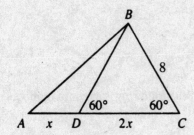

   A.  4
   B.  8
   C.  12
   D.  18
   E.  24

14. During a certain shift, a quality-control inspector inspects six out of every 30 items produced. What was the ratio of inspected to uninspected items during the shift?

   F.  1:4
   G.  1:5
   H.  1:6
   J.  5:1
   K.  6:1

15. Which of the following is a factorization of $36 - 12x + x^2$?

   A.  $(x - 6)(x + 3)$
   B.  $(x - 6)(x - 6)$
   C.  $(x + 6)(x + 6)$
   D.  $(x + 12)(x + 3)$
   E.  $(x - 12)(x + 1)$

16. Initially, 24 people apply for jobs with a firm, and $\frac{1}{3}$ of those are turned down without being given an interview. If $\frac{1}{4}$ of the remaining applicants are hired, how many applicants were given jobs?

   F.  2
   G.  4
   H.  6
   J.  8
   K.  12

17. In the figures below, if the area of the rectangle is equal to the area of the triangle, then $h = $?

   A.  2
   B.  3
   C.  4
   D.  6
   E.  9

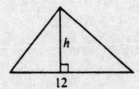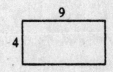

18. If eight francs equal one pound, and two pounds equal three dollars, then six dollars are equal to how many francs?

   F.  48
   G.  32
   H.  16
   J.  8
   K.  4

19. The price of a book, after it was reduced by $\frac{1}{3}$, is $B$ dollars. Which of the following equations can be used to determine $P$, the original price of the book?

A. $P = \dfrac{2B}{3}$

B. $P = \dfrac{3B}{4}$

C. $P = \dfrac{6B}{5}$

D. $P = \dfrac{4B}{3}$

E. $P = \dfrac{3B}{2}$

20. $Y$ years ago, Tom was three times as old as Julie was. If Julie is now 20 years old, how old in Tom in terms of $Y$?

F. $60 + 2Y$
G. $30 + 2Y$
H. $30 - 2Y$
J. $60 - 2Y$
K. $60 - 3Y$

21. If $S$ is the sum of $x$ consecutive integers, then $S$ must be even if $x$ is a multiple of:

A. 6.
B. 5.
C. 4.
D. 3.
E. 2.

22. If the radius of circle $O$ is 20 percent less than the radius of circle $P$, the area of circle $O$ is what percent of the area of circle $P$?

F. 60%
G. 64%
H. 72%
J. 80%
K. 120%

23. If the average (arithmetic mean) of 20, 23, 24, $x$, and $y$ is 26 and $\dfrac{x}{y} = \dfrac{3}{4}$, then $x = ?$

A. 25
B. 27
C. 36
D. 41
E. 63

24. The price of five boxes of candy is $d$ dollars. If each box contains 30 pieces of candy, what is the price, in *cents*, of 12 pieces of candy?

F. $8d$
G. $12d$
H. $\dfrac{25d}{2}$
J. $50d$
K. $72d$

25. If a cube has a side of length 2, what is the distance from any vertex to the center of the cube?

A. $\dfrac{\sqrt{2}}{2}$
B. $\sqrt{3}$
C. $2\sqrt{2}$
D. $2\sqrt{3}$
E. $\dfrac{3}{2}$

26. If $x + 1 + 2x + 2 + 3x + 3 = 6$, then $x = ?$

F. $-2$
G. 0
H. 1
J. 6
K. 12

27. If a horse gallops at an average speed of 40 feet per second, how many seconds will it take for the horse to gallop 500 feet?

A. 8
B. 9.5
C. 12.5
D. 20
E. 40

28. If $n$ is a positive integer greater than four, and if the remainder is the same when 13 and 21 are divided by $n$, then $n = ?$

F. 5
G. 6
H. 7
J. 8
K. 9

29. If 1 mill = 0.1 cents, how many mills are there in $3.13?

A. 0.313
B. 3.13
C. 31.3
D. 313
E. 3,130

30. Which of the following is a pair of numbers that are not equal?

F. $\dfrac{63}{6}, \dfrac{21}{2}$

G. $0.3\%, 0.003$

H. $\dfrac{44}{77}, \dfrac{4}{7}$

J. $\dfrac{3}{8}, 0.375$

K. $\sqrt{3^2}, 9$

31. If $\frac{64}{x} - 6 = 2$, then $x = ?$

    A. 8
    B. 12
    C. 16
    D. 24
    E. 31

32. If $x$, $y$, and $z$ are consecutive integers, and $x > y > z$, then $(x - y)(x - z)(y - z) = ?$

    F. $-2$
    G. $-1$
    H. 0
    J. 1
    K. 2

33. If $x$ and $y$ are different positive integers and $\frac{x}{y}$ is an integer, then which of the following must be true?

    I. $x > y$
    II. $xy > 0$
    III. $y - x < 0$

    A. I only
    B. II only
    C. III only
    D. I and II only
    E. I, II, and III

34. Which of the following is a factorization of $2x^2 - x - 3$?

    F. $(2x + 3)(x - 1)$
    G. $(2x - 3)(x + 1)$
    H. $(2x + 1)(x + 3)$
    J. $(x + 3)(2x + 3)$
    K. $(x - 3)(2x - 3)$

35. An article is on sale for 25 percent off its regular price of $64. If the merchant must also collect a 5-percent sales tax on this reduced price, what is the total cost of the article including sales tax?

    A. $42.10
    B. $44.20
    C. $49.60
    D. $50.40
    E. $56.70

36. If $\frac{x}{z} = k$ and $\frac{y}{z} = k - 1$, then $x = ?$

    F. $y - 1$
    G. $y + 1$
    H. $y + z$
    J. $z - y$
    K. $\frac{y}{z}$

37. In the figure below, $0$ is the center of the circle. What is the ratio of the area of the shaded portion of the figure to the area of the unshaded portion of the figure?

    A. $\frac{4}{1}$
    B. $\frac{\pi}{1}$
    C. $\frac{3}{1}$
    D. $\frac{5}{2}$
    E. $\frac{2}{1}$

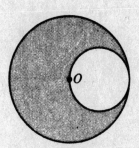

38. If a cube has a surface area of $54x^2$, what is the volume?

    F. $3x$
    G. $3x^2$
    H. $3x^3$
    J. $9x^3$
    K. $27x^3$

39. If $x$ is 25 percent of $y$, then $y$ is what percent of $x$?

    A. 400%
    B. 300%
    C. 250%
    D. 125%
    E. 75%

40. If $x$ is an integer that is a multiple of both 9 and 5, which of the following must be true?

    I. $x$ is equal to 45.
    II. $x$ is a multiple of 15.
    III. $x$ is odd.

    F. I only
    G. II only
    H. III only
    J. II and III only
    K. I, II, and III

# Answer Key

| | | | | | | | | | |
|---|---|---|---|---|---|---|---|---|---|
| 1. | A | 9. | D | 17. | D | 25. | B | 33. | E |
| 2. | G | 10. | K | 18. | G | 26. | G | 34. | G |
| 3. | D | 11. | C | 19. | E | 27. | C | 35. | E |
| 4. | H | 12. | K | 20. | J | 28. | J | 36. | H |
| 5. | E | 13. | C | 21. | C | 29. | E | 37. | C |
| 6. | H | 14. | F | 22. | G | 30. | K | 38. | K |
| 7. | B | 15. | B | 23. | B | 31. | A | 39. | A |
| 8. | H | 16. | G | 24. | F | 32. | K | 40. | G |

# Explanatory Answers

**1.** (A) Here you have a simple equation, so you can just solve for $N$:

$\frac{1}{2} N + \frac{1}{2} N = 4$

$N = 4$

**2.** (G) $x + 90 + x = 180$

$2x = 90$

$x = 45$

**3.** (D) You can set up an equation:

$\frac{2J}{3} = 12$

$2J = 36$

$J = 18$

Or, you could just test answer choices until you found one that worked. 18 times two is 36, and 36 divided by three is 12.

**4.** (H) One way of attacking this item is to use a fractional exponent, $\frac{1}{2}$, in place of the radical:

$\sqrt{24x^7 y^5} = \sqrt{24}(x^7 y^5)^{\frac{1}{2}} =$

$\sqrt{4 \times 6} \, (x^{\frac{7}{2}} y^{\frac{5}{2}}) =$

$2\sqrt{6}(x^3) (x^{\frac{1}{2}}) (y^2) (y^{\frac{1}{2}}) =$

$2\sqrt{6}(x^3) (\sqrt{x}) (y^2) (\sqrt{y}) =$

$2x^3 y^2 \sqrt{6xy}$

**5.** (E) Factor and find the solution:

$x^2 - 5x + 6 = 0$

$(x - 3) (x - 2) = 0$

So either $x - 3 = 0$ and $x = 3$ or $x - 2 = 0$ and $x = 2$. So the solutions to the equation are 3 and 2, and the sum of the solution is $2 + 3 = 5$.

**6.** (H) You can do the multiplication very easily:

$(a - b) (b - c) = ab - ac - b^2 + bc$

$(b - a) (c - b) = bc - b^2 - ac + ab$

Now subtract:     $ab - ac - b^2 + bc$

$\underline{- (ab - ac - b^2 + bc)}$

$0 - 0 - 0 - 0$

18

**7.** (B) Just test choices until you find the smallest available value that is divisible by both 6 and 9. The answer is 18.

**8.** (H) Just substitute 2 for $x$ in the function:

$$f(2) = 2^2 - 2 = 4 - 2 =$$

**9.** (D) The easiest way to handle the problem is to recognize that the shaded area takes up half of five of the squares. So the shaded area is $\frac{5}{2} \times 9 = \frac{5}{18}$ of the entire piece of land. Since $\frac{5}{18}$ of the total is equal to 5, the total is equal to 18 square miles.

**10.** (K) Just count the pairs that fit the requirement:

(2,1), (3,1), (3,2), (4,1), (4,2), (4,3)

**11.** (C) This question becomes easy once you recognize that C is the only expression that generates a positive result.

**12.** (K) Use the technique for finding a missing element in an average. Since the three scores average 75, she earned a total score of $3 \times 75 = 225$. We know that one score is 75, and $225 - 75 = 150$. The maximum she could receive on any test is 100, and $150 - 100 = 50$. So the lowest score she could receive (and still maintain a 75 average) is 50.

**13.** (C) The triangle on the right is an equilateral triangle, so $2x = 8$, which means that $x = 4$. So the length $AC$ is $8 + 4 = 12$.

**14.** (F) Since six items out of 30 are inspected, $30 - 6 = 24$ are not inspected, and the ratio 6:24 is equal to 1:4.

**15.** (B) Just multiply the answer choices to find the one that gives the desired result:
  **A.** $(x - 6)(x + 3) = x^2 - 3x - 18$ (Wrong.)
  **B.** $(x - 6)(x - 6) = x^2 - 12x + 36$ (Right!)
  **C.** $(x + 6)(x + 6) = x^2 + 12x + 36$ (Wrong.)
  **D.** $(x + 12)(x + 3) = x^2 + 15x + 36$ (Wrong.)
  **E.** $(x - 12)(x + 1) = x^2 - 11x - 12$ (Wrong.)

**16.** (G) Just work the calculation. Out of the 24, $\frac{1}{3}$, or 8, are rejected without an interview, leaving only 16. If $\frac{1}{4}$ of those are hired, then $\frac{1}{4}$ of $16 = 4$ are hired.

**17.** (D) The rectangle has an area of $4 \times 9 = 36$. Since the triangle also has that area:

$$\frac{1}{2} \times h \times 12 = 36$$

$$12h = 72$$

$$h = 6$$

**18.** (G) Use "*pounds*" as a common term. Since eight francs is equal to one pound, 16 francs is equal to two pounds. So 16 francs is equal to two pounds is equal to three dollars. Since three dollars is equal to 16 francs, six dollars is equal to 32 francs.

**19.** (E)  Set up the equation:

Original Price $-\frac{1}{3}$ Original Price $= B$

$$P - \frac{1}{3P} = B$$

$$\frac{2}{3}P = B$$

$$P = \frac{3B}{2}$$

Or you can assume some numbers, a technique we have often used.

**20.** (J)  You can set up the formula by reasoning as follows.  Tom's age minus $y$ years is equal to 3 times Julie's age minus $y$ years:

$$T - Y = 3(20 - Y)$$

$$T - Y = 60 - 3Y$$

$$T = 60 - 2Y$$

You can reach the same conclusion by assuming some values and substituting them into the formulas.

**21.** (C)  The sum of four consecutive integers must always be even.  You have two even numbers and an odd number added to an odd number, which yields another even number.

**22.** (G)  Let $r$ be the radius $P$, the larger circle.  It has an area of $\pi r^2$.  Then the radius of $O$, the smaller circle will be $0.8r$, and it will have an area of $\pi(0.8r)^2 = 0.64\pi r$.  So the area of the smaller circle is only 64 percent of that of the larger circle.

**23.** (B)  Solve using the technique for finding the missing elements of an average.  Since the average of the five numbers is 26, their sum is $26 \times 5 = 130$.  The sum of 20, 23, and 24 is 67, and $130 - 67$ is 63.  So $x + y = 63$.  Now you can use the method for solving simultaneous equations.  $x$ is equal to 27 and $y$ is equal to 36.

**24.** (F)  You can set up the formula in the following way.  If the price of five boxes of the candy is $d$ dollars, the price of five boxes of candy is $100d$ cents.  Since each box contains 30 pieces of candy, the price is $100d$ cents per $5 \times 30 = 150$ pieces, or $\frac{100d}{150}$ cents each.  The cost of 12 pieces of candy is 12 times that, $\frac{100d(12)}{150} = 8d$.  You can reach the same result without the algebra by assuming some value and testing the answer choices.

18

**25. (B)** This problem really needs a diagram:

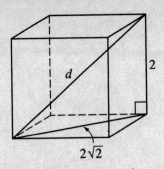

Notice that the diagonal of the face, the edge of the cube, and the diagonal of the cube form a right triangle, the hypotenuse of which is the diagonal of the cube. Since the edge has a length of 2, the diagonal of the face has a length of $2\sqrt{2}$. Now use the Pythagorean Theorem:

$$2^2 + (2\sqrt{2})^2 = d^2$$

$$4 + 8 = d^2$$

$$d^2 = 12$$

$$d = \sqrt{12} = 2\sqrt{3}$$

This is the length of the diagonal. The distance from any vertex to the center of the cube is one half of that, or $\sqrt{3}$.

**26. (G)** Just do the indicated operations:

$$x + 1 + 2x + 2 + 3x + 3 = 6$$

$$6x + 6 = 6$$

$$6x = 0$$

$$x = 0$$

**27. (C)** The easiest solution is to use a direct proportion.

$$\frac{40 \text{ feet}}{500 \text{ feet}} = \frac{1 \text{ second}}{x \text{ seconds}}$$

$$\frac{4}{50} = \frac{1}{x}$$

$$x = 12.5 \text{ seconds}$$

**28. (J)** Just test the test. $13 \div 8 = 1$ with a remainder of 5 and $21 \div 8 = 2$ with a remainder of 5. None of the other choices produces a similar result.

**29. (E)** This question just asks you to manipulate the decimal point: $3.13 = 333$ cents, and $313 \div 0.1 = 3,130$.

**30. (K)** Don't bother with any fancy mathematical theorizing. Just test the test. $\sqrt{3}^2 = 3$, which is not equal to 9.

**31.** (A) Here is a simple equation with one variable, so solve for $x$:

$$\frac{64}{x} - 6 = 2$$

$$\frac{64}{x} = 8$$

$$8x = 64$$

$$x = 8$$

**32.** (K) You can solve this by setting up equations. Since $x$, $y$, and $z$ are consecutive integers, and since $x > y > z$, $y = x - 1$ and $z = x - 2$.

$$(x - (x - 1))\,(x - (x - 2))\,((x - 1) - (x - 2)) =$$

$$(x - x + 1)\,(x - x + 2)\,(x - 1 - x + 2) =$$

$$(1)\,(2)\,(1) = 2$$

You can reach the same conclusion with a lot less effort just by assuming some numbers for $x$, $y$, and $z$. Say $x = 3$, $y = 2$, and $z = 1$. The result of substituting those numbers into the expression in the problem is 2.

**33.** (E) Since $\frac{x}{y}$ is an integer (and $x$ and $y$ are different integers and can't both be 1), $x$ must be greater than $y$ (otherwise $x$ would not be evenly divisible by $y$). So I is part of the correct answer. As for II, since $x$ and $y$ are positive integers, their product is greater then zero. Finally, $y - x < 0$ is equivalent to $y < x$, which is really statement I again. So all three statements belong in the correct choices.

**34.** (G) Just multiply each answer choice until you find the one that produces the desired result:

**F.** $(2x + 3)\,(x - 1) = 2x^2 + x - 3$   (Wrong.)
**G.** $(2x - 3)\,(x + 1) = 2x^2 - x - 3$   (Right!)
**H.** $(2x + 1)\,(x + 3) = 2x^2 + 7x + 3$   (Wrong.)
**J.** $(x + 2)\,(2x + 3) = 2x^2 + 7x + 6$   (Wrong.)
**K.** $(x - 3)\,(2x - 3) = 2x^2 - 9x + 9$   (Wrong.)

**35.** (D) First find the reduced price:

$\$64 - (25\% \text{ of } \$64) = \$64 - (0.25 \times \$64) = \$64 - \$16 = \$48$

Next, calculate the sales tax on $48:

$5\% \text{ of } \$48 = 0.05 \times \$48 = \$2.40$

Now find the total cost:

$\$48.00 + \$2.40 = \$50.20$

18

**36.** (H)  Use the method for solving simultaneous equations.  Since $\frac{y}{z} = k - 1$, $k = \frac{y}{z} + 1$.  And since $\frac{x}{z} = k$:

$$\frac{x}{z} = \frac{y}{z} + 1$$

$$x = z\left(\frac{y}{z} + 1\right)$$

$$x = y + z$$

**37.** (C)  Let $r$ be the radius of the smaller circle.  Its area is $\pi r^2$.  Then the radius of the larger circle is $2r$, and its area is $\pi(2r)^2 = 4\pi r^2$.  The shaded part of the diagram is the larger circle minus the smaller one.  So the area of the shaded part of the diagram is $4\pi r^2 - \pi r^2 = 3\pi r^2$.  And the ratio of the shaded area to the unshaded area is $\frac{3}{1}$.

**38.** (K)  Since a cube has six faces, the area of each face is:

$$6(\text{edge} \times \text{edge}) = 54x^2$$

$$\text{edge}^2 = 9x^2$$

$$\text{edge} = \sqrt{9x^2} = 3x$$

So the volume of the cube is $(3x)(3x)(3x) = 27x^3$.

**39.** (A)  If $x = 0.25y$, then $y = \frac{x}{0.25} = 4x$.  So $y$ is 400 percent of $x$.

**40.** (G)  Since 3 is a factor of 9 and 5 is a factor of 5, any multiple of both 9 and 5 will be a multiple of 15.  So II belongs in the correct choice.  I, however, is not correct.  $x$ could be any multiple of 45, e.g., 90, which also proves that III does not belong in the correct choice.

# Social Studies Review

The Social Studies Reading Test of your ACT will contain 52 questions and have a time limit of 35 minutes. The Social Studies test will contain two different types of questions: reading comprehension questions and free-standing, factual recall questions.

The reading comprehension questions are based on reading selections three to five paragraphs long. The selections treat material from history, government, economics, sociology, psychology, and anthropology that you are likely to encounter in introductory survey courses in college on those topics. Most of the reading comprehension questions are answerable on the basis of information provided in the text. A few, however, require some prior knowledge of the topic.

The free-standing factual recall items depend entirely on the knowledge of a topic you have gained from your coursework. To help you refresh your memory about some of the important points covered in high school social science courses, here is a substantive outline of those areas. The outline is organized according to the following topics:

* Psychology
* Sociology
* History
* Government
* Economics
* Anthropology

As you answer questions on the Social Studies Test, be sure to use the Holmesian strategy of eliminating answer choices wherever possible, even if you are unsure of a particular question.

# PSYCHOLOGY

## I.  Growth and Development

**A.**  Studies of Development

**1.**  Research Method
A primary issue in developmental psychology is the way people acquire their personalities, abilities, and social behaviors.  Developmental studies seek to connect changes in behavioral and psychological functioning with changes in age.  *Naturalistic observation*, which collects information from real-life settings, is the basic research method.

**2.**  Types of Studies
Two types of studies are commonly used.  In *longitudinal studies*, the same subjects are observed and data are collected over a long period of time.  In *cross-sectional studies*, subjects of different ages are studied at the same time.

**B.**  Principles of Development

**1.**  Development is orderly and predictable and proceeds in unvarying sequence. Development typically begins with *mass activity*—general, nongoal-directed movements involving large segments of the body.  This is followed by *specific activity*—more refined and differentiated movements directed toward specific goals.

**2.**  Although development is continuous, it is not necessarily smooth or gradual.  There are spurts in psychological and intellectual growth, just as there are spurts in physical growth.  Dramatic changes can occur in specific stages of development.

**3.**  Experience at early stages may affect later development.  Development can best be characterized as an accumulation of past experiences, with earlier experiences affecting later ones.

**4.**  There are critical or sensitive periods in development.  During the critical periods when certain organs or functions mature, the young person is most ready for development.  Interruption of or interference in this process may result in permanent psychological impairment or malfunctioning.

**5.**  Experience and maturation are involved in all stages.  Experience means learning and practice.  Maturation entails physical and biochemical changes.  Both interact to cause development.

**6.**  Development continues throughout the life cycle.  The process of development applies not only to childhood but to all stages in the life cycle.  Adulthood and old age present other stages and corresponding *life crises*, such as retirement, the death of a spouse, and the empty nest syndrome.

**C.**  Piaget's Cognitive Stages of Development
Swiss psychologist Jean Piaget maintained that certain inborn characteristics determine how human beings interact with the environment at each stage of development.  He proposed the following four stages of intellectual development from infancy to adulthood.

**1.**  Sensorimotor (birth to 2 yrs.)
During the first 24 months of life, infants adapt to the environment as their patterns of thought and action become more complex.  Initially vague and simple patterns (such as gross reflexes) are gradually refined into well-coordinated motor responses and more distinct and accurate perceptions of the environment.

**2.**  Preoperational (2 to 7 yrs.)
Between the ages of two and seven, the child's thoughts and actions are no longer tied to real objects and events.  Rather, the child begins to manipulate objects and events symbolically,

often in terms of images and words.  Thought during this period is usually egocentric, with the child unable to understand the point of view of others.

**3.** Concrete Operational (7 to 11 yrs.)
By age seven, children are able to focus on several dimensions of a problem at the same time. They become capable of logical processes and begin to comprehend relationships between things in their environment.  They are also able to create and follow rules.

**4.** Formal Operational (over 11 yrs.)
The fourth stage of development, which extends into adulthood, includes the ability to make abstractions and to reason by hypothesis and logic.  Children become concerned with belief and value systems and begin to evaluate their ideas and thoughts in relation to those of others.

## II. Personality and Behavior

**A.** Psychoanalytic Theories

**1.** Freud's Theories
Sigmund Freud was the originator of *psychoanalysis*, a method of treating personality disorders that has influenced much of modern psychology.  Through a process called *free association*, Freud encouraged patients to speak freely about anything that came to mind.  He believed that past events, particularly those repressed during childhood, exerted a significant influence over a current behavior.  Breakthroughs occurred when patients could bring those repressed events to consciousness and deal with them directly.  Key components of Freud's theories included the psychosexual stages of development, the tripartite nature of personality (id, ego, and superego), and the development of defense mechanisms.

    **a.** Psychosexual stages of development
Freud proposed four stages of psychosexual development.  Failure to pass through any of the stages successfully could lead to neurotic symptoms or antisocial behavior.  The first stage is the *oral* stage, during the first year of life, when infants seek gratification through the mouth.  The second stage is the *anal* stage, usually during years two and three, in which pleasure stemming from excretion and retention of feces dominates.  Starting at approximately the fourth year, children enter the *phallic* stage, in which excitation or stimulation of the genital regions are a primary source of pleasure.  After a latency period, children pass into the *genital* phase, where they remain through adulthood.

    **b.** Id, ego, and superego
According to Freud, the human personality is divided into three parts—the id, ego, and superego.  Each part represents a force that combines and competes with the other two to determine day-to-day behavior.  The *id* consists of unconscious impulses that seek immediate expression and gratification.  The id impulse leads a person to think only of immediate desires for pleasure.  The *superego* represents social and moral rules internalized from childhood.  Through feelings of guilt, the superego prevents the enjoyment of simple, socially acceptable pleasures.  The *ego* mediates between the id and the superego and focuses on the immediate and future consequences of behavior.  The ego attempts to balance the driving pressures of the id and superego with the realities of the environment.

    **c.** Defense mechanisms
Defense mechanisms enable people to resolve internal conflicts.  According to Freud, everyone uses defense mechanisms in daily life.  One common defense mechanism is *denial*, in which people refuse to believe they have unacceptable impulses.  *Reaction formation* is present when people behave in a manner that is completely opposite from their true feelings or attitudes.  In *projection*, people attribute to others their own unacceptable, repressed feelings and ideas.  In *sublimation*, people display unsatisfied or unacceptable impulses in socially acceptable ways.

**19**

**2.** Alternative Theories

Although many theorists agreed with the central elements of Freud's theories, they placed an increasing emphasis on the social and cultural influences on personality development. Erik Erikson, for example, viewed the stages of development chiefly in terms of developing a sense of individual identity and interpersonal relationships rather than in the more sexual terms of Freud.

**B.** Actualization Theories (Rogers)

*Actualization* theories take a humanistic approach to describing personality development. In general, they hold that people have an inherent ability to develop their personalities to their own benefit and that the development of a healthy personality requires unconditional positive regard from others. Carl Rogers is one of the primary proponents of actualization theories.

Actualization theories are based on five principles:
1. Human beings strive to fulfill their aims, goals, and potential.
2. Present experience is the main determinant of behavior.
3. Understanding people's thoughts and perceptions is essential to understanding behavior.
4. Emphasis should be placed on the positive aspects of personality development.
5. The love relationship is a positive force with a special role in personality development.

**C.** Learning Theories

**1.** Classical Conditioning (Pavlov)

**a.** Introduction

The idea of forming a simple relationship or association between two events is one of the oldest and most basic explanations of learning. In psychology, an association represents the connection between a stimulus and a response, such as braking a car when a stop sign comes in view. Simple associations were initially explored by Ivan Pavlov, who studied *classical conditioning*.

**b.** Experiment

According to Pavlov, classical conditioning occurs in three stages. The first stage involves an unconditioned stimulus (US) that by itself causes an innate or unconditioned response (UR). With a dog as his subject, Pavlov used meat powder (US) to make the dog salivate (UR). The second stage involves a neutral stimulus (NS) that by itself results in no automatic response. Pavlov used the sound of a bell. The third stage involves pairing the neutral stimulus with the unconditioned stimulus. In Pavlov's experiments, after repeated pairings the sound of the bell made the dog salivate even when the meat powder was no longer present. However, when the bell was rung repeatedly without occasional pairing with the meat powder, it soon lost its power to cause salivation in the dog. This process is called *extinction*.

**c.** Implications

Classical conditioning is considered to be responsible for many aspects of human behavior, particularly the development of phobias (fears). For example, if a loud noise or other frightening unconditioned stimulus is accidently paired with being in a high place, a child may develop a phobia of high places. A common treatment for phobias is continued exposure to the stimulus without pairing to the unconditioned stimulus.

**2.** Behavior Modification (Skinner)

**a.** Introduction

Classical conditioning explains some, but not all, of the ways that behavior can be learned. Building on the foundation of classical conditioning as well as on other research findings, B.F. Skinner suggested operant conditioning as a primary method for learning behavior.

**b.** Operant conditioning
The theory of *operant conditioning*, often known as behaviorism or *behavior modification*, states that future behavior is determined by the consequences experienced for similar behavior in the past. Stated more simply, behavior is controlled by its consequences. For instance, if in the past when you were thirsty you put coins in a soda pop machine (behavior) and got a can of soda in return (consequence), you will be more likely to put coins in the machine in the future when you are thirsty. However, if you put coins in the machine several times and no soda cans come out, you will probably be less likely to place coins in the machine in the future. The effect of consequences on behavior is determined both by their nature and by the schedule through which they are given.

**c.** Types of consequences
Depending on their effect, consequences may be either *reinforcers* or *punishers*. If a consequence results in a behavior occurring more frequently in the future, it is considered a reinforcer. A reinforcer can be either giving something positive or taking away something aversive (undesirable). Correspondingly, a punisher is a consequence that results in a behavior occurring less frequently in the future. A punisher can be either giving something aversive or taking away something positive. For example, if employees work hard, an employer might reinforce their behavior by raising their pay. This should increase hard-working behavior in the future. If employees have been lazy, the employer might reduce their pay, as a punisher. This should result in a decrease of lazy behavior in the future.

**d.** Schedules of reinforcement
The effectiveness of consequences is also determined by how frequently they are given—that is, by the schedule of reinforcement. In general, if a behavior is reinforced on a *continuous* basis, then it will be learned quickly but also disappear quickly once the reinforcers are no longer given. However, if a behavior is reinforced only on an occasional or *intermittent* basis, it will take longer to learn but last considerably longer once the reinforcer is removed. The most effective type of reinforcement schedule is the *variable-ratio* schedule, in which the reinforcer is given after a changing number of correct responses (after the third correct response, then the fifth, then the second, and so on). Slot machines are an example of the power of the variable-ratio schedule to motivate behavior.

**e.** Shaping
Skinner suggested that new, complex sets of behaviors are learned through *shaping*, or rewarding successive approximations of the behavior. For example, if you wanted to teach a child mathematics, you would break the parts of math down into smaller pieces (addition, multiplication, and so forth) and reward the child with praise as he or she successfully completed each part.

**3.** Social-Learning Theory

**a.** Introduction
While Skinner's approach focuses exclusively on consequences external to the individual, social-learning theory investigates the processes that occur within the individual. The belief that individuals can learn not only through trial and error (behaviorism) but also through watching the behavior of others is the foundation of social learning.

**b.** Modeling
According to social-learning theory, complex behavior is learned through *modeling*. The process involves a social situation in which at least two people are present—the "model" and the "imitator." Unlike behaviorism, modeling does not require the direct reinforcement of imitated behaviors. For example, watching others get reinforced for displaying certain behaviors will result in an increase in similar behaviors in the observer.

19

**c.** Importance of modeling in development
Modeling represents the primary way people learn such complex behaviors as social interaction and language skills. The effects of media modeling, such as the behaviors displayed on television, are still being investigated.

# SOCIOLOGY

## I. Socialization

**A.** Definition

*Socialization* is the process by which an individual, usually during childhood, learns and adopts patterns of behavior and norms that are appropriate for his or her social environment. Even when behavior is driven by biological impulses, the culture ultimately shapes these impulses into socially acceptable patterns of behavior. The development of moral standards is considered to be a key aspect of socialization. Several different theories attempt to explain how the socialization process works.

**B.** Theories of Socialization

**1.** Looking Glass

Through interactions with others in the environment, people develop a sense of *self-identity*, an awareness of who they are as individuals. Children develop images of themselves that are largely a reflection of the way others see them. This image is called the looking-glass self. As people mature and biological and emotional needs are satisfied, they learn to distinguish between themselves and others.

**2.** Psychoanalytic

Psychoanalytic theory (Freud) focuses on the importance of inner biological and emotional drives in the process of socialization. Many aspects of socialization are incorporated in the part of the personality called the superego, which acts as the conscience. This part of the personality is developed as an individual learns of society's demands for self-control, largely through instruction from the parents. The superego competes with the id, inborn sexual and aggressive drives. This conflict is regulated by the ego, which determines the pattern of our final behavior.

**3.** Behavioral

Behaviorist theory (Skinner) suggests that all human behavior is learned and is the result of the presence or absence of consequences, such as rewards and punishers. Socialization takes place as socially appropriate behaviors are rewarded and inappropriate ones are punished.

## II. Social Stratification

**A.** Definition

*Social stratification* is the ordering of groups of people according to their share in such social variables as wealth, power, and status. Historically, the principal forms of stratification have been estates, caste systems, and classes. People are considered to belong to the same social class when they possess similar amounts of wealth, power, or status.

**B.** The American Class System

Researchers suggest that the American social structure can be divided into five classes, based primarily on earning power and wealth.

**1.** Upper Class

The American upper class includes approximately 3 percent of the population but owns at least one-fourth of the nation's wealth. Its main sources of income are dividends and interest from stocks and bonds and revenues from other business investments. Much of the wealth is inherited.

19

**2.** Upper Middle Class

The upper middle class includes about 10 percent of the American population and includes business executives and professionals, such as physicians and lawyers. Its income is derived mainly from salaries, fees, and profits. Members of this class have valued occupational success and respectability.

**3.** Lower Middle Class

The lower middle class comprises about 28 percent of the population and consists mainly of small business owners, sales representatives, craftspeople, and office workers. Members of this class share many of the values of the upper middle class.

**4.** Working Class

The working class includes 34 percent of the population and consists of skilled and semi-skilled laborers and service workers. Members of this class may take great pride in working with their hands. They represent the largest class in terms of size.

**5.** Poor

The poor comprise 25 percent of the population. They include unskilled workers with a high rate of unemployment, welfare recipients, and others with little or no means of independent support. Many of the poor feel hopeless about their position and isolated from the mainstream of society.

**C.** Social Mobility

*Social mobility* is the movement from one social class to another. Many people believe that American society provides more opportunities than other societies for upward mobility. This is primarily because of widespread industrialization and automation as well as the availability of educational opportunities.

**D.** Communism (Karl Marx)

Opposed to capitalism (the system prevalent in the United States), which promotes a class system, is the concept of communism, first advanced by Karl Marx in 1849. Underlying communist theory is the belief that wealth and prosperity should be shared by all people equally, rather than being centralized among just a few. Because capitalism promoted conflict among the classes, Marx believed that it was doomed and would ultimately be replaced by worldwide communism. The exploited working class, or *proletariat*, would overthrow the owners of business, or *bourgeoisie*, and introduce a society in which the means and results of production were publicly owned.

## III. Population Growth

**A.** Definition

The study of human population is known as *demography*. Demographic studies examine a population's size, distribution, and composition through statistical data on birth, death, immigration, and emigration. The nature and size of a population have a significant impact on social behavior, organizations, and institutions.

**B.** World Growth

The world population grew slowly for centuries but doubled between 1650 and 1850. By the beginning of the twentieth century, the rate of population growth increased dramatically in unindustrialized countries but tended to decrease in industrialized nations. The world population was estimated to be 1 billion by 1850, 2 billion by 1930, and 4 billion by 1976. At the present rate, it is estimated that the population will double every 35 years.

**C.** Growth in the United States

A high birth rate and massive influx of immigrants have characterized much of the history of the United States. Both factors made rapid expansion of the country and its economy possible. Recently, the birth rate in the United States has declined to an all-time low of 1.8 children per couple. Even if the birth rate stays the same, however, the population of the United States will continue to grow because of the large number of women of child-bearing age. The American population is also getting older, with the average age increasing every year.

**D.** Population Explosion

Explosive population growth produces great pressure for social change. As more and more people share a limited number of resources, the amount of resources per person declines, causing the standard of living to decrease. The rapid growth of the world population is considered to be cause for alarm.

## IV. Crime

**A.** Definition

*Criminal behavior* is a form of social conduct that is negatively evaluated and likely to receive punitive responses from organized society. Criminologists study the causes, development, and effects of criminal behavior.

**B.** Types of Crime

   **1.** Juvenile Delinquency
   Juvenile delinquency refers to crimes committed by people under the age of 18. It represents approximately 40 percent of all serious crimes.

   **2.** Organized Crime
   Organized crime refers to supplying illegal goods and services through a confederation of underworld criminals. Typical businesses include gambling, drugs, and prostitution.

   **3.** White-Collar Crime
   White-collar crime refers to crimes committed by normally "respectable" people such as professionals and government officials. Common crimes include bribery, embezzlement, and cheating on income taxes.

   **4.** Victimless Crime
   Victimless crime refers to violations of the law that affect only the person committing the crime. Examples are drug use, prostitution, and adultery.

**C.** Causes of Crime

There are many theories on the causes of crime. Some sociologists attribute crime to adverse social conditions such as high unemployment and discrimination and to the number of young people in a population. Others suggest that crime is the result of contact with criminals. Still others suggest that people engage in criminal behavior because it is highly rewarded and because the possibility of punitive consequences is often remote.

## V. The Changing City

**A.** From Cities to Suburbs

The post-World-War-II movement of the American population from big cities to the suburbs represents one of the greatest mass migrations in the nation's history. By 1970 the United States was primarily a suburban society, with 37.6 percent of the nation's population living in the suburbs as compared to 31 percent in cities.

19

**B.** Growth of Suburbs

The growth of the suburbs has been attributed to a number of factors. Massive road-building programs made it easier to commute into the cities. The postwar baby boom created a great demand for housing that required more land than was available in urban areas. Finally, the postwar economic boom enabled millions of Americans to afford a house for the first time.

## VI. Sex Roles and Relationships

A *sex role* is a pattern of behavior expected of the males or females in a particular society. These patterns include sexual behavior, personality attributes, and expected work and social behavior. Throughout the world gender (sex) distinctions are used for assigning work activities; determining rights, duties, and property; and conferring social status. Although great progress has been made toward equality for women, particularly in the industrialized countries, their status is still considered lower than that of men. Even in the United States, where sex roles are changing rapidly, full equality for women remains an important goal.

## VII. Groups

**A.** Terminology

Groups are defined as two or more people who interact with each other and participate in at least one common activity. People who feel they belong to a group and can identify with it are called *in-group*. Usually a symbolic boundary, such as special clothes or haircuts, separates insiders from outsiders. Becoming an insider involves going through *initiation rites*, which can be a very simple or elaborate process. Any group that serves as a standard against which others are measured is called a *reference group*. *Primary groups* are characterized by close emotional ties, such as those that exist within families. *Secondary groups*, usually formed to complete a task, are characterized by impersonal, formal relationships.

**B.** Leadership

Each group usually has at least one member who can influence group behavior more than the other members. This person is called the leader. *Task leaders* are concerned primarily with getting tasks accomplished and gain power and satisfaction through this process. *Maintenance leaders* are concerned primarily with promoting good morale among group members.

**C.** Patterns of Interaction

Patterns of interaction, or social processes, exist among virtually all groups. *Cooperation* exists when members work together toward a common goal; *competition* exists when members try to outdo one another in pursuit of a reward.

## VIII. Social Conflict

**A.** Definition

*Social conflict* is a struggle over values, claims to status, power, or scarce resources. The conflicting parties often seek not only to gain their desired ends but also to neutralize, injure, or eliminate their adversaries. Conflict is an ever-present part of human existence. Understanding its nature is essential to attaining peaceful relationships among groups of people and among nations.

**B.** Relationship between Conflict and Violence

*Conflict* and *violence* are distinct concepts. Conflict situations can occur regardless of whether violence is present. Wars, riots, rebellions, and murders are all examples of violent conflict. Labor strikes and the "cold war" between the Soviet Union and the United States are examples of conflicts that do not necessarily involve violence. By the same token, violence can occur in the absence of conflict. Examples include accidental death or injury and international incidents such as plane or boat disasters that are not intentional.

**C.** Causes of Conflict

Conflict originates as a result of three interacting variables: shared resources, dependency, and incompatible goals. For example, in a marriage husband and wife usually share resources (money and property) and are dependent on each other for emotional, financial, and physical support. If their goals are not compatible, the stage is set for conflict.

**D.** Solutions to Conflict

Conflict is often resolved when conflicting parties or outsiders find a superordinate cause, or "supergoal," that binds the opponents together. For example, conflicts between labor and management are often set aside if the survival of a company depends on cooperative action. Conflict may also be resolved through compromise, with enlightened members of competing groups finding ways to satisfy most of the concerns of both groups.

## IX. Norms and Collective Behavior

**A.** Definition

Norms, or *normative behavior*, refer to common or expected patterns of social conduct. The opposite phenomenon, *collective behavior*, occurs when large numbers of people engage in conduct that is spontaneous, unpredictable, brief, and irregular.

**B.** Basic Conditions

Sociologists suggest that several conditions must exist for collective behavior to occur. A society must be structured to permit spontaneous behavior. The society must be strained by pressures such as discrimination, uncertainty about the future, and even boredom. A large number of people must share a common belief about a situation, and an incident must occur that serves as a trigger for collective action. Finally, news of the incident must be spread so that people are mobilized to act. Whether collective behavior goes out of control or is quickly checked depends on the strength and reaction of agents of social control, such as the police.

# HISTORY

## I. Ancient Period (Prehistory–A.D. 475)

### A. The Prehistoric Period

**1. Description**

Human beings made important advances in the period known as prehistory, defined as the time before written records existed. Knowledge of this period comes from a variety of sources identified by archaeologists and other scientists. Because most of the weapons, tools, and other artifacts that remain from prehistoric times are made of stone, this period is usually called the Stone Age.

**2. Stone Age**

The longest part of the Stone Age is called the Old Stone Age, which includes the time before 8000 B.C. People in this period lived by hunting and gathering their food. Significant developments of this period include making tools for specific uses, controlling and using fire, and developing a spoken language. The people of Europe and Asia created paintings, sculpture, and jewelry. Evidence of the development of religious beliefs is also present.

**3. New Stone Age (Neolithic Age)**

The New Stone Age, also called the Neolithic Age, began about 8000 B.C., which corresponds with the end of the Ice Age. The changes in climate after the Ice Age enabled people in some parts of the world to plant crops, domesticate animals, and group together in villages. Artisans of the period made pottery, wove cloth, and improved on the tools and weapons developed during earlier times. New tools of the period include the plow, the wheel, and the sail. Later in the period craftspeople in the Near East learned to work with metals and incorporate them into their tools, weapons, and decorative artwork.

### B. River Civilizations

**1. Origins**

Small farming villages that developed during the New Stone Age gradually grew into cities. Four great civilizations emerged around 3000 B.C. in river valleys in Asia and Africa. The first, Mesopotamia, arose in the region between the Tigris and Euphrates rivers in the area now known as the Middle East. The second, Egypt, developed along the banks of the Nile River in Africa. The third, India, emerged in the valley of the Indus River. The fourth, China, took shape along the Yellow River.

As these civilizations emerged, significant advances took place in organized government, religion, specialized skills and technology, and systems for record-keeping and writing.

**2. Mesopotamia**

The Sumerians inhabited the area between the Tigris and Euphrates called Mesopotamia. To make use of the rivers, they developed irrigation systems and devised building techniques that used baked clay bricks. Written records were kept in *cuneiform*, a writing system composed primarily of wedge-shaped symbols that were impressed on damp clay. Completed tablets of cuneiform were dried or baked and then stored in a library.

Other significant advances were made in the areas of technology, mathematics, and astronomy. In the *Code of Hammurabi*, one of the best-known legacies of the era, a system of laws was established and set down in written form. Many of the Sumerian traditions of law, religion (the worship of many gods), art, and government were adopted by later peoples of Mesopotamia.

**3.** Egypt

    **a.** Development
    The Egyptian civilization endured for almost 3000 years because of its strong traditions. The Egyptians were ruled by *pharaohs*, who were considered to be gods on earth. The pharaohs of the Old Kingdom, before Egypt was torn by civil war, built tombs in the form of pyramids, many of which still stand today. After the civil war, trade flourished in Egypt during the prosperous Middle Kingdom; the New Kingdom pharaohs who followed built substantial empires by conquering territories along Egypt's borders.

    Numerous officials ran the complex government and economy that developed in Egypt. During the period of prosperity, Egypt developed into a society with distinct classes of people, with priests and government officials at the top; skilled workers, scribes, and artisans in the middle; and peasants—the great majority of Egyptians—at the bottom. Outstanding pharaohs of the period, such as Thutmose, Akhenaton, and Ramses, made a significant impact on both Egyptian society and the world.

    Gradually, the pharaohs' power at home began to weaken, and invasions from the outside threatened the existence of the empire. By about 1200 B.C., Egyptian civilization had passed from its period of greatness. In succeeding centuries, Egypt came under the rule of many different peoples. With the conquests of Alexander the Great in the fourth century B.C., native rule finally ended in Egypt.

    **b.** Advances
    Egyptians are credited with making significant advances in medicine, engineering, and astronomy. They created a sun-based calendar and developed a form of picture writing called *hieroglyphics*. Many of their records are preserved on scrolls made from papyrus.

**C.** Greek Civilization

    **1.** Development
    Greek civilization is believed to have begun on the island of Crete as early as 2600 B.C. The development of city-states around 800 B.C. marked the beginning of the great period in Greek civilization known as the *Hellenic Age*. Two of the city-states, Athens to the north and Sparta to the south, played primary roles in Greek history. The military city-state of Sparta prided itself on its soldiers and its ability to wage war. By contrast, Athens was famous for its statesmen, thinkers, writers, and artists, and developed one of the first democratic forms of government.

    **2.** Persian Wars
    Because of their differences, the city-states often fought with one another. When the mighty Persian Empire threatened to conquer Greece in the fifth century B.C., the city-states united to preserve their way of life. The Persians attacked by land and later by sea and were defeated by the Greeks. The victory over Persia led to a golden age in Athens.

    **3.** Golden Age of Athenian Democracy
    After the defeat of the Persians, the Greek city-states formed alliances to protect themselves against outside enemies. With its powerful fleet and great wealth, Athens came to dominate one alliance, which soon turned into the Athenian empire. During this period Athens made significant advances in government and education. However, democracy in Athens was limited, with only about 10 percent of the population allowed full citizen status.

        **a.** Plato
        Plato, a student of Socrates, is one of the best-known philosophers of this period. Plato stressed the importance of knowledge and character and believed society as a whole should be regulated by reason. He questioned existing ideas about government and

democracy, arguing that government should be led by *philosopher-kings*, who would have the knowledge to govern in the whole society's best interest. Plato was the first thinker to analyze political systems.

**b.** Hippocrates

Hippocrates is considered to be the father of medicine. He taught Greek physicians to use a scientific approach in treating illness, urging them to find the causes for disease through reason, rather than blaming angry gods. His ideas about physicians' responsibilities were put in the form of the *Hippocratic oath*, which is still used as a guide in medicine today.

**4.** Alexander the Great

Eventually Sparta challenged Athens in the *Peloponnesian War*, which resulted in the weakening of both city-states. They were easily conquered by Philip of Macedonia in 338 B.C. Philip's son, Alexander the Great, made Greece part of a larger empire that stretched from Egypt to India. In 323 B.C., at the age of 33, Alexander died of fever, and his empire gradually disintegrated. His conquests, however, had the lasting effect of spreading Greek culture throughout the world.

**D.** Roman Civilization

**1.** Development

Starting as a small town in central Italy, Rome built the greatest empire of the ancient world. Ruled at first by kings, the Romans set up a republican form of government in 509 B.C. Over several hundred years the common people, or *plebeians*, were able to gain power, but by and large the Roman government was ruled by a small, wealthy upper class called the *patricians*.

**2.** Republic

**a.** Growth

The Roman republic became a great military power and conquered the rest of Italy through diplomacy, alliances, and war. Rome gained control in the western Mediterranean by defeating Carthage in the Punic Wars. With its victory in the First Punic War, Rome acquired Sicily as its first *province*. Its conquest of the Greek states to the east resulted in widespread Greek influence on the Roman culture.

**b.** Decline

While Rome's wars brought it new lands and power, social and political problems developed at home. Because many farms were destroyed during the wars, farmers sold out to large landowners who used foreign slaves for laborers, leaving much of the local population unemployed. In addition, Roman politics became corrupt and violent, resulting in deep divisions and conflicts between the rich and the poor. In 73 B.C. the slaves rebelled, and for two years they battered the Roman armies and devastated southern Italy. Julius Caesar, an ambitious general, reunited the republic, but his power, success, and popularity alarmed many nobles and senators, who feared that he would overturn the republic and declare himself king. Caesar's assassination in 44 B.C. plunged Rome into civil war.

**3.** Empire

**a.** Growth

In 27 B.C. the Roman republic was transformed into an empire under the rule of Octavian, later called Augustus, the first Roman emperor. Augustus' rule marked the start of 200 years of peace and stability in the Mediterranean world. The Roman Empire united various peoples with different customs and traditions under a common ruler and set of laws.  Trade expanded and cities thrived.  Greek-influenced Roman culture spread through-out Europe and North Africa.

**b.** Decline

By the third century A.D. a series of crises weakened the Roman Empire.  Civil wars and attacks by Germanic tribes disrupted the economy and caused people to flee from cities and take refuge in the country.  Although attempts were made to tighten control through taxes and laws, many Romans lost faith in the Empire.  The collapse of Rome to invading Germanic tribes in 476 A.D. marked the end of the ancient world.

## II. Medieval Period (476–1500)

### A. Frankish Empire

The decline of the Roman Empire left Europe in confusion.  Any semblance of strong govern-ment had vanished and economic life was in turmoil.  By the fifth century, Germanic peoples (the Franks) had established kingdoms in many of the lands that had previously belonged to Rome.  Germanic culture, laws, and political realities were very different from Roman rule.  The Frankish kingdoms were eventually united in 687 A.D. under a single king.  The Pope supported the Franks in order to protect the Christian Church from other groups in Europe.

### B. Dark Ages

During the sixth to eighth centuries, commonly referred to as the Dark Ages, few people except the clergy learned to read or write.  The Christian Church was the dominant social influence and closely regulated the growth and distribution of knowledge.

### C. Charlemagne

In 768 A.D. Charlemagne became king of the Franks.  Hoping to improve the training of his officials and clergy, he brought some of the finest scholars in Europe to his palace.  Charlemagne was a German whose government grew out of Germanic customs, but he was also a devout Christian who sought to spread the Christian faith and protect the Church against its enemies.  He was crowned emperor by the Pope.  This blending of Germanic and Christian elements, paired with a desire to preserve the Greco-Roman past, came to characterize the civilization of the Middle Ages.  The death of Charlemagne in 814 brought his empire to an end.

### D. The Roman Catholic Church

The Catholic Church had a dramatic influence on medieval civilization.  Headquartered in Rome and led by the Pope, it exercised power over most of Europe, and kings and princes obeyed its decrees.  As the leading institution of the age, the Church served as a unifying force for the new civilizations that arose in Europe.

### E. Crusades

**1.** Causes

At the end of the eleventh century, the Church waged a struggle against Islam because the Turkish Muslims had captured control of Jerusalem in the Holy Land.  In 1095, Pope Urban II appealed to the lords and knights of Europe to liberate the Holy Land and place Jerusalem back into Christian hands.  The appeal not only enabled the lords and knights to act as armed pilgrims for Christianity.  It also met their needs for adventure and wealth and helped to reduce the warring between the rulers in Christian lands.

**2.** Results

In 1099, after suffering incredible hardship on their journey, the Christian army captured Jerusalem in what became known as the *First Crusade*.  In later crusades, the Turks were able to recapture their lost lands and the Christian armies had a difficult time maintaining control. In 1291, almost 200 years after the initial call to arms, the last Christian outpost in Palestine fell to the Muslims.

### 3. Changes

The devastating results of the Crusades led to substantial changes throughout Europe. Initially, the Crusades served to strengthen the power of the Church and to unify Christian rulers. But as criticism of the effort grew, the prestige and power of the papacy and the Church declined. By contrast, trade flourished as Europeans who participated in the Crusades were exposed to products from the East. In particular, Italian cities benefited from the increased trade between East and West. Italian traders invested their profits in long journeys to India and the Orient and carried the goods back to eager buyers in Europe.

## F. Feudalism

### 1. Beginnings

Feudalism began as a result of the disintegration of Charlemagne's great empire. In the warfare and disorder that followed, medieval lords sought allies among the lesser nobles. The basis for the alliances was land, which the lords offered in exchange for military assistance and other services. A lord would grant a piece of land, called a *fief*, to a noble who was called a *vassal*. This relationship, called feudalism, was based on the system through which the vassal pledged loyalty to the lord.

### 2. Class System

Feudalism affected all classes of people in medieval society. In return for a pledge of loyalty, the vassal received the lord's protection and a grant of land, including the peasants who lived on the land. The peasants raised the crops that supported the vassal and in return were given protection. Vassals had to aid the lord in wartime and were supposed to raise money for ransom if the lord was captured. Lords were primarily warriors who protected their land.

### 3. Medieval Manor

The wealth of feudal lords came from the produce of the peasants who occupied their lands. The overwhelming majority of people were peasants. Most were *serfs*, who did not have the freedom to leave the land where they were born and lived in small villages on the lord's *manor*. Manors were largely self-sufficient worlds in which peasants and serfs accepted their plight. Open rebellion was rare until the fourteenth century.

## G. Byzantium

Even before Rome fell to invaders in 476 A.D., it had been divided into two different empires. The civilization that took shape in the eastern half of the Roman Empire was called *Byzantium*. Based on Greek language and culture, it endured for over a thousand years. The Byzantine civilization preserved many Greco-Roman customs, and its religion and culture spread to Eastern Europe, particularly Russia.

# III. Modern Period (after 1500)

## A. World History

### 1. The Renaissance

#### a. Description

In the centuries following the end of the Middle Ages, society, politics, and intellectual life in Europe underwent substantial changes, exploding from the restricted atmosphere that governed medieval life. This rebirth in thought and growth, known as the *Renaissance*, began in approximately 1350 in the city-states of northern Italy and lasted into the 1600s. The Renaissance spread from Italy to other parts of Europe.

**b.** Rediscovery of classical learning

The Renaissance was characterized by a high value placed on achievements, particularly in the arts and humanities. Wealthy Italian merchants and bankers encouraged the arts and the study of Greek and Latin language and culture. Support by the wealthy fostered greater freedom and creativity in painting, sculpture, and literature. Critical studies in history and politics also flourished during this time. *Niccolo Machiavelli*, a diplomat and student of politics, embodied the critical Renaissance spirit with the publication of his political treatise *The Prince*. The development of the printing press in the 1450s was instrumental in making new ideas available to much larger numbers of people. Before the printing press, only 100,000 books were available in all of Europe. Within a span of 50 years, more than 9 million books became available.

**2.** Reformation

**a.** Changes in Church practice

The Catholic Church played an extremely powerful role during the Middle Ages in determining the culture, lifestyle, and knowledge of people in Europe. A number of Church practices and traditions drew criticism as early as the 1300s, and an increasing number of people demanded reforms. Major changes did not occur until the 1500s, when the German scholar *Martin Luther* challenged basic Catholic teachings in his 95 theses (arguments), which he nailed to a church door in Wittenburg in 1517. Luther's speeches and writings won him many followers, including powerful princes who protected him. The Pope ordered Luther to give up his beliefs, but in an act of defiance cheered by many, Luther burned the papal order. In 1521 the Pope excommunicated him. Those who followed Luther in protesting against Catholic teachings and practices became known as *Protestants*. The movement was called the *Reformation*.

**b.** Spread to Northern Europe

The Protestant Reformation found supporters in other European countries. *John Calvin*, a Swiss theologian, and *John Knox*, a reformer from Scotland, became significant leaders in the process. In England, Reformation became part of the struggle for political power. When the Catholic Church refused to grant King Henry VIII a divorce, the English Parliament created the Church of England, headed by the king, not the Pope. In response to the spread of Protestantism, the Catholic Church made internal changes and reforms in administration. The Reformation, however, had gained a solid foothold in Europe.

**3.** Explorations and Discoveries

**a.** New routes to Asia

The desire for wealth motivated Europeans to make long voyages of exploration. The people of Europe sought such luxury goods as gold, silver, sugar, and silk, as well as spices needed to preserve food, particularly meat. All these resources were available in Asia. For a long period of time Muslim traders had controlled both the land and the sea routes from the Indian Ocean to the Mediterranean Sea, blocking direct access to Asia. In addition, Venice held exclusive control over trade with the Muslims.

European explorers sought more than wealth as a result of their travels. They were also looking for adventure and the opportunity to spread Christianity to other lands. Portugal took the lead in exploration. In 1498 Portuguese explorers found a sea route around Africa to India and soon established trading posts and plantations on the coasts of Africa and Asia. While Portugal explored to the east, Spain looked for a westward passage to Asia. Sailing under Spain's flag, *Christopher Columbus* failed to reach Asia on his westward trip across the Atlantic Ocean, landing instead on the islands of the Caribbean in 1492. Another notable explorer of the time, *Ferdinand Magellan*, circled the world in the early 1500s, thereby discovering a westward route from Europe to Asia.

19

**b.** Colonizing the Americas

In their search for gold, the Spanish moved from the Caribbean islands onto the mainland of the Americas, claiming vast amounts of territory. The Spanish conquerors brought with them the gun, the horse, and the wheel, all new developments in the Americas. Eventually, almost all of Central and South America became part of the Spanish colonial empire. The British, Dutch, and French explored northward and claimed much of the eastern seaboard of North America. All three countries claimed islands in the Caribbean.

**c.** Changes in trade and commerce

The rapid exploration and opening of new lands and resources brought about changes in European political and economic life. Following the theory of *mercantilism*, the powers in Europe determined that the purpose of these new-found lands was to provide wealth for the home countries. Rivalry over these resources led to a variety of armed conflicts between the home countries. The wealth and produce resulting from the explorations also set the stage for the rise of capitalism.

**4.** Scientific Revolution

**a.** Study of the universe

In the early 1500s, *Copernicus* challenged ancient beliefs about the moon, sun, and planets with his proposal that the earth revolves around the sun (rather than the sun revolving around the earth). Although contested by the Church, the theory gained popularity through *Galileo*, who used mathematics to support Copernicus's observations. *Isaac Newton* further contributed to the new awakening of scientific thought by demonstrating that all physical bodies, whether on earth or in the sky, behave according to a fixed set of natural laws.

**b.** Study of society

Newton's description of natural laws in physics led others to look for similar laws governing human society. One of the most influential philosophers of the time, *John Locke*, believed the purpose of government was to protect the rights of citizens to life, liberty, and property. In France, *Voltaire* wrote about the free expression of ideas.

**5.** French Revolution

**a.** Causes

A variety of problems led to revolution in France in 1789. French society was divided into three classes—an outgrowth of the feudalism of the Middle Ages. The nobility and the clergy were granted special privileges, while most of the rest of France lived in poverty. France's absolute monarchy prided itself on the display of wealth and extravagance. The standard of living of the king, wars among the European countries, and military assistance to the colonists during the American Revolution—all emptied the royal treasury. A financial crisis led the monarch, *Louis XVI*, to ask the nobility and clergy to agree to a tax on their lands. They refused. This forced the king to call a meeting of the elected legislature, the States General, a representative body that had not met for over 100 years. Members of this group decided to establish a National Assembly and to draft a constitution, and they were soon supported by popular revolts.

**b.** Stages

(1) *First phase (1789)*: On July 14, 1789, the people of Paris stormed the *Bastille* (a prison that was a hated symbol of the repression of the monarchy). In October a mob invaded the royal palace at Versailles. At about the same time, peasants in various parts of France rose up against their feudal lords. During the next two years, the National Assembly passed laws to deal with the abuses of the monarchy. The main areas of

change included equality and individual rights, government administration, religious influence, aid to business, and a constitutional form of government.

(2) *Second phase (1792)*: In 1792, in an effort to stop the revolution, Prussia and Austria went to war against France in support of the French king. In response, the French elected radical delegates to a national convention, which then abolished the monarchy, declared France a republic, and executed the king. A *Reign of Terror* followed and thousands of people who were believed to be enemies of the new republic were executed on the guillotine. The excesses and violence of the Reign of Terror led to its eventual end, and a new constitution was adopted in 1795.

  **c.** Change in society

The French Revolution transformed French society by ending feudalism, the absolute monarchy, and the special privileges of nobles and the clergy. It also represented the beginnings of *nationalism*, or devotion to a country rather than smaller special-interest groups.

**6.** Napoleonic Era

  **a.** Establishment of an empire

The republican government of France was overthrown in 1799 by *Napoleon Bonaparte*, a well-known and respected military commander who had previously brought France several military victories. A skilled politician, Napoleon brought order to the country and established a one-man rule. He was supported by both the working class and the owners of businesses. His code of laws incorporated many of the reforms initiated during the revolution. However, although great strides were made in social reform, many political liberties were lost. In 1804 Napoleon assumed the title of emperor.

An outstanding organizational, political, and military strategist, Napoleon sought to rule all of Europe—and was nearly successful in obtaining his goal. Between 1805 and 1807 Napoleon's armies won victories over Austria, Prussia, and Russia and extended the reforms of the revolution to the newly conquered territories. Of the great European powers of the time, only England was able to resist his advances because of its superior power at sea.

  **b.** Defeat of Napoleon

In 1812 Napoleon invaded Russia and captured Moscow. However, the severe Russian winter (with temperatures as low as 30° below zero) forced his army to retreat and resulted in severe losses. Following this disaster, the major powers of Europe united and eventually defeated Napoleon, exiling him to the Mediterranean island of Elba.

Napoleon returned to France in 1815 and regained control of the country for a period called the *Hundred Days*. His return renewed Europe's war against France and resulted in his defeat by the allied Europeans at Waterloo (Belgium). He was exiled again to St. Helena in the South Atlantic, where he died six years later.

**7.** Industrial Revolution

  **a.** Advancements

The *Industrial Revolution* represented a dramatic change in the way in which goods were produced. It began in Britain about 1750, fostered by that nation's large labor supply, plentiful natural resources, effective transportation system, and overseas market for manufactured goods. The textile industry was the first to adopt the new "factory" system, in which large numbers of people worked together running machines rather than producing goods individually. Under the *division of labor*, a prominent part of the new system, each worker did only one step in the manufacture of a product. The new

19

system allowed goods to be produced more quickly and more cheaply than the old domestic system.

The advent of the steam engine for railway transportation and machines for agriculture propelled the burst in production during the early to mid-1800s. Other nations followed England's lead, and soon Germany, France, and the United States joined the ranks of industrial powers. Cities grew rapidly to accommodate the new work force. The U.S. population boomed as millions of immigrants crossed the Atlantic in search of employment.

**b.** Social changes

The rapid industrialization and subsequent urbanization of the work force brought many problems. Overcoming the bitter opposition of employers, workers grouped together to form *labor unions*, which allowed them to bargain collectively for better wages and working conditions. The German government was the first to enact laws that provided workers with accident and old-age benefits. Other reform movements of the time focused on child labor and the right to vote and placed limits on the power exerted by large businesses.

The problems associated with urbanization became a focal point for economists and political philosophers. In Britain, *Adam Smith* argued for a *laissez-faire* economy, with minimal interference in business matters. In Germany, *Karl Marx* developed the ideas of communism and socialism, predicting that the working class would eventually overthrow the owners of business and establish a society without classes. In this class-free society the means and results of production would be owned equally by all the people rather than by the wealthy few.

**8.** Romanticism

At the same time that industrialization and nationalism were sweeping through Europe, a third movement called *romanticism* emerged in the field of the arts. The movement also had an impact on the social and political reforms of the time. Romanticism stressed feelings over reason through the expression of intense individual emotions and imagination. Romantic writers focused on the beauty and mystery of nature and found it a source of inspiration and emotion. Writers and composers of the period tied this new form of expression with strong themes of nationalism.

**9.** Imperialism

**a.** Causes

As the Industrial Revolution progressed, new markets were needed for the goods that were being developed. The powers of Europe entered the *Age of Imperialism*, scrambling to gain control over new lands for economic influence, national prestige, and strategic advantage. Imperialism frequently meant the disruption and exploitation of the traditional ways of the people in the conquered territories. It also brought with it opportunities for education, economic development, and the influence of European ideas.

**b.** India

The British East India Company established British power in India in the 1800s after defeating the French there and driving them from the country. After the British assumed direct control in 1857 as a result of an Indian rebellion, India became Britain's most valued colony because it served as a source for cotton and a market for the textiles produced in British factories.

A movement toward independence began to gain strength in the late 1800s as the Hindu-dominated Indian National Congress sought reform of British rule and more self-government. But it was only after World War II that India truly gained independence.

**c.** China

Led by Britain, the Europeans persuaded China to open the port city of Canton to foreign trade in 1834. Internal struggles weakened the ruling party in China, and the failure of the *Boxer Rebellion* of 1899 to rid the country of Western influence allowed the Europeans to gain even more control. Japan gained a foothold in the area through an expanding industrial economy and a powerful army and navy, and by 1910 it had become the major power in Asia.

**d.** Africa

Because of its abundance of natural and human resources, Africa was a primary target for the expansion of European powers. In the early 1800s, 90 percent of Africa was ruled by Africans; by 1914, only two African nations remained independent. Britain gained control of the eastern part from South Africa to Egypt, the French dominated the western African territories, the Belgians controlled the Congo in the middle of the continent, and Germany and Portugal ruled rich areas in the south.

**10.** World War I

**a.** Causes

The late 1800s and early 1900s brought significant advances to Europe in economics, politics, and the arts and sciences. Yet many social problems had gone unnoticed and were becoming more serious. Europe was plagued with deep rivalries between nations, intense nationalistic feelings, and inclinations toward war.

Nationalistic rivalries and militarism brought about an armaments race between the major countries of Europe. Several nations formed alliances to consolidate their strength. The *Triple Alliance* (later called the *Central Powers*) included Germany, Austria-Hungary, and Italy. The *Triple Entente* (later called the *Allies*) was made up of Britain, France, and Russia.

A nationalistic movement among the Slavs of Serbia led to the assassination of the heir to the Austrian throne, *Archduke Francis Ferdinand*. In killing the archduke and his wife, the Serbian nationalists hoped to increase tensions and pave the way for a Slavic revolution. The Austrian authorities, however, retaliated with military force. On July 28, 1914, Austria declared war on Serbia, marking the beginning of World War I.

**b.** European nations drawn into the war

The conflict escalated rapidly and became a battle for territory throughout Europe. Within one week Russia, Germany, France, and Britain entered the war. Shortly afterward, all major European powers were involved. When the conflict initially broke out, most military and political leaders, as well as the public, believed that it would be short-lived. The opposing sides represented the systems of alliances that had developed earlier. Turkey and Bulgaria eventually joined the Central Powers and Italy changed sides to join the Allies. In 1917 the United States entered the war alongside the Allies.

**c.** The war

The war centered around Germany and was fought primarily on two fronts—against the countries of Western Europe to the west and against the Russians to the east. The German army invaded Belgium in August 1914, hoping to sweep through Belgium into France while holding off the Russians to the east. However, the Russians were more aggressive than the Germans expected, requiring them to pull some of their troops off of the western front. The Germans were stopped in both France and Belgium, and the war reached a stalemate in the west in 1916 and 1917.

The war continued against the Russians on the eastern front. Although the Russians won early victories in eastern Germany, by 1916 their war effort was near collapse and they

19

were forced out of the war. Russia signed a treaty with the Germans in 1918. Poorly trained and financed troops, as well as a revolution at home, were the primary causes of Russia's withdrawal.

Trench warfare, chemical weapons, tanks, airplanes, and machine guns were the primary developments in war technology during World War I.

**d.** Entry of the United States

Although the United States attempted to play a neutral role early in the war, political and economic forces as well as Germany's attempted alliance with Mexico forced the Americans to enter the conflict. Early in 1917 the United States declared war on Germany.

Germany now tried to end the war quickly, before the large number of American troops and supplies could be sent for combat in France. The introduction of American troops in 1918 eroded the Germans' position, and on November 11, 1918, an armistice was signed.

**e.** Peace treaty

The war ended in 1918, yet a peace treaty was not signed until 1919. The Allies had difficulty agreeing on the terms. As a result, five separate treaties were signed in Paris. The settlement with Germany, the *Treaty of Versailles*, was the most important of the agreements.

The Versailles Treaty reduced German land and power, demilitarized German territory on both sides of the Rhine River, and required the Germans to pay *reparations* to the other countries for factories, farms, and other property destroyed in the war. The reparations totaled approximately $33 billion and placed an unbearable load on the German economy. New nations were created and a *League of Nations* was established in the hope of avoiding another world war. However, bitter feelings in many nations would serve to work against a permanent peace.

**11.** Revolution in Russia

In 1917, as the war was still raging, defeats and economic hardship sharpened discontent among Russians with the autocratic regime of Czar Nicholas II. In February an uprising at St. Petersburg, the capital, forced the Czar to abdicate, and a republican government was established. However, this new regime persisted in the war effort, and as a result, economic conditions worsened.

**a.** Lenin and the Bolsheviks

Widespread discontent with the new government increased the following of the Bolsheviks, the radical wing of the prewar socialist movement. This group, under its leader V.I. Lenin, called for an end to the war and a revolutionary transformation of society. In October the Bolsheviks led a successful coup that ousted the republican government. In its place they installed a revolutionary communist regime in which all power was exercised by Lenin and the other Bolshevik leaders. An armistice was then signed with Germany by which Russia withdrew from the war. The country, henceforth called the Soviet Union, then underwent radical changes. Private enterprise was abolished, opposition political parties were outlawed, individual freedoms were curtailed, and all economic activity was placed under state control.

**b.** Stalin

In 1924, Lenin died, and his place as Soviet leader was taken by Joseph Stalin. Under Stalin, ambitious five-year plans were implemented in an effort to transform the backward country into an industrial power. However, the regime grew still more dictatorial; a particularly brutal program forced the peasants onto collective farms; thousands were killed and millions more died in famines as agriculture stagnated. By the 1930s great progress in industrialization had been achieved, but the Soviet Union had evolved into a brutal dictatorship.

**12.** Fascism

In the years after the end of the war, many of the nations of Europe faced economic and political problems. Fascism, a political ideology based on extreme nationalism and militarism, gained popularity. It first emerged as a political force in 1919, when *Benito Mussolini* founded the Fascist Party in Italy. He soon established a dictatorship that controlled both social and economic life.

Fascist ideas continued to spread throughout Europe through the 1930s. New democracies that had been established after World War I collapsed and were replaced by authoritarian regimes. Civil War in Spain ended with victory for the fascists, who were led by *General Francisco Franco.*

**13.** Hitler

**a.** The Weimar Republic

After the end of World War I the Germans elected a national assembly, which met in the city of Weimar in 1919. The assembly set up a democratic form of government, adopted a republican constitution, and elected a president. This elective form of government, called the Weimar Republic, was new to the German people. Many considered democracy a weak form of rule.

**b.** The Nazi Party

(1) *Origins*: One of the most outspoken critics of the Weimar Republic was *Adolf Hitler*. Born in 1889 in Austria, Hitler served in the German army in World War I and was twice decorated for bravery. He adopted the extreme nationalistic positions and racist ideas that had been widespread in Europe in the late 1800s. After the war, he joined a small nationalist political group in Munich named the *National Socialist German Workers Party*, or the Nazi Party. Because of his extraordinary talents as an organizer and persuasive public speaker, Hitler quickly became the leader of the Nazi Party.

(2) *Philosophy of racism*: Hitler made racism a tenet of the Nazi way of thought and outlook on the world. He claimed that the Germans were a *master race*, direct descendants from the Aryan and Nordic peoples. He considered Jews, Slavs, and others inferior people who weakened the nation's social fiber. Taking advantage of the anti-Semitism that already existed in Germany, Hitler focused racial hatred on the Jews. He accused the Jews in Germany of being responsible for all the nation's problems—high unemployment, the spread of communism, even the defeat of Germany in World War I.

After Hitler gained power, the persecution of Germany's Jews grew worse. Anti-Semitism became official government policy: Jews lost their citizenship and were forbidden to hold jobs, own businesses, or carry on their professions. Later, terror and physical violence were also initiated against the Jews, culminating at last, during World War II in the 1940s, in a brutal policy of extermination in concentration camps. These terrible events, in which up to six million Jews were killed, are known to history as the *Holocaust*.

(3) *Nazis gain support*: With Hitler as its new leader, the Nazi Party flourished. Popular support grew as Hitler attacked the Versailles Treaty and the Weimar government. In 1923, after an unsuccessful attempt to overthrow the government, Hitler was sent to jail for nine months. It was during this time that he wrote *Mein Kampf*, a book expressing his dream of a German empire that stretched across Europe and into Russia.

19

The hard economic and political times that befell Germany as a result of World War I and the terms imposed by the Treaty of Versailles made the German people particularly vulnerable to movements like Nazism. Unemployment, insecurity, and inflation were common features of German life. In the fall of 1929, when the world tumbled into serious economic depression, Germany was particularly hard hit.

To win popular support, Hitler used *propaganda* that provided simple explanations for Germany's problems and emphasized his role as *Der Führer*, or the leader, who would restore Germany to power. Over and over he repeated what the German people wanted to hear, playing on their emotions with spellbinding speeches, while the Nazi Party committed acts of violence as a demonstration of strong rule.

**c.** Hitler as chancellor of Germany

By the end of 1932 the Nazis had become the strongest political party in Germany. In 1933 infiuential Germans persuaded the president of the Weimar Republic to make Hitler chancellor. A newly elected *Reichstag*, or German parliament, gave Hitler the powers of an absolute dictator and turned Germany into a totalitarian state. Hitler proclaimed the beginning of the *Third Reich* as the third great empire in German history.

The new Nazi government worked quickly to deal with many of the economic problems faced by Germany. The government set up programs to aid business, initiated public works projects to spur employment, and secretly began to build armaments on a large scale. As a result, unemployment nearly vanished, and workers' standard of living rose substantially. This new-found prosperity brought Hitler the loyalty of both the working people and the industrialists.

**14.** World War II

**a.** Beginnings

After World War I, many nations took part in efforts to preserve world peace. However, the rise of dictators in Germany and Italy, as well as the increasing influence of the military in Japan, led to acts of aggression in both Europe and Asia. In the face of Germany's aggressive acts in particular, the leaders of other European countries, eager to keep their nations out of conflict, did little to protest and followed a policy of *appeasement*.

In September 1938, the leaders of Britain, Germany, Italy, and France met in Munich to discuss the fate of Czechoslovakia, a land that the Germans wanted to control. Despite agreements to the contrary, Hitler invaded Czechoslovakia and then moved into Poland. A pact between Germany and the Soviet Union, in which the Soviets agreed not to interfere with Hitler's invasion in return for half of Poland, proved too much for the British and the French to ignore. Britain and France declared war against Germany in 1939.

**b.** European war

(1) *Early German success*: At the time of the invasion of Poland, Germany was far better prepared than either France or Britain for war. Germany and Italy formed the *Axis powers*, and by 1941 all the countries of Western Europe except Britain had fallen to Germany. Using a tactic called *blitzkreig*, a combination of heavy bombing and surprise offensives at great speed, the Germans accumulated rapid victories.

(2) *The Battle of Britain*: With the fall of France in 1940, Hitler began to apply pressure on Britain to surrender through massive bombings of British factories, airfields, seaports, and cities. The blitz continued for almost one year, destroying large sections of British cities and killing thousands of civilians. The British, however, stubbornly resisted and Hitler eventually stopped.

In addition to the air blitz, Germany installed a naval blockade around Britain, preventing the shipment of food and supplies. When Britain could no longer afford to buy supplies and military equipment, the United States began to provide equipment and supplies to Britain and other countries who fought against Germany through the *Lend-Lease Act* of March 1941.

(3) *German invasion of the Soviet Union*: While British resistance continued, Hitler opened a second front and invaded the Soviet Union, violating a treaty between the two countries. The Germans drove deep into the Soviet Union, and by October 1941 German troops were only 50 miles from Moscow. Soviet troops suffered enormous losses in the first months of the German attack.

That fall German forces also surrounded Leningrad, trapping some three million people in a city that had only minimal food and supplies. The siege lasted over two years, and nearly a million people died from starvation and disease.

However, harsh Russian winters and a *scorched-earth policy* (burning crops and fields and destroying equipment as Soviet troops withdrew) took its toll on the German army. The Soviets' introduction of new troops and strategy finally started to turn the tide in 1943. This new Soviet offensive would eventually take the Soviets to Berlin and the end of the war.

(4) *Victories for the Allies*: The entry of the United States into the war in 1941, combined with the massive supplies and equipment provided to the Allies through the Lend-Lease Act, exerted a substantial impact on the war. By the end of 1942, victories in Eastern Europe, the Mediterranean, and the Pacific turned the momentum of the war against the Germans. In Western Europe, massive Allied invasions concentrated on ending Hitler's control.

One of the crucial battles was the landing of Allied troops on the beaches of France on *D-Day*, June 6, 1944. D-Day caught the Germans by surprise. Less than a month after the invasion, over a million Allied soldiers were in France. By the end of August, Paris was liberated and the Allies moved toward Germany.

In December 1944, Hitler made one last attempt to stop the Allied advance in the *Battle of the Bulge*. German troops and tanks took the Allies by surprise, and the Germans scored early successes. However, the shortage of gasoline for tanks and trucks soon halted the German offensive, and the Allies quickly regained the lost territory.

(5) *Surrender of Germany*: The Allies on both the eastern and western fronts quickly advanced on Germany, with the Soviet troops reaching Berlin first on April 21, 1945. On April 30, with the Soviets only blocks away from his underground headquarters in Berlin, Hitler committed suicide. A demoralized and devastated German army surrendered unconditionally on *V-E Day*, May 8, 1945. Because of strong feelings against the Germans who had led the world into such devastating war, many of the surviving Nazi leaders were arrested and put on trial for "crimes against humanity." The trials began in 1945 in *Nuremberg*, Germany, and brought to light many of the atrocities committed by the Nazis during the war.

c.  Asian war
    (1) *Japanese expansion*: The war in Europe left many of the European colonies in Asia undefended. Japan quickly conquered these territories and took its place alongside Italy and Germany as the third member of the Axis powers. The United States tried to put an end to Japanese expansion through negotiating, limiting trade, and banning the export of war materials.

19

(2) *Pearl Harbor*: Japanese leaders, however, decided to cripple American naval bases in the Pacific and make it impossible for the Americans to interfere in Asia. On December 7, 1941, Japanese planes attacked Pearl Harbor, virtually destroying the American fleet in Hawaii. At almost the same time, Japanese planes attacked other American and British bases. Both countries immediately declared war against Japan.

(3) *The Pacific*: During the next year, while the United States attempted to rebuild its naval forces, Japan conquered a number of Asian countries. To bring the war closer to home for the Japanese, American forces began bombing raids on the capital city of Tokyo in 1942. One month later, Japan suffered its most serious defeat of the war near the island of Midway, a battle that marked a turning point in Japanese momentum. With the end of the war in Europe, the United States was able to divert more resources to the Pacific and started to liberate strategic islands on the way to Japan.

(4) *New weapon to end the war*: The United States decided to drop the first atomic bomb in history in an effort to accelerate the end of the war. Early in August 1945, a bomb was dropped on the Japanese city of Hiroshima, resulting in the death of over 80,000 people and the destruction of over 60 percent of the city. A second bomb was dropped shortly afterward on the city of Nagasaki, with equally devastating results.

The world was horrified by the destructiveness of this new weapon. The Soviet Union declared war on Japan and invaded Manchuria to increase pressure on the Japanese to surrender. On *V-J Day*, August 15, 1945, Japan's emperor announced the defeat of the Japanese people. Documents of surrender were signed on September 2, 1945.

**d.** Postwar developments

(1) *United Nations*: When Allied leaders met during the closing days of World War II, they began to make plans for the postwar years. The plans included establishing a world organization to help maintain world peace and prevent a third world war. By the fall of 1945, the Charter of the United Nations was ratified by the primary powers of the postwar world (the United States, Great Britain, China, France, and the Soviet Union) and by a majority of other member nations. The United Nations eventually established its headquarters in New York City.

(2) *Cold war*: The United States and the Soviet Union emerged as the two strongest nations in the postwar world. Although relations between the two countries had never been very friendly, and their political systems were diametrically opposed, they had both been members of the alliance that fought against Germany. However, after the war, rivalry and suspicion came to characterize their relationship. The result was an atmosphere of tension in which the two countries competed for influence through military aid, economic aid, and military strategy. This period became known as the cold war.

Germany served as a focal point for many of the tensions between the two *superpowers*. After the end of the war, sections of Germany were occupied by the Allies. When France, Britain, and the United States agreed to consolidate their areas to form a West German state, the Soviets reacted with a blockade of Berlin. Germany became divided between West Germany, representative of the United States' influence over Western Europe, and East Germany, symbolic of the Soviet Union's control over Eastern Europe. Tension again flared between the two powers in 1961, when the East German government built a wall closing off East Berlin from the western part of the city.

(3) *Revolution in China*: In China a revolution in 1912 had replaced the rule of the emperor with a republican, "nationalist" regime. However, this new government failed to control many regions, and its power was challenged by other political groups, including a growing communist party. Following invasion by Japan in the 1930s, the country united in the war effort. However, after the Japanese defeat in 1945, China entered a

period of civil war between the nationalist government and the communists. The war ended in 1949 when the communists, led by Mao Zedong, captured Beijing. The nationalists, led by Chiang Kai-shek, fled to the offshore island of Taiwan, where they established a government in exile.

The communists in China set up a Soviet-style regime, outlawing private enterprise and opposition political parties, centralizing control of the economy, and attempting rapid industrialization. At first aided by the Soviet Union, by the end of the 1950s China had broken relations with the other great communist power. Thereafter, China pursued an independent course in world affairs. By the 1980s many traditional communist goals had been abandoned in favor of attempts at rapid economic modernization.

(4) *Africa*: At the end of World War II there were only four independent nations in Africa. Within the next 30 years, almost all the countries on the continent would gain self-rule. Although many African nations made steady, peaceful progress toward majority rule, others met with violence in the transition from colony to independent nation.

After independence, the nations of Africa began the process of self-development. Besides the problems of building a sense of national unity, they had to find ways to deal with political instability, weak economies, and low levels of education. The emphasis on industry for economic development hurt their agriculture and, combined with famines in the 1980s, served to bring hardship and poverty to many African nations.

South Africa remained distinct from the rest. South Africa maintains a policy of *apartheid*, segregation of whites from nonwhites in society. Other countries in Africa as well as those around the world have denounced this official policy and have sought ways to encourage majority rule in South Africa.

**B.** American History

**1.** Colonial Period

    **a.** Origins
After Christopher Columbus's discovery of the Caribbean, the voyages of *John Cabot* beginning in 1497 established England's claim to North America. Not until the 1580s, with the defeat of Spain, was Great Britain strong enough to follow up on Cabot's explorations and begin to establish settlements in North America. At the same time, Spain established a huge empire in the southern and western parts of America, and the French and the Dutch settled in the northern parts of the continent.

England established its first successful colony at Jamestown, Virginia, in 1607. Although the colonists faced several difficult years because of poor organization and severe winters, the introduction of tobacco as a major crop helped the settlement to prosper. *Captain John Smith* is largely credited with saving the Jamestown settlement.

In 1619 the first representative government in America began with the creation of the *House of Burgesses* in Virginia. King James I of England made Virginia a royal colony in 1624.

    **b.** The colonies
By 1733 a total of 13 colonies had developed along the Atlantic seaboard. Many of the colonies were formed as a result of religious or political belief. Whatever their origin, and whatever the intent of their individual founders, eventually they grew to resemble one another in culture and politics.

    **c.** Economy
The economies of the colonies varied with their geographical region. In New England agriculture was limited to subsistence farming, with little surplus. Much of the wealth in New England came from trading through the West Indies, Africa, and Britain. The

19

middle colonies were largely agricultural and produced fruit, grains, and vegetables for trade. This area also served as a center for shipping, commerce, and flour milling. The southern colonies consisted mainly of large plantations that produced tobacco, rice, and indigo.

The colonies were sparsely populated. To meet their demands for labor, colonists used *apprentices*, *indentured servants*, and *slaves*. There was little opposition to slavery among the colonists, although slave rebellions were fairly common. Considerable upward social mobility did exist in the colonies, though there were limitations on blacks, native American Indians, and women.

**d.** Government

The democracy that existed in the colonies reflected the democratic nature of government in England in the mid-1700s. The system consisted of a governor, a council, and an assembly. The governor was appointed by the king and was responsible for carrying out the monarch's interests. The council was appointed by the governor and provided him with support and advice. Members of the assembly were elected by popular vote of the male colonists. As time progressed, the assemblies gained more and more power in determining local government.

**2.** American Revolution

**a.** Causes

In the mid-1700s, Britain and France fought the *French and Indian War* for control of North America. Although Britain was largely victorious, the conduct of war so distant from home caused a significant drain on the country's resources. In addition, as British-controlled territory expanded, governing the colonies became increasingly difficult.

To deal with the issues of finance and control, the British enacted the *Proclamation of 1763*, the *Sugar Act*, and the *Stamp Act*. The purpose of the first piece of legislation was to limit westward colonization; the purpose of the latter two acts was to raise revenue from the colonists. The colonists were opposed to taxation, believing the British should shoulder the cost for troops stationed in America in return for the great wealth that flowed back to England from the colonies. When the determined colonists refused to import British goods, the Stamp Act was eventually repealed.

The British enacted additional pieces of legislation both to gain revenue and to suppress acts of rebellion by the colonists. In one of the most famous rebellions, the *Boston Tea Party*, colonists destroyed shiploads of tea. Britain retaliated with the *Coercive Acts*, which closed Boston Harbor. To strengthen their position, colonial leaders organized the *First Continental Congress* in 1774. Conditions worsened, however, and British soldiers and colonial *minutemen* fired on each other at Lexington and Concord in 1775.

A *Second Continental Congress* met in May 1775 to begin preparations for war and also to petition the King of England, *George III*, to repeal the Coercive Acts and restore peace. The colonists eventually broke from Britain with the *Declaration of Independence* in 1776. *George Washington* became the commander in chief of the army (representing the Congress) that would fight the Revolutionary War.

**b.** The Revolutionary War

In general, the war progressed from north to south, with early battles taking place in New England and later ones erupting in the middle and southern colonies. Hostilities initially centered on Boston, where the British defeated the colonists at *Bunker Hill*. Later, the Americans captured *Fort Ticonderoga*, and with the military equipment acquired there, American troops drove the British from Boston.

In 1777, after battles in the Carolinas, New York, and New Jersey, the British attempted to isolate New England in a three-pronged attack. The victories of American troops and the capture of British troops in New York encouraged the French to join the Americans openly as allies. France's entrance provided the Americans with badly needed supplies and money.

During the last two years of the war, the British concentrated their efforts on the southern colonies. At first successful, the British suffered major defeats. In 1781 a combined American–French force defeated the British at *Yorktown*, Virginia. This battle effectively ended the war.

**c.** Treaty of Paris

The peace treaty signed in Paris in 1783 provided the Americans with significant gains. They won recognition as an independent, *sovereign* nation. They gained most of the land from the Appalachian Mountains to the Mississippi River. They were guaranteed continued fishing rights off the coast of Canada. In return, they agreed to honor all debts owed to British merchants before the war and to return or purchase lands confiscated from British loyalists.

**3.** Constitution

**a.** Articles of Confederation

As the Revolutionary War progressed, Americans moved to create a government of their own. In 1781 the colonists signed the *Articles of Confederation*, the first constitution for the new government. The document provided for a loose alliance that preserved the independence of each of the states.

When economic problems at home as well as rivalries between the states reached a critical stage, the Congress called for a convention to revise the Articles of Confederation.

**b.** Constitutional Convention

In secret proceedings, the delegates to the Constitutional Convention, held in Philadelphia during the summer of 1787, agreed to develop a new constitution rather than revise the Articles of Confederation. The final *Constitution*, approved by the delegates later that year, was the result of a series of compromises between large and small states, north and south, and centralized versus decentralized views of government. George Washington was unanimously elected chairman of the convention.

Plans proposed by Virginia and New Jersey illustrate the key differences between the interests of the various states at the convention. The *Virginia Plan* called for a strong central government with three branches (a judiciary and a legislature with two houses). Election to either of the legislative houses was to be determined primarily by the size of each state's population. In contrast, the *New Jersey Plan*, representing the interests of smaller states, called for seats in the legislature to be divided equally among the states regardless of population. The *Great Compromise*, proposed by Connecticut and later adopted by members of the convention, suggested that representation in the lower house be based on population and membership in the upper house, or Senate, be equally divided between the states.

Eleven states had ratified the Constitution by 1788, and in 1789 national elections were held to choose a new government. Ratification was a difficult process that emphasized critical differences in opinion on the role and strength of government in the new United States.

19

**4.** Jacksonianism

    **a.** Changes in the country

    Several significant cultural and economic changes took place across the United States in the early 1800s. It was an era of dramatic economic growth, fostering the American "rags to riches" dream. America's rapid westward movement created new centers of wealth and political power. These changes encouraged ordinary people to believe that the nation's leadership could come from one of their own rather than from America's traditional elite.

    **b.** Andrew Jackson as President

    The election of Andrew Jackson in 1828 marked a significant change in the style and conduct of the presidency. Representing the "self-made man," Jackson exerted strong, if at times unconventional, control over the government. He promoted a system of *patronage*, giving his loyal supporters jobs in the government in the place of existing office-holders. He greatly expanded presidential powers and was the first President to use the veto to block undesirable legislation. His opposition to rechartering the Bank of the United States in 1832 was considered a major cause of the Panic of 1837 and the start of a depression in the United States.

    During Jackson's administration, thousands of native American Indians were driven from their homes in the east and pushed across the Mississippi River. In 1838 the American army uprooted the Cherokees in Georgia and placed them in detention camps, later moving them on foot to Oklahoma. More than 15,000 Indians made the brutal westward journey, which came to be known as the *Trail of Tears*. Over a quarter of them died en route.

**5.** Westward Movement

The opening of new lands to the west and the settlement of new territory characterized much of the 1800s. The defeat of the Mexican army in Texas, compromises with the British for the Oregon territory, and the California Gold Rush in 1848 were all key events that spurred the movement west.

**6.** Civil War

    **a.** Causes

    Divisions between the Northern and Southern states, dating back to the Constitutional Convention, deepened during the mid-1800s. The key issue was the right of each state to determine its laws and future, particularly in regard to the institution of slavery in the South. The conflict reached a crisis stage in 1850 when California sought entrance into the Union. The *Compromise of 1850* established an uneasy truce between North and South by admitting California as a free (nonslave) state, balanced with the enactment of a strong *Fugitive Slave Law*.

    The conflict again deepened with the U.S. Supreme Court ruling in 1858 in the *Dred Scott case*, which permitted slaveholders to take their slaves into new territories without restriction. The 1860 election of *Abraham Lincoln*, with his strong antislavery stand, triggered the secession of seven states from the Union. These Southern states, eventually joined by four others, formed the *Confederacy*.

    Congress attempted to enact laws to stop the breakup of the Union. Lincoln opposed such legislation, however, because it permitted the expansion of slavery. In April 1861, Confederate forces attacked Fort Sumter in South Carolina, marking the beginning of the Civil War.

**b.** Early Battles

The *Battle of Bull Run* (Virginia), the first major conflict of the Civil War, ended in a Northern defeat. The war shifted to the west, where the North won several victories. In the east, the South won a second battle at Bull Run. The Battle of Antietam, in Maryland, represented the South's first invasion of the North and ended in a draw.

In 1863 the battles of *Fredericksburg* and *Chancellorsville*, in Virginia and close to Washington, D.C., ended in Union defeat and left the Union demoralized. Taking advantage of this momentum, *General Robert E. Lee* continued to advance to *Gettysburg*, Pennsylvania. This battle marked a turning point in the war, ending in a massive defeat of the South.

**c.** Emancipation Proclamation

At the start of his presidency, Lincoln had intended not to abolish slavery but rather to confine it to the Southern states. As the war progressed, he changed his views. In 1863 he issued the Emancipation Proclamation, officially ending slavery in the United States. Thousands of black men enlisted in the Union army and made a significant contribution to the war effort.

**d.** Surrender

After a series of successful battles against the South, including Sherman's destructive march through Georgia in 1864, *General Ulysses Grant* pursued the armies of the Confederacy into Virginia. After a long and costly battle, Lee met with Grant at the *Appomattox Court House* and arranged the formal terms of surrender. This step effectively marked the end of the Civil War.

**7.** America's Industrial Revolution

Several events contributed to the surge in industry in the United States in the late 1800s. A railroad line was built from coast to coast in 1869, uniting different parts of the nation. The invention of the telegraph and telephone revolutionized communication. The steel industry, which sold many of its products to the railroads, underwent enormous expansion.

The rapid growth that followed dramatically changed American business and put the United States on the road to becoming a major industrial power. In order to raise the large amounts of capital necessary to finance large factories, *corporations*, a new type of business structure, were formed. To reduce competition and increase profits, corporations grouped together into *trusts* and held monopoly power over some markets. Growth was rapid but uneven, and the economy experienced many ups and downs.

The success of the new industrial system depended on *mass production*, which required large numbers of workers. The demand was filled by thousands of immigrants from Europe and Asia. Opposition to the influx of foreign workers led the government to enact laws restricting immigration.

**8.** World War I

**a.** The war in Europe

The assassination of Austrian Archduke Ferdinand and his wife in 1914 ignited hostilities between the nations of Europe and marked the beginning of World War I. The war was a result of rivalries between countries, increased militarism, and a rising sense of nationalism. Europe became divided into two major alliances. The Central Powers included Germany, Austria-Hungary, Bulgaria, and the Ottoman Empire (Turkey). The Allies included Britain, France, Russia, Italy, and several other countries.

**b.** American neutrality

At the beginning of World War I, President *Woodrow Wilson* struggled to maintain the neutrality of the United States. However, with the years of prolonged battle in Europe and the growing loss of American lives to German U-boats in the Atlantic, Wilson asked Congress to declare war on Germany in 1917.

**c.** American participation

The American decision to enter the war came at a crucial time. Allied forces in Europe were reaching a point of exhaustion and were running out of supplies. American naval forces, followed by American army troops, made a substantial difference in the war, stopping and then driving back German offensives. More than 2 million American soldiers, called *doughboys*, served in France. An armistice ended World War I in 1918. The peace treaty imposed harsh terms on the Germans.

**d.** League of Nations

Woodrow Wilson proposed a plan to Congress called the *Fourteen Points* that he believed would help achieve a lasting world peace through the establishment of a League of Nations. However, Wilson was not able to get the U.S. Senate to approve of his idea, and the United States never became a member of the League.

**9.** Great Depression

**a.** Causes

A recession followed the end of World War I and lasted until 1922. The rapid growth in the American economy through the 1920s ended with the *stock market crash of 1929*. Although economists disagree on the specific causes of the market crash, several factors are believed to have contributed. They include agricultural problems, high tariffs and war debts, a frail banking system, overproduction, excessive credit, and failure to increase the country's money supply. The crash was followed in the 1930s by the Great Depression.

The Great Depression had a tremendous effect on the nation. The value of assets like houses and land plummeted, and over one-fourth of the nation's workers were unemployed. One bad event contributed to another in domino fashion. As a result, many Americans lost faith in the country's business leaders, though they remained loyal to long-standing political traditions.

**b.** Franklin D. Roosevelt

President *Herbert Hoover's* efforts to end the Great Depression met with little success. By the time of the national elections of 1932, the country was ready for a change in leadership.

*Franklin D. Roosevelt*, the Democratic Party's candidate, won the election by a landslide. Roosevelt came from a wealthy and distinguished New York family. His charismatic personality, as well as his valiant fight against polio, gave him strong popular appeal.

(1) *First New Deal*: Upon taking office in 1933, Roosevelt assembled a group of advisers to develop a "new deal" for America. When the country's banking system appeared close to collapse, Roosevelt declared a temporary bank holiday. To begin industrial recovery, Roosevelt signed the *National Industrial Recovery Act* (which was later declared unconstitutional by the U.S. Supreme Court). To provide employment for the great number of jobless Americans, he created a variety of public works projects and agencies, including the Civilian Conservation Corps (CCC) and the Tennessee Valley Authority (TVA).

Despite its effectiveness in reducing economic problems, the New Deal came under attack from both the conservative right and the radical left. The conservatives believed that the programs were too expensive and provided for too much government interference in business. The radicals criticized the programs for not doing enough and suggested more extreme measures.

(2) *Second New Deal*: Building on many of the gains of the first New Deal, Roosevelt increased the government's efforts through the *Social Security Act* of 1935 (which provided pensions for retired workers), the *Works Progress Administration* (whose goal was to employ five million Americans), and the *Agricultural Adjustment Administration*, or *AAA* (designed to help rural areas).

(3) *Results*: Roosevelt's efforts during the Great Depression had mixed results. He was successful in bolstering employment and raising the standard of living, although not to pre-Depression levels. However, accomplishing these goals required rapid government expansion and increased public debt, which tripled during the 1930s. Even with these costs, the New Deal is credited with helping more Americans socially and economically than any other program in the nation's history.

10. World War II

   a. America's entry
      Although Europe was clearly on the brink of war in the late 1930s, the United States pursued a policy of *isolationism* from the affairs of Europe. Even as Germany's armies conquered Poland and France, Roosevelt kept the United States neutral. In the Far East, however, Japanese expansion to the west aroused concern, and the United States issued economic sanctions against Japan.

      American participation in the war began with the *Lend-Lease Act* of 1941, which allowed the United States to supply arms, machines, food, and medicine to the Allied countries of Europe. Japan's attack on Pearl Harbor on December 7, 1941, brought the United States officially into the war against both Japan and Germany.

   b. The United States during the war
      Though it had hoped to avoid war and was largely unprepared, the United States geared up quickly to contribute arms and supplies and later millions of troops to the war effort. Government agencies were set up to control production and inflation.

   c. European war
      At the beginning of the war, the bulk of America's military forces were pitted against Germany and the other Axis powers of Europe. By 1943 the Allies had liberated North Africa from the Germans. The Allies then attacked the "soft underbelly of Europe," landing in southern Italy in 1943. By the summer of 1944, the Allies had progressed only to Rome, but they were successful in engaging and holding hundreds of thousands of German troops there.

      On June 6, 1944, under the command of *General Dwight Eisenhower*, Allied troops landed on French beaches and began their assault of Western Europe. This massive invasion became known as *D-Day*. Allied forces continued to advance eastward and, in alliance with Soviet forces moving westward, in May 1945 forced the Germans to surrender, ending the war in Europe.

   d. Pacific war
      After crippling American naval forces during the attack on Pearl Harbor, the Japanese rapidly conquered new territory in the Pacific. The *Battle of Midway* in 1942, the first major victory for the American forces, became a turning point in the war. *General Douglas MacArthur*, commander of the American troops in the Pacific, used a policy of island hopping (conquering only strategically placed islands) to reach Japan. Early in

1945 American troops captured *Iwo Jima* and *Okinawa*, two islands near Japan that had been held by the Japanese for centuries.

For several years the United States had been secretly developing an atomic superweapon through the *Manhattan Project*. In August 1945, hoping to end the war quickly, *President Harry Truman* ordered that atomic bombs be dropped on the Japanese cities of *Hiroshima* and *Nagasaki*. After the second bomb was dropped, Japanese leaders sued for peace. A ceasefire went into effect, ending the war in the Pacific.

**11.** Korean War

Fears of a worldwide communist revolution prevailed in the late 1940s and increased with the success of the communist revolution in China in 1949. When communist North Korea invaded South Korea in 1950, President Truman decided to intervene with American troops under the guidance of the United Nations. Although technically called a *police action*, the confrontation in Korea escalated quickly into war.

The United States, largely unprepared for combat, offered little initial help to the South Koreans. They had been pushed far back to a small southeastern section of Korea called *Pusan* before the Americans, under the command of General Douglas MacArthur, were able to turn the war around. Encouraged by early successes, MacArthur and Truman determined to drive the communists out of all Korea (both North and South). American troops pursued the Korean communists all the way to the *Yalu River* on the border of China.

Threatened, the Chinese struck back. Over 200,000 Chinese troops crossed the Yalu River to fight against the Americans. In the retreat that followed, the communists temporarily recaptured Seoul, South Korea's capital city. The war became a virtual stalemate for the next three years. In 1951 Truman relieved MacArthur of his command when the general insisted on using American forces against China. An armistice was signed in 1953 under President Dwight Eisenhower.

**12.** Vietnam War

Vietnam, a southeast Asian country that had been a colony of France, was partitioned in 1954 between the communist regime in the north and a noncommunist regime in the south. Fighting broke out between the two sides, and in the south, communist guerrillas, aided by the communist north, fought the noncommunist government. Soon President Dwight Eisenhower sent U.S. military advisors to aid the noncommunists; additional help was later sent by President John F. Kennedy. However, the fighting continued, and in 1965 President Lyndon B. Johnson sent U.S. combat troops to battle the guerrillas; by the end of the 1960s more than 400,000 U.S. troops were fighting in Vietnam, and the United States also staged bombing raids on targets in the north.

As the cost of the war mounted, antiwar sentiment developed in the United States. The issue polarized national opinion, especially as no victory appeared in sight and as the fighting spread into other countries of Southeast Asia. Following the election of Richard Nixon to the presidency in 1968, negotiations were begun with the communist regime in the north, and over a period of several years U.S. troops were gradually withdrawn. Later, in 1975, the forces of the communist north seized power throughout Vietnam and the country was reunited.

**13.** Struggle for Human Rights

**a.** Rights for black Americans

Civil rights for black Americans, a long-standing issue in American politics, reached a peak in the 1960s. Bus boycotts by blacks in Montgomery, Alabama, *sit-ins* at segregated lunch counters throughout the South, *Freedom Riders* attempting to integrate previously all-white buses—these and other acts of protest prompted the administration of President *John Kennedy* to take action by vigorously enforcing the civil rights laws already in effect.

A crisis in Kennedy's civil rights program came in 1962 when *James Meredith* sought admission to the University of Mississippi, which previously had never admitted blacks. The governor of the state personally blocked the doorway, and President Kennedy eventually called in U.S. marshalls to escort Meredith onto campus.

The following year, a leader of the civil rights movement, the Rev. *Martin Luther King, Jr.*, led 250,000 people on a march on Washington, D.C., calling for jobs and an end to segregation and racial intolerance. His address marked a high point of black civil rights activism in America.

In 1964 and 1965 riots erupted in the *ghettos* of several major cities across the United States. The riots were a violent protest against entrenched unemployment for blacks and a low standard of living. The radical leader *Malcolm X* called for blacks to separate from white society and control their own destiny ("black power"). Other black leaders favored the nonviolent forms of protest initiated by Martin Luther King.

The *Civil Rights Act of 1964* and the *Voting Rights Act of 1965* brought down the final legal barriers to black equality in the United States. Although these acts in themselves did not end discrimination, they set the stage for the social reforms of the years to come.

The assassination of Martin Luther King in 1968 weakened the civil rights movement. At the same time, the black power movement lost momentum. Although all problems were not solved, substantial gains had been made. With segregation officially ended, many blacks won political office and made economic gains. Blacks became a political power in the country.

**b.** Women's rights

In terms of population, women are a majority in the United States. Yet in matters of social and economic equality, they have much in common with minority groups. In the 1970s, as women entered the job market in increasing numbers, they encountered discrimination and narrow views about the place of women in society.

Proponents of the *women's movement* argued that women should be allowed to pursue their own interests, that they should be given the same job opportunities as men, and that work at home should be shared evenly between the sexes.

Aided by equal opportunity laws and by affirmative action programs mandated by the government, women have gained jobs in industries and professions that had previously been closed to them. But even today most women-held jobs pay only about two-thirds as much as jobs dominated by men.

19

# GOVERNMENT

## I. American Documents

**A.** Articles of Confederation

    **1.** Background
The *Second Continental Congress* served as the nation's first national government from 1775 to the adoption of the Articles of Confederation in 1781. Although the Second Continental Congress was instrumental in preparing the Declaration of Independence and serving as a central authority for the War of Independence from Great Britain, it became apparent that a new government was needed with stronger authority, primarily in domestic affairs. Not until 1781 was unanimous consent obtained from the 13 states to the provisions of this new government.

    **2.** Characteristics

        **a.** Under the *Articles of Confederation*, all the functions of a national government were to be performed by the legislature. No separate executive or judicial branches were designated, perhaps because of the colonists' poor experience with Great Britain's executive and judicial administration of the colonies.

        **b.** Each state had one vote, with unanimous consent required for all important decisions and three-fourths consent required for all other decisions. Each state cast its vote on decisions according to specific instructions from the state legislature.

    **3.** Weaknesses

        **a.** The national legislature, called the *Confederation Congress*, was not capable of effectively performing the executive and judicial functions of a national government.

        **b.** The Congress had no independent authority to enforce whatever decisions it might reach. All enforcement power remained with the individual states, and the Congress could not punish the states if they failed to implement decisions.

        **c.** In response to the concerns raised by Great Britain's taxation policies in the colonies, the Confederation Congress had deliberately not been granted the authority to tax or in any other way regulate the financial affairs of the states. Worthless government paper currency and the erection of barriers to interstate commerce were problems the Congress was powerless to correct.

        **d.** The fact that individual states retained considerable freedom in national defense and relations with foreign powers inhibited the Confederation Congress's ability to operate as a central authority.

        **e.** The rule of unanimous consent for all important decisions made such decisions almost impossible to implement. Potential amendments to the Articles of Confederation were endlessly debated but never agreed upon because of the various competing interests of the states. The situation deteriorated so badly that the only viable solution was a complete overhaul of the system, resulting in the Constitution in 1787.

**B.** Constitution

    **1.** Article I: Legislative Powers

        **a.** Express powers
All legislative powers of the national government are vested in the *Congress* of the United States. The Constitution enumerates several powers, including two important ones

absent under the Articles of Confederation: the power to collect taxes and the power to regulate all commerce between the states as well as with foreign nations.

**b.** Implied powers
Congress has the authority to make all laws necessary and proper to carry out the general powers given to it by the Constitution, even if such powers are not specifically stated. Only powers expressly prohibited to Congress by the Constitution are excluded.

**c.** Structure
Congress is divided into (1) a *House of Representatives* chosen by direct vote of the people, with each state represented in proportion to its population, and (2) a *Senate* in which each state has the equal representation of two senators.

Members of Congress cannot be removed on the basis of unpopular decisions (thereby correcting a problem under the Articles of Confederation), but serve for a specified length of time. Only death and certain specified crimes warrant removal of a member of Congress from office before a term expires.

**2.** Article II: Executive Power
The *President* of the United States of America is given the *executive authority* to implement the laws passed by Congress. The President is also designated as the Commander in Chief of the armed forces of the national government and of the militia of the various states when called into national service.

Provision is made for the President to establish an executive staff (Cabinet) to assist in the faithful execution of the laws.

Additional executive responsibilities include maintaining relationships with foreign nations and making treaties with other nations, such treaties to be effective only upon two-thirds approval of the Senate.

**3.** Article III: Judicial Power
A system of federal courts has the power to enforce federal laws. (Under the Articles of Confederation, there were no federal courts. Enforcement was in the hands of the various state courts.) Federal courts also have the power to overrule any state laws deemed to be incompatible with the Constitution and supporting federal laws. Disputes between the states as well as any disputes with the federal government are within the authority of the federal courts to rule upon.

Judges on the federal court cannot be removed on the basis of unpopular decisions, but only in the event of a commission of a crime. Their pay cannot be reduced in the event of unpopular decisions. (Both of these changes served to correct deficiencies present in the states' judicial systems, which exercised the real judicial power under the Articles of Confederation.)

**4.** Articles IV, V, VI: Federal–State Relations
The supremacy of the federal government over the various state governments in certain key areas is specified.

**a.** The Constitution and laws enacted by Congress are designated as the supreme law of the land, superseding any conflicting state laws or state judicial decisions.

**b.** The federal government is responsible for the protection of the several states from invasion or threats to a republican form of government.

**c.** Formation and admittance of new states into the United States are based on procedures adopted by the federal government.

19

**d.** Each state is required to respect the laws and the rights of the other states. No state may discriminate against citizens of other states in order to benefit its own citizens.

**e.** Changes to the Constitution can be made by the several states only under the procedures outlined in the Constitution. Unanimous consent is not required, but three-fourths of the states must agree to any change.

**C.** The Bill of Rights

One of the primary reasons Americans fought for independence from Great Britain was to protect their personal freedoms. Yet the original Constitution was largely silent on this important issue. Adoption of the Constitution was made contingent upon adding specific protections for civil liberties as soon as possible after ratification.

The first ten amendments to the Constitution, collectively known as the *Bill of Rights*, were approved by the states in 1791. Individuals are guaranteed that government will not infringe on their personal rights in several crucial areas, provided an appropriate balance is maintained between an individual's rights and the rights of society as a whole.

**1.** Freedom of Religion

Americans are provided the freedom to practice the religion of their choice, or to practice no religion at all. Government is prohibited from giving preference to one religion or religious group over all others.

**2.** Freedom of Speech and Press

Although the Bill of Rights specifically prohibits the enactment of laws restricting the freedom of speech or the press, an individual does not have an absolute right to say or publish anything he or she wishes. This freedom may be restricted if it produces a "clear and present danger." Restriction will occur only if the chance for danger is so imminent that the prohibition must be immediate.

**3.** Freedom of Assembly and Petition

Americans have the right to gather into groups, provided such assembly is peaceful. Police retain the right to disband any meeting that could reasonably be expected to turn into a riot. The freedom to petition gives every individual the right to make his or her grievances known to the appropriate government official for consideration without fear of being arrested for simply complaining, provided the approach is peaceful.

**4.** Right to Bear Arms

Although the Constitution appears to confirm "the right of the people to keep and bear arms," the more consistent interpretation has been that the protection extends to the right of the states to maintain a militia. Individuals do not have the absolute freedom to own or use whatever weapons they desire.

**5.** Freedom from Unreasonable Search and Seizure

Police may search and seize an individual's person, house, papers, and effects only so long as there is "probable cause" that a crime has been committed or that the public safety is endangered. A person may be arrested through a warrant issued under the proper procedures.

**6.** Freedom from Loss of Life, Liberty, and Property

An individual is protected from having to stand trial for a major crime unless a formal charge (an indictment) is made by a grand jury. Such an indictment will be made only when the grand jury has been persuaded there is a reasonable chance of conviction.

Individuals may not be forced to testify against themselves, and silence may not be interpreted as guilt. In addition, an individual is protected against *double jeopardy* (being tried twice for the same crime), although the interpretation of what actually constitutes double jeopardy is complex.

A broad protection exists so that an individual may not be deprived of life, liberty, or property by the government without *due process of law*. There is no precise definition of due process. In general, the concept means that an individual is presumed innocent until proved guilty. The government must consistently apply proper legal procedures in all cases where an individual's life, liberty, or property may be taken away.

7. Right to a Jury Trial
The right to a jury trial is guaranteed in all criminal cases and in all common-law civil suits where the amount in contention is over $20. Jurors must be impartial and render a decision based solely on the facts presented during the trial.

Defendants are guaranteed that the trial will begin as soon as possible after the indictment has been made. Normally, the trial is held in the area where the alleged crime was committed. During the trial, the defendant has a right to secure his or her own witnesses, to cross-examine the prosecution's witnesses, and to have an attorney assist in his or her defense.

8. Freedom from Unreasonable Punishment
Government is prohibited from inflicting on an individual (a) excessive bail, (b) excessive fines, or (c) cruel and unusual punishment during the trial process.

In practice, there is no fixed standard as to what constitutes excessive bail. Defendants accused of certain major crimes may even be denied the opportunity of posting bail to gain temporary freedom. An excessive fine is one that is out of proportion to the damage caused by the crime or civil violation.

The prohibition against cruel and unusual punishment is designed to prevent an individual convicted of a crime from enduring torture or serving a long prison term for a relatively minor crime.

9. Implied Rights of the Individual
Individuals are not denied personal rights simply because such rights are not specifically protected by the Constitution. Government must extend its protection beyond the expressed freedoms contained in the Bills of Rights.

10. Implied Rights of the States
The states are not denied rights simply because such rights are not specifically mentioned in the Constitution.

D. Other Important Constitutional Amendments

The Thirteenth Amendment (1865) formally abolishes slavery within the United States or any place subject to its jurisdiction. Congress has the authority to enact appropriate legislation to enforce abolition.

The Fourteenth Amendment (1868) protects the individual's life, liberty, and property from being taken by the states without due process of law. It also requires the states to give equal protection to all citizens under the law and prohibits discrimination against certain classes.

The Fifteenth Amendment (1870) guarantees the vote to all citizens regardless of race, color, or previous status as a slave. Neither the federal government nor the various states can abridge this right to vote.

The Sixteenth Amendment (1913) gives the federal government the power to collect an income tax.

The Seventeenth Amendment (1913) provides for United States senators to be elected directly by the people in the various states, replacing the earlier method of electing senators in the state legislatures.

19

The Nineteenth Amendment (1919) guarantees the vote to all citizens regardless of sex. Neither the federal government nor the various states can restrict this right.

The Twenty-fourth Amendment (1964) provides that citizens shall not be required to pay a fee to be able to vote in federal elections.

The Twenty-sixth Amendment (1971) provides that citizens over 18 years old shall not be prohibited from voting because of age.

**E.** Major Court Interpretations of the Constitution

The framers of the Constitution deliberately stated concepts in broad terms to keep the document flexible in the face of changing events. Consequently, few statutes are as imprecise as the key phrases of the Constitution. The continuing relevance of the document stems from the interpretations by the Supreme Court in key cases brought before that body. Following are nine major Supreme Court cases that have had a significant effect on the interpretation of the Constitution over the last two centuries.

**1.** Marbury vs. Madison (1803)

The Constitution makes no mention of the concept of *judicial review*. The Supreme Court assigned itself that right in the Marbury decision. Under the doctrine of judicial review, the court has the power to determine the constitutionality of the actions of the executive and legislative branches of government. Any act determined by the Supreme Court to be in violation of the Constitution automatically becomes null and void.

**2.** McCulloch vs. Maryland (1819)

The Supreme Court established the supremacy of the federal government over the states in those areas in which the federal government has express responsibility under the Constitution. In such areas, the states cannot restrict or hamper the federal government from taking all "necessary and proper" actions to implement its constitutional mandates. Only the judicial review function of the Supreme Court can restrain the implied powers of the federal government.

In addition, the states are denied the authority to tax the federal government (and vice versa, since "the power to tax implies the power to destroy").

**3.** Dartmouth College vs. Woodward (1819)

The Dartmouth decision made an important contribution to the economic stability of the nation by prohibiting the states from negating legal contracts between individuals. A corporation has the same rights as an individual when entering into contracts.

**4.** Gibbons vs. Ogden (1824)

Equally important for the economic growth of the nation was the Supreme Court decision giving broad powers to the federal government to implement its constitutional mandate on interstate commerce. The court held that the power of the federal government to regulate interstate commerce implies the power to regulate commerce of any kind that involves the passage of goods or people between the states. With interstate commerce forever removed from interference by the states, the way was paved for increasing federal regulation.

**5.** Munn vs. Illinois (1876)

Opposed to the concept of judicial review is the concept of *judicial restraint*. The Supreme Court confirmed that it had no business interfering in matters properly left to the individual states. Application of judicial restraint often varies, however, depending on prevailing interpretations of which issues are solely within the jurisdiction of the several states.

**6.** Plessy vs. Ferguson (1896)

The Supreme Court ruled that the *equal protection* provision of the Fourteenth Amendment ensured all citizens political equality but not necessarily social equality. States could pass laws providing for the segregation of the races, thereby perpetuating discrimination in all forms of human exchange except such activities as voting and holding elective office. As long as the intent of such state laws was to establish "separate but equal" (nonpolitical) conditions, these laws would be viewed as constitutional.

**7.** Brown vs. Board of Education of Topeka (1954)
Formally overturning the Plessy vs. Ferguson ruling, the Supreme Court interpreted the Fourteenth Amendment as prohibiting "separate but equal" state legislation, specifically declaring racially segregated schools to be unconstitutional.

Although this decision was a milestone in directing the nation's attention to equal social protection under the laws, it constituted only a first step. Both enforcement of the decision and elimination of segregation in all its forms still face obstacles today.

**8.** Miranda vs. Arizona (1966)
The Bills of Rights is designed to protect the personal freedoms of the individual from infringement by the federal government. Included in these freedoms are the individual's right to counsel and the protection against self-incrimination. In the Miranda decision, the Supreme Court held that the states must also protect the personal freedoms of their citizens from infringement.

Regardless of whether a case is being handled by federal or state authorities, no confession obtained through interrogation can be used against the accused unless the accused is first warned of his or her right to counsel and the right to remain silent until an attorney is consulted. Convictions obtained through violations of an individual's personal rights as described above are unconstitutional, and the defendant must be set free even if guilty. In this instance, the right of the individual is considered more important than the right of society.

**9.** New York Times Company vs. United States (1971)
In a decision upholding the right of the press to publish government documents obtained through private sources, the Supreme Court interpreted the Bill of Rights as permitting the press to "be left free to publish views, whatever the source, without censorship, injunctions, or prior restraints," except in extreme cases of national danger.

## II. Levels of Government

**A.** Branches of the Federal Government

  **1.** Executive Branch

    **a.** President
      (1) Constitutional responsibilities
      Article II of the Constitution assigns the President the following functions:

      (a) responsibility to ensure that all laws are faithfully executed; (b) power to serve as Commander in Chief of the armed forces of the United States; (c) power to grant reprieves and pardons for offenses against the United States, except in cases of impeachment; (d) power to make treaties, provided two-thirds of the Senate concurs; (e) power to commission all officers of the United States; (f) power to appoint ambassadors, other public ministers and consuls, judges of the Supreme Court, and all other officers of the United States not otherwise provided for, with the consent of the Senate (the Senate may waive the consent requirement for lesser officers); (g) power to fill vacancies in the above-named categories during the recess of the Senate; (h) responsibility to give Congress information on the *state of the union*, including the recommendations for necessary actions to be taken by the legislative branch; (i) power to call Congress into extraordinary session to consider matters of extreme

19

importance; and (j) power to obtain the written opinion of the principal officers of the various executive departments regarding any matter within their jurisdiction.

(2) Additional powers

Over the last two centuries, the President has gained additional executive power—as well as legislative and judicial power—in the execution of these constitutional responsibilities.

(a) Executive authority: Although technically the President must secure the Senate's approval for all appointments, the Senate does not require the President to seek its approval for numerous top-level positions. The President does not need Senate approval to dismiss an appointed officeholder. Treaties with foreign nations require approval of two-thirds of the Senate. In practice, however, relations with foreign nations are determined less often by formal treaties than by executive agreements. These executive agreements are negotiated by the President (and his staff) without ultimate Senate approval.

(b) Judicial authority: Senate approval is required for all presidential appointments to federal courts. However, Senate approval is usually automatic if the candidate is deemed competent. Thus the President can select people who closely reflect his views on the interpretation of the law and exert a long-lasting (although indirect) influence on judicial decisions.

(c) Legislative authority: Early in the nation's history, the President's state of the union report to Congress emphasized past achievements, offering only general advice as to what Congress should consider doing in the future. No other specific mention is made in the Constitution about the President's impact on proposed legislation. Today the President has become a major initiator of proposed legislation, sending Congress detailed proposals capable of being approved without alteration (although Congress always introduces some changes).

Article I of the Constitution, which details legislative responsibilities, permits the President to override congressional legislation through the *veto power*. Presidential vetoes can in turn be overridden by Congress.

**b.** Vice President

Other than becoming President upon the death, resignation, impeachment, or incapacity of the incumbent President, the *Vice President* is assigned only one official duty under the Constitution: "The Vice President of the United States shall be President of the Senate, but shall have no vote, unless the Senate be equally divided."

Modern Presidents have significantly enhanced the authority of their Vice Presidents by assigning them responsibility for coordination of key aspects of executive authority, such as chairing important presidential councils and committees.

**c.** Executive Office of the President

Established in 1939, the *Executive Office* of the President consists of a number of agencies and councils that are directly responsible to the President in assisting him in carrying out executive powers. Key components of the Executive Office include:

(1) The White House staff, which is responsible for handling the daily affairs of the White House and serving as liaison with all branches of government as well as with the public.

(2) The Office of Management and Budget, with responsibility for preparing, administering, and evaluating the immense fiscal program of the federal government.

(3) The National Security Council, which coordinates military activities and advises the President on all matters relating to national security.

(4) The Domestic Council, with responsibility for formulating and coordinating domestic policy recommendations to the President, as assisted by the Council of Economic Advisers.

**d.** Cabinet

The Constitution does not specify how the President "shall take care that the laws be faithfully executed." Congress has approved of the creation of several executive *Cabinet* departments to assist the President in this overall task.

Secretaries of the various Cabinet departments perform three major duties: (1) managing the department, (2) representing the department in its relationship with Congress, and (3) advising the President on issues of relevance to the particular department. Presidents tend to rely on Cabinet secretaries more for the execution of presidential policy than for the formulation of policy.

Cabinet departments are regularly created and abolished. The current list includes the Departments of State, Treasury, Defense, Justice, Interior, Agriculture, Commerce, Labor, Health and Human Services, Housing and Urban Development, Transportation, and Education.

**2.** Legislative Branch

**a.** Structure

As provided for in the Constitution, the Congress is responsible for creating the nation's laws. Congress consists of a House of Representatives and a Senate. Representatives are elected for a term of two years and senators for a term of six years, with one-third of the Senate seats up for election every two years. There are minimum age and citizenship requirements for those desiring to be elected to Congress.

The Senate consists of 100 members, with each state electing two senators. There are 435 members of the House of Representatives, all chosen by popular vote from districts within each state. To win a seat in Congress, a candidate needs to receive a plurality of the votes cast.

Both the Senate and the House of Representatives elect majority and minority leaders to coordinate congressional responsibilities. The Constitution provides for the House to elect one representative as its presiding officer, or *Speaker of the House*. Under the Constitution the Vice President is the *President of the Senate*, but real power within the Senate is concentrated in other Senate offices.

**b.** Expressed powers

Unlike its vague description of the duties of the executive branch, the Constitution is quite specific in listing the responsibilities of Congress.

(1) Legislative

Congress's prime responsibility is to enact laws that will enable the federal government to (a) collect taxes; (b) borrow money; (c) regulate interstate commerce; (d) regulate bankruptcy; (e) regulate the coining and printing of money; (f) establish and maintain the postal system; (g) control the granting of copyrights and patents; (h) establish a federal court system in support of the Supreme Court; (i) declare war and provide for the national defense; (j) govern the District of Columbia; and (k) make all laws necessary and proper for the implementation of the above responsibilities, unless otherwise prohibited by the Constitution.

(2) Judicial

The judicial powers of Congress include the right to (a) define federal offenses; (b) specify the punishment for each category of federal offense; and (c) impeach and remove federal officials who are found to have violated their oaths of office.

19

(3) Executive

Executive powers of Congress are exercised primarily through the *advice and consent* responsibility regarding presidential appointments and treaties.

(4) Constitutional

Congress plays a key role in amending the Constitution. Any proposed change must pass both the Senate and the House of Representatives by a two-thirds vote before being sent to the states for approval by three-quarters of the state legislatures.

**c.** Delegated powers

Congress has often been accused of informally delegating its legislative powers to the executive branch by responding to detailed presidential legislative proposals instead of creating laws on its own initiative.

Congress has formally delegated some of its constitutional powers to independent *government agencies* created through congressional legislation. Members of these agencies are appointed by the President with the approval of the Senate. Many of these independent government agencies have legislative authority to enact their own regulations, executive authority to enforce their own regulations, and judicial authority to punish (through fines and sanctions, not jail terms) those who violate their regulations.

Independent government agencies may serve either a regulatory function or an administrative function. Examples of the former include the Interstate Commerce Commission, the Federal Trade Commission, and the Securities and Exchange Commission. Examples of the latter include the Veterans Administration and the U.S. Postal Service.

**3.** Judicial Branch

**a.** Structure

The Constitution states that "the judicial power of the United States shall be vested in one Supreme Court, and in such inferior Courts as the Congress may from time to time ordain and establish." The constitutionally specified *Supreme Court* consists of a chief justice and eight associate justices appointed by the President (for life) with the consent of the Senate.

Congress has established federal *district courts* to try almost all cases arising under federal law. Eleven federal *courts of appeals* serve as a last appeal for most district court decisions. Specialized federal courts and courts of appeals handle certain categories of cases. Examples are the Tax Court and the Court of Military Appeals.

Like the Supreme Court justices, all federal judges are appointed by the President with the consent of the Senate. Each appointment is for life, subject to the "good behavior" of the judge.

**b.** Function

(1) Original jurisdiction

A court has *original jurisdiction* when a certain type of case must be brought before it first. The Constitution gives the Supreme Court original jurisdiction over only two types of cases: (a) those affecting foreign diplomats and (b) those in which a state is a party. The other federal courts, primarily the district courts, have original jurisdiction over all other cases involving the Constitution, federal issues, and relations with foreign entities.

(2) Appellate jurisdiction

A court has *appellate jurisdiction* when it has the authority to redecide a case already heard by another court. The process is usually initiated only when one of the parties in the case has appealed the decision of the first court. The function of an appeals court is not to rehear the facts of a particular case, but rather to determine whether the law was applied correctly to those facts.

The various federal appeals courts have appellate jurisdiction over the decisions of the federal district courts and administrative rulings of federal agencies. An appeals court does not have to hear a case whose decision has been appealed if it believes courtroom procedures were correctly followed and the law was correctly applied.

The U.S. Supreme Court has appellate jurisdiction over every other court in the nation. The Supreme Court exercises this jurisdiction, however, only when it believes a case involves a basic principle of constitutional or federal law that it wishes to examine.

Usually the Supreme Court will accept only those cases that have already been decided by a federal appellate court or a state supreme court. The Supreme Court ultimately hears less than 5 percent of the cases that are appealed to it.

**B.** State and Local Governments

**1.** State Government

**a.** Constitution

*State constitutions* take precedence over all nonfederal laws and have the following basic elements in common:

(1) A preamble outlining the power of the state government.

(2) A bill of rights and other procedural rights, usually paralleling those in the federal Constitution.

(3) Provision for a separation of powers into the executive, legislative, and judicial branches, with an emphasis on legislative power quite similar in intent to that of the federal Constitution.

(4) Articles on voting rights, elections, taxation, and spending, including restrictions on taxation and spending methods.

(5) Provision for amending the state constitution, a process that varies widely among the several states.

(6) Provision for the organization and powers of local governments as subdivisions of state government.

**b.** Executive branch

(1) Governor

The chief executive official in each of the states is called the *governor*. All states elect governors by direct vote of the citizens, with the usual term of office being four years. Each state has minimum age, citizenship, and residency requirements for those desiring to be governor.

Official powers of the governor closely resemble those accorded the President by the federal Constitution: (a) the role of commander in chief of the state's law enforcement, militia, and emergency personnel; (b) responsibility for ensuring that all state laws are faithfully executed; (c) duty to provide a "state of the state" message to the legislature; and (d) power to require any subordinate state or local official to provide information on matters relating to official duties.

Additional responsibilities and powers may include (a) submission of an annual proposed state budget to the legislature; (b) power to veto a bill or even parts of a bill (the "line item" veto); (c) power to appoint high-level administrative officials, although usually not unilateral freedom to remove such officials; and (d) power to pardon or alter the sentences of criminals convicted under state law.

State constitutions provide for the involuntary removal of governors. Virtually all the states specify an impeachment process for "high crimes and misdemeanors" not unlike that outlined in the federal Constitution. Over one-fourth of the states permit the electorate to remove a governor (as well as other state officials) via the *recall*, whereby a certain percentage of voters indicate they want the governor to leave office before the end of the term because of dissatisfaction with the governor's conduct of office.

(2) Additional executive positions
(a) Elected officials

Most states require the governor to share executive authority with several other officials who are elected at the same time and for the same term as the governor. Such elected state officials usually include (i) a lieutenant governor, who serves as acting chief executive when the governor is out of the state; (ii) an attorney general, who functions as the state's chief law officer; (iii) a secretary of state, who is responsible for the certification of elections and maintenance of the state administrative code; (iv) a state treasurer, who supervises the tax collection and revenue spending tasks of the state; and (v) a state superintendent of public instruction, who supervises the state's administration of the public school system.

(b) Appointed officials

Often the governor of a state is given the authority to appoint, with the consent of the legislature (occasionally even without such consent), senior administrative officials who have responsibility for administering the various state departments regulating the following areas: agriculture, banking, civil defense, commerce, conservation, health and welfare, transportation, insurance, employment and human relations, law enforcement, and highways.

**c.** Legislative branch

All states except Nebraska have a legislative structure patterned after the U.S. Congress, with a senate and a house of representatives (sometimes referred to as the assembly) whose members are elected by local citizens. (Nebraska has a one-house legislature.) Senators usually serve four years and representatives two years. Salaries are relatively low. *State legislatures* meet in official session for only a small portion of the year.

Leadership of the state legislature is consistent with that of Congress. Most of the states grant the official post of president of the senate to the lieutenant governor, while the leader of the house of representatives is a speaker of the house elected by the representatives.

Because state legislatures convene in official session for only a few months a year (some state bodies convene once every two years), committees of the legislature play an even more crucial role than those in the federal Congress to ensure that legislative functions are carried out.

A state legislature has the authority to enact legislation in any area not prohibited to it by either the federal Constitution or the constitution of the state. Legislation usually springs from one of the following broad areas of state authority:

(1) The police power of the state to promote the public safety, health, and welfare of its residents.

(2) The responsibility of the state to provide for the public education of all the state's residents.

(3) The regulation of all business activity within the state (such as the chartering of corporations).

(4) The authority to tax residents of the state in order to implement its several duties.

Several states permit voters to become directly involved in the legislative process through the *initiative* and the *referendum*. The initiative process enables private citizens to construct proposed legislation and submit the proposal directly to the voters. If a majority of the voters approve, the proposal becomes law. In many states certain laws cannot be enforced until voters specifically approve of the legislation through a referendum.

**d.** Judicial branch

Most state court systems can be divided into four categories or levels, as follows.

(1) Local courts

Local courts, or courts of *limited jurisdiction*, handle traffic cases, small claims, misdemeanors, and preliminary hearings for felony cases. A "justice of the peace" renders decisions in such cases without a jury and typically has no formal training in the law.

(2) District courts

District courts, or courts of *general jurisdiction*, are responsible for handling larger cases that arise within the geographic jurisdiction of a county or a city. A district court usually has authority over criminal cases involving felonies, important civil cases, and some appeals from courts of limited jurisdiction. In general, the district court makes the original decision in most cases involving state law or the state constitution.

District court judges have formal legal training and experience as lawyers and can be appointed or elected, depending on the state. District courts operate under the jury system.

(3) Appellate courts

Several states have intermediate appellate courts to handle appeals from the lower courts and thereby relieve the load of the state supreme court. As in the federal system, state appellate courts limit their involvement to those cases where the law may have been incorrectly applied to the given facts. Appellate judges are members of the legal profession and render decisions without a jury. Most states provide for the election of such judges.

(4) Supreme court

Every state has a supreme court to serve as the ultimate court of appeals for the various lower courts in the state judicial system. *State supreme courts* have the final say on interpretations of the state constitution and state statutes. Some states also permit the supreme court to exercise original jurisdiction over a limited category of cases.

There are up to nine justices on a state supreme court. The vast majority of the states provide for the popular election of these justices, although incumbents usually win reelection and thus may serve for life. Normally, a candidate for state supreme court justice must have an approval rating from the state bar association demonstrating exemplary prior experience as a judge.

State supreme court decisions are based on the interpretation of state law or the state constitution as applied to the facts established at the lower court level. Such decisions are reached without a jury. There is no appeal from a state supreme court decision, unless the U.S. Supreme Court decides to hear the case on federal constitutional grounds.

**19**

**2.** Local Government

Local government units have no authority beyond that granted specifically by the state government. The U.S. Bureau of the Census identifies five basic types of local government: (a) county, (b) municipality, (c) township, (d) school district, and (e) special district. County and municipal governments constitute the most influential forms of local government.

**a.** County government

Virtually all the state governments have delegated certain administrative functions to local *county* governments, organized by geographic regions within the state. The most common delegated responsibilities include administering the public library system, maintaining the public welfare system, maintaining roads and parks, implementing property zoning rules, providing agricultural assistance, enforcing the law, and ensuring the public safety.

A *board of supervisors* elected by county voters serves as the overall governing body. Executive authority is shared with such elected officials as the county sheriff, prosecutor, coroner, treasurer, clerk, and property assessor. The board usually delegates a substantial amount of the daily administrative workload to special committees and commissions, each of which has its own mandate (e.g., public welfare).

**b.** Municipal government

A municipality is a discrete geographic entity within a state (such as a city, village, or town) that has received a specific delegation of authority from the state in the form of a *corporate charter*. State governments are usually quite precise about the structure, function, authority, and boundaries that municipal corporations can have. Cities, villages, and towns possess only those powers specifically granted by the state.

Municipal governments are typically delegated the same authority and responsibility as that granted to county government. However, this authority is restricted to the geographic boundaries of the city, town, or village. Outside those limits, the county governments are also required to implement applicable state law within their boundaries.

The most influential form of municipal government is the city. Under the authority granted by the state, city governments execute their responsibilities through one of four major organizational forms.

(1) Council/manager

Voters elect a *city council*. The council then elects a *mayor* from its own ranks to serve as a policymaking executive and also hires a professional manager to run the daily affairs of government. The manager in turn hires department heads.

(2) Commission

City voters elect commissioners who both decide on regulations and implement the regulations within their spheres of authority (e.g., Commissioner of Public Works). A mayor may also be elected, but the office has relatively limited power to influence the actions of the various commissioners.

(3) "Strong" mayor/council

City voters elect both the council and the mayor. The council's primary responsibility is legislative, while the mayor is the chief executive authority of the city. The mayor appoints department heads to assist in the implementation of daily responsibilities.

(4) "Weak" mayor/council

City voters elect the council, the mayor, and all the important department heads who administer city government. The mayor has little ultimate control over any of these elected officials and hence has quite limited executive authority overall.

**C.** Balance of Power

No one component of the American government system has overriding power over all the others. Authority is divided among the executive, legislative, and judicial branches of government at all levels. Some forms of authority may be exclusive to one of the branches, while other forms may be shared by them. An example is the presidential power to appoint officials with the advice and consent of the Senate.

In a representative democracy, power is also shared with the people. Most important officials are elected by the people for a limited term of office. This holds for officials of federal, state, or local government and for those in the executive, legislative, or judicial branch. Public dissatisfaction with elected officials can result in their removal from office through the recall. In addition, voters have direct influence over the enactment and enforcement of legislation via the initiative and the referendum.

The heart of American government lies in the division of power between the federal and state governments, a system known as *federalism*. The balance of power between these entities today is a function of three elements: (1) the framework specified by the Constitution; (2) the subsequent interpretation of that framework by the courts; and (3) the implementation of that framework in the modern era.

**1.** Constitutional Federalism

In his explanation of the rationale behind the constitutional *separation of power* between federal and state governments, James Madison provided the most concise summary of federalism:

The powers delegated by the proposed Constitution to the federal government are few and defined. Those which are to remain in the state governments are numerous and indefinite. The former will be exercised principally on external objects, such as war, peace, negotiation, and foreign commerce; the last with which the power of taxation will, for the most part, be connected. The powers reserved for the several states will extend to all the objects which, in the ordinary course of affairs, concern the lives, liberties, and properties of the people and the internal order, improvement, and property of the state.

The Constitution specifies 17 areas in which the federal government has ultimate authority —among them war, taxation, national defense, interstate commerce, and the federal court system. In addition, Congress has the power "to make all laws which shall be necessary and proper for carrying into execution the foregoing powers, and all other powers vested by this Constitution in the government of the United States or in any department or officer thereof." The Constitution and all federal laws are the supreme law of the land.

Both the federal and state governments are denied powers that would infringe upon certain individual rights—most notably, the freedoms preserved in the Bill of Rights.

In this federalist framework, state governments are granted authority in all areas not delegated to the federal government or preserved by the individual. Such authority has historically included control of intrastate commerce; organization and control of local government; power to tax and spend for the general welfare of the residents of the state; control over the ownership and use of property; and public education.

**2.** Interpretation of Constitutional Federalism

In asserting its role as arbiter of the U.S. Constitution, the Supreme Court has been instrumental in shaping federalism to meet the changing demands of history. Landmark cases, discussed earlier in detail, have interpreted the Constitution as meaning the following.

**a.** The Supreme Court has the sole authority to determine the "supreme law of the land" to which state government must subordinate itself.

19

    **b.** The federal government has authority not only over those areas expressly mentioned in the Constitution but also over the states in any area "necessary and proper" to carry out its expressed authority.

    **c.** Constitutional protection against infringement of individual civil rights by the federal government extends to protection against similar infringement by state government.

    **d.** Once Congress enacts legislation in an area in which federal authority is appropriate, states must refrain from enacting legislation in this area, even if the Constitution permits both federal and state jurisdiction (unless Congress provides for supplemental state legislation).

  **3.** Modern Federalism

Relations between the federal government and the governments of the several states (and local communities) have evolved in a manner not anticipated by the writers of the Constitution.

The Sixteenth Amendment to the Constitution, ratified in 1913, gives the federal government the power to raise large sums of money through the income tax. Not only does the federal government spend this money in areas in which the Constitution expressly gives it supreme authority (e.g., on national defense); it also makes some of the money available to the states.

Such federal funds usually come with "conditions"—that is, the state government must spend the money as mandated by federal regulations. State governments are thus faced with a dilemma: They may take the unpopular step of raising state taxes in order to retain complete freedom of action in areas designated by the Constitution, or they may lower state taxes by taking the federal money, albeit with federal "strings" attached.

No state is required to take the available *federal grants*. To do so gives the federal government indirect power over many areas in which state authority is supposed to be preeminent, such as highways, welfare, education, housing, natural resources, employment, and health. But all the states have to some degree availed themselves of federal money and have thus contributed to the dominance of the federal government over the daily activities of citizens.

Political conservatives decry modern federalism as distorting the balance between state and federal power envisioned by the Constitution. Political liberals do not view the expansion of federal power as an infringement on existing state authority. Rather, they believe federal involvement has engendered state (and local) participation in improving the welfare of citizens in areas where such concern previously did not exist.

## III. Political Parties

**A.** Historical Development

Although the Constitution is silent on the role of political parties in the governing process, the Constitution itself is partially responsible for the development of the party system. Debate over ratification of the Constitution coalesced around the *Federalists*, who approved of a strong national government, and the *Anti-Federalists*, who wished to preserve strong state autonomy. Federalists tended to represent the financial interests of banking and commerce, while Anti-Federalists consisted of laborers, small farmers, Southern aristocrats, and frontier settlers.

The first half of the nineteenth century saw the *Whigs* replace the Federalists and the *Democrats* replace the Anti-Federalists, but the basic division into a two-party system remained along original lines.

In the mid-nineteenth century, as national tensions mounted toward civil war, the Whigs were supplanted by the *Republicans*. Antislavery at its origin, the Republican Party appealed to the nonslaveholding farmers of the Midwest, to Northern business and financial interests, and (particularly after the Civil War) to the emerging West.

The Civil War caused the Democratic Party to split into a northern and a southern wing, thereby contributing to Republican dominance of the American political scene for the next 75 years. Only when the Republicans themselves became divided early in the twentieth century were the Democrats able to sustain increased influence over national affairs (through the election of Woodrow Wilson).

A major realignment of political allegiance occurred later in the century as a result of the failure of the Republicans to adequately address the problems of the Great Depression. The Democrats became the nation's majority party, appealing to labor, minorities, and all other elements of society that sought expanded federal involvement in economic affairs.

Today, Americans perceive themselves as being evenly divided between Democrats, Republicans, and independents, with independents more likely to cast votes for Democrats.

**B.** Purpose and Campaigns

A *political party* exists to capture control of public office for its nominees. To do so, party members need to embrace the same political philosophy and work together to achieve goals consistent with that philosophy. These goals include a legislative program to be enacted once political office is won. Most important, the party must be able to win enough elections to government office to acquire the power and influence needed to enact its programs.

Getting elected to public office is an expensive undertaking that few private citizens can afford. The financial burden of getting elected has fallen primarily on the political parties, which obtain funds from the public through campaigning.

*Campaign committees*, often formed only for the purpose of raising money, are organized by political parties for their respective candidates. Campaign activities usually include such fundraisers as rallies, dinners, and speaking engagements featuring the candidate and/or the candidate's family.

The federal government has attempted to control the misuse of party campaign funds through such measures as mandatory financial reports on sources and uses of campaign funds, limits on spending, and prohibitions on who can contribute to a campaign (corporations may not) as well as how much any one person can contribute. The Federal Elections Commission provides campaign funds for presidential candidates, with specific safeguards and restrictions on how the money may be used.

Campaign financing does enhance the loyalty of political candidates, since the party provides invaluable assistance in raising needed funds through its campaign efforts. Yet the vast sums required to elect officeholders in the modern era have raised concern about the undue influence contributors may expect to exert by virtue of their campaign support.

**C.** Primary System

In some states, the political parties hold nominating conventions to determine who their candidates for elective office will be. Most other states allow voters to select a party's candidates for office through the *primary system*.

In "open primary" states the voter does not have to be a member of any party to enter the voting booth. In "closed primary" states, voting for a political party's candidates is limited to registered voters of that party. Some states declare that whoever wins a plurality of the votes wins the primary. Other states require the winner to receive a majority of the votes cast. If no candidate attains a majority, a runoff primary is held between the two most popular candidates.

The primary (and nominating convention) system produces one party candidate for each office open in the general election. In states where one political party is preeminent, winning the primary is tantamount to winning the general election.

19

**D.** General Elections and the Electoral College

A candidate needs only a *plurality* of the votes cast to win a general election. Since many elections involve candidates from just the Republican and Democratic parties, winning the general election usually involves winning the *majority* of all votes cast for that office.

The Constitution provides for a somewhat different method of electing the President and Vice President. Following is a summary of the *electoral college* system.

1. Each state is assigned a number of electors equal to its representation in the U.S. Senate and the House of Representatives.

2. The candidate winning a plurality of the votes cast within the state wins all the electoral votes for that state. Different totals are maintained for the President and the Vice President.

3. A candidate for either President or Vice President must obtain a majority of the total electoral votes for the respective office in order to win the general election.

4. Should no candidate gain a majority of the electoral votes for either of the two offices, Congress determines the winner.

   a. If no candidate for President wins a majority of the votes of the electoral college, the House of Representatives votes on the top three candidates, with each state having one vote. The candidate winning the majority of these votes is the next President.

   b. If no candidate for Vice President wins a majority of the votes of the electoral college, the Senate votes for the top two candidates, with each state having two votes. The candidate winning the majority of the Senate votes cast is the next Vice President.

   There are two primary criticisms of this constitutionally specified method of electing the President and Vice President: (1) A candidate who has won either the majority or the plurality of the total popular votes can be denied office by virtue of the distribution of the votes within the electoral college. (2) If more than two candidates are running for either office, the possibility exists that no one will win a majority within the electoral college. The nation's top officials will then be elected by Congress instead of by the "direct will of the people."

**E.** Presidential Nominating Conventions

The presidential *nominating convention* is perhaps the only political event in which parties function visibly on a national level.

Convention delegates are chosen on the basis of complex formulas that assign each state a proportion of the total delegates. Conventions organize standing committees on such party business matters as credentials, rules, resolutions, and permanent organization. The primary purposes of the convention are to adopt the party philosophy or *platform* for the upcoming campaign and to nominate the presidential candidate. The party's candidate for President is then permitted to nominate a candidate for Vice President.

Each state is allotted a proportion of the total votes to be cast, again on the basis of complex formulas. Legislation in several states requires delegates to vote for the candidates who have won the presidential primaries in those states.

To become a party's candidate for President or Vice President, an individual must win a majority of the votes cast by the delegates to that party's national nominating convention.

# ECONOMICS

## I. Labor and Trade

### A. Production

**1.** Definition and Measurement

*Production* is the means by which input resource factors are transformed into the output of goods and services. Gross national product (GNP) is the measure of the total production of goods and services in a nation during a calendar year.

**2.** Input Resource Factors

**a.** *Natural resources* consist of all natural resources and raw materials used in production (e.g., land, water).

**b.** *Capital* denotes the man-made physical improvements that increase the ability of the other factors to aid in the production process.

**c.** *Labor* is the physical and mental human effort employed in the production process.

**d.** *Entrepreneurship* (also called management) is the risk-taking function that combines the other factors to produce goods and services at a profit.

### B. Distribution

**1.** Definition

*Distribution* is the method of compensating the owners of an input resource factor for its use in the production of goods and services.

**2.** Compensation

Owners of natural resources are paid rent. Owners of capital are paid interest. Labor is paid wages. Entrepreneurs are compensated via profit.

### C. Exchange of Goods and Services

**1.** Definition

An *exchange of goods or services* (commodities) occurs when the seller supplies a commodity the buyer is demanding, in return for the buyer's commodity (usually money) at an agreed-upon price.

**2.** Demand

**a.** *Demand* is the amount of a commodity the buyer desires at a given price over a specified period of time. The quantity demanded should increase as the price falls and decrease as the price rises, all other aspects remaining constant.

**b.** Demand may also rise or fall due to a change in other, nonprice factors.

**3.** Supply

**a.** *Supply* is the amount of a commodity offered for sale at a given price for a specified period of time. The quantity supplied should increase as the price that can be obtained goes up and decrease as that price goes down, all other aspects remaining constant.

**b.** Supply may also rise or fall due to a change in other, nonprice factors.

**4.** Equilibrium

*Equilibrium* refers to that quantity and price at which the supply for a commodity equals the demand. Supply greater than demand means a surplus; demand greater than supply means shortage. Disruption of equilibrium may stem from inappropriate pricing as well as from other, nonprice considerations.

19

**D.** Media of Exchange

   **1.** Definition
*Money* refers to anything generally accepted in exchange; specifically, money is the medium of exchange for goods and services.

   **2.** Types

      **a.** Commodity money has intrinsic value independent of what it can buy (e.g., a pure silver dollar).

      **b.** Fiat money is valuable only as an acceptable medium of exchange (e.g., all paper money).

**E.** International Trade

In no one country will the demand for specific commodities be equal to the supply, hence the need to supplement demand via exports or supply via imports.

   **1.** Approaches

      **a.** *Free trade* is the complete absence of restrictions on exports or imports and serves to raise total world production.

      **b.** *Protectionism* involves restricting international trade (particularly imports) via tariffs, quotas, and regulations. Countries justify their use of protectionist measures for national security and employment reasons.

   **2.** Economic Concerns
A country practicing free trade can find itself at a disadvantage when foreign competitors engage in protectionism. One country's protectionist measures often invite protectionist retaliation from international trading partners, thereby lowering world production.

**F.** Wages

   **1.** Definition
*Wages* are the compensation paid to workers for their physical and mental input in the production process.

   **2.** Labor Productivity
*Labor productivity*, the output per unit of labor input, is the key to differing wage levels. The more productive the work force, the higher the real wage the employer will be capable of paying. Lower labor productivity lowers wages.

   **3.** Mandated Wage Levels
Wages mandated at levels higher than would otherwise be established through the interaction of the supply and demand often cause a reduction in the quantity of labor demanded at the artificially high price. Minimum wage laws and unions are often cited as examples of this phenomenon.

**G.** Labor Unions

   **1.** Definition
A *labor union* is an organization of employees that negotiates with management as the representative of the employees in a process called *collective bargaining*.

   **2.** Development

      **a.** American Federation of Labor (AFL)
The AFL was organized in 1886 as a federation of several craft unions in which skilled workers doing the same type of work (e.g., carpentry) were organized into a separate

union regardless of their employers. Unskilled workers were ignored in this effort to restrict supply and raise the wages of labor.

    **b.** Congress of Industrial Organizations (CIO)
Formed initially in 1935 as an entity within the AFL, the CIO officially separated in 1938 to become a rival federation of industrial unions, in which all the workers in a given industry (e.g., autos, steel) were organized into a separate union. Work stoppages, or *strikes*, were the primary mechanism used to raise wages and promote job security.

    **c.** AFL/CIO
The two rival federations reunited in 1955; in the interim independent unions, such as the International Brotherhood of Teamsters, developed outside this framework.

**3.** Major Legislation

    **a.** National Labor Relations Act (1935)
Also known as the Wagner Act, the *NLRA* recognized the legitimacy of the collective bargaining process and established the National Labor Relations Board to ensure that management did not interfere with the formation of unions or discriminate against employees who belonged to a union.

    **b.** Taft-Hartley Act (1947)
In response to aggressive union tactics immediately following World War II, the *Taft-Hartley Act* restricted discrimination in favor of union employees and curtailed the ability of unions to engage in strikes.

**4.** Current Status

    **a.** Although total union membership is declining, groups previously resistant to unionization, such as government employees, white-collar professionals, and migrant farm workers, have made striking gains in union membership.

    **b.** Job security has replaced increased pay and fringe benefits as the dominant union demand, with unions agreeing to wage concessions in order to enhance this security.

    **c.** Unions have become the economic equals of the industries with which they bargain. Monetary pressure via political contributions and pension investments has supplanted the strike as the unions' most-favored tool of influence. The potential corrupting influence of this economic factor remains a concern within the union system.

**H.** Use of Human and Natural Resources

**1.** Human Resources
Increasing the productivity of human input involves both improving the health of workers and enhancing their skills through education and training. There is no consensus, however, on the best methods of implementing this "investment in human capital."

**2.** Natural Resources
Conservation of the finite supply of natural resources makes long-term economic sense in order to ensure future economic production and the mental and physical health (i.e., productivity) of the labor force.

## II. Consumption

**A.** Consumerism

**1.** Definition
*Consumerism* is the belief that companies should not produce items that will impair the health or safety of the individual consumer or the public at large, even if the consumer is

**19**

willing to purchase such items. Government should intervene whenever companies are lax in self-regulation.

**2.** Analysis

Consumers do need protection in this technologically advanced age where the effects of purchase are not often fully understood. Yet regulation can raise costs (and thus prices), delay the introduction of new products, and even reduce competition.

**B.** Competition

**1.** Definition

*Competition* exists when the prices that suppliers demand and consumers pay are constrained by the actions of other suppliers and consumers in the market for a given commodity.

**2.** Effect on Price

**a.** In the long run, if the market price is high relative to the costs of efficient production, new suppliers will enter the market, thereby raising total supply. Assuming constant demand, an increase in supply will cause a reduction in the equilibrium market price until excess profits are eliminated.

**b.** In the long run, if the market price is low relative to the costs of efficient production, existing suppliers will leave the market, thereby lowering total supply. Again assuming constant demand, a decrease in supply will cause an increase in the equilibrium market price until losses are eliminated.

**C.** Free-Enterprise System

**1.** Definition

A *free-enterprise system* is one in which the allocation of resources is based on the voluntary decisions of individuals and companies, not central (governmental) authorities.

**2.** Effect

Acting out of self-interest in a voluntary economic exchange may result in the best interests of all concerned being met via the total of all such voluntary economic exchanges. Government intrusion for the collective well-being is thus perceived as being both unnecessary and counterproductive.

**3.** Current Practice

All economies are to some extent a mix of systems, with a private sector in which economic exchanges remain primarily voluntary and a public sector in which government prescribes the nature and/or extent of economic exchange.

**D.** Protection Agencies

**1.** Need for Protection

The free-enterprise system can adversely affect portions of society even though benefiting society as a whole. Government is an external force that can restrain counterproductive acts of noncompetitive producers. In addition, consumerism has had its best success by seeking government regulation rather than by relying upon producer self-regulation when the need for protection comes into conflict with the profit-maximization objective.

**2.** Selected Federal Agencies

**a.** The Federal Trade Commission (FTC) restrains unfair methods of competition and deceptive trading practices.

**b.** The Environmental Protection Agency (EPA) administers regulations to restrict pollution of the environment.

    **c.** The Occupational Health and Safety Administration (OSHA) enforces standards relating to appropriate conditions in the workplace.

**E.** Monopolies and Other Types of Imperfect Competition

    **1.** Definitions

        **a.** A *pure monopoly* exists when there is only one supplier of a given commodity (e.g., public utilities).

        **b.** An *oligopoly* exists when there are only a few suppliers of a given commodity (e.g., automobiles); thus an individual supplier can change the price for the entire industry.

        **c.** *Monopolistic competition* exists in a given industry when an entrenched supplier is able to inhibit new firms from competing in the industry.

    **2.** Disadvantages to Consumers
    Imperfect competition can lower the supply and thus raise the price for a given commodity.

## III. Savings and Investment

**A.** Securities

Securities are the *stocks* and *bonds* a corporation issues to the public to finance its production activities; the public becomes either an owner (stocks) or a lender (bonds) to the production effort.

**B.** Types of Stocks and Bonds

    **1.** Stocks

        **a.** *Common stockholders* own the common stock of the corporation and exercise control over the management of the company primarily through the election of a board of directors. Such stockholders may also be eligible to receive a pro rata share of the profits of the corporation through the distribution of the dividends.

        **b.** *Preferred stockholders* own the preferred stock of the corporation and have preferential rights over common stockholders on such issues as receiving dividends and recapturing their investment should the corporation become insolvent.

    **2.** Bonds
    Although all bonds require payment of a principal amount at a specified date in the future, there is considerable variation as to whether periodic interest payments are required, whether corporate assets can be repossessed if bond payments are missed, and whether bondholders have the option of converting the bonds into shares of the corporation's stock.

**C.** Stock Market

Corporations seeking greater marketability for their securities will list those securities on the various stock exchanges where securities are publicly traded. Trading on the New York Stock Exchange and the American Stock Exchange, the dominant stock markets in the country, is regulated by the *Securities and Exchange Commission (SEC)*. SEC regulations are designed to protect investors in stocks and bonds from manipulation of prices and misrepresentation of financial data on which investments in securities are made.

**D.** Loans

    **1.** Sources
    Larger companies borrow directly from the public (through the issuance of bonds) as well as from banks. Smaller companies borrow from banks and other financial institutions such as insurance companies.

**19**

**2.** Cost

In addition to paying back the amount borrowed, the company obtaining the loan is normally required to pay periodic interest to the lender. The interest paid is based on the interest rate established by the forces of supply and demand for that type of loan. Lower interest rates reflect a supply of loanable funds that exceeds existing demand; higher interest rates reflect a demand for loanable funds that exceeds the supply available.

**E.** Federal Reserve System

**1.** Structure

The *Federal Reserve System* consists of a Federal Reserve Bank for each of the 12 districts in the United States. Each bank has its own board of directors. The entire system is governed by a national board of governors appointed by the President.

**2.** Function

Acting as the nation's central bank, the Federal Reserve is charged primarily with controlling the nation's supply of money and thus, indirectly, the interest rate cost of borrowing money. The actions of the Federal Reserve are based on specific monetary policies designed to adjust the money supply to meet the nation's economic goals of full employment, stable prices, and growth.

**F.** Taxes

**1.** Sources

The federal government obtains the largest portion of revenue for its operations from individual and corporate income taxes. State governments obtain revenue primarily from sales, property, and income taxes, as well as from federal government grants. Local governments derive revenue from property taxes and federal or state government grants.

**2.** Relationship to Income

Federal taxes are slightly *progressive*, in that higher incomes are taxed at increasingly higher rates. Conversely, state and local taxes tend to be *regressive*; that is, the lower a person's income, the larger the share paid in taxes.

**G.** Tax Laws

**1.** Purposes

Federal, state, and local governments collect taxes for several competing purposes: to pay for government operations; to promote consumerist objectives; to implement policies designed to improve the well-being of society as a whole; and to move resources from the private to the public sector. Rarely does tax law attempt to encourage economic efficiency as an end in itself.

**2.** Distortions

Taxpayers often make economic decisions on the basis of the perceived tax effect rather than on the basis of efficient economic growth. The *Tax Reform Act of 1986* took a major step toward reducing such economic distortions, which can undermine the efficient production and exchange of commodities. The act was not as successful in reducing the complexity of the nation's tax code.

## IV. Economic Theories

**A.** Early Theories

**1.** Laissez Faire

Writing at the beginning of the Industrial Revolution, Adam Smith was the earliest and one of the most influential advocates of the philosophy that government should take a *laissez-faire* (hands off) role by minimizing its interference in the economy. The voluntary exchange inherent in a free-enterprise system should serve the best interests of all concerned through the total of all such economic exchanges. Government is thus best suited to enforce economic contracts and to provide for the public defense, and it should not attempt to regulate the economy.

**2.** Market Failure

John Stuart Mill took the position that government intervention might be warranted in cases of *market failure* (e.g., where innocent third parties are injured by the enforcement of an economic agreement). Government involvement should be permitted when the collective benefits of such regulation can be expected to exceed the collective costs.

**3.** Population Limits

T.R. Malthus believed the growth in population would eventually outstrip humanity's ability to produce food. When that occurred, economic growth and living standards would begin to fall until the population drastically declined. Although the Industrial Revolution greatly increased the ability to produce food, Malthusian concerns have reemerged today in the developing countries of the world.

**4.** Business Cycles

Over the last few centuries, business activity in general has repeated the cycle of growth, decline/growth, decline. Several prominent writers have explored possible underlying reasons for this cyclical phenomenon.

Kondratieff believed the economy was destined to rise and fall in "long waves" of up to 60 years each. Schumpeter felt business cycles were generated by the advent of major inventions and innovations.

Karl Marx postulated the cause as the nature of the capitalist free-enterprise system itself. Wealth becomes concentrated in the hands of producers instead of consumers, inevitably leading to an oversupply. Such oversupply is then "corrected" through a business downturn or through imperialistic wars designed to open up new markets. Then the cycle begins again.

**B.** Classical Theory

*Classical theory* refers to a combination of ideas on the functioning of the overall economy that dominated economic thinking from the mid-1800s to the Great Depression of the 1930s.

**1.** Premises

**a.** Aggregate supply, the supply for all commodities in an economy, will create an aggregate demand for that supply. According to *Say's Law*, the equilibrium price/quantity level for aggregate supply and demand for the overall economy will be at the level of full employment.

**b.** Any imbalances in the equilibrium short of full employment will only be temporary, provided the government ensures a stable money supply and avoids regulating interest rates, prices, or wages.

**c.** Equilibrium concepts applicable to individual exchanges of commodities can therefore be applied to the economy as a whole. Given enough patience, disruptions in equilibrium will eventually self-correct.

**2.** Weaknesses

The Great Depression demonstrated in dramatic fashion the problem with Say's Law: Aggregate supply and aggregate demand could fall to a new equilibrium far short of full employment. Falling interest rates, prices, and wages did not generate increased demand, but rather further decreased supply until the new (lower) equilibrium generated massive unemployment.

19

**C.** Keynesian Fiscal Theory

In 1936 a British economist, John Maynard Keynes, published a treatise attempting to explain why classical economic theory was so ill-equipped to deal with the Great Depression. He proposed a new economic theory to deal with the situation.

**1.** Premises

    **a.** Reversing Say's Law, Keynes held that aggregate demand will create its own aggregate supply. Efficient full employment will occur when aggregate demand is adequate for the use of all resource input factors, including labor.

    **b.** Equilibrium between aggregate demand and supply at the full employment level is the primary goal. A stable money supply and flexible (unregulated) interest rates, wages, and prices should all be subordinate to the primary goal, to be deferred until the proper equilibrium is reached.

    **c.** Aggregate demand can be controlled by fiscal policy. A *stimulative fiscal policy* is one in which government spending exceeds tax revenues (i.e., deficit spending). A *restrictive fiscal policy* is one in which taxes exceed spending.

    **d.** The government should adopt stimulative fiscal policies during a business downturn, thereby raising aggregate demand. Soon aggregate supply will rise in response to the increased demand. Such stimulative policies should be discontinued when aggregate demand and supply reach a new equilibrium at approximately the full employment level.

    **e.** The government should adopt restrictive fiscal policies to curtail an overheated economy and to pay off the deficits incurred under stimulative fiscal policies.

    **f.** Once equilibrium at the full employment level is reached, it will be maintained if the government then pursues a stable money supply and flexible interest rates, wages, and prices.

**2.** Weaknesses
Stimulative fiscal policies are very popular with politicians, for constituents perceive themselves to be receiving the benefits of increased government spending without individually having to pay the full cost. Thus restrictive fiscal policies are rarely adopted, even though the failure to adopt them will lead to inflation as the economy approaches the full employment level.

**D.** Monetary Theory

Over the past several decades, implementation of Keynesian *demand-side theories* has too often resulted in inflation and excessive government involvement in the economy. Milton Friedman, an American economist, is a leading proponent of *monetarist theories* designed to correct this situation.

**1.** Premises

    **a.** Changes in the money supply are the real cause of changes in both employment and inflation for the economy as a whole. Allowing the money supply to grow faster than the rate of normal economic growth will lead to inflation; slowing the money supply will generate deflation through lower prices.

    **b.** Inflation results in a new equilibrium between aggregate demand and supply at a level of higher prices but an overall lower supply. The lower quantity of commodities produced involves lower use of the labor resource input factor, thus lower employment.

   **c.** Stimulative fiscal policies, although attractive in the short term, ultimately cause government spending to supplant private economic exchanges. Instead of stimulating overall economic growth, these policies only result in a reallocation of available resources.

   **d.** Not only is the economy reasonably stable over the long run; it can be stable over shorter periods of time if (1) the government restricts its intervention in the economy by adopting neutral (balanced budget) fiscal policies, and (2) the Federal Reserve pursues a monetary policy that makes growth in the nation's money supply equal to the basic growth rate of the overall economy.

  **2.** Weaknesses

The money supply does appear to play a crucial role in the generation of inflation and deflation. However, the monetarist school of thought ignores the significant effect of fiscal policies on overall production and employment.

Monetary theory also seems ill-equipped to deal with periods of economic *stagflation*, characterized by the simultaneous presence of inflation and economic stagnation. Lowering the monetary supply to combat inflation can deepen the business downturn, making the pressure for relief more intense.

**E.** Neo-Keynesian Theories

  **1.** Premises

Neo-Keynesians, of which American economist John Kenneth Galbraith is perhaps the most noted, believe the answer lies in even more government involvement in the economy. Extensive *wage-price controls* can combat inflation, while public service jobs can reduce unemployment. The government should thus constantly seek to "control" the economy.

  **2.** Weaknesses

Government attempts to control the economy for more than a brief period of time appear to be counterproductive. Such is the case whether the controls are mandatory (Nixon's wage–price controls) or voluntary (Carter's wage–price guidelines). Moreover, politicians are rarely unanimous or even consistent in detailing specific programs to meet the economic objectives.

Other than during extreme cases of market failure such as the Great Depression, government attempts to control the economy (as opposed to merely "stabilizing" it) have produced more disruptions than benefits overall.

**F.** Supply-Side Theory

American economist Arthur Laffer and others have advanced *supply-side theories* to overcome the problems associated with earlier economic thought.

  **1.** Premises

   **a.** The best way to achieve higher employment without higher inflation is to raise aggregate supply. Increasing the production of commodities will bring about increased employment. The new equilibrium will be achieved without inflation since the higher quantity of goods can be sold only at lower prices for any given level of aggregate demand.

   **b.** Reduction in taxes—most importantly, in the federal income tax—will provide an incentive to invest and raise aggregate supply. Tax rates should therefore be reduced for those most likely to channel the resulting savings into producing an increased supply of commodities rather than into increased consumer demand.

   **c.** The proper role of the government in supply-side theory is to (1) lower personal income taxes to encourage work effort; (2) lower business taxes to stimulate investment; (3) reduce stimulative (demand-side) government fiscal policies; and (4) reduce government

19

regulation and control over the economy, which serves only to raise prices and reduce production.

**2.** Recent Implementation

In the 1980s, the Reagan administration implemented supply-side theory primarily through tax reduction. However, simultaneous increases in overall government spending produced stimulative fiscal policies, in direct opposition to supply-side tenets.

The Federal Reserve initially pursued restrictive monetary policies to combat inflation, then adopted more liberal monetary policies to combat worldwide recession. Thus monetary policy was not consistently directed to increasing supply.

After the recession of the early 1980s, economic recovery was driven largely by consumer demand rather than by increased domestic production. Foreign suppliers played an increasing role in meeting this demand.

**3.** Conclusion

Economic events in the United States during the 1980s more convincingly demonstrated the ability of stimulative fiscal policy to increase aggregate demand than the ability of tax cuts to increase aggregate supply.

# ANTHROPOLOGY

## I. Racial Groups

**A.** Scientific Classifications

   **1.** Geographic Races

   Anthropologists often classify people into racial groups on the basis of place of origin. One such classification divides humanity into seven races: Americans, Australians, Africans, Europeans, Indians, Melanesians, and Polynesians.

   **2.** Physical-Characteristic Races

   Anthropologists have also attempted to describe racial groups on the basis of a combination of physical characteristics or traits. Skin color, hair texture, height, skull shape, and even blood type have all assumed importance in such studies.

   Under this approach, a Nordic might be defined as having straight hair, blue or gray eyes, tall stature, and a round skull. A Negro might be classified as having curly hair, dark skin, and a longish skull structure.

**B.** Disadvantages of Scientific Classifications

   **1.** Humanity continues to demonstrate a remarkable capacity for migration and for exchanging mates between groups, thus rendering any classification scheme obsolete.

   **2.** Over time, environmental factors alter the physical characteristics of human groups, with different geographic regions being affected in different ways. Nature itself thus defeats any attempt to establish unvarying criteria for dividing humanity into groups.

**C.** Cultural Perspectives

   **1.** Although concepts of race are very much a product of cultural bias, anthropologists generally agree that culturally defined racial categories cannot be translated into objective classifications of humanity.

   **2.** The cultural results of races living together stem from social, not biological, factors.

   **3.** There is no scientific basis for believing that human groups differ in their innate capacity for intellectual and emotional development. The capacity to develop culture is not tied to racial characteristics.

## II. Cultures

**A.** Definition

A *culture* is the way of life of a group of people. It includes patterns of learned behavior that are handed down from one generation to the next through language and imitation. Culture consists not only of all the learned behavior of the group but also of rules and guidelines for the behavior of individuals within the group.

**B.** Elements of Culture

Elements of culture include (1) the techniques established for the production, consumption, and distribution of food; (2) the buildings in which members of the group live and work; (3) the clothes that members of the group wear; (4) the kinds of art with which the group is familiar; (5) the language used for communication; (6) the group's kinship structures; (7) the myths and religion the group members learn; and (8) the social systems group members participate in.

**C.** Prehistoric Cultures

Prehistoric cultures are those that existed before the advent of writing. The earliest such culture identified by anthropologists arose in the *Paleolithic Age*. It was marked by food obtained through hunting and foraging, tools made of stone, and evidence of religious beliefs.

The next cultural stage, the *Neolithic Age*, saw cultivation replace hunting and foraging as the means of obtaining sustenance. Permanent housing and woven clothing made their appearance.

A third prehistoric cultural stage, the *Metal Age*, was characterized by the development of tools made of iron and bronze; surplus agricultural production through the use of irrigation and animal-powered plows; specialization of labor into occupations other than farming; stratification of society into urban and rural; and increasing trade and warfare between societies.

**D.** Cultural Evolution

   **1.** Language
   Most anthropologists agree that language is the primary means by which cultural requirements are taught and understood. However, anthropologists do not agree on the nature of the relationship between language and culture. Some have suggested that language *is* culture, inseparable from how native speakers perceive the environment in which they live.

   **2.** Art
   Dancing, music, and decorative art are components of every society's culture. The overall function of these artistic forms is to communicate symbolically, thereby reinforcing the cultural views of the group. Art is intertwined with other cultural elements, such as language and religion, to achieve communication.

   **3.** Individual Personality
   Personality infused with cultural expectations determines how a person behaves within society. Although culture is a major factor in the formation of personality, there are other influences, including physical factors and unique experiences. Acceptable behavior in one culture may well be aberrant in another.

## III.  Kinship Structures

**A.** Definition

*Kinship* refers to relationships based on biological descent and marriage. Kin acquired through marriage are *affinal kin*; biological relatives are *consanguineal kin*. A kinship structure is not merely an aggregate of relatives; it also includes the culturally specified ways of behaving toward different categories of relatives.

**B.** Marriage

   **1.** *Marriage* is a culturally sanctioned relationship between males and females that provides for the fulfillment of sexual needs and the legitimacy of children. All cultures recognize marriage when the concept is defined in its broadest terms.

   **2.** All cultures have restrictions on who may marry whom and limitations on what constitutes an appropriate sexual partner. Normally, either or both parties must change residence when a marriage occurs.

   **3.** Although virtually all cultures allow for the dissolution of marriage, they vary greatly in defining grounds for divorce, accompanying economic transactions, disposition of children, and other considerations.

**C.** Family

**1.** Type of Marriage Arrangement

**a.** *Monogamy*, involving one man and one woman, is common among industrialized nations but exists in only one-fourth of the world's cultures.

**b.** *Polygyny*, involving one man and more than one woman, is the most common family structure among the world's cultures.

**c.** *Polyandry*, involving one woman and more than one man, is practiced primarily in parts of southern Asia.

**d.** *Group marriage*, involving more than one man and more than one woman, is rare and is often an outgrowth of polyandrous arrangements.

**2.** Functions
The universal functions of the family include (a) sexual mating leading to children, (b) economic division of labor between spouses, (c) establishment of kinship structure, and (d) provision of culture to children. The family is a more successful instrument than other social structures in providing for the care and enculturation of the young.

**D.** Descent

Every culture has rules of descent that recognize links between generations. In cultures based on *patrilineal descent*, men are the linkages between generations. In those based on *matrilineal descent*, women are the links. In cultures with *unilineal descent*, ancestry is traced through either the male or the female line, but not both.

Patrilineal descent is the most common kinship structure not only in industrialized cultures but in the world as a whole.

## IV. Religion

**A.** Definition

*Religion* may be defined as the set of human beliefs relating to the meaning of life, and more specifically as the relationship of human beings to spiritual forces.

**B.** Components

**1.** Beliefs
Belief in the supernatural is a part of every known culture and can be divided into two broad categories.

**a.** *Animism* is the belief in the existence of specific spiritual beings.

**b.** *Animatism* is the belief that supernatural power can reside in animate as well as inanimate objects. An example is the Polynesian concept of *mana*, a power that pervades the universe but resides in some people and objects more than others.

**2.** Mythology
*Mythology* is a symbolic explanation of the character and activities of sacred beings. It also provides the cultural answers to the seeming contradictions of life, thereby justifying the existing order of society.

**3.** Ritual
Belief in the supernatural and acceptance of the culture's mythology are demonstrated by the performance of specific acts or *rituals*. Sacred symbols play an important role in ritual by embodying the imperatives of the religion for all members of the culture.

19

**4.** Leadership
Most societies recognize at least one kind of religious leader whose role is to advance and defend the religious component of the culture.

**a.** Shamans and prophets
*Shamans* or *prophets* act as intermediaries between the society and the supernatural world through direct communication with the supernatural. Their leadership derives from the communicative ability given to them by the supernatural — or at least such ability as members of the society believe them to have.

**b.** Priests
*Priests* are elected or appointed by the members of a society to master its rituals and "defend the faith." Direct communication with the supernatural is not essential, as leadership authority has been granted by the society itself.

**5.** Taboos
*Taboos* are constraints imposed on members of the society by the supernatural. The religious culture warns that violation of any taboo is a sin, with certain supernatural punishment as the inevitable result.

Taboos are part of all cultures and are essential (1) to sustain the proper respect for the all-important belief in the supernatural; (2) to separate the believers in one culture from those in other cultures; and (3) to control social behavior.

**C.** Magic

*Magic* is the perception that the supernatural can be controlled by mortal beings through certain procedures. This is a contrast to the religious approach of prayerful subordination to the almighty spirit. Although religion is generally antagonistic to magic, in practice it can be difficult to separate the two.

Magic in itself is neither good nor bad; the purpose it is used for determines its nature. *Sorcery* is magic used against other human beings (or their possessions) in ways the society specifically disapproves of.

# V. Social Systems

**A.** Definitions

A *social system* is the grouping of people in society according to their perceived status. Ascribed status is assigned at birth and cannot be changed; achieved status is brought about by the individual's own actions or the passage of time. A *social role* is the behavior associated with a particular status.

**B.** Status Classifications

**1.** Marriage and Kinship
All societies provide for and distinguish members by grouping them according to marital status and associated kinship structure.

**2.** Age
All societies categorize members by means of age, providing for a code of rules governing the conduct within and among the various age sets. Important matters pertaining to the society as a whole are often restricted to certain age sets.

**3.** Gender
Still dominant in several of the world's cultures is the explicit separation of and preference given to men's societies. These male-only groupings often serve to perpetuate male control of the community. Many societies contain both male and female groupings.

**4.** Ethnic Origin

A social group that shares the same ethnic origin can also be expected to share common cultural values and will usually be biologically stable over time.

**5.** Voluntary Associations

People often join or form groups by choice in order to accomplish a given purpose. These voluntary groupings are more numerous and powerful in industrialized, urbanized nations than in other societies. Such groupings encourage feelings of solidarity and provide protection from other groupings within the society.

**6.** Secret Societies

Secret societies often develop when established groupings do not accomplish what people desire. The groupings are secret either because they are illegal or because secrecy makes desired goals easier to achieve. Complex initiation rites bind the members of the group and instill respect for the group's power.

**C.** Social Classes and Castes

A *social class* is a grouping of people who share several related statuses and thus develop an awareness of common interests and privileges.

A *caste* is a self-perpetuating social class whose members are not permitted to marry outside the group. Caste systems can be either (1) a pariah system, in which segregation is due mainly to occupation; or (2) an ethnic system, in which segregation is imposed on conquered peoples, foreign immigrants, or ethnic groups.

# Social Studies Reading Walk-Through Test

In this lesson you will find a Social Studies Reading Test. There is no time limit for the test. In the columns to the right of the questions, you will find answers and explanations, so that you can "walk through" the test.

# Walk-Through

**DIRECTIONS:** Below each of the following reading passages is a series of questions. Choose the *best* answer to each question, interpreting what is stated or implied by the passage in the light of your own background in the subject. You may refer back to the passage as often as necessary, though the answers to some questions may not be found expressly in the passage.

*Status* is the term used by sociologists to denote any one of the many socially defined positions in a large social group. The concept of status includes almost any categorized position within a social group. Status groups include such groupings as that of a high school student, a mother, a teenager, a senior citizen, a resident of Maryland, or an apartment dweller. Each of these positions constitutes a particular status. It is obvious that everyone belongs to more than one status group. One might be a teenage resident of Maryland who lives in an apartment.

Status is categorized in two basic ways. *Ascribed status* is assigned by the society itself without regard to any special ability or performance. It is based on characteristics such as age, sex, body type, race, and ethnic heritage. One may, for example, be a teenager of Swedish extraction or a black elderly citizen. Such status groups are defined by biological characteristics. Some of these characteristics are fixed; others, such as age, vary over time. They are significant only by virtue of the meaning or importance given them within a particular culture.

*Achieved status* refers to a social position attained by an individual through personal talent and effort. Literally, one must do something to earn achieved status. Whether one is a criminal, a philanthropist, or a professional athlete, one achieves status by what one does.

Status is not a neutral concept. Implicit in the concept of status is a ranking according to a value system. A chief executive of a corporation obviously has a higher social status than a clerk in the executive's office. The ranking of status groups is a function of prestige. *Prestige* is the evaluation of status per se. If you are a surgeon, you have the prestige of the position regardless of whether you are an excellent surgeon. If you are a nurse's aide, you have the prestige accorded that position. Every individual has the prestige of the occupational group to which he or she belongs.

Individuals may achieve recognition within a status group regardless of the prestige associated with the group. They are evaluated by the way in which they perform their roles. Such evaluation is called *esteem*. The esteem a person is accorded is in direct relation to how well he or she performs. A filing clerk, for example, may be highly esteemed by other workers in an office. One has prestige regardless of performance. Only performance determines whether one is held in high esteem.

1.  The term *achieved status* would characterize:

    I.   a Nobel prize winner.
    II.  an Asian high school student.
    III. an elderly white parent.

    A. I and III
    B. II and III
    C. I, II, and III
    D. I only

2.  The difference in prestige associated with one professional status group such as physicians and another status group such as actors is often associated with:

    F. individual recognition given by members of the group.
    G. average age of the members of the group.
    H. monetary rewards associated with the position.
    J. ethnic heritage.

3.  According to the passage, ascribed status is defined by:

    I.   biological characteristics.
    II.  educational achievements.
    III. cultural awareness.

    A. II only
    B. II and III
    C. I, II, and III
    D. I only

4.  For a dentist, the probable effect of study, increased efficiency in performance, and concern for patients' comfort would be to:

    F. deny the dentist's achieved status.
    G. add to the dentist's esteem.
    H. add to the dentist's prestige.
    J. blur the distinction between esteem and prestige.

5.  According to the passage, which statement about prestige is true?

    A. A good surgeon has greater prestige than an average one.
    B. All members of the same professional group are accorded a similar degree of prestige.
    C. Prestige is a matter of education *and* achievement.
    D. Esteem can affect prestige.

1.  (D) A Nobel prize winner is one whose talents and efforts have enabled him to achieve such a prestigious status. Therefore, the conferring of the prize underscores his achieved status. The other examples illustrate ascribed status.

2.  (H) Monetary rewards constitute the difference in prestige associated with one professional status group with that of another. Prestige is conferred by a society as a whole, not by members of a single group. The correct answer cannot be inferred from the passage alone.

3.  (D) By definition, ascribed status emanates from biological characteristics.

4.  (G) Esteem recognizes individual performance. The tangible results of study, increased efficiency in performance, and a palpable concern for the comforts of patients would add to the esteem accorded to a dentist.

5.  (B) Because prestige is a manifestation of the status accorded to an entire professional group, all members of the group possess the same degree of prestige.

**6.** Some factors associated with ascribed status can influence the possibilities for achieved status. Illustration of this fact might include:

    I. the number of people who contract terminal illnesses.

    II. the number of people who retire early.

    III. the number of professional basketball players who are tall.

    **F.** I, II, and III

    **G.** III only

    **H.** I and II

    **J.** II and III

**6.** (G) Ascribed status is defined by biological characteristics. Of the possible answers listed, only height is a biological characteristic, or an aspect of ascribed status that could influence the achieved status of professional basketball players, who usually are tall.

**7.** It is clear that the servant of a king might have:

    **A.** great prestige but little esteem.

    **B.** great prestige and much esteem.

    **C.** great esteem but little prestige.

    **D.** None of the above.

**7.** (C) The servant of a king probably has great esteem because his good performance is recognized by the king and other servants. On the other hand, the servant of the king has little prestige because the position is a low status group in society.

**8.** According to the passage, which statement about status is true?

    **F.** All characteristics that determine ascribed status are fixed.

    **G.** Status groups are always the same from one culture to another.

    **H.** Each person belongs to several status groups.

    **J.** No person belongs to more than one status group.

**8.** (H) As explained in the first paragraph of the passage, each person belongs to several status groups.

**9.** The irony associated with prestige is that:

    **A.** societies sometime accord high status to groups who in reality do very little for the betterment of society.

    **B.** societies never accord prestige to the most important status groups.

    **C.** societies rarely recognize those who have esteem as well as prestige.

    **D.** prestige groups never vary from society to society.

**9.** (A) It is ironical that societies sometimes accord high status to groups that do very little for the betterment of society. For example, rock stars and professional athletes are paid huge sums of money, whereas sanitation workers, whose services are essential to the preservation of the health of the community, receive comparatively low wages. The answer cannot be inferred from the passage alone.

**10.** Instances of the significance attached by society to ascribed status would include:

    I. Jews in Nazi Germany.

    II. Palestinians in Israel.

    III. blacks in South Africa.

   **F.**   I and II

   **G.**   II and III

   **H.**   I only

   **J.**   I, II, and III

**10.** (J) The persecution of all three groups based on their biological characteristics underscores the significance that some societies have attached to ascribed status. The genocide of the Jews was the ultimate solution that the Nazis devised to terminate the lives of a race of people whom they considered to be inferior. Similarly, apartheid in South Africa reflects the racist beliefs of the white minority ruling class that black South Africans are inferior and are incapable of governing themselves. The suppression of the Palestinian demands for an independent homeland of their own reflects the belief on the part of the Israeli authorities that the Palestinians are no different in ethnic origin from the people of Jordan and therefore Jordan is their true homeland.

Special interest groups are so common and powerful today that many political leaders fear that the American two-party system is coming to an end. An interest group consists of people who are organized to further the special concerns of their members. The goal of an interest group is to influence public policy about a special issue. For example, members of a right-to-life interest group are concerned with lobbying for antiabortion legislation and for funding to educate people against the practice of abortion.

The range of goals of special interest groups is as broad as the concerns of people. As one might expect, there are numerous special interest groups, many of which compete against other groups that have conflicting concerns—that is, for every antiabortion group, there is a proabortion group; for every antinuclear power group, there is a pronuclear power group. Many political party leaders point out that the struggle between special interest groups has taken its toll on the traditional party system. They charge that the activities of special interest groups often polarize the general public around one particular issue. Thus a special interest group may succeed in defeating a candidate for reelection based on his or her views about an issue. Yet the candidate's views on other issues might be quite acceptable to many members of the group. Many critics of special interest groups argue that these groups, in fact, are producing a stalemated society in which effective government action has become less and less possible.

These critics assert that special interest groups are especially effective in *blocking* government action, such as stopping the passage of a bill. They point out that special interest groups are much less successful in promoting government action. Interest groups generally have little tolerance for solutions that involve compromise between the objectives of groups that have opposing views; this is true despite the fact that compromise is the essence of a viable democratic political system.

On the other hand, people who support the work of special interest groups point out that political party members must deal with the concerns of a particular region, whereas the issue that concerns the interest group may in fact concern many areas of the nation. Supporters of interest groups further argue that their work is supplemental to the normal political process and that their right to try to influence the work of politicians is a vital part of a working democracy.

**11.** According to the passage, the goals of a particular special interest group always are:

A. as broad as the concerns of all of the members of the group.
B. supported by the members of other special interest groups.
C. limited to an issue or a group of related issues.
D. related to finding a reasonable compromise solution to a particular problem.

**11.** (C) By definition, a special interest group is organized to influence public policy about an issue or a group of related issues. For example, members of a special interest group that is opposed to abortion might be expected to support social services for unwed mothers.

**12.** Which of the following statements describes an action that you would not expect from a special interest group?

F. A special interest group publishes literature that explains its position on the issue.
G. A special interest group holds a fund-raising dinner to get the money it needs to operate.
H. A special interest group nominates a candidate for a political office.
J. A special interest group supports a candidate for political office who agrees with its position on the issue.

**12.** (H) Interest groups are not political parties. In the United States, only political parties have a legal right to nominate candidates for political office.

13. According to the passage, which statement about the negative effects of special interest groups is true?

   A. Special interest groups are most effective at promoting political action and not at blocking it.

   B. Special interest groups usually do not deal with an issue that is of concern to a particular region of the country but with issues that may involve several regions or the whole nation.

   C. Special interest groups only do work that is supplemental to the work done by political parties.

   D. Special interest groups are more effective at blocking political action than at promoting it.

14. The concerns of an antiabortion special interest group would include:

   I. working to get antiabortion legislation passed.

   II. working to get funding for antiabortion education programs.

   III. working for the election of a proabortion politician.

   F. II only

   G. I and II

   H. II and III

   J. I, II, and III

15. According to the passage, promoters of special interest groups believe that:

   A. the concerns of a special interest group are supplemental to the concerns of political leaders and their parties.

   B. the concerns of a special interest group may have a wider geopolitical basis than the concerns of a particular political leader.

   C. special interest groups enjoy the right to influence the political process.

   D. All of the above.

13. (D) Because they are deeply committed to their goals, interest groups are not interested in compromise. Their unswerving dedication to changing public policy in favor of their interests prevents compromise.

14. (G) In order to shape the content of public policy, an interest group organized to end legal abortions works to get antiabortion legislation passed. It also seeks funding for antiabortion education programs to convince other citizens that abortion is immoral and therefore ought to be made illegal.

15. (D) As highly visible operatives in the political systems of democratic polities, promoters of special interest groups believe that their concerns and their activities complement the concerns and the activities of political leaders by redirecting the attention of political leaders to the special concerns of the population at large. Unlike political leaders who are elected by statewide constituencies, special interest groups in many cases represent a broad, national constituency of citizens who share their points of view. The laws of democratic political systems reflect the belief articulated by promoters of special interest groups that such groups do indeed have the right to contend in the political arena in order to influence the political process.

**16.** Special interest groups must engage in which of the following activities?

    I. Raise money to operate
    II. Sign up members who support the cause
    III. Campaign to get their views across and influence political leaders

  **F.** III only
  **G.** I and II
  **H.** II and III
  **J.** I, II, and III

**17.** According to the passage, which of the following would not be classified as a special interest group?

  **A.** A group of mothers concerned with raising education funds to teach teenagers about the perils of drunk driving
  **B.** Members of a chess club who meet once a week to play
  **C.** Members of the recording industry lobbying for the passage of legislation to prevent illegal duplication of music
  **D.** Members of a group who wish to stop the passage of a law that would fund the building of a missile base near their community

**18.** A political leader would likely respond favorably to the appeal of a pressure group:

  **F.** if the politician thought that his constituency disagreed with the position of the pressure group.
  **G.** if the politician thought that his constituency supported the position of the pressure group.
  **H.** if the politician had no strong opinions about the issue.
  **J.** if the politician understood the issue as well as the members of the pressure group.

**19.** Which of the following techniques do special interest groups use to influence public officials?

    I. Appear before leaders to present information about the issue and their position
    II. Use propaganda to convince others to support their views about the issue
    III. Write legislation to be approved by political leaders

  **A.** I and II
  **B.** I only
  **C.** II only
  **D.** I, II, and III

**16.** (J) In order to influence public policy, special interest groups must raise money to maintain and expand their operations. Public relations activities are expensive to mount. TV ads and mass mailings designed to recruit members, solicit funds, and maintain lobbying efforts in national, state, and local capitals require sophisticated organizational networks and the expenditure of vast sums of money. Therefore, all these activities are essential to the achievement of the goals of special interest groups.

**17.** (B) Members of a chess club who meet once a week to play cannot be classified as a special interest group because as a group of chess players they do not contend in the public arena in order to influence public policy. As members of the club, their special interest is confined to playing chess.

**18.** (G) A political leader is elected to represent the interests of his constituents. Political leaders who ignore or disregard the concerns of those who elect them frequently face defeat in the next election. Therefore, a political leader would likely respond favorably to the appeal of a pressure group if he thought that his constituency supported the appeal of the group.

**19.** (A) Special interest groups, which rely on lobbying and public relations to achieve their goals, appear before leaders to present information about the issues that they support and use propaganda to convince others to support their views about the issues. They do not have the legal status to write and officially propose legislation.

20. Which of the following would you expect to oppose a special interest group?

F. Another special interest group with a differing view of the issue

G. A politician whose constituency supports the concern of the special interest group

H. The political party not represented in the White House at the time the issue arises

J. A member of the special interest group

20. (F) A special interest group will always be opposed by another special interest group that propounds a differing view of the issue.

American financial markets are regulated by the federal government through the Securities and Exchange Commission and by various state agencies. In recent years, there has been considerable discussion of the need for more regulation because of the increased number of corporate takeovers. Many observers of the economic scene argue that much of this activity has had harmful effects not only on stockholders but on the economy as a whole.

Many corporate takeovers are hostile; that is, an outside group or company tries to seize control of an existing company whose management opposes the takeover. Most hostile takeovers begin with a tender offer in which the outside raiders offer to buy a sufficient amount of the company's outstanding stock at a stated price — usually well above the current market price. Another takeover strategy is to orchestrate a proxy battle in which a vote of shareholders of record on a specific date is taken to approve or reject a new slate of directors put forth by the raiders. The raiders generally argue that the new directors will make the company more profitable and thereby enhance the value of the stock for the existing stockholders.

Regardless of the takeover strategy employed, most raiders must purchase a significant portion of the company's stock at a price above its current market value. Outsiders usually finance such large purchases of stock through the sale of bonds that pay a very high rate of interest. The raiders argue that the debt to be incurred can easily be paid off by selling parts of the targeted company or by drawing on the additional profits that the new management insists it can make.

In 1986 and 1987, charges came to light that individuals within Wall Street firms specializing in raising capital for corporate takeovers were, in fact, selling inside information about future takeover attempts. Some of the individuals involved have already been sentenced to jail terms. In addition, such scandals have added to pressure on Congress and the Securities and Exchange Commission to provide more effective regulation of the financial aspects of attempted corporate takeovers.

Critics of hostile corporate takeovers believe that the managers of the company to be taken over usually engage in short-term activities that have very negative long-term effects. In order to avoid hostile takeovers, managers of companies generally take measures to make the takeovers less desirable. For instance, they may insert a *golden parachute clause* in employment contracts. This clause requires a company to pay very large bonuses to any management members who are fired after a takeover. Another tactic, the *poison pill*, restructures the financial base of the corporation so that an attempted takeover would make the company less profitable. Yet another antiraid tactic is to pay *greenmail* to the raiders; that is, the target of the takeover pays the raiders, who have acquired a significant percentage of the stock at a premium, to sell those shares back to the targeted company at a much higher price. This prevents the takeover, but it usually adds a substantial sum to the company's debt.

Supporters of corporate raiders counterargue that, in fact, it is the threat of a takeover that makes managers more efficient. For instance, it may cause managers to sell parts of the corporation that they are not managing well in order to raise the money to fend off the takeover. In addition, those who believe that takeovers are good argue that the existing shareholders always do better in a hostile takeover, since they invariably get a higher price for each share of stock than the current market value.

21. Which statement expresses the main idea of this passage?

A. The government is regulating the financial aspects of corporate takeovers adequately.

B. There has been recent debate over the need for additional government regulation of corporate takeovers.

C. Hostile corporate takeovers are beneficial to the targeted corporation.

D. Trading insider secrets has become a common problem in hostile corporate takeovers.

21. (B) This is the only statement general enough to cover the specific information in the piece. Statement (A) is contradicted by the text. Statements (C) and (D) are specific details and, therefore, too narrow in scope to be the main idea of the passage.

22. A corporation's board of directors votes to approve a new company policy. According to the plan, each member of the board and of upper management would receive severance of from two to five years' pay if the member was fired by the new owner after a corporate takeover. This action would be considered:

    F. a poison pill.
    G. a golden parachute.
    H. greenmail.
    J. a hostile takeover.

22. **(G)** Since the policy approved by the board involves the payment of large bonuses to any management member who is fired after a takeover, the policy by definition is a golden parachute.

23. One of the most powerful figures convicted on charges of insider trading was:

    A. Harry Helmsley.
    B. Bess Myerson.
    C. Ivan Boesky.
    D. Oliver North.

23. **(C)** Boesky was one of the richest and most influential financiers on Wall Street. He was convicted of insider trading in 1987 and was sentenced to prison. All of the other choices are people who have been indicted on other charges.

24. According to the passage, which of the following parties in a hostile takeover will likely incur new debt?

    F. The raiders, because they need money to buy large blocks of stock
    G. The Securities and Exchange Commission, because it must oversee the transactions more closely
    H. The stockholders, because they must furnish additional funds
    J. The critics of hostile takeovers, because they make less money in the stock market

24. **(F)** This statement is supported by the beginning of paragraph 3, which tells of the methods used by raiders to raise the cash they need to buy a targeted company's stock.

25. According to the passage, a poison pill strategy involves:

    A. paying the raiders high prices to buy back the company's stock from them.
    B. paying high bonuses to the members of the old management who are fired by the new management.
    C. more regulation by the Securities and Exchange Commission.
    D. restructuring the financial base of the company so that it will be less profitable or valuable to the raiders.

25. **(D)** Paragraph 2 defines the three antitakeover strategies. Statement (A) defines the greenmail strategy. Statement (B) defines the golden parachute theory, and statement (C) is not supported by anything in the passage.

26. According to the passage, supporters of corporate takeovers believe that:

    F. the shareholders always lose money because a takeover profits only the raiders.
    G. fear of being targeted for a takeover makes managers more efficient.
    H. insider trading should be made legal.
    J. a proxy fight is the best way to win control.

26. **(G)** This argument is made at the beginning of the last paragraph. The topics of statements (F), (H), and (J) are all mentioned in the passage, but the text does not support any of these statements.

**27.** According to the passage, in a proxy fight:

   **A.** the raiders sell bonds to buy the targeted company's stock.

   **B.** the raiders offer to buy stock at a higher-than-market price.

   **C.** insider information is sometimes traded illegally.

   **D.** a stockholders' meeting is called to vote for approval or rejection of a new board of directors put forth by the raiders.

**28.** The management of a business recently targeted for takeover decides to sell two of its unprofitable subsidiaries to raise cash and cut expenses. Supporters of corporate takeovers would say that this action:

   **F.** is an example of how the greenmail strategy works.

   **G.** is an example of how a golden parachute strategy works.

   **H.** is an example of how the fear of a takeover makes managers more efficient.

   **J.** is an example of how the poison pill strategy works.

**29.** Bonds with very high interest rates sold to raise cash to buy a large amount of a targeted company for takeover are called:

   **A.** greenmail.
   **B.** junk bonds.
   **C.** common stocks.
   **D.** golden parachutes.

**27.** (D) The meaning of a proxy fight is presented in paragraph 2. The other choices are all true but do not involve a proxy battle.

**28.** (H) This point is explicitly made at the beginning of the last paragraph. All the other choices are properly defined in the paragraph before the last.

**29.** (B) This question requires information beyond the scope of the passage. Choices (A) and (D) are properly defined within the passage. Choice (C) clearly contradicts the stem of the question since bonds are not stock.

**DIRECTIONS:** Questions 30–42 are not based on a reading passage. Choose the *best* answer to each question in accordance with your background and understanding in social studies.

30. Sigmund Freud developed a theory of the stages of psychosexual development in individuals. In this theory, the first stage is called the:

   F. anal stage.
   G. phallic stage.
   H. latency stage.
   J. oral stage.

30. (J) In Freud's theory, the first stage was called the oral stage. In this stage, the child seeks gratification through his or her mouth.

31. The invention of cuneiform is considered to be one of the major cultural achievements of the Sumerians. Cuneiform is:

   A. a system of writing.
   B. a type of painting.
   C. a process for making clothing.
   D. a type of building material.

31. (A) The writing system invented by the Sumerians is called cuneiform. It is composed primarily of wedge-shaped symbols that were impressed on damp clay.

32. In labor relations, a worker's "right to work" is:

   F. the right to join a union.
   G. the right to engage in collective bargaining.
   H. the right to a permanent job.
   J. the right not to join a union.

32. (J) In labor relations, the "right to work" is a worker's legal right not to join a union that represents the worker's co-workers. This right, guaranteed by law in certain states, has sometimes been supported by employers as a way of discouraging membership among workers.

33. The individual rights guaranteed by the Bill of Rights are:

   A. absolute.
   B. subject to interpretation by the President.
   C. balanced against the welfare of society as a whole.
   D. subject to review by Congress.

33. (C) The individual rights guaranteed by the Bill of Rights are not absolute, but typically are balanced against the welfare of society as a whole. An individual does not have the unrestricted right to assemble anywhere, anytime, or in any manner if society as a whole will be endangered by such actions.

34. The first openly active role that the United States took in World War II was:

   F. landing troops on the beaches of France.
   G. providing air support to protect Great Britain.
   H. providing Red Cross supplies to German POWs.
   J. providing supplies and equipment to Great Britain under the Lend-Lease Act.

34. (J) When Great Britain began having difficulty affording supplies and military equipment, the United States, under the Lend-Lease Act of March 1941, began providing equipment and supplies to Britain and to other countries that were fighting against Germany.

**35.** The philosophy of communism asserts that the wealth produced through labor rightly belongs to the workers rather than to their capitalist employers. The originator of modern communist theory was:

- **A.** Vladimir Lenin.
- **B.** Adam Smith.
- **C.** Karl Marx.
- **D.** Joseph Stalin.

**36.** The executive branch officials provided for in the Constitution include the President and also:

- **F.** the Vice-President only.
- **G.** the Vice-President and the Cabinet.
- **H.** the Vice-President, the Cabinet, and the National Security Council.
- **J.** the Vice-President and the Secretary of State.

**37.** The federal agency that enforces standards for workplace conditions is called the:

- **A.** Federal Trade Commission.
- **B.** Environmental Protection Agency.
- **C.** Occupational Safety and Health Administration.
- **D.** Securities and Exchange Commission.

**38.** The Treaty of Paris, which ended the American Revolutionary War in 1783, did not provide for:

- **F.** American fishing rights off the coast of Canada.
- **G.** American repayment of all debts owed to British merchants.
- **H.** restoration or government purchase of lands confiscated from British Loyalists.
- **J.** American ownership of lands west of the Mississippi River.

**39.** Polyandry is a marriage arrangement involving:

- **A.** one man and one woman.
- **B.** one man and more than one woman.
- **C.** one woman and more than one man.
- **D.** more than one man and more than one woman.

**40.** The consumer movement in the United States has had its greatest success in achieving its goals by relying on:

- **F.** government regulation.
- **G.** the free-enterprise system.
- **H.** voluntary self-regulation by producers.
- **J.** None of the above.

**35.** (C) Karl Marx, a German philosopher, produced the first works of modern "scientific" communist theory in the late 1840s. A central tenet of Marx's theory is that capitalist employers exploit workers by appropriating the wealth produced by their labor.

**36.** (F) Of all the choices, only the Vice-President is mentioned in the Constitution, and his or her only official function is to serve as President of the Senate.

**37.** (C) The Occupational Safety and Health Administration (OSHA) enforces standards for proper workplace conditions.

**38.** (J) Under the Treaty of Paris, the Americans gained control of most of the area between the Appalachian Mountains and the Mississippi River. They were also guaranteed fishing rights off the coast of Canada. In return, they agreed to honor all debts owed to British merchants before the war and to restore or purchase lands confiscated from British Loyalists.

**39.** (C) Polyandry, a marriage arrangement involving one woman and more than one man, is practiced primarily in parts of southern Asia.

**40.** (F) The consumer movement has come to rely on government regulation to achieve its goals, since government is the most powerful external force able to restrain the counterproductive acts of producers.

**41.** The share of the vote needed to win a seat in Congress is at least a:

**A.** three-fifths majority.
**B.** plurality.
**C.** two-thirds majority.
**D.** three-fourths majority.

**42.** Plato was the first great thinker to analyze political systems. He believed that people should be ruled by:

**F.** elected representatives.
**G.** officials chosen by lot.
**H.** an emperor appointed by the senate.
**J.** philosopher-kings.

**41.** (B) To win a seat in Congress, a candidate must receive at least a plurality of the votes cast for that seat.

**42.** (J) Plato questioned existing ideas about government and democracy, and he believed that the best government would be one led by philosopher-kings, who would have the knowledge needed to govern in the whole society's best interest.

In July of 1893 Frederick Jackson Turner, a historian from the University of Wisconsin, presented a paper to a group of historians convening in Chicago during the Columbian Exposition. Entitled "The Significance of the American Frontier in History," Turner's paper drew little immediate reaction. Yet no theory of history has had a greater influence on the direction and methodology of inquiry and the issues of debate in American history. Later historians took issue with some of Turner's interpretations; some of his own students were among those whose research proved certain of his views wrong. Yet these debates merely serve to illustrate the importance of Turner's hypothesis.

Turner's was an overarching hypothesis about how the settlement of the frontier had shaped the American experience and character. As with all general hypotheses in any field of study, it gave a coherent interpretation to many facts that had been largely ignored by historians up to that time.

Turner used statistical evidence from the 1880 census as the basis for a startling conclusion: Prior to 1880 there had been a frontier to be settled. By 1890, Turner pointed out, there was no longer any area of wilderness completely untouched by settlements. The frontier had disappeared. The passing of the frontier, Turner concluded, was a historic moment.

Turner further claimed that the frontier experience had produced a distinctively American character, which was not explainable simply as the predictable behavioral traits molded by English political institutions. Frontier settlers developed inquisitiveness, inventiveness, energy, and a great passion for freedom. These attributes defined a new American character, one evidenced in nationalism, independence, and democracy. This new sense of national identity derived from the fact that people from every section of the country mixed at the Western frontier. Economic independence could be traced to the fact that the settlers no longer depended on England for goods but had become self-sufficient. In addition, the frontier settlers, whose basic social unit was the family, enjoyed freedom from direct governmental interference. Frontier life thus reinforced the fundamental ideals of populist democracy.

Turner also argued that the frontier fostered democracy in the cities of the East. The availability of free land at the frontier provided a "safety-valve" against possible social unrest: Those discontented with social inequities and economic injustice could strike out and settle the free land available in frontier territories.

Turner's thesis was thus original in both what it said and in the methodology that Turner used in formulating it. Up to the time of Turner's essay, history had been essentially the history of politics. A Midwesterner, Turner challenged this traditional approach of Eastern historians by incorporating techniques of the social sciences, showing how factors of geography, economics, climate, and society influenced the development of the American West. Although now common among historians, at the time this interdisciplinary approach was novel.

---

**43.** Turner's essay challenged the views of:

   **A.** frontier writers such as Mark Twain.
   **B.** other American historians of his time.
   **C.** sociologists.
   **D.** European critics of America.

**44.** Turner's methods were original in that he:

   **F.** utilized research techniques from a variety of other academic fields.
   **G.** insulted other historians.
   **H.** refused to encourage further research.
   **J.** ignored the need for a unifying view.

**43.** (B) As stated in the last paragraph of the passage, Turner's essay challenged the views of other American historians of his time.

**44.** (F) Turner was the first historian to use the techniques of the social sciences to formulate and investigate historical questions. He studied the effects of economic, geographical, and sociological factors on the settlement of the American West. In addition, Turner redirected the focus of historical inquiry away from politics and political leaders, centering it instead on the lives of people in a national setting. In doing so, Turner identified what he considered to be the attributes of the American character.

45. Turner's evidence for the disappearance of the American frontier drew on:

A. interviews with settlers.
B. his reading of Karl Marx.
C. diaries.
D. the census of 1880.

45. (D) As noted in the third paragraph of the passage, Turner's evidence for the disappearance of the American frontier drew on the census of 1880.

46. Turner's essay affected:

F. the reputations of American historians in Europe.
G. future settlements in the West.
H. the way in which population was counted.
J. the subsequent focus of inquiry in American history.

46. (J) As stated in the first paragraph of the passage, Turner's essay affected the subsequent direction and methodology of inquiry in American history.

47. One fact that casts a doubtful light on Turner's view that the West was settled by individuals looking for escape from the pressures of Eastern city life is that:

A. many Western towns had few inhabitants.
B. few people settled in mountain country.
C. much of the land in the West and Midwest was actually bought by wealthy land speculators from the East.
D. many people chose to settle along the banks of the Mississippi.

47. (C) The fact that much of the land in the West and Midwest was bought by wealthy land speculators from the East cast doubt on Turner's view that the West was settled by individuals looking to escape from the pressure of city life in the East.

48. Which of the following items proves that Turner's "safety-valve" theory was false?

F. Population movements showed that more people actually left the farms for the cities than left cities to move to the frontier.
G. Much of the West had a desert climate.
H. The transcontinental railroad was completed in 1869.
J. The numbers of buffalo dropped markedly during the late nineteenth century.

48. (F) In contrast to Turner's theory that the West served as a safety valve by providing a means for the dissipation of social dissatisfaction stemming from the frustration of city life, demographic data show that more people actually left the farms for the cities than left the cities to move to the frontier.

49. A theory would best be defined as:

A. a foolish notion founded on questionable data.
B. an idle speculation that may have no basis in fact.
C. a hypothesis that explains a large number of isolated facts.
D. a somewhat questionable view of factual data.

49. (C) A theory can be defined as a hypothesis that contains an assumed explanation of a large number of isolated facts. A theory can be tested and thus can be proved or disproved.

**50.** The frontier line of America moved essentially from:

    **F.**   the South to the East.

    **G.**   the West to the East.

    **H.**   the East to the West.

    **J.**   the North to the South.

**51.** The economic independence of Americans arose, Turner said, from the fact that:

    **A.**   Americans rarely bought anything.

    **B.**   many pioneers had few relatives left in Europe.

    **C.**   Americans were buying American goods rather than English goods.

    **D.**   few settlers ever voted in local elections.

**52.** Which of the following quotations captures the approach of historians at the time when Turner read his paper?

    **F.**   "This history of the world is but the biography of great men."

    **G.**   "History is past Politics and Politics is present History."

    **H.**   "Those who do not heed the lessons of history are doomed to repeat them."

    **J.**   "Anybody can make history. Only a great man can write it."

**50.** (H) The frontier line of America moved from the East, where the first English colonies were founded, to the West, where the last settlements were established.

**51.** (C) According to Turner, the change from the American pattern of buying goods made in England to buying goods made in the United States culminated in the economic independence of Americans.

**52.** (G) As stated in the last paragraph of the passage, before Turner turned his attention to studying the people and the settlements of the American frontier, American historians had restricted the boundaries of American history to the history of politics and the roles played by past American political leaders.

# Social Studies Reading Warm-Up Test 1

Now that you have "walked through" a Social Studies Reading Test, it is time for you to do a full-length practice exercise under timed conditions.

Set aside at least an hour during which you won't be interrupted. Use a watch to time yourself. After time has expired, but before you check the answer key and explanations on page 440, finish any questions you did not have time to finish. Then check your work.

# SOCIAL STUDIES READING

*35 Minutes—52 Questions*

**DIRECTIONS:** Below each of the following reading passages is a series of questions. Choose the *best* answer to each question, interpreting what is stated or implied by the passage in the light of your own background in the subject. You may refer back to the passage as often as necessary, though the answers to some questions may not be found expressly in the passage.

---

What is the object of the People's Charter? The undoubted answer is to obtain social and political equality. Some wiseacres may, perhaps, drop in a question, ask what is meant by social and political equality, thinking (the stupid knaves) to overthrow the whole theory by simply asking the question. However, to show the coxcombs that the question is not only easily answered, but that equality is not quite so visionary as interested people have been in the habit of maintaining, I beg to give, in a few words, what I consider to be its true definition: —Political equality means that every individual in any given state, has the right not only to take part in all political proceedings whatever, whether it be to give a vote for a member of Parliament or for a parish officer, but also that he has the right to fill any office of state, if the majority of his fellow citizens will and approve that he should do so—in other words, political equality means that no one individual man is better than another one, unless the majority of his fellow citizens declare him to be so. Political equality means that the minority must submit to the will of the majority, at the same time that freedom of speech and opinion is secured to all. Social equality means, that the mountains of wealth must be pulled down, and the valleys of want filled up. Social equality means that thousands of heads of cattle and swine must not be exported from Ireland annually, whilst her population are dying from want of food, and perishing for want of shelter and clothing. Social equality means, that the four courses to a meal, viz., fish, flesh, fowl and pudding, with a drop of something afterwards, is rather too barefaced, whilst the poor labourer, through whose sweat and toil all these good things are produced, is dragging on a wretched existence in want of even the common necessaries of life; in short, social equality means, that all shall have a good house to live in with a garden at the back or front, just as the occupier likes; good clothing to keep him warm, and to make him look respectable, and plenty of good food and drink to make him look and *feel* happy. Yes, my friends, social equality means, that though *all* must work, yet all must be happy. And now, having answered the inquirer as to what I consider social and political equality to mean, just let me ask you, kind reader, one single question, do you expect that such a state of things will ever come to pass, by going down on your bended knees and praying for it? Be not deceived, your tyrants, will never concede justice till they are compelled; never will they yield to your *demands* even till they are overcome by the fire and sword, driven or exterminated from the face of the earth.

1. One would most likely read the above passage in:
   A. a high school textbook.
   B. a political science journal.
   C. an historical novel.
   D. a radical newspaper.

2. The main purpose of this passage is to:
   F. discuss the theory of communism.
   G. incite a riot amongst the populace.
   H. define the nature of basic human rights.
   J. All of the above.

3. The author would most likely agree that:
   A. the government always looks after the welfare of the disadvantaged.
   B. all individuals need four course meals.
   C. social and political equality are basic human rights.
   D. the prayers of the masses will always be answered.

4. As used in this passage, the word *visionary* (line 5) means:

F. impractical.
G. far-seeing.
H. pragmatic.
J. genuine.

5. The "People's Charter" referred to in line 1 is most likely:

A. an individual who represents the masses in dealings with the government.
B. a document setting forth aims for social and political reform.
C. a radical journal intended to cause riots among the poor.
D. a piece of legislation detailing certain privileges enjoyed by the ruling classes.

6. The type of government the author implies would be most receptive to the principles in this passage is a:

F. communist regime.
G. absolute monarchy.
H. democracy.
J. oligarchy.

7. The tone of this passage can be described as:

A. detached.
B. amused.
C. impassioned.
D. pedantic.

8. To achieve the ends stated in the passage, the author seems to approve:

F. armed rebellion.
G. boycotting Irish goods.
H. voting for members of Parliament.
J. giving the laborer "the common necessaries of life."

9. In this passage social equality is defined as:

A. the workers owning the means of production.
B. the population controlling exportation.
C. each laborer providing his own goods.
D. all individuals having the right to adequate food, clothing and shelter.

10. This passage is most likely addressed to:

F. members of Parliament.
G. the ruling monarch.
H. poor laborers.
J. parish officers.

Anthropology is the study of human beings and the diverse manifestations of human culture. Culture can be defined as the way of life of a particular race or of a large social group. An aspect of social group existence peculiar to man alone, culture includes all behavior that is learned and passed on from generation to generation. What is meant by culture varies widely from place to place as well as from period to period during people's existence on earth.

The two basic divisions of anthropology are physical anthropology and cultural anthropology. Physical anthropology is the study of the human race as a biological organism. It includes the comparative study of differences in human size and form, as exhibited both by contemporary races and by fossilized specimens of earlier human and primate forms. The focus of contemporary physical anthropology is on biological evolution, in particular on the relationship between humans and other mammals and between humans and other primates. Physical anthropologists now employ techniques of modern science, which include genetics and biochemistry, disciplines that have made it possible to study subtle distinctions of blood type and genetic susceptibility to or immunity from disease.

Cultural anthropology concerns itself with the study of human cultures, both historically and geographically. It encompasses three disciplines: archeology, ethnology, and linguistics. Archeology is the attempt to describe and analyze the material remains of earlier cultures. The archeologist is the historian of anthropology. Archeology reaches far beyond recorded human history, however. It deals with evidence accumulated over a great span of time. Man's culture preceded the development of writing systems by thousands of years. The focus of archeology is on the discovery of artifacts, including tools, pottery, and weapons—objects fashioned or altered by human beings in order to achieve a goal. From such evidence the specific facts about the culture of a group of human beings can be inferred.

Just as the archeologist studies cultures of the past, the ethnologist studies contemporary cultures in depth. To study a culture properly, the ethnologist must engage in field work, living among the people whose culture he desires to study, learning their customs and habits, their language, and their religious belief systems.

Linguistics is the study of language as a phenomenon of human culture. Descriptive linguistics is the study of the grammatical and lexical structures of a language, as well as its vocabulary. Comparative linguistics focuses on the relationship between contemporary language systems and between the historical variations within and between the language families of the world. The relationship between language and culture is complex. One of the basic questions in anthropological linguistics concerns just how language and culture interact. In what way is one responsible for the other? Which plays a primary role? For example, Western languages have relatively few words to describe camels and the activities associated with them. The Arabic dialects of nomadic Bedouins, however, reveal an amazing wealth of terms for naming camels, their behavior, and other things related to a way of life in which the camel is the central animal for travel and the movement of goods across the desert.

**11.** From the information in this passage, one can conclude that:

**A.** learned behavior is important for a definition of culture.

**B.** variations in behavior among cultures can be ascribed to relative size of the brain.

**C.** blood type directly affects learned behavior.

**D.** genetics will someday replace anthropology as a discipline.

**12.** One of the ways in which archeology can contribute to advances in physical anthropology is through the:

**F.** unearthing of human and primate fossils.

**G.** unearthing of human artifacts such as pottery.

**H.** study of written records.

**J.** comparative study of the languages of a culture.

**13.** Discoveries at the site of an archeological dig might yield evidence about:

I. the stage of the biological development of the people who lived in that region.

II. the relative importance of weapons in the daily life of the community.

III. the effect of climate on the life of the community.

**A.** I, II, and III

**B.** III only

**C.** II and III

**D.** I and III

**14.** The degree of sophistication of prehistoric tools might offer a clue to:

**F.** the language spoken by the people.

**G.** the comparative size of the brain at that time.

**H.** the number of language families in the world.

**J.** the governmental structure of the social unit.

**15.** According to the passage, ethnology is:

**A.** the study of contemporary human cultures across the world.

**B.** the study of past cultures across the world.

**C.** the study of lost cities of the world.

**D.** the study of the written record of commerce and industry.

**16.** The primary focus of the first paragraph is on:

**F.** a definition of cultural anthropology.

**G.** a definition of physical anthropology.

**H.** a definition of culture.

**J.** the distinction between history and archeology.

**17.** The fact that Eskimos have more than 20 words to describe snow suggests that:

**A.** Eskimo customs influenced their history.

**B.** Eskimo language is unlike other language.

**C.** knowledge of snow was important to Eskimo survival.

**D.** Eskimo poetry developed primarily apart from nature.

**18.** The fact that ethnologists must learn the language of the people they are studying suggests that:

I. ethnology has contributed to the development of linguistics.

II. ethnologists need to study Latin or Greek first.

III. ethnologists need training in linguistic methods.

**F.** I and II

**G.** I and III

**H.** I only

**J.** II and III

**19.** Which of the following items of information is important for an ethnologist?

I. the religious practices of a people

II. the oral literature of a people

III. the family structure of a people

**A.** I and II

**B.** II and III

**C.** I, II, and III

**D.** II only

**20.** The province of cultural anthropology includes the study of:

**F.** biological variations in brain sizes.

**G.** the blood of humans and primates.

**H.** language as a social and cultural phenomenon.

**J.** comparative description of the bone structure of hands and feet.

One of the most dramatic examples of post-war inflation and the panic it could create was demonstrated by the events in Europe in the years following World War I.

The war had left virtually all of Europe bankrupt, and most countries were faced with rebuilding their own economies as well as paying off debts to other nations. Germany was required to make reparations to France, and virtually every Allied country in Western Europe was indebted to the United States, which had been a chief supplier of war munitions at high prices.

Since countries had exhausted their reserves of precious metals for use as hard currency, in paying off foreign debts they resorted to the "printing press" solution by making paper money widely available. As this money began to circulate, each country's unit of currency began to devaluate rapidly since paper currency lacked the stability inherent to gold currency. Before Germany abandoned the gold standard, one American dollar bought five German marks. By early 1923, after the paper mark had been introduced, one American dollar bought over 21,000 paper marks. Other European countries also experienced currency devaluations, although not to the same extent as Germany.

American insistence on the repayment of the Europeans' outstanding war debts slowed economic recovery there, although at home it prompted one of the greatest periods of economic expansion in United States history, commonly known as the "Roaring Twenties."

The economic stagnation in Europe, made even worse with the onset of the Great Depression in 1929, had inevitable political ramifications leading up to World War II. Fascist leaders came to power in Germany and Italy, promising a restoration of prosperity on the basis of tremendous military expansion.

The aftermath of World War II presents a marked contrast to United States policy in Europe following World War I. Instead of merely collecting wartime repayments like before, the United States implemented the Marshall Plan, which provided the necessary capital to virtually rebuild Western Europe. Not only did this policy help the Western Europeans; it provided jobs for Americans and helped to prevent an anticipated postwar depression. With the restored economic prosperity in Europe came political stability, which has lasted for more than forty years.

21. One of the primary aims of the passage is to link economic events with:

  A. post-war peace conferences.
  B. the Great Depression.
  C. the Roaring Twenties.
  D. political consequences.

22. The introduction of paper-based currency caused rampant inflation in Europe because:

  F. paper currency was less valuable than gold.
  G. paper currency fluctuated in value, whereas the value of gold had remained stable.
  H. European exports to the United States decreased dramatically.
  J. military expansion in Germany and Italy was draining resources that could be put to other uses.

23. According to the passage, when economic crisis overwhelmed Europe after World War I, U.S. economic policy:

  A. mollified it.
  B. remedied it.
  C. exacerbated it.
  D. delayed it.

24. Fascist leaders came to power in Germany and Italy through:

  F. popular support.
  G. threats against the population.
  H. foreign conquest.
  J. abdication of the monarch.

25. It can be inferred from the context of the second paragraph that the Allied countries were those which were fighting:

  A. against France.
  B. on the side of the Germans.
  C. on the side of the United States.
  D. with war munitions.

26. The characterization of the Roaring Twenties as American prosperity at the expense of the Europeans is:

  F. accurate since the Europeans helped rebuild the United States after the war.
  G. inaccurate since it was the United States which made its European allies victorious.
  H. accurate since the transfer of European gold reserves to the United States as war payments infused large amounts of cash into the United States.
  J. inaccurate since the United States actually wound up receiving no payment whatsoever from the debtor nations.

27. In which way was the Marshall Plan *similar* to United States policy toward Europe after World War I?

A. It helped to rebuild war-devastated nations.
B. It collected war debts owed to the United States by the Europeans.
C. It created a climate of political stability.
D. It created conditions of economic prosperity in the United States.

28. Which of the following can be regarded as a reason for the shift in the United States' European policy after the Second World War?

F. The United States was not devastated after the Second World War as it was after the first; therefore, it could afford to help other nations rebuild.
G. The United States realized that its policy after the First World War did not produce lasting stability in Europe; therefore, it sought to pursue a policy after the Second World War which would have the opposite effect.
H. The United States wanted to eventually hegemonize, or take over its Western European allies, and the economic interdependency created by the Marshall Plan was seen as the best way to do so.
J. The United States wanted to prepare its Western European allies for what it saw as an inevitable Third World War.

29. The "Roaring Twenties" were characterized by:

A. United States isolation from the political turmoil in Europe.
B. economic stagnation at home.
C. repudiation of European war debts by the United States.
D. abandonment of the gold standard in the United States.

**DIRECTIONS:** Questions 30–42 are not based on a reading passage. Choose the *best* answer to each question in accordance with your background and understanding in social studies.

30. Actualization theories take a relatively humanistic approach to describing personality development. In general, according to these theories:

F. individual behavior is entirely determined by external events.
G. people have an inherent capability to develop their abilities to their own benefit.
H. individual behavior is determined by the struggle between the id and the superego.
J. interpersonal relationships change as people pass through different stages of psychological development.

31. City-states played a dominant role in Greek life during the Hellenic Age beginning about 800 B.C. Which of the following was a Greek city-state with a reputation for democratic government?

A. Athens
B. Sparta
C. Carthage
D. Tyre

32. State governments obtain their revenues primarily from:

F. income taxes.
G. sales taxes.
H. property taxes.
J. All of the above.

33. Not all state constitutions provide for:

    **A.** separation of executive, legislative, and judicial powers.

    **B.** a governor as chief executive.

    **C.** a way to amend the constitution.

    **D.** a one-house legislature.

34. During the Age of Exploration, many European countries with overseas colonies followed an economic policy called mercantilism, according to which:

    **F.** the role of trade was to encourage self-sufficiency in the colonies.

    **G.** the purpose of the colonies was to provide wealth for the home country.

    **H.** the most important goal was the development of industry in the colonies.

    **J.** emigration from the home country was discouraged.

35. The total population of the world:

    **A.** was estimated at approximately 2 billion in the mid-1980s.

    **B.** is slowly declining.

    **C.** is expected to reach 20 billion by 1990.

    **D.** was estimated at approximately 4 billion in the mid-1970s and is expected to double every 35 years.

36. Both the President and the state governors can be involuntarily removed from office before the end of a term by:

    **F.** impeachment.

    **G.** recall.

    **H.** resignation.

    **J.** referendum.

37. The theory that the government should take a "hands-off" role in the nation's economy is called:

    **A.** supply-side economics.

    **B.** the business cycle.

    **C.** socialism.

    **D.** laissez-faire.

38. In the "Reign of Terror" that occurred during the French Revolution, many people were executed because:

    **F.** the king feared they would rebel against him.

    **G.** they were caught stealing from the government.

    **H.** they were believed to be enemies of the newly established republic.

    **J.** their wealth aroused the jealousy of the poor.

39. The earliest people to reach North America are thought to have arrived:

    **A.** from Asia via a land bridge at the Bering Strait.

    **B.** from South America via Panama.

    **C.** from Europe by sailing ship.

    **D.** from Asia by raft.

40. A noted political economist who believed that population growth would eventually outstrip the world's food supplies was:

    **F.** Thomas Hobbes.

    **G.** John Locke.

    **H.** Thomas Malthus.

    **J.** Karl Marx.

41. The procedure by which a state may delay enforcing a law until that law is approved by the voters is called the:

    **A.** initiative.

    **B.** referendum.

    **C.** recall.

    **D.** recount.

42. The first successful English colony in the New World was established at:

    **F.** New Orleans.

    **G.** New York.

    **H.** Jamestown.

    **J.** Toronto.

The events of the decade following the Russian revolution of 1917 show that the Communist leadership actually furthered the very notion of the autocrat it had promised to defeat before coming to power.

From 1917 until his death, Lenin ran his newly formed Soviet government under the principle of what he called "democratic centralism," meaning that the chairman of the Communist Party resolved issues and implemented policy through debate among other senior members of the party, although Lenin was not one to take kindly to opposition and would quickly stamp out any views that differed from his own. There was hardly anything democratic about an elite group of nonelected officials running the country in total isolation from the masses, yet "democratic centralism" seems benign when compared to government under Stalin, who took on the responsibilities of leadership after Lenin's death.

While Lenin reluctantly tolerated opposition from within the Communist Party, Stalin eliminated it altogether and in the process became one of history's most notorious dictators. Stalin utilized what became known as "salami tactics" to cultivate alliances within the party and form a coalition to eliminate potential opposition to his quest for leadership. Once this person was effectively defeated, Stalin would proceed to "slice off" those who had sided with him. This cycle of events continued for several years until Stalin emerged as the undisputed leader of the Soviet Union in 1929, impervious to any pressure from within the Communist Party.

Victorious on the political front, Stalin now proceeded to implement policy virtually singlehandedly to fortify the nation, which had never returned to the conditions of economic growth that had preceded the outbreak of World War I in 1914. The most urgent domestic problem was the need for a remedy to the food shortage. In contrast to Lenin, who saw the necessity of making concessions to peasants and other small merchants by allowing them to sell their wares for a profit, Stalin proceeded to collectivize all Soviet farms into a single state-owned entity, and the results were a fiasco; enraged peasants hoarded crops and killed livestock, and famine became even more widespread.

The peasants were not the only group Stalin turned against; a massive campaign was begun in the mid - 1930s to eliminate all those who were perceived by Stalin as "enemies of the state." Trials were staged with forced confessions by the accused, resulting in numerous killings. Hence, a trend can be seen in which Stalin's initial quest for power evolved into full-scale paranoia about keeping his position intact.

43. From the context of the passage, it can be concluded that an "autocrat" is:

A. a democratically elected official.
B. a one-man ruler with absolute power.
C. a cabinet minister who advises the leader.
D. an underground movement.

44. When Lenin's government is described as "benign" compared to Stalin's in the second paragraph, this means that it seemed:

F. cordial.
G. convivial.
H. harmless.
J. erudite.

45. This passage paints a general picture of the Soviet government which is:

A. defensive.
B. critical.
C. flattering.
D. unbiased.

46. The passage conveys that the government in power before World War I:

F. prevailed over more prosperous economic conditions than the Communist government.
G. did a worse job at running the country than the Communist government.
H. voluntarily transferred power to the Communists.
J. used "salami tactics" which enabled the Communists to come to power.

47. The passage conveys the notion that "democratic centralism" was:

A. a way for the population to voice its concerns to the government.
B. a method of diplomatic maneuvers aimed at reaching a compromise within the party.
C. one-man dictatorship in disguise.
D. a method of governing that was imitated by Stalin.

**48.** The passage implies that Stalin's ascent to the leadership after Lenin's death was:

    **F.** accomplished quickly and easily.

    **G.** endorsed by others within the Communist Party.

    **H.** accomplished through popular elections.

    **J.** a complex political process which took time to fully achieve.

**49.** The passage depicts Lenin as a leader who was:

    **A.** always open to suggestions.

    **B.** intent on achieving his goals through violence.

    **C.** more realistic than Stalin in tackling certain problems.

    **D.** able to come to power without bloodshed.

**50.** The passage depicts the Communist Party as:

    **F.** a cooperative, efficient decisionmaking body.

    **G.** an open, democratically elected institution.

    **H.** a government with satellite offices throughout the country which maintained close ties to the citizenry.

    **J.** a political entity that was subject to internal power struggles and potential conflict.

**51.** Which of the following activities would Stalin's regime have been likely to sanction?

    **A.** A straw poll to elect candidates for regional government posts.

    **B.** A voluntary campaign to improve the quality of consumer goods.

    **C.** A forced program of industrialization.

    **D.** A deal granting concessions to rebellious peasants in return for donated livestock.

**52.** The passage strongly implies that those perceived by Stalin to be "enemies of the state":

    **F.** were plotting to overthrow Stalin.

    **G.** were probably innocent.

    **H.** confessed to their crimes voluntarily.

    **J.** were sent to prisons and eventually released by Stalin.

# Answer Key

| | | | | | |
|---|---|---|---|---|---|
| 1. D | 11. A | 21. D | 31. A | 41. B | 51. C |
| 2. H | 12. F | 22. G | 32. J | 42. H | 52. G |
| 3. C | 13. A | 23. C | 33. D | 43. B | |
| 4. F | 14. G | 24. F | 34. G | 44. H | |
| 5. B | 15. A | 25. C | 35. D | 45. B | |
| 6. H | 16. H | 26. H | 36. F | 46. F | |
| 7. C | 17. C | 27. D | 37. D | 47. C | |
| 8. F | 18. G | 28. G | 38. H | 48. J | |
| 9. D | 19. C | 29. A | 39. A | 49. C | |
| 10. H | 20. H | 30. G | 40. H | 50. J | |

# Explanatory Answers

1. **(D)** From the tone and content, it seems most likely that this passage is from a fairly widely distributed publication, possibly a radical newspaper.

2. **(H)** While there is an implication of possible violence in the final sentence, the main purpose of the passage appears to be a discussion of the social and political rights of the individual.

3. **(C)** As previously stated, the author sees social and political equality as human necessities.

4. **(F)** The author implies that many people view the possibility of equality as impractical.

5. **(B)** From the passage, it seems likely that the People's Charter is a document which demands reforms to achieve social and political equality.

6. **(H)** The principles in this passage relate most closely to the basic theory of democracy.

7. **(C)** Its intense expression and sense of justice (and particularly the call to arms in the final sentence) give this passage an impassioned tone.

8. **(F)** Again, in the final sentence, the author seems to advocate armed rebellion.

9. **(D)** The author demands that "all shall have a good house to live in. . . . good clothing to keep him warm, . . . . and plenty of good food and drink to make him look and *feel* happy."

10. **(H)** The author refers to the "kind reader" who is most likely sympathetic to his cause. The workers are the most likely candidates.

11. **(A)** By definition, culture includes all behavior that is learned and passed on from generation to generation.

12. **(F)** Archeologists perform an invaluable service to physical anthropologists by unearthing human and primate fossils. Physical anthropologists use such fossils to study the differences in human size and form and thus to enhance their knowledge of the discipline which is focused on biological evolution.

13. **(A)** Discoveries of both fossils and artifacts yield evidence about the stage of the biological development of the people who lived in the region of the dig, the relative importance of weapons in their daily lives, and the effect of climate on the life of the community. Fossils are studied to determine the stage of biological development, and artifacts are examined to determine atmospheric effects as well as to ascertain the significance of specific tools to the community.

14. **(G)** Because physical anthropologists have hypothesized that brain size correlates with the capacity to forge tools, the degree of sophistication of prehistoric tools might offer a clue about the size of the brain of the prehistoric people who fashioned the tools.

15. (A) As stated in the fourth paragraph of the passage, ethnology is the study of contemporary human cultures across the world.

16. (H) The first paragraph of the passage is focused on a definition of culture.

17. (C) It can be inferred from the last paragraph of the passage that the number of words used to name a specific person, place, or thing indicates the centrality of that person, place, or thing to the society that developed those words. The fact that Eskimos have more than 20 words to describe snow suggests that knowledge of snow was important to their survival.

18. (G) In order to study cultures in depth, ethnologists must learn the languages of various peoples. Ethnologists, therefore, need training in linguistic methods to help them acquire such knowledge. In studying language as a phenomenon of culture, ethnologists have contributed to the study of linguistics.

19. (C) Because an ethnologist is concerned with studying contemporary cultures in depth, knowledge of the religious practices, oral literature, and family structure of a people is essential to the success of his field work.

20. (H) As stated in the third paragraph of the passage, linguistics is one of the disciplines of cultural anthropology. Linguistics is defined in the fifth paragraph: It is the study of language as a phenomenon of human culture.

21. (D) Taken as a whole, the passage contrasts American economic policy toward European allies following the First and Second World Wars, and points out the political events which resulted from these differing policies.

22. (G) The correct answer is stated in the third paragraph.

23. (C) The passage blames the United States for worsening, or *exacerbating*, the plight of European countries by enforcing the payment of war debts when these countries were already struggling to rebuild at home.

24. (F) The fifth paragraph states that Fascist leaders came to power by *promising a restoration of prosperity*. It is logical to assume that such promises allowed them to rise with widespread popular support.

25. (C) Since the Allied countries were provided military equipment by the United States, it is logical to assume that they were fighting on the same side as the United States.

26. (H) The correct answer is stated in the fourth paragraph.

27. (D) The last choice is the only one which is a *similarity* between the two policies.

28. (G) The fact that the United States willingly helped rebuild Western Europe, noted in the last paragraph, lends credence to choice G . No mention is made in the passage of any facts supporting either choices F , H , or J .

29. (A) No mention is made of any turmoil within the United States during the Roaring Twenties, making A the best choice.

30. (G) One of the central tenets of actualization theories is the belief that, when encouraged, individuals can find ways to develop their inherent abilities.

31. (A) Ancient Athens — famous for its statesmen, thinkers, writers, and artists —had a democratic form of government. However, power was restricted to adult male citizens; women, slaves, and those of non-Athenian descent were barred from participation.

32. (J) State governments obtain their revenues from income taxes, sales taxes, and property taxes, as well as from federal grants.

**33.** (D) Of all the state constitutions, only that of Nebraska provides for a one-house legislature.

**34.** (G) According to the policy of mercantilism that the European powers followed during the Age of Exploration, the sole purpose of overseas colonies was to provide wealth for the home country.

**35.** (D) The world's population is estimated to have totaled approximately 1 billion in 1850, 2 billion in 1930, and 4 billion in 1976. At the present growth rate, it is expected that the population will double every 35 years.

**36.** (F) The possibility of removing an elected official via a recall is provided for in only a few state constitutions. However, both the President and any state governor can be removed from office by impeachment. Resignation is the voluntary relinquishing of an office.

**37.** (D) The British economist Adam Smith was an early proponent of the "laissez-faire" economic theory, which holds that government should not attempt to regulate the economy other than through the enforcement of private economic contracts.

**38.** (H) During the Reign of Terror, large numbers of people were executed because they were believed to be enemies of the newly established republic.

**39.** (A) The earliest people to have reached North America are thought to have walked from northeastern Asia across a land bridge at what is now the Bering Strait. The date of this crossing is a subject of intense dispute.

**40.** (H) Thomas Malthus (1766–1834) believed that human population growth, if left unchecked, would eventually outstrip the world's food supplies. The result would be a famine that would reduce the population to a more economically viable size.

**41.** (B) In certain states a law passed by the state legislature may be subject to a referendum; that is, the law will not be enforced until the voters specifically approve it.

**42.** (H) England established its first successful colony in the New World at Jamestown (Virginia) in 1607.

**43.** (B) The discussion emphasizes the fact that both Lenin and Stalin ran their governments virtually singlehandedly. Since the passage says the Communists "continued the notion of the autocrat," it is logical to conclude that an autocrat is also one who rules singlehandedly.

**44.** (H) The passage cynically describes Lenin's notion of "democratic centralism," yet it goes on to describe how Stalin's way of governing was even worse. "Harmless" is the best available choice, closest in meaning to the word *benign*.

**45.** (B) The passage says virtually nothing nice about either Lenin's or Stalin's regime, and it certainly says nothing to defend either regime. *Critical* best describes the tone of this passage.

**46.** (F) Reference in the fourth paragraph to the fact that the country "never returned to the conditions of economic growth" that had existed before the Communists came to power means that conditions were more prosperous before they came to power.

**47.** (C) The second paragraph describes the Communist Party as "an elite group of nonelected officials" with Lenin, as chairman, quick to "stamp out any views that differed from his own." These characteristics are most consistent with the notion of dictatorship.

**48.** (J) The third paragraph describes Stalin's "salami tactics" which involved repeated maneuvers to form alliances within the party to eliminate opposition, with the process taking several years to complete.

**49.** (C) The fourth paragraph notes that Lenin "saw the necessity of making concessions" to certain groups of people, while Stalin went ahead with his own agenda regardless of the reaction to it.

**50.** (J) The passage as a whole emphasizes the opposition faced by both Lenin and Stalin during their tenure as leader, and how Stalin in particular had to manipulate people in order to achieve full power. No evidence can be found to support any of the other choices.

**51.** (C) The passage makes no mention of Stalin's regime being democratic; nor does it mention any tendency to grant concessions to any interest groups. Choice (C) is most consistent with the facets of Stalin's regime that are discussed.

**52.** (G) The last paragraph says that the confessions by the accused were *forced*, implying that these people were probably innocent.

# Social Studies Reading Warm-Up Test 2

Here is another full-length Social Studies Reading Test to be done under timed conditions. Set aside at least an hour during which you won't be interrupted. Use a watch to time yourself. After time has expired, but before you check the answer key and explanations on page 454, finish any questions you did not have time to finish. Then check your work.

# SOCIAL STUDIES READING

*35 minutes—52 questions*

**DIRECTIONS:** Below each of the following reading passages is a series of questions. Choose the *best* answer to each question, interpreting what is stated or implied by the passage in the light of your own background in the subject. You may refer back to the passage as often as necessary, though the answers to some questions may not be found expressly in the passage.

---

The primary cause of emotion is a stimulus, either an external one, such as an accident, or an internal one, such as a sharp pain. During an emotion-producing experience, physiological changes occur in the body, each of which produces a condition that allows a person to react swiftly to the stimulus. The heart beats faster and blood pressure increases in order to increase the supply of oxygen to the brain, making faster cognitive response possible. The level of sugar in the blood also increases, adding needed energy for physical action in response to the stimulus. The supply of blood-clotting factor increases to help prevent possible blood loss due to injury. Digestive processes also slow, making more blood available for both mental and physical reactions.

Clearly, psychologists know how the body reacts to an emotion-producing stimulus. What they do not know, however, is whether the bodily changes precede the awareness of emotion or result from it. One theory of emotion, first proposed by William James and Carl Lange in the 1890s, expressed the view that bodily reactions to a stimulus precede the cognitive awareness of the emotion. According to this theory, if something frightening occurs, the first reaction is in the body. Only after the physiological changes have occurred does one sense fear. Emotions thus are one's conscious awareness of the bodily changes.

The Cannon-Bard theory, which was formulated in the 1920s, proposed that both the bodily changes that signal the body's reaction to a stimulus and the conscious awareness of emotion occur simultaneously. The basis for this view lay in the fact that the hypothalamus, a gland in the brain, sends messages to the nervous system. These messages initiate bodily responses and at the same time send messages to the brain itself, which result in the feeling or emotion.

A third and more recent theory takes an entirely different perspective on the problem by focusing on the cognitive awareness of emotion. It was discovered that when asked to describe an emotion recently experienced, a person usually describes not physiological changes but the situation, person, or object that was the stimulus of the emotion. The labeling of the emotion as happiness, sorrow, or anger comes *after* the description of the stimulus situation. Experiments supporting the theory suggested strongly that how one *interprets* the physiological reaction is a crucial element. When people do not actually know what is causing the physiological reactions, they turn to the environment in which the situations occurred and from that decide how to name the emotions they feel.

**1.** The basic question answered by each of the three theories of emotion concerns:

**A.** whether sensed emotions are anything more than the body's physiological reactions to a stimulus.

**B.** whether a stimulus is necessary in order to experience an emotion.

**C.** the relationship between stimulus, bodily reactions to it, and felt emotion.

**D.** whether glands actually play a key role in emotion.

**2.** The effect of increased heart rate and blood pressure is to:

**F.** hasten the digestive process.

**G.** hasten the action of the hypothalamus.

**H.** increase the supply of oxygen to the brain.

**J.** increase the level of sugar in the blood.

3. During a response to an emotion-causing situation, the digestive process:

   A. stops.
   B. increases.
   C. slows.
   D. remains the same.

4. The James-Lange theory of emotion states that:

   I. emotional awareness follows physiological re-actions to a stimulus.
   II physiological reactions arise after emotional awareness.
   III. both physiological reactions and emotional awareness occur simultaneously.

   F. I only
   G. II only
   H. III only
   J. None of the above.

5. The Cannon-Bard theory of emotion states that:

   I. emotional awareness follows physiological re-actions to a stimulus.
   II. physiological reactions arise after emotional awareness.
   III. both physiological reactions and emotional awareness occur simultaneously.

   A. I only
   B. II only
   C. III only
   D. None of the above.

6. The cognitive theory of emotion takes the view that in an emotional experience people tend to focus on:

   F. the environmental context in which the emo-tion occurred and not on the physiological reactions.
   G. the physiological responses and not the envi-ronmental context.
   H. the quality of the emotion itself and not the context of it.
   J. None of the above.

7. Objections that could be raised to the James-Lange theory might include:

   I. a person pleasantly surprised is less likely to faint than one who is frightened.
   II. physiological reactions do not differ significantly from one emotion to another.
   III. emotions are sensed in different degrees by different people.

   A. I and II
   B. II only
   C. II and II
   D. III only

8. Arguments that tend to disprove the Cannon-Bard theory include the following:

   I. Because it is difficult to determine when a stimulus actually occurs, it is not possible to determine exactly when the emotional aware-ness and the physiological reactions actually take place.
   II. If the stimulus is internal, it is difficult to determine exactly when such a stimulus begins to produce reactions.
   III. Because emotions tend to heighten physiologi-cal reactions, which in turn cause heightened emotional awareness, it is difficult to say which is cause and which is effect.

   F. I only
   G. II and III
   H. I and II
   J. I, II, and III

9. Which of the following statements is true?

   A. The James-Lange theory preceded the Cannon-Bard theory.
   B. The James-Lange theory depends on the Cannon-Bard theory.
   C. The cognitive theory of emotions preceded the Cannon-Bard theory.
   D. The cognitive theory preceded the James-Lange theory.

10. The bodily changes that occur in response to an emotion-producing stimulus:

   F. lessen the ability to react to the stimulus.
   G. heighten the ability to react to the stimulus.
   H. heighten a person's ability to describe the emotion.
   J. prevent a person from describing the emotion.

In addition to providing essential services to their residents, the municipal governments of thousands of towns, cities, and villages across the United States also are empowered to exercise executive and legislative authority. The organization of the government of a municipality is decided by the type of charter it has adopted. In the United States, there are three basic kinds of municipal government: the mayor-council plan, the commission plan, and the council-manager plan.

The *mayor-council plan* is by far the most popular; it is used in about half the American cities with populations of more than 5,000. In fact, there are really two mayor-council plans, depending on the actual powers given to the mayor. Under both mayor-council plans, the citizens elect a mayor and a city council.

Under the *strong mayor plan* favored by most large cities, the mayor has substantial or full executive authority. A strong mayor directs all the services of the city and has hiring and firing power over the administrators of the various service agencies and departments.

Under the *weak mayor plan*, the mayor has much more limited powers, and in some variations on the plan, the mayor's position is largely ceremonial. The City Council controls the various city departments and services and has the power to hire and fire. In some municipalities, a weak mayor has certain veto powers over the City Council; nevertheless, it is clear that it is the council, not the mayor, who is responsible for running the government day to day.

The *commission plan* enjoyed some popularity in the early twentieth century. The plan was first used in Galveston, Texas, in 1908 and became popular among reformers for a decade or two. In a commission government, the citizens elect commissioners who perform both executive and legislative functions. Each commissioner heads a city agency, and together the commissioners form the City Council. In most cities that operate under a commission plan, the voters do not elect a mayor, although the City Council may appoint one of its own members to be mayor. When this occurs, the additional title usually brings only ceremonial duties. Only a few hundred municipalities currently use a commission plan.

Another type of municipal government in the United States is the council-manager plan. This type of government began in Staunton, Virginia, in 1908. It was soon adopted in places where there were serious problems facing the citizens of the municipality. Under the *council-manager plan*, the citizens elect a number of people as a council to carry out legislative duties. The council is empowered to hire a professional manager to handle the day-to-day business of the municipality.

In most municipalities that are governed under a council-manager plan, the manager can appoint or fire department heads and other municipal officials. Although the council is not supposed to interfere with the day-to-day operations of the municipality, it does have the right to hire and fire the city manager. About one-third of the cities with populations of fewer than 500,000 currently have a council-manager plan. A large number of these places are in the West, especially California.

11. The most common type of municipal government in the United States is:

   A. the mayor-council plan.
   B. the commission plan.
   C. the council-manager plan.
   D. the metropolis plan.

12. Under which municipal system of government might the mayor hold an essentially ceremonial position?

   I. the commission plan
   II. the weak mayor variation of the mayor-council plan
   III. the strong mayor variation of the mayor-council plan

   F. I only
   G. II only
   H. III only
   J. I and II

13. Under the commission plan, *each* commissioner performs which functions?

   I. executive functions such as heading a municipal agency
   II. legislative functions such as serving on the City Council and passing new ordinances
   III. ceremonial functions of the mayor such as attending awards dinners

   A. I only
   B. II only
   C. I and II
   D. I, II, and III

14. The mayor of a large city fires his commissioner of transportation after a series of accidents involving buses reveals that there has been poor maintenance of the vehicles. The mayor in this example is properly governing under a:

    F. commission plan.
    G. mayor-council plan.
    H. council-manager plan.
    J. None of the above.

15. Which of the following would you expect not to be a function of the City Council under a weak mayor variation of the mayor-council plan?

    A. the right to hire and fire the mayor
    B. the right to appoint the heads of municipal agencies
    C. the right to pass new local laws
    D. the right to establish public policy for the city

16. Which of the following would you expect to be the chief defect of the commission plan?

    F. inability to pass new laws
    G. inability to manage the administration of services to the public
    H. lack of strong leadership from a chief administrator
    J. lack of money to provide municipal services

17. Under the mayor-council plan, weak and strong mayors both:

    A. may make recommendations to the council.
    B. may fire the heads of municipal agencies.
    C. may fire members of the City Council.
    D. may enact new municipal ordinances.

18. A comparatively recent innovation in connection with the strong mayor plan is:

    F. the removal of the deputy mayor.
    G. the addition of a commission that reports to the mayor.
    H. the removal of all legislative functions from the City Council.
    J. the addition of a managing director selected by and responsible to the mayor.

19. The controlling principle of the council-manager plan is the:

    A. diffusion of authority and responsibility among the members of the council.
    B. concentration of authority and responsibility in the mayor.
    C. concentration of authority and responsibility in the council.
    D. concentration of authority and responsibility in the council in conjunction with a division of functions between the council and the manager.

20. Which of the following is not a power usually possessed by the manager under a council-manager plan?

    I. the direction, control, supervision, and coordination of the city services
    II. the appointment and removal of department heads
    III. the preparation and execution of the city budget

    F. I only
    G. II only
    H. II and III
    J. I, II, and II

Many people who are concerned with the size of the current federal budget deficit, or national debt, think that a substantial reduction in the deficit can be achieved by various kinds of tax remedies. Among these are two types of taxes that are new to the United States.

*Consumption Tax.* This type of tax is applied directly to the consumer. It is a tax calculated on the total sum of dollar expenditures during a year. At present, people in the United States are not taxed directly on expenditures but on income only. A consumption tax would thus become a kind of national sales tax. At present the federal government does not tax sales as do states and local communities.

A consumption tax is based on what are termed "consumption expenditures," which are defined as the difference between yearly income and the amount of yearly savings. An example makes clear the method of calculating this tax. First, one would determine one's net worth—the difference between the value of one's assets and one's debt, or liabilities. Let us suppose that one's net worth for the given year came out to $4,000 more than it did the previous year. One's consumption expenditures would then be the difference between total income and net worth for the year, for example, $37,000 less $4,000, or $33,000. This is the amount on which the consumption tax would be levied. If the tax rate were 10 percent, the tax would come to $3,300.

*Value-Added Tax.* This tax is paid directly by the manufacturer, not the individual consumer. "Value added" is defined as the difference between the amount of money a manufacturer actually gets from the sale of a product and the amount of money the manufacturer paid for the raw materials from which the product was made. The tax has the effect of raising the price of manufactured goods. In theory, the buyer does not bear the full amount of the tax. Part is borne by the shareholders of the company, who may receive a lower rate of return on their investments. Part is also borne by employees, whose wages and salaries may be lowered. The disadvantage of a value-added tax to the consumer is that unlike the consumption tax, the tax is indirect. Although the individual consumer ends up paying more for the product, it is not clear just how much of the price is actually tax. The mode of collection makes the tax a hidden one.

Those who argue for both types of taxes say that such taxes add incentive to savings. It is only fair to this argument to point out that at present, taxpayers are in effect taxed twice on savings dollars, once as earned income and again on the dollars of interest that money earns. The benefit of either a consumption or a value-added tax to the taxpayer would not be great unless the federal government changed its treatment of savings, either by a significant reduction in the rate of taxation or by eliminating the tax on interest and dividends.

21. Consumption taxes are levied against:

 A. an individual's liabilities.
 B. an individual's net worth.
 C. an individual's total consumption expenditures.
 D. an individual's savings.

22. Consumption expenditures do *not* include:

 F. food costs.
 G. savings dollars.
 H. clothing costs.
 J. interest on loans.

23. In consumption taxes, one's tax is levied:

 I. directly on the individual.
 II. indirectly on the individual.
 III. directly on the manufacturer of goods sold.

 A. I only
 B. II only
 C. III only
 D. II and III

24. Value-added tax is a tax:

 I. on the cost of producing goods.
 II. on the cost of raw materials needed to produce goods.
 III. on the final price of a product.

 F. I only
 G. II and III
 H. II only
 J. I and III

25. The disadvantage of a value-added tax is that:

 A. companies do not know the labor cost of individual items.
 B. companies rarely know the exact cost of raw materials.
 C. what individuals actually pay in taxes is hidden.
 D. what individuals actually pay as tax is too high.

26. The following can be considered to be a national sales tax:

 F. tax on savings interest.
 G. value-added tax.
 H. consumption tax.
 J. both value-added and consumption taxes.

27. The individual taxpayer might be better off with a consumption tax if the:

 A. tax on savings interest were slightly increased.
 B. tax on savings interest were kept as it is at present.
 C. tax on savings interest were eliminated entirely.
 D. tax on savings interest were greatly increased.

28. According to the proposed method of applying consumption tax, if one's income remains constant while one's net worth increases:

 I. one's consumer tax would drop.
 II. one's consumer tax would rise.
 III. one's consumer tax would remain the same.

 F. I only
 G. II only
 H. III only
 J. II or III

29. The consumption tax would produce a probable increase in the rate at which people save money only if:

 A. it were levied in addition to current income taxes.
 B. it replaced the current method of taxing income.
 C. it were levied in addition to a value-added tax.
 D. it were added to a poll tax similar to that recently enacted by the British Parliament.

30. According to Sigmund Freud, defense mechanisms allow people to resolve inner conflicts. The defense mechanism called *sublimination* represents the process whereby individuals:

    F. display unacceptable impulses in socially acceptable ways.
    G. behave in a manner completely opposite from their true feelings.
    H. refuse to believe they have unacceptable impulses.
    J. attribute to others their own unacceptable feelings.

31. Which of the following statements best characterizes ancient Egyptian society?

    A. Egypt was a classless society in which everyone was equal.
    B. Egypt developed into a society with distinct classes of people; the great majority of Egyptians were in the lowest class.
    C. Only the pharaohs were socially distinct from other Egyptians. All other Egyptians had equal status.
    D. Skilled workers were held in the highest esteem because they were needed to build the Pyramids.

32. In labor relations, a picket line is:

    F. a barricade built by workers to block a factory entrance.
    G. a barricade built by an employer at a factory entrance to keep workers out.
    H. a workers' demonstration at a workplace entrance in support of a strike.
    J. a line of guards who prevent striking workers from entering a workplace.

33. Amendments to the Constitution provide that an individual connot be barred from voting on the basis of:

    A. race or sex.
    B. income or education.
    C. place of residence or place of birth.
    D. All of the above.

34. The first European voyage around the world was led by:

    F. Christopher Columbus.
    G. Ferdinand Magellan.
    H. Amerigo Vespucci.
    J. Vasco Balboa

35. Demography is the study of:

    A. the size and distribution of the human population.
    B. the formation of the oceans.
    C. weather patterns.
    D. changes in government.

36. The Speaker of the House of Representatives is:

    F. not a member of the House.
    G. appointed to that post.
    H. barred from voting on legislation.
    J. elected to that post.

37. A state of imperfect competition in which there are only a few suppliers of a given commodity is called:

    A. oligopoly
    B. monopoly.
    C. scarcity.
    D. elasticity.

38. Which of the following was not a characteristic of the fascist regime established in Germany by the Nazis?

    F. extreme nationalism
    G. militarism and massive expenditures on armaments
    H. persecution of Jews and other minorities
    J. a foreign policy based on peaceful coexistence

39. A traditional tribal priest or medicine man who claims to influence the actions of good or evil spirits is generally termed a(n):

    A. animist.
    B. wizard.
    C. lama.
    D. shaman.

40. Control over the management of a corporation is usually vested in the corporation's:

    F. bondholders.
    G. common stockholders.
    H. preferred stockholders.
    J. chief executive officer.

41. The Supreme Court hears most of its cases as a result of its:

    A. original jurisdiction.
    B. appellate jurisdiction.
    C. Constitutional obligation to hear the case.
    D. concern over the facts of the case.

**42.** Napoleon's armies lost their final battle at Waterloo in Belgium. After this defeat, Napoleon:

F. was executed as a war criminal.

G. was exiled to the Mediterranean island of Elba.

H. was killed in battle.

J. was exiled to St. Helena in the South Atlantic.

The event that touched off World War I occurred in Sarajevo, the capital of the Austro-Hungarian province of Bosnia, on June 28, 1914. There the Archduke Francis Ferdinand, the Hapsburg heir to the throne of the Austro-Hungarian Empire, was shot and killed by a young Serbian nationalist seeking revenge against the Austrians for their annexation of Bosnia. Austria issued an ultimatum to Serbia. The Serbians acquiesced, in an attempt to stave off war. Austria, however, was intent on exacting retribution and in July of that year declared war on Serbia.

For almost a century, since the Congress of Vienna in 1815, European diplomats had prevented any real threat to the delicate balance of power achieved by the Congress. This time, though, they seemed powerless to stop the movement toward war. The assassination provoked a fateful series of responses that led Russia to support its ally Serbia. Austria sought and received the aid of its ally Germany. The other members of the Triple Entente, France and Great Britain, soon joined their ally Russia against Austria. In 1917 the United States was drawn into the battle as an ally of France and Great Britain.

World War I was unlike any other war fought before or since then. The profound shock it generated dramatically affected the progression of life in Europe and America and changed the course of world politics. Moreover, the war shocked millions of people throughout Europe into confronting the terrible losses and the grim and brutal realities of modern war. The few wars that had been fought since 1815 were distant colonial wars. Europeans had always been victorious, and the battles seemed nothing more than skirmishes that offered chances to experience adventure and to demonstrate bravery and heroism. The trenches and battlefields of Europe introduced millions of young men and women to a world of pain and death that they had never imagined.

The war altered the collective social sensibility of the people of Europe. It destroyed the spirit of optimism that had prevailed in the nineteenth century. Civilized, polite behavior now seemed archaic and utterly hypocritical. Moreover, the impression that there appeared to be no sane way to end the carnage only added to the sense of futility. The war changed relationships between members of the same social class. Before the war, the upper classes of Europe felt a common bond that united them across national borders. After the war, national boundaries defined social consciousness in a way that destroyed the solidarity of class.

World War I produced several dramatic changes in the political landscape of Europe. The breakup of the Austro-Hungarian, Russian, and German empires led to the reemergence of the state of Poland and the formation of other independent nation states in Europe. The war acted as a catalyst for European revolutionaries. The Russian Revolution of 1917 set the stage for the Bolshevik seizure of power, the exercise of total power by the Communist party, and the rise of Stalin as the absolute dictator of the Russian state (renamed the Union of Soviet Socialist Republics). World War I bore bitter fruit in Central and Southern Europe as well. The rise of Nazism in Germany and fascism in Italy led many historians to conclude that World War II, which was begun by Nazi Germany in 1939, was in actuality the continuation of the Great War that destroyed the social fabric of Europe in 1914.

**43.** The precipitating cause of World War I was:

A. an assassination.

B. a coronation.

C. a rebellion.

D. a plebiscite.

**44.** The event occurred in the city of:

F. Sarajevo in Bosnia.

G. Vienna in Austria.

H. Trieste in Italy.

J. Budapest in Hungary.

45. Before World War I, a balance of power had existed for:

    **A.**  nearly 15 years.
    **B.**  almost a quarter century.
    **C.**  almost 100 years.
    **D.**  nearly 10 years.

46. The chief reason European countries other than Austria and Serbia were drawn into the conflict was that:

    **F.**  they were members of the two alliance systems to which the combatants belonged.
    **G.**  they feared the Hapsburgs.
    **H.**  they wanted to ensure freedom of the seas.
    **J.**  they wanted the land of neighboring countries.

47. Mobilization for war resulted swiftly when:

    **A.**  the United States declared war.
    **B.**  attempts at diplomacy failed.
    **C.**  Russia refused to help Serbia.
    **D.**  Italy joined the conflict.

48. The way in which class relationships changed as a result of the outbreak of World War I suggests that:

    **F.**  nationalism might have weakened had the war never occurred.
    **G.**  the middle classes had no real love of country.
    **H.**  the upper classes had eagerly anticipated war.
    **J.**  everyone sanctioned the war.

49. The forces of militant nationalism that were unleashed during World War I culminated in the breakup of the Russian Empire and the German Empire. The political regimes that came to power in Germany and the Soviet Union before World War II were:

    **A.**  democracies that isolated themselves from world politics.
    **B.**  ruthless dictatorships dedicated to world conquest.
    **C.**  weak states allied with the United States.
    **D.**  members of a Europe-wide common market.

50. The sense of futility felt throughout Europe during and after World War I would be evident in a study of:

    **F.**  American investment policies.
    **G.**  statistics concerning foreign language study in America.
    **H.**  European literature of the 1920s, 1930s, and 1940s.
    **J.**  the number of transatlantic voyages between 1920 and 1930.

51. World War I and its aftermath suggest the idea that:

    **A.**  nationalism has little to do with world conflict.
    **B.**  war feeds on nationalist sympathies.
    **C.**  the cause of peace is best aided by reinvigorating the spirit of nationalism.
    **D.**  diplomacy never works.

52. Archduke Francis Ferdinand, as the heir to the Austro-Hungarian Empire, was a member of the:

    **F.**  Hohenzollern family.
    **G.**  Hanover family.
    **H.**  Hapsburg family.
    **J.**  Stuart family.

# Answer Key

| | | | | | |
|---|---|---|---|---|---|
| 1. C | 11. A | 21. C | 31. B | 41. B | 51. B |
| 2. H | 12. J | 22. G | 32. H | 42. G | 52. H |
| 3. C | 13. C | 23. A | 33. A | 43. A | |
| 4. F | 14. G | 24. F | 34. G | 44. B | |
| 5. C | 15. A | 25. C | 35. A | 45. C | |
| 6. F | 16. H | 26. H | 36. J | 46. F | |
| 7. B | 17. A | 27. C | 37. A | 47. G | |
| 8. J | 18. J | 28. F | 38. J | 48. J | |
| 9. A | 19. D | 29. B | 39. D | 49. B | |
| 10. C | 20. J | 30. F | 40. G | 50. H | |

# Explanatory Answers

1. (C) Each theory discussed is concerned with the question of the sequence of responses to a stimulus. (A) and (B) state positions contrary to any of the theories. (D) is a concern of only one theory, the Cannon-Bard theory.

2. (H) Information about increased blood flow is given in the first paragraph.

3. (C) Information about the digestive process is given in the first paragraph.

4. (F) Item I states the view of the James-Lange theory, which is discussed in the second paragraph.

5. (C) Item III states the view of the Cannon-Bard theory, which is discussed in the third paragraph.

6. (F) This item states the view of the cognitive theory, as discussed in the fourth paragraph.

7. (B) Only Item II is relevant to the question. II would suggest that physiological reactions alone would not account for the sensed difference in the emotions felt in reaction to a specific stimulus. Neither I nor III relates to the central issue of the order in which emotions and bodily reactions occur.

8. (J) Items I, II, and III present observations that would tend to weaken the Cannon-Bard theory. Each presents a reason why it would be difficult, if not impossible, to determine whether emotion or bodily reactions was the truly causal factor involved.

9. (A) The James-Lange theory was formulated in the 1890s. The Cannon-Bard theory was not formulated until the 1920s.

10. (C) The reactions described in the first paragraph produce conditions that would enable a person to react swiftly to an emotion-causing stimulus.

11. (A) This fact is made clear in the first sentence of paragraph 3. The article does not mention any type of municipal government called the metropolis plan.

12. (J) Paragraphs 3 and 4 of the passage make it clear that the ceremonial position of mayor is possible under the weak mayor variation of the mayor-council plan and the commission plan. The strong mayor variation of the mayor-council plan always calls for a powerful executive in the position of mayor.

13. (C) Under the commission plan, *each* commissioner performs both executive functions as a head of a municipal agency and legislative functions as a member of the council. Only *one* of the commissioners, if any, is appointed mayor.

14. (G) Only under a strong mayor-council plan does the mayor have the authority to fire the commissioner of transportation.

15. (A) Under the mayor-council plan, the citizens of the municipality elect the mayor. B, C, and D are mentioned as functions of the council under this plan in paragraph 3 of the passage.

**16.** (H) The passage mentions that in many cases municipalities governed under the commission plan do not have a mayor at all. If they do have a mayor, he usually has very limited power. This suggests that the commission plan might suffer from a lack of strong leadership from an overseer. A government could not exist with F, G and J.

**17.** (A) This point is not explicitly stated in the passage but can be inferred from it. The passage does indicate that weak mayors do not have the right to dismiss heads of municipal departments, and so choice B cannot be correct. Under no plan may the mayor fire members of the City Council, and choice C is not correct. Choice D is incorrect since the mayor alone does not have the right to enact new laws.

**18.** (J) The information to answer this question is not contained in the passage. Philadelphia is one of the major American cities that has added a managing director to the basic mayor-council plan. The managing director supervises the departments whose heads he appoints and the boards and commissions connected with those departments. The managing director's actions are subject to the approval of the mayor.

**19.** (D) Although not explicitly stated in the passage, the correct choice is D. Choices A, B, and C are contradicted by the information presented and, therefore, cannot be correct.

**20.** (J) The information required to answer this question may be inferred from the description of the council-manager plan presented in the passage.

**21.** (C) As paragraph 3 explains, consumption tax is calculated on the difference between one's net worth and one's total income for any given year. Net worth is calculated as the difference between one's assets and liabilities. Savings are part of one's assets.

**22.** (G) It is clear that savings dollars are not part of consumption expenditures. Each of the other items, however, is.

**23.** (A) Items II and III would be true of value-added tax. Only I is true of consumption tax.

**24.** (F) I is the correct answer. Value-added tax is not based on the cost of raw materials (II) or on the final price (III) alone or on II and III individually, but is calculated on III minus II, which would be the cost of production (I).

**25.** (C) A and B are clearly false. D is speculative and not necessarily true at all. C is true, inasmuch as the consumer does not know what part of the price of a product reflects value-added tax.

**26.** (H) H is the only correct answer. Consumption expenditures obviously represent things bought, whether products or services. Thus a tax on such amounts is actually a sales tax levied at the federal level. The value-added tax, although it may seem similar to a sales tax, is actually a tax on the manufacturer's cost of production.

**27.** (C) Only under the condition that savings taxes were eliminated would the taxpayer be better off. Under any of the other three conditions, the taxpayer would be paying tax twice on savings, in addition to paying a consumption tax.

**28.** (F) An increase in net worth implies a corresponding decrease in expenditures relative to a given yearly income. Thus if consumer expenditures decrease, one's consumption tax would decrease also.

29. (B)  For savings to increase nationally, a consumption tax would have to replace the present income tax procedures.  A or C state conditions that would place too great a tax burden on the individual taxpayer.  The British poll tax, which has provoked much opposition, is an attempt to replace local real estate taxes by levying a tax on each individual, who will continue to pay income tax.

30. (F)  The defense mechanism called sublimation is the process whereby a person finds socially acceptable ways to display otherwise unacceptable impulses.

31. (B)  Ancient Egypt developed into a society with distinct classes of people, with priests and government officials at the top, skilled workers, scribes, and artisans in the middle, and the peasants—the great majority of the population—at the bottom.

32. (H)  In labor relations, a picket line is a workers' demonstration at a workplace entrance in support of a strike.  The workers on the line may be those on strike, or they may be others who agree with the strikers' aims.

33. (A)  The 15th and 19th Amendments to the Constitution provide that an individual cannot be barred from voting on the basis of race or sex.  Individuals under the age of 18 are still denied the right to vote, as are non-citizens.

34. (G)  Ferdinand Magellan, who in the early 1500s led the first European voyage around the world, thereby discovered a westward route from Europe to Asia.

35. (A)  The study of human population is called demography.  Demographic studies focus on a population's size, its distribution, and its composition by analyzing statistics on births, deaths, immigration, and emigration.

36. (J)  The members of the majority party in the House elect one among their number to be Speaker.  The Speaker presides over House debates and also takes part in voting on legislation.

37. (A)  An oligopoly exists when there are only a few suppliers of a given commodity.  In this situation an individual supplier has the power to change the product price for the entire market.

38. (J)  The fascist regime established in Germany by the Nazis was characterized by nationalism, militarism, and violent persecution of minorities.

39. (D)  Certain Siberian and Eskimo tribes included a traditional tribal medicine man called a shaman, who claimed to be able to influence good or evil spirits.  The word is now used as a general term for similar persons in many different traditional societies.

40. (G)  Common stockholders exercise control over the management of a corporation through the election of a board of directors, which is responsible for overseeing senior management.

41. (B)  The Constitution gives the Supreme Court original jurisdiction only over cases involving foreign diplomats and cases to which a state is a party. However, it hears a much larger number of cases as a result of its appellate jurisdiction, or power to judge cases that are appealed from a lower court.

42. (G)  After Waterloo, Napoleon was exiled for the second time, this time to St. Helena in the South Atlantic, where he died six years later.

43. (A)  The precipitating cause of World War I was an assassination.  On June 28, 1914, Archduke Francis Ferdinand, the heir to the throne of the Austro-Hungarian Empire, was assassinated by a Serbian nationalist.

44. (B) The assassination occurred in the city of Sarajevo in Bosnia. Claimed by Serbia, Bosnia was annexed by Austria, provoking the ire of the government and the people of Bosnia and Serbia.

45. (C) Before the outbreak of World War I, a balance of power had existed for almost 100 years. World War I shattered the balance of power that had been established by the Congress of Vienna in 1815.

46. (F) Russia, the protector of Serbia, and Austria were members of competing alliance systems. When war broke out between them, the member states of their alliances were drawn into the conflict. Germany intervened on the side of Austria, its alliance member, and Great Britain and France joined forces with Russia, with which both countries were allied.

47. (G) The summer of 1914 was marred by the repeated failure of diplomatic missions undertaken to persuade the Austrians to moderate the terms of the ultimatum that they were planning to issue to Serbia. The suspicions enkindled by the failure of diplomacy sparked the order to mobilize the Russian armed forces. German mobilization was ordered after the Russian order was issued.

48. (J) A spirit of nationalism, not class solidarity, animated the people of the individual nation states that fought against one another in World War I. No longer did the upper classes of Europe act as a unified class. Instead, they joined with their compatriots of the middle and lower classes to wage war against people in other countries with whom they had once shared values, beliefs, and a way of life.

49. (B) The Nazi regime that came to power in Germany in 1933 and the regime of Stalin that tyrannized the Soviet people from 1927 to 1953 were ruthless dictatorships dedicated to world conquest.

50. (H) The sense of futility felt throughout Europe during and after World War I would be evident in a study of European literature of the 1920s, 1930s, and 1940s. T. S. Eliot's poem *The Wasteland* and Erich Maria Remarque's novel *All Quiet on the Western Front* exemplify that spirit. As leading critics have always maintained, the art of a particular period mirrors as well as illuminates the spirit of the age.

51. (B) World War I and its aftermath suggest the idea that war feeds on nationalist sympathies. The sense of affront felt by the Austrian people when the heir to the throne of their empire was assassinated did not allow the Austrian leaders to adopt a moderate stance in their dealings with the government of Serbia. Similarly, the sympathies evident in the pan-slavic brand of nationalism that animated the rulers of Russia to undertake the protection of Serbia led the Russians to perceive the Austrians as their implacable enemies, setting in motion the chain of events that led to the outbreak of war. Moreover, the militantly nationalistic forces that came to power in Germany, Italy, and Japan in the period between the two world wars undertook conquests that precipitated World War II.

52. (H) Archduke Francis Ferdinand, as the heir to the Austro-Hungarian Empire, was a member of the Hapsburg family.

# Natural Sciences Review

The Natural Sciences Reading Test of your ACT will contain 52 questions and have a time limit of 35 minutes. The Natural Sciences Test will contain two different types of questions: reading comprehension questions and free-standing, factual recall questions.

The reading comprehension questions are based on reading selections three to five paragraphs long. The selections treat material from physics, chemistry, biology, and the physical sciences that you are likely to encounter in introductory survey courses in college on those topics. Most of the reading comprehension questions are answerable on the basis of information provided in the text. A few, however, require some prior knowledge of the topic.

The free-standing factual recall items depend entirely on the knowledge of a topic you have gained from your coursework. To help you refresh your memory about some of the important points covered in high school natural science courses, here is a substantive outline of those areas. The outline is organized according to the following topics:

* Earth Science
* Biology
* Chemistry
* Physics

As you answer questions on the Natural Sciences Test, be sure to use the Holmesian strategy of eliminating answer choices wherever possible. Even if you are unsure of a particular question, eliminate as many choices as possible and enter your guess on your answer sheet.

# Earth Science

## I. The study of earth science

**A.** The scientific method
  1. The problem: identification and statement of the problem, and the gathering of information related to it
  2. The hypothesis: explanatory statement about the problem
  3. The experiment: testing the hypothesis; involves controlling for variables, observing, recording, and analyzing data
  4. The conclusion: agreement or disagreement as to the validity of the hypothesis
  5. The theory: generally accepted hypothesis used to explain events; subject to revision or rejection based on new data

**B.** Earth science fields
  1. Astronomy: the study of objects in space
  2. Geology: the study of the earth
  3. Oceanography: the study of the oceans
  4. Meteorology: the study of the atmosphere

**C.** Earth science instruments
  1. Telescopes
     a) Optical: detect visible light; may be refracting or reflecting
     b) Infrared: detect infrared energy
     c) Radio: detect radio waves
     d) X-ray: detect X-rays
  2. Spectroscopes: use prisms to break light into colors of the spectrum
  3. Microscopes: magnify small particles of matter
  4. Satellites: carry instruments for use in astronomy, meteorology, geology, and oceanography

## II. The universe

**A.** Matter in the universe
  1. Properties of matter
     a) Mass: the amount of matter in an object
     b) Volume: the amount of space an object takes up
     c) Density: the amount of matter in a given amount of substance; density = mass/volume
  2. Phases of matter
     a) Solid: matter with a definite shape
     b) Liquid: matter with a definite volume but an indefinite shape
     c) Gas: matter with no definite volume or shape
  3. Structure of matter
     a) Molecules: smallest atomic unit capable of a stable independent existence
     b) Atoms: smallest unit of an element
     c) Subatomic particles: include protons, electrons, and neutrons
     d) Isotopes: atoms that have the same number of protons but differ in the number of neutrons
     e) Ions: charged atoms that differ in the number of electrons
  4. Forms of matter
     a) Elements: substances which cannot be decomposed by ordinary chemical means
     b) Compounds: combinations of different atoms
     c) Mixtures: combinations of substances

**B.** Energy in the universe
   **1.** Nuclear energy: produced in the nuclei of atoms; released by fission or fusion
   **2.** Heat energy: produced by the internal motion of particles
   **3.** Electromagnetic energy: produced by moving electrical charges; includes light, X-rays, and radio waves
   **4.** Chemical energy: produced by atomic bonds
   **5.** Mechanical energy: produced by matter in motion
**C.** The origin of the universe: the big bang theory states that the universe exploded and expanded from a central point of concentrated matter and energy; gravitational attraction of this matter creates galaxies, stars, and planets
**D.** Stars
   **1.** Galaxies: groups of stars
      **a)** Spiral galaxies: star groups with a central cluster and flattened arms that spiral out from the center; the Milky Way Galaxy is a spiral galaxy
      **b)** Elliptical galaxies: star groups with a definite (but varied) shape; generally contain older stars, little gas or dust
      **c)** Irregular galaxies: star groups with no definite shape
   **2.** Star clusters: groups of stars found within galaxies
      **a)** Globular clusters: tight spherical clusters
      **b)** Open clusters: less organized clusters
   **3.** Star systems
      **a)** Solitary stars: the sun is a solitary star
      **b)** Multiple systems: includes paired binary stars
   **4.** Constellations: star groups that form patterns
   **5.** Star composition: determined by spectroscopy
      **a)** Hydrogen: makes up 60 to 80 percent of a star
      **b)** Helium: combines with hydrogen to make up 96 to 99 percent of a star
      **c)** Other elements: include oxygen, neon, carbon, and nitrogen
   **6.** Nuclear fusion: occurs when a star's gravity forces hydrogen atoms to fuse, forming helium atoms and energy in the form of heat and light

## III.  The solar system

**A.** The sun
   **1.** Sun layers
      **a)** Corona: outermost layer
      **b)** Chromosphere: second layer
      **c)** Photosphere: inner layer of the sun's atmosphere
      **d)** Core: center of the sun where nuclear fusion occurs
   **2.** Sun activity
      **a)** Prominences: gaseous eruptions from the sun's surface
      **b)** Solar flares: bursts of light on the sun's surface
      **c)** Sunspots: dark, cool storms in the sun's inner atmosphere
      **d)** Solar wind: stream of high-energy particles released by the sun into space

**B.** Planets: define the limit of the solar system
1. Mercury
2. Venus
3. Earth
4. Mars
5. Jupiter
6. Saturn
7. Uranus
8. Neptune
9. Pluto

**C.** Moons: large objects that revolve around planets

**D.** Meteoroids: small rocklike objects that orbit the sun; a meteor is the trail produced by friction with the earth's atmosphere; a meteorite is a meteoroid that has reached the earth's surface

**E.** Asteroids: large rocklike objects that orbit the sun; many are found in a belt between Mars and Jupiter

**F.** Comets: chunks of ice, rocks, and dust that orbit the sun; many are located in the Oort Cloud

**G.** The earth and the moon
1. The earth's features
   a) The hydrosphere: 70 percent of the earth's surface
   b) The atmosphere: 78 percent nitrogen, 21 percent oxygen
   c) The crust
2. The earth's motion
   a) Orbit: 365.25 days
   b) Rotation: about 24 hours; day and night are affected by the tilt of the earth's axis
3. The earth's magnetism: produces magnetosphere oriented around the magnetic poles
4. The moon's features
   a) Highlands: moon mountain ranges
   b) Maria: dry sea-like plains
   c) Rilles: long valleys formed by volcanic activity
   d) Craters: created by meteorite impacts
5. The moon's motion
   a) Orbit: an elliptical shape taking 27½ days; perigee is the point of orbit closest to the earth; apogee is the point farthest away
   b) Rotation: 27½ days; one side always faces the earth
6. The moon's phases: caused by reflected light from the sun
   a) New moon: not visible on earth
   b) Crescent: less than half visible
   c) Gibbous: more than half visible
   d) Full moon: one side entirely visible
   e) Waxing: the lighted area is increasing in size
   f) Waning: the lighted area is decreasing in size
7. Tides: caused on earth by the moon's gravitational pull
   a) High tides: occur on both the side facing and opposite to the moon
   b) Low tides: occur on the sides at a perpendicular angle to the moon
   c) Spring tides: occur during new and full moon phases
   d) Neap tides: occur during moon's first and last quarter phases
8. Eclipses
   a) Lunar eclipses: the moon passes through the earth's shadow
   b) Solar eclipses: the earth passes through the sun's shadow
   c) Umbra: area of complete shadow
   d) Penumbra: area of partial shadow

## IV. The earth

A. The earth's composition
  1. Minerals: naturally occurring crystalline solids formed from magma
     a) Mineral properties
        i. Color
        ii. Luster
        iii. Hardness
        iv. Density
        v. Crystal shape
        vi. Cleavage and fracture
        vii. Streak
     b) Mineral groups: determined by their composition
        i. Elements
        ii. Silicates
        iii. Carbonates
        iv. Oxides
        v. Sulphides
        vi. Sulphates
        vii. Halides
     c) Mineral types: determined by their scarcity and use
        i. Ores: include metals and nonmetals
        ii. Gems: include precious and semiprecious stones
  2. Rocks
     a) Igneous rock: formed from magma
        i. Intrusive rock: formed beneath the surface; includes stock, batholith, laccolith, sill, and dike formations
        ii. Extrusive rock: formed at the surface; includes lava plateaus
     b) Sedimentary rock: formed from compaction or cementation of mud, sand, gravel, bones, and shells into strata
        i. Clastic rock: formed from rocks or rock fragments; includes conglomerate, breccia, sandstone, siltstone, and shale
        ii. Organic rock: formed from organic materials; includes limestone and chalk
     c) Metamorphic rock: formed from other rocks due to pressure, heat, or chemical reactions; includes contact and regional metamorphism
        i. Foliated rock: layered rock formed from pressure or density differences; includes slate, schist, and gneiss
        ii. Unfoliated rock: formed when grains change size and shape; includes quartzite and marble

B. The earth's interior
  1. The core: composed of iron and nickel
     a) The inner core: solid due to pressure
     b) The outer core: liquid
  2. The mantle: makes up 80 percent of the earth's volume; separated from the crust by the Moho Discontinuity
  3. The crust: on average 8–32 kilometers thick
     a) Continental crust: thicker, composed of granite and basalt rock
     b) Oceanic crust: thinner; composed of basalt rock

**4.** Motion: creates mountains, domes, and plateaus
   **a)** Stress: action of rocks upon each other
      **i.** Compression
      **ii.** Tension
      **iii.** Shearing
   **b)** Folding: change in the shape of rocks
      **i.** anticline
      **ii.** syncline
   **c)** Faults: breaks in rocks where movement occurs
      **i.** Normal faults
      **ii.** Reverse faults
      **iii.** Thrust faults
      **iv.** Lateral faults
      **v.** Fault-block mountains
      **vi.** Rift valleys
**5.** Earthquakes: caused by sudden movements of the crust
   **a)** The focus: point of origin
   **b)** The epicenter: surface area directly above the focus
   **c)** Seismic waves: Shock waves produced by an earthquake
      **i.** Primary waves or P waves: move rocks forward and back
      **ii.** Secondary waves or S waves: slower than P waves; do not travel through liquids; move rocks side to side
      **iii.** Surface waves or L waves: move along surface from epicenter
   **d)** Tsunamis: giant ocean waves caused by oceanfloor earthquakes
   **e)** The seismograph: detects seismic waves and records them on a seismogram
   **f)** The Richter scale: measures an earthquake's strength on a scale of 1 to 10
**6.** Volcanoes: openings in the earth where lava reaches the surface
   **a)** Magma: hot liquid rock
   **b)** Lava: magma that reaches the surface
   **c)** Volcanic rocks: formed from hardened lava; include dust, ash, cinders, and volcanic bombs
   **d)** Vents: openings in a volcano
   **e)** Craters: pits formed at the top of volcanoes; calderas are large craters
   **f)** Cinder cones: formed from explosive volcanoes
   **g)** Shield volcanoes: formed from lava flows
   **h)** Composite volcanoes: formed from alternating explosions and lava flows
**7.** Plate tectonics
   **a)** Continental drift: movement of the continents throughout earth's history; original super-continent is called Pangea
   **b)** Ocean-floor spreading: lava flow from ocean floor rifts moves the ocean floor; the floor is subducted at ocean floor trenches
   **c)** Plates: compose the lithosphere; divided by plate boundaries; moved by convection currents in the mantle; cause continents to separate, move, and re-form; movement at plate boundaries produces mountains, earthquakes, and volcanoes
**C.** Soils
   **1.** Soil formation
      **a)** Mechanical weathering: breakdown of rock caused by changes in temperature, collisions, or root action
      **b)** Chemical weathering: decomposition of rock through chemical interactions with water, oxygen, or acids
      **c)** Organic decomposition: produces humus

    **2.** Soil layers
       **a)** Topsoil: the A horizon
       **b)** Subsoil: the B horizon
       **c)** Weathered rock: the C horizon
       **d)** Bedrock: parent rock from which soil is produced
    **3.** Soil motion
       **a)** Mass wasting: movement of soil down a slope due to gravity
       **b)** Wind erosion: forms dunes and loess
       **c)** Water erosion: forms deltas, alluvial fans, flood plains, and levees
       **d)** Glacial erosion: produces till which forms moraines and drumlins
       **e)** Wave erosion: forms beaches, sandbars, spits, cliffs, terraces, stacks, and caves
**D.** Landmasses
    **1.** Continents: large land masses
       **a)** North America
       **b)** South America
       **c)** Europe
       **d)** Africa
       **e)** Asia
       **f)** Australia
       **g)** Antarctica
    **2.** Islands: small land masses
    **3.** Topography: a measure of elevation and relief
       **a)** Mountains: may be isolated or part of a range, system, or belt
       **b)** Plains: may be coastal or interior
       **c)** Plateaus: high-altitude plains
    **4.** Mapping
       **a)** Meridians: run between the North and South poles; the prime meridian is 0° longitude
       **b)** Parallels: run perpendicular to meridians; the equator is 0° latitude
       **c)** Time zones: 24 zones, 15° each
       **d)** Globes: three-dimensional representations
       **e)** Mercator projections: direction and shape are accurate but size and distance are distorted
       **f)** Equal-area projections: distance is accurate but size and shape are distorted
       **g)** Topographic maps: use contour lines to show relief
**E.** Fresh water: 3 percent of the earth's water, of which 85 percent is ice
    **1.** The hydrologic cycle
       **a)** Evaporation: most water evaporates from the oceans
       **b)** Condensation: occurs when air cools
       **c)** Precipitation: can occur as rain, sleet, snow, or hail
    **2.** Running water: includes rivers and streams
    **3.** Standing water: includes lakes, ponds, and reservoirs
    **4.** Groundwater: water located underground in openings or permeable soil and rock
       **a)** The zone of aeration: layer of earth that water passes through
       **b)** The zone of saturation: layer of earth where water is held
       **c)** The water table: surface of the zone of saturation
       **d)** Aquifers: layers of permeable soil or rock containing water
    **5.** Ice: includes glaciers and icebergs

**F.** Oceans
  **1.** The oceans
    **a)** The Pacific: largest ocean
    **b)** The Atlantic: second largest ocean
    **c)** The Indian: smallest ocean
    **d)** The Arctic Ocean: considered part of the Atlantic Ocean
    **e)** Seas: parts of oceans partially enclosed by land
  **2.** Ocean properties
    **a)** Salt: mainly sodium chloride; described in terms of salinity
    **b)** Gases: mainly nitrogen, carbon dioxide, and oxygen; amounts vary with depth
    **c)** Temperature: varies with location and depth outside of polar areas, vertical zones include well-mixed surface zone, variable thermocline, and cold deep zone
  **3.** Ocean topography
    **a)** Continental margin: where a continent meets the ocean floor; includes the continental shelf, slope, and rise
    **b)** Continental shelf: shallow slope from the shelf to the ocean floor
    **c)** Continental slope: sharp slope from the shelf to the ocean floor
    **d)** Submarine canyons: deep valleys in the continental shelf and slope
    **e)** Abyssal plains: large, flat areas on the ocean floor
    **f)** Seamounts: underwater volcanic mountains that may form islands
    **g)** Guyots: flat-topped seamounts created by wave erosion
    **h)** Trenches: deep canyons in the ocean floor
    **i)** Midocean ridges: long lava mountain belts
    **j)** Reefs: limestone ridges formed by small animals and their shell remains; include fringing reefs, barrier reefs, and atolls
  **4.** Ocean motion
    **a)** Waves: formed by wind, the moon's gravitational pull, and earthquakes
    **b)** Currents: formed by wind and differences in water density; include surface and deep currents
    **c)** Tides: caused by the moon's gravitational pull
  **5.** Ocean zones: associated with plankton, nekton, and benthos organisms
    **a)** Intertidal zone: between low and high-tide lines
    **b)** Neritic zone: extends along continental shelf
    **c)** Bathyal zone: extends from upper edge of continental slope to about 2000 meters
    **d)** Abyssal zone: found below bathyal zone
**G.** The atmosphere
  **1.** Composition
    **a)** Historical composition: originally mainly methane and ammonia; chemical reactions produced ozone layer and other changes; autotrophic organisms produced oxygen
    **b)** Modern composition
      **i.** Nitrogen: 78 percent
      **ii.** Oxygen: 21 percent
      **iii.** Other: includes carbon dioxide, water vapor, argon, and trace gases

2. Layers
   a) The troposphere: lowest level; mixed by convection currents
   b) The stratosphere: separated from the troposphere by the tropopause; includes most atmospheric ozone
   c) The mesosphere: separated from the stratosphere by the stratopause; coldest region of the atmosphere
   d) The thermosphere: separated into the ionosphere and the exosphere
   e) The magnetosphere: magnetic field above the atmosphere; ions from the solar wind are arranged into the Van Allen belts

**H.** Earth history
1. Radioactive dating: uses the half-life of a radioactive element to determine the age of an object
2. Geologic eras: include period and epoch divisions
   a) Precambrian era: dates back to the formation of the earth 4.6 billion years ago; 4,040 million years long
   b) Paleozoic era: 345 million years long
   c) Mesozoic era: includes the Triassic, Jurrasic, and Cretaceous periods; 160 million years long
   d) Cenozoic era; includes the Tertiary and Quaternary periods to the present; 65 million years long

## V. Activity on the earth

**A.** Weather
1. Seasons: caused by the tilt of the earth's axis
   a) Solstices: the summer solstice is the longest day of the year; the winter solstice is the shortest
   b) Equinoxes: vernal and autumnal; periods when day and night are of equal length throughout the world
2. Weather factors
   a) Radiant energy: from the sun; most is absorbed by ozone, water molecules, and carbon dioxide, or by the earth
   b) Conduction: transfer of heat energy from the earth's surface to the air
   c) Convection: atmospheric heat transfer through convection currents
   d) Radiation: transfer of heat energy in waves; ultraviolet energy from the sun, infrared energy from the earth
   e) Greenhouse effect: infrared energy radiated from the earth is trapped by the atmosphere
3. Pressure: affected by elevation, temperature, and water vapor
4. Wind: produced by heat and pressure differences
   a) Sea breezes: from the sea to the land, usually during the day
   b) Land breezes: from the land to the sea, usually during the night
   c) The Coriolis effect: wind direction changes due to the earth's rotation
   d) Doldrums: calm air around the equator
   e) Trade winds: move between 30° latitude and the equator
   f) Prevailing westerlies: move between 40° and 60° latitude
   g) Polar easterlies: move between the poles and 60° latitude
   h) Jet streams: high pressure belts in the upper atmosphere

5. Moisture: measured as relative humidity
   a) Clouds: formed when moisture reaches the dew point
      i. Cumulus
      ii. Cumulonimbus
      iii. Stratus
      iv. Cirrus
      v. Fog
   b) Precipitation: movement of water from the atmosphere to the earth's surface
      i. Rain
      ii. Sleet
      iii. Snow
      iv. Hail
6. Air masses: similar bodies of air
   a) Maritime tropical: forms over oceans around the equator
   b) Maritime polar: forms over northern oceans
   c) Continental tropical: forms over Mexico
   d) Continental polar: forms over northern Canada
7. Fronts: form where air masses meet
   a) Cold fronts: form when a cold air mass undercuts a warm air mass
   b) Warm fronts: form when a warm air mass moves over a cold air mass
   c) Occluded fronts: form when a cold air mass overtakes a warm air mass
   d) Stationary fronts: form when no movement occurs after a warm and cold air mass meet
8. Storms
   a) Normal storms: can occur when fronts collide; include rainstorms, snowstorms, thunderstorms, and blizzards
   b) Cyclones: occur in low pressure areas with rising warm air; spin inward and counterclockwise in the north
   c) Anticyclones: occur in high pressure areas with cold air; spin outward and clockwise in the north
   d) Hurricanes: giant cyclones occurring over tropical oceans
   e) Tornadoes: funnel-shaped clouds that spin at high speeds
9. Weather forecasting: performed by meteorologists and presented on weather maps
   a) Isotherms: define areas of equal temperature on a weather map
   b) Isobars: define areas of equal pressure on a weather map
B. Climate
   1. Climate factors
      a) Temperature: affected by latitude, altitude, and ocean currents
      b) Precipitation: affected by prevailing winds and mountain ranges
   2. Climate zones
      a) Polar zones: located from the poles to 60° latitude; yearly temperatures are below freezing
      b) Temperate zones: located from 60° to 30° latitude; seasonal temperatures
      c) Tropical zones; located from 30° latitude to the equator, high temperatures
      d) Marine zones: areas near the ocean: less varied temperatures
      e) Continental zones: areas within a large landmass; more varied temperatures
   3. Climate changes: usually occur over geologic time; may be caused by continental drift, changes in the position of the earth's tilt or orbit, or changes in the sun's energy output; can also be caused by changes in ocean currents such as El Nino
      a) Ice ages: periods of major glaciation
      b) Interglacial periods: occur between ice ages

# Biology

## I. The study of biology

**A.** The scientific method

   **1.** The problem: identification and statement of the problem, and the gathering of information related to it

   **2.** The hypothesis: explanatory statement about the problem

   **3.** The experiment: testing the hypothesis; involves controlling for variables, observing, recording, and analyzing data

   **4.** The conclusion: agreement or disagreement as to the validity of the hypothesis

   **5.** The theory: generally accepted hypothesis used to explain events; subject to revision or rejection based on new data

**B.** Biology fields

   **1.** Zoology: the study of animals; includes microbiology and marine biology

   **2.** Botany: the study of plants

   **3.** Anatomy: the study of structures; includes cytology

   **4.** Physiology: the study of function

   **5.** Ecology: the study of relationships

   **6.** Taxonomy: the study of classification

**C.** Biology instruments

   **1.** Magnifying glass: enlarges the image through a lens

   **2.** Compound light microscope: enlarges the image through more than one lens; contains a mirror, objectives, and an eyepiece; magnification is described by a number and an X

   **3.** Electron microscope: uses electrons to form an image

## II. The cell

**A.** Cell types

   **1.** Prokaryotes: simple cells with few organelles and no nuclear membrane

   **2.** Eukaryotes: complex cells with many organelles and a nuclear membrane; multicellular organisms are composed of eukaryotic cells

**B.** Cell structure

   **1.** Cell membrane: surrounds cell; selectively permeable to control homeostasis

   **2.** Cell wall: found in plant cells; external to cell membrane

   **3.** Nucleus: controls cell activity

   **4.** Nuclear membrane: semi-permeable membrane surrounding the nucleus

   **5.** Nucleolus: found in some nuclei; involved in protein synthesis

   **6.** Cytoplasm: protoplasm found between cell membrane and nucleus

   **7.** Ribosomes: organelles involved in protein synthesis

   **8.** Rough endoplasmic reticulum: intercellular canal containing ribosomes; involved in protein synthesis and material transport

   **9.** Smooth endoplasmic reticulum: intercellular canal containing enzymes; involved in cell metabolism

   **10.** Mitochondria: rod-shaped organelles; produce energy through the breakdown of sugars

   **11.** Vacuoles: storage organelles; small vacuoles are called vesicles

   **12.** Lysosomes: organelles containing enzymes; involved in molecular digestion

   **13.** Golgi apparatus: organelles that package protein and waste materials

   **14.** Plastids: organelles that make or store food

   **15.** Microtubules: animal cell organelles; involved in transport and maintaining cell shape

   **16.** Microfilaments: involved in changing cell shape

   **17.** Chloroplasts: organelles found in plants, algae, and some protists; involved in photosynthesis

**C.** Cell function

1. Absorption: intake of substances from the external environment
2. Synthesis: building of larger compounds from smaller ones
3. Transport: translocation of substances within a cell
4. Digestion: breakdown of food molecules
5. Excretion: removal of waste products
6. Respiration: chemical process of breaking down organic compound bonds to release energy
7. Reproduction: creation of new cells
8. Secretion: release of substances from a cell for use elsewhere in multicellular organisms
9. Response: activity of a cell to external stimuli

**D.** Nucleic acids

1. DNA or deoxyribonucleic acid: double-stranded nucleic acid found in the nucleus or nuclear region of a cell
   a) Nucleotide: the basic component of DNA; composed of a deoxyribose sugar, a phosphate group, and a nitrogen base
   b) Nitrogen bases: bond with sugars and complementary bases to form a double helix
      i. Adenine: a purine; bonds with thymine
      ii. Guanine: a purine; bonds with cytosine
      iii. Cytosine: a pyrimidine; bonds with guanine
      iv. Thymine: a pyrimidine; bonds with adenine
   c) Replication: creation of an identical copy of DNA; helix strands split and two new strands are formed from nitrogen bases in the cytoplasm; occurs before cell division
2. RNA or ribonucleic acid: single-stranded nucleic acid involved in protein synthesis; the nitrogen base uracil replaces thymine
   a) rRNA or ribosomal RNA: located on the ribosomes
   b) mRNA or messenger RNA: carries the DNA code from the nucleus to the ribosomes
   c) tRNA or transfer RNA: carries amino acids to mRNA

**E.** Cell transport

1. Passive transport: movement of substances without energy expenditure
   a) Diffusion: passive transport of a substance from a higher concentration to a lower one
   b) Osmosis: movement of water through a selectively permeable membrane
      i. Isotonic solution: concentration is equal; no water movement
      ii. Hypertonic solution: concentration is higher; water moves out
      iii. Hypotonic solution: concentration is lower; water moves in
2. Active transport: movement of substances against a diffusion gradient using energy
   a) Endocytosis: active transport of particles into a cell through cell membrane pockets
      i. Phagocytosis: cell membrane extends outwards
      ii. Pinocytosis: cell membrane folds inward
   b) Exocytosis: active transport of substances out of a cell

**F.** Cell metabolism

1. Catabolic reactions: biochemical breakdown of molecules
2. Anabolic reactions: synthesis of new molecules
3. Enzymes: catalytic protein molecules that increase reaction rates; affected by pH, temperature, and the relative amounts of enzyme and substrate
   a) Substrate: substance on which an enzyme acts
   b) Active site: part of the enzyme that reacts with a substrate's reactive site
   c) Coenzymes: molecules that help enzymes act; many are vitamins
   d) Lock and key hypothesis: each enzyme molecule is shaped to fit the substrate it acts upon
   e) Induced fit theory: enzyme active site changes to fit the substrate reactive site

**4.** Dehydration synthesis: the bonding of smaller molecules to form larger ones through the formation of water molecules; involves enzymes as catalysts

**5.** Hydrolysis: the breakdown of larger molecules into smaller ones by adding water molecules; occurs in cell vacuoles; uses enzymes as catalysts

**6.** The ATP cycle: releases and stores energy for cellular reactions

    **a)** ATP: adenosine triphosphate coenzyme composed of the nitrogen base adenine, the sugar molecule ribose, and three phosphate groups; when a phosphate bond is broken, ADP is formed and energy is released for anabolic reactions

    **b)** ADP: adenosine diphosphate; catabolic reaction energy is stored by the cell through the addition of a phosphate group to ADP, forming ATP

    **c)** AMP: adenosine monophosphate; formed when a phosphate bond is broken from ADP; rarely occurs, as the energy released is minimal

**7.** Protein synthesis: creation of proteins by RNA using DNA base codes

    **a)** Transcription: creation of mRNA using a DNA template; three-base sequences are codons for specific amino acids

    **b)** Translation: building of proteins using mRNA and tRNA; tRNA picks up amino acids in cytoplasm, tRNA anticodon bonds to mRNA codon of the ribosomes and amino acids are sequenced into proteins using peptide bonds

**G.** Cellular reproduction

    **1.** Mitosis: simple cell division resulting in diploid ($2n$) cells

        **a)** Interphase: cell growth phase; includes DNA replication of homologous chromosomes

        **b)** Prophase: chromosomes appear as doubled chromatids held by a centromere; spindle forms; nuclear membrane disappears

        **c)** Metaphase: chromosomes line up at cell equator; centromeres attach to spindle microtubules

        **d)** Anaphase: centromeres divide; chromatids separate and move toward the poles; cytoplasmic separation begins

            **i.** Cleavage furrow: separates cytoplasm in animal cells

            **ii.** Cell plate: separates cytoplasm in plant cells

        **e)** Telophase: nuclear membranes form around chromosomes; other organelles disappear; cytoplasm completes division

    **2.** Meiosis: reproductive cell division resulting in monoploid ($n$) gametes

        **a)** Interphase: DNA is replicated

        **b)** Prophase 1: double-stranded homologous chromosomes pair up in synapsis

        **c)** Metaphase 1: paired chromosomes line up on equatorial plane

        **d)** Anaphase 1: homologous chromosomes move, remaining double-stranded

        **e)** Telophase 1: nuclear membranes form around chromosomes, cell divides

        **f)** Interkenesis: similar to interphase, but DNA is not replicated

        **g)** Second meiotic division: similar to mitosis

**H.** Cellular respiration

    **1.** Definition: chemical bond energy in food molecules is converted through the synthesis of ATP to a form usable by the cell

    **2.** Anaerobic respiration: occurs in the cytoplasm; does not use free oxygen; two molecules of ATP are produced

        **a)** Alcoholic fermentation: in yeast and certain bacteria; breaks down $NADH_2$ to NAD; produces ethyl alcohol:

$$C_6H_{12}O_6 \rightarrow 2C_2H_5OH + 2CO_2 + 2ATP$$

        **b)** Lactic acid fermentation: in certain bacteria, molds, and muscle cells; produces lactic acid:

$$C_6H_{12}O_6 \rightarrow 2CH_3CHOHCOOH + 2ATP$$

**3.** Aerobic respiration: uses oxygen; 38 molecules of ATP are produced:
$$C_6H_{12}O_6 + 6O_2 \rightarrow 6CO_2 + 6H_2O + 38ATP$$
   **a)** Glycolysis: anaerobic phase occurring in cytoplasm; similar to alcoholic fermentation; produces pyruvic acid and 2ATP
   **b)** Aerobic phase: occurs in mitochondria
       **i.** Citric acid cycle: produces citric acid and 2ATP
       **ii.** Electron transport cycle: produces 34ATP
**4.** Organismal respiration
   **a)** Obligate aerobic: cannot live without oxygen
   **b)** Obligate anaerobic: cannot live in the presence of oxygen
   **c)** Facultative: can perform aerobic or anaerobic respiration

## III. Nutrition

**A.** Autotrophic nutrition
   **1.** Photosynthesis: the conversion of light energy to chemical bond energy; occurs in cells containing chlorophyll:
$$6CO_2 + 12H_2O \rightarrow C_6H_{12}O_6 + 6H_2O + 6O_2$$
       **a)** Light reactions: occur in the grana of chloroplasts; use light energy; produce ATP and NADPH$_2$
       **b)** Dark reactions: occur in the stroma of chloroplasts; do not use light energy; produce glucose
   **2.** Chemosynthesis: the use of chemical reaction energy to produce organic compounds
**B.** Heterotrophic nutrition
   **1.** Ingestion: movement of food into an organism's body
   **2.** Digestion: breakdown of large food molecules for use within cells
       **a)** Physical breakdown: distortion of food to increase surface area
       **b)** Chemical breakdown: hydrolysis of food molecules using digestive enzymes for use in cells
           **i.** Extracellular
           **ii.** Intracellular
   **3.** Egestion: removal of undigested food from an organism

## IV. Reproduction

**A.** Asexual reproduction
   **1.** Binary fission: equal division of a parent cell resulting in the production of two daughter cells; binary fission involves mitotic division
   **2.** Budding
       **a)** Unicellular budding: unequal division of a parent cell's cytoplasm resulting in the production of a smaller cell or bud
       **b)** Multicellular budding: multicellular outgrowth of a parent organism resulting in the development of a new organism
   **3.** Sporulation: production of haploid cells called spores; may develop into multicellular organisms or undergo mitosis and produce gametes (sexual reproduction)
   **4.** Vegetative propagation: development of a new organism from a section of the parent organism
   **5.** Regeneration: development of a new organism from a part or segment of the parent organism
   **6.** Parthenogenesis: development of an egg without fertilization

**B.** Sexual reproduction
   1. Conjugation: passage of genetic material between cells
   2. Sporulation: gamete development from spores
   3. Alternation of generations: occurs in plants; development of an asexual stage (the sporophyte) and a sexual stage (the gametophyte)
   4. Hermaphroditism: development of both male and female sex cells within an organism; may involve self- or cross-fertilization
   5. Cross-fertilization: occurs between male organisms containing sperm and female organisms containing eggs; may be external or internal

## V. Viruses

**A.** Description
   1. Features: composed of a protein capsid coat and a nucleic acid core
   2. Reproduction: takes over host cells by injecting genetic material or entering cell whole; controls host cell's chemical activities to produce virions
      **a)** Bacteriophage lytic cycle: invasion, replication, and release of virions from a bacteria cell by a phage
         **i.** Attachment: occurs on cell wall receptor sites
         **ii.** Entry: DNA is injected into the cell
         **iii.** Replication: viral DNA uses cell's system for replication
         **iv.** Release: cell lysis occurs and virions are released
      **b)** Bacteriophage lysogenic cycle: invasion of a bacteria cell by a temperate phage and attachment to cell chromosome; replication occurs during cell mitosis; non-active virus
   3. Transduction: transfer of cellular DNA by virions
**B.** Examples
   1. RNA viruses: contain RNA; may replicate using RNA, or create DNA through RNA reverse transcription
   2. DNA viruses: contain DNA

## VI. Monerans

**A.** Bacteria: Schizophyta
   1. Description
      **a)** Features: prokaryotic; unicellular; may be cocci, spirilli, or bacilli; have a cell wall and nuclear area; some have a capsule, flagella, and pilli
      **b)** Reproduction: asexual fission or endosporulation; DNA can be transferred through conjugation, transformation, or transduction
   2. Example: *Escherichia*
**B.** Blue-green algae or bacteria: Cyanophyta
   1. Description
      **a)** Features: prokaryotic; unicellular; photosynthetic; have a cell wall and nuclear area; involved in nitrogen fixation
      **b)** Reproduction: asexual fission or sporulation
   2. Example: *Nostoc*

## VII. Protists

**A.** Sarcodinians: Sarcodina
   1. Description
      **a)** Features: eukaryotic; unicellular; cytoplasm divided into ectoplasm and endoplasm; pseudopodia; some produce cysts
      **b)** Reproduction: binary or multiple fission
   2. Example: *Amoeba*

**B.** Ciliates: Ciliophora
    **1.** Description
        **a)** Features: eukaryotic; unicellular; contain a micronucleus and a macronucleus; pellicle; cilia; trichocysts; digestive system includes an oral groove, gullet, and anal pore
        **b)** Reproduction: binary fission or conjugation
    **2.** Example: *Paramecium*
**C.** Flagellates: Mastigophora
    **1.** Description
        **a)** Features: eukaryotic; unicellular; pellicle; flagellum; eyespot; some contain chloroplasts with chlorophyll
        **b)** Reproduction: longitudinal binary fission
    **2.** Example: *Euglena*
**D.** Sporozoans: Sporozoa
    **1.** Description
        **a)** Features: eukaryotic; unicellular
        **b)** Reproduction: in stages; sexual sporulation followed by binary fission
    **2.** Example: *Plasmodium*

## VIII. Fungi

**A.** Bread molds: Zygomycetes
    **1.** Description
        **a)** Features: eukaryotic; multicellular; hyphae include stolons and rhizoids; sporangia produce spores
        **b)** Reproduction: asexual sporulation or sexual conjugation
    **2.** Example: *Rhizopus*
**B.** Sac fungi: Ascomycetes
    **1.** Description
        **a)** Features: eukaryotic; unicellular or multicellular; ascus produces ascospores
        **b)** Reproduction: sexual sporulation, binary fission, or budding
    **2.** Examples: yeasts, mildews
**C.** Molds: Deuteromycetes
    **1.** Description
        **a)** Features: eukaryotic; produce conidia
        **b)** Reproduction: asexual or sexual
    **2.** Example: *Penicillium*
**D.** Club fungi: Basidiomycetes
    **1.** Description
        **a)** Features: eukaryotic; multicellular; produce mycelia, basidia, and fruiting bodies
        **b)** Reproduction: usually sexual sporulation
    **2.** Example: mushrooms

## IX. Non-seed-bearing plants

**A.** Green algae: Chlorophyta
    **1.** Description
        **a)** Features: eukaryotic; photosynthetic; may be unicellular, filamentous, or colonial
        **b)** Reproduction: asexual fission or sporulation; sexual isogamy or heterogamy
    **2.** Examples: *Spyrogyra*, *Protococcus*, desmids

**B.** Golden algae: Chrysophyta
  **1.** Description
    **a)** Features: eukaryotic; photosynthetic; unicellular or multicellular
    **b)** Reproduction: asexual fission or sexual isogamy
  **2.** Example: Diatoms
**C.** Brown algae: Phaeophyta
  **1.** Description: marine seaweeds
    **a)** Features: varied; some are very large and contain air bladders
    **b)** Reproduction: asexual zoospore production or regeneration; sexual alternation of generations
  **2.** Examples: *Laminaria, Sargassum*, kelp
**D.** Red algae: Rhodophyta
  **1.** Description
    **a)** Features: unicellular or filamentous
    **b)** Reproduction: asexual or sexual
  **2.** Examples: coralline algae, *Polysiphonia*
**E.** Dinoflagellates: Pyrrophyta
  **1.** Description
    **a)** Features: unicellular; contain two flagella; some are biolumenescent; may produce red tides
    **b)** Reproduction: primarily binary fission
  **2.** Examples: *Noctiluca, Gonyaulax*
**F.** Mosses: Bryophyta
  **1.** Description
    **a)** Features: lack true roots, stems, and vascular tissue
    **b)** Reproduction: alternation of generations; antheridia are male organs, archegonia are female organs
  **2.** Examples: *Sphagnum, Polytrichum, Andreaea*
**G.** Liverworts: Bryophyta
  **1.** Description
    **a)** Features: lack true roots, stems, and vascular tissue
    **b)** Reproduction: alternation of generations, vegetative propagation
  **2.** Example: *Marchantia*
**H.** Club mosses: Tracheophyta
  **1.** Description
    **a)** Features: contain vascular tissue, true roots, stems, and leaves
    **b)** Reproduction: alternation of generations
  **2.** Example: *Selaginella*
**I.** Horsetails: Tracheophyta
  **1.** Description
    **a)** Features: contain vascular tissue, true roots, stems, and leaves.
    **b)** Reproduction: alternation of generations
  **2.** Example: *Equisetum*
**J.** Ferns: Tracheophyta
  **1.** Description
    **a)** Features: contain vascular tissue, true roots, stems (underground rhizomes), and leaves (fronds)
    **b)** Reproduction: alternation of generations

## X. Seed-bearing plants

**A.** Structure
  **1.** Tissues
     **a)** Epidermal tissue: outer cell layer
     **b)** Meristematic tissue: differentiates into specialized tissues
         **i.** Meristem: found on stem and root tips; involved in plant growth
         **ii.** Cambium: found within stems and roots
     **c)** Parenchyma tissue: involved in storage and photosynthesis
     **d)** Vascular tissue: conducts substances
         **i.** Xylem: transports water; composed of tracheids or vessel elements
         **ii.** Phloem: transports food; composed of sieve elements and companion cells
     **e)** Schlerenchyma tissue: supports plants
  **2.** Roots: absorb, move, and store materials, and anchor plant; may be underground, aerial, aquatic, or adventitious
     **a)** Primary root or taproot: major part of the root; stores food
     **b)** Secondary roots: grow out from the primary root
     **c)** Root tip
         **i.** Meristematic region: division of cells occurs
         **ii.** Elongation region: growth of cells occurs
         **iii.** Maturation region: differentiation of cells occurs
         **iv.** Root hairs: increase surface area for absorption
         **v.** Root cap: protects root tip
     **d)** Primary tissues
         **i.** Epidermis: outer layer of cells
         **ii.** Cortex: controls absorption rate and stores food
         **iii.** Vascular cylinder: includes xylem, phloem, and vascular cambium
     **e)** Secondary tissues: the cork cambium
  **3.** Stems: support shoot and produce new cells
     **a)** Herbaceous: supported by turgor pressure
     **b)** Woody: supported by fibers, tracheids, and vessel elements
         **i.** Bark: includes cork, cork cambium, cortex, and phloem
         **ii.** Vascular cambium: forms phloem and xylem
         **iii.** Wood: composed of xylem cells
         **iv.** Pith: composes the central core
     **c)** Others: include bulbs, tubers, rhizomes, corms, and stolons or runners
  **4.** Leaves: simple, compound pinnate, or compound palmate; may have parallel, net, or pinnate venation
     **a)** Petiole: the leaf stalk; absent in sessile leaves
     **b)** Blade: flat part of a leaf where majority of photosynthesis occurs
     **c)** Stipule: protects leaf, may support the stem
     **d)** Tissues
         **i.** Epidermis: outer cell layer; contains cuticle, epidermal hairs, and guard cells with stomata
         **ii.** Mesophyll: middle cell layer; consists of spongy and palisade cells with chloroplasts
         **iii.** Fibrovascular bundles; provide support and transport

     **5.** Flowers: reproductive structures
       **a)** Pedicel: flower stalk
       **b)** Receptacle: produces flower organs
       **c)** Sepals: combine to form the calyx
       **d)** Stamen: male organ; composed of the filament and anther
       **e)** Pistil: female organ; composed of the ovary, style, and stigma
       **f)** Petals: combine to form the corolla

**B.** Transport
     **1.** Cohesion and transpiration pull: evaporation of water in the leaves causes cohesive water molecules to move upward through the plant
     **2.** Root pressure: osmotic pressure in the roots
     **3.** Capillary action: attraction of water molecules to the sides of a column

**C.** Responses
     **1.** Plant hormones
       **a)** Auxins: involved in apical dominance, cell elongation, and cell development
       **b)** Giberellins: involved in cell elongation and division
       **c)** Cytokinins: involved in cell growth and division
       **d)** Abscisic acid: retards seed growth
       **e)** Ethelyne: involved in fruit ripening and abscission of leaves and fruits

**D.** Reproduction
     **1.** Asexual propagation
       **a)** Adventitious budding: plant development from stolons and runners
       **b)** Multicellular budding: produces plantlets
       **c)** Artificial propagation
         **i.** Cutting
         **ii.** Layering
         **iii.** Grafting
         **iv.** Budding
     **2.** Sexual reproduction
       **a)** Spermatogenesis: occurs in anther pollen sacs; microspores develop into pollen grains, each containing a tube and generative nucleus; second stage occurs after pollination
       **b)** Oogenesis: occurs in the ovuole; megaspore divides into embryo sac, egg, and two cells with polar nuclei
       **c)** Pollination: pollen from the anther is transferred to the stigma
         **i.** Tube formation: controlled by pollen tube nucleus
         **ii.** Sperm formation: produced by meiotic division of pollen generative nucleus; sperm travel down tube to ovary
         **iii.** Endosperm formation: produced by uniting of one sperm nucleus with both polar nuclei
         **iv.** Fertilization: other sperm nucleus unites with egg

**E.** Development
     **1.** Cones: produced by gymnosperms
     **2.** Fruits: produced by angiosperms
     **3.** Seeds: plant embryos
       **a)** Monocot seeds: contain one cotyledon, as well as endosperm, epicotyl, hypocotyl, and radicle
       **b)** Dicot seeds: contain two cotyledons, as well as epicotyl, hypocotyl, and radicle

## XI. Animals

**A.** Sponges: Porifera

    **1.** Description

        **a)** Features: cell layers composed of epithelial cells, amoebocytes, and collar cells; skeleton consists of spicules or spongin; pores include ostia and osculum; flagella

        **b)** Reproduction: asexual budding or regeneration; hermaphroditic

**B.** Coelenterates: Coelenterata

    **1.** Description

        **a)** Features: radially symmetrical; form may be polyp or medusa; tissues include exoderm, mesoglia, and gastrodermis; coelenteron; nerve net; cnidoblasts contain nematocysts

        **b)** Reproduction: budding or cross-fertilization

    **2.** Examples: hydra, jellyfish, corals, sea anemones

**C.** Flatworms: Platyhelminthes

    **1.** Description

        **a)** Features: bilaterally symmetrical; have a dorsal and ventral surface; cell layers include exoderm, mesoderm, and ectoderm; ciliated flame bulbs are involved in excretion

        **b)** Reproduction: primarily hermaphroditic; may have parasitic reproductive cycles

    **2.** Examples: planarians, flukes, tapeworms

**D.** Roundworms: Nematoda

    **1.** Description

        **a)** Features: have a mouth, digestive tube, and anus; reproductive systems feature ovaries or testes and a cloaca

        **b)** Reproduction: cross-fertilization

    **2.** Examples: hookworms, trichina

**E.** Rotifers: Rotifera

    **1.** Description

        **a)** Features: pseudocoelom; cilia; foot; digestive system consists of a mouth, mastax, and anus; simple two-nerve system; eyespots are light-sensitive

        **b)** Reproduction: cross-fertilization

    **2.** Example: rotifer

**F.** Segmented worms: Annelida

    **1.** Description

        **a)** Features: bilaterally symmetrical; segmented; coelom; complete organ systems; most have setae

        **b)** Reproduction: hermaphroditic cross-fertilization

    **2.** Example: earthworms

        **a)** Digestive system

            **i.** Prostomium: liplike swelling

            **ii.** Mouth: located under prostomium

            **iii.** Pharynx: muscular tube

            **iv.** Esophagus: extension of the pharynx

            **v.** Gizzard: grinds up food through muscle wall action

            **vi.** Intestine: digestive area

            **vii.** Anus: excretes undigested food as castings

        **b)** Excretory system: nephridia tubes located on most segments; excretes wastes from the coelom through pores

      **c)** Circulatory system: closed

          **i.** Dorsal blood vessel: carries blood toward the anterior

          **ii.** Ventral blood vessel: carries blood toward the posterior

          **iii.** Paired vessels: connect dorsal and ventral blood vessels

          **iv.** Aortic arches: five vessels connecting dorsal and ventral vessels; move blood by contracting

      **d)** Respiratory system: gas exchange occurs through the skin

          **i.** Mucus: epidermal cell secretion to enhance gas exchange

          **ii.** Cuticle: epidermal cell secretion to protect the skin

      **e)** Nervous system: coordinates movement and reaction through nerve impulses

          **i.** Ventral nervous cord: runs the length of the body

          **ii.** Ganglia: enlargements of the ventral nervous cord found in each segment; include the cerebral ganglion and the esophageal ganglion

      **f)** Muscle system: used with setae for movement

          **i.** Longitudinal muscles: shorten body

          **ii.** Circular muscles: lengthen body

      **g)** Reproductive system: hermaphroditic cross-fertilization

          **i.** Testes: produce sperm

          **ii.** Seminal vesicles: store sperm

          **iii.** Sperm duct: transfers sperm to the male genital pore

          **iv.** Seminal receptacle: receives sperm from another individual and releases it to fertilize eggs

          **v.** Ovaries: produce eggs

          **vi.** Oviducts: carry eggs to the female genital pore

          **vii.** Clitellum: posterior swelling that produces slime ring

          **viii.** Slime ring: moves forward to receive eggs and sperm; released from anterior end; protects developing zygotes

**G.** Echinoderms: Echinodermata

    **1.** Description

      **a)** Features: radially symmetrical; coelom; endoskeleton includes spines; water-vascular system

      **b)** Reproduction: regeneration; cross-fertilization

    **2.** Examples: starfish, sea urchin, sea cucumber

**H.** Mollusks: Mollusca

    **1.** Description

      **a)** Features: bilaterally symmetrical; coelom; regions include head, mantled visceral mass, and foot; may be bivalve, univalve, or have no shell; most have a radula

      **b)** Reproduction: cross-fertilization

    **2.** Examples: clams, snails, squids

**I.** Arthropods: Arthropoda

    **1.** Description: includes crustaceans, arachnids, and insects

      **a)** Features: chitinous exoskeleton; jointed legs; body region divided into the head, thorax, and abdomen; breathe with tracheae

      **b)** Reproduction: cross-fertilization; parthenogenesis; includes incomplete and complete metamorphic development; may use pheromones during courtship

    **2.** Examples: grasshoppers

      **a)** Features

          **i.** Head: contains a pair of antennae, eyes, and mouth

          **ii.** Thorax: divided into prothorax, mesothorax, and metathorax; each section contains a pair of legs; mesothorax contains wings

          **iii.** Abdomen: involved in reproduction

    **b)** Digestive system

       **i.** Lips: include upper labrum and lower labium

       **ii.** Jaws: include outer mandibles and inner maxillae

       **iii.** Esophagus: tube for food passage

       **iv.** Crop: storage chamber containing salivary glands

       **v.** Gizzard: breaks up food

       **vi.** Midgut: contains gastric caeca

       **vii.** Hindgut: contains intestines and anus; blood wastes are emptied by Malphigian tubules

    **c)** Circulatory system

       **i.** Heart: blood enters through the ostia and leaves through the aorta

       **ii.** Body cavity: open area where blood flows

    **d)** Nervous system

       **i.** Brain: controls functions

       **ii.** Nerve cord: transmits nerve impulses

       **iii.** Eyes: consist of three simple and two compound eyes

       **iv.** Tympanum: found on the abdomen; involved in hearing

    **e)** Reproductive system

       **i.** Testes: produce sperm

       **ii.** Ovaries: produce eggs

       **iii.** Seminal receptacle: stores sperm in females

       **iv.** Ovipositor: deposits eggs

**J.** Fish: Chordata

  **1.** Description

    **a)** Features: cold-blooded; two-chambered heart; fins; gills, cartilaginous or bony skeleton

    **b)** Reproduction: cross-fertilization

  **2.** Examples: lamprey, shark, perch

**K.** Amphibians: Chordata

  **1.** Description

    **a)** Features: cold-blooded; three-chambered heart; bony skeleton; respiration—juvenile stage usually has gills, adult stage usually has lungs

    **b)** Reproduction: cross-fertilization; most deposit eggs in water; development involves metamorphosis

  **2.** Example: frogs

    **a)** Digestive system

       **i.** Tongue: sticky organ used to catch prey

       **ii.** Teeth: include vomarine and maxillary teeth

       **iii.** Esophagus: connects mouth to stomach

       **iv.** Stomach: involved in digestion; empties through the pylorus

       **v.** Small intestine: attached by mesentery; duodenum receives enzymes from pancreas and bile from liver; ileum empties into large intestine

       **vi.** Large intestine: stores food waste

       **vii.** Cloaca: stores and excretes food waste

    **b)** Excretory system

       **i.** Skin: excretes carbon dioxide

       **ii.** Kidneys: remove waste products from blood

       **iii.** Bladder: receives urine waste from kidneys through urinary ducts

       **iv.** Cloaca: excretes urine

       **v.** Liver: forms urea waste

      **c)** Circulatory system
         **i.** Heart: three-chambered
         **ii.** Arteries: transport blood through body; include truncus arteriosus, dorsal aorta, and carotids
         **iii.** Veins: return blood to heart and lungs; include pulmonary ventral, abdominal, and hepatic portal veins
      **d)** Nervous system
         **i.** Brain: includes cerebrum, cerebellum, medulla oblongata, and optic and olfactory bulbs
         **ii.** Vision: eyes include immobile lids and nictitating membrane
         **iii.** Hearing: ears include tympanum and inner ear
         **iv.** Smell: involves external and internal nares
      **e)** Reproductive system
         **i.** Testes: produce sperm which are transported by sperm ducts
         **ii.** Urinary ducts: store sperm in seminal vesicles and transport to cloaca
         **iii.** Ovaries: produce eggs
         **iv.** Oviduct: coats, stores (in ovisac), and transports eggs to cloaca

**L.** Reptiles: Chordata
   **1.** Description
      **a)** Features: cold-blooded; three-chambered heart; scales
      **b)** Reproduction: cross-fertilization, may be oviparous, ovoviviparous, or viviparous; produce an amniotic egg consisting of a shell, chorion, allantois, and yolk
   **2.** Examples: snakes, lizards, turtles, crocodiles, tuatara

**M.** Birds: Chordata
   **1.** Description
      **a)** Features: warm-blooded; four-chambered heart; wings; toothless beaks; feathers may be down, contour, filoplumes, or bristles; hollow bones; lungs contain parabronchi and air sacs; syrinx produces sound
      **b)** Reproduction: cross-fertilization; internal fertilization; females have only one ovary; egg is amniotic and hard-shelled; young may be altricial or precocial
   **2.** Examples: sparrow, hawk, duck, ostrich

**N.** Mammals: Chordata
   **1.** Description
      **a)** Features: warm-blooded; four-chambered heart; fur; diaphragm; lungs contain bronchioles and alveoli; larynx produces sound
      **b)** Reproduction: cross-fertilization; internal fertilization; most are viviparous; mammary glands produce milk; monotremes lay eggs, marsupials have pouches, placentals have complete embryo development in uterus
   **2.** Examples: duck-billed platypus, oppossum, human

## XII. Humans

**A.** Structure
   **1.** Tissues
      **a)** Epithelial: protective covering
      **b)** Connective: connects and supports body
      **c)** Muscle: moves body by contraction
      **d)** Nerve: conducts electronic messages

**2.** Skeleton: supports and shapes body; stores minerals; produces blood cells
   **a)** Axial skeleton: includes skull, vertebral column, and thorax
   **b)** Appendicular skeleton: includes girdles and bones of arms and legs
   **c)** Bones: formed by ossification; composed of spongy tissue, compact tissue with periosteum and haversian canals, and marrow
   **d)** Joints: allow skeleton to move; cartilage, synovial fluid, and bursae reduce friction; include pivot, hinge, gliding, and ball-and-socket joints
   **e)** Cartilage: fibrous tissue found between bones
   **f)** Ligaments: fibrous tissue connecting bones
**3.** Integument
   **a)** Epidermis: outer layer composed of epithelial cells
   **b)** Glands: include sweat and oil glands
   **c)** Hair: strands of dead epithelial cells; originate from follicles
   **d)** Nails: composed of keratin
**4.** Muscles: composed of myosin and actin
   **a)** Skeletal muscle: voluntary striated fibers attached to bones
   **b)** Smooth muscle: involuntary tissue found in blood vessels and digestive tract
   **c)** Cardiac muscle: automatic tissue found in the heart
**5.** Digestive system
   **a)** Mouth: includes hard and soft palate; contains salivary glands, tongue, and teeth composed of cementum, enamel and dentine
   **b)** Stomach: digests food that passes through esophagus and pharynx by peristalsis
   **c)** Small intestine: contains villi; divided into duodenum, jejunum, and ileum; digests, absorbs, and stores food received through stomach pyloric valve
   **d)** Large intestine: divided into ascending, transverse, descending, and sigmoid colons, and the rectum; moves waste to the anus
   **e)** Liver: produces bile which is stored in the gall bladder
   **f)** Pancreas: produces digestive enzymes
**6.** Excretory system
   **a)** Sweat glands: found in skin; release perspiration
   **b)** Kidneys: composed of nephrons, the Bowman's capsule, and glomerulus capillaries from the renal artery; purify blood and form urine
**7.** Circulation
   **a)** The heart: divided into atria and ventricles separated by the septum; systole contraction of ventricles sends blood into arteries, diastole relaxation of ventricles causes blood to flow from atria
   **b)** Arteries: move blood into body; branch into arterioles and capillaries
   **c)** Veins: return blood to the heart
   **d)** Lymph vessels: form lymph nodes; move tissue fluid to the bloodstream
   **e)** Blood: consists of plasma, red corpuscles, and white corpuscles, as well as protein, antibodies, Rh factor, and antigens which determine blood type
**8.** Respiratory system
   **a)** Trachea: receives air past protective epiglottis from the pharynx; divides into bronchi
   **b)** Lungs: divide from bronchioles into alveoli; exchange gases between alveoli and capillaries; diaphragm and intercostal muscles cause inhalation and exhalation
   **c)** Hemoglobin: pigment found in red corpuscles; helps transport oxygen and carbon dioxide

23

9. Nervous system: divided into peripheral and autonomic systems
    a) The brain: composed of grey and white matter
        i. Cerebrum: divided into right and left hemispheres, and frontal, parietal, and temporal lobes; controls voluntary activity
        ii. Cerebellum: divided into two hemispheres; controls involuntary activity
        iii. Brain stem: divided into the pons and the medulla oblongata; involved in involuntary activity and cranial nerve transmission
    b) The spinal cord: protected by vertebrae; transmits messages and controls reflexes
    c) Neurons: composed of a cell body, dendrites, and axons; separated by synapses; may be sensory, motor or mixed
    d) Sense organs
        i. The eye: composed of a cornea, iris, pupil, lens, and retina with cones and rods
        ii. Smell receptors: connect the nasal cavity to olfactory bulbs
        iii. Taste buds: located on the tongue
        iv. The ear: divided into the external, middle, and inner ears; involved in hearing and balance
        v. The skin: contains touch and pressure receptors
10. Endocrine system: ductless glands that secrete hormones into the bloodstream
    a) The thyroid: secretes thyroxine and calcitonin; affects metabolism and calcium and phosphate levels
    b) The pituitary: secretes variety of hormones; human growth hormone affects growth, vasopressin affects kidney activity, oxytonin affects blood pressure and childbirth
    c) Adrenals: secrete adrenalin and corticoids; increase physiological rates, affect glycogen, salt, and water levels, and reduce inflammation
    d) Pancreas: isles of Langerhans secrete glucagon and insulin; affects glycogen levels and conversion
    e) Thymus: secretes thymosin; affects immune system
11. Reproductive system
    a) The male system
        i. Scrotum: contains testes
        ii. Testes: seminiferous tubules produce sperm
        iii. Vas deferens: transports sperm from epididymis to urethra
        iv. Glands: include seminal vesicle, prostate gland, and Cowper's gland; secretions combine with sperm to form semen
    b) The female system
        i. Ovaries: produce eggs
        ii. Fallopian tube: transports egg
        iii. Uterus: site of zygote development; if fertilization does not take place, menstruation occurs
B. Development
    1. Embryonic stage: zygote undergoes cleavage; includes morula, blastula, and gastrula stages; primary germ layers form
    2. Gestation stage: embryo develops within uterus wall; chorion, amnion, yolksac, and allantois membranes form; placenta and umbilical cord transport nutrients, oxygen, and waste
    3. Birth stage: ejection of the fetus through the vagina by uterine contractions

**C.** Health
  **1.** Nutrition: involves nutrients for metabolism, growth, and repair
   **a)** Proteins: composed of amino acids
   **b)** Carbohydrates: include sugars and starches
   **c)** Fats: also called lipids
   **d)** Vitamins: may be fat-soluble or water soluble
   **e)** Minerals: inorganic substances
   **f)** Water: composes 60 to 80 percent of the body
  **2.** Infectious diseases
   **a)** Defenses
    **i.** Skin: protective barrier
    **ii.** Secretions: includes perspiration, oils, tears, mucus, and enzymes
    **iii.** Phagocytes: white blood cells; include leukocytes and macrophages
    **iv.** Antibodies: produced by lymphocytes; respond to antigens
    **v.** Interferon: acts on viruses
    **vi.** Immunity: may be inborn, active or passive
    **vii.** Medical: includes vaccines and antibiotics
   **b)** Causes: pathogens may be contagious
    **i.** Viruses: infect and disrupt cells
    **ii.** Bacteria: disrupt metabolic activity; release toxins
    **iii.** Protozoans: often transmitted by a primary host

## XIII. Genetics

**A.** Mendelian genetics: developed by Gregor Mendel in the 19th century; discovered that inheritance is controlled by paired factors (genes)
  **1.** Law of dominance: one factor may mask and prevent the effect of the other
  **2.** Law of segregation: paired factors separate during gamete formation
  **3.** Law of independent assortment: paired factors separate independently
**B.** Modern genetics
  **1.** Gene-chromosome theory
   **a)** Genes: segments of DNA found on chromosomes
   **b)** Loci: location of a gene on a chromosome
   **c)** Alleles: alternate forms of a gene
   **d)** Multiple alleles: sets of genes that affect the same trait
   **e)** Genotype: genetic makeup of an organism
    **i.** Homozygous: paired genes are the same
    **ii.** Heterozygous: paired genes are different
   **f)** Phenotype: effect of the genetic makeup on the organism
   **g)** Gene linkage: occurrence of different genes on a chromosome that are inherited together
   **h)** Crossing-over: replacement of one allele on a chromosome by the contrasting allele from the homologous chromosome
   **i)** Sex chromosomes: pair of chromosomes that determine sex; other chromosomes are autosomal
   **j)** Sex-linked genes: genes carried on the X chromosome; expression is affected by the sex of the individual

23

**2.** Dominance: occurs in a heterozygous pairing of alleles where only one allele is expressed: the other allele is recessive

   **a)** Definitions

      **i.** Parental generation: P1

      **ii.** First generation: F1

      **iii.** Second generation: F2

      **iv.** Dominant allele: capital letter (T)

      **v.** Recessive allele: lower case letter (t)

      **vi.** Paired alleles: homozygous dominant (TT); homozygous recessive (tt); heterozygous (Tt)

   **b)** Punnett squares: charts used to determine the results of a cross

|       | T      | t      |
|-------|--------|--------|
| **T** | TT     | Tt     |
| **t** | Tt     | tt     |

**Punnett Square**
**(hybrid cross)**

   **c)** Hybrid cross: breeding of two heterozygous individuals, resulting in a genotype of 1:2:1 and a phenotype of 3:1

   **d)** Test cross: test to determine if a dominant trait is homozygous or heterozygous by breeding the organism with a homozygous recessive

   **e)** Dihybrid cross: breeding of individuals with two different traits involving two pairs of alleles

   **f)** Incomplete dominance: partly dominant allele resulting in an intermediate heterozygous form

**C.** Mutations

   **1.** Somatic mutations: occur in body cells; nonheritable

   **2.** Germ mutations: occur in sex cells; inheritable

   **3.** Chromosomal mutations

      **a)** Nondisjunction: the failure of homologous chromosomes to separate properly during meiosis, resulting in a chromosome number different from normal (*n*)

         **i.** Addition/deletion: the addition or loss of a chromosome section

         **ii.** Translocation: a section of one chromosome attaches to a nonhomologous chromosome

   **4.** Gene mutations: changes in the base sequence of DNA; often recessive and disadvantageous

   **5.** Mutagenic agents: cause mutations; include radiation, chemicals, and viruses

**D.** Human genetics: 23 pairs of chromosomes; includes XX (female) or XY (male) pair

   **1.** Multiple alleles: control blood type

   **2.** Inherited diseases

      **a)** Sickle-cell disease: affects red blood cells

      **b)** Phenylketonuria or PKU: involves a missing enzyme

   **3.** Sex-linked traits

      **a)** Hemophilia: affects blood clotting

      **b)** Color-blindness: affects color vision

**4.** Nondisjunction
   **a)** Down's syndrome: extra twenty-first chromosome
   **b)** Turner's syndrome: only one X chromosome
   **c)** Klinefelter's syndrome: one Y and multiple X chromosomes

## XIV. Evolution

**A.** Evolutionary theory: existing organisms evolved from earlier forms over a long period of time
**B.** Support for evolution
   **1.** Geologic evidence: rocks have been shown to be layered by age according to radioactive dating
   **2.** Fossil evidence: fossils found in differently aged rock layers show similarities suggesting organisms developed from earlier forms
   **3.** Comparative structure: similarity in organisms that suggest a common ancestor
      **a)** Homologous structures: similarity of anatomy
      **b)** Cell structure: similarity of cell organelles
      **c)** Biochemistry: similarity of biochemical compounds
      **d)** Development: similarity of embryo developmental stages
**C.** Heterotroph hypothesis: theory of the development of life on earth; environmental energy created organic aggregates, anaerobic respiration released carbon dioxide, autotrophs developed by utilizing carbon dioxide and released oxygen, leading to aerobic respiration
**D.** History of evolution
   **1.** Lamarck: theorized that acquired traits developed over an organism's lifetime could be inherited
   **2.** Darwin: developed the idea of natural selection, where organisms best suited to their environment survive and reproduce; based on overproduction of offspring, variation among individuals, and competition over resources
**E.** Modern evolutionary theory
   **1.** Hardy-Weinberg principle: gene frequency in a large population does not change unless one of five conditions occur
      **a)** Nonrandom mating: selective or disproportionate mating
      **b)** Mutation: change in the genetic makeup of a cell
      **c)** Genetic drift: random shift in gene frequency
      **d)** Migration: movement of genes into or out of a population
      **e)** Natural selection: environmental effect on a population's gene pool
   **2.** Speciation
      **a)** Species: a group of organisms that interbreed
      **b)** Reproductive isolation: new species may develop if populations are separated by geographic or other barriers
      **c)** Divergent evolution: or adaptive radiation; development from a common ancestor
      **d)** Convergent evolution: development of similar analogous characteristics by unrelated organisms
   **3.** The rate of evolution
      **a)** Gradualism: theory of slow, gradual change
      **b)** Punctuated equilibrium: theory of long periods where no or little change occurs followed by periods of sudden change

23

## XV.  Ecology

**A.** Ecological divisions
  **1.** The biosphere: thin layer about the earth's surface containing life
  **2.** Ecosystem: interacting biotic and abiotic factors within an area of the biosphere
  **3.** Community: group of interacting organisms within an ecosystem
  **4.** Population: group of organisms of the same species within a community
  **5.** Habitat: area where an organism lives
  **6.** Niche: role of an organism in the ecosystem
**B.** Ecological factors
  **1.** Abiotic: non-living factors such as light, temperature, water, and soil
  **2.** Biotic: living factors
    **a)** Autotrophs: green plants and some bacteria that derive energy from inorganic matter
    **b)** Heterotrophs: obtain energy from organic matter
      **i.** Saprophytes: derive energy from decaying organic matter
      **ii.** Herbivores: derive energy from ingesting plant matter
      **iii.** Carnivores: derive energy from ingesting animal matter; include predators, omnivores, and scavengers
**C.** Ecological cycles
  **1.** The carbon-oxygen cycle
    **a)** Photosynthesis: intake of carbon dioxide and water to form glucose
    **b)** Cellular respiration: breakdown of glucose to form carbon dioxide
    **c)** Ingestion: involves organismal respiration and digestion
    **d)** Organic breakdown: release of carbon dioxide trapped in organic matter through decomposition
  **2.** The nitrogen cycle
    **a)** Nitrogen fixation: formation of nitrogen compounds from atmospheric nitrogen; performed by some algae, soil bacteria, and bacteria living symbiotically in plant roots
    **b)** Nitrification: conversion of organic compounds into nitrates which are used by plants; performed by nitrifying bacteria
    **c)** Denitrification: release of nitrogen from nitrates into the atmosphere by soil bacteria
    **d)** Lightning: forms nitrate ions from atmospheric nitrogen
    **e)** Erosion: breakdown of nitrate-rich rock
  **3.** The water cycle
    **a)** Evaporation: movement of water molecules into the atmosphere; caused by the sun's energy
    **b)** Precipitation: movement of water droplets or frozen water back to the earth's surface; caused by condensation
    **c)** Organic: movement of water through organisms
**D.** Energy flow
  **1.** Food chains: show the movement of energy and materials from organism to organism
  **2.** Food web: complex of overlapping food chains
    **a)** Producers: organisms that produce their own food
    **b)** Consumers: feed on producers (primary) or other consumers (secondary and tertiary)
    **c)** Decomposers: break down organic matter
  **3.** Energy pyramid: describes the energy transfer at each trophic level of a food chain

**E.** Ecological relationships
  **1.** Succession: sequence of changes in plant (and animal) species over time
   **a)** Primary succession: community development in an area where no or little life existed
   **b)** Secondary succession: community development in an area where the original community has been partially destroyed
   **c)** Climax community: long-lasting community dominated by a single plant type
   **d)** Eutrophication: aquatic succession due to sedimentation and decay
  **2.** Competition: interactions by members of a community over resources
   **a)** Interspecific competition: between members of different species
   **b)** Intraspecific competition: between members of the same species
  **3.** Predation: the feeding upon of prey items by predators
  **4.** Symbiosis: interaction between organisms that affects the survival of one or both
   **a)** Commensalism: one organism is benefited, the other is not harmed
   **b)** Mutualism: both organisms are benefited
   **c)** Parasitism: one organism is benefited, the other is harmed
  **5.** Population factors
   **a)** Immigration: movement of individuals into a population
   **b)** Emigration: movement of individuals out of a population
   **c)** Population growth: (birth + immigration) − (death + emigration)
   **d)** Carrying capacity: maximum population size an environment can support
   **e)** Density dependent factors: include predation and disease
   **f)** Density independent factors: include storms and drought
   **g)** Dispersal: movement of individuals into a new habitat
   **h)** Barriers to dispersal
     **i.** Geographic
     **ii.** Ecological
     **iii.** Behavioral
**F.** Ecological rhythms
  **1.** Annual: related to seasons or rainfall; affects hibernation, estivation, and migration
  **2.** Lunar: related to tidal patterns; affects coastal organisms
  **3.** Circadian: 24-hour biological clock; affects diurnal or nocturnal activities and physiological changes
**G.** Biomes: geographic areas determined by climate and biological characteristics
  **1.** Terrestrial Biomes
   **a)** Tundra: area with permafrost and stunted vegetation
   **b)** Taiga: area with extensive coniferous forest
   **c)** Temperate: area with deciduous forest
   **d)** Grassland: area with grasses and sparse or no woody vegetation
   **e)** Desert: area with low rainfall and sparse vegetation
   **f)** Tropical forest: area with high rainfall and great plant diversity
  **2.** Aquatic biomes
   **a)** Marine: includes coastal, pelagic, and benthic environments; organisms divided into plankton, nekton, and benthos
     **i.** Intertidal zone
     **ii.** Neritic zone
     **iii.** Bathyal zone
     **iv.** Abyssal zone
   **b)** Freshwater: may be eutrophic or oligotrophic
     **i.** Lakes and ponds
     **ii.** Rivers and streams
   **c)** Estuaries: regions where fresh and salt waters meet

# Chemistry

## I.  The study of chemistry

**A.**  The scientific method

**1.** The problem: identification and statement of the problem, and the gathering of information related to it

**2.** The hypothesis: explanatory statement about the problem

**3.** The experiment: testing the hypothesis; involves controlling for variables, observing, recording, and analyzing data

**4.** The conclusion: agreement or disagreement as to the validity of the hypothesis

**5.** The theory: generally accepted hypothesis used to explain events; subject to revision or rejection based on new data

**B.**  Chemistry fields

**1.** Analytic chemistry: the study of material composition and classification

**2.** Physical chemistry: the study of material characteristics and reactions

**3.** Inorganic chemistry: the study of nonorganic materials

**4.** Organic chemistry: the study of carbon compounds

**5.** Nuclear chemistry: the study of subatomic particles and nuclear reactions

**6.** Biochemistry: the study of living materials and processes

**C.**  Chemical measurements

**1.** Weight: measure of the earth's attraction for an object

**2.** Mass: measure of an object's inertia; $m = D \times V$

**3.** Volume: amount of space occupied by an object; measured in cubic units; $V = m/D$

**4.** Density: measure of the mass of a unit volume of a material; $D = m/V$

**5.** Metric system: decimal unit system

   **a)** Length: in meter units

   **b)** Mass: in gram units

   **c)** Capacity: volume of liquids and gases; in liter units

**6.** Heat: energy transferred between two systems

   **a)** Kinetic energy: $E_k = \frac{1}{2}(mv^2)$

   **b)** Joule: $J = kgm^2/s^2$

   **c)** Calorie: quantity of heat required to raise the temperature of 1 gram of water 1° Celsius; 1 cal = 4.19 J

**7.** Temperature: measure of heat

   **a)** Fahrenheit

   **b)** Celsius

   **c)** Kelvin: $°K = °C + 273$

**8.** Scientific notation: exponential system; $M \times 10^n$

**9.** Uncertainty

   **a)** Accuracy: nearness of measurement to an accepted value

     **i.** Absolute error: $E_a = |O - A|$

     **ii.** Relative error: $E_r = E_a/A \times 100\%$

   **b)** Precision: agreement of similar measurements

     **i.** Absolute deviation: $D_a = |O - M|$

     **ii.** Relative deviation

   **c)** Significant figures: express digits known with certainty, plus the first digit that is uncertain; shown by a $\pm$ notation; product or quotient of significant figures is rounded to the first point of uncertainty in the significant figures

## II. Matter

**A.** Definition: anything that occupies space and has mass
  **1.** Homogeneous: matter with similar properties
  **2.** Heterogeneous: matter containing parts with different properties
**B.** Substances: homogeneous material consisting of one kind of matter; has a definite chemical composition; described by chemical formulas
**C.** Elements: cannot be further decomposed by normal chemical means; there are 92 natural elements and 17 synthetic or transuranium elements
  **1.** Metals: electropositive elements with good conducting properties
  **2.** Nonmetals: electronegative elements with poor conducting properties
  **3.** Metalloids: elements containing properties intermediate between metals and nonmetals
  **4.** Noble metals: elements that exhibit low chemical activity
**D.** Molecules: smallest chemical unit of a substance capable of a stable, independent existence
  **1.** Molecular formula: indicates the actual molecular composition
  **2.** Empirical formula: indicates the constitutent elements of a substance; uses simplest whole-number ratio of atoms
  **3.** Structural formula: indicates molecular bond structure
  **4.** Electron-dot formula: indicates molecular electron structure
**E.** Compounds: can be decomposed into two or more simpler substances by normal chemical means; always composed of the same elements in a definite mass relationship
**F.** Mixtures: heterogeneous material consisting of two or more kinds of matter, each retaining its own characteristic properties

## III. Energy

**A.** Definition: the capacity to do work
**B.** Types of energy
  **1.** Mechanical energy
    **a)** Potential energy: energy of position
    **b)** Kinetic energy: energy of motion
  **2.** Heat energy
  **3.** Chemical energy
  **4.** Radiant energy
  **5.** Electric energy
  **6.** Nuclear energy
**C.** Electromagnetic radiation: travels in waves
  **1.** Speed of light: $3.00 \times 10^8$ m/s; $c = f\lambda$
  **2.** Photons: energy units transmitted to matter; $E = hf$
**D.** The law of conservation: the amount of energy and matter in the universe is constant; energy and matter are interchangeable

## IV. The atom

**A.** Definition: smallest unit of an element that can exist either alone or in combination with atoms of the same or different elements
**B.** Structure
  **1.** The nucleus: composed of neutrons and protons
    **a)** Neutrons: neutral particles
    **b)** Protons: positively charged particles
  **2.** The electron cloud: composed of identical negatively charged electrons
  **3.** Nuclides: atom varieties; determined by the number of protons and neutrons in the nucleus
  **4.** Isotopes: nuclides differing only in the number of neutrons

**C.** Atomic measures
   **1.** Atomic number: number of protons in a nucleus
   **2.** Mass number: sum of protons and neutrons in a nucleus
   **3.** Atomic mass: expressed in atomic mass units, amu; one amu = $\frac{1}{12}$ mass of a carbon-12 atom
   **4.** Atomic weight: ratio of an element's average atomic mass to one amu
   **5.** Avogadro's number: number of atoms in 12 grams of carbon-12; $6.02 \times 10^{23}$
   **6.** Mole: amount of a substance containing $6.02 \times 10^{23}$ units of the substance
   **7.** Gram-atomic weight: contains one mole of atoms of an element
**D.** Electrons
   **1.** Quantum numbers: Four numbers used to describe an electron's distance from the nucleus, shape, position, and direction of spin
      **a)** Principal quantum number: describes distance ($n$); expressed in whole numbers (1, 2, 3, 4, . . .$n$)
      **b)** Orbital quantum number: describes orbital shape; expressed in letters ($s$, $p$, $d$, $f$, . . .$n$)
      **c)** Magnetic quantum number: describes orbital position; orbital quantum number $s = 1$, $p = 3$, $d = 5$, $f = 7$; principal quantum number $1 = 1$, $2 = 4$, $3 = 9$, $4 = 16$, . . .$n = n^2$
      **d)** Spin quantum number: describes electron spin; principal quantum number $1 = 2$, $2 = 8$, $3 = 18$, $4 = 32$, . . .$n = 2n^2$
   **2.** Electron configuration: arrangement of electrons
      **a)** Orbital notation: describes orbitals, electron numbers, and spin
      **b)** Electron-dot notation: describes highest energy level electrons
   **3.** Ionization energy: energy required to remove an electron from an atom, resulting in the formation of an ion
      **a)** Metals: have a low ionization energy
      **b)** Nonmetals: have a high ionization energy
   **4.** Electron affinity: energy change that occurs when a neutral atom acquires an electron, resulting in the formation of an ion

## V. Periodic law

**A.** Definition: physical and chemical properties of the elements are periodic functions of their atomic numbers
**B.** The periodic table: arranges in periods or series and groups or families
   **1.** Periods or series: element properties pass from strong metallic to metalloid to strong nonmetallic nature, ending with a noble gas containing an octet in its highest numbered energy level
      **a)** First series: contains hydrogen ($1s^1$)and the noble gas helium ($1s^2$)
      **b)** Second series: contains eight elements with electrons in the first and second energy levels
      **c)** Third series: contains eight elements with electrons in the third energy level
      **d)** Fourth series: contains eighteen elements including transition elements
      **e)** Fifth series: contains eighteen elements including transition elements
      **f)** Sixth series: contains thirty-two elements including transition and lanthanide rare earth elements
      **g)** Seventh series: contains twenty-three reported elements including transition and actinide rare earth elements

2. Groups or families: elements with similar properties and arrangements of electrons in their highest energy level
   a) Group I: sodium family or alkali metals; very active metallic elements with one $s$ electron in the highest energy level
   b) Group II: calcium family or alkaline-earth metals; active metallic elements with two $s$ electrons in the highest energy level
   c) Group III: contain two $s$ and one $p$ electrons in the highest energy level
   d) Group IV: contain two $s$ and two $p$ electrons in the highest energy level
   e) Group V: nitrogen family; contain two $s$ and three $p$ electrons in the highest energy level
   f) Group VI: oxygen family; contain two $s$ and four $p$ electrons in the highest energy level
   g) Group VII: halogen family; contain two $s$ and five $p$ electrons in the highest energy level
   h) Group VIII: noble-gas family: contain two $s$ and six $p$ electrons in the highest energy level
3. Transition elements: subgroup of elements found between groups II and III
4. Metalloids: include boron, silicon, germanium, arsenic, antimony, tellurium, and polonium

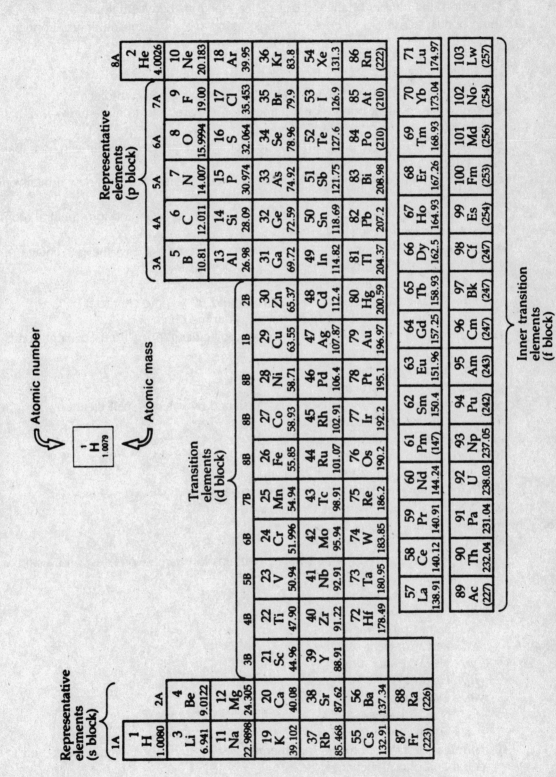

PERIODIC TABLE OF THE ELEMENTS

## VI. Chemical formulas

**A.** Chemical bonds
  **1.** Definition: the transfer or sharing of valence electrons between atoms
  **2.** Ionic bonds: transfer of valence electrons; atoms usually attain noble-gas configurations; form ions
    **a)** Cations: positive ions
    **b)** Anions: negative ions
  **3.** Covalent bonds: sharing of valence electrons and formation of molecules
    **a)** Nonpolar covalent bond: equal attraction for shared electrons resulting in a balanced charge
    **b)** Polar covalent bond: unequal attraction for shared electrons resulting in an unbalanced charge
    **c)** Hybridization: combining orbitals of nearly equal energy to form new orbitals of equal energy
    **d)** Bond energy: energy necessary to break a chemical bond and form neutral atoms; expressed in kcal/mole
    **e)** Electronegativity: attraction of an atom for shared electrons; the percentage of ionic character of a bond A—B = $X_A - X_B/X_A \times 100\%$
      **i.** Ionic bonds: more than 50% ionic character
      **ii.** Polar covalent bonds: between 5% and 50% ionic character
      **iii.** Nonpolar covalent bonds: below 5% ionic character
    **f)** Formulas: used to show the structure of molecules formed from covalent bonds
      **i.** Structural formula
      **ii.** Electron-dot formula
      **iii.** Resonance structure
  **4.** Molecular geometry: bond angles are determined by valence shell electron-pair repulsion theory
    **a)** Linear: contains two electron pairs
    **b)** Trigonal planar: contains three electron pairs
    **c)** Tetrahedral: contains four electron pairs
    **d)** Trigonal bipyramidal: contains five electron pairs
    **e)** Octahedral: contains six electron pairs
**B.** Chemical compounds
  **1.** Naming
    **a)** Compounds: derived from formulas; contains ion names, prefixes, and a suffix
      **i.** Mono-: prefix for 1
      **ii.** Di-: prefix for 2
      **iii.** Tri-: prefix for 3
      **iv.** Tetra-: prefix for 4
      **v.** Penta- or pent-: prefix for 5
      **vi.** Hexa-: prefix for 6
      **vii.** Hepta-: prefix for 7
      **viii.** Octa-: prefix for 8
      **ix.** Nona-: prefix for 9
      **x.** Deca-: prefix for 10
    **b)** Formulas: derived from the ion charges; lowest common multiples are used to form equal and opposite charges
      **i.** Empirical formula calculations: moles of atoms of an element = (element mass) /(mass of 1 mole of the element)
      **ii.** Molecular formula calculations: (empirical formula weight)$_x$ = molecular weight

**2.** Weights
- **a)** Formula weight: sum of the atomic weights of all atoms in the formula
- **b)** Molecular weight: formula weight for molecular substances

**3.** Percentage composition:

$$\% \text{ element} = \frac{\text{element atomic weight} \times \text{number of atoms}}{\text{compound formula weight}} \times 100\% \text{ of compound}$$

## VII. Reactions

**A.** Thermochemistry: changes in heat energy that accompany reactions
  **1.** Heat: thermal energy added to or released from a substance during a reaction
  **2.** Enthalpy: $H$; heat content of a substance; described in terms of kcal/mole
  - **a)** Endothermic reaction: products have a higher $H$ than reactants
  - **b)** Exothermic reaction: reactants have a higher $H$ than products
  - **c)** Change in heat content: $\Delta H = H$ of product $- H$ of reactants
  **3.** Molar heat of formation: $H$ released or absorbed when 1 mole of a compound is formed
  **4.** Heat of combustion: $H$ released by the complete combustion of 1 mole of a substance
  **5.** Entropy: $S$; tendency of disorder in a system to increase
  **6.** Free energy: $G$; includes change in energy and change in entropy
  **7.** Free-energy change: $\Delta G = \Delta H - T\Delta S$
**B.** Collision theory: particle collisions result in chemical interactions
  **1.** Activation energy: minimum energy needed for a collision to produce a reaction; involves removal of a reactant from an energy trough
  **2.** Activated complex: transitional structure resulting from activation energy input
  **3.** Rate-influencing factors: dependent on collision frequency and efficiency
  - **a)** Reactant nature
  - **b)** Surface area
  - **c)** Concentration level
  - **d)** Temperature
  - **e)** Catalytic action
  **4.** Reaction rate law: reaction rate is directly proportional to the frequency of collision; determined experimentally
**C.** Types of reactions
  **1.** Composition reactions: two or more substances react to form a more complex substance
  **2.** Decomposition reactions: one substance reacts with heat or electricity to form two or more simpler substances
  **3.** Replacement reactions: one substance in a compound is displaced by another substance; depends on the relative activities of the substances
  **4.** Ionic reactions: ions in solution react to form a substance that leaves the reaction environment
**D.** Equations: describe reactions
  **1.** Law of conservation of atoms: mass of reactants must equal the mass of products
  **2.** Balancing equations
  - **a)** Oxidation numbers: needed to produce the correct element or ion ratios in the formulas
  - **b)** Mass: used to balance reactants and products in the lowest ratio of whole-number coefficients
  **3.** Phase symbols
  - **a)** Solid: $(s)$
  - **b)** Liquid: $(l)$
  - **c)** Gas: $(g)$
  - **d)** Water solution: $(aq)$

**E.** Stoichiometry: involves mass relations of reactants and products to determine quantitative relationships in terms of molecules, moles, or volumes

**F.** Chemical equilibrium

    **1.** Definition: balanced state in which opposing reaction rates are exactly equal; entropy is balanced by energy; dynamic reversible reactions

    **2.** The equilibrium constant:

$$K = \frac{(C)^x \times (D)^y}{(A)^n \times (B)^m}$$

    when $K$ is greater than 1, products are favored; when $K$ is less than one, reactants are favored

    **a)** Ionization constant: $K_a = K(H_2O)$

    **b)** Ionization constant for water: $K_w = (H_3O^+)(OH^-)$

    **3.** Equilibrium factors: involve Le Chatelier's principle

        **a)** Concentration

        **b)** Pressure

        **c)** Temperature

        **d)** Catalysts

    **4.** Reaction completions: remove ions from the solution

        **a)** Products

            **i.** Gases

            **ii.** Precipitates

            **iii.** Slightly ionized products

        **b)** Solubility-product constant: $K_{sp}$

**G.** Oxidation and reduction

    **1.** Oxidation: reaction causing atoms or ions to attain a more positive state through loss of electrons

        **a)** Rules of oxidation numbers

            **i.** Oxidation number is 0 for a substance in elemental form

            **ii.** Oxidation number of a monotomic ion is the net charge of that ion

            **iii.** Oxidation number of a compound is the sum of the oxidation numbers of its elements

            **iv.** Oxidation number of oxygen is $-2$ in compounds, except in peroxides where it is $-1$

            **v.** Oxidation number of alkali metals is $+1$

            **vi.** Oxidation number of alkaline metals is $+2$

        **b)** Redox reactions: oxidation and reduction occur simultaneously and equally

            **i.** Oxidizing agent: substance that is reduced

            **ii.** Reducing agent: substance that is oxidized

            **iii.** Autooxidizing agent: substance that can be reduced or oxidized ($H_2O_2$)

    **2.** Electrochemistry: involves spontaneous oxidation-reduction reactions which transform chemical energy to electrical energy

        **a)** Electrochemical cells: transfer of electrons through a wire conductor

            **i.** Anode: electrode where oxidation occurs

            **ii.** Cathode: electrode where reduction occurs

        **b)** Electrolysis: oxidation-reduction reactions are driven by an electric current

        **c)** Electrode potential: potential difference between an electrode and its solution in a half-reaction

## VIII. Solutions
**A.** Types
1. Solution: homogeneous mixture of two or more substances
   a) Solute: substance that dissolves
   b) Solvent: substance in which the solute dissolves
2. Colloidal suspension: two-phase heterogeneous mixture having dispersed particles suspended in a medium
3. Electrolytes: soluble ionic substances that conduct an electric charge
4. Saturated solution: contains maximum proportion of dissolved solute to solvent; affected by temperature
5. Supersaturated solution: cooled solution that does not crystallize

**B.** Activity
1. Dissolving: increased by heating the solvent, stirring, or powdering the solid
2. Solubility: maximum amount of a substance that can dissolve in a specific amount of solvent
3. Solution equilibrium: dissolving and crystallizing of a solute occurs at equal rates
4. Henry's law: solubility of a gas in a liquid is directly proportional to the pressure of the gas above the liquid
5. Heat of solution: difference between heat content of a solution and that of its components
   a) Endothermic: solubility increases with a rise in temperature;
      solute + solvent → solution + heat
   b) Exothermic: solubility decreases with a rise in temperature;
      solute + solvent → solution + heat

**C.** Measures
1. Molality: concentration expressed in moles of solute per kilogram of solvent
2. Molarity: concentration expressed in moles of solute per liter of solution
3. Normality: concentration expressed in equivalents of solute per liter of solution
4. Freezing-point depression: $\Delta T_f = K_f M$
5. Gram-molecular weight:

$$\text{g-mol weight} = \frac{K_f \times \text{g solute}}{T_f \times \text{g solute}}$$

**D.** Ionization: formation of ions from solute molecules through the action of a solvent
1. Dissociation: separation of ions from crystals of an ionic compound during the solution process
2. Hydration: attachment of water molecules to ions of a solute

**E.** Acids and bases
1. Electrolytes: can be classified as acids, bases, or salts
2. Acids: substances that react to form hydronium ions ($H_3O^+$) in an aqueous solution
   a) Arrhenius' theory: an acid increases the concentration of hydrogen ions in aqueous solutions
   b) Brønsted-Lowry theory: an acid is a proton (hydrogen ion) donor
   c) Lewis theory: an acid is an electron-pair acceptor
3. Bases: substances that react to form hydroxide ions ($OH^-$) in an aqueous solution
   a) Arrhenius' theory: a base is a soluble hydroxide that neutralizes acids in a solution
   b) Brønsted-Lowry theory: a base is a proton (hydrogen ion) acceptor
4. Amphoteric substances: have acidic or basic properties under certain conditions
5. Salts: ionic compound composed of the positive ions from a base and the negative ions from an acid

23

**6.** Equivalents
   **a)** Acid: quantity that donates 1 mole of protons
   **b)** Base: quantity that accepts 1 mole of protons or supplies 1 mole of hydroxide ions
**7.** pH: common logarithm of the reciprocal of the hydronium ion concentration;

$$pH = \frac{1}{(H_3O^+)}$$

or pH $= -\log (H_3O^+)$
   **a)** Neutral solutions: pH equals 7
   **b)** Acidic solutions: pH is lower than 7
   **c)** Basic solutions: pH is higher than 7
**8.** Acid-base reactions
   **a)** Neutralization: an acid and a hydroxide react to cancel the properties of each other
   **b)** Titration: controlled addition of a measured amount of solution which reacts completely with a measured amount of a solution of unknown concentration

## IX. Kinetic theory

**A.** Definition
   **1.** Particles: compose matter
   **2.** Motion: the particles are in continual motion
   **3.** Elastic collisions: the particles collide and transfer energy, but the total kinetic energy remains the same
**B.** Gases
   **1.** Properties
      **a)** Expansion
      **b)** Pressure
      **c)** Low density
      **d)** Diffusion
   **2.** Ideal gas: imaginary gas whose behavior is described by the gas laws
   **3.** Kinetic energy of gas molecules: $E_k = \frac{1}{2}(mv^2)$
   **4.** Van der Waal forces: attractive force between molecules
      **a)** Dispersion interaction: occurs in all molecules; dependent on number and density of electrons in an atom
      **b)** Dipole-dipole attraction: occurs between polar molecules
   **5.** Gas volume: dependent on temperature and pressure
      **a)** STP: standard temperature (0°C) and pressure (1 atmosphere)
      **b)** Boyle's law: volume of a definite quantity of dry gas is inversely proportional to the pressure if the temperature is constant; $V/V' = p'/p$ or $V' = Vp/p'$
   **6.** Charles' law: volume of a definite quantity of dry gas varies directly with the Kelvin temperature if the pressure is constant; $V/V' = T/T'$ or $V' = VT'/T$
   **7.** Boyle's and Charles' law: $V' = V \times p/p' \times T'/T$
   **8.** Partial pressure: pressure exerted by each gas in a mixture if it were alone
   **9.** Dalton's law: the total pressure of a gas mixture is the sum of their partial pressures
   **10.** Measuring gas volume: uses an eudiometer
      **a)** Mercury displacement
      **b)** Water displacement
   **11.** Guy-Lussac's law: under similar pressure and temperature, the volumes of reacting gases and their gaseous products are expressed in ratios of small whole numbers
   **12.** Avogadro's principle: under similar pressure and temperature, equal volumes of all gases have the same number of molecules
   **13.** Molar volume: the volume of one mole of a gas at STP = 22.4 L

**23**

    **14.** Gram-molecular weight: at STP = density × 22.4 L

    **15.** The gas constant: $pV = nRT$

**C.** Liquids

    **1.** Properties

        **a)** Definite volume

        **b)** Fluidity

        **c)** Noncompressibility

        **d)** Diffusion

        **e)** Evaporation

    **2.** Liquid kinetic theory: liquid particles are more densely packed than gas particles, but still exhibit fluid movement

    **3.** Dynamic equilibrium: opposing changes occur at equal rates

        **a)** Physical equilibrium: dynamic state in which two opposing physical changes occur at equal rates in the same system

        **b)** Evaporative equilibrium: liquid + energy ⇌ vapor

        **c)** Equilibrium vapor pressure: pressure exerted by a vapor in equilibrium with its liquid; dependent on the nature of the liquid and the temperature

    **4.** Le Chatelier's principle: when stress is applied to a system in equilibrium, the equilibrium is displaced in the direction that relieves the stress

    **5.** Boiling point: temperature at which equilibrium vapor pressure of a liquid equals the atmospheric pressure

    **6.** Liquification point: below critical temperature and pressure

    **7.** Vapor: a gas at a temperature below critical temperature

**D.** Solids

    **1.** Properties

        **a)** Definite shape

        **b)** Definite volume

        **c)** Noncompressibility

        **d)** Very slow diffusion

        **e)** Crystal formation

            **i.** Crystalline

            **ii.** Amorphous

    **2.** Solid kinetic theory: solid particles are held closely together in fixed positions; movement is limited to particle vibrations

    **3.** Phase changes

        **a)** Melting and fusion: solid + energy ⇌ liquid

        **b)** Sublimation: solid + energy ⇌ vapor

## X. Organic chemistry

**A.** Organic compounds: contain carbon; differ from inorganic compounds

    **1.** Reactions: proceed at slower rates than inorganic compounds

    **2.** Decomposition: occurs more easily by heating than inorganic compounds

    **3.** Water: most do not dissolve in water as readily as inorganic compounds

**B.** Carbon: has four valence electrons in a tetrahedral arrangement; forms covalent bonds with other carbon atoms

    **1.** Allotropic forms: include diamond and graphite

    **2.** Carbon dioxide: gas at room temperature; at high pressure and low temperature may become a liquid or dry ice

       **a)** Structure: resonance hybrids of four electron-dot structures
       **b)** Preparation
          **i.** Burning carbon
          **ii.** Natural gas and steam reaction
          **iii.** Carbonate heating
          **iv.** Carbonate and acid reaction
          **v.** Molasses fermentation
          **vi.** Respiration and decay

**3.** Carbon monoxide
    **a)** Structure: unequal resonance hybrid of four electron-dot structures
    **b)** Preparation
       **i.** Carbon dioxide reduction
       **ii.** Hot coke and steam reaction
       **iii.** Formic acid decomposition

**4.** Hydrocarbons: composed of carbon and hydrogen; carbon properties produce isomers
    **a)** Saturated hydrocarbon: has only single covalent bonds between carbon atoms
       **i.** General formula: $C_nH_{2n}$
       **ii.** Reactions: include addition, polymerization, alkylation, and combustion
    **b)** Alkanes: or paraffin series; straight-chain or branched-chain hydrocarbons; saturated; have a low chemical reactivity; homologous series differing by $CH_2$ groups
       **i.** General formula: $C_nH_{2n} + 2$
       **ii.** Reactions: include combustion, substitution, and hydrogen preparation
    **c)** Alkenes: or olefin series; have double covalent bond between carbon atoms
       **i.** General formula: $C_nH_{2n}$
       **ii.** Reactions: include combustion addition, polymerization, and alkylation
    **d)** Alkynes: or acetylene series; have triple covalent bond between carbon atoms
       **i.** General formula: $C_nH_{2n-2}$
       **ii.** Reactions: include combustion, dimerization, and halogen addition
    **e)** Aromatic hydrocarbons: contain resonance hybrid bonds between carbon atoms
       **i.** General formula: described by benzene rings or phenyl groups; $C_6H_5-$
       **ii.** Reactions: include halogenation, Friedel-Crafts reactions, nitration, and sulfonation

**5.** Alcohols: have an alkane structure with hydroxyl groups substituted for hydrogen atoms
**6.** Ethers: contain alkyl groups in the formula ROR'
**7.** Aldehydes: contain a hydrocarbon group and formyl groups in the formula RCHO
**8.** Ketones: contain a carbonyl group in the formula RCOR'
**9.** Carboxylic acids: contain a carboxyl group in the formula RCOOH
**10.** Esters: formula is RCOOR'
    **a)** Esterification: formation of an ester through the reaction of an alcohol and an acid

## XI. Radioactivity

**A.** Natural radioactivity: the spontaneous breakdown of an unstable nucleus and the subsequent release of particles and rays
**B.** Nuclear reactions
    **1.** Radioactive decay: decay of radioactive materials into simpler atoms; the half-life of a radioactive material is the time necessary for one-half of a given amount of the material to decay
    **2.** Transmutation: change in the number of protons in a nucleus
    **3.** Nuclear disintegration: nuclear bombardment by particles causing emission of protons or neutrons
    **4.** Fusion: combination of nuclei
    **5.** Fission: splitting of nucleus

**C.** Radiation
   **1.** Alpha particles: helium nuclei
   **2.** Beta particles: electrons
   **3.** Gamma rays: electromagnetic waves
**D.** Radioactive nuclides: nuclides beyond element 83 of the periodic table
   **1.** Superscript: mass number
   **2.** Subscript: atomic number
**E.** Artificial radioactivity: forced transmutation
   **1.** Nuclear mass defect: difference between the mass of a nucleus and the mass of its constituent particles
   **2.** Nuclear binding energy: released when a nucleus forms from its constituent particles
   **3.** Radioactive devices
      **a)** Geiger counter: used to measure radioactivity
      **b)** Particle accelerators: used to bombard atomic nuclei
         **i.** Cyclotron
         **ii.** Synchrotron
         **iii.** Linear accelerator
      **c)** Nuclear reactors: use critical mass of a radioactive material to produce a controlled fission chain reaction

23

# Physics

## I. The study of physics

**A.** The scientific method

    **1.** The problem: identification and statement of the problem, and the gathering of information related to it

    **2.** The hypothesis: explanatory statement about the problem

    **3.** The experiment: testing the hypothesis; involves controlling for variables, observing, recording, and analyzing data

    **4.** The conclusion: agreement or disagreement as to the validity of the hypothesis

    **5.** The theory: generally accepted hypothesis used to explain events; subject to revision or rejection based on new data

**B.** Physics measurements

    **1.** Weight: measure of the earth's attraction for an object; $w = m \times g$

    **2.** Mass: measure of an object's inertia; $m = D \times V$

    **3.** Volume: amount of space occupied by an object; measured in cubic units; $V = m/D$

    **4.** Density: measure of the mass of a unit volume of a material; $D = m/V$

    **5.** Metric system: decimal unit system

        **a)** Length: in meter units

        **b)** Mass: in gram units

        **c)** Capacity: volume of liquids and gases; in liter units

    **6.** Heat: energy transferred between two systems

        **a)** Kinetic energy: $E_k = \frac{1}{2}(mv^2)$

        **b)** Joule: $J = kgm^2/s^2$

        **c)** Calorie: quantity of heat required to raise the temperature of 1 gram of water 1° Celsius; 1 cal = 4.19 J

    **7.** Temperature: measure of heat

        **a)** Celsius

        **b)** Kelvin: $°K = °C + 273$

    **8.** Scientific notation: exponential system; $M \times 10n$

    **9.** Uncertainty

        **a)** Accuracy: nearness of measurement to an accepted value

            **i.** Absolute error: $E_a = |O - A|$

            **ii.** Relative error: $E_r = E_a/A \times 100\%$

        **b)** Precision: agreement of similar measurements

            **i.** Absolute deviation: $D_a = |O - M|$

            **ii.** Relative deviation

        **c)** Significant figures: express digits known with certainty, plus the first digit that is uncertain; shown by a ± notation; product or quotient of significant figures is rounded to the first point of uncertainty in the significant figures

    **10.** Graphics: involve data placed within an $x$ axis and a $y$ axis

    **11.** Vectors: involve magnitude and direction

## II. Motion

**A.** Definition: change in position relative to a frame of reference

**B.** Speed: distance traveled by a moving object per unit of time; $s = d/t$

    **1.** Constant speed: the graph of (distance/time) in a straight line

    **2.** Average speed: (total distance)/(elapsed time)

    **3.** Instantaneous speed: slope of the line tangent to the curve at a given point

**C.** Velocity: speed in a given direction
   **1.** Average velocity: $v_{av} = \Delta d/\Delta t$
   **2.** Instantaneous velocity
**D.** Acceleration: rate of change in velocity; $a_{av} = \Delta v/\Delta t$
   **1.** Deceleration
   **2.** Free fall
   **3.** Circular motion
**E.** Momentum: mass × velocity

## III. Force

**A.** Definition: force = mass × acceleration; described in Newtons (N)
**B.** Laws of motion
   **1.** Law of inertia: an object at rest or in motion will remain that way unless an unbalanced force acts on it
   **2.** Law of acceleration: an applied force causes an object to accelerate in the direction of the force; acceleration is directly proportional to the object's mass
   **3.** Law of interaction: every force has an equal and opposite force
**C.** Types of forces
   **1.** Balanced forces: opposite in direction and equal in size; result in no change in motion
   **2.** Unbalanced forces: not opposite and equal; result in a change in motion
**D.** Resolution of forces: determination of force components
**E.** Friction: force that opposes the motion of an object
   **1.** Sliding: friction produced when two solid objects slide over one another
   **2.** Rolling: friction produced when a solid object rolls over a surface
   **3.** Fluid: friction produced when an object moves through a fluid
**F.** Gravity: force of attraction between two objects
   **1.** Law of universal gravitation: all objects in the universe attract each other by the force of gravity
   **2.** Orbital motion: combined motion of an object resulting from forward inertia and gravitational pull
   **3.** Projectile motion: combined motion of an object resulting from forward inertia and gravitational acceleration
   **4.** Weight: due to gravitational pull; weight = mass × acceleration
**G.** Pressure: force over a certain area; pressure = force/area
   **1.** Fluid pressure
      **a)** Buoyancy: dependent on density
      **b)** Bernoulli's principle: pressure in a moving stream of fluid is less than in the surrounding fluid
         **i.** Lift
         **ii.** Thrust
         **iii.** Drag

## IV. Work

**A.** Definition: force applied to an object and distance through which the force is applied; work = force × distance
**B.** Work measures
   **1.** Newton-meter
   **2.** Joule
**C.** Power: work done per unit time; power = work/time or $p = f \times (d/t)$; measured in watts

**D.** Machines: devices that perform work
  **1.** Work input: work done on a machine: $W_I = F_E \times d_E$
  **2.** Work output: work done by a machine; $W_O = F_R \times d_R$
  **3.** Efficiency: equals $(W_O/W_I) \times 100$; expressed as a percent
  **4.** Types of machines
    **a)** Inclined plane
    **b)** Lever
    **c)** Pulley
    **d)** Wedge
    **e)** Screw
    **f)** Wheel and axle
    **g)** Compound machine

## V. Energy

**A.** Classification
  **1.** Potential energy: energy of position; gravitational potential energy = weight × height
  **2.** Kinetic energy: energy of motion; K.E. = $(m \times v^2)/2$
**B.** Energy and mass
  **1.** Law of conservation of energy: energy may only be converted, not destroyed
  **2.** Einstein's theory: mass and energy are related; $E = mc^2$
**C.** Conversion: changes in the forms of energy; P.E. $\rightleftarrows$ K.E.
**D.** Heat energy: caused by internal motion of particles
  **1.** Heat measurement
    **a)** Temperature: measure of the average kinetic energy of molecules
    **b)** Calorie: measure of heat; 1 cal = 4.19 J
  **2.** Transfer
    **a)** Conduction: direct contact
    **b)** Convection: liquid or gas current
    **c)** Radiation: through space
  **3.** Exchange
    **a)** Heat capacity: quantity of heat necessary to raise an object's temperature 1°C; equals $Q/\Delta T$
    **b)** Specific heat: heat capacity of a material per unit mass; $c = Q/(m\Delta T)$
    **c)** Endothermic reaction: chemical reaction in which energy is absorbed
    **d)** Exothermic reaction: chemical reaction in which energy is released
  **4.** Thermal expansion
    **a)** Solids
    **b)** Liquids
    **c)** Gases
      **i.** Charles' law: volume of a definite quantity of dry gas varies directly with the Kelvin temperature if the pressure is constant; $V/V' = T/T'$ or $V' + VT/T'$
      **ii.** Boyle's law: volume of a definite quantity of dry gas is inversely proportional to the pressure if the temperature is constant; $V/V' = p'/p$ or $V' = Vp/p'$
      **iii.** Charles' and Boyle's law: $V' = V \times p/p' \times T'/T$
      **iv.** The gas constant: $pV = nRT$
      **v.** Avogadro's number: number of atoms in 12 grams of carbon−12; $6.02 \times 10^{23}$
      **vi.** Mole: amount of a substance containing $6.02 \times 10^{23}$ units of the substance
      **vii.** Gram-atomic weight: contains one mole of atoms of an element

23

    **5.** Phases
      **a)** Freezing
      **b)** Melting
      **c)** Vaporization
      **d)** Condensation
      **e)** Sublimation
      **f)** Triple point
      **g)** Critical point
    **6.** Laws of thermodynamics
      **a)** First law: the quantity of heat energy supplied to a system is equal to the work done plus the change in internal energy; energy is not lost when it is converted to or from heat
      **b)** Second law: a closed system loses available energy and gains in entropy unless work is performed
    **7.** Engines
      **a)** Internal combustion
      **b)** External combustion
      **c)** Types
        **i.** Steam
        **ii.** Gasoline
        **iii.** Turbine
        **iv.** Jet
        **v.** Rocket

## VI. Waves

**A.** Characteristics
    **1.** Amplitude: maximum distance molecules are displaced from their rest position
    **2.** Wavelength: distance between two consecutive crests or troughs of a wave
    **3.** Frequency: number of complete wave cycles per time
    **4.** Speed: equals frequency × wavelength
**B.** Movement
    **1.** Rectilinear propagation: movement of a wave in a straight line
    **2.** Reflection: return of a wave from a medium's boundary; the angle of incidence equals the angle of reflection
    **3.** Refraction: bending of waves due to change in speed
    **4.** Diffraction: bending of waves around a barrier
    **5.** Interference: meeting and combining of two waves to make one
      **a)** Constructive interference: amplitude of the new wave is the sum of the amplitudes of the original waves
      **b)** Destructive interference: amplitude of the new wave is the difference of the amplitudes of the original waves
      **c)** Standing wave: constructive and destructive interference produce wave nodes and antinodes
    **6.** Impedance: ratio of wave-producing force to displacement velocity
**C.** Types
    **1.** Electromagnetic: does not need a material medium
    **2.** Mechanical: involves a material medium
    **3.** Transverse: vibrations are at right angles to the direction of wave propagation
    **4.** Longitudinal: vibrations are parallel to the direction of wave propagation
    **5.** Periodic: involves repeated vibration periods

## VII. Sound

**A.** Sound waves: energy passed through a medium causing molecular vibrations
**B.** Transmission: dependent on elasticity of the medium
**C.** Speed: dependent on the medium and temperature; in air the speed of sound is equal to 340 m/s
   **1.** Intensity: amount of energy in a sound wave; dependent on wave amplitude; measured in decibels
   **2.** Frequency: speed of molecular vibration; dependent on wave speed; measured in hertz
   **3.** Quality: combinations of frequencies
**D.** Effects
   **1.** Loudness: a product of intensity
   **2.** Pitch: a product of frequency
   **3.** Timbre: a product of quality

## VIII. Electricity

**A.** Electric charge: described in coulombs
   **1.** Protons: have a positive charge
   **2.** Electrons: have a negative charge
**B.** Electric fields
   **1.** Force of attraction: occurs between oppositely charged particles
   **2.** Force of repulsion: occurs between similarly charged particles
**C.** Static electricity: buildup of electric charge on an object
   **1.** Friction: transfer of a charge through contact and motion
   **2.** Induction: transfer of a charge by bringing an object into the electric field of another charged object
   **3.** Conduction: transfer of an electric charge through a medium
      **a)** Conductors: allow electric charges to move easily
      **b)** Insulators: do not allow electric charges to move easily
**D.** Voltage: or potential difference; described in volts; $V = $ work/charge
**E.** Electric current: flow of electrons through a wire; described in amperes
   **1.** Resistance: opposition to electric flow; described in ohms
   **2.** Dry cell: involves a wire connecting positive and negative terminals; a series of dry cells is a battery
      **a)** Cathode: negative electrode
      **b)** Anode: positive electrode
      **c)** AC: alternating current
      **d)** DC: direct current
   **3.** Wet cell: involves placement of electrodes in an electrolyte
   **4.** Ohm's law: current = voltage/resistance
   **5.** Lenz's law: an induced current's direction opposes the change that induces it
**F.** Circuits: closed-loop conducting paths
   **1.** Parallel: provides separate conducting paths
      **a)** Current: is equal to the sum of the currents in the separate branches; $I_T = I_1 + I_2 + I_3 + $ etc.
      **b)** Potential: has the same magnitude throughout; $V = V_1 = V_2 = V_3 = $ etc.
      **c)** Resistance: the reciprocal is equal to the sum of the separate resistance reciprocals; $1/R_T = 1/R_1 + 1/R_2 + 1/R_3 + $ etc.
   **2.** Series: or battery; provides a single conducting path
      **a)** Current: has the same magnitude throughout; $I_T = I_1 = I_2 = I_3 = $ etc.
      **b)** Potential: is equal to the applied EMG; $E = V_1 + V_2 + V_3 + $ etc.
      **c)** Resistance: is equal to the sum of the separate resistances; $R_T = R_1 + R_2 + R_3 + $ etc.

**G.** Electric measures

    **1.** Power: measure of electric work; measured in watts; power = voltage × current

    **2.** Energy: measured in kilowatt-hours; energy = power × time

**H.** Magnetism

    **1.** Magnetic force: attraction or repulsion due to electron arrangement

    **2.** Magnetic field: region in which magnetic forces act

        **a)** Poles: N and S ends of a magnet

        **b)** Magnetic flux: line whose tangent represents the direction of a magnetic field

        **c)** Magnetic induction: or magnetic flux density; number of flux lines per unit area

**I.** Electromagnetism

    **1.** Conduction: production of a magnetic field caused by an electric current

        **a)** Straight conduction: direction of flux follows the left-hand rule

        **b)** Loop: flux moves through the inside of the loop in the same direction

        **c)** Solenoid: has magnetic properties of a bar magnet

        **d)** Galvanometer: instrument used to detect small currents

    **2.** Induction: production of an electric current caused by a magnetic field

        **a)** Generator: converts mechanical energy into electric energy

        **b)** Transformer: increases or decreases the voltage of alternating current

## IX. Light

**A.** Theories

    **1.** Particle theory: involved particles

    **2.** Wave theory: involved transverse waves

    **3.** Electromagnetic radiation theory: involves electricity and magnetism

    **4.** Quantum theory: involves energy bundles called photons

        **a)** Photon energy: involves Planck's constant; $E = hf$

        **b)** Bright line spectra: involves hydrogen electron energy

            **i.** Lyman series: ultraviolet

            **ii.** Balmer series: visible

            **iii.** Paschen series: infrared

    **5.** Modern theory: light consists of photon transported by a wave field

**B.** Speed: varies with the medium; in a vacuum = 299,792 km/s; in air = 299,729 km/s

**C.** Illumination

    **1.** Luminous object: gives off light

    **2.** Illuminated object: reflects light

**D.** Electromagnetic spectrum: produced by variation in wavelength and frequency

    **1.** Radio waves

        **a)** AM: varies in amplitude

        **b)** FM: varies in frequency

    **2.** Infrared rays

    **3.** Visible light: has a frequency between 430 trillion and 760 trillion hertz

        **a)** Primary colors: in combination produce all other colors

            **i.** Red

            **ii.** Green

            **iii.** Blue

         **b)** Complementary colors: combinations of colors that produce white light

    **4.** Ultraviolet

    **5.** X-rays

    **6.** Gamma rays

23

**E.** Production
  **1.** Incandescence: produced by heat
  **2.** Fluorescence: produced by electron bombardment of gas molecules
**F.** Reflection
  **1.** Law of reflection: the angle of incidence (i) is equal to the angle of reflection (r)
  **2.** Reflectance: ratio of light reflected to the light falling on a surface
  **3.** Regular: reflection from a polished surface with little scattering of light
  **4.** Diffuse: scattered light caused by irregular reflection
  **5.** Mirrors: opaque materials that reflect light
    **a)** Plane: produces a virtual image
    **b)** Concave: produces a real image; involves an optical axis and focal point
    **c)** Convex: produces a virtual image behind the mirror
**G.** Refraction: bending of light rays that pass from one medium to another of different optical density
  **1.** Index of refraction: ratio of speed of light in a vacuum to the speed of light in a substance
  **2.** Critical angle: limiting angle of incidence in an optically denser medium that results in an angle of refraction greater than 90°.
  **3.** Lenses: transparent materials that refract light
    **a)** Converging: thicker in the middle than at the edges
    **b)** Diverging: thicker at the edges than in the middle
**H.** Dispersion: process of separating polychromatic light into its component wavelengths
**I.** Interference: superimposition of two or more light waves
  **1.** Coherence: combination of two waves with identical wavelengths and constant phase relationships
  **2.** Destructive interference: results in loss of intensity
  **3.** Constructive interference; results in increase of intensity
**J.** Diffraction: spreading of light into a region behind an obstruction
  **1.** Double slit
  **2.** Single slit

## X. Atomic physics

**A.** Atom: smallest unit of an element that can exist either alone or in combination with atoms of the same or different elements
**B.** Structure
  **1.** The nucleus: composed of neutrons and protons
    **a)** Neutron: neutral particles
    **b)** Protons: positively charged particles
  **2.** The electron cloud: composed of identical negatively charged electrons
  **3.** Nuclides: atom varieties; determined by the number of protons and neutrons in the nucleus
  **4.** Isotopes: nuclides differing only in the number of neutrons
  **5.** Radioisotopes: radioactive isotopes
**C.** Atomic measures
  **1.** Atomic number: number of protons in a nucleus
  **2.** Mass number: sum of protons and neutrons in a nucleus
  **3.** Atomic mass: expressed in atomic mass units, amu; one amu = $\frac{1}{12}$ mass of a carbon$-12$ atom
  **4.** Atomic weight: ratio of an element's average atomic mass to one amu

**D.** Quantum mechanics
  **1.** The uncertainty principle: it is impossible to specify the exact position of an electron and its momentum at the same time
  **2.** Quantum numbers: four numbers used to describe an electron's distance from the nucleus, shape, position, and direction of spin
    **a)** Principal quantum number: describes distance ($n$); expressed in whole numbers (1, 2, 3, 4, ...$n$)
    **b)** Orbital quantum number: describes orbital shape; expressed in letters ($s$, $p$, $d$, $f$, ...$n$ etc.)
    **c)** Magnetic quantum number: describes orbital position; orbital quantum number $s = 1$, $p = 3$, $d = 5$, $f = 7$; principal quantum number $1 = 1$, $2 = 4$, $3 = 9$, $4 = 16$, ...$n = n^2$
    **d)** Spin quantum number: describes electron spin; principal quantum number $1 = 2$, $2 = 8$, $3 = 18$, $4 = 32$, ... $n = 2n^2$
  **3.** The exclusion principle: no two electrons can be described by the same set of quantum numbers
  **4.** Electron configuration: arrangement of electrons
    **a)** Orbital notation: describes orbitals, electron numbers, and spin
    **b)** Electron-dot notation: describes highest energy level electrons
  **5.** Ionization energy: energy required to remove an electron from an atom, resulting in the formation of an ion; used to describe the stability of an atom
  **6.** Electron affinity: energy change that occurs when a neutral atom acquires an electron, resulting in the formation of an ion

## XI. Nuclear physics

**A.** Natural radioactivity: the spontaneous breakdown of an unstable nucleus and the subsequent release of particles and rays
**B.** Nuclear reactions
  **1.** Radioactive decay: decay of radioactive materials into simpler atoms; the half-life of a radioactive material is the time necessary for one-half of a given amount of radioactive materials to decay
  **2.** Transmutation: change in the number of protons in a nucleus
  **3.** Nuclear disintegration: nuclear bombardment by particles causing emission of protons or neutrons
  **4.** Fusion: combination of nuclei
  **5.** Fission: splitting of nucleus
**C.** Radiation
  **1.** Alpha particles: helium nuclei
  **2.** Beta particles: electrons
  **3.** Gamma rays: electromagnetic waves
**D.** Radioactive nuclides: nuclides beyond element 83 of the periodic table
  **1.** Superscript: mass number
  **2.** Subscript: atomic number
**E.** Artificial radioactivity: forced transmutation
  **1.** Nuclear mass defect: difference between the mass of a nucleus and the mass of its constituent particles
  **2.** Nuclear binding energy: released when a nucleus forms from its constituent particles; expressed in electron-volts

**3.** Radioactive devices
   **a)** Geiger counter: used to measure radioactivity
   **b)** Particle accelerators: used to bombard atomic nuclei
        **i.**   Van de Graaff generator
        **ii.**  Cyclotron
        **iii.** Synchroton
        **iv.**  Linear accelerator
   **c)** Nuclear reactors: use critical mass of a radioactive material to produce a controlled fission chain reaction

# Natural Sciences Reading Walk-Through Test

In this lesson you will find a Natural Sciences Reading Test. There is no time limit for the test. On the pages facing the selections and questions, you will find answers and explanations, so that you can "walk through" the test.

# Walk-Through

**DIRECTIONS:** Below each of the following reading passages is a series of questions. Choose the *best* answer to each question, interpreting what is stated or implied by the passage in the light of your own background in the subject. You may refer back to the passage as often as necessary, though the answers to some questions may not be found expressly in the passage.

A knowledge of atomic structure provides an understanding of how various atoms combine. They form compounds. One group of the atoms (the positive atoms) tends to give up one or more planetary electrons, transferring the electrons to the planets of atoms of another group (negative atoms), which have a tendency to gain planetary atoms. When such an exchange occurs, the participating atoms tend to cling together to form a molecule. The number of planetary electrons which can be gained or lost during such a union is specified as the valence of the particular atom involved.

What causes atoms to combine? The electrons in the outermost shell of an atom play a very important part in the formation of compounds. For this reason, the electrons in an incomplete outer shell are called valence electrons. The remainder of the atom, excluding valence electrons, is called the "kernel" of the atom. In the formation of compounds from elements, the valence electrons are either transferred from the outer shell of one atom to the outer shell of another atom or shared among the outer shells of the combining atoms. This produces a chemical bond, with all the atoms involved attaining a stable outer shell.

The types of chemical bonding that are generally recognized are "ionic bonding" and "covalent bonding." In the formation of a compound by ionic bonding, electrons are actually transferred from the outer shell of one atom to the outer shell of a second atom. By this process, both atoms attain stable outer shells containing eight electrons. In the second type of bonding, covalent bonding, the electrons are not transferred from one atom to another, but the two atoms each share one of their electrons with the other. These two shared electrons effectively fill the outer shell in each element. It is important to note that while atoms transfer or share electrons to form chemical bonds, there are still equal numbers of protons and electrons in the group of atoms forming the molecule.

1. The last sentence implies that:
   A. a molecule of any compound is electrically neutral.
   B. a molecule of any compound has an electrically positive charge.
   C. a molecule of any compound has an electrically negative charge.
   D. the "kernel" of any molecule is electrically neutral.

1. (A) Protons are positively charged particles. Electrons are negatively charged particles. If the molecule has "equal numbers of protons and electrons," it is electrically neutral.

2.  Valence electrons are:

    F.   the electrons in the outer ring of any atom.

    G.   the electrons in the incomplete outer ring of an atom.

    H.   all the electrons in an atom.

    J.   all the electrons in the kernel of an atom.

3.  The part(s) of the atom involved in chemical bonding is (are) the:

    A.   nucleus.

    B.   valence electrons.

    C.   protons.

    D.   neutrons.

4.  If we let $V$ represent the number of valence electrons in an atom, $T$ represent the total number of planetary electrons, and $K$ represent the number of electrons in the kernel of the atom, then the formula that would best represent the kernel would be:

    F.   $K = V - T$

    G.   $K = V + T$

    H.   $K = T - V$

    J.   $K = TV$

5.  According to this passage, ionic bonding differs from covalent bonding because:

    A.   in ionic bonding, the number of electrons in the outer shell of the resulting compound is different from the number in a compound formed by covalent bonding.

    B.   in ionic bonding, the nucleus of the compound differs from the nucleus of a compound formed by covalent bonding by the addition of one or more protons.

    C.   in ionic bonding, the number of valence electrons in the outer shell is different from the number of valence electrons in covalent bonding.

    D.   in ionic bonding, electrons are actually given up or received, whereas in covalent bonding atoms have mutual electrons.

6.  In the noble gas argon, the outer shell of electrons is complete. Consequently, you would expect that:

    F.   argon can form only ionic bonds.

    G.   argon forms covalent bonds but not ionic bonds.

    H.   argon does not normally form compounds with other atoms.

    J.   argon can form covalent or ionic bonds.

2.  (G)  Valence electrons are those in an incomplete outer shell. Electrons in a complete outer shell are not valence electrons.

3.  (B)  Chemical bonds are formed when valence electrons are transferred or shared between atoms. The other parts of the atoms are not involved.

4.  (H)  The kernel includes all of the planetary electrons except the valence electrons. Therefore $K = T - V$.

5.  (D)  The difference between ionic and covalent bonding is that in the former, electrons are transferred, but in the latter, they are shared.

6.  (H)  Since in argon the outer shell of electrons is complete, no electrons are available for bonding. Consequently, argon normally does not form compounds with other atoms.

7. A certain atom has the following electron configuration: $1s2\ 2s2\ 2p6\ 3s1$. How many electrons are in the kernel of this atom?

   A. 2
   B. 4
   C. 10
   D. 11

7. (C) The kernel of an atom includes everything but the valence electrons in an incomplete outer shell. In the given atom, there is one valence electron. The sum of the electrons in the kernel is 10.

8. Every hydrogen atom consists of one proton and one electron. If water is formed when an oxygen atom bonds with two hydrogen atoms, you may conclude that the number of valence electrons in the outer shell of an oxygen atom is:

   F. 8.
   G. 6.
   H. 2.
   J. 1.

8. (G) According to the passage, a stable outer shell is one with eight electrons. When oxygen bonds with hydrogen, it can gain only a single electron. If it forms a stable outer shell by bonding with the two hydrogen atoms, it is gaining two electrons and must therefore have started with six in order to make a total of eight.

9. Two atoms of different substances combine by chemical bonding. Compared to the original two atoms, the resulting molecule will have:

   A. fewer total electrons.
   B. the opposite electrical charge.
   C. different chemical properties.
   D. fewer total protons.

9. (C) The resulting molecule will have the same total number of protons and electrons as the original two atoms, and like them, it will be electrically neutral. However, when atoms bond chemically, the resulting compound has a different set of chemical properties.

Certain animals are able to sense the presence of nearby objects through a remarkable ability called echolocation. This is the ability to emit extremely high-pitched sounds—often inaudible to the human ear—and to use the echoes made by those sounds to determine the location, size, and shape of objects in the surrounding area. Bats are one species that uses echolocation as a guide during flight. In many kinds of bats, mouths and breathing passages have developed peculiar shapes that are well adapted to producing supersonic sounds. Ears, too, are often relatively large in order to better hear the echoes.

In the sea, echolocation is widely used by whales and other seagoing mammals. Some of the noises produced by these animals can be heard by humans; many others can not. Echolocation is an invaluable guide to these animals as they swim through deep waters or among ice or rocks. In captivity, whales and porpoises continue to use their echolocation ability. Many studies of echolocation have been made using captive animals.

10. Echolocation gives bats the ability to:

    F. fly safely in darkness.
    G. fly safely during very cold weather.
    H. identify safe nesting sites.
    J. fly safely during strong winds.

10. (F) Echolocation enables bats to determine the location and shape of nearby objects. This helps them avoid obstacles while flying in darkness. None of the other choices refer to potential obstacles that could be identified by echolocation.

11. A scientist applying the theory of evolution might say that:

    A. bats grew larger ears in order to make better use of echolocation.
    B. bats born with larger ears had greater echolocation abilities and a better chance of surviving and producing large-eared offspring.
    C. bats grew specially shaped mouths in order to be better able to emit supersonic sounds.
    D. a bat that learned to emit supersonic sounds could pass this ability on genetically to its offspring.

12. Because most bats can use echolocation, which other sensory ability can they most likely survive without?

    F. Smell
    G. Touch
    H. Taste
    J. Sight

13. How might echolocation enable insect-eating bats to avoid competing with birds for food?

    A. The bats can cover a greater territory than birds can.
    B. The bats can find more insects than birds can.
    C. The bats can fly faster than birds can.
    D. The bats can hunt at night while the birds are asleep.

14. A captive porpoise in a large tank is blindfolded for an experiment. Using echolocation, the porpoise probably will be able to:

    F. tell a white floating tennis ball from a yellow floating tennis ball.
    G. tell whether a person outside the tank is holding a ball or a hoop.
    H. tell whether fish are swimming nearby.
    J. tell whether a seal in the tank is grey or brown.

15. For whales migrating long distances in groups, another use of echolocation might be to:

    A. maintain a consistent direction of travel.
    B. maintain communication in darkness or rough seas.
    C. determine the location of ocean currents.
    D. foretell the approach of stormy weather.

11. (B) According to evolutionary theory, an organism born with an advantageous trait has a better chance of surviving, reproducing, and passing the trait to its offspring. Traits that are acquired during the lifetime cannot be passed to the offspring.

12. (J) Bats that can use echolocation to determine the location and shape of nearby objects can likely survive without the sense of sight. In fact, many types of bats are almost blind.

13. (D) Echolocation allows the bats to hunt insects at night, while birds are asleep. None of the other choices relate to echolocation.

14. (H) The porpoise will be able to sense the location and shape of the nearby fish. It will be unable to tell the color of the tennis ball (choice F) or the seal (choice J), and its use of echolocation in the water will not tell anything about the objects outside of the tank.

15. (B) Echolocation will enable the whales to stay in contact with each other. It will provide no knowledge about the items mentioned in the other choices.

16. Scientists believe that porpoises have learned to use supersonic sounds as a means of catching fish for food. Which of the following fish behaviors would be evidence for this conclusion?

    F.    The fish swim slowly away as the porpoise approaches.

    G.    The fish gather close together as the porpoise approaches.

    H.    The fish scatter in different directions as the porpoise approaches.

    J.    The fish act stunned and lie motionless as the porpoise approaches.

16. (J) Supersonic sounds will most likely stun the fish and make them easy prey. None of the other behaviors indicate that the porpoise is doing anything to make the fish easy to catch.

17. Which of the following could disrupt a porpoise's echolocation system?

    A.    Rocks on the seabed

    B.    A sunken ship

    C.    A large, rapidly moving school of fish

    D.    A nearby powerboat

17. (D) A powerboat will make a loud underwater noise that could disrupt echolocation. None of the items in the other choices produce underwater noise.

18. Which of the following could NOT be detected by a porpoise's echolocation system?

    F.    A dangerous reef

    G.    A shark or other dangerous predator

    H.    Toxic chemicals in the water

    J.    A sailboat

18. (H) Echolocation enables the porpoise to determine the location and shape of solid objects in the water. It would not help detect toxic chemicals.

19. The man-made device that most resembles a porpoise's echolocation system is:

    A.    an automatic pilot.

    B.    sonar.

    C.    a computer.

    D.    an astrolabe.

19. (B) Sonar, a device that emits vibrations and detects their echoes under water, allows submarines to determine the location and shape of nearby objects in the sea.

**DIRECTIONS:** Questions 20–34 are not based on a reading passage. You are to answer these questions on the basis of your previous schoolwork in the natural sciences.

20. A biologist viewing a cell under a microscope could tell that the cell was from a plant rather than an animal if the cell had:

    F.    a cell membrane and a nucleus.

    G.    a cell wall and chloroplasts.

    H.    a contractile vacuole and mitochondria.

    J.    a cell membrane and cilia.

20. (G) Only plant cells have a cell wall and choloroplasts.

21. All water has mass and:

    A.    color.

    B.    occupies space.

    C.    is soluble.

    D.    is solid.

21. (B) This is the definition of matter.

22. The tissues of the human body that cause the legs to move are made up of:

    F.  muscle.
    G.  nerves.
    H.  cartilage.
    J.  skin.

23. The smallest particle of gold that still retains its characteristics is:

    A.  a molecule of gold.
    B.  a proton.
    C.  an electron.
    D.  an atom of gold.

24. "Opposites attract" is the fundamental law of:

    F.  momentum.
    G.  forces.
    H.  magnetism.
    J.  gravitation.

25. The motion of the earth as it turns from west to east on its axis is called:

    A.  revolution.
    B.  rotation.
    C.  tilting.
    D.  falling.

26. The nutrients that supply an animal with its main source of energy are:

    F.  proteins.
    G.  carbohydrates.
    H.  lipids.
    J.  nucleic acids.

27. All atoms contain protons and:

    A.  neutrons.
    B.  electrons.
    C.  compounds.
    D.  filled outer shells.

28. In a simple series circuit, if the voltage is doubled and the resistance remains the same, then the:

    F.  current halves.
    G.  power halves.
    H.  current remains the same.
    J.  current doubles.

29. During a solar eclipse:

    A.  the earth prevents the light of the sun from reaching the moon.
    B.  the shadow of the moon falls on the sun.
    C.  the moon prevents the light of the sun from reaching the earth.
    D.  the sun prevents reflected moonlight from reaching the earth.

22. (F) Muscles make the leg move.

23. (D) An atom is the smallest part of an element that retains the properties of that element.

24. (H) The like poles of different magnets repel each other and the unlike poles attract each other.

25. (B) The earth spins or rotates on its axis from west to east, but it revolves in orbit around the sun.

26. (G) Carbohydrates are the main source of energy for animals.

27. (B) All atoms have protons, electrons, and neutrons except for hydrogen, which has no neutrons.

28. (J) Ohm's Law: $E = I \times R$; if $E$ doubles, then $I$ must double ($R$ is constant).

29. (C) The moon is between the sun and the earth during a solar eclipse and so prevents the light of the sun from reaching the earth.

30. In a human being, the organ of the body that carries out most of the digestion process is the:

   F.  mouth.
   G.  stomach.
   H.  liver.
   J.  small intestine.

30. (J) In human beings, most digestion takes place in the small intestine.

31. Brass is:

   A.  an alloy.
   B.  a mixture.
   C.  a mineral.
   D.  an element.

31. (A) Brass is an alloy composed of a combination of copper and zinc.

32. In an electric wire, resistance:

   F.  increases with length and increases with thickness.
   G.  increases with length and decreases with thickness.
   H.  decreases with length and increases with thickness.
   J.  decreases with length and decreases with thickness.

32. (G) The longer and thinner the wire, the harder it is for electrons to travel through it.

33. A piece of paper is torn. This is an example of a:

   A.  chemical change.
   B.  combustion change.
   C.  nuclear change.
   D.  physical change.

33. (D) The paper is changed physically, not chemically.

34. A rocket takes off from earth and heads out into space. The attractive force between earth and the rocket is:

   F.  magnetic.
   G.  electric.
   H.  centripetal.
   J.  gravitational.

34. (J) Gravity is the attraction between any two objects.

Scientists classify volcanoes into five broad categories. These categories are:

1) *Hawaiian*. In this type of volcano, most eruptions consist of vast outpourings of lava from a central crater. The eruptions are rarely violent, although escaping gas often causes spectacular lava "fountains." Only small amounts of ash are produced. The great lava flows produce enormous, gently sloping mountains with a characteristic "shield" shape.

2) *Strombolian*. In this type of volcano, named for Stromboli in Italy, eruptions of moderate strength occur almost continuously. Lava in the crater constantly crusts over, then bursts as pent-up gases send lava fragments high in the air.

3) *Vulcanian*. In this type of volcano, named for Vulcano in Italy, thick lava forms a solid crust over the crater, blocking eruptions for many years. At last, however, gases beneath the crust burst forth in a violent explosion, sending a huge cloud of ash high in the air. Lava flows then issue from the crater to cover the slopes of the mountain.

4) *Pelean*. This type of volcano, named for Mount Pelee in Martinique, has the most violent eruptions of all. The crater is often blocked by a lava plug. An eruption occurs when a cloud of extremely hot gas and ash bursts through the side of the mountain and rushes down the slope, destroying everything in its path. Little lava is produced.

5) *Icelandic*. In this type of volcano, lava issues in vast flows not from a mountain crater but from huge fissures that may extend for many miles. The lava is very fluid and may flow long distances over a flat countryside.

**35.** In 1980 in the state of Washington, Mount St. Helens, a long-dormant volcano, erupted in a huge explosion. A white-hot cloud of gas broke through the side of the mountain and destroyed everything in its path. Mount St. Helens is a:

   **A.** Strombolian volcano.
   **B.** Vulcanian volcano.
   **C.** Hawaiian volcano.
   **D.** Pelean volcano.

**35.** (D) The white-hot cloud of gas that broke through the side of Mount St. Helens and destroyed everything in its path indicates a Pelean type of volcano.

**36.** In 79 A.D. the Roman writer Pliny the Younger watched from across the Bay of Naples as Vesuvius, a long-dormant volcano, erupted with tremendous violence. He later described the eruption cloud as resembling an enormous pine tree, extending high in the air and then gradually spreading out in the formation that looked like tree branches. Vesuvius is a:

   **F.** Strombolian volcano.
   **G.** Vulcanian volcano.
   **H.** Hawaiian volcano.
   **J.** Pelean volcano.

**36.** (G) Since Vesuvius had been long dormant, and since its eruption took the form of an enormous cloud projected upward from the crater, the correct classification is Vulcanian.

**37.** Mount Etna in Sicily has erupted repeatedly for thousands of years. Each time, huge quantities of lava have poured out, and today the mountain rises more than 10,000 feet high. Its long slopes extend outward from the crater almost 15 miles in all directions. Mount Etna is a:

   **A.** Strombolian volcano.
   **B.** Vulcanian volcano.
   **C.** Hawaiian volcano.
   **D.** Pelean volcano.

**37.** (C) Because Etna erupts frequently and emits large quantities of lava that created a large, gently sloping mountain, scientists classify it as a Hawaiian-type volcano.

**38.** In general, volcanoes are classified according to:
   **F.** destructiveness.
   **G.** length of the eruptive activity.
   **H.** type of eruption.
   **J.** composition of released gases.

**38.** (H) The basis for the classification system is the type of eruption.

**39.** The vast lava plateaus that cover thousands of square miles in Idaho, Oregon, and Washington were most likely created by:

   **A.** Strombolian volcanoes.
   **B.** Icelandic volcanoes.
   **C.** Pelean volcanoes.
   **D.** Vulcanian volcanoes.

**39.** (B) The great lava plateaus were created by Icelandic-type volcanoes consisting of huge fissures that released lava to cover a wide, flat plain.

**40.** In volcanoes, violent explosions typically result from:

  **F.** the collapse of the crater floor.
  **G.** the intense heat of the lava.
  **H.** the huge quantities of hot ash.
  **J.** the sudden release of hot gas.

**41.** In some parts of the world, lava flows have built large islands in the sea. These flows most likely came from which type(s) of volcanoes?

  I. Strombolian
  II. Hawaiian
  III. Icelandic

  **A.** I only
  **B.** I and II
  **C.** II only
  **D.** II and III

**42.** If you lived on the slopes of a Hawaiian-type volcano, your greatest danger would be from:

  **F.** clouds of hot gases.
  **G.** massive lava flows.
  **H.** violent explosions.
  **J.** huge falls of hot ash and cinders.

**43.** Scientists studying a Pelean-type volcano announce that an eruption is imminent. The strongest evidence is most likely:

  **A.** a perceptible bulge in one side of the mountain.
  **B.** an increase in ground temperature at the top of the mountain.
  **C.** emissions of ash from the crater.
  **D.** small flows of lava from the crater.

**40.** (J) In every type of volcano, the violence of the explosions is directly related to the sudden release of hot gases.

**41.** (D) The two types of volcanoes that release the most lava, and are thus capable of producing large islands, are the Hawaiian and the Icelandic.

**42.** (G) Hawaiian-type volcanoes produce great flows of lava. They do not produce hot gas clouds, violent explosions, or great falls of cinders and ash.

**43.** (A) In a Pelean-type volcano, eruptions occur when hot gases break through the side of the mountain. Before such an eruption, the side of the mountain might be expected to swell perceptibly.

Whether used to control airplane traffic, detect speeding automobiles, or track a hurricane, radar is a very useful tool. Developed during World War II, this technology allows for remote sensing, that is, locating objects that are not seen directly. The word *radar* is a contraction of "radio detection and ranging." It works in much the same way as an echo. When you shout toward a cliff or a large building, part of the sound bounces back. In radar, waves of electromagnetic radiation are sent out. When they strike an object, they bounce back and are picked up by a receiver. The returning signal indicates the direction of the object; the time it takes for the signal to return indicates the distance to the object. Radar waves detect objects by their varying densities. They are not deflected by atmospheric layers and therefore always travel in a straight line—in all weather, both day and night.

Radar waves are electromagnetic waves, as are light waves, electric waves, X-rays, cosmic rays, and radio waves. All electromagnetic waves travel at 300,000 kilometers per second—the speed of light. Waves differ from each other in the number of times they vibrate per second; this variable is known as frequency and is usually expressed as cycles per second. Waves also differ in their size, or wavelength. The speed, frequency, and wavelength of a wave are related by the wave equation in which:

$$\text{speed} = \text{frequency} \times \text{wavelength}$$

This shows that the product of the frequency and wavelength of any given wave is always a constant—the speed of light. To find the wavelength of a wave knowing the frequency, this formula is used:

$$\text{wavelength} = \text{speed/frequency}$$

For example, if a radio station broadcasts waves at 600,000 cycles per second (cps), wavelength would be calculated this way:

$$\text{wavelength} = 300,000 \text{ km per sec}/600,000 \text{ cps}$$
$$\text{wavelength} = 0.5 \text{ km or } 500 \text{ m}$$

If the frequency of the wave were doubled to 1,200,000 cycles per second, its wavelength would be cut in half to 250 meters. Since frequencies are so high, the unit *megahertz* is usually used; 1 megahertz = 1,000,000 cycles per second.

Wavelength within the electromagnetic spectrum varies greatly. Radar has wavelengths that measure from approximately one centimeter (0.01 m) up to one meter. Each kind of wave has a range of wavelengths. The table compares some sample wavelengths of several kinds of electromagnetic waves.

| Type of Wave | Sample Wavelength in Meters |
|---|---|
| cosmic rays | 0.0000000000000001 |
| X-rays | 0.0000000001 |
| ultraviolet rays | 0.00000001 |
| visible light | 0.000001 |
| infrared heat | 0.0001 |
| microwaves | 0.001 |
| radar | 0.1 |
| television | 1.0 |
| radio | 100 |
| long radio waves | 10,000 |
| electric power | 1,000,000 |

**44.** Radio waves and radar waves have the same:

F. frequency.
G. wavelength.
H. cycles per second.
J. speed.

**44.** (J) All electromagnetic waves, including radio waves and radar waves, travel at 300,000 kilometers per second, the speed of light. They differ according to their frequency and wavelength.

**45.** A radar signal having a frequency of 3,000 megahertz would have a wavelength of:

A. 0.001 km.
B. 0.01 km.
C. 10 m.
D. 0.1 m.

**45.** (A) Wavelength $= \dfrac{\text{speed}}{\text{frequency}}$

3,000 megahertz = 3,000,000,000 cps

Wavelength $= \dfrac{300,000 \text{ kps}}{3,000,000,000 \text{ cps}}$

Wavelength $= 0.001$ km or 1 m

All other choices are incorrect.

**46.** A radar set could not locate an airplane if it were flying:

F. faster than the speed of sound.
G. above a heavy storm.
H. above the atmosphere.
J. below the horizon.

**46.** (J) Radar waves travel in a straight line; therefore, they could not reach an airplane below the horizon. Radar can track an airplane traveling at supersonic speeds or in any atmospheric condition.

47.  It is possible to find the distance to an object from a radar set because the:

A.  wavelength of radar is known.
B.  frequency of radar is known.
C.  speed of radar is 300,000 kilometers per second.
D.  set operates at over 10 megahertz.

47.  (C) The speed of radar is constant. The time it takes for a signal to return indicates how far away an object is.

48.  The relationship between the frequency and wavelength of a wave is:

F.  constant.
G.  directly proportional.
H.  exponential.
J.  inverse.

48.  (J) As the frequency of a wave increases, its wavelength decreases. This is an inverse relationship between the variables.

49.  An antenna picks a signal that has a wavelength of about one meter. It is likely to be:

A.  in the visible spectrum.
B.  an ultraviolet ray.
C.  a television signal.
D.  an X-ray.

49.  (C) According to the table, a television signal has a wavelength of 1 meter. All the other choices have much shorter wavelengths.

50.  Radio waves will not penetrate the ionosphere, but microwaves will. Would you expect X-rays to penetrate the ionosphere?

F.  Yes, because they have a shorter wavelength than microwaves and radio waves.
G.  Yes, because they have a lower frequency than microwaves and radio waves.
H.  No, because they travel more slowly than microwaves.
J.  No, because they have fewer cycles per second than microwaves or radio waves.

50.  (F) If microwaves penetrate the ionosphere while radio waves cannot, it can be inferred that shorter wavelengths can penetrate the atmosphere. Since X-rays have a shorter wavelength than microwaves, they must also penetrate the atmosphere.

51.  Compared to cosmic rays, the frequency of visible light waves is:

A.  higher.
B.  lower.
C.  the same.
D.  impossible to determine from the information given.

51.  (B) According to the table, cosmic rays have much shorter wavelengths than do visible light rays. Therefore, cosmic rays must have higher frequencies according to the wave formula.

52.  Which factor would be most important in order for radar to detect and track storms?

F.  Radar signals travel in straight lines.
G.  The densities of moist air masses are different from those of dry air masses.
H.  Radar signals are not deflected by the atmosphere.
J.  Radar signals travel much faster than storm tracks.

52.  (G) Radar signals must bounce off something that has a density different from its surroundings. The differential densities of air masses allow meteorologists to employ weather radar. Although radar travels in straight lines and in all conditions, and at the speed of light, these factors are not as crucial as density.

# Natural Sciences Reading Warm-up Test 1

Now that you have "walked through" a Natural Sciences Reading Test, it is time for you to do a full-length practice exercise under timing conditions.

Set aside at least an hour during which you won't be interrupted. Use a watch to time yourself. After time has expired, but before you check the answer key and explanations on page 531, finish any questions you did not have time to finish. Then check your work.

# NATURAL SCIENCES READING

*35 Minutes—52 Questions*

**DIRECTIONS:** Each passage in this test is followed by several questions. After reading a passage, choose the best answer to each question. You may refer to the passage as often as necessary.

---

Every few years off the western coasts of North and South America, an unusual warming trend occurs in the waters of the Pacific Ocean. This curious phenomenon, known locally as "El Niño" or "The Child" because it often appears close to Christmas, may last several months or more. During this period the entire Pacific Coast environment is affected. Many ocean plants are killed by the higher-than-normal temperatures; local fish species die or migrate away, to be replaced by others that normally inhabit the tropics. The weather, too, is affected: the prevailing winds often shift direction, and violent Pacific storms move onshore, causing flooding and other damage. Finally, however, the El Niño wanes. Ocean temperatures return to normal, the winds resume their usual course, and the stormy weather ceases.

Scientists now know that El Niños are caused by temporary shifts in the whole pattern of water circulation in the Pacific. Normally, currents run in two huge circles, one clockwise around the edges of the North Pacific, the other counterclockwise around the edges of the South Pacific. In both circles, cold water from the poles is carried toward the equator, down the coast of North America in the North Pacific and up the coast of South America in the South Pacific. At the equator, where the circles meet, the currents in both turn westward, across the ocean toward Asia and Australia. As the water flows along the equator, its temperature rises; by the time it reaches Asia it is considerably warmer than when it left the Americas. Sometimes, however, this great flow reverses direction. Water runs eastward instead of westward, steadily warming as it approaches the Americas. The result is an El Niño. The El Niño ends only when the circulation at last reverts to its normal pattern.

1. When an El Niño is observed off the Americas, the waters off Asia are most likely:

   A. warmer than normal.
   B. cooler than normal.
   C. stagnant.
   D. flowing westward.

2. Warm water heats the air above it, causing it to rise. Colder air then flows in beneath the heated air to take its place. Based on this information, you would expect that in normal times, the air over the equatorial Pacific flows:

   F. from east to west.
   G. from west to east.
   H. in circles.
   J. toward the poles.

3. During an El Niño, the air over the equatorial Pacific most likely flows:

   A. from east to west.
   B. from west to east.
   C. in circles.
   D. toward the poles.

4. Coastal fog often forms where ocean-cooled air touches a warm land mass. During an El Niño, California will most likely have:

   F. the same amount of fog as usual.
   G. more fog than usual.
   H. less fog than usual.
   J. colder air temperatures than usual.

5. In normal years, the Pacific coasts of California, Mexico, and South America have a dry climate. From this fact, it can be inferred that:

   A. ocean-warmed air carries little moisture.
   B. ocean-cooled air carries large quantities of moisture.
   C. ocean-cooled air carries little moisture.
   D. subtropical and tropical regions are generally dry.

6. During an El Niño, the weather on the Asian Pacific coast is most likely:

   F. hotter than normal.
   G. wetter than normal.
   H. drier than normal.
   J. stormier than normal.

7. During an El Niño, a major problem on the Pacific coast of North America might be:

   A. drought.
   B. erosion.
   C. earthquakes.
   D. brush fires.

8. After an El Niño ends, the waters of the equatorial Pacific:

   F. resume flowing from east to west.
   G. resume flowing from west to east.
   H. flow north along the west coast of North America.
   J. flow south along the west coast of South America.

9. A scientist suspects that El Niños might result from major volcanic eruptions, which periodically hurl ashes into the upper atmosphere and disrupt global weather. Evidence to support this theory might be found in:

   A. maps showing average annual rainfall on each continent.
   B. ocean charts showing average summer and winter water temperatures.
   C. listings of record high temperatures for Asian cities.
   D. historical records of the dates of recorded El Niños during the past century.

We know that a small permanent magnet, such as a compass needle, will set itself parallel to a magnetic line of force. But an unmagnetized piece of soft iron will do the same thing and will, furthermore, be attracted to the pole of a permanent magnet just as a compass needle is. For example, suppose that a nail is brought near the south pole of a permanent magnet. A north pole is induced in the nail on the end nearer the south pole of a permanent magnet and the nail becomes a temporary magnet. But it loses most of its induced magnetism as soon as it is removed from the field of the permanent magnet.

Nearly all materials have weak magnetic properties that can be detected by a delicate apparatus. But a few materials—iron, cobalt, nickel, and several alloys—show outstandingly large magnetic effects. These ferromagnetic substances, as they are called, are essentially different from the common run of materials. They naturally contain a multitude of tiny magnets called domains which normally point in all different directions, so that their individual magnetic effects cancel out. When the material is placed in a magnetic field, all the domains in it turn about and tend to line up with the field and so with one another. Once the magnetic field is removed, the tiny magnets again become disorganized, and the material no longer acts as a magnet.

Permanent magnets are also made of ferromagnetic materials, but various tricks are employed to keep the tiny elementary magnets in them from getting out of alignment once they have been lined up in a magnetic field. In steel, for example, the elementary magnets can be aligned only with difficulty, but they rarely get out of line with one another after the magnetizing field is removed; a permanent magnet is the result. Even a steel magnet, however, will lose its magnetism if it is heated or severely jarred. In recent years, certain alloys have been used to make extremely powerful magnets.

The earth itself acts like a giant magnet. Many theories have been advanced to explain this behavior. The magnetism of both the sun and earth appears to be connected with the rotation of these bodies. For many reasons it seems unlikely that the earth's core actually contains a large iron magnet. But why aren't the magnetic poles located at the geographic poles? And why do the magnetic poles gradually shift their positions with the passage of years? At present, the north magnetic pole (that is, the place where a compass needle points vertically downward) is located north of Hudson Bay, well over a thousand miles from the north geographic pole. It is moving westward at the rate of a very few miles per year. The south magnetic pole is in the Antarctic, nearly opposite the north magnetic pole.

Because of the earth's magnetic poles, compass needles fail to point to true north. Furthermore, their error, or declination, changes slightly from year to year in any one locality. In Maine the compass points as much as 23° to the west of true north and in the state of Washington as much as 24° to the east of true north. There is one line in the United States (extending irregularly from South Carolina northward through the middle of Lake Superior) where the compass does point to the true north; but east or west of this line the declination varies between 0° and the maximum of 23° or 24°.

**10.** The south pole of a magnet attracts:

    **F.** the north pole of another magnet.
    **G.** the south pole of another magnet.
    **H.** both poles of another magnet.
    **J.** either pole, but not both poles, of another magnet.

**11.** In an ordinary piece of iron the domains are probably arranged:

    **A.** with all poles pointing in the same direction.
    **B.** with poles on either end pointing in the same direction.
    **C.** so that only the poles in the center neutralize each other.
    **D.** in a random order.

**12.** The reason a temporary magnet loses its magnetism is that the domains have:

    **F.** lost their magnetism.
    **G.** lost their alignment.
    **H.** become permanent magnets.
    **J.** become temporary magnets.

**13.** In order to make a light alloy of aluminum that would be magnetic, it might be best to combine it with:

    **A.** helium.
    **B.** silver.
    **C.** gold.
    **D.** nickel.

**14.** If two large magnets were placed together and heated:

    **F.** one magnet would increase in strength and one magnet would decrease.
    **G.** both magnets would increase in strength.
    **H.** both magnets would decrease in strength.
    **J.** both magnets would remain unchanged.

**15.** The causes for the magnetic fields of the earth are probably connected with:

    **A.** materials at the earth's core.
    **B.** materials located at the earth's poles.
    **C.** the orbiting of the moon around the earth.
    **D.** the daily rotation of the earth.

**16.** If someone living in the state of Washington corrects a compass so that it points to true north and then moves to Maine, the compass will:

    **F.** still be correct.
    **G.** point 23° west of true north.
    **H.** point 47° west of true north.
    **J.** be of no value.

**17.** If an explorer were to follow a compass south until it pointed directly down, he would be:

    **A.** at the south geographic pole.
    **B.** at the north geographic pole.
    **C.** 1,000 miles from the south geographic pole.
    **D.** 1,000 miles from the north geographic pole.

**18.** If a compass were corrected today for local use, when would it be necessary to correct it again if it is to be absolutely correct?

    **F.** Next month
    **G.** Next year
    **H.** Next century
    **J.** Never

**DIRECTIONS:** Questions 19–33 are not based on a reading passage. You are to answer these questions on the basis of your previous schoolwork in the natural sciences.

**19.** Of the following organs, which is specifically a part of the excretory system?

    **A.** Heart
    **B.** Salivary glands
    **C.** Kidney
    **D.** Stomach

**20.** Which of the following processes is responsible for clothes drying on the line on a warm summer day?

    **F.** Condensation
    **G.** Sublimation
    **H.** Evaporation
    **J.** Melting

21. When all the colors of the spectrum are fused, the resulting light is:

    A.   red.
    B.   white.
    C.   blue.
    D.   black.

22. In an atom of a given element, the proton is found in the:

    F.   K shell.
    G.   L shell.
    H.   nucleus.
    J.   electron cloud.

23. The process by which rocks are broken down into smaller fragments by the atmosphere and other factors in the environment is called:

    A.   sorting.
    B.   wind erosion.
    C.   glaciation.
    D.   weathering.

24. Which of the following facts is true about the DNA molecule?

    I. It takes the shape of a double helix.
    II. It is associated with chromosomes and reproduction.
    III. It determines the shape and structure of all living things.

    F.   I and II only
    G.   I and III only
    H.   II and III only
    J.   I, II, and III

25. An acid reacts with a base to form water and a salt. This is called:

    A.   neutralization.
    B.   esterification.
    C.   hydrolysis.
    D.   deamination.

26. How does the heat from the sun reach the earth?

    F.   Conduction
    G.   Convection
    H.   Condensation
    J.   Radiation

27. Cirrus, dew point, front, and isotherm are terms commonly associated with the field of:

    A.   meteorology.
    B.   oceanography.
    C.   mineralogy.
    D.   seismology.

28. Iron is essential in the structure of human:

    F.   cartilage.
    G.   muscles.
    H.   red blood cells.
    J.   bones.

29. The number of calories required to change the temperature of 250 grams of water from 22°C to 25°C is:

    A.   83.3.
    B.   250.
    C.   375.
    D.   750.

30. A 100-pound person weighs about:

    F.   100 kilograms.
    G.   45,000 kilograms.
    H.   45 kilograms.
    J.   0.45 kilograms.

31. Which of the following lacks a backbone?

    A.   Jellyfish
    B.   Tiger
    C.   Alligator
    D.   Baby panda

32. When a fuel is burned, it usually results in the production of:

    F.   oxygen.
    G.   hydrogen.
    H.   alcohol.
    J.   water.

33. Which is NOT a form of energy?

    A.   Light
    B.   Radio waves
    C.   Temperature
    D.   Heat

The life of every organism depends upon a steady supply of materials and energy. The materials are necessary to provide for the growth and repair of the organism, to maintain its structure in opposition to the tendency of all things to become randomly arranged and disordered. The living cell is intricately organized. Even its constituents, such as the cell membrane, the mitochondria, and the parts of the nucleus, reflect an orderly arrangement of the protein, lipid, and nucleic acid molecules of which they are composed. Cells, in turn, are organized into tissues, the tissues into organs, and so on. All these levels of organization depend ultimately upon energy to preserve their pattern. The maintenance of these complex, orderly patterns is one of the main features that distinguishes living from nonliving things. With additional energy, additional materials can be organized into these patterns, resulting in growth.

Energy is also necessary for living things to cope with changes in their environment. The activity of nerves and the contraction of muscles permit you to respond to changes in your environment. These activities require energy. Do you think that there is any connection between using energy to preserve the complex organization of matter and using additional energy for growth and interaction with the environment?

Heterotrophic organisms supply their needs for both matter and energy by taking in complex, energy-rich, organic molecules from their environment.

Where do these complex, energy-rich, organic molecules come from? They are manufactured by green plants and protists. These organisms are capable of synthesizing organic molecules from such simple, inorganic materials in the environment as $CO_2$ and $H_2O$. This type of nutrition is referred to as autotrophic. Organisms that are capable of autotrophic nutrition not only supply all their own needs for materials and energy but also, directly or indirectly, the needs of all heterotrophic organisms (including ourselves). The Bible's statement "All flesh is grass" reflects a crucial biological truth: heterotrophic organisms depend for their existence upon autotrophic organisms. We may dine on beefsteak, but the steer dined on grass.

The kind of autotrophic nutrition upon which almost all heterotrophic organisms (including ourselves) depend is photosynthesis of organic compounds from inorganic ones.

34. Heterotrophic organisms meet their requirements by:

F. taking in energy in the form of organic molecules.
G. taking in energy in the form of inorganic material.
H. taking in energy in the form of $CO_2$ and $H_2O$.
J. synthesizing membranes from mitochondria.

35. Green plants are capable of producing:

A. organic molecules from inorganic materials.
B. $H_2O$.
C. inorganic molecules from organic materials.
D. hemoglobin.

36. In paragraph 4, "All flesh is grass" most nearly means:

F. autotrophic organisms are the basis of life.
G. heterotrophic organisms are the basis of life.
H. heterotrophs all must eat grass to survive.
J. autotrophs cannot exist without heterotrophs.

37. From this passage, we may infer that the agent responsible for changing energy-poor inorganic molecules into energy-rich organic molecules is:

A. nucleic acid.
B. photosynthesis.
C. the ribosome.
D. the heterotroph.

38. Which of these is not a type of molecule found in a living cell?

F. $CO_2$
G. Mitochondrion
H. Organic
J. $H_2O$

39. Which organisms are autotrophs?

I. Green plants
II. Protists
III. Animals

A. I only
B. II only
C. I and II
D. II and III

40. Which of the following is not an organic compound?

F. Water
G. Lipid
H. Protein
J. Nucleic acid

41. Fungi, such as mushrooms, grow on the ground as plants do, yet they lack chlorophyll and get their nutrition from organic matter in soil. Fungi are:

A. autotrophs like green plants.
B. autotrophs like protists.
C. heterotrophs.
D. neither heterotrophs nor autotrophs.

**42.** What process is least likely to occur in a heterotrophic organism?

    **F.** Coping with the environment
    **G.** Photosynthesis
    **H.** Repair of cells
    **J.** Using new materials for growth

Certain elements are radioactive. That is, they emit various types of radiation from their atomic nuclei. Two common types of radiation are alpha particles and beta particles. An *alpha particle*—which is the equivalent of a helium nucleus—consists of two protons and two neutrons. It is written $^4_2He$ (note that the superscript $^4$ is the mass number of the particle, and the subscript $_2$ is its atomic number). A *beta particle* is an electron traveling at high speed. It is written $^0_{-1}e$. Both types of radiation are emitted at very high speed and can easily penetrate other substances.

When atoms of a substance emit radiation, they are said to undergo *radioactive decay*. When this happens, the result is a different element with a different atomic number and a different mass number. For example, when a radium atom emits an alpha particle, it decays into an atom of radon. This reaction is shown in the following equation:

$$^{226}_{88}Ra \rightarrow {}^4_2He + {}^{222}_{86}Rn$$

Note that the equation is *balanced*. That is, the atomic number of the original atom on the left side of the equation equals the sum of the atomic numbers of the products on the right side of the equation. Similarly, the mass number of the original atom equals the sum of the mass numbers of the products. Every nuclear reaction balances in this same manner.

Some types of nuclear radiation take place very slowly; other types are very rapid. The rate of radiation is measured in half-lives. A *half-life* is the time required for one-half the amount of a given radioactive substance to decay.

**43.** As radium emits alpha particles, the mass of radium will:

    **A.** increase.
    **B.** decrease.
    **C.** stay the same.
    **D.** either increase or decrease depending on conditions.

**44.** In nuclear chemistry notation, two isotopes (forms) of cobalt are written $^{59}_{27}Co$ and $^{60}_{22}Co$. The difference between the two isotopes is:

    **F.** an alpha particle.
    **G.** a beta particle.
    **H.** a proton.
    **J.** a neutron.

**45.** An alpha particle has:

    **A.** no electric charge.
    **B.** a positive electric charge.
    **C.** a negative electric charge.
    **D.** a variable electric charge.

**46.** A beta particle has:

    **F.** no electric charge.
    **G.** a positive electric charge.
    **H.** a negative electric charge.
    **J.** a variable electric charge.

**47.** When an atom emits a beta particle, the mass of the atom will:

    **A.** increase.
    **B.** decrease.
    **C.** stay the same.
    **D.** either increase or decrease depending on conditions.

**48.** In the nuclear equation $^{238}_{92}U \rightarrow {}^4_2He + X$, $X =$:

    **F.** $^{230}_{91}Pa$
    **G.** $^{234}_{90}Th$
    **H.** $^{232}_{93}Np$
    **J.** $^{236}_{94}Pu$

**49.** In the nuclear equation $^{55}_{24}Cr \rightarrow {}^0_{-1}e + X$, $X =$:

    **A.** $^{55}_{26}Fe$
    **B.** $^{50}_{22}Ti$
    **C.** $^{51}_{23}V$
    **D.** $^{55}_{25}Mn$

50. In the nuclear equation $X \rightarrow {}_{-1}^{0}e + {}_{7}^{14}N$, X = ?

    F.  ${}_{9}^{18}F$

    G.  ${}_{8}^{16}O$

    H.  ${}_{5}^{12}B$

    J.  ${}_{6}^{14}C$

51. At the end of three half-lives, the amount of an 8-g sample of ${}_{88}^{228}Ra$ that remains undecayed is:

    A.  1 g.
    B.  2 g.
    C.  3 g.
    D.  4 g.

52. At the end of 12 days, one-quarter of an original sample of a radioactive element remains undecayed. The half-life of the element is:

    F.  24 days.
    G.  48 days.
    H.  3 days.
    J.  6 days.

# Answer Key

| | | | | | | | | | | |
|---|---|---|---|---|---|---|---|---|---|---|
| 1. | B | 9. | D | 17. | C | 25. | A | 33. | C | 41. | C | 49. | D |
| 2. | F | 10. | F | 18. | F | 26. | J | 34. | F | 42. | G | 50. | H |
| 3. | B | 11. | D | 19. | C | 27. | A | 35. | A | 43. | B | 51. | A |
| 4. | H | 12. | G | 20. | H | 28. | H | 36. | F | 44. | J | 52. | J |
| 5. | C | 13. | D | 21. | B | 29. | D | 37. | B | 45. | B | | |
| 6. | H | 14. | H | 22. | H | 30. | H | 38. | G | 46. | H | | |
| 7. | B | 15. | D | 23. | D | 31. | A | 39. | C | 47. | C | | |
| 8. | F | 16. | H | 24. | J | 32. | J | 40. | F | 48. | G | | |

# Explanatory Answers

1. (B) Human beings generally hear frequencies ranging from 20 to 20,000 vibrations per second. Dogs can hear sounds above 20,000; dog whistles are designed to take advantage of this ability. Therefore A is incorrect. Choice C is irrelevant, and choice D is incorrect because a whistle would not vibrate at a low frequency.

2. (G) According to the passage, the three bones of the middle ear transmit vibrations to the liquid within the inner ear. The outer ears (F) gather the sound and the auditory nerves (J) are stimulated by the transmitted vibrations.

3. (D) Vibrations occur at all frequencies, making A incorrect. Vibrations above or below the human range can be detected by other animals or by machines; therefore B is incorrect. C is incorrect because individual ranges vary.

4. (F) A vibration of 4,000 per second is at the high end of the most sensitive range of human hearing, as stated in the second paragraph of the passage.

5. (B) According to the passage, sound arrives first at the ear closer to a sound, enabling the listener to detect the direction of the sound.

6. (J) The auditory nerve does not vibrate itself; therefore, F and G are incorrect. The nerves are stimulated by the vibrations that penetrate the liquid of the inner ear; they do not filter vibrations (H).

7. (D) The lower the frequency of a sound, the deeper it penetrates through the liquid of the inner ear. The bass drum vibrates at a lower frequency than choices A, B, or C. The loudness of the sound does not affect the depth of penetration.

8. (J) According to the passage, more vigorous oscillations are interpreted as louder sounds. Choice F would not be heard; the high pitch of a whistle (G) and the low pitch of a bass drum (H) would not be as loud as a cannon.

9. (D) The auditory nerve does not cause the brain to do any of the choices given. Rather, it is memories of previous experiences that are stored in the brain which enable sounds to be located and interpreted. This makes choices B and C incorrect. Choice A is untrue; the nerve endings in the cochlea are stimulated by vibrations.

10. (J) Since each new volcano forms to the east of the one before it, the next one to appear will likely be east of the easternmost island.

11. (C) As new islands form, the rest move slowly westward and undergo erosion. The westernmost island would be the oldest and most eroded.

12. (J) If the plate stopped moving west and started moving south, the older islands would be carried away to the south while newer islands would begin forming in a line north of the easternmost island.

13. (C) The volcanic activity is a sign that Yellowstone, which is being carried westward by the tectonic plate, is now directly over the "hot spot." Note that it is Yellowstone that is moving, not the "hot spot."

14. (J) Craters of the Moon has moved westward off the "hot spot" and is now dormant.

**16.** (H) A compass in the state of Washington would show north as being 24° east of true north. However, in Maine, a compass points 23° west of true north. If the same compass had been corrected for the Washington location and then brought to Maine, the correction would have an additive effect, causing the needle to point even farther west.

**17.** (C) According to the passage, magnetic north is located about 1,000 miles from the north geographic pole. The south magnetic pole is nearly opposite the north magnetic pole. Therefore, the south geographic pole must be 1,000 miles from the south magnetic pole.

**18.** (F) According to the passage, the north magnetic pole moves a few miles per year. Therefore, to be absolutely correct, a compass should be corrected each month.

**19.** (C) The kidney is the organ in the body in which wastes collect, so therefore it is an excretory organ. The heart is part of the circulatory system and the salivary glands and stomach are part of the digestive system.

**20.** (H) During the process of evaporation, liquid water changes state and becomes a gas. This would occur during drying. In sublimation, a solid becomes a gas. During condensation, a gas becomes a liquid and during melting, a solid becomes a liquid.

**21.** (B) The fusion of all the colors of the spectrum produces white light. Conversely, if white light is separated using a prism, all the colors of the spectrum can be seen.

**22.** (H) The nucleus of an atom contains the protons and neutrons. The shells or electron cloud is where electrons are found.

**23.** (D) Weathering occurs when rocks are broken down into smaller fragments by various factors in the environment including water, wind, and ice.

**24.** (J) All of the choices are true about DNA.

**25.** (A) Acids and bases neutralize each other by forming water and a salt. Esterification is the formation of organic esters; hydrolysis is the splitting of the water molecule, and deamination is the removal of a nitrogen group.

**26.** (J) Radiation is the only choice that requires no atmosphere through which to travel.

**27.** (A) All of these terms are associated with weather forecasting, the science of meteorology.

**28.** (H) Iron is an essential component of hemoglobin, the red pigment in red blood cells.

**29.** (D) It takes one calorie to raise the temperature of one gram of water one degree. Therefore, it takes 750 calories to raise 250 grams of water three degrees (from 22° C to 25° C).

**30.** (H) 1 pound = 454 grams; 100 lbs = 45,400 grams = 45.4 kilograms

**31.** (A) The jellyfish is the only invertebrate choice.

**32.** (J) During the burning of a fuel, the decomposition of the fuel often results in the release of water. For example, methane burns according to this equation: $CH_4 + 2O_2 \rightarrow CO_2 + 2H_2O$.

**33.** (C) Energy is defined as the capacity for doing work. Temperature is an indicator of the intensity of heat, but it is not a form of energy.

**34.** (F) It is clearly stated: "Heterotrophic organisms supply their needs for both matter and energy by taking in complex, energy-rich, organic molecules from their environment."

**35.** (A) The fourth paragraph states that green plants "are capable of synthesizing organic molecules from such simple, inorganic materials in the environment as $CO_2$ and $H_2O$."

**36.** (F) This paragraph states, "Heterotrophic organisms depend for their existence upon autotrophic organisms. We may dine on beefsteak, but the steer dined on grass." Life, as mentioned in this passage, includes autotrophs (green plants and protists) and heterotrophs.

**37.** (B) Choices (A) and (C) are neither mentioned nor implied in this passage. (D) is incorrect because, according to the last paragraph, heterotrophic organisms depend on photosynthesis and therefore cannot be catalysts, or agents, for it. But "autotrophic nutrition . . . is photosynthesis of organic compounds from inorganic ones."

**38.** (G) A mitochondrion is an organelle concerned with the intracellular respirational process; it is not a molecule. In any living cell you will find organic, inorganic, $H_2O$, and $CO_2$ molecules.

**39.** (C) According to the passage, green plant and protists are autotrophs. Animals, including humans, are heterotrophs.

**40.** (F) Water does not contain carbon and is not an organic compound. All the other choices are organic compounds found in the cell.

**41.** (C) Fungi do not make their own food and thereby are heterotrophs.

**42.** (G) Photosynthesis only occurs in autotrophs. The other processes listed all occur in heterotrophic organisms.

**43.** (B) An alpha particle consists of two protons and two neutrons. As the radium emits alpha particles, its atomic number and mass number will decrease; in other words, the radium will lose mass.

**44.** (J) The two isotopes have the same atomic number (i.e., number of protons), but different mass numbers (sums of protons and neutrons). The difference between them is one neutron.

**45.** (B) Since an alpha particle contains two protons but no electrons, it has a positive electric charge.

**46.** (H) Since a beta particle consists of an electron only, it has a negative electric charge.

**47.** (C) When an atom emits a beta particle, it is losing an electron. The atom's mass number (the sum of its protons and neutrons) stays the same, so its mass is unchanged.

**48.** (G) The balanced equation will read:

$$^{238}_{92}U \rightarrow \,^{4}_{2}He + \,^{234}_{90}T$$

Note that the sums of the atomic numbers and mass numbers of the products equal the atomic number and mass number of the original atom.

**49. (D)** The balanced equation will read:

$$_{24}^{55}Cr \rightarrow _{-1}^{0}e + _{25}^{55}Mn$$

Note that the sums of the atomic numbers and mass numbers of the products equal the atomic number and mass number of the original atom.

**50. (H)** The balanced equation will read:

$$_{6}^{14}C \rightarrow _{-1}^{0}e + _{7}^{14}N$$

Note that the atomic number and mass number of the carbon atom equal the sum of the atomic numbers and mass numbers of the two products.

**51. (A)** The half-life of a radioactive atom is the time required for one-half the atoms in a given sample to decay. In this sample, at the end of one half-life, 4 g of the radium will remain undecayed. At the end of two half-lives, 2 g will remain undecayed. At the end of three half-lives, only 1 g will remain undecayed.

**52. (J)** The half-life is the time required for one-half the atoms in a given sample to decay. If after 12 days one-quarter of the sample remains undecayed, the 12 days must represent two half-lives. Therefore, one half-life is six days.

25

# Natural Sciences Reading Warm-Up Test 2

Here is another full-length Natural Sciences Reading Test to be done under timed conditions. Set aside at least an hour during which you won't be interrupted. Use a watch to time yourself. After time has expired, but before you check the answer key and explanations on page 545, finish any questions you did not have time to finish. Then check your work.

# NATURAL SCIENCES READING

---

The ear is indeed a remarkable and sensitive mechanism. At the threshold of audibility, the power requirement is inconceivably tiny. If all people in the United States were listening simultaneously to a whisper (20 decibels), the power received by all of their eardrums together would total only a few millionths of a watt—far less than the flying power generated by a single mosquito.

The ear is remarkable, too, for its ability to distinguish between various pitches and qualities of sounds. In the range of frequencies where the ear is most sensitive (500 to 4,000 vibrations per second), changes in pitch of 0.3 percent can be detected. Thus if a singer trying to reach the octave above middle C (512 vibrations per second) is off key by only 1.5 vibrations per second, the fault can be detected. The normal ear can respond to frequencies ranging from 20 to 20,000 vibrations per second. In this range it is estimated that the ear can distinguish more than half a million separate pure tones: that is 500,000 differences in frequency, loudness or both.

The range varies somewhat from ear to ear and becomes considerably shorter for low-intensity sounds. Above the audible range, air vibrations similar to sound are called supersonic vibrations. Supersonic vibrations apparently can be heard by some animals, notably bats. Bats are guided during flight by supersonic "sounds" which they emit and reflect back to their ears from various surfaces and obstacles.

Because we have two ears instead of one, human beings are able to tell the direction from which sound comes. The sound arrives a split second later at one ear than at the other, and the brain by experience interprets this phase difference in terms of direction.

The ear is divided into three parts: the outer ear, the middle ear, and the inner ear. The outer ear consists of a canal closed at the inner end by the eardrum. The middle ear contains a system of three bone levers: the hammer, the anvil, and the stirrup. These bones transmit the sound vibrations from the eardrum to the membrane-window covering the inner ear. The principal feature of the inner ear is the cochlea, a peculiar spiral bony enclosure that looks like a snail shell. Contained in the cochlea is the vital organ of hearing, the basilar membrane, which is about 0.01 inch wide and, when uncoiled, is scarcely more than an inch in length.

Surrounding the basilar membrane is a liquid. The sound vibrations from the middle ear are transmitted to this liquid and then, apparently, through the liquid a certain distance depending on the frequency. Lower frequencies are transmitted to the farther end of the basilar membrane; higher frequencies penetrate only a short distance through the liquid. Along the basilar membrane are the auditory nerve endings. When a part of the basilar membrane is stimulated by the sound vibrations, the brain records the disturbance as a certain pitch. More vigorous oscillation is interpreted as a louder sound.

1. A dog might be able to hear a whistle that a human cannot hear because:

   A. the human hears sounds of a higher frequency.
   B. the dog hears sounds of a higher frequency.
   C. the human hears sounds of a lower frequency.
   D. the dog hears sounds of a lower frequency.

2. Ordinary sounds cause vibrations to be transmitted by:

   F. the outer ear.
   G. the middle ear.
   H. the auditory nerves.
   J. all of the above.

3. Which of the following statements about hearing is true?

   A. All vibrations occur at frequencies of between 20 and 20,000 vibrations per second.
   B. Vibrations below 20 or above 20,000 per second cannot be detected.
   C. All human beings can hear sounds if the vibrations are within a range of 20 to 20,000 vibrations per second.
   D. The average human being cannot hear sounds below 20 or above 20,000 vibrations per second.

4. If a musical instrument had the ability to make a sound at 4,000 vibrations per second, most people would consider the sound to be:

   F. high-pitched.
   G. medium-pitched.
   H. low-pitched.
   J. inaudible.

5. A sound coming from a person's left would:

   A. hit the right ear first.
   B. hit the left ear first.
   C. hit both ears at the same time.
   D. None of the above.

6. Sounds get from the ear to the brain because the auditory nerve:

   F. can vibrate faster than 20,000 times per second.
   G. vibrates between 20 and 20,000 times per second.
   H. filters out vibrations higher than 20,000 per second and lower than 20 per second.
   J. reacts to vibrations of between 20 and 20,000 per second.

7. Which of the following sounds would penetrate most deeply into the ear?

   A. A loud, high-pitched whistle
   B. The squeak of a fingernail on the blackboard
   C. A normal human voice
   D. A softly struck bass drum

8. Which of the following would cause the most vigorous vibration in the human ear?

   F. A supersonic vibration
   G. A police whistle
   H. A loud bass drum
   J. A shot from a cannon

9. The auditory nerve causes the brain to:

   A. stimulate the cochlea.
   B. correctly locate sounds.
   C. correctly interpret sounds.
   D. None of the above.

A much-debated geologic theory proposes that certain prominent landscape features that are plainly volcanic in origin are the product of so-called "hot spots." These are thought to be plumes of hot lava rising from Earth's mantle through a weak spot or opening in the crust and occasionally breaking forth in volcanic eruptions or other manifestations. A "spot" of this type is thought to remain stationary while the continents and seafloors above it move, carried along by the forces of plate tectonics. The result is generally a line of volcanic peaks extending in the direction of plate movement. As the plate continues moving, new, active volcanoes and other volcanic phenomena appear at one end of the line, where a new area has moved over the "hot spot." Meanwhile, the volcanic peaks elsewhere in the line, which are moving farther and farther away from the "hot spot," tend to become dormant and start to erode through the natural process of weathering.

Many sites have been suggested as the locations of "hot spots." Three in the United States are thought to illustrate the slow westward movement of North America and the Pacific seafloor. They are, respectively, the Hawaiian Island chain stretching westward from Hawaii out to Midway Island, the line of volcanic features stretching west from Yellowstone Park in Wyoming back through Montana and Idaho, and the line of peaks stretching from the White Mountains of New Hampshire east through the hills near Montreal and also including the undersea New England Seamounts east of the coast of Maine. In each of these cases, the tectonic plate is thought to have moved slowly west, while the stationary "hot spot" beneath "squirted out" volcanic peaks one by one to create a line of mountains stretching from west to east.

10. If the "hot spot" theory is correct, the next volcano to appear in the Hawaiian Islands will most likely be located:

    F.  in the center of the chain.
    G.  on the westernmost island.
    H.  west of the westernmost island.
    J.  east of the easternmost island.

11. As you travel along the Hawaiian Island chain from east to west, each island is smaller than the one before. According to the "hot spot" theory, this is most likely because:

    A.  the easternmost islands are the oldest and most eroded.
    B.  the easternmost islands are the youngest and most eroded.
    C.  the westernmost islands are the oldest and most eroded.
    D.  the westernmost islands are the youngest and most active.

12. Suppose that the tectonic plate carrying the Hawaiian Islands stopped moving westward and started heading directly south. In this case, if the "hot spot" theory is correct, the next volcano to appear in the chain will most likely be located:

    F.  west of the westernmost island.
    G.  south of the westernmost island.
    H.  south of the easternmost island.
    J.  north of the easternmost island.

13. Yellowstone Park, at the eastern end of the line of volcanic features stretching west into Idaho, contains numerous geysers, hot springs, and other signs of ongoing volcanic activity. According to "hot spot" theory, that is because:

    A.  a "hot spot" has moved westward under Yellowstone.
    B.  a "hot spot" has moved eastward under Yellowstone.
    C.  Yellowstone has moved westward over a "hot spot."
    D.  Yellowstone has moved eastward over a "hot spot."

14. Craters of the Moon National Monument, a volcanic area in Idaho, is thought to have been created by the "hot spot" now farther east under Yellowstone Park. Craters of the Moon is now most likely:

    F.  potentially still active, since the "hot spot" is moving toward it.
    G.  potentially still active, since it is moving toward the "hot spot."
    H.  dormant, since the "hot spot" is moving away from it.
    J.  dormant, since it is moving away from the "hot spot."

15. In the line of landscape features stretching eastward from the White Mountains through the Montreal hills to the New England Seamounts, the youngest terrain is most likely in:

    A.  the New England Seamounts.
    B.  the ocean floor near the New England Seamounts.
    C.  the Montreal hills.
    D.  the White Mountains.

16. Rock samples from different peaks in the White Mountains show ages that are scattered over 100 million years and do not grow progressively older from east to west. These samples may be evidence that:

    F.  new eruptions can be expected in the White Mountains.
    G.  the "hot spot" in this case moved from east to west.
    H.  the White Mountains may not have been formed by a "hot spot."
    J.  only the Montreal hills and the New England Seamounts are moving from east to west.

17. If the Montreal hills, White Mountains, and New England Seamounts were all formed by a single "hot spot," the next occurrence of volcanic activity will most likely take place:

    A.  west of the White Mountains.
    B.  east of the easternmost seamount.
    C.  west of the westernmost seamount.
    D.  west of the Montreal hills.

18. Based on the "hot spot" theory, the youngest volcanic peaks in the Hawaiian Island chain would be those:

    F.  on the easternmost island.
    G.  on the westernmost island.
    H.  in the center of the chain.
    J.  on Midway Island.

19. After performing strenuous muscular activity for a period of time, a person's muscles become tired. This fatigue is due to the presence of which one of the following chemicals?

   A. oxygen
   B. glucose
   C. lactic acid
   D. amino acids

20.

   In the above compound, methane, four hydrogen atoms are bonded to a carbon atom. The bonds are:

   F. electrovalent.
   G. ionic.
   H. covalent.
   J. nuclear.

21. The atmospheric pressure at the bottom of a mountain is measured at 14.7 pounds per square inch. At the top of the same mountain, the atmospheric pressure is:

   A. less because of a smaller amount of atmosphere pushing down.
   B. less because of the greater amount of atmosphere pushing down.
   C. greater since there is a greater proximity to the clouds.
   D. the same.

22. Objects that range in size from one to five hundred miles in diameter and revolve around the sun are:

   F. moons.
   G. meteors.
   H. satellites.
   J. asteroids.

23. Which of the following is true of photosynthesis and respiration in green plants?

   A. Both photosynthesis and respiration take place during the day and at night.
   B. Photosynthesis takes place only during the day and respiration takes place only at night.
   C. Photosynthesis takes place only during the day and respiration takes place both day and night.
   D. Photosynthesis takes place both day and night and respiration takes place only during the day.

24. The formula for converting Celsius (C) to Fahrenheit (F) temperature is $°C = (°F - 32) \times \frac{5}{9}$. If the Fahrenheit temperature is 212°F, then the Celsius temperature is:

   F. 10°.
   G. 32°.
   H. 100°.
   J. 180°.

25. All the following tend to purify water EXCEPT:

   A. bacteria.
   B. oxidation.
   C. sedimentation.
   D. chlorination.

26. The use of iodine in the body is most closely related to the function of:

   F. the carotid artery.
   G. the thyroid gland.
   H. the cornea.
   J. pancreatic fluid.

27. Sound travels faster when it moves through:

   A. steel.
   B. water.
   C. air.
   D. a vacuum.

28. Planting vegetation, terracing, and strip-cropping are common practices employed in the prevention of:

   F. mechanical weathering.
   G. soil erosion.
   H. irrigation.
   J. delta formation.

29. Which of the following determines the sex of a human?

   A. Egg cell
   B. Sperm cell
   C. Sex-linked traits
   D. Fertilization

30. An atom containing 19 protons, 20 neutrons, and 19 electrons has a mass number of:

   F. 19.
   G. 20.
   H. 39.
   J. 58.

31. The change from the solid state directly to the gaseous state is called:

    A. crystallization.
    B. sublimation.
    C. evaporation.
    D. condensation.

32. Which common electrical device contains an electromagnet?

    F. Telephone
    G. Electric iron
    H. Toaster
    J. Electrical outlet

33. At 30°C, 37 grams of salt will dissolve in 100 grams of water. At 100°C, 39 grams of salt will dissolve in the same amount of water. Which conclusion is correct?

    A. Solubility increases with volume.
    B. Solubility and temperature are inversely proportional.
    C. Solubility and temperature are directly proportional.
    D. None of the above.

The behavior of gases under different conditions can be described by a set of rules called the Gas Laws. The first of these, called Avogadro's Law, states that at a constant temperature and pressure, any gas will have a specific number $N$ of molecules per unit of volume $V$. Avogadro's Law is written:

$$N = kV$$

where $k$ is a proportionality constant expressing the idea that $N$ and $V$ are proportional to each other.

A second gas law, called Boyle's Law, states that the pressure $P$ exerted by a fixed amount of a gas on its container at a constant temperature is inversely proportional to the volume $V$ of that container. In other words, if the same amount of a gas is put into a larger container, it will exert less pressure on the container. If it is put into a smaller container, it will exert more pressure on the container. Boyle's Law is written:

$$PV = k$$

where $k$ is a constant.

A third law, called Charles' Law, states that the temperature $T$ of a fixed amount of gas at constant pressure is directly proportional to the volume $V$ of that gas. In other words, an increase in one will cause an increase in the other, and vice versa. Charles' Law is written:

$$V = cT$$

where $c$ is a proportionality constant. Note that in all calculations using Charles' Law, Celsius temperatures must be converted to the Kelvin scale by the formula $°K = °C + 273$.

34. Boyle's Law can be restated in part by saying that:

    F. as volume increases, pressure increases.
    G. as volume decreases, pressure decreases.
    H. as pressure increases, temperature increases.
    J. as volume increases, pressure decreases.

35. A gas has a volume of 150 mL at a pressure of 600 mmHg. At a pressure of 300 mmHg, this gas will occupy a volume of:

    A. 900 mL.
    B. 300 mL.
    C. 120 mL.
    D. 100 mL.

36. A gas has a volume of 400 mL at a pressure of 300 mmHg. At a volume of 300 mL, this gas will have a pressure of:

    F. 400 mmHg.
    G. 500 mmHg.
    H. 200 mmHg.
    J. 100 mmHg.

37. A gas has a volume of 937 mL at a pressure of 760 mmHg. If the pressure were changed to 740 mmHg, you would expect that:

    A. the volume of the gas would stay the same.
    B. the volume of the gas would decrease.
    C. the volume of the gas would increase.
    D. both the volume and the temperature of the gas would increase.

38. Charles' Law can be restated in part by saying that:

    F. as pressure increases, volume decreases.
    G. as temperature increases, pressure increases.
    H. as volume increases, temperature decreases.
    J. as temperature increases, volume increases.

39. A gas occupies a volume of 100 mL at a temperature of 280°K. If the temperature were changed until a Celsius thermometer read 27°C, you would expect that:

A. the volume of the gas would stay the same.
B. the volume of the gas would increase.
C. the volume of the gas would decrease.
D. both the volume and the pressure of the gas would decrease.

40. A gas has a volume of 200 mL at a temperature of 127°C. If the temperature were changed to 27°C at constant pressure, this gas would have a volume of:

F. 50 mL.
G. 100 mL.
H. 150 mL.
J. 200 mL.

41. A gas has a volume of 70 mL at a temperature of 77°C. If the gas was heated and increased in volume to 100 mL (under constant pressure), its new temperature must be:

A. 100°C.
B. 127°C.
C. 177°C.
D. 227°C.

42. A set amount of a gas has a volume of 100 mL at a pressure of 700 mmHg and a temperature of 20°C. At a new pressure of 600 mmHg and a new temperature of 25°C, the volume of the gas will:

F. stay the same.
G. increase.
H. decrease slightly, then increase.
J. decrease.

43. One cubic millimeter of a gas contains $x$ molecules. The number of molecules in 1 cubic centimeter of the gas (at constant temperature and pressure) is:

A. $x$.
B. $10x$.
C. $100x$.
D. $1000x$.

Most materials either conduct electricity or do not, thereby being classified as either conductors or insulators. However, even in a good conductor such as silver or copper, there is still resistance to the flow of electrons. The concept of resistance is basic to electricity and is expressed by a formula known as Ohm's Law:

$$\text{Resistance} = \frac{\text{Electric potential}}{\text{Current}}$$

$$\text{or: } R = \frac{V}{I}$$

where $R$ is measured in ohms, $V$ in volts, and $I$ in amperes. Also, the amount of resistance in any one material can vary with its temperature; the lower the temperature, the lower the resistance. In 1911 it was found that at low enough temperatures, some materials lose all resistance to the flow of electrons. When a material functions in this way, it is called a superconductor. Using superconductors to conduct electricity has a great benefit: no energy is lost on the heat that is usually produced by the conductor's resistance. However, to get a material such as aluminum to function in this way requires lowering its temperature close to absolute zero.

Research has concentrated on achieving superconductivity without using temperatures as low as absolute zero, since that temperature is difficult and impractical to maintain even in ideal laboratory conditions. A major goal of this research has been to find a material that will act as a superconductor at the rather "warm" temperature of −321°F, the temperature at which readily available and easy-to-use nitrogen becomes a liquid. In this way, liquid nitrogen could be used as a coolant.

After much time spent looking for the right material, a breakthrough occurred using an unlikely substance: ceramic. Ceramics, such as those commonly used in light sockets, are good insulators. But under low temperatures they act as superconductors. Using a ceramic containing copper oxide mixed with barium, all resistance may be lost at −293°F. Although not perfected yet, ceramic superconductors may someday be used in superefficient electrical motors, computer chips, and transmission wires. Also some superconductors generate strong magnetic fields. These superconductors are already being used to power experimental friction-free trains and may someday power the most powerful particle accelerator in the world.

44. A lamp is connected to a circuit that has a current of 0.25 amperes powered by a 4.5 V battery. The resistance in the lamp is:

    F.  0.0555 ohms.
    G.  1.125 ohms.
    H.  1.8 ohms.
    J.  18 ohms.

45. If the number of lamps in that same circuit were increased to two, what would happen to the circuit?

    A.  The current would double and the voltage would stay the same.
    B.  The current would be halved and the voltage would stay the same.
    C.  The current would be halved and the voltage would double.
    D.  The current would stay the same and the voltage would double.

46. Which of the following is an insulator at room temperature?

    F.  Gold
    G.  Silver
    H.  Ceramic
    J.  Copper

47. In general, what happens to the resistivity of a material as the temperature decreases?

    A.  It increases.
    B.  It decreases.
    C.  It stays the same.
    D.  It stays the same until the temperature reaches absolute zero and then it decreases.

48. It is desirable to use superconductors because they do NOT produce:

    F.  electric current.
    G.  colder temperatures.
    H.  heat of resistance.
    J.  magnetic fields.

49. According to the passage, which of the following is the highest temperature?

    A.  the temperature at which aluminum becomes a superconductor
    B.  the temperature at which nitrogen becomes a liquid
    C.  the temperature at which silver becomes a superconductor
    D.  the temperature at which ceramic becomes a superconductor

50. During the course of research, the first copper oxide and barium ceramic superconductors were made to function at −397°F. At this temperature:

    F.  researchers could easily use liquid nitrogen to keep the ceramic cold.
    G.  conditions are at absolute zero.
    H.  researchers must have used something like liquid helium as a coolant.
    J.  all materials would lose their resistance.

51. According to the passage:

    A.  all materials lose their resistance to the flow of electrons at the same temperature.
    B.  all materials can be made to be superconductors if the temperature is low enough.
    C.  even some insulators can be made into super conductors if the temperature is low enough.
    D.  all resistance to electron flow ceases at −293°F.

52. A super collider particle accelerator for atomic research will use the powerful magnets made by superconductors. It will require 250,000 gallons of liquid nitrogen. The nitrogen is for:

    F.  supercooling the particles to be accelerated.
    G.  keeping the magnets cool.
    H.  keeping superconducting cable cool.
    J.  keeping the temperature at absolute zero.

# Answer Key

| | | | | | | |
|---|---|---|---|---|---|---|
| 1. B | 9. D | 17. B | 25. A | 33. C | 41. G | 49. D |
| 2. G | 10. J | 18. F | 26. G | 34. J | 42. D | 50. H |
| 3. D | 11. C | 19. C | 27. A | 35. B | 43. G | 51. C |
| 4. F | 12. J | 20. H | 28. G | 36. F | 44. F | 52. H |
| 5. B | 13. C | 21. A | 29. G | 37. C | 45. B | |
| 6. J | 14. J | 22. J | 30. B | 38. J | 46. H | |
| 7. D | 15. A | 23. C | 31. H | 39. B | 47. B | |
| 8. J | 16. H | 24. J | 32. B | 40. H | 48. H | |

# Explanatory Answers

1. **(B)** Human beings generally hear frequencies ranging from 20 to 20,000 vibrations per second. Dogs can hear sounds above 20,000; dog whistles are designed to take advantage of this ability. Therefore A is incorrect. Choice C is irrelevant, and choice D is incorrect because a whistle would not vibrate at a low frequency.

2. **(G)** According to the passage, the three bones of the middle ear transmit vibrations to the liquid within the inner ear. The outer ears (F) gathers the sound and the auditory nerves (J) are stimulated by the transmitted vibrations.

3. **(D)** Vibrations occur at all frequencies, making A incorrect. Vibrations above or below the human range can be detected by other animals or by machines; therefore B is incorrect. C is incorrect because individual ranges vary.

4. **(F)** A vibration of 4,000 per second is at the high end of the most sensitive range of human hearing, as stated in the second paragraph of the passage.

5. **(B)** According to the passage, sound arrives first at the ear closer to a sound, enabling the listener to detect the direction of the sound.

6. **(J)** The auditory nerve does not vibrate itself; therefore, F and G are incorrect. The nerves are stimulated by the vibrations that penetrate the liquid of the inner ear; they do not filter vibrations (H).

7. **(D)** The lower the frequency of a sound, the deeper it penetrates through the liquid of the inner ear. The bass drum vibrates at a lower frequency than choices A, B, or C. The loudness of the sound does not affect the depth of penetration.

8. **(J)** According to the passage, more vigorous oscillations are interpreted as louder sounds. Choice F would not be heard; the high pitch of a whistle (G) and the low pitch of a bass drum (H) would not be as loud as a cannon.

9. (D) The auditory nerve does not cause the brain to do any of the choices given. Rather, it is memories of previous experiences that are stored in the brain which enable sounds to be located and interpreted. This makes choices B and C incorrect. Choice A is untrue; the nerve endings in the cochlea are stimulated by vibrations.

10. (J) Since each new volcano forms to the east of the one before it, the next one to appear will likely be east of the easternmost island.

11. (C) As new islands form, the rest move slowly westward and undergo erosion. The westernmost island would be the oldest and most eroded.

12. (J) If the plate stopped moving west and started moving south, the older islands would be carried away to the south while newer islands would begin forming in a line north of the easternmost island.

13. (C) The volcanic activity is a sign that Yellowstone, which is being carried westward by the tectonic plate, is now directly over the "hot spot." Note that it is Yellowstone that is moving, not the "hot spot."

14. (J) Craters of the Moon has moved westward off the "hot spot" and is now dormant.

15. (A) Since the tectonic plate is moving westward, the easternmost feature in the chain, the New England Seamounts, most likely contains the youngest terrain.

16. (H) Since "hot spot" theory calls for new volcanoes to appear in a sequence dictated by the movement of the tectonic plate, the evidence seems to indicate that the White Mountains were not formed by a "hot spot." Choice J is wrong because the evidence does not disprove the general westward movement of the North America plate.

17. (B) Since the plate is moving west, and the "hot spot" remains stationary, any new volcanic activity would be in the east or east of the easternmost seamount in the New England Seamount chain.

18. (F) Since the islands are moving from east to west, each new peak forms to the east of the one before it.

19. (C) Lactic acid is the chemical that builds up in tired muscles. Oxygen is needed for muscular activity; glucose is a carbohydrate that is used as a source of energy, and amino acids are the building blocks of proteins.

20. (H) The bonds are covalent because the electrons are shared.

21. (A) The farther up the mountain you climb, the less atmosphere is above you. Space has no atmosphere.

22. (J) Asteroids, also known as planetoids, are small, usually irregularly shaped bodies that orbit the sun. Moons are satellites that revolve around the planets.

23. (C) In green plants, photosynthesis takes place only during the day when there is sun, but respiration (burning food to make energy) takes place both day and night.

24. (J) By substituting values, $°C = (212 - 32) \times \frac{5}{9}$
$$°C = 180 \times \tfrac{5}{9} \text{ or } 100°C.$$

25. (A) The more bacteria in the water, the less pure it is. The other choices purify water.

26. (G) Iodine is used in the thyroid gland to make thyroxin, the hormone that is the gland's major product.

27. (A) Steel conducts sound faster than any of the other media.  Sound does not travel at all through a vacuum.

28. (G) The practices named help to prevent soil erosion.

29. (B) The sperm cell contains the X or Y chromosome that determines the sex of a human embryo.

30. (H) The mass number is the total number of neutrons and protons in an atomic nucleus.  Therefore, the 19 protons and 20 neutrons result in a mass number of 39.

31. (B) Sublimation is defined as the complete process of a solid passing directly into a vapor state without melting.

32. (F) The telephone is the only one of the electrical devices given that uses an electromagnet, which produces a force field.

33. (C) As the temperature increases, so does the amount of salt dissolved in the same volume of water.  Therefore, solubility and temperature are directly proportional.

34. (J) Boyle's Law states that the pressure and the volume of a fixed amount of a gas (at constant temperature) are inversely proportional.  In other words, as volume increases, pressure decreases.

35. (B) By the equation for Boyle's Law, $150 \times 600 = 90,000 = k$.  By substituting, we see that $300V = 90,000$, so $V = 300$.

36. (F) By the equation for Boyle's Law, $400 \times 300 = 12,000 = k$.  By substituting, we see that $300P = 12,000$, so $P = 400$.

37. (C) Boyle's Law states that volume and pressure (at constant temperature) are inversely proportional.  Consequently, if the pressure on the gas were decreased, the volume of the gas would increase.

38. (J) Charles' Law states that the volume and temperature of a gas (at constant pressure) are directly proportional.  In other words, as temperature increases, volume increases.

39. (B) $27°C = 300°K$.  Consequently, the temperature has risen by $20°K$.  By Charles' Law, you would expect that the volume of the gas would also increase.

40. (H) $127°C = 400°K$.  By Charles' Law, $200 = 400c$, so $c = \frac{1}{2}$.  $27°C = 300°K$; substituting into the equation for Charles' Law, we find that the new volume $V = \frac{1}{2}(300) = 150$ mL.

41. (D) $77°C = 350°K$.  By Charles' Law, $70 = 350c$, so $c = \frac{1}{5}$.  Substituting the new volume of 100 mL into the equation for Charles' Law, we find that $100 = \frac{1}{5}T$, so $T = 500°K = 227°C$.

42. (G) Since the pressure decreased and the temperature increased, by Boyle's Law and Charles' Law, the volume of the gas will increase.

43. (D) One cubic centimeter equals 1,000 cubic millimeters.  By Avogadro's Law, if there are x molecules of the gas in 1 cubic millimeter, there must be 1,000x molecules of the gas in 1 cubic centimeter.

44. (F) Substituting using Ohm's Law,

$$R = \frac{V}{I}$$
$$R = \frac{4.5 \text{ V}}{.25 \text{ amp.}} = 18 \text{ ohms.}$$

**45.** (B) The voltage supplied by the battery would remain constant. With the increase in the amount of resistance in the circuit, the current would be reduced by half.

**46.** (H) Ceramics are used for insulators as they do not conduct electricity at normal temperature. The other choices do.

**47.** (B) Generally, the resistivity decreases with the temperature until it reaches the temperature at which all resistance stops.

**48.** (H) Because no energy goes into the heat usually produced by resistance, superconductors are very efficient conductors of electrons. They do pass a current and produce magnetic fields (choices [F] and [J]), but they do not make the material colder (G).

**49.** (D) According to the passage, ceramic superconductors may lose resistance at −293°F. Aluminum loses its resistance close to absolute zero (−459°F), making A incorrect; liquid nitrogen forms at −321°F, making B incorrect. It can be inferred that silver must also lose resistivity at a low temperature comparable to other metals.

**50.** (H) Since liquid nitrogen forms at −321°F, it is not so easily used for much colder temperatures such as −397°F. It must be inferred that liquid helium, which forms at an even lower temperature, must have been used. Choices G and J are also incorrect.

**51.** (C) According to the passage, some materials can be made into superconductors, but the temperature at which this happens varies with materials.

**52.** (H) It is important for the cable carrying the superconductor to remain cool, not the particles or the magnet. However, the temperature need not be as cold as absolute zero.

# PART THREE
## The Practice Tests

# Practice Test 1

# ANSWER SHEET. PRACTICE TEST 1

## English Usage

| | | | | | | |
|---|---|---|---|---|---|---|
| 1 Ⓐ Ⓑ Ⓒ Ⓓ | 12 Ⓕ Ⓖ Ⓗ Ⓙ | 23 Ⓐ Ⓑ Ⓒ Ⓓ | 34 Ⓕ Ⓖ Ⓗ Ⓙ | 45 Ⓐ Ⓑ Ⓒ Ⓓ | 56 Ⓕ Ⓖ Ⓗ Ⓙ | 67 Ⓐ Ⓑ Ⓒ Ⓓ |
| 2 Ⓕ Ⓖ Ⓗ Ⓙ | 13 Ⓐ Ⓑ Ⓒ Ⓓ | 24 Ⓕ Ⓖ Ⓗ Ⓙ | 35 Ⓐ Ⓑ Ⓒ Ⓓ | 46 Ⓕ Ⓖ Ⓗ Ⓙ | 57 Ⓐ Ⓑ Ⓒ Ⓓ | 68 Ⓕ Ⓖ Ⓗ Ⓙ |
| 3 Ⓐ Ⓑ Ⓒ Ⓓ | 14 Ⓕ Ⓖ Ⓗ Ⓙ | 25 Ⓐ Ⓑ Ⓒ Ⓓ | 36 Ⓕ Ⓖ Ⓗ Ⓙ | 47 Ⓐ Ⓑ Ⓒ Ⓓ | 58 Ⓕ Ⓖ Ⓗ Ⓙ | 69 Ⓐ Ⓑ Ⓒ Ⓓ |
| 4 Ⓕ Ⓖ Ⓗ Ⓙ | 15 Ⓐ Ⓑ Ⓒ Ⓓ | 26 Ⓕ Ⓖ Ⓗ Ⓙ | 37 Ⓐ Ⓑ Ⓒ Ⓓ | 48 Ⓕ Ⓖ Ⓗ Ⓙ | 59 Ⓐ Ⓑ Ⓒ Ⓓ | 70 Ⓕ Ⓖ Ⓗ Ⓙ |
| 5 Ⓐ Ⓑ Ⓒ Ⓓ | 16 Ⓕ Ⓖ Ⓗ Ⓙ | 27 Ⓐ Ⓑ Ⓒ Ⓓ | 38 Ⓕ Ⓖ Ⓗ Ⓙ | 49 Ⓐ Ⓑ Ⓒ Ⓓ | 60 Ⓕ Ⓖ Ⓗ Ⓙ | 71 Ⓐ Ⓑ Ⓒ Ⓓ |
| 6 Ⓕ Ⓖ Ⓗ Ⓙ | 17 Ⓐ Ⓑ Ⓒ Ⓓ | 28 Ⓕ Ⓖ Ⓗ Ⓙ | 39 Ⓐ Ⓑ Ⓒ Ⓓ | 50 Ⓕ Ⓖ Ⓗ Ⓙ | 61 Ⓐ Ⓑ Ⓒ Ⓓ | 72 Ⓕ Ⓖ Ⓗ Ⓙ |
| 7 Ⓐ Ⓑ Ⓒ Ⓓ | 18 Ⓕ Ⓖ Ⓗ Ⓙ | 29 Ⓐ Ⓑ Ⓒ Ⓓ | 40 Ⓕ Ⓖ Ⓗ Ⓙ | 51 Ⓐ Ⓑ Ⓒ Ⓓ | 62 Ⓕ Ⓖ Ⓗ Ⓙ | 73 Ⓐ Ⓑ Ⓒ Ⓓ |
| 8 Ⓕ Ⓖ Ⓗ Ⓙ | 19 Ⓐ Ⓑ Ⓒ Ⓓ | 30 Ⓕ Ⓖ Ⓗ Ⓙ | 41 Ⓐ Ⓑ Ⓒ Ⓓ | 52 Ⓕ Ⓖ Ⓗ Ⓙ | 63 Ⓐ Ⓑ Ⓒ Ⓓ | 74 Ⓕ Ⓖ Ⓗ Ⓙ |
| 9 Ⓐ Ⓑ Ⓒ Ⓓ | 20 Ⓕ Ⓖ Ⓗ Ⓙ | 31 Ⓐ Ⓑ Ⓒ Ⓓ | 42 Ⓕ Ⓖ Ⓗ Ⓙ | 53 Ⓐ Ⓑ Ⓒ Ⓓ | 64 Ⓕ Ⓖ Ⓗ Ⓙ | 75 Ⓐ Ⓑ Ⓒ Ⓓ |
| 10 Ⓕ Ⓖ Ⓗ Ⓙ | 21 Ⓐ Ⓑ Ⓒ Ⓓ | 32 Ⓕ Ⓖ Ⓗ Ⓙ | 43 Ⓐ Ⓑ Ⓒ Ⓓ | 54 Ⓕ Ⓖ Ⓗ Ⓙ | 65 Ⓐ Ⓑ Ⓒ Ⓓ | |
| 11 Ⓐ Ⓑ Ⓒ Ⓓ | 22 Ⓕ Ⓖ Ⓗ Ⓙ | 33 Ⓐ Ⓑ Ⓒ Ⓓ | 44 Ⓕ Ⓖ Ⓗ Ⓙ | 55 Ⓐ Ⓑ Ⓒ Ⓓ | 66 Ⓕ Ⓖ Ⓗ Ⓙ | |

## Mathematics Usage

| | | | | | | |
|---|---|---|---|---|---|---|
| 1 Ⓐ Ⓑ Ⓒ Ⓓ Ⓔ | 7 Ⓐ Ⓑ Ⓒ Ⓓ Ⓔ | 13 Ⓐ Ⓑ Ⓒ Ⓓ Ⓔ | 19 Ⓐ Ⓑ Ⓒ Ⓓ Ⓔ | 25 Ⓐ Ⓑ Ⓒ Ⓓ Ⓔ | 31 Ⓐ Ⓑ Ⓒ Ⓓ Ⓔ | 37 Ⓐ Ⓑ Ⓒ Ⓓ Ⓔ |
| 2 Ⓕ Ⓖ Ⓗ Ⓙ Ⓚ | 8 Ⓕ Ⓖ Ⓗ Ⓙ Ⓚ | 14 Ⓕ Ⓖ Ⓗ Ⓙ Ⓚ | 20 Ⓕ Ⓖ Ⓗ Ⓙ Ⓚ | 26 Ⓕ Ⓖ Ⓗ Ⓙ Ⓚ | 32 Ⓕ Ⓖ Ⓗ Ⓙ Ⓚ | 38 Ⓕ Ⓖ Ⓗ Ⓙ Ⓚ |
| 3 Ⓐ Ⓑ Ⓒ Ⓓ Ⓔ | 9 Ⓐ Ⓑ Ⓒ Ⓓ Ⓔ | 15 Ⓐ Ⓑ Ⓒ Ⓓ Ⓔ | 21 Ⓐ Ⓑ Ⓒ Ⓓ Ⓔ | 27 Ⓐ Ⓑ Ⓒ Ⓓ Ⓔ | 33 Ⓐ Ⓑ Ⓒ Ⓓ Ⓔ | 39 Ⓐ Ⓑ Ⓒ Ⓓ Ⓔ |
| 4 Ⓕ Ⓖ Ⓗ Ⓙ Ⓚ | 10 Ⓕ Ⓖ Ⓗ Ⓙ Ⓚ | 16 Ⓕ Ⓖ Ⓗ Ⓙ Ⓚ | 22 Ⓕ Ⓖ Ⓗ Ⓙ Ⓚ | 28 Ⓕ Ⓖ Ⓗ Ⓙ Ⓚ | 34 Ⓕ Ⓖ Ⓗ Ⓙ Ⓚ | 40 Ⓕ Ⓖ Ⓗ Ⓙ Ⓚ |
| 5 Ⓐ Ⓑ Ⓒ Ⓓ Ⓔ | 11 Ⓐ Ⓑ Ⓒ Ⓓ Ⓔ | 17 Ⓐ Ⓑ Ⓒ Ⓓ Ⓔ | 23 Ⓐ Ⓑ Ⓒ Ⓓ Ⓔ | 29 Ⓐ Ⓑ Ⓒ Ⓓ Ⓔ | 35 Ⓐ Ⓑ Ⓒ Ⓓ Ⓔ | |
| 6 Ⓕ Ⓖ Ⓗ Ⓙ Ⓚ | 12 Ⓕ Ⓖ Ⓗ Ⓙ Ⓚ | 18 Ⓕ Ⓖ Ⓗ Ⓙ Ⓚ | 24 Ⓕ Ⓖ Ⓗ Ⓙ Ⓚ | 30 Ⓕ Ⓖ Ⓗ Ⓙ Ⓚ | 36 Ⓕ Ⓖ Ⓗ Ⓙ Ⓚ | |

## Social Studies Reading

| | | | | | | | |
|---|---|---|---|---|---|---|---|
| 1 Ⓐ Ⓑ Ⓒ Ⓓ | 8 Ⓕ Ⓖ Ⓗ Ⓙ | 15 Ⓐ Ⓑ Ⓒ Ⓓ | 22 Ⓕ Ⓖ Ⓗ Ⓙ | 29 Ⓐ Ⓑ Ⓒ Ⓓ | 36 Ⓕ Ⓖ Ⓗ Ⓙ | 43 Ⓐ Ⓑ Ⓒ Ⓓ | 50 Ⓕ Ⓖ Ⓗ Ⓙ |
| 2 Ⓕ Ⓖ Ⓗ Ⓙ | 9 Ⓐ Ⓑ Ⓒ Ⓓ | 16 Ⓕ Ⓖ Ⓗ Ⓙ | 23 Ⓐ Ⓑ Ⓒ Ⓓ | 30 Ⓕ Ⓖ Ⓗ Ⓙ | 37 Ⓐ Ⓑ Ⓒ Ⓓ | 44 Ⓕ Ⓖ Ⓗ Ⓙ | 51 Ⓐ Ⓑ Ⓒ Ⓓ |
| 3 Ⓐ Ⓑ Ⓒ Ⓓ | 10 Ⓕ Ⓖ Ⓗ Ⓙ | 17 Ⓐ Ⓑ Ⓒ Ⓓ | 24 Ⓕ Ⓖ Ⓗ Ⓙ | 31 Ⓐ Ⓑ Ⓒ Ⓓ | 38 Ⓕ Ⓖ Ⓗ Ⓙ | 45 Ⓐ Ⓑ Ⓒ Ⓓ | 52 Ⓕ Ⓖ Ⓗ Ⓙ |
| 4 Ⓕ Ⓖ Ⓗ Ⓙ | 11 Ⓐ Ⓑ Ⓒ Ⓓ | 18 Ⓕ Ⓖ Ⓗ Ⓙ | 25 Ⓐ Ⓑ Ⓒ Ⓓ | 32 Ⓕ Ⓖ Ⓗ Ⓙ | 39 Ⓐ Ⓑ Ⓒ Ⓓ | 46 Ⓕ Ⓖ Ⓗ Ⓙ | |
| 5 Ⓐ Ⓑ Ⓒ Ⓓ | 12 Ⓕ Ⓖ Ⓗ Ⓙ | 19 Ⓐ Ⓑ Ⓒ Ⓓ | 26 Ⓕ Ⓖ Ⓗ Ⓙ | 33 Ⓐ Ⓑ Ⓒ Ⓓ | 40 Ⓕ Ⓖ Ⓗ Ⓙ | 47 Ⓐ Ⓑ Ⓒ Ⓓ | |
| 6 Ⓕ Ⓖ Ⓗ Ⓙ | 13 Ⓐ Ⓑ Ⓒ Ⓓ | 20 Ⓕ Ⓖ Ⓗ Ⓙ | 27 Ⓐ Ⓑ Ⓒ Ⓓ | 34 Ⓕ Ⓖ Ⓗ Ⓙ | 41 Ⓐ Ⓑ Ⓒ Ⓓ | 48 Ⓕ Ⓖ Ⓗ Ⓙ | |
| 7 Ⓐ Ⓑ Ⓒ Ⓓ | 14 Ⓕ Ⓖ Ⓗ Ⓙ | 21 Ⓐ Ⓑ Ⓒ Ⓓ | 28 Ⓕ Ⓖ Ⓗ Ⓙ | 35 Ⓐ Ⓑ Ⓒ Ⓓ | 42 Ⓕ Ⓖ Ⓗ Ⓙ | 49 Ⓐ Ⓑ Ⓒ Ⓓ | |

## Natural Sciences Reading

| | | | | | | | |
|---|---|---|---|---|---|---|---|
| 1 Ⓐ Ⓑ Ⓒ Ⓓ | 8 Ⓕ Ⓖ Ⓗ Ⓙ | 15 Ⓐ Ⓑ Ⓒ Ⓓ | 22 Ⓕ Ⓖ Ⓗ Ⓙ | 29 Ⓐ Ⓑ Ⓒ Ⓓ | 36 Ⓕ Ⓖ Ⓗ Ⓙ | 43 Ⓐ Ⓑ Ⓒ Ⓓ | 50 Ⓕ Ⓖ Ⓗ Ⓙ |
| 2 Ⓕ Ⓖ Ⓗ Ⓙ | 9 Ⓐ Ⓑ Ⓒ Ⓓ | 16 Ⓕ Ⓖ Ⓗ Ⓙ | 23 Ⓐ Ⓑ Ⓒ Ⓓ | 30 Ⓕ Ⓖ Ⓗ Ⓙ | 37 Ⓐ Ⓑ Ⓒ Ⓓ | 44 Ⓕ Ⓖ Ⓗ Ⓙ | 51 Ⓐ Ⓑ Ⓒ Ⓓ |
| 3 Ⓐ Ⓑ Ⓒ Ⓓ | 10 Ⓕ Ⓖ Ⓗ Ⓙ | 17 Ⓐ Ⓑ Ⓒ Ⓓ | 24 Ⓕ Ⓖ Ⓗ Ⓙ | 31 Ⓐ Ⓑ Ⓒ Ⓓ | 38 Ⓕ Ⓖ Ⓗ Ⓙ | 45 Ⓐ Ⓑ Ⓒ Ⓓ | 52 Ⓕ Ⓖ Ⓗ Ⓙ |
| 4 Ⓕ Ⓖ Ⓗ Ⓙ | 11 Ⓐ Ⓑ Ⓒ Ⓓ | 18 Ⓕ Ⓖ Ⓗ Ⓙ | 25 Ⓐ Ⓑ Ⓒ Ⓓ | 32 Ⓕ Ⓖ Ⓗ Ⓙ | 39 Ⓐ Ⓑ Ⓒ Ⓓ | 46 Ⓕ Ⓖ Ⓗ Ⓙ | |
| 5 Ⓐ Ⓑ Ⓒ Ⓓ | 12 Ⓕ Ⓖ Ⓗ Ⓙ | 19 Ⓐ Ⓑ Ⓒ Ⓓ | 26 Ⓕ Ⓖ Ⓗ Ⓙ | 33 Ⓐ Ⓑ Ⓒ Ⓓ | 40 Ⓕ Ⓖ Ⓗ Ⓙ | 47 Ⓐ Ⓑ Ⓒ Ⓓ | |
| 6 Ⓕ Ⓖ Ⓗ Ⓙ | 13 Ⓐ Ⓑ Ⓒ Ⓓ | 20 Ⓕ Ⓖ Ⓗ Ⓙ | 27 Ⓐ Ⓑ Ⓒ Ⓓ | 34 Ⓕ Ⓖ Ⓗ Ⓙ | 41 Ⓐ Ⓑ Ⓒ Ⓓ | 48 Ⓕ Ⓖ Ⓗ Ⓙ | |
| 7 Ⓐ Ⓑ Ⓒ Ⓓ | 14 Ⓕ Ⓖ Ⓗ Ⓙ | 21 Ⓐ Ⓑ Ⓒ Ⓓ | 28 Ⓕ Ⓖ Ⓗ Ⓙ | 35 Ⓐ Ⓑ Ⓒ Ⓓ | 42 Ⓕ Ⓖ Ⓗ Ⓙ | 49 Ⓐ Ⓑ Ⓒ Ⓓ | |

# TEST 1. ENGLISH USAGE

*40 Minutes—75 Questions*

**DIRECTIONS:** In the reading selections below, certain parts of the sentences have been underlined and numbered. In the right-hand column, you will find different ways of writing each underlined part. Choose the one that best expresses the idea and uses standard written English. If you think the original version is the best, choose "NO CHANGE." The answers to many questions depend upon material that follows the underlined part. So be sure that you have read far enough ahead before you select your answer choice.

## Passage 1

The Puerto Rican community is one of the ethnic groups subsumed under the general rubric "Hispanic," a category which <u>erroneous implies</u> that the Hispanic population in the United States is a single, homogeneous

group, in fact, Hispanic communities include a number

of ethnic subgroups, each <u>with it's</u> own unique character. One such subgroup is the Puerto Rican community.

The island of Puerto Rico was "discovered" and colonized by the Spanish conquistadors. During the colonization process, the original inhabitants, the Taino Indians, eventually disappeared. <u>Although</u> there are some Indian features found among Puerto Ricans today,

for all practical purposes their culture <u>having been</u> completely destroyed. As the Indian population dwindled,

1. A. NO CHANGE
   B. erroneously implies
   C. erroneous, implies
   D. erroneously, implies

2. F. NO CHANGE
   G. group in fact
   H. group. In fact
   J. group, however, in fact

3. A. NO CHANGE
   B. having their
   C. with its
   D. on having its

4. F. NO CHANGE
   G. Since
   H. Because
   J. Furthermore

5. A. NO CHANGE
   B. was
   C. is being
   D. were

GO ON TO THE NEXT PAGE

black slaves were transported from Africa in large num-

bers. The Africans <u>brung</u> with them their own culture,
6

with some remaining in evidence in Puerto Rico today.
7

## Passage 2

The strategy of large-scale modern warfare, which

relies heavily upon the Intercontinental Ballistic Missile,

<u>may well have begun</u> with the epic attack of the Doolittle
8

Raiders against Tokyo in April 1942.

The Americans <u>knowing that</u> the bomb loads of
9

sixteen B-25 bombers could not do enough physical

damage to cause any permanent delay of the war.

But there <u>was</u> high hopes that the appearance of
10

American planes over Japanese home islands

<u>would be such a psychological blow</u> that the enemies
11

might change <u>his</u> strategy of conquest to the benefit
12

of the Allies.

The raid did hasten the end of the war by encourag-

ing the Japanese to engage the Americans at Midway

where they <u>lose</u> disastrously. Then, in a desperate at-
13

tempt <u>of finding</u> a means of reprisal, the Japanese
14

conceived a method to strike directly at the American

6.  F.  NO CHANGE
    G.  have brought
    H.  had brung
    J.  brought

7.  A.  NO CHANGE
    B.  some of which is remaining evident
    C.  some elements of which remain evident
    D.  of which many remain

8.  F.  NO CHANGE
    G.  may well have began
    H.  might have begun well
    J.  may have begun well

9.  A.  NO CHANGE
    B.  having known that
    C.  knew that
    D.  knew about how

10. F.  NO CHANGE
    G.  were
    H.  having been
    J.  are

11. A.  NO CHANGE
    B.  had been such a psychological blow
    C.  would of been such a blow psychologically
    D.  being such a psychological blow

12. F.  NO CHANGE
    G.  its
    H.  their
    J.  OMIT

13. A.  NO CHANGE
    B.  are losing
    C.  lost
    D.  have lost

14. F.  NO CHANGE
    G.  to find
    H.  to finding
    J.  for finding

GO ON TO THE NEXT PAGE

continent, they planned to launch balloons carrying
15

incendiary and anti-personnel bombs.  The balloons

would cross the Pacific on the prevailing winds and drop

the bombs on American cities, forests, and drop them on
16

farmlands.

In November 1944 the first few of more than

9,000 bombs was released.  An estimated 1,000 reached
17

the North American continent.  If the extent of this

remote bombing had been generally known, the shock to

the American people might have been worse than the

potential material damage.  Although historians tend to

make light of this incident, it was a significant develop-

ment in military concepts and it prefigured today's inter-
18

continental ballistic missiles.

### Passage 3

One problem in labor-management relations is the

"us/them" mentality.  Fiscal constraints, continuing prob-
19

lems with the Fair Labor Standards Act, bad faith

negotiations, bad management practices, poor union

leadership, and a continued losing of management pre-
20

rogatives will all combine to produce forces that

having caused a significant increase in disruptive job
21

actions in the near future.  Neither side is blameless,
22

the tragedy of the situation is that the impact of poor

15. A. NO CHANGE
    B. continent.  They planned
    C. continent they planned
    D. continent but planning

16. F. NO CHANGE
    G. then drop them
    H. drop them
    J. OMIT

17. A. NO CHANGE
    B. have been released
    C. were released
    D. had been releasing

18. F. NO CHANGE
    G. todays
    H. todays'
    J. today

19. A. NO CHANGE
    B. mentality—fiscal
    C. mentality fiscal
    D. mentality, furthermore fiscal

20. F. NO CHANGE
    G. with a continued loss
    H. and a continued loss
    J. and continually losing

21. A. NO CHANGE
    B. are causing
    C. will cause
    D. having caused

22. F. NO CHANGE
    G. has no blame,
    H. blameless the
    J. blameless, and the

GO ON TO THE NEXT PAGE

labor–management relations are relative predictable and
23

it can thus be avoidable.
24

Moreover, the economic situation will not improve
25
significantly in the next few years, so the pressure on the

part of union leaders to obtain more benefits, for its
26

members will be frustrated.  As a result of the
27

Patco strike, management has learned that times

being conducive to regaining prerogatives lost during the
28

previous decade.  In many areas, even the slightest

disagreement could precipitate a disruptive job action.

The only solution to this seemingly intractable problem
29

lays in the the area of skilled negotiations and good-faith
30

bargaining.  This requires commitment on the part of

management and labor to live up to the term of existing
31

contracts.

## Passage 4

Galaxies come in a variety of sizes and

shapes: majestic spirals, ruddy disks, elliptical dwarfs
32

and giants, and a menagerie of other, more bizarre

forms.  Most currently popular theories suggesting that
33

conditions prior to birth—mass of the protogalactic

23. A.  NO CHANGE
    B.  is relatively
    C.  are relatively
    D.  being relative

24. F.  NO CHANGE
    G.  is thus avoidably
    H.  it can be avoided thus
    J.  thus avoidable

25. A.  NO CHANGE
    B.  (Begin a new paragraph) Since
    C.  (Do NOT begin a new paragraph) Since
    D.  (Do NOT begin a new paragraph) Moreover

26. F.  NO CHANGE
    G.  benefits, for their
    H.  benefits; for its
    J.  benefits for their

27. A.  NO CHANGE
    B.  had been frustrated
    C.  are frustrating
    D.  have been frustrating

28. F.  NO CHANGE
    G.  are conducive to
    H.  are conducive with
    J.  were conducive to

29. A.  NO CHANGE
    B.  of this seemingly
    C.  to this seeming
    D.  to these seemingly

30. F.  NO CHANGE
    G.  lies in
    H.  laid in
    J.  lay in

31. A.  NO CHANGE
    B.  living up to
    C.  having lived up to
    D.  in order to live up to

32. F.  NO CHANGE
    G.  shapes, majestic
    H.  shapes; majestic
    J.  shapes, with

33. A.  NO CHANGE
    B.  suggest
    C.  suggested
    D.  suggests

GO ON TO THE NEXT PAGE

cloud, its size, its rotation—determines whether or not
<u>34</u>
a galaxy will be large or small, spiral or elliptical.

To a certain extent these theories must be incorrect.
About 10 percent of all galaxies are members of rich
clusters of thousands of galaxies. Galaxies in the crowded
central region of rich clusters <u>are constantly distorted</u> by
<u>35</u>
the gravitational force fields of nearby galaxies. Addi-

tionally, rich clusters of galaxies are <u>pervaded with</u> a
<u>36</u>
tenuous gas with a temperature of up to 100 million
degrees. Galaxies are blasted and scoured by a hot wind
created <u>by its motion</u> through the gas. In crowded
<u>37</u>

conditions such as these, environment <u>becomes</u> a more
<u>38</u>
important determinant of the size and shape of a galaxy
<u>as heredity.</u> In fact, if our galaxy had happened to form
<u>39</u>
well within the core of a cluster such as Virgo, the Sun

would probably never <u>be formed,</u> because the Sun, a
<u>40</u>

second- or third-generation star <u>with its location in</u> the
<u>41</u>
disk of the galaxy, was formed from leftover gas, 5 billion

years or so after the initial period of star formation.

34. F. NO CHANGE
    G. determine whether or not
    H. determines if
    J. determining if

35. A. NO CHANGE
    B. is distorted constantly
    C. is constantly distorted
    D. constantly are distorted

36. F. NO CHANGE
    G. pervasive with
    H. pervaded by
    J. pervasive by

37. A. NO CHANGE
    B. from their motion
    C. by it's motion
    D. by their motion

38. F. NO CHANGE
    G. would become
    H. will become
    J. had become

39. A. NO CHANGE
    B. than heredity
    C. than was heredity
    D. as was heredity

40. F. NO CHANGE
    G. have been formed
    H. be forming
    J. formed

41. A. NO CHANGE
    B. having its location in
    C. located in
    D. being situated in

GO ON TO THE NEXT PAGE

## Passage 5

Public general hospitals <u>originating</u> in the almshouse
<sub>42</sub>

infirmaries established <u>as early than</u> colonial times by
<sub>43</sub>

local governments to care for the <u>poor.  Later</u> in the 18th
<sub>44</sub>

and early 19th centuries, the infirmary separated from

the almshouse and became an independent institution

supported by local tax monies.  At the same time,

private charity hospitals <u>are beginning to develop.</u>  Both
<sub>45</sub>

private and public hospitals mainly provided food and

shelter for the impoverished sick, since there was little

that medicine <u>could do actually curing illness</u>, and the
<sub>46</sub>

middle class was treated at home by private physicians.

Later in the 19th century the private charity

hospitals <u>began trying attracting</u> middle-class patients.
<sub>47</sub>

The depression of 1890 stimulated the growth of
<sub>48</sub>

charitable institutions, and an expanding urban popula-

tion <u>became dependent of</u> assistance.  Because of a
<sub>49</sub>

decline in private contributions, these organizations

<u>which were forced</u> to look to local government for
<sub>50</sub>

financial support.  Since private institutions had also

lost <u>benefactors; one</u> began to charge patients.
<sub>51</sub>

42. **F.** NO CHANGE
    **G.** originated
    **H.** having originated
    **J.** originating

43. **A.** NO CHANGE
    **B.** as early as
    **C.** early like in
    **D.** earlier as in

44. **F.** NO CHANGE
    **G.** poor, meanwhile, later
    **H.** poor, later
    **J.** poor later

45. **A.** NO CHANGE
    **B.** began to develop
    **C.** had began to develop
    **D.** are developing

46. **F.** NO CHANGE
    **G.** can do about the curing of illness
    **H.** could do actually curing illness
    **J.** could actually do to cure illness

47. **A.** NO CHANGE
    **B.** had begun trying attracting
    **C.** began trying to attract
    **D.** began an attempt at the attraction of

48. **F.** NO CHANGE
    **G.** While the
    **H.** Since the
    **J.** Though the

49. **A.** NO CHANGE
    **B.** becomes dependent on
    **C.** became dependent on
    **D.** becoming dependent of

50. **F.** NO CHANGE
    **G.** that was forced
    **H.** having been forced
    **J.** were forced

51. **A.** NO CHANGE
    **B.** benefactors and they
    **C.** benefactors, they
    **D.** benefactors; they

GO ON TO THE NEXT PAGE

Owing to the fact that paying patients became more
52

necessary to the survival of the private hospital, the

public hospitals slowly became the only place for the

poor to get treatment.

### Passage 6

Ultrasonography works much as sonar.  High-
53

frequency sound waves are bounced off surfaces

in order that it create a two-dimensional picture of
54

anatomical structure.  Since it became generally avail-
55

able about 10 years ago, diagnostic ultrasound has gained

increasing exceptence in the American medical commu-
56

nity.  The lower cost and apparent safety have made it
57

one of the most frequently used methods of imaging in

the United States: rivaling conventional radiography in
58

popularity.  And because ultrasonography does not uti-

lize ionizing radiation, diagnostic ultrasound is particu-

larly attracted to obstetricians and gynecologists.  This
59

aspect of ultrasound, however, can also be a disadvantage.

Because X-rays pass through every type of tissue,
60

images show the varying absorption of radiation—more

for bones, less for soft tissue.  But virtually all of the

ultrasonic waves that encounter bone or an air pocket

52. F.  NO CHANGE
G.  As
H.  With that
J.  Being that

53. A.  NO CHANGE
B.  pretty much as
C.  much like
D.  about like

54. F.  NO CHANGE
G.  in order for it to create
H.  and are created into
J.  to create

55. A.  NO CHANGE
B.  Place before *Since*
C.  Place after *ago*
D.  Place after *Since*

56. F.  NO CHANGE
G.  excepting
H.  accepting
J.  acceptance

57. A.  NO CHANGE
B.  Their low
C.  It's low
D.  Its low

58. F.  NO CHANGE
G.  States and rivaling
H.  States; rivaling
J.  States, rivaling

59. A.  NO CHANGE
B.  attractive for
C.  attractive to
D.  attracting to

60. F.  NO CHANGE
G.  (Do NOT begin a new paragraph) Because
H.  (Do NOT begin a new paragraph) Since
J.  (Begin a new paragraph) Furthermore

GO ON TO THE NEXT PAGE

get reflected. Therefore, the adult brain cannot be
61
imaged because ultrasound cannot penetrate the com-

pletely formed skull similarly, the lungs cannot be imaged
62
because the ultrasonic waves are almost totally reflected

by the air passages.

## Passage 7

An earthquake struck Kingston, Jamaica, and the
63
surrounding countryside on January 14, 1907, at

3:40 p.m. The shock and the fires that followed
64
destroyed thousands of houses and took more than a

thousand lives. The quake lasted a mere 40 seconds,
65

and its destructive power was enormous in its magnitude.
66

News of the disaster was slow about reaching the
67

outside world, the quake had cut the cable connecting
68
Jamaica to other islands in the West Indies, and precise

information was forthcoming only when ships reached

Cuba the following day. The news was not reported

in the American press until some 48 hours

after the event that took place. Newpapers in London
69

61. A. NO CHANGE
    B. are reflected
    C. get reflecting
    D. are reflecting

62. F. NO CHANGE
    G. skull—similarly
    H. skull, similarly
    J. skull. Similarly

63. A. NO CHANGE
    B. striking
    C. had stricken
    D. that struck

64. F. NO CHANGE
    G. that followed it
    H. (that followed it)
    J. (following)

65. A. NO CHANGE
    B. seconds, but its
    C. seconds but it's
    D. seconds, and it's

66. F. NO CHANGE
    G. was enormous
    H. is enormous
    J. was enormously

67. A. NO CHANGE
    B. was slow to reaching
    C. was slow to reach
    D. were slow to reach

68. F. NO CHANGE
    G. world; the
    H. world the
    J. world and

69. A. NO CHANGE
    B. event was over
    C. event
    D. incident occurred

GO ON TO THE NEXT PAGE

were similarly handicapped by its reporting.
70

    On January 18, the American press began to publish

details of the loss of lives and to what extent things were
71

damaged.  According to the report, Kingston was in ruins.

The British army's hospital camp destroyed by fire,
72

and many soldiers were dead.  Part of the town's
73

waterfront was under the water, and its defensive batter-

ies sank eight feet.  A visitor to Kingston described

thousands of panic-stricken residents taking to the streets.

Fortunately, there was no tidal wave after the earthquake

and the weather continued good for some time, sparing
74

the thousands who were forced to sleep outdoors

no further misery.
75

70. F. NO CHANGE
    G. by their
    H. in their
    J. OMIT

71. A. NO CHANGE
    B. to what extent things had been damaged
    C. the extent of the damage
    D. the extent that things are damaged

72. F. NO CHANGE
    G. Fire destroys the British Army's hospital camp
    H. The British Army's hospital camp had been destroyed by fire
    J. With fire destroying the British Army's hospital camp

73. A. NO CHANGE
    B. (Begin a new paragraph) Part of the town's
    C. (Begin a new paragraph) Part of the towns'
    D. Part of the towns

74. F. NO CHANGE
    G. continuing
    H. continues
    J. continually

75. A. NO CHANGE
    B. any further
    C. having any more
    D. no other

## END OF TEST

If you complete this test before the time is up, check
back over the questions on this test only.  Do not go back
to the previous test.  Do not proceed to the next test until
you are told to do so.

# TEST 2. MATHEMATICS USAGE

*50 Minutes—40 Questions*

**DIRECTIONS:** Solve each of the following problems. Choose the correct answer.

Solve as many problems as you can. Do not spend too much time on any one problem. You may return to problems so long as you have time left in this section.

Note: The figures that accompany the problems are not necessarily drawn to scale. Figures are assumed to lie in a plane unless a note states otherwise.

---

1. If $\dfrac{1}{x} + \dfrac{1}{x} = 8$, then $x = ?$

   A. $\dfrac{1}{4}$

   B. $\dfrac{1}{2}$

   C. 1

   D. 2

   E. 4

2. If $x = 2$ and $y = -1$, then $3x - 4y = ?$

   F. $-5$

   G. $-1$

   H. 0

   J. 2

   K. 10

3. In a certain school, there are 600 boys and 400 girls. If 20 percent of the boys and 30 percent of the girls are on the honor roll, how many of the students are on the honor roll?

   A. 120

   B. 175

   C. 240

   D. 250

   E. 280

4. If $p, q, r, s,$ and $t$ are whole numbers, the expression $t(r(p + q) + s))$ *must* be an even number when which of the five numbers is even?

   F. $p$

   G. $q$

   H. $r$

   J. $s$

   K. $t$

5. A student conducting a lab experiment finds that the population of flies in a bottle increases by a certain multiple from week to week. If the pattern shown in the table continues, how many flies can the student expect to find in the bottle in week 5?

   RESULTS OF BIOLOGY PROJECT
   CONDUCTED BY STUDENT X

   | Week | 1 | 2 | 3 | 4 | 5 |
   |------|---|---|---|---|---|
   | No. of flies in bottle | 3 | 12 | 48 | 192 | |

   A. 195

   B. 240

   C. 384

   D. 564

   E. 768

6. Three students are each scheduled to give a short speech at an assembly. In how many different orders can the speeches be scheduled?

   F. 12

   G. 9

   H. 6

   J. 4

   K. 3

GO ON TO THE NEXT PAGE

7. If points $P$ and $Q$ lie in the $xy$-plane and have the coordinates shown below, what is the midpoint of $PQ$?

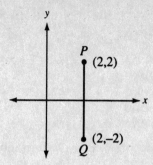

A. $(-2,0)$
B. $(-2,2)$
C. $(0,2)$
D. $(2,0)$
E. $(2,2)$

8. If $xy = |xy|$ and $xy \neq 0$, which of the following CANNOT be true?

F. $x > y > 0$
G. $y > x > 0$
H. $x > 0 > y$
J. $0 > x > y$
K. $0 > y > x$

9. In the scale drawing of the floor of a rectangular room shown below, the scale used was 1 centimeter = 4 meters. What is the actual area, in square meters, of the floor of the room?

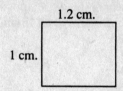

A. 9.6
B. 13.6
C. 15
D. 19.2
E. 38.4

10. If $30,000 \times 20 = 6 \times 10^n$, then $n = ?$

F. 4
G. 5
H. 6
J. 7
K. 8

11. Karen purchased a total of 4 pounds of candy, some of which was chocolates and some of which was caramels. If chocolates cost $3 per pound and caramels cost $2 per pound, and if Karen spent a total of $10.00, how many pounds of chocolates did she buy?

A. 1
B. 2
C. 2.5
D. 3
E. 3.5

12. The average (arithmetic mean) of Al's scores on three tests was 80. If the average of his scores on the first two tests was also 80, what was his score on the third test?

F. 90
G. 85
H. 80
J. 75
K. 72

13. A book contains 10 photographs, some in color and some in black and white. Each of the following could be the ratio of color to black-and-white photographs EXCEPT:

A. 9:1
B. 4:1
C. 5:2
D. 3:2
E. 1:1

14. If $\frac{4}{5} = \frac{x}{4}$, then $x = ?$

F. 5
G. $\frac{16}{5}$
H. $\frac{5}{4}$
J. $\frac{4}{5}$
K. $\frac{5}{16}$

GO ON TO THE NEXT PAGE

**15.** In the figure below, three equilateral triangles have a common vertex. $x + y + z = ?$

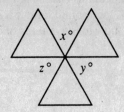

- **A.** 60
- **B.** 90
- **C.** 120
- **D.** 180
- **E.** 240

**16.** Peter spent $\frac{1}{4}$ of his allowance on Monday and $\frac{1}{3}$ of the *remainder* on Tuesday. What part of the allowance does Peter still have?

- **F.** $\frac{1}{12}$
- **G.** $\frac{1}{4}$
- **H.** $\frac{1}{2}$
- **J.** $\frac{3}{4}$
- **K.** $\frac{11}{12}$

**17.** If 100 identical bricks weigh $p$ pounds, then in terms of $p$, 20 of these bricks weigh how many pounds?

- **A.** $\frac{p}{20}$
- **B.** $\frac{p}{5}$
- **C.** $20p$
- **D.** $\frac{5}{p}$
- **E.** $\frac{20}{p}$

**18.** If the distances between points $P$, $Q$, and $R$ are equal, which of the following could be true?

- I. $P$, $Q$, and $R$ are points on a circle with center $O$.
- II. $P$ and $Q$ are points on a circle with center $R$.
- III. $P$, $Q$ and $R$ are vertices of an equilateral triangle.

- **F.** I only
- **G.** I and II only
- **H.** I and III only
- **J.** II and III only
- **K.** I, II, and III

**19.** In the table below, the percent increase in the price of the item was greatest during which of the following periods?

| Year | 1950 | 1955 | 1960 | 1965 | 1970 | 1975 |
|---|---|---|---|---|---|---|
| Price of Item | $2 | $4 | $7 | $12 | $20 | $30 |

- **A.** 1950–1955
- **B.** 1955–1960
- **C.** 1960–1965
- **D.** 1965–1970
- **E.** 1970–1975

**20.** Which of the following is a factorization of $x^2 + 4x - 12$?

- **F.** $(x - 6)(x + 2)$
- **G.** $(x - 4)(x + 3)$
- **H.** $(x - 2)(x + 6)$
- **J.** $(x + 2)(x + 6)$
- **K.** $(x + 3)(x + 4)$

**21.** Two cartons weigh $3x - 2$ and $2x - 3$. If the average weight of the cartons is 10, the heavier carton weighs how much more than the lighter carton?

- **A.** 2
- **B.** 4
- **C.** 5
- **D.** 6
- **E.** 10

**22.** A group of 15 students took a test that was scored from 0 to 100. If exactly 10 students scored 75 or more on the test, what is the *lowest* possible value for the average of the scores of all 15 students?

- **F.** 25
- **G.** 50
- **H.** 70
- **J.** 75
- **K.** 90

**23.** For all real numbers $x$, $16^x$ is equal to which of the following expressions?

- **A.** $x^{16}$
- **B.** $2^{3x}$
- **C.** $4^{2x}$
- **D.** $8^{2x}$
- **E.** $8^{4x}$

GO ON TO THE NEXT PAGE

**24.** If the figure below is a square, what is the perimeter of the figure?

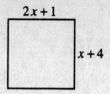

2x + 1

x + 4

F. 28
G. 16
H. 9
J. 3
K. 2

**25.** If a certain rectangle has a length that is twice its width, what is the ratio of the area of the rectangle to an isosceles right triangle with hypotenuse equal to the width of the rectangle?

A. $\frac{1}{8}$

B. $\frac{1}{4}$

C. $\frac{1}{2}$

D. $\frac{4}{1}$

E. $\frac{8}{1}$

**26.** In the coordinate plane, what is the shortest distance between the point with $(x, y)$ coordinates $(1, 3)$ and the line with the equation $x = -2$?

F. 1
G. 3
H. 4
J. 6
K. 9

**27.** If 5 pounds of coffee cost $12, how many pounds of coffee can be purchased for $30?

A. 7.2
B. 10
C. 12.5
D. 15
E. 18

**28.** If the two triangles below are equilateral, what is the ratio of the perimeter of the smaller to that of the larger?

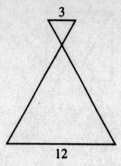

3

12

F. $\frac{1}{36}$

G. $\frac{1}{15}$

H. $\frac{1}{9}$

J. $\frac{1}{4}$

K. $\frac{1}{3}$

**29.** If $f(x) = -3x^3 + 3x^2 - 4x + 8$, then $f(-2) = ?$

A. 16
B. 22
C. 28
D. 36
E. 52

**30.** A merchant pays $120 wholesale for a dress and then adds a 30-percent markup. Two weeks later, the dress is put on sale at 40-percent off the retail price. What is the sale price of the dress?

F. $102.40
G. $97.30
H. $93.60
J. $89.40
K. $87.00

**31.** If $\frac{1}{3}$ of a number is 2 more than $\frac{1}{5}$ of the number, then which of the equations can be used to find the number $x$?

A. $\frac{1}{3}x + 2 = \frac{1}{5}x$

B. $\frac{1}{3}x - 2 = \frac{1}{5}x$

C. $\frac{1}{3}x - \frac{1}{5}x = 2$

D. $\frac{1}{3}x - \frac{1}{5}x = -2$

E. $5\left(\frac{1}{3}x + 2\right) = 0$

GO ON TO THE NEXT PAGE

**32.** In the figure below, if the triangle is equilateral and has a perimeter of 12, then the perimeter of the square = ?

F. 9
G. 12
H. 16
J. 20
K. 24

**33.** If one solution of the equation $12x^2 + kx = 6$ is $\frac{2}{3}$, then $k = ?$

A. 1
B. $\frac{3}{2}$
C. 2
D. 5
E. 9

**34.** If a six-sided polygon has two sides of length $x - 2y$ each and four sides of length $2x + y$ each, what is its perimeter?

F. $6x - 6y$
G. $6x - y$
H. $5x$
J. $6x$
K. $10x$

**35.** At the first stop on her route, a driver unloaded $\frac{2}{5}$ of the packages in her van. After she unloaded another three packages at her next stop, $\frac{1}{2}$ of the original number of packages in the van remained. How many packages were in the van before the first delivery?

A. 10
B. 18
C. 25
D. 30
E. 36

**36.** For all $x$ and $y$, $12x^3 y^2 - 8x^2 y^3 = ?$

F. $4x^2 y^2(2xy)$
G. $4x^2 y^2(3xy)$
H. $4x^2 y^2(3x - 2y)$
J. $2x^2 y^2(4x - y)$
K. $x^3 y^3(12xy - 8xy)$

**37.** $\dfrac{1}{1 + \dfrac{1}{x}}$ is equal to which of the following?

A. $x + 1$
B. $\dfrac{1}{x + 1}$
C. $\dfrac{x}{x + 1}$
D. $\dfrac{x + 1}{x}$
E. $x^2 + x$

**38.** If $S$ is 150% of $T$, then $T$ is what percent of $S + T$?

F. $33\frac{1}{3}\%$
G. 40%
H. 50%
J. 75%
K. 80%

**39.** In $\triangle PQR$, the lengths of $PQ$ and $QR$ are equal, and the measure of $\angle Q$ is 3 times that of $\angle P$. What is the measure of $\angle R$?

A. 24°
B. 30°
C. 36°
D. 45°
E. 60°

**40.** If the cost of $b$ books is $d$ dollars, which of the following equations can be used to find the cost, $C$, in dollars, of $x$ books at the same rate?

F. $C = xd$
G. $C = \dfrac{dx}{b}$
H. $C = \dfrac{bd}{x}$
J. $C = bx$
K. $C = \dfrac{bx}{d}$

## END OF TEST

If you complete this test before the time is up, check back over the questions on this test only. Do not go back to the previous test. Do not proceed to the next test until you are told to do so.

# TEST 3. SOCIAL STUDIES READING

*35 Minutes—52 Questions*

**DIRECTIONS:** Below each of the following reading passages is a series of questions. Choose the *best* answer to each question, interpreting what is stated or implied by the passage in the light of your own background in the subject. You may refer back to the passage as often as necessary, though the answers to some questions may not be found expressly in the passage.

---

Mayors are distinctive as American political executives because they are in close proximity to their constituents (which makes it easier to fight city hall than the state house or the White House); because they have daily involvement in the administrative details of service delivery; and because the public presumes that the mayor is directly responsible and accountable for street-level service problems. Presidents take credit for their foreign-policy accomplishments, and governors may focus on and take credit for their new highways and community colleges. But the people in city hall are the custodians of the sidewalks, who must deal every day with the most ordinary and personal needs of their constituents. It is the mayor's job to make an increasingly ungovernable city work.

The first point to be made is that the mayor works in closer physical proximity to his constituents than Presidents and governors do. For many urban residents, city hall is no farther from their homes than their places of work. Residents can reach city hall or the board of education or the police department by picking up their telephone and making a local call. By contrast, the governor's office and the White House are relatively removed in both physical distance and citizen perception.

More important, the mayor is a highly visible political figure. Many urban residents have seen their mayor and spoken with him. He spends a considerable amount of his time out in public—out in the neighborhoods. Fiorello LaGuardia of New York City created a small legend for himself by reading the Sunday comics on the radio. Local newspapers often give the impression that the mayor does nothing but attend ground-breaking ceremonies, visit schools and hospitals, review parades, and sit on the dais at the community functions. For this reason and because local government is the least mysterious level of government, the mayor is a more ordinary, less aloof political figure than the governor or the President. The ennobling and highly symbolic aura that surrounds the President and the Presidency does not attach to the mayor and the idea of city hall. The President is concerned with the loftiest questions of war and peace and national purpose; the mayor collects the garbage. Thus the man in city hall cannot rely to the same extent on powerful symbols of office to give him a valuable cushion of authority, respect, and deference.

1. The author of the passage compares the mayor to the President in terms of:

   A. visibility.
   B. prestige.
   C. daily responsibilities.
   D. all of the above.

2. The author of the passage conveys the impression that mayors are:

   F. aloof.
   G. accessible.
   H. improvident.
   J. unimportant.

3. The tone in which this passage is written could be best described as:

   A. laudatory.
   B. critical.
   C. lugubrious.
   D. ambivalent.

4. The author depicts the task of running a city as:

   F. futile.
   G. unstrenuous.
   H. obnoxious.
   J. therapeutic.

GO ON TO THE NEXT PAGE

5. According to the passage, mayors spend much of their time:

A. greeting dignitaries.
B. repairing bridges.
C. brandishing power.
D. meeting constituents.

6. The role of the governor is characterized by:

F. high visibility.
G. menial daily tasks.
H. insulation from the public.
J. administrative details.

7. The passage is primarily which of the following?

A. An analysis of the problems facing cities
B. A glorification of governors and presidents
C. A one-sided picture of the duties and role of the mayor
D. A vindication of urban politics

8. According to the passage, the mayor is viewed by his constituents as:

F. awe-inspiring.
G. ordinary.
H. reckless.
J. respectable.

9. The passage depicts local governments in general as:

A. meticulously organized.
B. hierarchical.
C. exclusive.
D. unmysterious.

10. Which of the following would NOT be a good title for this passage?

F. Fundamental Dilemmas in Urban Government
G. You, Too, Can Fight City Hall
H. Ineffective City Management: Diversion of Responsibility to Higher Levels of Government
J. Street-Level Democracy: The Unglamorous Side of Urban Politics

Never had a President tried to achieve so much in the world with so little understanding or support from the people. If a gap had opened between the President and the public, its origin was here; for while he had been growing ever more determined to uphold the nation's image, the public had been growing ever more tired and confused. His solution was to try to take on himself the responsibility for pursuing the strategy. Since the demonstrations of will that were crucial to the policy were not forthcoming from the country, he apparently felt all the more obliged to make it clear to the world that his own will, at least, was firm.

In the closing passages of his speech, President Nixon turned his attention to the domestic scene. At the beginning of the speech, when he said that immediate withdrawal would be the "popular and easy course," he had seemed to acknowledge that the country still wanted to get out of the war quickly. But then he went on to define two groups of Americans — a "minority" who were trying to "impose" their point of view "by mounting demonstrations in the street" in order to end the war immediately, and a "majority" who, presumably, supported the secret plan whose existence he was now revealing. The Constitution, he said, required him to comply with the wishes of those he defined as being in the majority. "For almost two hundred years," he said, "the policy of this nation has been made under our Constitution by those leaders in the Congress and the White House elected by all of the people. If a vocal minority, however fervent its cause, prevails over reason and the will of the majority, this nation has no future as a free society." Having defined the movement against the war as an anti-democratic force that would, if it succeeded, overthrow the Constitution and put an end to freedom in America, he made a final appeal, not to the nation as a whole but the part of it that supported him and that he said was a majority. "So tonight, to you, the great silent majority of my fellow Americans, I ask for your support," he said. In reference to others — the minority — he said, "North Vietnam cannot defeat or humiliate the United States. Only Americans can do that." His assertion marked a significant shift. He had identified a foe within the United States more dangerous to the country than the one it was fighting in Vietnam. As he now saw things, therefore, the war had two fronts — a primary front at home, where the government struggled against a foe who could not only

GO ON TO THE NEXT PAGE

overthrow the Constitution but also "defeat" and "humiliate" the United States, and a secondary front in Vietnam, where the government struggled against a less formidable foe, unable to accomplish any of these dread things. He had already deployed forces on this primary front. His Administration had brought the indictment against the Chicago demonstrators. It had launched its covert attacks on the press. The Vice-President and other members of the Administration were giving the anti-war movement an almost daily lashing. The Nixon Big Charge was on. A year earlier, the war had been widely viewed as an international struggle that had some important domestic consequences. Now, in the eyes of the President, the war was a domestic struggle with some serious international consequences. Thereafter, the Vietnam War would be waged primarily in the United States.

11. In the passage, President Nixon is depicted as using his speech primarily to:

   A. rationalize the United States involvement in the Vietnam War.
   B. humiliate the North Vietnamese.
   C. end United States involvement in the Vietnam War.
   D. extol the virtues of the United States Constitution.

12. According to the passage, which of the following did President Nixon view to be the biggest threat to the United States?

   F. The "great silent majority" of Americans
   G. The North Vietnamese
   H. The United States Constitution
   J. The "vocal minority" of Americans opposed to the Vietnam War

13. President Nixon's perception of public opinion is depicted by the passage as:

   A. accurate.
   B. presumptuous.
   C. influenced by Congress and the Vice-President.
   D. influenced by the "great silent majority" of Americans.

14. The tone in which this passage was written could be best described as:

   F. optimistic about the eventual outcome of the Vietnam War.
   G. indifferent toward the chaos within the United States as a result of the war.
   H. critical toward the actions of President Nixon.
   J. None of the above.

15. The author depicts the anti-war movement in the United States as:

   A. a group that was rapidly losing momentum.
   B. a powerful force that President Nixon viewed as a threat to the nation and therefore his Presidency.
   C. a movement totally in agreement with the "silent majority" of Americans.
   D. supportive of the Constitution of the United States.

16. The passage ends with the sentiment that:

   F. the Vietnam War was a bitter, divisive issue whose force was being felt just as severely at home as it was on the battlefront.
   G. the Vietnam War would be won eventually if the United States continued to fight.
   H. President Nixon's actions were heavily influenced by the Vice President and Congress.
   J. the North Vietnamese, not the anti-war movement, were really the ones who could "defeat and humiliate" the United States.

17. According to the passage, President Nixon's primary reason for wanting to win the Vietnam War was:

   A. to comply with the wishes of the anti-war movement.
   B. to comply with the wishes of the "great silent majority" of Americans.
   C. to uphold the image of the United States internationally.
   D. to acquiesce to world opinion that was heavily against the North Vietnamese.

18. Generally speaking, President Nixon is depicted by the author as:

   F. a President who fervently wanted to uphold the principles of the United States Constitution.
   G. a President who was trying hard to please all of the various and competing interest groups in the United States.
   H. an isolated leader, with no genuine regard for public opinion, who went ahead with his own agenda.
   J. a leader rendered powerless by Congressional restraints.

GO ON TO THE NEXT PAGE

19. President Nixon's actions during the Vietnam War are depicted in the beginning of the passage as:

A. audacious.
B. flippant.
C. benevolent.
D. inconsequential.

20. Given the tone of the entire passage, it is logical to assume that an extension of it would go on to do which of the following?

F. Summarize the most significant accomplishments of President Nixon
G. Describe in detail North Vietnamese efforts to "defeat and humiliate" the United States
H. Discuss related situations where the author viewed President Nixon's actions as improvident
J. Describe how the United States Constitution would be eventually overthrown by the "vocal minority" against the Vietnam War

In discussing the causes of inflation, two basic but opposing theories can be cited.

The *monetarist* theory adheres to the tenet that the rate of inflation is tied directly to the supply of money. The more money there is in circulation, the less valuable it becomes, and therefore prices must rise. An example of this phenomenon is the period following the Spanish exploration of North and South America during the sixteenth century. Gold and silver were brought back to Europe in large quantities, thereby increasing the supply of currency and causing inflation. Given this theory, the monetarists believe that inflation can be kept under control simply by placing constraints on the money supply. This must be done by the government, which should ensure that any increase in the money supply conforms to the rate of increase in economic output.

The *cost-push* theory espouses the belief that inflation is tied to political and social factors that are symptoms of class warfare. An example used to support this theory is the effect of trade unions and strikes on the economy. The unions demand higher wages for the workers, and if higher wages are granted, this cost will be passed along to consumers in the form of higher prices. As a remedy for inflation, advocates of the cost-push theory would resist granting union demands that the economy cannot support.

Although these two theories differ radically, it is difficult to justify categorizing them as belonging to opposite ends of the political spectrum. Many writers try to classify the monetarists as politically conservative because they focus on economic implications and not social ones, yet true conservatives traditionally argue against government regulation of the economy. Those in favor of the cost-push theory, more cognizant of social factors than economic ones, are typically classified as liberals, yet they are clearly in favor of placing constraints on trade unions and other interest groups which are traditionally liberal in orientation. This said, however, it is impossible to refute the fact that there do happen to be many monetarists who would classify themselves as politically conservative; likewise, many cost-push advocates undoubtedly think of themselves as liberals.

Therefore; in this case at any rate, it seems as if the connection between politics and economics is an uncertain one at best.

21. To control inflation, a proponent of the monetarist theory would rely on the actions of the:

A. Congress.
B. Justice Department.
C. State Department.
D. Federal Reserve Board.

22. To control inflation, a proponent of the cost-push theory might rely on:

F. high tariffs.
G. import quotas.
H. wage and price controls.
J. a balanced-budget amendment.

23. To control the growth of the money supply, one effective action the government might take would be to:

A. pass a balanced-budget amendment.
B. raise interest rates on loans to banks.
C. institute price controls.
D. encourage banks to make overseas loans.

GO ON TO THE NEXT PAGE

24. It can be inferred from the passage that if trade unions did not exist:

F. workers' wages would most likely be higher than they are.
G. the prices of most goods would most likely rise.
H. the money supply would increase.
J. workers' wages would most likely be lower than they are.

25. In a time of inflation, non-union workers:

A. will not be affected.
B. will prosper because jobs will be plentiful.
C. may suffer because they have no effective way of winning wage increases.
D. will see their buying power increase.

26. Inflation will cause the value of a nation's currency to:

F. rise as the supply of money grows.
G. stay approximately the same.
H. fall as it takes less money to buy the same amount of goods.
J. fall as it takes more money to buy the same amount of goods.

27. A country that is experiencing severe inflation may also experience:

A. an enormous increase in expensive imports.
B. an enormous increase in the inflow of foreign investments.
C. massive emigration of population.
D. recurrent strikes by unionized workers.

28. One group of people who may benefit from inflation are:

F. debtors.
G. retired people on fixed incomes.
H. lenders.
J. non-union workers.

29. Some economists favor a policy of indexing, or linking regular wage increases to the rate of inflation. This policy would most likely:

A. end inflation permanently.
B. not end inflation, but it would probably mitigate its effects.
C. worsen the plight of working people.
D. drastically increase the inflation rate.

---

**DIRECTIONS:** Questions 30–42 are not based on a reading passage. Choose the *best* answer to each question in accordance with your background and understanding in social studies.

---

30. Social-learning theory differs from strict behaviorism in that it:

F. places more emphasis on interpersonal relationships.
G. focuses on developing social behaviors.
H. asserts that although direct reinforcement is important, people can also learn new behaviors by watching others.
J. suggests that positive consequences are not important in developing new behavior, and may in fact block behavior development.

31. After the collapse of the Western Roman Empire under the pressure of barbarian invasions, the Eastern Roman (Byzantine) Empire continued to flourish for another thousand years. The capital city of this empire was:

A. Damascus.
B. Constantinople.
C. Alexandria.
D. Athens.

32. Monetarists believe that allowing the money supply to grow faster than the output of real goods and services will lead to:

F. inflation.
G. deflation.
H. recession.
J. greater productivity.

33. Today the relationship between the federal and state governments is characterized by:

A. total federal control of state policies.
B. total state independence of federal policies.
C. partial federal control of state policies through the use of guidelines specifying how the states may spend federal money.
D. partial state control of federal policies through selective state enforcement of federal laws.

GO ON TO THE NEXT PAGE $\Rightarrow$

34. In 768 A.D., Charlemagne became king of the Franks. Which of the following is not true about this leader?

F. His kingdom was divided after his death.
G. He encouraged preservation of ancient Greco-Roman literature and art.
H. He sought to diminish the role of the Church because it inhibited learning.
J. He sought guidance from some of the finest scholars of Europe.

35. Which of the following is not considered to be a primary reason for the enormous growth of suburbs after World War II?

A. The only housing available in the cities was prohibitively expensive.
B. Road-building programs made commuting easier.
C. "Baby boom" families wanted more space than was available in city apartments.
D. Federal mortgage policies favored single-family dwellings.

36. Major realignment of political party loyalties in the United States has occurred during:

F. the Civil War and the Great Depression.
G. World War I and World War II.
H. the 1920s and the 1950s.
J. the Mexican War and the Spanish-American War.

37. The economic condition called "stagflation" is characterized by the simultaneous presence of inflation and:

A. an increasing money supply.
B. economic growth.
C. equilibrium between supply and demand.
D. recession.

38. Which of the following was not a motive for undertaking the medieval Crusades to the Holy Land (Palestine)?

F. European Christians wanted to expel the Turkish Muslims from Jerusalem.
G. The Pope hoped that by focusing on an external enemy, European Christian rulers would cease warring among themselves.
H. European Christians hoped to avert a Turkish attack on Rome itself.
J. The Crusades were an opportunity to seek adventure and to gain wealth.

39. Which of the following was not a contributor to the European scientific revolution that began in the 1500s?

A. Copernicus
B. Hippocrates
C. Galileo Galilei
D. Sir Isaac Newton

40. Extensive government controls on wages and prices would most likely be advocated by:

F. classical economists.
G. monetarist economists.
H. supply-side economists.
J. neo-Keynesian economists.

41. The most important function of a political party is to:

A. recruit members who share the same political philosophy.
B. draft a program for enactment by the legislature.
C. capture important public offices through successful election campaigns.
D. maintain unity despite divisive primary campaigns.

42. The immediate cause for U.S. entry into World War I in 1917 was:

F. loss of American lives due to German submarine attacks on shipping.
G. the length of the war in Europe and the toll it was taking on the European countries.
H. the increasing weakness of the Allied forces.
J. a surprise attack on U.S. naval forces in the Pacific.

GO ON TO THE NEXT PAGE

In the twentieth century the notion of "obedience" has come to take on far-reaching and distressing social implications. Consider the psychological study conducted by Stanley Milgram. Subjects representing a wide range of social and economic backgrounds were recruited to participate in an experiment which purported to measure the effects of punishment on learning. The recruited subjects were given the roles of "teachers," who would each be testing the memory of a pre-selected "learner."

The teacher-subject was told by the experimenter that he was to administer electric shocks to the learner as punishment for any incorrect answers given. The subject saw the learner being strapped into the contraption through which the shocks were to be administered; then the subject and the experimenter moved to a different room to begin administering the "test." Communication between the teacher and the learner was conducted through an intercom. The subject was also told that the shocks he administered would increase in intensity for each successive incorrect answer.

Unknown to the teacher-subject, no shocks were actually administered; the "learners" were actually professional actors who were playing their role. The learners' screams increased in intensity with successively stronger "shocks," and the real aim of the experiment was to test the subjects' willingness to administer increasing amounts of punishment that they knew to be painful.

What was found at the conclusion of this study was that almost two-thirds of the subjects willingly administered shocks in increasing intensity, even as they were hearing the screams of their "victims." The significant fact to be noted, however, is not that the subjects were cruel people who enjoyed hurting their victims; many of the subjects expressed repugnance to administering the shocks even as they were doing it. They continued the punishment primarily because they were told by the experimenter that they should do so. Acting as an "agent" for the experimenter effectively nullified the moral implications of what the subjects themselves were doing.

The consequences of this type of behavior go far beyond the laboratory. Parallels can be seen when one examines the deaths of millions of people in concentration camps during the Second World War. When chief executors of this massacre were brought to trial after the war, they based their defense on the notion that they were simply carrying out orders given by their superiors. As has been written by H. Arendt, many of those overseeing the mass executions were "terribly and terrifyingly normal."

43. The experiment by Stanley Milgram was conducted to prove:
   A. that punishment has definite effects on peoples' ability to learn.
   B. that people, when given orders to carry out, frequently do not question the validity or morality of what they are doing.
   C. that people can be unnecessarily punitive when they are in the mood to do so.
   D. that people who participate in psychological experiments are easily fooled.

44. The tone of this passage could be best described as:
   F. prejudiced.
   G. patronizing.
   H. dramatic.
   J. concerned.

45. According to the passage, the tendency to place the blame on someone else for one's own wrongdoings is:
   A. repugnant.
   B. typical.
   C. malevolent.
   D. judicious.

46. Milgram's experiment could be described as a study of human beings':
   F. cognitive processes.
   G. intellectual capacities.
   H. subconscious perceptions.
   J. None of the above.

47. According to the author of the passage, the findings of Milgram's experiment were:
   A. valid.
   B. inconclusive.
   C. fabricated.
   D. unintelligible.

48. The recruitment of people from a "wide range of social and economic backgrounds" was done to ensure:
   F. opportunity for everyone to participate.
   G. a forum that would promote lively interaction while the experiment was being conducted.
   H. representation of an authentic cross-section of society.
   J. that certain types of people were less willing to administer punishment than others.

GO ON TO THE NEXT PAGE

49. In the experiment, the "shocks" were increased in intensity in order to:

   A. punish bad behavior while rewarding good behavior.

   B. administer the test in an efficient and impartial manner.

   C. embarrass the "learner" for any incorrect answers.

   D. provide a gauge to determine the extent to which people will obey an order.

50. The "teacher" and the "learner" were moved to different rooms *primarily* because:

   F. it would have been inhumane for the subjects to watch their "victims" suffer.

   G. a certain degree of anonymity and distance needed to be kept between teacher and learner.

   H. the subject otherwise would have noticed that the "victim" was in fact not receiving any shocks.

   J. the shocking device operated by remote control.

51. Milgram's experiment seems to prove the hypothesis that:

   A. human beings are happy and willing to carry out orders from their superiors.

   B. human beings seldom carry out the orders of their superiors without putting up a fight.

   C. human beings are not as distressed when their harmful actions reflect the motives of others and not themselves.

   D. there is an indubitable correlation between a human being's motives and actions.

52. The passage conveys the message that the behavioral tendencies shown by Milgram's experiment are:

   F. widely diffused throughout the population and insignificant.

   G. universal in nature.

   H. not as distressing as Milgram thought them to be.

   J. exhibited only among certain groups within the population.

**END OF TEST**

If you complete this test before the time is up, check
back over the questions on this test only. Do not go back
to the previous test. Do not proceed to the next test until
you are told to do so.

# TEST 4. NATURAL SCIENCES READING

*35 Minutes—52 Questions*

**DIRECTIONS:** Each passage in this test is followed by several questions. After reading a passage, choose the best answer to each question and blacken the corresponding space on your answer sheet. You may refer to the passage as often as necessary.

---

A laser is a beam of light so intense that it can cut through dense materials or produce searing heat with pinpoint accuracy. The name *laser* is derived from its meaning: **l**ight **a**mplification by **s**timulated **e**mission of **r**adiation. The term that explains why a laser works is *stimulated emission*. Electrons in atoms may exist in a low-energy, unexcited state or in a higher-energy, excited state. If unexcited atoms are given enough energy, some electrons will jump to a higher-energy state, exciting the atoms. The excited state is not a stable one, so the electrons soon drop back to the low-energy state. As they do so, a packet of light, or photon, is released. Usually, the light released is random, not of any particular color or wavelength. However, if the excited atom is exposed to light of a particular wavelength, it will emit a photon of the same wavelength as the one that stimulated it. The new emission amplifies the light wave. If many atoms carry out this same event simultaneously, the resulting beam is made of light of the same wavelength. This light is called coherent light and is extremely powerful.

All lasers have basically the same three components: a medium that will emit photons of light, an energy source or pump that will stimulate the medium to emit light, and a way of controlling the direction of the beam. This is usually done by two facing parallel mirrors that form an optical cavity.

The first laser was a ruby laser. The ends of a pink ruby rod were cut flat, polished, and then coated with mirrors, forming an optical cavity to reflect light. The rod's sides were left clear to let in light from a flash lamp that was wound around the rod. When the light flashed, a powerful beam of red light was produced. Since that time garnets and many artificial crystals have been used in solid-state lasers. Today, some lasers use a liquid or gas for a medium.

Lasers have adapted to fields as diverse as automobile-making and medicine. Carbon dioxide lasers are used to weld pipelines and automobile parts. A laser's advantage is that the heat energy needed for a job is aimed precisely where it is needed without heating up the other parts. Lasers are also used to cut and drill wood, leather, textiles, plastic, rubber, ceramics, quartz, and glass. In medicine, lasers are used in delicate eye surgery and for the removal of kidney stones, the plaque around arteries, scar tissue, and even tattoos.

1. The radiation emitted by a laser is:
   A. thermonuclear.
   B. electromagnetic.
   C. sympathetic.
   D. piezoelectric.

2. A photon of light is released when:
   F. an electron jumps from a low-energy state to a high-energy state.
   G. an electron is exposed to one wavelength of light.
   H. an atom becomes excited.
   J. an electron drops back to a low-energy state.

3. If a laser beam has formed, then excited atoms must have been:
   A. exposed to red light.
   B. exposed to a single wavelength of light.
   C. exposed to all wavelengths of light.
   D. made to jump to a higher energy level.

GO ON TO THE NEXT PAGE

4. The light amplification referred to in the name *laser* means that:

F. many wavelengths combine to make a single strong beam of coherent light.
G. the same beam of light is reflected many times by the mirrors of the optical cavity.
H. many atoms emit photons at the same time.
J. all of these events occur simultaneously.

5. All of the following could be found in a laser EXCEPT:

A. mirrors.
B. carbon dioxide.
C. a flash lamp.
D. an electron gun.

6. Ordinary light that we see all the time is:

F. coherent light.
G. incoherent light.
H. both coherent and incoherent light.
J. neither coherent nor incoherent light.

7. A medium used in the first laser was:

A. a solid.
B. a liquid.
C. a gas.
D. all of the above.

8. In industry, lasers are used to weld metal parts together because:

F. they efficiently conduct heat through the metal.
G. there is always an excess of carbon dioxide to be used as a medium.
H. they heat only the area being welded.
J. metals have an excess of electrons.

9. Which would be the most important factor in using a laser to remove a cataract from an eye?

A. The precision with which the beam can be directed
B. The medium used as a source of photons
C. The amount of heat produced by the beam
D. The size of the optical cavity

The pituitary gland is a gland about the size of an acorn that lies at the base of the brain. It was once thought to be the "master gland" of the body, since its secretions appeared to influence all other endocrine glands. However, it is now known that other glands, especially the thyroid and adrenal glands, influence the pituitary gland.

The pituitary gland consists of two lobes: anterior and posterior. The anterior lobe secretes several hormones, including the somatotropic, or growth, hormone, which regulates the growth of the skeleton. If an oversecretion of this hormone occurs during the growing years, tremendous height may be attained, resulting in giantism. Circus giants over 8 feet tall and weighing over 300 pounds are examples of this disorder. If the oversecretion occurs during adult life, the bones of the face and hands thicken and the soft tissues enlarge tremendously. This condition, known as acromegaly, is characterized by greatly enlarged jawbones, noses, hands and fingers. Somatotropic hormone deficiency results in a pituitary dwarf, or midget. These individuals are perfectly proportioned and, unlike the thyroid dwarf, have normal intelligence.

Another hormone of the anterior lobe of the pituitary gland, the gonadotropic hormone, influences the development of the reproductive organs. It also influences hormone secretion of the ovaries and testes. The gonadotropic hormone and sex hormones cause the sweeping changes that occur during adolescence.

Other secretions of the anterior lobe of the pituitary gland include hormones that stimulate the secretion of milk in the mammary glands (lactogenic hormone) and the activity of the thyroid gland (thyrotropic hormone) and the parathyrotropic glands (parathyrotropic hormone).

ACTH is a secretion of the anterior lobe of the pituitary gland and stimulates the outer part, or cortex, of the adrenal glands. The adrenals, in turn, secrete hormones that are responsible for the control of certain phases of metabolism and water balance in the body.

The adrenal cortex also yields hormones that control the production of some types of white corpuscles. When ACTH is given to leukemia patients, a dramatic, but unfortunately temporary, improvement occurs.

The posterior lobe of the pituitary gland produces two hormones: (1) pitressin, which helps regulate the amount of water in the blood and the blood pressure; and (2) pitocin, which stimulates smooth muscles. It is sometimes administered during childbirth to cause contraction of the muscles of the uterus, thus preventing blood loss.

GO ON TO THE NEXT PAGE

10. A hormone is

    F.  an important gland.
    G.  a type of medicine.
    H.  a chemical secretion.
    J.  a type of germ.

11. Which of the following is not a secretion of the pituitary gland?

    A.  Somatotropic hormone
    B.  Gonadotropic hormone
    C.  Pitocin
    D.  Adrenalin

12. Which of the following will affect the age at which a person reaches puberty?

    F.  Sex hormones
    G.  Gonadotropic hormone
    H.  Lactogenic hormone
    J.  None of the above

13. Cretinism results in a stunted body and low intelligence. It is caused by a defect in which gland?

    A.  Pituitary
    B.  Adrenal
    C.  Thyroid
    D.  Parathyroid

14. The circus giant who is over 8 feet tall probably got too much somatotropic hormone when he was:

    F.  an infant.
    G.  a teenager.
    H.  a young adult.
    J.  an older adult.

15. A cure for leukemia is:

    A.  a pituitary hormone.
    B.  an adrenal hormone.
    C.  a cortexial hormone.
    D.  none of the above.

16. A cow that lacked the normal amount of lactogenic hormone would probably:

    F.  fail to become pregnant.
    G.  become overly fat.
    H.  lose a lot of weight.
    J.  not give any milk.

17. A person admitted to a hospital with swollen limbs due to too much water in the joints may be suffering from:

    A.  improper functioning of the adrenal gland.
    B.  overactivity of the pituitary gland.
    C.  underactivity of the pituitary gland.
    D.  too much pitressin.

18. The hormones of the pituitary gland reach the necessary parts of the body by means of:

    F.  a special duct system.
    G.  the respiratory system.
    H.  the nervous system.
    J.  blood vessels.

**DIRECTIONS:** Questions 19-33 are not based on a reading passage. You are to answer these questions on the basis of your previous schoolwork in the natural sciences.

19. Calcium has an atomic weight of 40. Which of the following arrangements represents the correct number of protons, electrons, and neutrons for this element?

    A.  19, 21, 19
    B.  22, 14, 14
    C.  13, 14, 13
    D.  20, 20, 20

20. Life processes which take place in most animals include all of the following EXCEPT:

    F.  using energy for metabolism.
    G.  elimination of water and waste.
    H.  reproduction.
    J.  giving off oxygen.

21. The Second Law of Thermodynamics is best summarized as follows:

    A.  Energy transformations are not 100% efficient.
    B.  The ultimate energy source in the biosphere is our sun.
    C.  Energy cannot be created or destroyed.
    D.  For each action there exists an equal and opposite reaction.

22. Ursa Major, Orion, and Andromeda are fixed groups of stars called:

    F.  galaxies.
    G.  constellations.
    H.  satellites.
    J.  quasars.

GO ON TO THE NEXT PAGE

23. Polar molecules:

    A.   are cryogenic.
    B.   have different charges at either end.
    C.   are chlorogenic.
    D.   have an excess of electrons.

24. A compound that is quickly absorbed through the walls of the stomach is:

    F.   alcohol.
    G.   sugar.
    H.   fat.
    J.   protein.

25. Sound waves are best described as:

    A.   electromechanical.
    B.   transverse.
    C.   longitudinal.
    D.   polarized.

26. The isotope $^{14}_{6}C$ has:

    F.   6 electrons.
    G.   8 protons.
    H.   20 atoms.
    J.   6 carbons.

27. Cities located along the eastern seaboard consistently record higher temperatures than inland cities in the same states during the winter season. Which of the following statements might explain this situation?

    A.   Eastern cities receive more sun than inland cities.
    B.   The average amount of daylight is greater in the winter than in the summer.
    C.   The angle of the sunlight is greater in inland cities.
    D.   The winter weather along the coast is milder due to the influence of the ocean.

28. A decrease in the number of red blood corpuscles will seriously impair the body's ability to:

    F.   transport oxygen.
    G.   clot blood.
    H.   retain water.
    J.   eliminate waste.

29. If water is electrolyzed, which of the following best describes the products obtained?

    A.   $H^+$ and $OH^-$.
    B.   $H_2$ and $OH$.
    C.   $H_2$ and $O_2$.
    D.   $H_2O_2$ and $H_2$.

30. Suppose a man in a sealed boxcar drops a steel ball as the car moves horizontally at a constant velocity. We can assume that:

    F.   the man will see the ball drop straight down to the floor.
    G.   the man will see the ball move backward in an arc as it falls to the floor.
    H.   the man will see the ball move horizontally briefly.
    J.   none of the above will occur.

31. Grasses are usually pollinated by:

    A.   birds.
    B.   water.
    C.   humans.
    D.   wind.

32. If it requires two joules of work to move 20 coulombs from point $A$ to point $B$, a distance of 0.2 meter, the potential difference between points $A$ and $B$, in volts, is:

    F.   $2 \times 10^{-2}$.
    G.   $4 \times 10^{-2}$.
    H.   $4 \times 10^{-1}$.
    J.   $1 \times 10^{-1}$.

33. When a beam of light is passed through a beaker filled with a clear liquid, the beam can be seen in the solution. This describes a characteristic of what type of system?

    A.   A true solution
    B.   A colloidal system
    C.   A thermally unstable system
    D.   A mixture

      The western part of the state of Washington is the site of an extraordinary landform called the "scablands." In this area, a vast network of wide, deep channels has been carved out of the earth, in many cases right down to the bare bedrock. These channels—some many miles across—trend generally northeast to southwest; between them are high soil hills that stand out like "islands." Within the channels are many areas that look to have been scoured out by tremendous rapids; there are also great escarpments that, from their position, must have been the sites of gigantic waterfalls.

      How these channels were formed—located as they are on an arid plateau—was long a mystery. Today, however, we know that they are the result of a complicated series of events that took

GO ON TO THE NEXT PAGE

place at the end of the last Ice Age. At that time a huge glacier extended south into what is now northern Montana and Idaho. One lobe of that glacier created a huge dam cross the Clark Fork River, blocking drainage from all of western Montana. Behind the dam glacial meltwater formed an enormous lake: Ice Age Lake Missoula, filling 3000 square miles to a depth of 2,000 feet.

Eventually, as melting occurred, the ice dam burst, instantly releasing 500 cubic miles of water. A 1,000-foot-high wall of water raced southwestward across the Washington plateau, sweeping away the soil and gouging out the huge scabland channels. The colossal torrent poured over ridges in its way, creating rapids and tremendous waterfalls. At what is now Coulee City, the water dropped over an 800-foot-high cliff of soft sandstone; the tremendous cataract rapidly eroded the cliff face by undermining it at the bottom, completely changing the landscape but leaving an enormous escarpment to show what had happened.

At last, in south-central Washington, the water reached the narrow canyon of the Columbia River, into which it poured in four mighty waterfalls. The flood then drained westward down the Columbia. Where the river reached the Pacific coast, it began dropping the huge load of sediment swept off the plateau by the flood; soon some 900 square miles were buried under a broad, level delta at the river's mouth.

34. Based on the way they were formed, the "islands" between the scabland channels most likely:

F. are completely round in shape.
G. taper to a point at their southwest ends.
H. taper to a point at their northeast ends.
J. were once covered by water.

35. In the valleys of western Montana, you would expect to find:

A. huge channels cut into the bedrock.
B. an ice dam cross the Clark Fork River.
C. "beach" lines 2,000 feet up the mountain slopes.
D. a broad delta deposited by the Ice Age flood.

36. For the great Ice Age flood to have been possible, the eastern part of Washington State:

F. must be uniformly level.
G. must generally tilt downhill from northeast to southwest.
H. must generally tilt downhill from southwest to northeast.
J. must be generally higher than western Montana.

37. The flood sediment began settling out of the Columbia River near the river's mouth most likely because at that point:

A. the river speeds up as it nears the ocean.
B. the river slows down as it crosses level country near the coast.
C. the river narrows at the western end of its canyon.
D. the sediment load was heavier than it had been upstream.

38. As the great Coulee City waterfall eroded, it most likely:

F. increased in height.
G. grew steeper and steeper.
H. "advanced" downstream.
J. "retreated" upstream.

39. An earth scientist could prove that the four waterfalls into the Columbia canyon were all formed at the same time by showing that:

A. they were all the same width.
B. they all carried the same amount of water.
C. they were all created by the overflow of water from the same height.
D. they were all located on the north rim of the canyon.

40. The amount of sediment deposited by the floodwater on the Washington plateau would have been:

F. very small, because the water was traveling so fast.
G. very large, because the water was traveling so fast.
H. about the same as the amount deposited at the mouth of the Columbia River.
J. much greater than the amount deposited at the mouth of the Columbia River.

41. The deep sediment layer deposited by the flood at the mouth of the Columbia River most likely consists of:

A. fine silt at the bottom and heavy boulders on top.
B. fine silt at the bottom and gravel on top.
C. gravel at the bottom and heavy boulders on top.
D. gravel at the bottom and fine silt on top.

42. Today the only land suitable for agriculture in the scablands region is most likely:

F. the deep flood channels.
G. the areas where rapids had formed.
H. the "islands" between the channels.
J. the areas where waterfalls had formed.

GO ON TO THE NEXT PAGE →

The three basic types of chemical bonding are metallic, ionic, and covalent. Each involves a different type of electron behavior.

In metallic bonds, metal atoms give up the electrons in their outermost shells to a surrounding "sea" of free electrons. The bonding consists of the attraction between those atoms—which have now become positively charged ions—and the free electrons.

In an ionic bond, one or more electrons are transferred from the outer shell of one atom to the outer shell of another. For example, the single electron in the outer shell of a sodium (Na) atom may be transferred to the outer shell of a chlorine (Cl) atom. Since there are already seven electrons in that outer shell, this transfer "completes" the outer shell. The chlorine atom must expend a small amount of energy to acquire the extra electron. Once the transfer is complete, however, the Na and Cl atoms remain linked together by their opposite charges.

Atoms that form ionic bonds tend to be those that easily lose or gain electrons one from the other. Usually this results from the fact that one has very few electrons in its outer shell, while the other's outer shell is almost complete. This difference gives the two atoms very different electron-attracting potentials (electronegativities).

Covalent bonds are made by atoms that, because of their electron configurations, do not easily lose or gain electrons one from the other. These atoms, instead of transferring electrons between them, share one or more electron pairs. By sharing, each atom completes its outer electron shell. For example, in water ($H_2O$), an oxygen atom with six electrons in its outer shell forms two covalent bonds with two hydrogen atoms. In each bond, one electron pair is shared. In this way the oxygen atom "gains" one electron from each of the two hydrogen atoms, thus completing its outer shell. Some atoms must form double or even triple covalent bonds in order to complete their outer electron shells.

43. When an Na atom forms an ionic bond, it gives up the single electron in its outermost shell. It then assumes the electron configuration of a:

   A.  metal.
   B.  halogen.
   C.  hydrocarbon.
   D.  noble gas.

44. An Na atom that gives up the electron in its outermost shell then becomes a:

   F.  metal.
   G.  positive ion.
   H.  negative ion.
   J.  neon atom.

45. When a Cl atom forms an ionic bond, it adds a single electron to the seven already in its outermost shell. It then assumes the electron configuration of a:

   A.  metal.
   B.  halogen.
   C.  hydrocarbon.
   D.  noble gas.

46. A Cl atom that adds an electron to its outermost shell becomes a(n):

   F.  metal.
   G.  positive ion.
   H.  negative ion.
   J.  argon atom.

47. Ionic bonds involving the transfer of one or two electrons are far more common than those involving the transfer of three or more electrons. This is most likely because:

   A.  it takes less energy to acquire each additional electron.
   B.  the atoms involved have similar electronegativities.
   C.  it takes more energy to acquire each additional electron.
   D.  three or more electrons cannot complete an atom's outermost shell.

48. Atoms that form covalent bonds rather than ionic bonds tend to be those that:

   F.  have similar electronegativities.
   G.  have very different numbers of electrons in their outermost shells.
   H.  have very different electronegativities.
   J.  easily lose or gain electrons one from the other.

49. The bond in $O_2$, represented in Lewis symbols as $:\ddot{O}::\ddot{O}:$, is a(n):

   A.  ionic bond.
   B.  single covalent bond.
   C.  double covalent bond.
   D.  triple covalent bond.

GO ON TO THE NEXT PAGE

**50.** The bonds in $CH_4$, expressed in Lewis symbols as

$$H:\overset{\cdot\cdot}{C}:H$$

with H above and H below, are:

   **F.** ionic bonds.
   **G.** single covalent bonds.
   **H.** double covalent bonds.
   **J.** triple covalent bonds.

**51.** The bond in $N_2$, represented in Lewis symbols as $\overset{\cdot}{N}:::\overset{\cdot}{N}$, is a(n):

   **A.** ionic bond.
   **B.** single covalent bond.
   **C.** double covalent bond.
   **D.** triple covalent bond.

**52.** In general, atoms form bonds in order to completely fill the outermost electron shell. Based on the number of electrons in that shell, this principle is most likely called the:

   **F.** unit rule.
   **G.** pair rule.
   **H.** quartet rule.
   **J.** octet rule.

**END OF TEST**

If you complete this test before the time is up, check
back over the questions on this test only. Do not go
back to the previous test.

# Answer Key

## English Usage

| | | | | |
|---|---|---|---|---|
| 1. B | 16. J | 31. A | 46. J | 61. B |
| 2. H | 17. C | 32. F | 47. C | 62. J |
| 3. C | 18. F | 33. B | 48. F | 63. A |
| 4. F | 19. A | 34. G | 49. C | 64. F |
| 5. B | 20. H | 35. A | 50. J | 65. B |
| 6. J | 21. C | 36. K | 51. C | 66. G |
| 7. C | 22. J | 37. D | 52. G | 67. C |
| 8. F | 23. B | 38. F | 53. C | 68. B |
| 9. C | 24. J | 39. B | 54. J | 69. C |
| 10. G | 25. A | 40. G | 55. A | 70. J |
| 11. A | 26. J | 41. C | 56. J | 71. C |
| 12. H | 27. A | 42. G | 57. D | 72. H |
| 13. C | 28. G | 43. B | 58. J | 73. A |
| 14. G | 29. A | 44. F | 59. C | 74. F |
| 15. B | 30. G | 45. B | 60. F | 75. B |

## Mathematics Usage

| | | | | |
|---|---|---|---|---|
| 1. A | 9. D | 17. B | 25. E | 33. A |
| 2. K | 10. G | 18. K | 26. G | 34. K |
| 3. C | 11. B | 19. A | 27. C | 35. D |
| 4. K | 12. H | 20. H | 28. J | 36. H |
| 5. E | 13. C | 21. D | 29. E | 37. C |
| 6. H | 14. G | 22. G | 30. H | 38. B |
| 7. D | 15. D | 23. C | 31. C | 39. C |
| 8. H | 16. H | 24. F | 32. H | 40. B |

## Social Studies Reading

| | | | | | |
|---|---|---|---|---|---|
| 1. D | 10. H | 19. A | 28. F | 37. D | 46. J |
| 2. G | 11. A | 20. H | 29. B | 38. H | 47. A |
| 3. B | 12. J | 21. D | 30. H | 39. B | 48. H |
| 4. F | 13. B | 22. H | 31. B | 40. J | 49. D |
| 5. D | 14. H | 23. B | 32. F | 41. C | 50. H |
| 6. H | 15. B | 24. J | 33. C | 42. F | 51. C |
| 7. C | 16. F | 25. C | 34. H | 43. B | 52. G |
| 8. G | 17. C | 26. J | 35. A | 44. J | |
| 9. D | 18. H | 27. D | 36. F | 45. B | |

## Natural Sciences Reading

| | | | | | |
|---|---|---|---|---|---|
| 1. B | 10. H | 19. D | 28. F | 37. B | 46. H |
| 2. J | 11. D | 20. J | 29. C | 38. J | 47. C |
| 3. B | 12. G | 21. A | 30. F | 39. C | 48. F |
| 4. H | 13. C | 22. G | 31. D | 40. F | 49. C |
| 5. D | 14. G | 23. B | 32. J | 41. D | 50. G |
| 6. G | 15. D | 24. F | 33. B | 42. H | 51. D |
| 7. A | 16. J | 25. C | 34. H | 43. D | 52. J |
| 8. H | 17. A | 26. F | 35. C | 44. G | |
| 9. A | 18. J | 27. D | 36. G | 45. D | |

# Explanatory Answers

### English Usage

1. **(B)** *Erroneous* is intended to modify the verb *implies*, but *erroneous* is an adjective—and that is erroneous. You need the adverb *erroneously*. C fails to correct the error of the original. D does correct the error but introduces a new error. The comma in D isolates the subject of the clause (*which*) from its verb (*implies*) and distorts the logical structure of the sentence.

2. **(H)** The original is a run-on sentence. H solves the problem by correctly beginning a new sentence when a new idea is introduced. G and J fail to correct the problem of the run-on sentence.

3. **(C)** *It's* is the contraction for *it is*. Here you need the possessive pronoun *its*. B is incorrect because *their* is plural and does not agree with its singular antecedent, *each*. H is simply not idiomatic English.

4. **(F)** The original is correct as written. G and H are both incorrect because they imply a causal connection where none is intended. They incorrectly imply that the fact that some Indian features survive was the cause of the destruction of the Taino culture. As for J, *furthermore* cannot be used to introduce a dependent clause. Additionally, *furthermore* signals a continuation of a thought, but the two ideas in this sentence imply a contrast of thoughts.

5. **(B)** *Having been* is not a conjugated verb, so it cannot be used as the main verb in a clause. As written, the clause that follows the comma has no main verb, and B supplies one. Although C and D also supply a main verb, C is wrong because the present progressive *is being* suggests that the Taino culture is at this time being destroyed; but the sense of the paragraph is that it was destroyed some time in the past. As for D, *were* is plural and does not agree with the subject, *culture*.

6. **(J)** *Brought*, not *brung*, is the past tense of *bring*. Thus, the original and H are both wrong. Both G and J supply possible forms of *bring*, but the use of the present perfect (*have brought*) is incorrect. *Have brought* implies a past action continuing into the present, but the sense of the paragraph is that the action was completed at some time in the past.

7. **(C)** The original contains two errors. First, *remaining* is a participle and, as such, seems to be an adjective modifying *some*. This structure, however, is not idiomatic. Second, *some* refers to *culture*, but the phrase *some culture remains* is not idiomatic. B solves the first problem but at the cost of creating an awkward and wordy sentence. D eliminates both errors in the original but introduces a new mistake: *many* is plural, but its antecedent, *culture*, is singular. Only C eliminates both errors of the original without making any new mistake.

8. **(F)** The original is correct as written. In each of the alternatives, the placement of *well* is such that the resulting sentence would not be idiomatic.

9. **(C)** *Knowing* is a participle that seems to be an adjective modifying *Americans* (as in "The Americans, knowing they would win, proposed a surrender plan to the enemy."). Since *knowing* functions as an adjective, the original sentence is missing a main verb and is thus a fragment rather than a complete sentence. B fails to solve this problem because *having known* is also a participle form. C and D both correct the error of the original. D is wrong, however, because the phrase *knew about how* is not idiomatic English.

10. **(G)** This is an inverted sentence in which the verb comes before the subject. The subject of the sentence is the plural noun *hopes*. Therefore, the verb should be the plural *were* rather than the singular *was*. H is wrong because the resulting main clause would lack a conjugated verb. (*There were high hopes* is the independent clause in this sentence. *That* introduces a dependent clause, which cannot stand alone.) J does have the merit of supplying a main verb, but the present tense *are* conflicts with the other verbs in the selection. The passage describes actions that occurred in the past.

11. **(A)** The original is acceptable as written. The use of *would be* (the subjunctive) correctly implies that, at the time the raid was planned, the American leaders were not sure that it would have its desired consequence. B is incorrect because the sense of doubt is missing from *had been* (the past perfect tense of the indicative mood). Additionally, the past perfect *had been* suggests a past action that was completed before some other past action but that incorrectly implies that the effect of the raid occurred even before the raid itself. C makes two errors. First, the phrase *would of been* is not idiomatic. It is a confused rendering of *would have been*. Second, C is awkward. (*Psychologically* is an adverb, but it is difficult to understand how it modifies the verb *would have been*.) Finally, D is the participle of *to be*, but the use of the participle would leave the dependent clause introduced by *that* without a main verb.

12. **(H)** *His* is a singular pronoun intended to refer to *enemies*. Since *enemies* is plural, you must use a plural pronoun. Thus, H is correct. As for G, *its*, too, is singular and therefore incorrect. Finally, as for J, if the pronoun is omitted altogether, the resulting construction is: "might change strategy of . . . ." But that is not idiomatic.

13. (C) The present tense *lose* is out of place in this selection, which describes past actions. The correct tense is the past tense *lost*. Thus, C is correct. B is wrong because it, too, refers to actions occurring in the present. (*Are losing* is the present progressive tense. In English, we often use the progressive tenses for special emphasis.) As for D, *have lost* is in the present perfect tense. It implies that an action was begun in the past but continues into the present. The sense of the selection, however, is that the action of the battle was not only begun but completed at some time in the past.

14. (G) The original is simply not idiomatic. Here you should use the infinitive, *to find,* rather than the gerund, *finding.* H is wrong because *to finding* is not a verb form that exists in English. Finally, J is wrong because *for* is not a possible choice of prepositions here.

15. (B) The original is a run-on sentence. You cannot use a comma—with no accompanying conjunction—to splice together two independent clauses. B is one way of correcting the problem: just start a new sentence. C is wrong because the sentence is still a run-on sentence. D does solve the problem of the comma splice but is wrong for several reasons. One, the *but* signals a contrast of thoughts where none is intended. Second, *planning* is a participle that seems to be used an adjective. But what noun (or pronoun) does it modify? None. So the phrase has no unambiguous logical relationship to the rest of the sentence.

16. (J) The sentence suffers from a lack of parallelism. When you have a series of elements in a sentence that have the same logical function, those elements should have similar or parallel forms: *American cities, forests, and farmlands.* By omitting the repeated verb, you restore the parallelism. G and H are incorrect because they fail to bring the third element of the series into conformity with the first two.

17. (C) The subject of the sentence is *few,* which is plural, so you must use a plural verb such as *were.* B does use a plural, but the present perfect tense is out of place. The release of the balloons is an act completed entirely in the past. D, too, uses a verb tense that is inappropriate and is, in any case, incorrect for the further reason that the compound tenses are formed using the past participle (*released*), not the present participle (*releasing*). C is correct. *Were* is a plural verb, and the past tense *were released* is consistent with the other verbs in the paragraph.

18. (F) The sentence is correct as written. Since *today's* is intended to modify *missiles,* it must be in the possessive case. G and J are incorrect because a noun cannot modify another noun (unless it shows possession). Finally, since H is plural, it illogically implies that there is more than one today.

19. (A) The sentence is correct as written. B is incorrect because the dash seems to signal a parenthetical remark, but what follows the dash is an independent clause expressing an important idea. C and D are

wrong because by eliminating the sentence break, they create run-on sentences.

20. (H) The sentence suffers from a lack of parallelism. The underlined part is the last in a series of elements all of which are nouns, so you need a noun rather than a verb form such as *losing.* Thus, H is correct. G does supply a noun form but is incorrect because *with* is a preposition and cannot be substituted for the conjunction *and.* Such a substitution destroys the logic of the sentence. Finally, J fails to correct the original error.

21. (C) *Which* introduces a relative clause and requires a conjugated verb. *Having caused* is a participle form, not a conjugated verb. C solves this problem by supplying a conjugated verb. Further, C correctly uses the future tense. B is wrong because the present tense is inconsistent with the logic of the sentence, which is referring to events that will occur sometime in the future. Finally, D fails to correct the problem of the original.

22. (J) The original is a run-on sentence. The comma splices together two independent clauses with no conjunction. J corrects the problem by supplying the conjunction *and.* G fails to solve this problem and is wrong for the further reason that it is not idiomatic. Finally, H fails to solve the problem of the run-on sentence even though it does eliminate the comma.

23. (B) The original contains two errors. First, the plural verb *are* does not agree with the singular subject *impact.* Second, the adjective *relative* cannot modify the adjective *predictable.* B corrects both errors. It uses a singular verb, *is,* and it uses an adverb, *relatively,* to modify the adjective *predictable.* C corrects the second error but not the first. D fails to correct the second error. Additionally, D leaves the noun *impact* with no verb.

24. (J) The original is not idiomatic. It mixes together two idioms: *it can be avoided* and *it is avoidable.* (Since the *-able* suffix means "having the property of something," the original is equivalent to "it can can be avoided.") J solves this by eliminating one of the *cans.* In the sentence created by J, *avoidable* is an adjective modifying *impact* and is governed by the verb *are* (which also governs *predictable*). G is wrong because *avoidable* is intended to be an adjective describing *impact,* not an adverb modifying *is.* Finally, the placement of *thus* in H is just not idiomatic.

25. (A) The original is correct. This is a good point to begin a new paragraph since the author is taking up a new topic. He is moving from a general discussion to a discussion of particular problems. C and D eliminate the paragraphing and are therefore wrong. As for B, the use of the conjunction *since* reduces what is in the original an independent clause to a dependent clause. As a consequence, the resulting sentence has no main clause.

26. (J) The original is wrong for two reasons. First, the possessive pronoun *their* does not agree in number with its antecedent, *leaders.* Second, the comma isolates the prepositional phrase introduced by *with*

from the rest of the sentence, thus disrupting the logical structure of the sentence. J corrects both errors. G corrects the first but not the second error. H corrects neither error and actually compounds the second error by even more sharply isolating the prepositional phrase from the noun it modifies.

27. (A) The original is correct. The phrase "in the next few years" clearly refers to future events, so you must use the future tenses. B and C, which are the past perfect and future tenses, respectively, are wrong. Finally, D is not even a correct verb form. The compound tenses in English are formed using the past participle (*frustrated*).

28. (G) The original sentence lacks a main verb. (*Being* is the participle of *to be* and cannot function as a main verb.) G correctly supplies a main verb. As for H, the correct English idiom is *conducive to*, not *conducive with*. As for J, the use of the past tense *were* is inconsistent with the other verb in the sentence. The present perfect *has been* implies a condition that began in the past and continues into the present. Thus, that condition should be described with the present tense *are*, not the past tense *were*.

29. (A) The original is correct. As for B, the correct idiom is *solution to*, not *solution of*. As for C, *seemingly* modifies the adjective *intractable*, so you must use the adverb and not the adjective, *seeming*. Finally, D is wrong because *these* (a demonstrative adjective) does not agree in number with *problem*.

30. (G) The original contains an error of diction. *Lays* is a form of the verb *to lay*, but what is required here is a form of the verb *to lie*, meaning "located." G supplies the correct verb. H is the past tense of *to lay* and must be wrong. Finally, J is the past tense of *to lie*, the right verb, but the past tense is out of place in this paragraph, which discusses present events.

31. (A) The original is correct. B and C are simply not idiomatic. (You need the infinitive, not a participle.) Finally, D deviates from the intended meaning of the original.

32. (F) The original is correct. One use of a colon is to introduce a listing of the sort you have here. G is wrong because the comma suggests that *shapes* is the first element of the series. But the sense of the sentence is that *majestic spirals,* etc., are all examples of shapes. H is wrong because a semicolon would be used to separate one main clause from another, but what follows is not a clause. Finally, as for J, *with* is a preposition, but it is not clear what the resulting prepositional phrase is supposed to modify. In any event, you should not separate a prepositional phrase from the rest of the sentence with a comma.

33. (B) Since *suggesting* is a participle and not a conjugated verb, the original sentence lacks a main verb. B, C, and D could each function as a main verb. But C is wrong because the author is describing current theories, so you should use the present rather than the past tense. As for D, *suggests* is singular, but the subject of the sentence, *theories*, is plural.

34. (G) The subject of the clause introduced by *that* is *conditions,* a plural noun. So the original verb, *determines,* which is singular, is incorrect. G corrects this error. H fails to correct the problem of subject–verb agreement and contains an error of diction as well. *If* does not mean "whether." Finally, J suffers from this last problem and from the further defect that it leaves the subject, *conditions,* without a conjugated verb.

35. (A) The original is correct. B and C are wrong because the singular verb, *is distorted,* does not agree with the plural subject, *galaxies.* Finally, D is wrong because the placement of *constantly* is not as idiomatic as that of the original.

36. (H) The original is not idiomatic. The correct idiom is *pervaded by,* not *pervaded with.* G and J are also not idiomatic. *Pervasive* is an adjective meaning "widespread," but that meaning is not appropriate in this sentence.

37. (D) In the original, the singular pronoun, *its,* does not agree with its antecedent, *galaxies.* D makes the needed correction. B makes the correction also, but B is not idiomatic. The correct preposition here is *by,* not *from.* As for C, *it's* is not a pronoun at all, but a contraction for *it is.*

38. (F) The original is correct as written. You need the present tense *becomes* because the paragraph is describing conditions that exist at this time. G is wrong because *would* (the subjunctive) implies that one event is contingent upon another event, but that is not the intended meaning of the original. And H and J are wrong because their tenses conflict with the other verbs in the passage.

39. (B) The original is not idiomatic: "more important determinant . . . as heredity." B supplies the correct idiom: "more important determinant . . . than heredity." C eliminates the problem of idiom but is needlessly wordy. (Additionally, the use of *was* is illogical, since the effect of heredity continues even into the present.) Finally, D combines the worst aspects of the original and C.

40. (G) The formation of the Sun is a past event, so it must be described using some kind of past tense verb. G provides the correct tense. As for H, this verb would be used to describe a present event, not a past event. As for J, without the auxiliary (helping) verb *have,* the resulting construction is not idiomatic: *would never formed.*

41. (C) The original is needlessly wordy and awkward, as you can see by comparing the original to C. Additionally, C is better than B or D for the same reason.

42. (G) The original sentence lacks a main verb. Only G is a conjugated form of the verb *to originate,* so only G can serve as a main verb.

43. (B) The original is simply not idiomatic. The correct idiom is *as early as,* not *as early than.* As for C, *as early like* is not idiomatic. Finally, as for D, the *in* is superfluous. (Additionally, the *in* distorts the logic of the sentence.)

**44.** (F) The original sentence is correct. This is an appropriate point to begin a new sentence. The other three choices all create run-on sentences and must be incorrect.

**45.** (B) The verb tense of the original is incorrect. The passage describes events that belong to the past, so the present tense *are beginning* is out of place. As for C, though this verb form would be used to describe a past action, it is reserved to describe a past action that occurred before some other past action. But the phrase "at the same time" indicates the two past actions were simultaneous. Finally, D is wrong because you need a past tense verb.

**46.** (J) The original is not idiomatic. You should use the infinitive *to cure* rather than the gerund *curing*. Only J makes the needed change.

**47.** (C) Again, the original is not idiomatic because you should use the infinitive *to attract* rather than the gerund *attracting*. B fails to make the needed correction and introduces yet another error. The past perfect *had begun* implies that this event occurred in the past before some other past event, but that is not the sense of the original. Finally, D is awkward.

**48.** (F) The sentence is correct as written. Each of the other choices makes the same error. *While, since,* and *though* are all conjunctions that introduce dependent clauses. The *and,* however, joins two independent clauses. So you would wind up with a problem of illogical subordination and coordination.

**49.** (C) The original is not idiomatic. The correct idiom is *dependent on* (or *dependent upon*), not *dependent of*. Although B corrects this problem, B is wrong because you need a past tense verb to describe the past action being discussed. Finally, D fails to correct the problem of idiom and contains another error. *Becoming* is not a conjugated verb, so it cannot function as the main verb of that clause.

**50.** (J) The *which* in the original seems to introduce a relative clause modifying *organizations*. But if what follows *which* is read as a dependent clause, then *organizations,* which seems to be the subject of the main clause, lacks a verb. The *which,* therefore, disrupts the logic of the sentence. J solves the problem by eliminating the offending word. Now *were forced* functions as the main verb of the sentence. G is wrong because *that* creates the same problem of logical expression as *which*. Finally, as for H, *having been forced* is not a conjugated verb, so the resulting construction would be a sentence fragment.

**51.** (C) The original contains two errors. First, a semicolon cannot be used to separate an introductory dependent clause from the main clause of the sentence. (You need a comma for that.) Second, *one* is singular and does not agree with its antecedent, *institutions*. Every choice corrects this second problem. D, however, fails to correct the first problem. As for B, *and* creates a problem of subordination. You have a sentence with a dependent clause introduced by *since,* which is in turn joined to the independent clause by *and*.

**52.** (G) The original contains a low-level usage. The phrase "owing to the fact that" should not be used in place of *because*. Similarly, J is low-level usage. Finally, H is not idiomatic. *With* is a preposition, not a conjunction. So *with* cannot be used to introduce a clause. G is correct, for *as* is a conjunction and can be used to introduce the introductory, dependent clause.

**53.** (C) The original and the wrong choices are simply not idiomatic. The correct idiom, as provided by C, is *much like*.

**54.** (J) The original is wrong for two reasons. First, *it* must refer to *waves,* but *waves* is plural while *it* is singular. Second, the construction *in order that* is not idiomatic. *In order to.* would be better. J avoids both problems altogether and has the additional advantage of being concise. Although G solves the problem of unidiomatic expression, the resulting construction is very awkward and still contains the offending pronoun. As for H, the resulting sentence would be awkward.

**55.** (A) In general, a modifier should be placed as close to what it modifies as possible. Since *generally* is intended to modify *available,* the original is correct.

**56.** (J) The original contains an error of diction. The word intended by the sentence is *acceptance*. (There is an English word *exceptance,* but it is archaic and, in any event, has the meaning *exception*.) G, which is another form of *except,* doesn't have a meaning required by this sentence. Finally, H is wrong because idiomatic expression would use the noun here rather than the gerund.

**57.** (D) The original is wrong on two counts. First, the word *lower* implies a comparison, but the cost of ultrasound has not been compared in the passage to the cost of anything else. Second, the use of the definite article (*the*) implies that *cost* has already been mentioned. Since cost has not yet been mentioned, the reader is left wondering about a particular cost that has never been introduced. Cost doesn't seem to have a logical connection to anything that has come before. D corrects both problems. First, *low* simply describes the cost of ultrasound without implying a comparison to any other particular cost. Second, substituting *its* for *the* gives the reader a clue as to how to connect cost with the information that has come before. B makes the two corrections but fails because *their* is plural and cannot be used to refer to *ultrasonography,* a singular noun. C is incorrect because *it's* is not a pronoun but the contraction for *it is*.

**58.** (J) The original is incorrectly punctuated. What follows the colon is not a listing but a participial phrase, so the colon is incorrect. *Rivaling* is a participle that is intended to modify *one,* which in turn ultimately refers to *ultrasonography*. Since the information it introduces is not essential to the definition of *ultrasonograph,* it should be set off by a comma. G is incorrect because the nonessential information should be set off by a comma. H is wrong because the semicolon cannot be used in place of the comma here.

(Although there are some jobs that can be done by either a comma or a semicolon, this is not one of them.)

59. (C) The original contains a diction error. *Attracted to* implies that the ultrasound likes or finds attractive the doctors. The correct phrase is *attractive to.* B and D are not idiomatic.

60. (F) The original is correct. You should begin a new paragraph here because the author is taking up a new topic: a disadvantage of ultrasound. Thus, G and H are incorrect. As for J, *furthermore* is an adverb, not a conjunction. If you replace *because* with *furthermore,* you no longer have a dependent clause introduced by a conjunction. You have an independent clause introduced by an adverb. But then the sentence becomes a run-on sentence because its independent clauses are joined only by a comma.

61. (B) The use of *get* to suggest the passive voice is not acceptable in standard written English. Instead, you should use some form of the verb *to be.* Although both B and D use *are,* D is incorrect because the form *are reflecting* is the active voice, not the passive voice. Thus, D implies that the sound was doing the reflecting rather than being reflected.

62. (J) The original is a run-on sentence. The best move is simply to start a new sentence with *similarly.* J does this. G is incorrect because the dash cannot be used to join two independent clauses. Finally, H would result in a comma splice.

63. (A) The original is correct. The rest of the passage describes events in the past, so the use of the past tense in this sentence is correct. B is incorrect since *striking* is not a conjugated verb and the resulting construction would lack a main verb. C is wrong because the use of the past perfect (*had struck*) implies that the earthquake preceded some other event, but the author doesn't mention any other such event. Finally, D is wrong because *that* seems to introduce a dependent clause. But the resulting structure would lack a main verb.

64. (F) The original is correct as written. As for G, the *it* is superfluous, so F is preferable. As for H and J, the phrase *that followed* is essential to the meaning of the sentence. It shows that the shock and fires were caused by the earthquake. Therefore, the phrase should not be placed in parentheses.

65. (B) The original contains one error. *And* is used to join two ideas that are similar. *But* is used to join two ideas that contrast. The two ideas here should be joined by *but.* As for C, *it's* is not a possessive pronoun. D makes this mistake too and fails to correct the original error.

66. (G) The original is redundant. *Enormous* necessarily describes magnitude. G is better than the original because it is more concise. While H is more concise than the original, the use of the present tense *is* is inconsistent with the other verbs in the passage (which are in the past tense). As for J, *enormously* is an adverb, so it must modify *was,* but then you have no predicate complement to finish off the *was.*

67. (C) The original is not idiomatic. The correct idiom is *slow to reach,* not *slow about reaching.* For this reason C is correct and B is incorrect. D uses the correct idiom, but the verb does not agree with its subject. Although *news* ends in *s,* it is singular, not plural.

68. (G) The original sentence contains a comma splice. You need something else to separate the two independent clauses, either a comma plus a conjunction or a semicolon. G uses the latter alternative. H and J both fail to correct the problem of the run-on sentence.

69. (C) The original is awkward. *That* seems to introduce a relative clause that is intended to provide essential information about *event.* (For example, *I live in the house that has a chimney. That* introduces a vital piece of information that identifies the house indicated.) But it is part of the definition of *event* that it occurred, so the additional information is really superfluous. C is the best choice because it is the most concise.

70. (J) The original is wrong in at least two respects. First, *its* must refer to *newspapers,* which is plural, not singular. Second, *by* is not the correct preposition. In any event, the entire phrase is superfluous, so the best course of action is simply to omit it altogether.

71. (C) The original is needlessly wordy, as you can see by comparing it to the correct choice, C. B and D are also needlessly wordy and are awkward as well.

72. (H) The first clause of the sentence lacks a main verb. At first, you might think that *destroyed* is the main verb. But *destroyed* is a transitive verb and requires an object: destroyed what? The sentence intends, however, that the hospital camp was destroyed. Since *hospital camp* is the subject of the sentence, you need the passive voice. Thus, H is correct. G is wrong because the present tense *destroys* is inconsistent with the other verbs in the selection. Finally, J creates a prepositional phrase. A prepositional phrase must have a logical connection to some other element in the sentence. But it is not clear what the prepositional phrase created by J would modify.

73. (A) You should not begin a new paragraph here. This sentence describes one of several effects of the quake and so belongs in this paragraph with other sentences describing other effects. Thus, B and D are wrong. As for C, *towns'* is a plural noun, but the passage refers to only one town.

74. (F) The original is correct. You need a past tense verb here because the other verbs are in the past tense. For this reason, the alternative choices are wrong.

75. (B) The original contains a phrase that is very much like a double negative: *sparing no further misery.* This really says the people did suffer further misery, but that is not what the sentence means to say. B makes the needed correction. D fails to correct the error, and C is awkward.

## Mathematics Usage

1. (A) Here you have a single equation with one variable, so you might as well solve for $x$:

$$\frac{1}{x} + \frac{1}{x} = 8$$

$$\frac{2}{x} = 8$$

$$x = \frac{1}{4}$$

Or, you might have reasoned that $\frac{1}{x}$ and $\frac{1}{x}$ are equal, and since their sum is 8, $\frac{1}{x}$ must be 4. So the value of $x$ must be $\frac{1}{4}$. And, of course, you could have substituted numbers; but this is such a simple equation, one of the two techniques just described is more effective.

2. (K) This question asks that you evaluate the expression $3x - 4y$. It requires only a simple calculation, so the correct approach is just to do it.

$$3x - 4y = 3(2) - 4(-1) = 6 - (-4) = 6 + 4 = 10$$

3. (C) This question asks about percents. You must take a percent of a number:

20% of 600 boys = 120 boys on the honor roll

30% of 400 girls = 120 girls on the honor roll

120 boys + 120 girls = 240 students on the honor roll

4. (K) This question tests the even and odd properties of numbers. Since an even number times any other whole number yields an even number, the correct answer is K. None of the other letters guarantees an even result. If this insight escapes you, you can experiment with some values. For each letter, assume that that letter only is even and that all other numbers are odd. Only $t$ generates an even result under those circumstances.

5. (E) This is a long question but is not that difficult. You must see that the number of flies in each successive week is four times the number of the previous week. So the final count should be $4 \times 192 = 768$.

6. (H) You can use the formula for finding the number of permutations to solve this question:

$$3! = 3 \times 2 \times 1 = 6$$

But you can also count the number of possibilities on your fingers: ABC, ACB, BAC, BCA, CAB, CBA.

7. (D) This question tests basic coordinate geometry. Since the $x$ coordinate of both points is 2, the line runs parallel to the $y$ axis. The $x$ coordinate of the midpoint will also be 2. As for the $y$ coordinate, the midpoint is halfway between 2 and $-2$, which is zero.

8. (H) Since the absolute value of $xy$ is positive, $xy$ itself must be positive (since $|xy| = xy$). Therefore, both $x$ and $y$ both have the same sign. They might both be positive, or they might both be negative. And it doesn't make any difference which is larger. So F, G, J, and K can all be true. $x$ and $y$ cannot, however, have different signs, because a positive times a negative yields a negative result. And, of course, you could have tried substituting numbers. If $x > 0 > y$, then $x$ could be 1 and $y$ could be $-1$, and $1 \times -1 = -1$.

9. (D) Just convert the dimensions shown to real dimensions. Since 1 centimeter is equal to 4 meters, the width of the room is 4 meters, and the length is 4.8. So the area of the room is $4 \times 4.8 = 19.2$.

10. (G) This question tests powers. $30,000 \times 20 = 600,000 = 6 \times 10^5$. (One power of ten for each zero.)

11. (B) You can solve this problem with simultaneous equations. Let $x$ be the quantity of chocolates and $y$ the quantity of caramels:

$$x + y = 4 \text{ and } 3x + 2y = 10$$

$$y = 4 - x$$

$$3x + 2(4 - x) = 10$$

$$3x + 8 - 2x = 10$$

$$x = 10 - 8 = 2$$

Or you can test the answers, starting with C. If Karen buys 2.5 pounds of chocolates, she bought $4 - 2.5 = 1.5$ pounds of caramels and the total cost would be $(2.5 \times 3) + (1.5 \times 2) = 7.50 + 3 = \$10.50$. Too much money and wrong. Since chocolates are more expensive than caramels, Karen bought less than 2.5 pounds of chocolates. So try B: 2 pounds of chocolates and 2 pounds of caramels would cost $(2 \times 3) + (2 \times 2) = 10$. B is correct.

12. (H) You can use the procedure you learned for finding a missing element of an average. The total of all three numbers is $3 \times 80 = 240$. The total of the two numbers you know is $2 \times 80 = 160$. So the missing number is $240 - 160 = 80$. Or, you might have used the "above and below" method. Since 80 is neither above nor below the average, the first two 80s are equal to the average, so the final number can be neither above nor below the average. It must be 80.

13. (C) This question tests your understanding of ratio parts. The total number of ratio parts in the ratio 5:2 is 7, and 10 is not evenly divisible by 7.

**14.** (G) You can treat this equation as a proportion. Cross-multiply and solve for $x$:

$$\frac{4}{5} = \frac{x}{4}$$

$$4(4) = 5x$$

$$x = \frac{16}{5}$$

Yes, you could have substituted numbers here, and it is good to see that as a possibility. But substitution would have taken much more time than simply solving for $x$.

**15.** (D) Let us label the unlabeled angles:

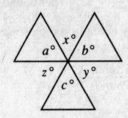

Since the measure of the degrees in a circle is 360, the sum of $x$, $y$, and $z$ plus the sum of $a$, $b$, and $c$ is 360. What is the value of the angles inside the triangles? Since those are equilateral triangles, each of the angles is 60°.

$$3(60) + x + y + z = 360$$

$$x + y + z = 180$$

**16.** (H) This is just an exercise in multiplying fractions. If Peter spent $\frac{1}{4}$ of his allowance on Monday, he had $\frac{3}{4}$ of his allowance left. Then, he spent $\frac{1}{3}$ of that $\frac{3}{4}$ on Tuesday: $\frac{1}{3}$ of $\frac{3}{4} = \frac{1}{3} \times \frac{3}{4} = \frac{1}{4}$. After spending the additional $\frac{1}{4}$, he has left $\frac{3}{4} - \frac{1}{4} = \frac{1}{2}$ of the original allowance. Of course, you could have substituted numbers but the arithmetic would have been the same.

**17.** (B) There are three ways of arriving at the solution. The simplest and most direct is to reason that if 100 bricks weigh $p$ pounds, 20 bricks, which is $\frac{1}{5}$ of 100, must weigh $\frac{1}{5}$ of $p$.

This same reasoning can be expressed using a direct proportion. The more bricks, the greater the weight, so

$$\frac{100}{20} = \frac{p}{x}$$

$$100x = 20p$$

$$x = \frac{20p}{100} = \frac{p}{5}$$

Finally, you could have substituted numbers. Assume that 100 bricks weigh 100 pounds, which is 1 pound apiece. 20 bricks weigh 20 pounds. On the assumption that $p = 100$, the correct formula will generate the number 20.

**18.** (K) The following drawings show that I, II, and III are possible.

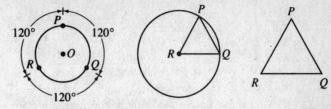

The thing to watch out for here is the Watson blunder. Both I and III are fairly obvious possibilities; II is more subtle.

**19.** (A) This problem can be solved with the "change-over" principle. But, you object, that is five different calculations. True, so look for an escape route: approximation. The percent increase in the period 1950–1955 was $\frac{(4-2)}{2} = 100\%$. For the next period it was $\frac{3}{4}$, which is less than 100 percent. For the next, $\frac{5}{7}$, which is less than 100 percent. For the next, $\frac{8}{12} = \frac{2}{3}$, which is less than 100 percent. And for the last it was $\frac{10}{20}$, 50 percent less than 100 percent. So the correct answer is A.

**20.** (H) The easiest approach is just to perform the multiplication for the answer choices:

**F.** $(x - 6)(x + 2) = x^2 - 4x - 12$ (Wrong.)
**G.** $(x - 4)(x + 3) = x^2 - x - 12$ (Wrong.)
**H.** $(x - 2)(x + 6) = x^2 + 4x - 12$ (Right!)
**J.** $(x + 2)(x + 6) = x^2 + 8x + 12$ (Wrong.)
**K.** $(x + 3)(x + 4) = x^2 + 7x + 12$ (Wrong.)

**21.** (D) The best approach to this question is just to do the algebra. Since the average of $3x - 2$ and $2x - 3$ is 10, their sum is 20:

$$3x - 2 + 2x - 3 = 20$$

$$5x - 5 = 20$$

$$5x = 25$$

$$x = 5$$

So one of the packages weighs $3(5) - 2 = 13$ pounds and the other weighs $2(5) - 3 = 7$ pounds. So the difference between their weights is 6.

Testing choices would not be a good strategy for this question, because the question asks for the *difference* between the weights. So the choices do not represent possible weights of an individual package.

**22.** (G) This question is a variation on the theme of an average with missing elements. Since ten students have scores of 75 or more, the total of their scores is at minimum $10 \times 75 = 750$. Then, even assuming the other five students each scored zero, the average for the 15 would be at least $750 \div 15 = 50$.

**23.** (C) Since $16 = 4^2$, $16^x = (4^2)^x = 4^{2x}$. You could reach the same conclusion by assuming a value for $x$, say, 1. On that assumption, $16^x = 16^1 = 16$. Now substitute 1 for $x$ in the answer choices. The correct choice will yield the value 16:

  **A.** $1^{16} = 1$ (Wrong.)
  **B.** $2^{3(1)} = 2^3 = 8$ (Wrong.)
  **C.** $4^{2(1)} = 4^2 = 16$ (Right!)
  **D.** $8^{2(1)} = 8^2 = 64$ (Wrong.)
  **E.** $8^{4(1)} = 8^4$ (Wrong.)

**24.** (F) Since the figure is a square, the two sides are equal:

$$2x + 1 = x + 4$$

$$x = 3$$

So each side is $x + 4 = 3 + 4 = 7$, and the perimeter is $4(7) = 28$.

**25.** (E) You can work this out algebraically. Let $w$ be the width of the rectangle. The length of the rectangle is twice that, or $2w$. So the rectangle has an area of $w \times 2w = 2w^2$. Then, $w$ is also the length of the hypotenuse of a 45-45-90 triangle. Each of the other two sides (the ones that form the right angle) is $\frac{1}{2} \times w \times \sqrt{2} = \frac{\sqrt{2}w}{2}$. (Since the two sides form a right angle, they can be the altitude and base). So the area of the triangle is $\frac{1}{2} \times$ altitude $\times$ base $= \frac{1}{2}(\frac{\sqrt{2}w}{2})(\frac{\sqrt{2}w}{2}) = \frac{1}{2}(\frac{2w^2}{4}) = \frac{w^2}{4}$. And the ratio of the area of the rectangle to that of the triangle is $\frac{2w^2}{\frac{w^2}{4}} = \frac{2}{\frac{1}{4}} = \frac{8}{1}$.

It's true the explanation above is difficult to follow without a diagram, which is why you are encouraged to draw a figure when one is not provided.

Now the explanation will not only be easier to follow; you can dispense with it altogether.

In the first place, the rectangle is obviously bigger than the triangle, so you can eliminate three choices: A, B, and C. Next, a quick addition to the figure shows that the area of the triangle is less than $\frac{1}{4}$ of the area of the rectangle:

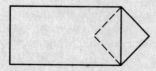

By the process of elimination, E must be correct.

**26.** (G) No diagram is provided, so sketch one:

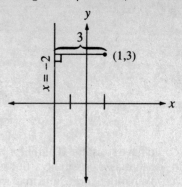

**27.** (C) This question can be answered using "supermarket math." You find out how much coffee costs per pound: $\frac{\$12}{5 \text{ pounds}} = \$2.40$ per pound. Then you divide $30 by $2.40: $\$30 \div \$2.40 = 12.5$. The steps of the process can all be represented in a single proportion:

$$\frac{\text{Cost X}}{\text{Cost Y}} = \frac{\text{Pounds X}}{\text{Pounds Y}}$$

$$\frac{\$12}{\$30} = \frac{5}{x}$$

$$12x = 5(30)$$

$$x = \frac{150}{12} = 12.5$$

**28.** (J) Attack the question directly. Find the perimeter of each triangle. Since the triangles are equilateral, the smaller one has a perimeter of $3 + 3 + 3 = 9$, and the larger one has a perimeter of $12 + 12 + 12 = 36$. And $\frac{9}{36} = \frac{1}{4}$.

You might also have reasoned that since the triangles are equilateral, the ratio of their perimeters is the same as the ratio of their sides. So the ratio of their perimeters will also be $\frac{3}{12}$, or $\frac{1}{4}$.

The second line of reasoning is more elegant (simpler), but who needs elegance when the first line of attack is easily managed anyway?

**29.** (E) Substitute $-2$ for $x$ in the function:

$$f(-2) = -3(-2)^3 + 3(-2)^2 - 4(-2) + 8 =$$

$$-3(-8) + 3(4) - (-8) + 8 =$$

$$24 + 12 + 8 + 8 = 52$$

**30.** (H) First add 30 percent to the $120 wholesale price:

$$\$120 + (0.30 \times \$120) = \$120 + \$36 = \$156$$

Now find the sale price:

$$\$156 - (0.40 \times \$156) = \$156 - \$62.40 = \$93.60$$

**31.** (C) You reason in English:

$\frac{1}{3}$ of the number is equal to $\frac{1}{5}$ of the number plus 2:

$$\tfrac{1}{3}x = \tfrac{1}{5}x + 2$$

Therefore:

$$\tfrac{1}{3}x - 2 = \tfrac{1}{5}x \text{ or } \tfrac{1}{3}x - \tfrac{1}{5}x = 2$$

**32.** (H) This is a composite figure. One side of the equilateral triangle is also a side of the square. The triangle has a perimeter of 12, so each side is 4. If the square has a side of 4, then it has a perimeter of $4 + 4 + 4 + 4 = 16$.

**33.** (A) Subsitute $\frac{2}{3}$ for $x$ and solve for $k$:

$$12\left(\frac{2}{3}\right)^2 + k\left(\frac{2}{3}\right) = 6$$

$$12\left(\frac{4}{9}\right) + k\left(\frac{2}{3}\right) = 6$$

$$4\left(\frac{4}{3}\right) + k\left(\frac{2}{3}\right) = 6$$

$$k\left(\frac{2}{3}\right) = 6 - \frac{16}{3}$$

$$k\left(\frac{2}{3}\right) = \frac{18}{3} - \frac{16}{3} = \frac{2}{3}$$

$$k\left(\frac{2}{3}\right) = \frac{2}{3}$$

$$k = 1$$

**34.** (K) To find the perimeter of a figure, you add the lengths of the sides:

$$2(x - 2y) + 4(2x + y) =$$

$$(2x - 4y) + (8x + 4y) =$$

$$2x + 8x - 4y + 4y = 10x$$

You can, if you prefer, substitute numbers. Assume that $x = 3$ and $y = 1$. The two short sides are each $3 - 2(1) = 1$, for a total of 2. And the four long sides are $2(3) + 1 = 7$, for a total of 28. The perimeter is $28 + 2 = 30$. So if $x = 3$ and $y = 1$, the correct formula will generate the number 30. Only K produces the correct value.

**35.** (D) Set up an equation. Let $x$ be the number of packages in the van before the driver makes her first delivery:

$$\left(x - \frac{2}{5}x\right) - 3 = \frac{1}{2}x$$

$$\frac{3}{5}x - 3 = \frac{1}{2}x$$

$$\frac{3}{5}x - \frac{1}{2}x = 3$$

$$\frac{1}{10}x = 3$$

$$x = 30$$

**36.** (H) The largest common factor of 12 and 8 is 4, so you can factor out a 4 from the coefficients of the two terms. Then, you can also factor an $x^2$ and a $y^2$. The result is:

$$4x^2 y^2 (3x - 2y)$$

**37.** (C) This question asks you to rewrite the expression:

$$\frac{1}{1 + \frac{1}{x}} = \frac{1}{\frac{x + 1}{x}} = 1\left(\frac{x}{x + 1}\right) = \frac{x}{x + 1}$$

Or you could have substituted numbers. If $x = 1$, then

$$\frac{1}{1 + \frac{1}{x}} = \frac{1}{1 + \frac{1}{1}} = \frac{1}{1 + 1} = \frac{1}{2}$$

On the assumption that $x = 1$, two answer choices generate the result $\frac{1}{2}$—B and C. So try another number, say, $x = 2$. If $x = 2$, the correct answer should generate the value $\frac{2}{3}$. Now you eliminate B, and C must be correct.

**38.** (G) You can solve this problem using $S$ and $T$ as unknowns. Since $S$ is 150 percent of $T$, $S$ equals $1.5T$. Then the question asks you to express $\frac{T}{(S + T)}$ as a percent. Just substitute $1.5T$ for $S$: $\frac{T}{(1.5T + T)} = \frac{T}{2.5T} = \frac{1}{2.5}$ $= 40$ percent. If you don't like working with letters, then pick some numbers. Let $S$ be 10 and $T$ be 15. Then $\frac{T}{(S + T)} = \frac{15}{(10 + 15)} = \frac{10}{25} = 40\%$.

**39.** (C) No figure is provided, so sketch one:

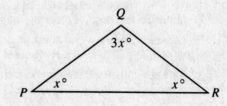

$$x + x + 3x = 180$$

$$5x = 180$$

$$x = 36$$

**40.** (B) Use a direct proportion:

$$\frac{b}{x} = \frac{d}{C}$$

Cross-multiply:

$$bC = dx$$

Divide by $b$:

$$C = \frac{dx}{b}$$

Or, you can assume numbers to test answer choices, a procedure you are familiar with by now.

## Social Studies Reading

**1.** (D) All of the first three factors are mentioned in the context of both mayoral and Presidential jobs. Therefore, *all of the above* is the best choice.

**2.** (G) The passage states, "Residents can reach city hall by picking up a telephone," conveying the impression of the *accessibility* of the mayor. This automatically disqualifies choice F, and choices H and J are not conveyed anywhere else in the passage.

**3.** (B) The passage is consistently *critical* about the role of mayors. A *laudatory* passage would praise the role of mayor; a *lugubrious* passage would be mournful; and an *ambivalent* passage would not express a clearly defined opinion.

**4.** (F) The passage consistently emphasizes the difficulties involved in "making an increasingly ungovernable city work." Therefore, *futility* is the best choice.

**5.** (D) The passage emphasizes that the mayor "works in closer physical proximity to constituents" and he is a "highly visible political figure ... spend(ing) a considerable amount of his time out in public." This makes D the best choice.

**6.** (H) The passage states that "the governor's office ... (is) relatively removed in both physical distance and citizen perception." This makes H the best choice.

**7.** (C) The passage maintains a critical view of the mayor's role throughout. Choice B is mentioned only incidentally and is not the main point of the passage; choice A is also only an incidental factor; and choice D is incorrect because a *vindication* would emphasize the positive over the negative.

**8.** (G) The passage's emphasis on the mayor's closeness to the people makes *ordinary* the best choice.

**9.** (D) The passage calls local government the "least mysterious level of government," making D the best choice.

**10.** (H) Only choice H offers something which is NOT conveyed by the passage; no mention is made about the problems of cities being handled by higher levels of government.

**11.** (A) The second paragraph tells how President Nixon revealed his secret plan in Vietnam as a fait accompli and how he asked what he saw as the "silent majority" of Americans to support his policy. No evidence can be found to support choices B and C, and citing the United States Constitution was used only as an accessory for Nixon to accomplish what is stated in choice A.

**12.** (J) No evidence can be found to support choices G and H; choice F is incorrect since Nixon was not urgently worried about those who were "silent." Nixon's derisive comments about the "minority" who were "mounting demonstrations in the street," along with his remark that only Americans could "defeat and humiliate" the United States, makes J the best choice.

**13.** (B) From the very first sentence of the passage, the author consistently emphasizes ways in which President Nixon was out of touch with public opinion with regard to the Vietnam War. Therefore, President Nixon was *presumptuous* in believing he could persuade the public to support his policy.

**14.** (H) The tone of this passage is consistently critical about the actions of President Nixon that are discussed. Neither optimism nor indifference is expressed anywhere in the passage.

**15.** (B) President Nixon's defensive attitude toward the "vocal minority" (the anti-war movement) and his implication that this group could "defeat and humiliate" the United States make B the best choice.

**16.** (F) None of the last three choices is stated or implied in the passage. Choice F is stated outright at the end of the passage.

**17.** (C) The correct answer is stated in the first paragraph of the passage.

**18.** (H) The passage, toward the beginning, states that Nixon "tried to achieve so much with so little understanding or support from the people." This sentiment is supported with the example of Nixon's "silent majority" speech. This makes H the best choice.

**19.** (A) The first statement of the passage conveys that Nixon was overly ambitious and that he carried out his plans without public support. All of these factors make his actions appear *audacious* or bold.

**20.** (H) The passage does not purport to be an objective, chronological summary; it is clearly an opinionated tirade against President Nixon's actions. Therefore, it would be logical for any further material to be written in the same point of view as the original material, making H the best choice.

**21.** (D) Monetarists advocate an inflation control policy that is tied directly to influencing the money supply. The *Federal Reserve Board* is the only government agency that could effect such a policy. The other three agencies are concerned with lawmaking, law enforcement, and foreign relations.

**22.** (H) Proponents of the cost-push theory advocate controlling inflation by constraining the demands of the trade unions. H is the only choice in agreement with this theory.

23. (B) If the government raises interest rates on loans to banks, banks in turn will raise lending rates to customers, making it harder for people to borrow. Growth in the money supply will thereby be curtailed.

24. (J) If trade unions did not exist, there would be no organization to articulate the demands of the workers. It is logical to assume that workers' wages would be lower under these circumstances.

25. (C) Without any organization to help them win wage increases, non-union workers will suffer during periods of inflation.

26. (J) Inflation is characterized by rising prices, which imply a fall in the value of a nation's currency.

27. (D) A country experiencing severe inflation would be likely to be beset by strikes since workers will inevitably be demanding higher wages to keep up with rising prices.

28. (F) Debtors (people paying back loans) are the ones most likely to benefit from inflation since the money they are paying back, which is set at a fixed amount, is actually *less* in value in relative terms than it was when the loan was taken.

29. (B) Indexing workers' wages to the rate of inflation is implemented primarily to help people cope with inflation and meet their basic needs. It is only a temporary solution, since increased wages will cause an increase in the money supply and yet more inflation.

30. (H) Social-learning theory suggests that people learn much of their behavior through watching what other people do and what happens to those people as a result.

31. (B) Constantinople (now called Istanbul), located on the Bosporus where Europe meets Asia, was the capital of the Eastern Roman (Byzantine) Empire.

32. (F) Monetarists believe that inflation is generated when the money supply is allowed to grow faster than the output of real goods and services.

33. (C) The relationship between the federal and state governments has evolved in a manner not anticipated by the Constitution. Today the federal government controls many state government policies and programs by issuing guidelines specifying how the states may spend the federal monies that make up a very large share of state budgets.

34. (H) Charlemagne, a ruler of Germanic descent, established a kingdom that eventually included much of modern France, West Germany, and northern Italy. He encouraged preservation of ancient Greco-Roman literature and art, but he was also a devout Christian and sought to protect the Church against its enemies. After his death his kingdom was divided among his sons.

35. (A) The growth of the suburbs after World War II has been attributed to a number of factors. Massive road-building programs made it easier to commute into the cities from the suburbs. The postwar "baby boom" families wanted more living space than was available in city apartments. Inexpensive city apartments were available, but federal mortgage policies instead influenced people to buy single-family suburban houses.

36. (F) During the Civil War era the Republican Party emerged as the dominant political party, while during the Great Depression of the 1930s the Democratic Party became dominant.

37. (D) The simultaneous occurrence of inflation and economic stagnation, or recession, is termed "stagflation." This condition afflicted many industrialized countries during the 1970s.

38. (H) In 1095, Pope Urban II appealed to the Christian rulers and knights of Europe to launch a Crusade to expel the Turkish Muslims from the Holy Land. The Crusade was immediately popular and the Pope also hoped it would divert the European rulers away from their ceaseless wars among themselves. The nobles and knights of Europe were attracted to the Crusade because of the opportunity it offered for adventure and for gaining wealth in the countries of the Near East.

39. (B) Hippocrates lived in ancient Greece and is credited with being the founder of the medical profession.

40. (J) Neo-Keynesian economists believe in extensive government regulation of the economy, including wage and price controls if necessary to control inflation without producing unemployment.

41. (C) A political party exists to wage successful election campaigns that bring control of important public offices.

42. (F) During the early years of World War I, President Woodrow Wilson struggled to maintain the neutrality of the United States. However, neutrality was difficult when German submarine attacks on Allied shipping began costing American lives. Following a particularly deadly series of such attacks in early 1917, Wilson asked Congress to declare war on Germany.

43. (B) The passage starts off by saying that "the notion of *obedience*" has far-reaching implications. This is the main point of the passage; all of the other choices are only peripheral factors.

44. (J) The author is clearly upset about the implications of Milgram's experiment; therefore the best answer choice is *concerned*.

45. (B) Milgram's experiment showed that two-thirds of his subjects obeyed the orders of their superiors even when they thought they were doing wrong. The author of the passage provides similar information, citing occurrences during the Second World War. All of this material shows that it is typical to blame the person who conceived the idea of the wrongdoing.

46. (J) The experiment was first and foremost a study of *human behavior*. None of the first three choices adequately characterizes what the experiment was about.

47. (A) The author of the passage makes no effort to deride or refute the findings of the experiment; therefore it can be concluded that he accepts the information as valid.

48. (H) The designer of a psychological experiment such as the one discussed would obviously want to make sure that the people he is observing are a normal, authentic representation of society. Otherwise the findings would not be regarded as accurate.

49. (D) The experiment was conducted primarily to test how readily people will carry out orders given by their superiors. The subjects' perception of increasingly severe shocks showed to what extent they were willing to obey orders given by the experimenter.

50. (H) While choices F, G, and J might have been *contributing* factors to this decision, the *primary* reason for separating teacher and learner had to be to ensure that the subject thought the ''learner'' was actually receiving shocks.

51. (C) This question is similar to questions 3 and 7. A main point of the experiment was to show that when human beings carry out the orders of their superiors, even when the actions are wrong, they are less likely to blame themselves for the wrongdoing and more likely to blame the one who told them to do it.

52. (G) The final paragraph conveys the message that this type of behavior is found in other places besides the laboratory, implying that it is universal in nature. No evidence can be found to support any of the other choices.

## Natural Sciences Reading

1. (B) Lasers emit coherent light; light is a form of radiant energy and part of the electromagnetic spectrum.

2. (J) As stated in the passage, a photon is released when an electron of an excited atom drops back to a low-energy state from a high-energy state. Both G and H may occur when a photon is released, but J is the source of the energy.

3. (B) An important characteristic of lasers is that excited atoms be exposed to only one wavelength. It is the stimulated emission of many photons at the same wavelength that forms the laser beam.

4. (H) The stimulated emissions that occur simultaneously form a laser beam composed of coherent light of one wavelength. The mirrors reflect light, causing a multiplying effect as more and more atoms are stimulated to emit light.

5. (D) The three parts of a laser are a medium (a solid, liquid, or gas), an energy source (such as a flash lamp), and a way of controlling the beam (mirrors).

6. (G) Only laser light is coherent; that is, its waves are in phase with one another. Under normal circumstances, light waves are not in phase with one another and are therefore incoherent.

7. (A) The first lasers were ruby lasers. Rubies and other crystals are solids. Today, solids, liquids, and gases are media for lasers.

8. (H) An advantage of laser welding is the ability to heat one area while leaving the surrounding area cool; heat is not conducted through the metal, thereby making the operation easier to contain.

9. (A) Precision would be more important than the size, medium, or power of the laser because of the delicate nature of microsurgery.

10. (H) Hormones are the chemicals secreted by the endocrine or ductless glands.

11. (D) Adrenalin is secreted by the adrenal cortex; all the other hormones, as stated in the passage, are secretions of the pituitary.

12. (G) The gonadotropic hormone influences the development of the reproductive organs; thus it would most affect the onset of sexual maturity. Sex hormones are not effective until the sex organs themselves are developed.

13. (C) According to the passage, a thyroid dwarf has less than normal intelligence. It can be inferred that the secretions of the thyroid affect intelligence.

14. (G) As stated in the passage, giantism results if there is an oversecretion of growth hormone during the growing years.

15. (D) Although some leukemia patients have been treated with ACTH, a secretion of the adrenals, it is not a cure.

16. (J) According to the passage, lactogenic hormone, a secretion of the anterior lobe of the pituitary, stimulates the secretion of milk in the mammary glands. Without enough hormone, a cow would probably not produce milk.

17. (A) According to the passage, water balance in the body is controlled by a hormone secreted by the adrenal glands. The pituitary gland does not have this function. It does secrete pitressin, but this hormone regulates the water in the blood and blood pressure.

18. (J) The hormones of all the endocrine or ductless glands are released directly into the blood vessels; the glands lack any specialized ducts for the transport of hormones.

19. (D) The atomic weight of an element is calculated by adding the number of protons and neutrons. The electrons, because of their small size and insignificant weight, are not generally factored in the atomic weight.

20. (J) Most life processes require the utilization of oxygen; it is eliminated only in excess.

21. (A) According to the First Law of Thermodynamics, energy is neither created nor destroyed but is transformed from one type to another. When energy changes form, according to the Second Law of Thermodynamics, some energy is always dispersed or lost. Thus the transformation is not 100-percent efficient.

22. (G) Each is a named constellation of the recognized 88 constellations in the sky.

23. (B) A polar molecule has a positive charge at one end and a negative charge at the opposite end.

24. (F) Alcohol is one of a very few substances very quickly absorbed after being ingested. The other substances require digestion.

25. (C) During sound production the vibratory motion of the molecules of the transmitting medium is in the same direction as the traveling wave front. The waves are therefore longitudinal.

26. (F) Isotopes are forms of the same element that differ only in neutron number. The atomic number represents the number of protons in the atom. Since atoms are electrically neutral, the number of electrons equals the number of protons in the atom. The atomic weight of an atom is equal to the sum of protons and neutrons. Therefore, the correct answer is F.

27. (D) Bodies of water are slower than land in absorbing heat, but they are also slower than land in giving heat up.

28. (F) The major function of the red blood corpuscles is to carry oxygen to various parts of the body.

29. (C) When a sample of water is placed in an electrical circuit, the water is said to be electrolyzed. The action of the electricity converts water to hydrogen ($H_2$) and oxygen ($O_2$). These two molecules can then be reconverted to water.

30. (F) Since the horizontal velocities of the man, the ball, and the car were the same, the man could not detect the horizontal motion of the ball with respect to the earth's surface. An observer outside of the boxcar would see the ball fall along a typical trajectory.

31. (D) The most common form of pollination of grasses is caused by the wind.

32. (J) The potential difference is the work required to move a test charge from point $A$ to $B$ divided by the magnitude of the test charge.

$V$     = 2 joule/20 coulomb

$V$     = 0.1 joule/coulomb

one volt = one joule/coulomb

$V$     = $1 \times 10^{-1}$ volt

33. (B) This question concerns a type of behavior characteristic of colloidal solutions. These are not true solutions but dispersions of very fine particles in a liquid so that the liquid appears clear but in actuality contains solid material. The effect described in the question is called the Tyndall effect.

34. (H) Since the floodwaters passing them were racing from northeast to southwest, the "islands" most likely became tapered to a point at their northeast, or upstream, ends.

35. (C) In the valleys of western Montana, where the glacial meltwaters backed up to form Ice Age Lake Missoula, you would expect to find "beach" lines on the mountain slopes. No flood channels were cut there by moving water, nor was a delta deposited.

36. (G) Since the floodwaters flowed downhill from northeast to southwest, you can infer that eastern Washington generally tilts downhill from northeast to southwest.

37. (B) Sediment tends to settle out of rivers when they reach level ground and lose velocity. Since the sediment in the Columbia was deposited near the river's mouth, you can infer that the river slows down as it crosses level country near the coast.

38. (J) The great Coulee City waterfall was formed where the floodwaters dropped over a cliff of soft sandstone. The erosion that occurred as the rapidly moving water undermined the cliff face would most likely cause the waterfall to "retreat" upstream.

39. (C) If all four waterfalls were created by the overflow of water from the same height, it is extremely unlikely that they could have been formed at different times. None of the other choices would prove anything about when the waterfalls were formed.

40. (F) Sediment tends not to settle out of water that is moving very fast. Since the floodwaters "raced" across the Washington plateau, it is unlikely that they dropped much sediment there.

41. (D) As sediment settles out of water, the heavier portions, such as rocks and gravel, are deposited first. The lighter portions, such as fine silt, are deposited last.

42. (H) Since the only places in the scablands that still retain their topsoil are the "islands," these are most likely the only areas suitable for agriculture.

43. (D) When an Na atom gives up the single electron in its outermost shell, the shell just beneath becomes the new outermost shell. Since this shell is complete, the Na atom now has the electron configuration of a noble gas.

44. (G) When an Na atom gives up the single electron in its outermost shell, it then has one more proton than it has electrons. Consequently, it becomes a positively charged ion.

45. (D) When a Cl atom adds an electron to the seven atoms already in its outermost shell, it completes that shell. Consequently, it thus assumes the electron configuration of a noble gas.

46. (H) When a Cl atom adds an electron to its outermost shell, it then has one more electron than it has protons. Consequently, it becomes a negatively charged ion.

47. (C) It takes a certain amount of energy for one atom to "free" an electron from the outermost shell of another. It therefore stands to reason that it takes more energy to free two electrons, and still more to free three. This accounts for the fact that ionic bonds involving the transfer of three or more electrons are relatively rare.

**48.** (F) Atoms that form ionic bonds are those that gain or lose electrons easily one from the other since they have very different electronegativities. Atoms that form covalent bonds, however, do not easily lose or gain electrons one from the other. You may conclude from this that these atoms most likely have similar electronegativities.

**49.** (C) The two shared electron pairs make up a double covalent bond.

**50.** (G) Each shared electron pair is a single covalent bond.

**51.** (D) The three shared electron pairs make up a triple covalent bond.

**52.** (J) The number of electrons usually required to complete an electron shell is eight. This principle is the basis for the so-called "octet rule."

# Practice Test 2

# ANSWER SHEET. PRACTICE TEST 2

## English Usage

1 Ⓐ Ⓑ Ⓒ Ⓓ  12 Ⓕ Ⓖ Ⓗ Ⓙ  23 Ⓐ Ⓑ Ⓒ Ⓓ  34 Ⓕ Ⓖ Ⓗ Ⓙ  45 Ⓐ Ⓑ Ⓒ Ⓓ  56 Ⓕ Ⓖ Ⓗ Ⓙ  67 Ⓐ Ⓑ Ⓒ Ⓓ
2 Ⓕ Ⓖ Ⓗ Ⓙ  13 Ⓐ Ⓑ Ⓒ Ⓓ  24 Ⓕ Ⓖ Ⓗ Ⓙ  35 Ⓐ Ⓑ Ⓒ Ⓓ  46 Ⓕ Ⓖ Ⓗ Ⓙ  57 Ⓐ Ⓑ Ⓒ Ⓓ  68 Ⓕ Ⓖ Ⓗ Ⓙ
3 Ⓐ Ⓑ Ⓒ Ⓓ  14 Ⓕ Ⓖ Ⓗ Ⓙ  25 Ⓐ Ⓑ Ⓒ Ⓓ  36 Ⓕ Ⓖ Ⓗ Ⓙ  47 Ⓐ Ⓑ Ⓒ Ⓓ  58 Ⓕ Ⓖ Ⓗ Ⓙ  69 Ⓐ Ⓑ Ⓒ Ⓓ
4 Ⓕ Ⓖ Ⓗ Ⓙ  15 Ⓐ Ⓑ Ⓒ Ⓓ  26 Ⓕ Ⓖ Ⓗ Ⓙ  37 Ⓐ Ⓑ Ⓒ Ⓓ  48 Ⓕ Ⓖ Ⓗ Ⓙ  59 Ⓐ Ⓑ Ⓒ Ⓓ  70 Ⓕ Ⓖ Ⓗ Ⓙ
5 Ⓐ Ⓑ Ⓒ Ⓓ  16 Ⓕ Ⓖ Ⓗ Ⓙ  27 Ⓐ Ⓑ Ⓒ Ⓓ  38 Ⓕ Ⓖ Ⓗ Ⓙ  49 Ⓐ Ⓑ Ⓒ Ⓓ  60 Ⓕ Ⓖ Ⓗ Ⓙ  71 Ⓐ Ⓑ Ⓒ Ⓓ
6 Ⓕ Ⓖ Ⓗ Ⓙ  17 Ⓐ Ⓑ Ⓒ Ⓓ  28 Ⓕ Ⓖ Ⓗ Ⓙ  39 Ⓐ Ⓑ Ⓒ Ⓓ  50 Ⓕ Ⓖ Ⓗ Ⓙ  61 Ⓐ Ⓑ Ⓒ Ⓓ  72 Ⓕ Ⓖ Ⓗ Ⓙ
7 Ⓐ Ⓑ Ⓒ Ⓓ  18 Ⓕ Ⓖ Ⓗ Ⓙ  29 Ⓐ Ⓑ Ⓒ Ⓓ  40 Ⓕ Ⓖ Ⓗ Ⓙ  51 Ⓐ Ⓑ Ⓒ Ⓓ  62 Ⓕ Ⓖ Ⓗ Ⓙ  73 Ⓐ Ⓑ Ⓒ Ⓓ
8 Ⓕ Ⓖ Ⓗ Ⓙ  19 Ⓐ Ⓑ Ⓒ Ⓓ  30 Ⓕ Ⓖ Ⓗ Ⓙ  41 Ⓐ Ⓑ Ⓒ Ⓓ  52 Ⓕ Ⓖ Ⓗ Ⓙ  63 Ⓐ Ⓑ Ⓒ Ⓓ  74 Ⓕ Ⓖ Ⓗ Ⓙ
9 Ⓐ Ⓑ Ⓒ Ⓓ  20 Ⓕ Ⓖ Ⓗ Ⓙ  31 Ⓐ Ⓑ Ⓒ Ⓓ  42 Ⓕ Ⓖ Ⓗ Ⓙ  53 Ⓐ Ⓑ Ⓒ Ⓓ  64 Ⓕ Ⓖ Ⓗ Ⓙ  75 Ⓐ Ⓑ Ⓒ Ⓓ
10 Ⓕ Ⓖ Ⓗ Ⓙ  21 Ⓐ Ⓑ Ⓒ Ⓓ  32 Ⓕ Ⓖ Ⓗ Ⓙ  43 Ⓐ Ⓑ Ⓒ Ⓓ  54 Ⓕ Ⓖ Ⓗ Ⓙ  65 Ⓐ Ⓑ Ⓒ Ⓓ
11 Ⓐ Ⓑ Ⓒ Ⓓ  22 Ⓕ Ⓖ Ⓗ Ⓙ  33 Ⓐ Ⓑ Ⓒ Ⓓ  44 Ⓕ Ⓖ Ⓗ Ⓙ  55 Ⓐ Ⓑ Ⓒ Ⓓ  66 Ⓕ Ⓖ Ⓗ Ⓙ

## Mathematics Usage

1 Ⓐ Ⓑ Ⓒ Ⓓ Ⓔ  7 Ⓐ Ⓑ Ⓒ Ⓓ Ⓔ  13 Ⓐ Ⓑ Ⓒ Ⓓ Ⓔ  19 Ⓐ Ⓑ Ⓒ Ⓓ Ⓔ  25 Ⓐ Ⓑ Ⓒ Ⓓ Ⓔ  31 Ⓐ Ⓑ Ⓒ Ⓓ Ⓔ  37 Ⓐ Ⓑ Ⓒ Ⓓ Ⓔ
2 Ⓕ Ⓖ Ⓗ Ⓙ Ⓚ  8 Ⓕ Ⓖ Ⓗ Ⓙ Ⓚ  14 Ⓕ Ⓖ Ⓗ Ⓙ Ⓚ  20 Ⓕ Ⓖ Ⓗ Ⓙ Ⓚ  26 Ⓕ Ⓖ Ⓗ Ⓙ Ⓚ  32 Ⓕ Ⓖ Ⓗ Ⓙ Ⓚ  38 Ⓕ Ⓖ Ⓗ Ⓙ Ⓚ
3 Ⓐ Ⓑ Ⓒ Ⓓ Ⓔ  9 Ⓐ Ⓑ Ⓒ Ⓓ Ⓔ  15 Ⓐ Ⓑ Ⓒ Ⓓ Ⓔ  21 Ⓐ Ⓑ Ⓒ Ⓓ Ⓔ  27 Ⓐ Ⓑ Ⓒ Ⓓ Ⓔ  33 Ⓐ Ⓑ Ⓒ Ⓓ Ⓔ  39 Ⓐ Ⓑ Ⓒ Ⓓ Ⓔ
4 Ⓕ Ⓖ Ⓗ Ⓙ Ⓚ  10 Ⓕ Ⓖ Ⓗ Ⓙ Ⓚ  16 Ⓕ Ⓖ Ⓗ Ⓙ Ⓚ  22 Ⓕ Ⓖ Ⓗ Ⓙ Ⓚ  28 Ⓕ Ⓖ Ⓗ Ⓙ Ⓚ  34 Ⓕ Ⓖ Ⓗ Ⓙ Ⓚ  40 Ⓕ Ⓖ Ⓗ Ⓙ Ⓚ
5 Ⓐ Ⓑ Ⓒ Ⓓ Ⓔ  11 Ⓐ Ⓑ Ⓒ Ⓓ Ⓔ  17 Ⓐ Ⓑ Ⓒ Ⓓ Ⓔ  23 Ⓐ Ⓑ Ⓒ Ⓓ Ⓔ  29 Ⓐ Ⓑ Ⓒ Ⓓ Ⓔ  35 Ⓐ Ⓑ Ⓒ Ⓓ Ⓔ
6 Ⓕ Ⓖ Ⓗ Ⓙ Ⓚ  12 Ⓕ Ⓖ Ⓗ Ⓙ Ⓚ  18 Ⓕ Ⓖ Ⓗ Ⓙ Ⓚ  24 Ⓕ Ⓖ Ⓗ Ⓙ Ⓚ  30 Ⓕ Ⓖ Ⓗ Ⓙ Ⓚ  36 Ⓕ Ⓖ Ⓗ Ⓙ Ⓚ

## Social Studies Reading

1 Ⓐ Ⓑ Ⓒ Ⓓ  8 Ⓕ Ⓖ Ⓗ Ⓙ  15 Ⓐ Ⓑ Ⓒ Ⓓ  22 Ⓕ Ⓖ Ⓗ Ⓙ  29 Ⓐ Ⓑ Ⓒ Ⓓ  36 Ⓕ Ⓖ Ⓗ Ⓙ  43 Ⓐ Ⓑ Ⓒ Ⓓ  50 Ⓕ Ⓖ Ⓗ Ⓙ
2 Ⓕ Ⓖ Ⓗ Ⓙ  9 Ⓐ Ⓑ Ⓒ Ⓓ  16 Ⓕ Ⓖ Ⓗ Ⓙ  23 Ⓐ Ⓑ Ⓒ Ⓓ  30 Ⓕ Ⓖ Ⓗ Ⓙ  37 Ⓐ Ⓑ Ⓒ Ⓓ  44 Ⓕ Ⓖ Ⓗ Ⓙ  51 Ⓐ Ⓑ Ⓒ Ⓓ
3 Ⓐ Ⓑ Ⓒ Ⓓ  10 Ⓕ Ⓖ Ⓗ Ⓙ  17 Ⓐ Ⓑ Ⓒ Ⓓ  24 Ⓕ Ⓖ Ⓗ Ⓙ  31 Ⓐ Ⓑ Ⓒ Ⓓ  38 Ⓕ Ⓖ Ⓗ Ⓙ  45 Ⓐ Ⓑ Ⓒ Ⓓ  52 Ⓕ Ⓖ Ⓗ Ⓙ
4 Ⓕ Ⓖ Ⓗ Ⓙ  11 Ⓐ Ⓑ Ⓒ Ⓓ  18 Ⓕ Ⓖ Ⓗ Ⓙ  25 Ⓐ Ⓑ Ⓒ Ⓓ  32 Ⓕ Ⓖ Ⓗ Ⓙ  39 Ⓐ Ⓑ Ⓒ Ⓓ  46 Ⓕ Ⓖ Ⓗ Ⓙ
5 Ⓐ Ⓑ Ⓒ Ⓓ  12 Ⓕ Ⓖ Ⓗ Ⓙ  19 Ⓐ Ⓑ Ⓒ Ⓓ  26 Ⓕ Ⓖ Ⓗ Ⓙ  33 Ⓐ Ⓑ Ⓒ Ⓓ  40 Ⓕ Ⓖ Ⓗ Ⓙ  47 Ⓐ Ⓑ Ⓒ Ⓓ
6 Ⓕ Ⓖ Ⓗ Ⓙ  13 Ⓐ Ⓑ Ⓒ Ⓓ  20 Ⓕ Ⓖ Ⓗ Ⓙ  27 Ⓐ Ⓑ Ⓒ Ⓓ  34 Ⓕ Ⓖ Ⓗ Ⓙ  41 Ⓐ Ⓑ Ⓒ Ⓓ  48 Ⓕ Ⓖ Ⓗ Ⓙ
7 Ⓐ Ⓑ Ⓒ Ⓓ  14 Ⓕ Ⓖ Ⓗ Ⓙ  21 Ⓐ Ⓑ Ⓒ Ⓓ  28 Ⓕ Ⓖ Ⓗ Ⓙ  35 Ⓐ Ⓑ Ⓒ Ⓓ  42 Ⓕ Ⓖ Ⓗ Ⓙ  49 Ⓐ Ⓑ Ⓒ Ⓓ

## Natural Sciences Reading

1 Ⓐ Ⓑ Ⓒ Ⓓ  8 Ⓕ Ⓖ Ⓗ Ⓙ  15 Ⓐ Ⓑ Ⓒ Ⓓ  22 Ⓕ Ⓖ Ⓗ Ⓙ  29 Ⓐ Ⓑ Ⓒ Ⓓ  36 Ⓕ Ⓖ Ⓗ Ⓙ  43 Ⓐ Ⓑ Ⓒ Ⓓ  50 Ⓕ Ⓖ Ⓗ Ⓙ
2 Ⓕ Ⓖ Ⓗ Ⓙ  9 Ⓐ Ⓑ Ⓒ Ⓓ  16 Ⓕ Ⓖ Ⓗ Ⓙ  23 Ⓐ Ⓑ Ⓒ Ⓓ  30 Ⓕ Ⓖ Ⓗ Ⓙ  37 Ⓐ Ⓑ Ⓒ Ⓓ  44 Ⓕ Ⓖ Ⓗ Ⓙ  51 Ⓐ Ⓑ Ⓒ Ⓓ
3 Ⓐ Ⓑ Ⓒ Ⓓ  10 Ⓕ Ⓖ Ⓗ Ⓙ  17 Ⓐ Ⓑ Ⓒ Ⓓ  24 Ⓕ Ⓖ Ⓗ Ⓙ  31 Ⓐ Ⓑ Ⓒ Ⓓ  38 Ⓕ Ⓖ Ⓗ Ⓙ  45 Ⓐ Ⓑ Ⓒ Ⓓ  52 Ⓕ Ⓖ Ⓗ Ⓙ
4 Ⓕ Ⓖ Ⓗ Ⓙ  11 Ⓐ Ⓑ Ⓒ Ⓓ  18 Ⓕ Ⓖ Ⓗ Ⓙ  25 Ⓐ Ⓑ Ⓒ Ⓓ  32 Ⓕ Ⓖ Ⓗ Ⓙ  39 Ⓐ Ⓑ Ⓒ Ⓓ  46 Ⓕ Ⓖ Ⓗ Ⓙ
5 Ⓐ Ⓑ Ⓒ Ⓓ  12 Ⓕ Ⓖ Ⓗ Ⓙ  19 Ⓐ Ⓑ Ⓒ Ⓓ  26 Ⓕ Ⓖ Ⓗ Ⓙ  33 Ⓐ Ⓑ Ⓒ Ⓓ  40 Ⓕ Ⓖ Ⓗ Ⓙ  47 Ⓐ Ⓑ Ⓒ Ⓓ
6 Ⓕ Ⓖ Ⓗ Ⓙ  13 Ⓐ Ⓑ Ⓒ Ⓓ  20 Ⓕ Ⓖ Ⓗ Ⓙ  27 Ⓐ Ⓑ Ⓒ Ⓓ  34 Ⓕ Ⓖ Ⓗ Ⓙ  41 Ⓐ Ⓑ Ⓒ Ⓓ  48 Ⓕ Ⓖ Ⓗ Ⓙ
7 Ⓐ Ⓑ Ⓒ Ⓓ  14 Ⓕ Ⓖ Ⓗ Ⓙ  21 Ⓐ Ⓑ Ⓒ Ⓓ  28 Ⓕ Ⓖ Ⓗ Ⓙ  35 Ⓐ Ⓑ Ⓒ Ⓓ  42 Ⓕ Ⓖ Ⓗ Ⓙ  49 Ⓐ Ⓑ Ⓒ Ⓓ

# TEST 1.  ENGLISH USAGE

*40 Minutes—75 Questions*

**DIRECTIONS:** In the reading selections below, certain parts of the sentences have been underlined and numbered. In the right-hand column, you will find different ways of writing each underlined part. Choose the one that best expresses the idea and uses standard written English. If you think the original version is the best, choose "NO CHANGE." The answers to many questions depend upon material that follows the underlined part. So be sure that you have read far enough ahead before you select your answer choice.

---

### Passage 1

The challenge <u>beginning to make</u> timely progress
                  1
toward removing the threat of nuclear war is today the

most important challenge in international relations.

Three general principles guide our defense and negotiat-

ing policies toward such a goal, principles based on the

technical realities of nuclear war.

First, nuclear weapons are <u>fundamentally different</u>
                                              2
<u>than</u> non-nuclear weapons.  These are weapons of mass

destruction, and they have a long and deadly radioactive

<u>memory, moreover</u> the unknowns of nuclear conflict
      3
dwarf the predictable consequences.  The number of

deaths resulting from injuries and the unavailability of

medical care and the economic damage <u>as a result from</u>
                                                      4
disruption and disorganization <u>would be even more</u>
                                              5
<u>devastating than</u> the direct loss of life and property.

Nuclear war <u>could have</u> no winners.
                    6
Second, the sole purpose of nuclear weapons must

be to deter nuclear <u>war, it is</u> neither a substitute for
                          7
maintaining adequate conventional military forces to

1. **A.** NO CHANGE
   **B.** to begin making
   **C.** to begin the making of
   **D.** of beginning the making of

2. **F.** NO CHANGE
   **G.** different than fundamentally
   **H.** different from fundamentally
   **J.** fundamentally different from

3. **A.** NO CHANGE
   **B.** memory.  Moreover,
   **C.** memory moreover,
   **D.** memory.  Since

4. **F.** NO CHANGE
   **G.** as a result to
   **H.** resulting from
   **J.** with a result of

5. **A.** NO CHANGE
   **B.** is even more devastating than
   **C.** are even more devastating as
   **D.** might be more devastating even as

6. **F.** NO CHANGE
   **G.** can't have no
   **H.** hasn't no
   **J.** can have no

7. **A.** NO CHANGE
   **B.** war.  They are
   **C.** war they are
   **D.** war; it is

GO ON TO THE NEXT PAGE →

meet vital national security goals <u>but</u> an effective defense

against the almost total mutual annihilation and devasta-

tion that would result from a full-scale nuclear war.

<u>Third,</u> arms control is an essential part of our national

security.  Thus far, we have had no effective controls on

offensive nuclear weaponry, and it is clear that each step

forward in the arms race toward more and improved

weapons <u>has made less</u> our security.  Before deploying

additional weapons, <u>it will be necessary developing</u> a

coherent arms control strategy.

### Passage 2

The founders of the Republic <u>viewing their</u> revolu-

tion primarily in political terms <u>rather as in</u> economic

terms. Therefore they viewed the kind of education

needed for the new Republic largely in political terms

rather than <u>as a means to</u> academic excellence or

individual self-fulfillment.  <u>Talking about</u> education

as a bulwark for liberty, equality, popular consent,

and devotion to the public <u>good goals</u> which

<u>took precedence over</u> the uses of knowledge for self-

improvement or occupational preparation.  Over and

over again, the Revolutionary generation, both liberal

8. **F.** NO CHANGE
   **G.** and
   **H.** nor
   **J.** including

9. **A.** NO CHANGE
   **B.** (Do NOT begin a new paragraph.) Third
   **C.** (Begin a new paragraph.) Third
   **D.** (Begin a new paragraph.) Third,

10. **F.** NO CHANGE
    **G.** has lessened
    **H.** have lessened
    **J.** have made less of

11. **A.** NO CHANGE
    **B.** the development will be necessary of
    **C.** it will be necessary to develop
    **D.** it will be necessarily developed,

12. **F.** NO CHANGE
    **G.** having viewed its
    **H.** viewed its
    **J.** viewed their

13. **A.** NO CHANGE
    **B.** rather than in
    **C.** but in
    **D.** to the contrary of

14. **F.** NO CHANGE
    **G.** as a means or a way to
    **H.** to
    **J.** as

15. **A.** NO CHANGE
    **B.** Talking
    **C.** With the talking about
    **D.** They talked about

16. **F.** NO CHANGE
    **G.** good.  Goals
    **H.** good, goals
    **J.** good; goals are

17. **A.** NO CHANGE
    **B.** precede
    **C.** precede over
    **D.** took precedence on

GO ON TO THE NEXT PAGE

and conservative in outlook— assert their faith that the

welfare of the Republic rested upon an educated citizenry.

All agreed that the principal ingredients of a civic

education was literacy and inculcation of patriotic and

moral virtues some others added the study of history and

the study of the principles of the republican government

itself.  The founders, as was the case with almost all their

successors, were long on exhortation and rhetoric re-

garding the value of civic education; since they left it to

the textbook writers to distill the essence of those values

for school children.  Texts in American history and

government appeared as early as the 1790s.  The text-

book writers turned out being very largely of conserva-

tive persuasion, more likely Federalist in outlook than

Jeffersonian, and universally almost agreed that political

virtue must rest upon moral and religious precepts.

In the first half of the Republic, civic education

in the schools emphasized the inculcation of civic

values, put less emphasis on political knowledge, and

no attempt to develop political skills.  This was left to the

local parties, the town meetings, the churches, coffee

houses, and ale houses where men gathered to talk.

18. F. NO CHANGE
    G. outlook, asserted its
    H. outlook; asserted its
    J. outlook asserts their

19. A. NO CHANGE
    B. being
    C. were
    D. were like

20. F. NO CHANGE
    G. virtues—some
    H. virtues, some
    J. virtues; some

21. A. NO CHANGE
    B. education.  And
    C. education.  Since
    D. education.  But

22. F. NO CHANGE
    G. turned out to be
    H. turning out to be
    J. having turned out to be

23. A. NO CHANGE
    B. almost, agreed universally
    C. almost universally agreed
    D. almost universally, agreed

24. F. NO CHANGE
    G. made no attempt to develop
    H. none at all on the development of
    J. none was put at all on developing

GO ON TO THE NEXT PAGE

**(1)**

The contribution of women on the home front
25

during World War I was varied.  It included a large range

of activities from knitting and the operation of drill
26

presses and engaged a cross section of the female popula-

tion from housewives to society girls.  World War I

marked the first time in the history of the United States
27

that a systematic effort was made, through organizations

like the League for Women's Service, to utilize the
28

capabilities of women in all regions of the country.

**(2)**

While much of this volunteer work falls within the
29

established bounds of women's club work, many women

entered areas of industrial work previously reserved by
30

for the male population.  Women put on the uniforms of

elevator operators, streetcar conductors, postmen and

industrial workers.  However, they were employed in
31

aircraft and munitions plants as well as in shipbuilding

yards and steel mills.

**(3)**

Much of the work fell into the traditional realm of

volunteer activity knitting garments for the boys over-
32

seas, canning for Uncle Sam, planting Victory gardens,

25.  A.  NO CHANGE
     B.  Womens' contribution
     C.  The contribution of woman
     D.  Womans' contribution

26.  F.  NO CHANGE
     G.  from knitting with the operation of
     H.  from knitting and operating
     J.  from knitting to operating

27.  A.  NO CHANGE
     B.  has marked the first time
     C.  is the first time it is marked
     D.  was marked, the first time

28.  F.  NO CHANGE
     G.  being able to utilize
     H.  utilizing
     J.  and utilize

29.  A.  NO CHANGE
     B.  fell within
     C.  having fallen within
     D.  fell in

30.  F.  NO CHANGE
     G.  having previously been reserved
     H.  previously reserved
     J.  reserved previous to then

31.  A.  NO CHANGE
     B.  workers.  They were employed
     C.  workers, but they were employed
     D.  workers.  Employing themselves

32.  F.  NO CHANGE
     G.  activity: to knit
     H.  activity: knitting
     J.  activity, to knit

GO ON TO THE NEXT PAGE

etc. Through these activities, every homemaker could

demonstrate their patriotism while still fulfilling her role
___33___

as homemaker. Women with more time volunteered to

hostess at canteens; make bandages, and organize food
___34___

and clothing drives. The Women's Land Army, dressed

in bloomer uniforms and armed with such slogans as

"The Woman with the Hoe Must Defend the Man with

the Musket" was dispatched to assist farmers in process-
___35___

ing crops.

<br>

**(4)**

Women performed ably during the war and

laid the foundation for more specialized jobs, increased
___36___

wages, better working conditions, and a more competi-

tive job status in the labor market.

<br>

*Passage 4*

In the year 982, Eric the Red was banished from

Iceland for a period of three years. About 900, a

Norwegian named Gunnbiorn has been blown off his
___38___

course on the way from his own country to Iceland, and

he discovered some islands to the west. Eric directed his

course there, reached the coast of Greenland, and,

rounding its southernmost point, discovering the more
___39___

habitable parts of the island. When the period of his

exile was over; he returns to Iceland with such flattering
___40___

<br>

33. **A.** NO CHANGE
    **B.** be demonstrating
    **C.** have demonstrated their
    **D.** demonstrate her

34. **F.** NO CHANGE
    **G.** canteens make
    **H.** canteens, make
    **J.** canteens making

35. **A.** NO CHANGE
    **B.** musket—was dispatched
    **C.** musket," were dispatched
    **D.** musket," was dispatched

36. **F.** NO CHANGE
    **G.** the foundation was laid
    **H.** the foundation was lain
    **J.** laying the foundation

37. Which of the following represents the most logical
sequence for the paragraphs?
    **A.** 1, 4, 3, 2
    **B.** 1, 3, 4, 2
    **C.** 1, 3, 2, 4
    **D.** 2, 4, 3, 1

38. **F.** NO CHANGE
    **G.** was
    **H.** had been
    **J.** is

39. **A.** NO CHANGE
    **B.** point, discovered
    **C.** point, discovers
    **D.** point with the discovery of

40. **F.** NO CHANGE
    **G.** over, he having returned
    **H.** over he, returning
    **J.** over, he returned

GO ON TO THE NEXT PAGE

accounts of the new land that <u>intended colonists</u> began
<sub>41</sub>

flocking there.  Only 14 actually arrived; the rest

<u>having been forced to return or lost.</u>  More soon followed,
<sub>42</sub>

<u>and therefore</u> two main settlements were formed.
<sub>43</sub>

    In the summer of 999 Leif voyaged to Norway, where

he <u>had spent</u> the following winter with King Olaf.
<sub>44</sub>

On his departure he was commissioned by the king

<u>for carrying</u> Christianity to Greenland. It is possibly on
<sub>45</sub>

this return voyage to Greenland that he discovered

America.

### Passage 5

    Following the end of World War II, substantial

changes <u>undertaken</u> in Japan to liberate the individual
<sub>46</sub>

from authoritarian restraints.  The new democratic value

system was <u>acceptable by</u> many teachers, students, intel-
<sub>47</sub>

lectuals, and old <u>liberals, and it</u> was not immediately
<sub>48</sub>

embraced by the society as a whole.  Japanese traditions

were dominated by group values, and notions of personal

freedom and individual rights <u>being</u> unfamiliar.
<sub>49</sub>

---

**41.** **A.** NO CHANGE
    **B.** those intended as colonists
    **C.** intending colonists
    **D.** people who wished to become colonists

**42.** **F.** NO CHANGE
    **G.** being lost or having been forced to return
    **H.** were lost or forced to return
    **J.** but the rest were lost or forced to return

**43.** **A.** NO CHANGE
    **B.** so therefore
    **C.** and, so,
    **D.** and

**44.** **F.** NO CHANGE
    **G.** having spent
    **H.** spending
    **J.** spent

**45.** **A.** NO CHANGE
    **B.** to carry
    **C.** with the carrying of
    **D.** and carry

**46.** **F.** NO CHANGE
    **G.** will be undertaken
    **H.** have been undertaken
    **J.** were undertaken

**47.** **A.** NO CHANGE
    **B.** accepted by
    **C.** excepted by
    **D.** excepted to

**48.** **F.** NO CHANGE
    **G.** liberals, since
    **H.** liberals; but
    **J.** liberals; consequently

**49.** **A.** NO CHANGE
    **B.** were
    **C.** was
    **D.** are

GO ON TO THE NEXT PAGE

Today, the triumph of democratic processes
50

is clear evident in the widespread participation of the
51

Japanese in social and political life, furthermore, there is
52

no universally accepted and stable value system,
53

values being constantly modified by strong infusions of

Western ideas.  School textbooks expound democratic

principles, and so emphasizing equality over hierarchy
54

and rationalism over tradition; but in practice these

values are often sometimes distorted, particularly by the
55

youth that translated the individualistic and humanistic
56

goals of democracy into egoistic and materialistic ones.

## Passage 6

From the beginning, humankind always has shared
57

some sort of link with the animal world.  The earliest

and most primitive was surely that of hunter and prey—

with humans possibly playing the fatal role of victim.

Later, of course, humans reversed the roles as they

became more skillful and intelligenter.  The later domes-
58

50. **F.** NO CHANGE
    **G.** (Do NOT begin a new paragraph) Today the triumph,
    **H.** (Begin a new paragraph) Today, the triumph,
    **J.** (Do NOT begin a new paragraph) Today, owing to the fact that

51. **A.** NO CHANGE
    **B.** is clearly
    **C.** is clear and also
    **D.** are clearly

52. **F.** NO CHANGE
    **G.** life,
    **H.** life; yet
    **J.** life, yet

53. **A.** NO CHANGE
    **B.** system with that
    **C.** system.  Values are
    **D.** system, values are

54. **F.** NO CHANGE
    **G.** principles, emphasizing
    **H.** principles and the emphasis of
    **J.** principles with the emphasis that

55. **A.** NO CHANGE
    **B.** had been misinterpreted and distorted often
    **C.** often misinterpreted and distorted
    **D.** are often misinterpreted and distorted

56. **F.** NO CHANGE
    **G.** that translate
    **H.** who translate
    **J.** translate

57. **A.** NO CHANGE
    **B.** have always shared
    **C.** is always sharing
    **D.** has always shared

58. **F.** NO CHANGE
    **G.** so intelligent
    **H.** and more intelligent
    **J.** but intelligent

GO ON TO THE NEXT PAGE

tication of certain animals and also the discovery of
59

agriculture, made for a more settled and stable existence

and was an essential step in the not-so-orderly process of

becoming civilized.  However, the intellectual distance

between regarding an animal as the source of dinner or

of material comfort and to consider them a worthy
60

subject for study is considerable.

Not until Aristotle did the animal world become a

subject for serious scientific study.  Although he seem-
61

ingly writes on every subject, Aristotle's work in zoology
62

—studying animals as animals—is considered his most

successful.  He seemed to have had a natural affinity for

and curiosity about the living creatures of the world, and

he took special interest in marine life.

Aristotle's zoological writings reveal him to be a

remarkably astute observer of the natural world,

wedding his observations to what might be called specu-
63

lative reason.  He was therefore a theorist as well.  His

overall theory was simple.  In the works of Nature," he
64

said, "purpose and not accident is predominant." A

thing is known, then, when we know what it is for.  He

linked and combined theory and practice by saying that
65

interpretation of an observed phenomenon must always

be made in light of its purpose.  His zoological theory
66

was thus a reflection of the essentially teleological nature

of his overall philosophy.

59. A.   NO CHANGE
    B.   animals, also
    C.   animals, along with
    D.   animals; along with

60. F.   NO CHANGE
    G.   considering it
    H.   considering them
    J.   then to consider them

61. A.   NO CHANGE
    B.   he wrote (seemingly) on
    C.   writing seemingly on
    D.   he wrote on seemingly

62. F.   NO CHANGE
    G.   subject; Aristotles work
    H.   subject Aristotles' work
    J.   subject: Aristotle's work

63. A.   NO CHANGE
    B.   who was wedded to
    C.   in that he wedded
    D.   with the wedding of

64. F.   NO CHANGE
    G.   simple—in
    H.   simple.  "In
    J.   simply.  "In

65. A.   NO CHANGE
    B.   combining
    C.   to combine
    D.   OMIT

66. F.   NO CHANGE
    G.   in light of their purpose
    H.   given their purpose
    J.   because of its purpose

GO ON TO THE NEXT PAGE

**Passage 7**

Someday the Sun will run out of fuel. According to the projections of astrophysical theory, this will happen <u>67</u> in about five billion years, and the Sun will turn into a degenerate dwarf star. Nuclear fusion reactions in the central <u>part's of the Sun supplying</u> the energy that keeps <u>68</u> the Sun shining. The raw material for these reactions is hydrogen gas. When the hydrogen in the central parts of the Sun <u>had been used up,</u> the Sun will have a brief <u>69</u> career as a red giant star. During this time the core of the Sun will <u>collapse a shell</u> of hydrogen gas on the edge of <u>70</u> this collapsed core will be compressed and heated by the collapse of the core. Thermonuclear reactions involving the fusion of hydrogen nucleii and helium nucleii will produce a new surge of power in the central regions of the star. The outer layers of the Sun <u>expands</u> until the <u>71</u> Sun has a diameter a hundred times <u>of what its present</u> <u>72</u> value is. The oceans will boil and the mountains will <u>melt, then,</u> in a few hundred million years, the shell of <u>73</u> hydrogen gas will be used up, and the Sun will collapse to form a white dwarf star about the size of the earth. <u>When</u> this happens, the sun will be at most a few percent <u>74</u> as bright <u>like it is now.</u> <u>75</u>

67. **A.** NO CHANGE
    **B.** theory, happening
    **C.** theory, and it will happen
    **D.** theory. This will happen

68. **F.** NO CHANGE
    **G.** parts of the Sun supply
    **H.** parts of the Sun supplied
    **J.** part's of the Sun having supplied

69. **A.** NO CHANGE
    **B.** has been used up
    **C.** used up
    **D.** is getting used up

70. **F.** NO CHANGE
    **G.** collapse; a shell
    **H.** collapse but, a shell
    **J.** collapse, a shell

71. **A.** NO CHANGE
    **B.** would have expanded
    **C.** will expand
    **D.** had expanded

72. **F.** NO CHANGE
    **G.** it's present value
    **H.** its value at the present time
    **J.** its present value

73. **A.** NO CHANGE
    **B.** melt then
    **C.** melt. Then,
    **D.** melt, but

74. **F.** NO CHANGE
    **G.** So
    **H.** For
    **J.** Of course,

75. **A.** NO CHANGE
    **B.** as bright as
    **C.** bright like
    **D.** bright as

## END OF TEST

If you complete this test before the time is up, check
back over the questions on this test only. Do not go
back to the previous test. Do not proceed to the next
test until you are told to do so.

# TEST 2. MATHEMATICS USAGE

*50 Minutes—40 Questions*

**DIRECTIONS:** Solve each of the following problems. Choose the correct answer.

Solve as many problems as you can. Do not spend too much time on any one problem. You may return to problems so long as you have time left in this section.

Note: The figures that accompany the problems are not necessarily drawn to scale. Figures are assumed to lie in a plane unless a note states otherwise.

---

1. $121{,}212 + (2 \times 10^4) = ?$

   A. 312,212
   B. 141,212
   C. 123,212
   D. 121,412
   E. 121,232

2. If $6x + 3 = 21$, then $2x + 1 = ?$

   F. 1
   G. 2
   H. 3
   J. 6
   K. 7

3. At a recreation center, it costs \$3 per hour to rent a ping-pong table and \$12 per hour to rent a lane for bowling. For the cost of renting a bowling lane for two hours, it is possible to rent a ping-pong table for how many hours?

   A. 4
   B. 6
   C. 8
   D. 18
   E. 36

4. If $j < k < l < m$, which of the following *could* be true?

   F. $k = k + l$
   G. $j = l + m$
   H. $j + k = l + m$
   J. $j + k + m = l$
   K. $j + m = k + l$

5. Of the following, which is greater than $\frac{1}{2}$?

   A. $\frac{9}{19}$
   B. $\frac{7}{15}$
   C. $\frac{4}{9}$
   D. $\frac{6}{11}$
   E. $\frac{3}{7}$

6. Out of a group of 360 students, exactly 18 are on the track team. What percent of the students are on the track team?

   F. 5%
   G. 10%
   H. 12%
   J. 20%
   K. 25%

GO ON TO THE NEXT PAGE

**7.** In the figure below, three lines intersect as shown. Which of the following must be true?

I. $a = x$
II. $y + z = b + c$
III. $x + a = y + b$

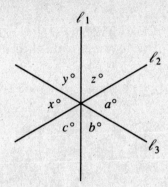

**A.** I only
**B.** II only
**C.** I and II only
**D.** I and III only
**E.** I, II, and III only

**8.** In the figure below, $x = ?$

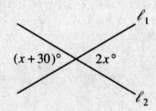

**F.** 15
**G.** 30
**H.** 45
**J.** 60
**K.** 90

**9.** Which of the following is the prime factorization of 60?

**A.** (2)(3)(10)
**B.** (3)(4)(5)
**C.** (2)(2)(3)(5)
**D.** (2)(2)(3)(6)
**E.** (3)(3)(3)(5)

**10.** The average (arithmetic mean) height of four buildings is 20 meters. If three of the buildings have a height of 16 meters, what is the height, in meters, of the fourth building?

**F.** 32
**G.** 28
**H.** 24
**J.** 22
**K.** 18

**11.** In the figure below, what is the value of $x$?

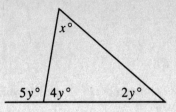

**A.** 15
**B.** 20
**C.** 30
**D.** 45
**E.** 60

**12.** In the figure below, what is the length of PQ?

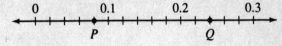

**F.** 0.12
**G.** 0.16
**H.** 0.13
**J.** 0.11
**K.** 0.01

**13.** What is the perimeter of the rectangle shown below?

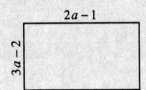

**A.** $10a - 6$
**B.** $10a - 3$
**C.** $6a - 2$
**D.** $5a - 6$
**E.** $5a - 3$

**14.** If the average (arithmetic mean) of $x, x, x, 56$, and 58 is 51, then $x = ?$

**F.** 43
**G.** 47
**H.** 49
**J.** 51
**K.** 53

GO ON TO THE NEXT PAGE

613

15. For how many integers $x$ is $-2 \le 2x \le 2$ ?
   A. 1
   B. 2
   C. 3
   D. 4
   E. 5

16. For all real numbers $x$, $8^x$ equals which of the following?
   F. $8x$
   G. $x^8$
   H. $2^{2x}$
   J. $x^{\frac{2}{3}}$
   K. $2^{3x}$

17. What is the sum of the areas of two squares with sides of 2 and 3, respectively?
   A. 1
   B. 5
   C. 13
   D. 25
   E. 36

18. If the rectangular solid shown below has a volume of 54, then $x = ?$

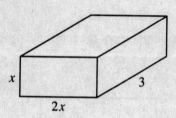

   F. 2
   G. 3
   H. 6
   J. 9
   K. 12

19. If $x$ is 80 percent of $y$, then $y$ is what percent of $x$?
   A. $133\frac{1}{3}\%$
   B. 125%
   C. 120%
   D. 90%
   E. 80%

20. From which of the following statements can it be deduced that $m > n$ ?
   F. $m + 1 = n$
   G. $2m = n$
   H. $m + n > 0$
   J. $m - n > 0$
   K. $mn > 0$

21. If $f(x) = x^2 + x$, then what is the value of $f(f(2))$?
   A. 42
   B. 38
   C. 32
   D. 18
   E. 4

22. The circle below with center $O$ has a radius of length 2. If the total area of the shaded regions is $3\pi$, then $x = ?$

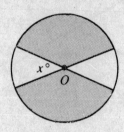

   F. 270
   G. 180
   H. 120
   J. 90
   K. 45

23. If a bar of metal alloy consists of 100 grams of tin and 150 grams of lead, what percent of the entire bar, by weight, is tin?
   A. 10%
   B. 15%
   C. $33\frac{1}{3}\%$
   D. 40%
   E. $66\frac{2}{3}\%$

24. If $\dfrac{1}{x} + \dfrac{1}{y} = \dfrac{1}{z}$, then $z = ?$
   F. $\dfrac{1}{xy}$
   G. $xy$
   H. $\dfrac{x+y}{xy}$
   J. $\dfrac{xy}{x+y}$
   K. $\dfrac{2xy}{x+y}$

25. $|-5| + |-12| - |-2| + (-6) = ?$
   A. 2
   B. 3
   C. 6
   D. 9
   E. 14

GO ON TO THE NEXT PAGE

**26.** If the average of $2x$, $2x + 1$, and $2x + 2$ is $x - 1$, which of the following equations could be used to find $x$?

   **F.**  $6x + 3 = x - 1$
   **G.**  $6x + 3 = 3(x - 1)$
   **H.**  $3(6x + 3) = x - 1$
   **J.**  $(6x + 3) + (x - 1) = 3$
   **K.**  $(6x + 3)(x - 1) = 3$

**27.** Members of a civic organization purchase boxes of candy for $1 apiece and sell them for $2 apiece. If no other expenses are incurred, how many boxes of candy must they sell to earn a net profit of $500?

   **A.**  250
   **B.**  500
   **C.**  1,000
   **D.**  1,500
   **E.**  2,000

**28.** $(-2)^2 - (-2)^3 = ?$

   **F.**  16
   **G.**  12
   **H.**  2
   **J.**  $-2$
   **K.**  $-8$

**29.** The sum, the product, and the average (arithmetic mean) of three different integers are equal. If two of the integers are $x$ and $-x$, the third integer is:

   **A.**  $\dfrac{x}{2}$.
   **B.**  $2x$.
   **C.**  $-1$.
   **D.**  $0$.
   **E.**  $1$.

**30.** In a school with a total enrollment of 360, 90 students are seniors. What percent of all students enrolled in the school are seniors?

   **F.**  25%
   **G.**  $33\frac{1}{3}\%$
   **H.**  50%
   **J.**  $66\frac{2}{3}\%$
   **K.**  75%

**31.** The perimeter of the square below is:

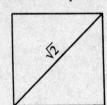

   **A.**  1.
   **B.**  $\sqrt{2}$.
   **C.**  4.
   **D.**  $4\sqrt{2}$.
   **E.**  8.

**32.** The figure below is a scale drawing of the floor of a dining hall. If 1 centimeter on the drawing represents 5 meters, what is the area, in square meters, of the floor?

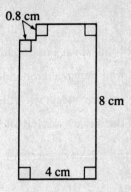

   **F.**  144
   **G.**  156
   **H.**  784
   **J.**  796
   **K.**  800

**33.** If two straight lines intersect as shown, what is the value of $x$?

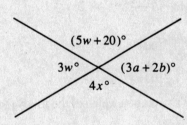

   **A.**  15
   **B.**  30
   **C.**  45
   **D.**  60
   **E.**  75

**34.** A triangle has one side of length 4 and another side of length 11. What are the greatest and least possible *integer* values for the length of the remaining side?

   **F.**  7 and 4
   **G.**  11 and 4
   **H.**  14 and 8
   **J.**  15 and 7
   **K.**  16 and 7

GO ON TO THE NEXT PAGE

**35.** Which of the following is the solution set for the equation $x^2 = 3 - 4x$ ?

   **A.** $(-3, -1)$
   **B.** $(-3, 1)$
   **C.** $(1, 3)$
   **D.** $(1, 4)$
   **E.** $(3, 5)$

**36.** A school club spent $\frac{2}{5}$ of its budget for one project and $\frac{1}{3}$ of what remained for another project. If the club's entire budget was equal to $300, how much of the budget was left after the two projects?

   **F.** $60
   **G.** $90
   **H.** $120
   **J.** $180
   **K.** $240

**37.** If the cost of $n$ nails is $c$ cents, which of the following equations could be used to determine $d$, the cost in dollars, of $x$ nails?

   **A.** $d = 100cnx$
   **B.** $d = 100\frac{cx}{n}$
   **C.** $d = \frac{100nx}{c}$
   **D.** $d = \frac{nx}{100c}$
   **E.** $d = \frac{cx}{100n}$

**38.** If $a^2 b^3 c < 0$, then which of the following must be true?

   **F.** $b^3 < 0$
   **G.** $b^2 < 0$
   **H.** $b < 0$
   **J.** $c < 0$
   **K.** $bc < 0$

**39.** If the figure below is an equilateral triangle, what is its perimeter?

   **A.** 1
   **B.** 3
   **C.** 9
   **D.** 12
   **E.** 15

**40.** In the coordinate plane, what is the distance between the point with $(x,y)$ coordinates $(2,1)$ and the point with $(x,y)$ coordinates $(5,5)$?

   **F.** $\sqrt{3}$
   **G.** $2\sqrt{3}$
   **H.** 5
   **J.** $3\sqrt{2}$
   **K.** 6

**END OF TEST**

If you complete this test before the time is up, check back over the questions on this test only. Do not go back to the previous test. Do not proceed to the next test until you are told to do so.

# TEST 3. SOCIAL STUDIES READING

*35 Minutes—52 Questions*

**DIRECTIONS:** Below each of the following reading passages is a series of questions. Choose the *best* answer to each question, interpreting what is stated or implied by the passage in the light of your own background in the subject. You may refer back to the passage as often as necessary, though the answers to some questions may not be found expressly in the passage.

---

The forces that generate conditions conducive to crime and riots are stronger in urban communities than in rural areas. Urban living is more anonymous living. It often releases the individual from community restraints more common in tradition-oriented societies. But more freedom from constraints and controls also provides greater freedom to deviate. And living in the more impersonalized, formally controlled urban society means that regulatory orders of conduct are often directed by distant bureaucrats. The police are strangers executing these prescriptions on, at worst, an alien subcommunity and, at best, an anonymous set of subjects. Minor offenses in a small town or village are often handled without resort to official police action. As disputable as such action may seem to be, it nonetheless results in fewer recorded violations of the law compared to the city. Although perhaps causing some decision difficulties for the police in small towns, formal and objective law enforcement is not always acceptable to villagers.

Urban areas with mass populations, greater wealth, more commercial establishments, and more products of our technology also provide more frequent opportunities for theft. Victims are impersonalized, property is insured, consumer goods in more abundance are vividly displayed and are more portable.

Urban life is commonly characterized by population density, spatial mobility, ethnic and class heterogeneity, reduced family functions, and a greater anonymity. All of these traits are expressed in comparison to nonurban life, or varying degrees of urbanism and urbanization. When, on a scale, these traits are found in high degree, and when they are combined with poverty, physical deterioration, low education, residence in industrial and commercial centers, unemployment or unskilled labor, economic dependency, marital instability, poor or absent male models for young boys, overcrowding, lack of legitimate opportunities to make a better life, the absence of positive anticriminal behavior patterns, higher frequency of organic diseases, and a cultural minority status of inferiority, it is generally assumed that social-psychological mechanisms leading to deviance are more likely to emerge.

These include frustration, lack of motivation to obey external demands, internalized cultural strains of inconsistency between means available and ends desired, conflicting norms, and anomie. The link between these two conditions—physical features of subparts of a city and the social-psychological aspects—has not been fully researched to the point when the latter can be safely said to be invariable or highly probable consequences of the former. Thus, to move onto a third level—namely, a tradition of lawlessness, of delinquent or criminal behavior, as a further consequence of the physical and social-psychological conditions of much urban life—is an even more tenuous scientific position. Nonetheless, these are the assumptions under which the community of scholars and public administrators operate today. The assumptions are the most justified and logically adequate we can make unless, or until, successfully refuted.

GO ON TO THE NEXT PAGE

1. The title that best expresses the main idea of the article is:

   A. Causes of Juvenile Crime.
   B. Ways of Preventing Crime in the City.
   C. What Urban Centers Can Learn from Suburban Crime Control Techniques.
   D. The Causes of Crime in Our Urban Centers.

2. All of the following are mentioned as reasons for a high crime rate in the city EXCEPT:

   F. cultural background.
   G. amount of personal freedom.
   H. amount of education.
   J. individual intelligence.

3. The article would place the causes of crime in the following order of predictability:

   A. physical, traditional, social.
   B. physical, social, traditional.
   C. social, physical, traditional.
   D. social, traditional, physical.

4. In the author's opinion, to say that a city environment leads to a tradition of lawlessness is:

   F. not logical.
   G. justified.
   H. scientific.
   J. inadequate.

5. It can be inferred from the article that in comparison with the city police, the village police must be:

   A. more impersonal.
   B. more personal.
   C. better educated.
   D. more honest.

6. According to the passage, crime in small towns and villages is lower despite a lack of police presence because:

   F. rural residents possess more inherent respect for the law than urban residents have.
   G. sparse settlement in rural areas gives residents more freedom to deviate.
   H. a rural resident who perpetrates a crime is likely to be punished by friends or relatives, creating a stigma that would not be present in a more anonymous society.
   J. rural police are better known to the residents they serve, making the residents more hesitant to break the law.

7. The author concludes the passage on a note that is:

   A. confrontational.
   B. tentative.
   C. complacent.
   D. vitriolic.

8. A purely demographic reason cited by the author for higher crime rates in urban areas is:

   F. lack of motivation among urban dwellers.
   G. marital instability.
   H. anomie.
   J. population density.

9. A paragraph *preceding* this passage might logically mention:

   A. the high incidence of crime in urban areas.
   B. sociological causes of crime in urban areas.
   C. demographic conditions in rural areas.
   D. contrasting types of police protection in urban and rural areas.

10. A most logical occupation for the author of this passage would be:

    F. a lawyer.
    G. a criminologist.
    H. an urban planner.
    J. a welfare worker.

GO ON TO THE NEXT PAGE

The concept of democratic citizenship can be traced back to the classical Greeks, who believed that uniquely human capacities could be completely developed only through full participation in the political community of the city-state. Aristotle argued that outside of the *polis* man must be either beast or god; human capacities could not be developed apart from political community. The Greek notion of citizenship required direct participation of citizens in deliberations on public issues. The status of citizen in the early Greek *polis* was limited to the few who possessed the economic means and the leisure to devote their attention to public matters. The classical Greek concept of citizenship emphasized the predominance of public obligations over the pursuit of private interests.

The liberal view of democratic citizenship that developed in the 17th and 18th centuries was fundamentally different from that of the Greeks. The pursuit of private interests with as little interference as possible from government was seen as the road to human happiness and progress. Public obligations and involvement in the collective community were not given the importance they had in the Greek concept. Freedom was not to be realized through immersion in the collective life of the political community but rather by limiting the scope of governmental activity and political obligation. The basic participatory role of the citizen was to select governmental leaders and keep the powers and scope of public authority in check. The rights of the citizen against the state were given particular emphasis.

Over time the liberal democratic notion of citizenship developed in two directions. First, a movement to increase the proportion of members of the society who were eligible to participate as citizens—especially through extending the right of suffrage—and to ensure the basic political equality of all citizens was begun. Second, there was a broadening of the legitimate activities of government and a use of governmental power to redress imbalances in social and economic life. Political citizenship became an instrument through which groups and classes with sufficient numbers of votes could use the state power to enhance their social and economic well-being.

Within the general liberal view of democratic citizenship, tensions have developed over the degree to which government can and should be used as an instrument for promoting happiness and well-being. Political philosopher Martin Diamond has categorized two views of democracy as follows. On the one hand, there is the "libertarian" perspective that stresses the private pursuit of happiness and emphasizes the necessity for restraint on government and protection of individual liberties. On the other hand, there is the "majoritarian" view that emphasizes "the task of government to uplift and aid the common man against the malefactors of great wealth." The tensions between these two views are very evident today. Taxpayer revolts and calls for smaller government and less government regulation clash with advocation of greater government involvement in the economic marketplace and the social sphere.

11. A common denominator between the classical and the original liberal view of democratic citizenship is:

   A. the belief that the state exists for the purpose of pleasing the community.
   B. the belief that government and the public should work together toward a common cause.
   C. the belief that the public should have a role in community affairs by selecting leaders.
   D. None of the above.

12. The attitude of the passage's author toward the differing views of democratic citizenship can best be described as:

   F. biased.
   G. incensed.
   H. cavalier.
   J. detached.

13. Of the following statements, which represents a CORRECT interpretation of the original liberal view of democratic citizenship?

   A. There is a strong correlation between politics and the common good.
   B. Private issues are subservient to issues of public concern.
   C. There is an inherent tension between the citizenry and those who are elected to lead them.
   D. None of the above.

GO ON TO THE NEXT PAGE

14. The evolution of the liberal view discussed in the third paragraph represents:

F. increased polarization between citizens and government.

G. a movement back to the classical view of the relative priorities of public and private interests.

H. the combination of citizens' increased awareness of public issues with the desire for self-enhancement.

J. the subservience of government to social interest groups.

15. From the discussion in the fourth paragraph of the libertarian and majoritarian views of citizenship, one can conclude that:

A. the libertarian view is most closely aligned with the original liberal view, while the majoritarian view is most closely aligned with the classical view.

B. the libertarian view is most closely aligned with the classical view, while the majoritarian view is most closely aligned with the original liberal view.

C. the libertarian view represents the original liberal view, while the majoritarian view represents the more developed liberal view.

D. both the libertarian view and the majoritarian view represent a totally new variation on the original liberal view.

16. An appropriate title for this passage might be:

F. Evolving Views of Democratic Citizenship: Have Public Issues Become Privatized?

G. The Decreasing Influence of Public Participation in Democratic Government.

H. Continuing Tension Between Classical and Liberal Views of Democratic Government.

J. None of the above.

17. In classical Greek society, the *polis* consisted of:

A. the elite governing body of a city-state.

B. the predominance of public obligations over private pursuits.

C. all citizens of the city-state.

D. human behavior developed outside of the political community.

18. At the outset of the passage, the author sets out to:

F. describe all aspects of the Greek view of democratic citizenship.

G. trace the history of various views of democratic citizenship.

H. elaborate on Aristotle's concept of the *polis*.

J. provide a definition of what is a political community.

19. One could conclude that the reason for the radical transformation in views of citizenship between the classical and modern eras is due to the:

A. disintegration of the *polis*.

B. increased importance of capitalistic and other property-oriented endeavors.

C. lessening importance of public obligations.

D. decreasing role of citizens in selecting their leaders.

20. Tensions between the libertarian and majoritarian views discussed in the fourth paragraph are:

F. exclusively political in nature.

G. exclusively economic in nature.

H. both political and economic in nature.

J. only superficial; the basic tenets of both philosophies are more similar than different.

A simple reductionist theory of international economic affairs could hold that they are merely reflections of political-military developments. Changes in international economic relations would therefore be explained by shifts in military power. This explanation, however, does not hold up well against the pattern of recent events. The United States position in the world economy and its dominance in policymaking have clearly declined since 1944. At Bretton Woods the United States could construct the system largely according to its specifications; now it can only veto proposals it dislikes. Yet during this period, the United States has remained, militarily, the most powerful state in the world, and its lead in this respect over its major economic partners, Japan and Europe, has been maintained. Although it has become more costly for the United States to intervene effectively in other countries over the past 30 years, American deterrent power has remained intact. Thus, although the distribution of military power is an important underlying factor affecting the international economic order, by itself it provides only a partial explanation. Two other major factors particularly must be taken into account to explain changes in international economic relations: changes in perceptions of the threat of military aggression, and changes in the relative economic strength of countries within U.S.-led alliances.

GO ON TO THE NEXT PAGE

21. In the first paragraph the author states that the United States has weakened to a degree as an economic power while:

    A. weakening militarily.
    B. its allies have weakened economically.
    C. remaining strong militarily.
    D. its allies have strengthened militarily.

22. From the context of the first paragraph, one can assume that Bretton Woods was:

    F. a military invasion.
    G. an economic policymaking conference.
    H. a treaty in which the United States granted economic concessions to its allies.
    J. a trade barrier.

23. The subject matter of a paragraph immediately following the last would logically address:

    A. changes in the economic strength of U.S. allies.
    B. economic conditions existing before the time of Bretton Woods.
    C. the decrease in U.S. military power.
    D. changes in perceptions of the threat of military aggression.

24. The reductionist theory of international economic affairs espouses the notion that:

    F. the global economy determines the relative military strength of all participating countries.
    G. the prevailing framework of the global economy was laid out at Bretton Woods.
    H. U.S. military power has weakened in the last 30 years.
    J. the global economy is subservient to the prevailing political and military balance in the world.

25. According to the first paragraph, U.S. military power has remained strong since Bretton Woods because:

    A. the United States invested heavily in advanced military technology following the end of World War II.
    B. U.S. alliances with strengthening European countries have compensated for whatever decline might have taken place.
    C. the U.S. economy has remained strong.
    D. None of the above reasons are mentioned.

26. One can conclude that the author regards the reductionist theory as:

    F. valid.
    G. incomplete.
    H. invalid.
    J. nebulous.

27. The first paragraph emphasizes that since 1944:

    A. the United States has become weaker than its allies both militarily and economically.
    B. the United States has remained a world power economically, but it has significantly declined militarily.
    C. the United States has remained a world power both militarily and economically.
    D. the United States has remained a world power militarily, but it has become weaker economically than its allies.

28. The tone of this passage can be best described as:

    F. didactic.
    G. condescending.
    H. maudlin.
    J. esoteric.

29. Countries that participate in an international economic conference might be hoping to achieve:

    A. an agreement on currency exchange rates.
    B. a tariff and trade agreement.
    C. both A and B.
    D. neither A nor B.

GO ON TO THE NEXT PAGE

**DIRECTIONS:** Questions 30–42 are not based on a reading passage. Choose the *best* answer to each question in accordance with your background and understanding in social studies.

30. Which of the following is not considered to be one of the primary principles of psychological development?

    F. Development is orderly and predictable.
    G. Development continues throughout the life cycle.
    H. Maturation takes place only during the earlier stages of the life cycle.
    J. Experiences at earlier stages may affect later development.

31. Which of the following people sparked the Reformation in Europe by openly challenging certain basic Roman Catholic teachings?

    A. Martin Luther
    B. Galileo Galilei
    C. John Locke
    D. Augustus Caesar

32. In international trade, a quota is an example of:

    F. free trade.
    G. protectionism.
    H. monopoly.
    J. regulation.

33. To be elected governor of a state, a candidate must win at least a:

    A. two-thirds majority of the total votes cast.
    B. plurality of the total votes cast.
    C. three-fifths majority of the total votes cast.
    D. three-fourths majority of the total votes cast.

34. Which of the following is not generally considered to have been a cause of the stock market crash of 1929?

    F. Overproduction of manufactured goods
    G. An excess of credit
    H. Difficult economic conditions for farmers
    J. Cessation of trade between the United States and Europe

35. The most common measure used to determine a person's social class is:

    A. the amount of wealth the person has.
    B. the part of the country in which the person resides.
    C. the type of music that the person prefers.
    D. the amount of education that the person has received.

36. Under the Articles of Confederation adopted by the original thirteen states in 1781, a weakness of the national government was that:

    F. the government possessed too much authority.
    G. taxes were too high.
    H. the courts possessed too much authority.
    J. all important decisions required the unanimous consent of Congress.

37. The input resource factor that typically accounts for the largest share of production costs is:

    A. natural resources.
    B. capital.
    C. labor.
    D. entrepreneurship.

38. The incident that ignited World War I was:

    F. a surprise attack by Germany on Poland.
    G. an assassination attempt against the King of England.
    H. the assassination of the Austrian Archduke Francis Ferdinand.
    J. a change of rulers in Germany.

39. Anthropologists generally believe that Neanderthal people:

    A. were the ancestors of today's human race.
    B. were ill-adapted for survival and quickly became extinct.
    C. co-existed with Cro-Magnon people over a certain period of time.
    D. raised crops and domesticated cattle.

40. An example of a craft union is:

    F. the American Federation of Labor.
    G. the Congress of Industrial Organizations.
    H. the International Brotherhood of Teamsters.
    J. None of the above.

41. Under the Constitution, the responsibility for making treaties with foreign countries belongs to:

    A. the President.
    B. Congress.
    C. Both of the above.
    D. Neither of the above.

GO ON TO THE NEXT PAGE

**42.** Which of the following is not one of the four areas in which civilizations first developed in approximately 3000 B.C.?

F. Mesopotamia
G. The Nile River valley
H. The Indus River valley
J. The Amazon River valley

Under the original electoral system established by the Constitution, each presidential elector cast his ballot for two men without designating between them as to office. The candidate who received the greatest number of votes became President; the second highest became Vice-President. In the presidential election of 1796, Jefferson foresaw on the basis of his own calculations that the electoral vote would be close. He wrote to Madison that in the event of a tie, he wished for the choice to be in favor of Adams. The New Englander had always been his senior in public office, he explained, and the expression of public will being equal, he should be preferred for the higher honor and that he, Jefferson, could more easily accept the vice-presidency, a more "tranquil and unoffending station." A shrewd politician, he realized that the transition of power from the nearly mythical Washington to a lesser luminary in the midst of the deep and bitter political divisions facing the nation could be perilous, and he had no desire to be caught in the storm that had been brewing for four years and was about to break. "This is certainly not a moment to covet the helm," he wrote to Edward Rutledge.

When the electoral vote was tallied, Adams emerged the victor with 71 votes to Jefferson's 68. Jefferson, as the recipient of the second-highest vote, was elected Vice-President. Rejoicing at his "escape," he seemed completely satisfied with the decision. Despite their obvious and basic political differences, Jefferson genuinely respected John Adams as a friend and compatriot. Although he believed that Adams had deviated from the course set in 1776, Jefferson "never felt a diminution of confidence in his integrity" and was confident that the New Englander would not steer the nation too far off its republican tack. Within two years, Jefferson's views would be drastically altered as measures such as the Alien and Sedition Acts of 1798 convinced him of the need to wrest control of the government from the Federalists.

**43.** To which political party did John Adams belong?

A. Republican
B. Federalist
C. Democratic
D. None of the above

**44.** This passage most closely takes the form of:

F. a character portrait.
G. a eulogy.
H. an autobiography.
J. a biography.

**45.** A paragraph added to the end of this passage would most likely discuss:

A. changes in the presidential balloting system since 1796.
B. Jefferson's endeavor to win the presidency in the subsequent presidential election.
C. the accomplishments of John Adams during his tenure as President.
D. similarities and differences between the management styles of Presidents Washington and Adams.

**46.** In the passage, George Washington is depicted as:

F. a declining figurehead who would be quickly forgotten.
G. a controversial figure being ousted from the presidency.
H. a retiring President who was carefully grooming his choice as successor.
J. a deified figure who set the standard by which the next President would be judged.

**47.** The attitude of the author toward Jefferson is most likely one of:

A. worship.
B. equivocation.
C. admiration.
D. cynicism.

GO ON TO THE NEXT PAGE

48. Jefferson's quest for the presidency is depicted in the passage as:

   F.   a diehard attempt to achieve a lifelong ambition.
   G.   an attempt to humiliate a lifelong personal rival.
   H.   an attempt to fulfill what he saw as a necessary obligation to his country.
   J.   All of the above.

49. As a person, Jefferson is depicted in the passage as one who is:

   A.   accommodating.
   B.   anomalous.
   C.   apathetic.
   D.   manipulative.

50. During Jefferson's tenure as Vice-President, his attitude toward John Adams changed from:

   F.   one of contempt to one of complacency.
   G.   one of equivocation to one of respect.
   H.   one of criticism to one of fear.
   J.   one of respect to one of dissatisfaction.

51. Regarding the system of presidential balloting that existed in 1796, which of the following statements is true?

   A.   The candidate who was the most senior public official was elected President.
   B.   The President and Vice-President ran on a single ticket.
   C.   The President, after being elected, personally chose the Vice-President.
   D.   There was actually no candidate for Vice-President.

52. The general condition prevailing in the United States at the time of the 1796 election could be described as one of:

   F.   peace and prosperity among the citizenry.
   G.   political harmony within the government.
   H.   pronounced cleavages on a number of issues that threatened to ruin the nation.
   J.   wariness toward other nations.

## END OF TEST

If you complete this test before the time is up, check back over the questions on this test only. Do not go back to the previous test. Do not proceed to the next test until you are told to do so.

# TEST 4.  NATURAL SCIENCES READING

*35 Minutes—52 Questions*

**DIRECTIONS:** Each passage in this test is followed by several questions. After reading a passage, choose the best answer to each question and blacken the corresponding space on your answer sheet. You may refer to the passage as often as necessary.

---

Chemical reactions are usually reversible; that is, the products can react to re-form the original materials. In certain cases, both processes can go on simultaneously. In other words, while the original materials go through the so-called *forward* reaction to create the products, those products go through the reverse reaction to recreate the original materials. Sometimes a point is reached at which the forward reaction takes place at exactly the same rate as the reverse reaction. At this *equilibrium* point, the relative concentrations of all the substances—original materials as well as products—remain the same. In chemical notation, the symbol used for this situation is $\rightleftharpoons$.

In each such situation, changes in outside pressure or temperature can cause the different reactions to reach a new equilibrium at different concentrations of the various substances. These variations can be predicted using Le Chatelier's Principle, which states that when a stress such as pressure or heat is placed on a system at equilibrium, that system will react in the way that relieves that stress. For example, consider the forward and reverse reactions in which nitrogen and hydrogen combine to form ammonia, and ammonia breaks down into nitrogen and hydrogen:

$$N_2 + H_2 \rightleftharpoons 2HN_3 + \text{heat}$$

Suppose pressure is increased, so that the two reactions take place within a smaller volume. In this case, we can predict that the equilibrium will shift to a point where relatively more $NH_3$ exists and relatively less $N_2$ and $H_2$. The reason is that the two molecules in $2NH_3$ take up less space than the corresponding single molecule of $N_2$ plus the three molecules in $3H_2$. The system has shifted to relieve the stress caused by too much pressure.

Suppose instead that the temperature in the environment is increased. Again, the system will shift to relieve stress. The forward reaction creates heat, so the reverse reaction must necessarily absorb heat. If heat from outside is added, the system will shift to favor the reverse (heat-absorbing) reaction at the expense of the forward (heat-producing) reaction. The result will be equilibrium at a relatively greater concentration of $N_2$ and $H_2$ and a relatively lesser concentration of $NH_3$.

1. Equilibrium is possible only in chemical reactions that are:
   A. predictable.
   B. heat-absorbing.
   C. reversible.
   D. heat-producing.

2. According to Le Chatelier's Principle, if a system at equilibrium is stressed, that system will:
   F. become irreversible.
   G. tend to favor heat-absorbing reactions.
   H. shift until there is a greater concentration of the original materials.
   J. shift in a way that relieves the stress.

3. Chemical equilibrium can:
   A. occur only at one set of concentration levels for the various substances involved.
   B. occur at different concentration levels depending on pressure and temperature.
   C. occur at different concentration levels at the same temperature and pressure.
   D. occur only at one specific temperature and pressure for a given set of reactions.

GO ON TO THE NEXT PAGE

4. In the equilibrium system $H_2 + I_2 \rightleftharpoons 2HI + heat$, an increase in temperature will:

    F. destroy the equilibrium.
    G. increase the concentrations of $H_2$ and $I_2$.
    H. increase the concentration of HI.
    J. favor the heat-producing reaction.

5. In the equilibrium system $2SO_2 + O_2 \rightleftharpoons 2SO_3$, an increase in pressure will:

    A. destroy the equilibrium.
    B. increase the concentrations of $SO_2$ and $O_2$.
    C. increase the concentration of $SO_3$.
    D. decrease the concentration of $SO_3$.

6. In the equilibrium system $PCl_5 + heat \rightleftharpoons PCl_3 + Cl_2$, an increase in temperature will:

    F. destroy the equilibrium.
    G. increase the concentration of $PCl_5$.
    H. increase the concentrations of $PCl_3$ and $Cl_2$.
    J. favor the heat-producing reaction.

7. In the equilibrium system $H_2 + I_2 + heat \rightleftharpoons 2HI$, the concentration of HI will increase if there is an increase in:

    A. temperature.
    B. pressure.
    C. volume of the reaction container.
    D. reaction speed.

8. In the equilibrium system $N_2 + O_2 \rightleftharpoons 2NO + heat$, an increase in temperature would produce an increase in the concentration of:

    F. $N_2$ only.
    G. NO only.
    H. $N_2$ and $O_2$ only.
    J. $N_2$, $O_2$, and NO.

9. In the equilibrium system $X + Y = 2Z$, an increase in pressure at constant temperature would cause the concentration of Z to:

    A. decrease.
    B. increase.
    C. remain the same.
    D. first decrease, then increase.

10. In the equilibrium system $C_2H_4 + H_2 \rightleftharpoons C_2H_6 + heat$, an increase in pressure will:

    F. destroy the equilibrium.
    G. decrease the relative concentration of $C_2H_4$ and $H_2$.
    H. increase the relative concentration of $C_2H_4$ and $H_2$.
    J. decrease the relative concentration of $C_2H_6$.

Earth and the other planets are periodically bombarded by *meteoroids*, small fragments of matter from interplanetary space. When such an object hits Earth's atmosphere, the air in front of it becomes compressed and superheated. The object itself begins to melt, leaving a streak of light—called a *meteor*—across the sky. Whatever portion of the object that survives to reach the ground is called a *meteorite*. Large objects that plunge straight down are hardly slowed by their passage through the atmosphere; these objects form impact craters when they hit the ground.

Scientists theorize that meteoroids date from the time 4.6 billion years ago when the solar system formed out of a vast nebula surrounding the infant sun. Within that nebula, dust grains continually collided, slowly coalescing into the different planets, moons, smaller objects called planetesimals, and still smaller fragments. During the first billion years of their existence, the revolving planets and moons gradually swept up most of the small objects within their orbits. However, between the orbits of Jupiter and Mars there remained—and remains today—a vast revolving band of planetesimals and smaller fragments called the asteroid belt. Here the bits and chunks of ancient matter constantly collide with and grind against each other, creating a vast field of stony rubble. Most of these objects continue in orbit indefinitely. Sometimes, however, the strong gravity of nearby Jupiter pulls one of the objects out of its usual circuit and sends it on a new, irregular orbit across the paths of the inner planets, including that of Earth. Nothing may happen for millions of years; however, at some point the meteoroid and Earth may meet, and gravity will bring the meteoroid crashing to Earth's surface.

Today astronomers have identified more than 40 large meteoroids whose orbits regularly cross Earth's path. They estimate that there may be as many as 1000 such objects that are more than a kilometer in diameter. Several such objects will probably strike Earth every million years.

GO ON TO THE NEXT PAGE

11. During the first billion years of the solar system, meteoroids bombarded Earth and the other planets:

    A. about as frequently as they do today.
    B. much more frequently than they do today.
    C. much less frequently than they do today.
    D. very rarely.

12. Most of the craters visible today on the Moon most likely date from:

    F. the past billion years.
    G. the period when the solar system was forming.
    H. the first billion years of the solar system.
    J. the period when the asteroid belt was forming.

13. The meteorites that fall to Earth are:

    A. generally the same age as the rocks on Earth's surface.
    B. sometimes much younger than the rocks on Earth's surface.
    C. always much younger than the rocks on Earth's surface.
    D. always much older than the rocks on Earth's surface.

14. More impact craters are visible today on the Moon than on Earth because:

    F. the Moon has been struck more frequently by meteorites.
    G. the Moon is closer to the asteroid belt.
    H. the Moon is older than Earth.
    J. the Moon has no wind or rain to erode surface features.

15. To cross Earth's orbit, a meteoroid from the asteroid belt would also have to cross the orbit of:

    A. Mars.
    B. Jupiter.
    C. Venus.
    D. Mercury.

16. A meteoroid that crosses Earth's orbit is:

    F. never closer to the sun than Earth is.
    G. always closer to the sun than Earth is.
    H. sometimes closer to the sun than Earth is.
    J. always about the same distance from the sun as Earth is.

17. The number of meteorites striking the Earth's oceans is probably:

    A. slightly smaller than the number striking land.
    B. about the same as the number striking land.
    C. greater than the number striking land.
    D. about half the number striking land.

18. An observer watching a meteoroid fall to the Moon's surface would see:

    F. a flash of light streaking across the sky, then an impact.
    G. a light moving slowly across the sky, then an impact.
    H. only a light streaking across the sky.
    J. a dark object crossing the sky, then an impact.

19. The 66-ton Hoba meteorite, which fell to the ground in Africa, did not create an impact crater. This was most likely because:

    A. the meteorite was melting when it hit the ground.
    B. the ground where the meteorite struck was stony.
    C. the meteorite plunged straight down through the atmosphere.
    D. the meteorite entered the atmosphere at an angle, and its descent was slowed.

**DIRECTIONS:** Questions 20-34 are not based on a reading passage. You are to answer these questions on the basis of your previous schoolwork in the natural sciences.

20. The chemical properties of an atom are directly related to the:

    F. protons in the nucleus.
    G. electrons in the outer orbits.
    H. atomic weight of the atom.
    J. the number of neutrons in the k, l, and m orbitals.

21. In the solar system the correct sequence for five of the planets is:

    A. Venus, Neptune, Jupiter, Mars, Earth.
    B. Venus, Uranus, Saturn, Mercury, Earth.
    C. Earth, Mars, Jupiter, Saturn, Uranus.
    D. Pluto, Mercury, Earth, Venus, Mars.

GO ON TO THE NEXT PAGE

22. Opposition to the flow of electric current through a conductor is known as:

F. voltage.
G. amperage.
H. resistance.
J. wattage.

23. Of the following organisms, the one that has an incomplete, but functional, digestive system is:

A. the lobster.
B. the clam.
C. the grasshopper.
D. the planaria.

24. In order for an atom to become an anion, it must:

F. gain protons.
G. lose electrons.
H. lose protons.
J. gain electrons.

25. A leaf from a green-and-white variegated colleus that was placed in the sun for several hours was treated in the following manner: 1) placed in hot alcohol until colorless, 2) placed in a clean Petri dish and flooded with Lugol's iodine, 3) washed in distilled water, 4) spread out on clean white paper. The same procedure was followed with the leaf from a green-and-white variegated plant that was stored without light for twelve hours. The following chart shows the results.

| TREATMENT | WHITE AREA OF LEAF | | GREEN AREA OF LEAF | |
|---|---|---|---|---|
| | without light | with light | without light | with light |
| alcohol | white | white | white | white |
| Lugol's | brown | brown | brown | blue-black |
| water | no change | no change | no change | no change |

Which of the following statements best explains the observed results of the experiments?

A. In green plants, light plus the green pigment chlorophyll result in the presence of starch.
B. Plants must have chlorophyll in order to synthesize organic nutrients.
C. Plants cannot grow without light.
D. The green chlorophyll molecule uses light energy to split one molecule of water.

26. A parallel-plate capacitor is charged and then disconnected from the charging battery. If the plates of the capacitor are then moved farther apart by the use of insulated handles, which one of the following results?

F. The charge on the capacitor increases.
G. The charge on the capacitor decreases.
H. The voltage across the capacitor remains the same.
J. The voltage across the capacitor increases.

27.

| Solution | Color |
|---|---|
| 1 | red |
| 2 | red |
| 3 | blue |
| 4 | no change |
| 5 | red |

The table shows the results from five solutions tested with litmus paper to determine if they were acids or bases. How many of the solutions had a pH of less then 7?

A. 1
B. 2
C. 3
D. 4

28. Albert Einstein's special theory of relativity utilizes:

F. the basic laws of nature, which are the same in all inertial reference frames.
G. the fact that the measured speed of light in a vacuum is the same for observers in all inertial reference frames.
H. the fact that force is equal to mass times acceleration.
J. both F and G.

29. The location of earthquakes and volcanoes can best be described by which of the following statements?

A. They are basically random in location.
B. They usually occur where the inner core is leaking into the crust.
C. They usually occur at the junction of lithospheric plates.
D. They usually occur where the earth's mantle is weak.

30. The type of muscle tissue found within the walls of blood vessels and of other internal organs is:

F. smooth muscle.
G. skeletal muscle.
H. cardiac muscle.
J. voluntary muscle.

GO ON TO THE NEXT PAGE

**31.**

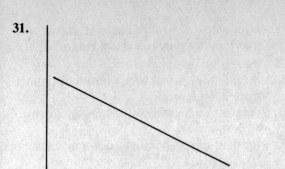

Which of the following could this graph represent?

A. A vibrating string at its fundamental frequency, where frequency of vibration is represented by the vertical axis and length of string by the horizontal axis

B. The relationship between force and acceleration, where force (measured in newtons) is represented by the vertical axis and acceleration (meters per second per second) is represented by the horizontal axis

C. The relationship between work and force, where work (measured in joules) is represented by the vertical axis and force (newtons) is represented by the horizontal axis

D. The relationship between the energy (represented by the vertical axis) and the wavelength (represented by the horizontal axis) of light waves

**32.** Which of the following statements best distinguishes electrolytes from non-electrolytes?

F. Electrolytes are always ionic compounds, while non-electrolytes are always covalent compounds.

G. Electrolytes are usually covalent compounds, while non-electrolytes are usually ionic compounds.

H. Electrolytes and non-electrolytes are both co-valent compounds soluble in water.

J. Electrolytes can be covalent or ionic compounds but must be ionic in solution.

**33.** Organisms in temperate zones are able to time their activities by cues given by the photoperiod, since:

A. light is a limiting factor.

B. all organisms have a biological clock.

C. day length is always constant for a specific locality and season.

D. some plants need long days in order to bloom.

**34.** Consider the following chemical formulae:

I. $CH_4$    II. $CCl_4$    III. $CHCl_3$

These formulae show that:

F. the carbon atom has four combining sites.

G. many compounds contain carbon.

H. carbon is important to living things.

J. ionic bonds have been formed.

Sir Isaac Newton formulated what are now known as the laws of motion during the seventeenth century. The first law, the law of inertia, states that if there is no net force acting on a body, it will stay at rest if already at rest, or, if in motion, a body will continue moving in a straight line. Thus, once something is moving, it will go on moving unless a force stops it, or if an object is not moving, it won't budge until a force acts on it. In everyday experience this would seem to be untrue, since it would mean that a moving object, such as an automobile, would continue moving without continuously being powered by a fuel engine. Upon closer inspection, however, it is observed that moving objects rarely have a net force of zero on them; the forces of friction and air resistance usually oppose the motion.

Newton's second law, the law of acceleration, explains what happens when a force is applied to something already moving. The greater the force, the greater it will accelerate the moving object in the direction of the force. The greater the mass of the object, the smaller the acceleration will be. This relationship can be expressed with the formula: $F = ma$, where $m$ is the mass of the object and $a$ is the acceleration expressed in distance per second per second (or second$^2$).

Newton's third law, the law of action and reaction, states that when one body exerts a force on another body, the second body exerts an equal force on the first body, but in the opposite direction. That is why the hot gases escaping downward from burning rocket fuel provide an upward force that thrusts a rocket into the air.

GO ON TO THE NEXT PAGE

35. According to Newton's first law, a bicycle should continue moving forever once it is in motion. This does not happen because:

    A. the net force on the moving bicycle is zero.
    B. the net force on the moving bicycle is not zero.
    C. friction provides a net force in the same direction as the motion.
    D. air resistance provides a net force in the same direction as the motion.

36. Which of the following is true about the second law?

    F. Acceleration is directly proportional to both the force exerted and the mass of the object.
    G. Acceleration is inversely proportional to both the force exerted and the mass of the object.
    H. Acceleration is inversely proportional to the force exerted and directly proportional to mass.
    J. Acceleration is directly proportional to the force exerted and inversely proportional to mass.

37. Presuming there are no other outside forces, how much force is necessary to accelerate a 1-kilogram brick 1 meter per second$^2$?

    A. 0.1 newton
    B. 1.0 newton
    C. 10 newtons
    D. 100 newtons

38. Presuming there are no other outside forces, what is the mass of an object accelerated 9 meters per second$^2$ by a force of 2.7 newtons?

    F. 0.3 kg
    G. 2.43 kg
    H. 3.33 kg
    J. 24.3 kg

39. Where might you observe Newton's first law with fewer forces acting upon objects?

    A. At atmospheric temperature and pressure
    B. At sea level
    C. In space
    D. None of the above

40. When you step down onto a platform with a force of 50 newtons (assuming ideal conditions):

    F. there is no reaction.
    G. the platform pushes back with a horizontal force of 50 newtons.
    H. the platform pushes with an upward force of 50 newtons.
    J. the platform pushes with a downward force of 50 newtons.

41. Which of the following does not represent a pair of action/reaction forces correctly?

    A. Action: A pile of books placed on a table has a gravitational force of 1 newton.
       Reaction: The table pushes up on the books with a force of 1 newton.
    B. Action: Person X tugs at a rope with a force of 25 newtons.
       Reaction: Person Y tugs at the other end of the rope with a force of 25 newtons.
    C. Action: A girl jumps out of a boat toward shore with a force of 40 newtons.
       Reaction: The boat moves away from shore with a force of 40 newtons.
    D. Action: The fuse from a lighted firecracker explodes downward with a force of 0.05 newton.
       Reaction: The firecracker moves upward with a force of 0.05 newton.

42. Which of the laws of motion must be taken into account when planning to launch a rocket out of the Earth's gravity?

    F. The law of inertia
    G. The laws of acceleration
    H. The law of action and reaction
    J. All of the laws

43. Which of the following would be affected LEAST by the forces of friction and air resistance?

    A. The force exerted on a body
    B. The mass of an object
    C. The acceleration of a moving object
    D. The upward reactive force of a rocket

   In the seventeenth century people believed that maggots arose spontaneously from decaying subtances. But Francesco Redi, a physician, could not believe this. "How could living things come from dead things?" he asked. Redi began to believe that all worms found in the meat were derived from the eggs of flies, and not from the decaying meat. This, of course, was a guess and not a conclusion. Scientists call a good guess like this a "working hypothesis," because it gives the scientist an idea of how and where to start work.

GO ON TO THE NEXT PAGE

Then Redi began to gather and record facts to find out if his hypothesis was correct. He did this by carrying out many experiments, which were designed to help him get the facts he needed.

Redi prepared several jars with a piece of meat in each. He left some jars open, and covered the others with cheesecloth. He observed not once, but many times that the flies flew to the open jars and laid their eggs on the meat. These eggs hatched into maggots.

Flies also flew to the jars covered with cheesecloth, but they could not get into those jars to lay their eggs on the meat. The meat in those jars rotted, but had no maggots. From many such observations, Redi concluded that maggots came from flies' eggs and not from the meat.

Redi was not satisfied with doing just one experiment. Rather, he performed this experiment many times before arriving at his conclusion. In this manner he eliminated the possibility that his results were due to chance.

44. In his experiment, Redi left some jars open:
   F. because he had run out of lids and cheesecloth.
   G. so that the flies would have access to the meat.
   H. only once.
   J. None of the above.

45. According to the passage, the belief of seventeenth-century people in the spontaneous generation of living things was:
   A. refuted by Redi.
   B. confirmed by Redi.
   C. observed by Redi.
   D. not discussed.

46. According to the passage, Redi's belief about the origin of maggots in flies' eggs was all of the following except:
   F. a guess.
   G. a working hypothesis.
   H. useful in constructing experiments.
   J. not his own idea.

47. From the passage it may be inferred that Redi used cheesecloth on the jars because it was:
   A. completely airtight.
   B. sterile.
   C. available.
   D. repulsive to flies.

48. From the description of the experiment and the results, we can infer that the meat in the cheesecloth-covered jars rotted because:
   F. of spontaneous generation.
   G. microscopic organisms came in through the cheesecloth.
   H. microscopic organisms were brought into the jars by flies.
   J. None of the above.

49. Flies are insects that undergo complete metamorphosis. How many of the stages in their life cycle are mentioned or implied in the passage?
   A. 1
   B. 2
   C. 3
   D. 4

50. Redi's experiments:
   F. confirmed his original hypothesis.
   G. confirmed the theory of spontaneous generation.
   H. did not confirm his original hypothesis.
   J. none of the above.

51. Another experimenter named Spallanzani tried to disprove spontaneous generation by corking, sealing, and heating flasks of nutrient broth and later examining them for microscopic organisms. Spallanzani's flasks were most similar to:
   A. Redi's uncovered jars.
   B. Redi's cheesecloth-covered jars.
   C. Redi's sterile covered jars.
   D. all of Redi's jars.

52. Because he compared the covered and uncovered jars, Redi's experiment:
   F. had no room for error.
   G. had a control.
   H. proved more than one hypothesis.
   J. eliminated results due to chance.

## END OF TEST

If you complete this test before the time is up, check back over the questions on this test only. Do not go back to the previous test. Do not proceed to the next test until you are told to do so.

# Answer Key

## English Usage

| | | | | |
|---|---|---|---|---|
| 1. B | 16. H | 31. B | 46. J | 61. D |
| 2. J | 17. A | 32. H | 47. B | 62. F |
| 3. B | 18. G | 33. D | 48. H | 63. A |
| 4. H | 19. C | 34. H | 49. B | 64. H |
| 5. A | 20. J | 35. D | 50. F | 65. D |
| 6. J | 21. D | 36. F | 51. B | 66. F |
| 7. B | 22. G | 37. C | 52. H | 67. A |
| 8. H | 23. C | 38. G | 53. C | 68. G |
| 9. D | 24. G | 39. B | 54. G | 69. B |
| 10. G | 25. A | 40. J | 55. D | 70. G |
| 11. C | 26. J | 41. D | 56. H | 71. C |
| 12. J | 27. A | 42. H | 57. D | 72. J |
| 13. B | 28. F | 43. D | 58. H | 73. C |
| 14. F | 29. B | 44. J | 59. C | 74. F |
| 15. D | 30. H | 45. B | 60. G | 75. B |

## Mathematics Usage

| | | | | |
|---|---|---|---|---|
| 1. B | 9. C | 17. C | 25. D | 33. B |
| 2. K | 10. F | 18. G | 26. G | 34. H |
| 3. C | 11. E | 19. B | 27. B | 35. C |
| 4. K | 12. G | 20. J | 28. G | 36. H |
| 5. D | 13. A | 21. A | 29. D | 37. E |
| 6. F | 14. G | 22. K | 30. F | 38. K |
| 7. C | 15. C | 23. D | 31. C | 39. C |
| 8. G | 16. K | 24. J | 32. H | 40. H |

## Social Studies Reading

| | | | | | | |
|---|---|---|---|---|---|---|
| 1. D | 9. A | 17. C | 25. D | 33. B | 41. C | 49. A |
| 2. J | 10. G | 18. G | 26. G | 34. J | 42. J | 50. J |
| 3. B | 11. D | 19. B | 27. C | 35. A | 43. B | 51. D |
| 4. G | 12. J | 20. H | 28. F | 36. J | 44. J | 52. H |
| 5. B | 13. C | 21. C | 29. C | 37. C | 45. B | |
| 6. H | 14. H | 22. G | 30. H | 38. H | 46. J | |
| 7. B | 15. C | 23. D | 31. A | 39. C | 47. C | |
| 8. J | 16. F | 24. J | 32. G | 40. F | 48. H | |

## Natural Sciences Reading

| | | | | | | |
|---|---|---|---|---|---|---|
| 1. C | 9. C | 17. C | 25. A | 33. C | 41. B | 49. C |
| 2. J | 10. G | 18. J | 26. J | 34. F | 42. J | 50. F |
| 3. B | 11. B | 19. D | 27. C | 35. B | 43. B | 51. B |
| 4. G | 12. H | 20. G | 28. J | 36. J | 44. G | 52. G |
| 5. C | 13. D | 21. C | 29. C | 37. B | 45. A | |
| 6. H | 14. J | 22. H | 30. F | 38. F | 46. J | |
| 7. A | 15. A | 23. D | 31. D | 39. C | 47. D | |
| 8. H | 16. H | 24. F | 32. J | 40. H | 48. G | |

# Explanatory Answers

## English Usage

1. (B) The original is not idiomatic. Correct expression requires the use of the infinitive (*to begin*) rather than the gerund (*beginning*). Both B and C make the needed correction, but C is needlessly wordy. And the additional verbiage in C gives it a stilted sound. Finally, D is awkward.

2. (J) The original contains an error of diction. The correct word for making the comparison intended by the original is *from*, not *than*. (*Than* is a conjunction, and conjunctions are used to introduce clauses. What follows the underlined part of the sentence is a noun phrase—not a clause.) G fails to make the needed correction. H makes the needed correction but introduces a new error. In general, a modifier should be placed as close as possible to what it modifies. Here, *fundamentally* must modify *are different*, but the placement of *fundamentally* after *from* suggests that it is intended to modify *weapons*. Thus, J would result in an ambiguous sentence.

3. (B) The original is a run-on sentence. B solves the problem by starting a new sentence at an appropriate point. Also, B correctly includes a comma after *moreover* to separate the introductory remark from the main body of the sentence. C fails to solve the problem of the run-on sentence. You must somehow separate *memory* from *moreover*. So the comma following *moreover* is needed, but you also need something else. D solves the run-on sentence problem but creates a new problem. *Moreover* is an adverb, but *since* is a conjunction. Thus, *since* introduces a dependent clause. But the result is a dependent clause with no independent clause to support it.

4. (H) The original is not idiomatic. You might use *as a result of*. Or you could also use, as H does, *resulting from*. G and J are simply not idiomatic.

5. (A) The original is correct as written. The use of the subjunctive *would* correctly suggests that a nuclear war might or might not occur. B and C are both wrong because the indicative mood (*is* and *are*) doesn't have this meaning. Additionally, either B or C must be wrong because one uses a singular and the other a plural verb. The subject of the sentence is the compound subject "Number of deaths . . . and economic damage," and a compound subject requires a plural verb. Thus B is wrong for yet another reason. As for D, although *might* preserves the element of contingency suggested by the subjunctive *would* (a war might or might not occur), the phrasing "more devastating even as" is not idiomatic.

6. (J) The original is incorrect because the use of *could* implies that a nuclear war might or might not have winners. But the author clearly means to assert that it is impossible for any country to win a nuclear war. J makes the needed correction. The indicative *can* makes it clear that no one can win a nuclear war. G and H are both incorrect because they contain double negatives.

7. (B) The original makes two mistakes. First, it is a run-on sentence; second, *it* is singular but must refer to *weapons*, which is plural. B makes both the needed corrections. C is wrong because the result is still a run-on sentence. D is wrong because *it* cannot refer to *weapons*.

8. (H) The original is not idiomatic. The correct idiom is "neither . . . nor" not "neither . . . but." Similarly, G and J are not correct idioms.

9. (D) The original is incorrect because a new paragraph should be started here. In the opening paragraph, the author announces that he will make three points. The second paragraph is devoted to the first point. So the other two points should also be presented in separate paragraphs. Since you need a new paragraph, B is wrong. As for C, you should use a comma after *third* so that the reader understands you are making the third in a series of points and are not referring to a "third arms control."

10. (G) The original is awkward. G is more concise and reads better than the original. H is incorrect because the subject of the sentence is *step*, a singular verb. And J suffers from the problems of the original and includes a plural verb.

11. (C) The original is not idiomatic. You should use the infinitive *to develop* rather than the gerund *developing*. C makes the needed change. B is extremely awkward because the prepositional phrase introduced by the *of* is separated from the noun it is intended to modify (*development*). D suffers from several problems. First, even setting aside problems of idiomatic expression and structure, D seems to assert that a coherent arms strategy will certainly be developed. But that is not the only intended meaning of the original. The author means that developing such a policy is a step that should be taken before deploying more weapons—not that such a strategy will necessarily be developed. Beyond this, the sentence that would result from using D would be extremely awkward. The phrase "a coherent arms control strategy" seems to be an appositive, but there is no noun in the sentence to which it can stand in apposition.

12. (J) The original sentence lacks a conjugated or main verb. H and J supply the needed verb, but G does not. (*Having viewed* is a participle form and cannot be a main verb.) As for H, *its* is intended to refer to *founders*, but *founders* is plural, not singular.

633

13. **(B)** The original is not idiomatic. The correct idiom is *rather than*, not *rather as*. Both C and D are wrong because they, too, are not idiomatic.

14. **(F)** The original is correct as written. G is needlessly wordy, so the original is preferable. H completely destroys the logical structure of the sentence. The resulting construction would read: "The Founders viewed education in political terms rather than to academic excellence." And J changes the intended meaning of the sentence by implying that the Founders could have chosen to view education as academic excellence— rather than as a means to academic excellence.

15. **(D)** The problem with the sentence as originally written is that it lacks a conjugated or main verb. *Talking* is a participle and cannot function as a main verb. Only D supplies a conjugated verb form.

16. **(H)** The original is incorrectly punctuated. *Goals* is an appositive that refers to liberty, etc. The correct punctuation is a comma preceding the appositive. G is wrong because the period completely isolates the appositive from the sentence that supports it and turns everything following the comma into a sentence fragment. J is also incorrectly punctuated. The semicolon is too powerful. It signals that an independent clause will follow. An appositive, however, is dependent for its existence on the nouns that come before it, so a comma provides enough separation from the main body of the sentence without being too powerful.

17. **(A)** The original is correct as written. *To take precedence over* is an English idiom meaning "to be more important than something else." B distorts the intended meaning of the original. *To precede* means "to come before in time," so the resulting sentence would make no sense. Finally, C is simply not idiomatic.

18. **(G)** The original contains three errors. First, the parenthetical expression signalled by the comma following *generation* must be closed by a comma, not a dash. (You can use dashes or commas to set off such remarks—but not a mixture of both.) Second, the subject of the sentence is *generation*, which is singular. So the plural noun *assert* is wrong. Third, *their* refers to *generation* and so fails to agree in number with its referent. G makes all three changes. H makes two of the changes, but the semicolon is a mistake. The semicolon would be used to separate two clauses, but what follows the semicolon used in H is not a clause. Finally, J fails to correct the third error mentioned above and is incorrectly punctuated. (You need that second comma.) Additionally, J uses the present tense verb *asserts*, which is inconsistent with the other verbs in the selection.

19. **(C)** The underlined verb, *was*, is singular and fails to agree with its plural subject, *ingredients*. C corrects this problem. B eliminates the problem of agreement. *Being* is a participle and doesn't show number. Unfortunately, because *being* is a participle, the resulting construction lacks a main verb, and the sentence becomes a sentence fragment. Finally, D distorts the intended meaning of the original. The author does not mean to say the principal ingredients of a civic education were similar to literacy and inculcation of patriotic and moral virtues.

20. **(J)** The original is a run-on sentence. You have two clauses run together without any punctuation and with no conjunction. J is one way of solving the problem: use a semicolon to separate the two clauses. (You could also use a comma and a coordinate conjunction such as *and*.) The dash cannot be used to separate two clauses, so G is wrong. As for H, a comma by itself is just not strong enough to do the job.

21. **(D)** The original contains an error of illogical subordination compounded by a punctuation mistake. The two ideas joined at the underlined part have equal importance. One should not be subordinated to the other, but *since* always signals a subordinate idea. Additionally, a semicolon cannot be used to join a subordinate clause to an independent or main clause. B solves the subordination problem, but *and* signals a continuation of a thought. The second idea here contrasts with the first and should be signalled by a word like *but*. C eliminates the punctuation mistake but creates a sentence fragment of the second half of the sentence. *Since* introduces a subordinate clause, which must be joined to an independent or main clause.

22. **(G)** The original sentence is not idiomatic. The correct idiom here requires the use of the infinitive *to be* rather than the gerund *being*. H and J both correct this error, but H and J also eliminate the only conjugated verb in the clause. The result is a fragment rather than a complete sentence.

23. **(C)** The placement of *almost* in the original is not idiomatic. Given its proximity to *agreed*, *almost* seems to modify *agreed* rather than *universally*. But the intended meaning of the sentence is that *almost* modifies *universally*. C provides the correct and idiomatic placement of *almost*. B is also not idiomatic. As for D, although the words are in the correct order, the comma between *universally*, an adverb, and the word it modifies, *agreed*, disrupts the logical flow of the sentence. (To prove this to yourself, read the sentence through, pausing at the comma.)

24. **(G)** The underlined part is incorrect because it destroys the parallelism of the sentence. You have a series of three elements: *emphasized*, *put*, and *attempt*. The third element is a noun rather than a verb. G restores the parallelism of the sentence by supplying a verb. H fails to provide a verb. Finally, although J includes a verb, it also includes a subject. The result is a clause, and the clause is not parallel to the verb forms.

25. **(A)** The original is correct as written. B is wrong because the word *womens* does not exist in English. *Women* is already plural, so you cannot add an *s* to it. C and D are illogical because the sentence intends to refer generally to the contribution of women as a whole—not to the contribution of any particular individual.

**26.** (J) The original is not idiomatic. The correct idiom is "range from . . . to," not "range from . . . and." G and H fail to correct this problem. Only J provides the correct idiom.

**27.** (A) The original is correct as written. It is idiomatic, and the past tense verb *marked* is consistent with the other past tense verbs in the selection. B is wrong because the present perfect *has marked* implies an action that began in the past but continues into the present. C is needlessly wordy and awkward. As for D, the use of the passive voice completely destroys the logic of the sentence.

**28.** (F) The original is correct as written: "effort was made . . . to utilize." G and H are simply not idiomatic: "effort was made . . . being able to utilize," "effort was made . . . utilizing." Finally, J destroys the logical structure of the sentence: "effort was made . . . and utilizing."

**29.** (B) The original uses an incorrect verb tense. The present tense *falls* conflicts with the other past tense verbs of the selection. Both B and D make the needed correction, but D is not idiomatic. The correct idiom is "falls within a category." Although *falls in* is a possible English phrase, it has a meaning that is not appropriate here. C is grammatically incorrect because it eliminates the only conjugated verb in the clause introduced by *while.*

**30.** (H) The original is not idiomatic. The correct idiom is *reserved for,* not *reserved by. Reserved by* has a meaning that is not appropriate here. G is needlessly wordy and ambiguous. G is ambiguous because it is not clear what the phrase is intended to modify. It seems to modify *women,* but the intent of the sentence is that the phrase modify *work.* J is wordy and awkward as well.

**31.** (B) The original uses an illogical transition word. *However* is used to signal a contrast, but the sentence that is introduced by "however" is actually a continuation of the thought contained in the previous sentence. B is correct because, since there is no transition word, the reader will naturally assume that the next sentence will continue the train of thought. C is wrong because the use of *but* tells the reader to expect a contrasting thought. Finally, D eliminates the only conjugated verb in the sentence, so the result is a fragment rather than a complete sentence.

**32.** (H) The original is incorrectly punctuated. Since there is no punctuation between *activity* and *knitting,* a reader won't pause after *activity.* Consequently, *knitting* seems to be a participle that somehow modifies *activity.* The author intends, however, for *knitting* to be a gerund in the series *knitting, canning,* and *planting.* The correct punctuation to introduce a series like this is the colon. Thus, H is correct and J is wrong. G does correctly use a colon, but the use of the infinitive *to knit* would destroy the parallelism of the series.

**33.** (D) The original contains an error of pronoun usage. The pronoun *their* refers to *homemaker.* Instead of the plural *their,* you should use the singular, *her.* B

eliminates the pronoun problem by using no pronoun at all. The resulting structure is a bit awkward ("demonstrate patriotism") but not incorrect. But the verb in B is not acceptable. The *could be demonstrating* is inconsistent with the other verbs in the paragraph. The verb in C is also incorrect. The verb *could have demonstrated* implies that a woman might or might not have demonstrated her patriotism, but this is not the intended meaning of the selection. The author means to assert definitely that women did demonstrate their patriotism. C is also wrong because it fails to correct the pronoun problem.

**34.** (H) The original is incorrectly punctuated. The colon seems to signal a clarification of the idea of hostessing at canteens. Instead, the hostessing is one of a group of activities women volunteered to do. So the correct punctuation is a comma. G is wrong because you do need a comma to separate the first element in a series of three or more elements from the following elements. And D is wrong because it destroys the parallelism of the series *hostess, makes,* and *organize.*

**35.** (D) The original is incorrectly punctuated. You need a comma following *musket* to close the parenthetical remark begun by the comma before *dressed.* B is wrong because you cannot mix commas and dashes in this way. If you signal the start of a parenthetical phrase with a comma, then you must also use a comma to signal its end. (Unless, of course, the parenthetical phrase is the last element of the sentence and ends with a period.) C is wrong because *were* does not agree in number with the subject of the sentence, *army.*

**36.** (F) The original is correct as written. The other choices disrupt the parallelism of the sentence. Since the two verbs *perform* and *laid* have a similar function in the sentence, they should both have similar forms. G and H use the passive voice and are not parallel to the active-voice *perform.* J is the participle and is not parallel to *perform,* which is a conjugated verb.

**37.** (C) One way of fixing the order of the paragraphs is to recognize that neither (2) nor (3) can be the first paragraph. The *this* in the first sentence of 2 clearly refers to something that has come before. Similarly, the phrase "much of the work" in the first sentence of (3) also refers to something that has come before. (1) appears the best choice for the first paragraph, because (4) seems to be a summary or conclusion. As for (2) and (3), (2) must follow (3) because (2) is intended to contrast with (3): most of the work was traditional but some was not. But a reader cannot understand the importance of the contrast suggested by (2) without the information provided by (3).

**38.** (G) The verb tense of the original is inconsistent with the other verbs in the selection. The author is describing events that occurred in the past and uses past tense verbs such as *discovered.* J is wrong for this reason as well. As for H, while *had been* refers to a past action, the past perfect implies an action that was completed in the past before some other past action. Thus, the sentence would suggest that Gunnbiorn was blown off course and then later discovered the islands. The intended meaning of the sentence, however, is that Gunnbiorn was blown off course and discovered the islands at that time, not later.

39. (B) The original suffers from a lack of parallelism. The action described is: directed course, reached the coast, and discovered something. Therefore, the last verb should be in the simple past tense to parallel the other verbs. The other two choices do not give you the parallelism you need.

40. (J) The original contains two errors. First, the present tense verb *returns* is inconsistent with the other verbs in the paragraph, which are in the past tense. Second, the semicolon is too strong. To set off an introductory dependent clause from the main body of the sentence, you need a comma. G is correctly punctuated, but by using the participle, G reduces the entire sentence to a sentence fragment. H is incorrectly punctuated. The placement of the comma in H is such that it not only fails to signal the end of the introductory subordinate clause; it also illogically isolates the subject of the sentence, *he*, from the verb *returned*.

41. (D) The original is not idiomatic. When *intended* precedes a noun, it implies that some agent has something in mind concerning the idea expressed by that noun, e.g., the criminal's intended victim. (The criminal has something in mind for the victim.) But here, it is the colonists who have an intention. Only D correctly renders the intended meaning of the original: that the people who returned with Eric themselves intended to become colonists.

42. (H) The original lacks a main verb. The semicolon signals that the second part of the sentence is a clause, so you need a conjugated verb. H provides one. Neither G nor J contains a verb form that can function as a main verb.

43. (D) The *therefore* is out of place in this sentence. *Therefore* is used to signal a logical sequence or connection. But there is nothing in the sentence to support this use; that is, there is no reason to believe that the creation of two main settlements was necessitated by the arrival of more colonists. Why not one settlement? Why not a dozen? (Here is an example of the correct use of the word: "I expect company for dinner. Therefore, I will buy two bottles of soda instead of just one.") B, of course, suffers from the same problem as the original. Additionally, *so* and *therefore* have similar meanings, so you don't need them both. C suffers from this problem as well and has the additional weakness of illogical punctuation.

44. (J) The use of the past perfect *had spent* implies that Eric spent the winter with King Olaf before the summer of 999. But the sentence clearly states he spent the following winter with King Olaf. J eliminates this problem. G and H are not conjugated verb forms, so neither can function as a verb for the subject *he*.

45. (B) The original is simply not idiomatic. B supplies the correct idiom. C is not idiomatic, and D destroys the logical structure of the sentence.

46. (J) *Undertaken* is the past participle of the verb *to undertake*. A past participle is not itself a complete verb. J solves this problem by creating a sentence that uses the passive voice: *changes were undertaken*. G and H are possible verb forms, but their tenses are inconsistent with the simple past tense used in the rest of the paragraph.

47. (B) The original is not idiomatic. The sentence means to say that the new values were embraced by some people, and that is the sense of B. C and D are also wrong because they are not idiomatic.

48. (H) The two ideas joined at the underlined part contrast with each other: these did something; the others did not. To signal this contrast, you must use something other than *and*. *But* is an acceptable choice, so H is correct. G and J are incorrect because *since* and *consequently* signal a relationship in which one idea follows from or is the consequence of another.

49. (B) The comma and *and* signal that the last half of the sentence must be a clause. The original, however, contains no main verb. B supplies a main verb that is in the right tense and agrees in number with its subject, *notions*.

50. (F) The original is correct. This is the proper place at which to begin a new paragraph since the author is shifting from talking about the past to a discussion of the present. Since you need a new paragraph here, G and J are wrong. And J is wrong for the additional reason that the use of *owing to* in place of *because* is low-level usage. Finally, although H correctly begins a new paragraph, the second comma illogically isolates the subject of the sentence from its verb.

51. (B) In the original, *clear* is intended to modify *evident*. But that is a job that can be done only by the adverb *clearly*. (Adverbs and not adjectives are used to modify adjectives.) C changes the intended meaning of the sentence: the triumph is clear and evident. Finally, D is wrong because *were* does not agree with the subject of the sentence *triumph*.

52. (H) The sentence contains two errors. First, the comma splices together two independent clauses. Those clauses should be separated either by a semicolon or by a comma plus a coordinate conjunction. Second, the *furthermore* is a poor choice for a transitional word, since the second idea of the sentence stands in contrast to the first idea. H supplies the correct punctuation and a logical transition word. G and J fail to correct the problem of the run-on sentence.

53. (C) The underlined part creates a run-on sentence. One way of solving the problem is simply to start a new sentence. C does this and correctly changes the participle "being" to a conjugated verb form that can function as the main verb of the sentence. B destroys the logical structure of the sentence, and D fails to correct the problem of the run-on sentence.

54. (G) The *and so* distorts the logical structure of the sentence. *And so* seems to introduce another

clause, but what follows lacks a main verb. By eliminating the *and so,* B allows *emphasizing,* a participle, to function as an adjective modifying *textbooks.* (Note: Although you ordinarily want your modifiers close to what they modify, here there is no possibility of misunderstanding.) H results in a sentence that is distorted because the *and* seems to join another verb to the first verb, *expound.* But *emphasis* is a noun, not a verb. Thus, with H you get: "textbooks expound . . . and emphasis." As for J, the *that* seems to introduce a relative clause, but no verb follows.

**55.** (D) *Often sometimes* is not a possible phrase in English, because the two words have opposite meanings. You have to eliminate one or the other. All of the choices make this correction. B, however, uses a verb tense that is inconsistent with the other tenses in the paragraph. As for C, *distorted* is a past participle and cannot stand alone. It requires another verb, such as *are.*

**56.** (H) The original contains two errors. First, the past tense *translated* is inconsistent with the present tense verbs in the rest of the paragraph. Second, *who* should replace *that,* since it refers to people. Only H makes both corrections.

**57.** (D) The original doesn't contain a grievous error, but on balance it is not as idiomatic as D. The placement of *always* directly before the main element of the verb instead of before the *have* is preferable to the original. B is wrong because *have* does not agree with the singular *humankind.* And C is wrong because the present tense is inconsistent with the introductory phrase "from the beginning."

**58.** (H) In English, if an adjective has more than two syllables, we form the comparative using *more* rather than by adding *-er.* H corrects the problem of the original. G and J are incorrect because they imply connections between the ideas of *skillful* and *intelligent* that are not intended by the original.

**59.** (C) The comma following *agriculture* a few words after the underlined portion has no logical function in the sentence as written. C solves this problem by allowing it to mark the close of a parenthetical expression introduced by a first comma in front of *along.* B attempts the correction, but B is wrong because the resulting phrase has no clear logical connection with the rest of the sentence. The resulting phrase consists of a noun modified by a prepositional phrase, but the noun can't just sit there—it has to do something. But because of the punctuation, the noun can't do its natural job, which would be to function as the subject of the sentence. (C doesn't have this problem. In C, the noun *discovery* is the object of a preposition, and the prepositional phrase is connected to the rest of the sentence as a modifier of *domestication.*) D destroys the logical structure of the sentence by isolating the subject from the verb. The semicolon is too strong.

**60.** (G) The original contains two errors. First, it lacks parallelism. It now reads: "between regarding . . . and to consider." Second, the pronoun *them* does

not agree in number with its antecedent, *animal.* Only G corrects both of these problems. H solves the problem of parallelism but fails to eliminate the wrong pronoun. And J doesn't correct either mistake.

**61.** (D) The original contains two errors. First, the placement of *seemingly* is incorrect. *Seemingly* is intended to modify *every* which in turn modifies *subject.* But its placement in the verb seems to suggest that Aristotle wrote in a style that could be called *seemingly.* Second, the present tense *writes* is inconsistent with the other verbs in the sentence, e.g., *seemed* and *was.* (Note: The present tense verbs are used to describe our attitudes today. Although Aristotle wrote in the past, we currently have certain attitudes about those writings.) B corrects the one problem but not the other. Simply putting *seemingly* into parentheses does not clarify what the word is supposed to modify. As for C, while this eliminates the problem of verb tense by reducing the verb to a participle modifying *Aristotle,* you still have the ambiguity created by *seemingly.*

**62.** (F) The original is correct as written. The comma following *subjects* marks the end of the introductory dependent clause. You do need punctuation at that point, so H is wrong. But the correct punctuation is a comma. The semicolon and the colon are both too powerful, so G and J are wrong as well.

**63.** (A) The original is correct as written. *Wedding* is a participle that modifies *observer.* B distorts the intended meaning of the original by suggesting that Aristotle himself was joined to something. The sentence means to say that Aristotle joined two ideas. C is needlessly wordy and awkward compared to the original. Finally, D creates a prepositional phrase that doesn't clearly modify any other element in the sentence.

**64.** (H) The original is incorrectly punctuated. You must use quotation marks to indicate the start of the quotation. G fails to make this correction and makes another error of punctuation. The dash cannot be used in place of the period. J is wrong because the adverb *simply* cannot be used as a predicate complement; that is, *simply* cannot modify the subject of the sentence.

**65.** (D) The original is needlessly wordy. *Link* and *combine* both have the meaning of *join,* so you should get rid of one or the other.

**66.** (F) The original is correct as written. G and H are wrong because the antecedent of the *their* is *phenomenon.* But *phenomenon* is singular, not plural. J distorts the intended meaning of the original by incorrectly suggesting a causal connection where none is possible.

**67.** (A) The original is correct as written. B eliminates both the subject and the conjugated verb of one of the main clauses of the sentence. The resulting material cannot stand on its own anymore, but it doesn't have any other logical role to play. It cannot, for example, be considered a participle used as an adjective because it has nothing to modify. C is wrong because the *and* incorrectly indicates the conjunction of two independent clauses, but the introductory material is not a clause at all. D is incorrect for a similar reason. Starting a new sentence at this point will result in a fragment.

**68.** (G) The original contains two errors. First, the *-'s* indicates possession, but there is no noun modified by *part's*. Second, *supplying* cannot be a main verb. G makes both the needed corrections. H, too, makes the corrections; but *supplied,* which is in the past tense, is inconsistent with the time frame of the selection. Finally, J doesn't correct either of the original errors.

**69.** (B) The verb tense of the original is incorrect. The *had been used* incorrectly implies that this event has already occurred. *Has been used* correctly indicates that the event is yet to come. C is wrong because the past participle *used* cannot by itself be a main verb. And D is wrong because it contains low-level usage. (Do not use a form of *get* to suggest the passive voice.)

**70.** (G) The original is a run-on sentence. G corrects this problem by joining the two independent clauses with a semicolon—a legitimate use of that mark. H is wrong because the placement of the comma is incorrect. It would be possible to join the two clauses with a coordinate conjunction and a comma, but the comma must be placed before the conjunction, not after it. Finally, J results in a comma splice, a form of run-on sentence.

**71.** (C) The verb tense in the underlined original is inconsistent with the other verbs used to sketch the course of future events. C is correct because the future tense *will expand* is consistent with the other verbs. B is wrong because the use of the subjunctive (*would have*) incorrectly suggests that the event is contingent on some other event. But the rest of the verbs are all in the indicative mood. Finally, D, which is in the past perfect tense, is inconsistent with the other verbs in the selection.

**72.** (J) The original is needlessly wordy and awkward, as you can see by comparing it with J. G is wrong because *it's* is a contraction for *it is,* not a pronoun. And H is needlessly wordy, as you can prove by comparing it with J.

**73.** (C) The underlined part contains a comma splice. Two independent clauses are joined by only a comma. C solves this problem by starting a new sentence. B fails to solve the problem of the run-on sentence. D solves that problem but creates another problem. *But* signals a contrast, but the author is talking about a sequence in which one event follows the other according to the laws of physics. So the *but* is out of place.

**74.** (F) The original is correct. G and J are wrong because they substitute adverbs for the subordinate conjunction, *when*. As a result, the introductory subordinate clause becomes an independent clause that is then incorrectly joined to the other independent clause only by a comma. As for H, although *for* is a subordinate conjunction, its meaning is not appropriate here.

**75.** (B) The original is not idiomatic. The correct idiom is *as bright as,* not *as bright like.* C and D are also not idiomatic.

## Mathematics Usage

**1.** (B) $2 \times 10^4 = 20,000$, and $121,212 + 20,000 = 141,212$

**2.** (K) Solve for $x$:

$$6x + 3 = 21$$
$$6x = 18$$
$$x = 3$$

So $2x + 1 = 2(3) + 1 = 7$.

**3.** (C) There is no trick to this question. Just use "supermarket" math. Find out how much the one thing would cost. Then, using that cost, find how much of the other you can buy.

The cost of renting a bowling lane for 2 hours is $2 \times \$12 = \$24$. And for $24 you can rent a ping-pong table for $\$24 \div \$3 = 8$ hours.

**4.** (K) You can reason in general terms to the correct answer. As for F, since $j$ is less than $k$, $j$ cannot be equal to $k$ plus something. The same reasoning applies to G, H, and J. K, however, could be true. For example, if $j$ is 5 and $k$ is 10, and if $l$ is 15 and $m$ is 20, then $5 + 20 = 10 + 15$.

**5.** (D) Use $\frac{1}{2}$ as a benchmark. And reason in this way: Eliminate A. Since $\frac{9}{18}$ is $\frac{1}{2}$, $\frac{9}{19}$ is less than $\frac{1}{2}$. Continue eliminating choices until you are left with D.

**6.** (F) Use the "this-of-that" strategy:

$$\frac{this}{of\ that} = \frac{student\ on\ track\ team}{total\ students} =$$

$$\frac{18}{360} = \frac{1}{20} = 5\%$$

**7.** (C) I must be true because $a$ and $x$ are vertically opposite each other. Similarly, II must be true because $y$ and $b$ are equal and $z$ and $c$ are equal. III, however, is not necessarily true. $x$ and $a$ are equal and $y$ and $b$ are equal, but you don't have information on which to base a conclusion about the relationship between $x$ and $y$ or the relationship between $z$ and $b$.

**8.** (G) You can set up an equation:

$$x + 30 = 2x$$
$$x = 30$$

**9.** (C) First eliminate any choice that contains a number that is not a prime. This eliminates A, B, and D. Then multiply the remaining choices:

**C.** $2 \times 2 \times 3 \times 5 = 60$ (Correct!)
**E.** $3 \times 3 \times 3 \times 5 = 135$ (Wrong.)

**10.** (F) Use the method for finding the missing element of an average. Since the average height of all four buildings is 20, the sum of the heights of all four is $4 \times 20 = 80$. The three known heights total $3 \times 16 = 48$. So the missing value is $80 - 48 = 32$.

**11.** (E) First find the value of $y$:

$$5y + 4y = 180$$
$$9y = 180$$
$$y = 20$$

Next find the value of $x$:

$$4y + 2y + x = 180$$
$$6y + x = 180$$
$$6(20) + x = 180$$
$$120 + x = 180$$
$$x = 60$$

**12.** (G) The trick here is to recognize that each of the marks between the numbered marks is $\frac{1}{5}$ of the distance between the numbered marks. The distance between each numbered mark is 0.1, so each of the others is worth $0.1 \div 5 = 0.02$. So $PQ = 0.02 + 0.1 + 2(0.02) = 0.16$.

**13.** (A) The perimeter is:

$$2(3a - 2) + 2(2a - 1) = 6a - 4 + 4a - 2 = 10a - 6$$

That's a fairly simple algebraic manipulation; but if you insist on avoiding algebra altogether, you can assume a value for $a$. For example, if $a = 2$, then the length of the figure is $3(2) - 2 = 4$, and the width of the figure is $2(2) - 1 = 3$. The perimeter would be $4 + 4 + 3 + 3 = 14$. Substituting 2 for $a$ into the correct formula yields the value 14. And only A does that.

**14.** (G) Use the technique for finding the missing elements of an average. The average of the five numbers is 51, so their sum is $5 \times 51 = 255$. The two known values total 114. So the remaining three numbers total $255 - 114 = 141$. And $141 \div 3 = 47$.

**15.** (C) $x$ could be $-1$, or zero, or $+1$.

**16.** (K) $8 = 2^3$, so $8^x = (2^3)^x = 2^{3x}$.

**17.** (C) Just do the indicated operations. One square has an area of $2 \times 2 = 4$, the other an area of $3 \times 3 = 9$, and the sum of their areas is $4 + 9 = 13$.

**18.** (G) You can set up an equation:

$$x(2x)(3) = 54$$
$$2x^2 = 18$$
$$x^2 = 9$$
$$x = \sqrt{9} = 3 \quad \text{(Distances are always positive.)}$$

Or, you can "test the test." Try each answer choice as the value of $x$ until you find one that generates a volume of 54.

**19.** (B) Since $x$ is 80 percent of $y$, $x = 0.8y$, and $y = \frac{x}{0.8} = 1.25x$. So $y$ is 125% of $x$. Or, you can just use some numbers. Assume that $y$ is 100. If $y = 100$, then $x = 80\%$ of $y = 80$. Finally, find what percent $y$ is of $x$: $\frac{100}{80} = \frac{5}{4} = 1.25 = 125\%$.

**20.** (J) You can rewrite $m - n > 0$ by adding $n$ to both sides: $m > n$. As for F, this proves that $m < n$. As for G, this proves nothing about $m$ and $n$, since $m$ and $n$ might be either negative or positive. The same is true of H, which is the equivalent of $m > -n$. Finally, as for K, you have neither relative values for $m$ and $n$ nor their signs.

**21.** (A) First, find $f(2)$:

$$f(2) = (2)^2 + 2 = 4 + 2 = 6$$

Next, find $f(6)$:

$$f(6) = (6)^2 + 6 = 36 + 6 = 42$$

So $f(f(2)) = 42$.

**22.** (K) First, find the area of the circle: $\pi r^2 = \pi(2)^2 = 4\pi$. Since the shaded area is equal to $3\pi$, it accounts for $\frac{3\pi}{4\pi} = \frac{3}{4}$ of the circle. So the unshaded area accounts for $\frac{1}{4}$ of the circle. This means that angle $x$ plus the angle vertically opposite $x$ are equal to $\frac{1}{4}$ of $360° = 90°$. So $2x = 90$, and $x = 45$.

**23.** (D) Use the "this-of-that" strategy:

$$\frac{\text{this}}{\text{of that}} = \frac{\text{tin}}{\text{entire bar}} = \frac{100}{(100 + 150)} = \frac{100}{250} =$$

$$\frac{2}{5} = 40\%$$

**24.** (J) Rewrite the equation:

$$\frac{1}{x} + \frac{1}{y} = \frac{1}{z}$$

Add the fractions using the "flying $x$":

$$\frac{y + x}{xy} = \frac{1}{z}$$

Multiply both sides by $z$:

$$z\left(\frac{y + x}{xy}\right) = 1$$

Multiply both sides by $\frac{xy}{y + x}$:

$$z = \frac{xy}{y + x} = \frac{xy}{x + y}$$

Or, just assume some values. Assume that $x = 1$ and $y = 1$. On that assumption, $z = \frac{1}{2}$. Then substitute 1 for $x$ and 1 for $y$ into the choices. Only D generates the value $\frac{1}{2}$.

**25.** (D) $|-5| = 5$, $|-12| = 12$, and $|-2| = 2$. So:

$$5 + 12 - 2 + (-6) = 15 - 6 = 9$$

**26.** (G) Treat this average as you would any other. Add the three elements and divide by 3:

$$\frac{(2x) + (2x + 1) + (2x + 2)}{3} = x - 1$$

$$\frac{(2x + 2x + 1 + 2x + 2)}{3} = x - 1$$

$$\frac{6x + 3}{3} = x - 1$$

$$6x + 3 = 3(x - 1)$$

**27.** (B) The profit on each box of candy is $2 - $1 = $1. To earn a total profit of $500, it will be necessary to sell $500 ÷ $1 = 500 boxes.

**28.** (G) Perform the indicated operations:

$$(-2)^2 - (-2)^3 = 4 - (-8) = 12$$

**29.** (D) You can arrive at the correct answer in several ways. First, you can reason that if the product of three different integers is zero, one of them is zero. Of $x$ and $-x$, one is positive and the other negative, so they cannot be zero. The missing number must be zero.

You can also set up equations, but that seems unnecessarily complicated. You would be better off using a third method, just substituting some values for $x$. You'll find that the missing number must be zero.

**30.** (F) This is a simple percent question. Use the "this-of-that" strategy. The "of that" is "of all students enrolled." The other number, the "this," is seniors:

$$\frac{\text{seniors}}{\text{total}} = \frac{90}{360} = \frac{1}{4} = 25\%$$

**31.** (C) The diagonal of a square creates an isosceles right triangle. So the side of the square is equal to $\frac{1}{2} \times \sqrt{2}$ x $\sqrt{2} = 1$. Since the side has a length of 1, the perimeter of the square is $4(1) = 4$.

**32.** (H) If the floor were a perfect rectangle, it would have a width of $4 \times 5 = 20$ meters, a length of $8 \times 5 = 40$ meters, and a total area of $20 \times 40 = 800$ square meters. But the floor is not a perfect rectangle. Its actual area is smaller. Subtract the area of the missing "corner." It has actual dimensions of $0.8 \times 5 = 4$. So its actual area is 16. $800 - 16 = 784$.

**33.** (B) The angles labeled $3w$ and $(5w + 20)$ form a straight line:

$$3w + (5w + 20) = 180$$

$$8w + 20 = 180$$

$$8w = 160$$

$$w = 20$$

And the angles labeled $3w$ and $4x$ also form a straight line:

$$3w + 4x = 180$$

$$3(20) + 4x = 180$$

$$60 + 4x = 180$$

$$4x = 120$$

$$x = 30$$

**34.** (H) The difference between 11 and 4 is 7, so 7 marks the limit of the shorter side of a triangle with sides of 11 and 4. But the side must be an integer. So the shortest possible side is 8. Conversely, the sum of 4 and 11 is 15. So 15 marks the limit of the longer side. Since the longer side must have an integral value, its maximum length is 14.

**35.** (C) One approach to this item is to put the equation in standard form, factor, and solve for $x$:

$$-x^2 = 3 - 4x$$

$$0 = 3 - 4x + x^2$$

$$x^2 - 4x + 3 = 0$$

$$(x - 3)(x - 1) = 0$$

So either $x - 3 = 0$ and $x = 3$ or $x - 1 = 0$ and $x = 1$. The solution set is (1, 3).

Alternatively, you could simply substitute the values given for $x$ back into the equation. The only values that work are 1 and 3.

**36.** (H) If the club spent $\frac{2}{5}$ of the budget on the first project, it was left with $\frac{3}{5}$ of $300 = $180. If it spent $\frac{1}{3}$ of $180, it was left with $180 - $60 = $120.

**37.** (E) Since $n$ nails cost $c$ cents, $x$ nails will cost $\frac{cx}{n}$ cents. And since a dollar contains 100 cents, the cost of $x$ nails in dollars is $\frac{cx}{100n}$: $d = \frac{cx}{100n}$.

Or, you can use the technique of assuming some values for the variables. Assume, for example, that nails cost 5 cents each and you want to buy 20 of them. On that assumption, the cost is $1. So if $n = 1$, $c = 5$, and $x = 20$, then $d = 1$:

**A.** $1 = 100(5)(1)(20)$   (Wrong.)

**B.** $1 = \dfrac{100(5)(20)}{1}$   (Wrong.)

**C.** $1 = \dfrac{100(1)(20)}{5}$   (Wrong.)

**D.** $1 = \dfrac{(1)(20)}{100(5)}$   (Wrong.)

**E.** $1 = \dfrac{(5)(20)}{100(1)}$ $100(1)$   (Right.)

**38.** (K) Since the expression is less than zero, either one or three of the factors must be negative. $a^2$ cannot be negative. So either $b^3$ is negative or $c$ is negative, but not both. And this means either $b$ or $c$ is negative but not both. So $bc$ must be negative. You can eliminate A, B, C, and D since they might be, but are not necessarily, true.

**39.** (C) Since this is an equilateral triangle, the sides are equal. Set up equations:

$$2x + 1 = 2x + y$$
$$y = 1$$

And

$$2x + y = 2y + 1$$
$$2x + (1) = 2(1) + 1$$
$$2x + 1 = 2 + 1$$
$$2x = 2$$
$$x = 1$$

Now pick any side: $2x + y = 2(1) + 1 = 3$. So the perimeter of the triangle is $3(3) = 9$.

**40.** (H) You can use the distance formula if you remember it, but you can also use the Pythagorean Theorem:

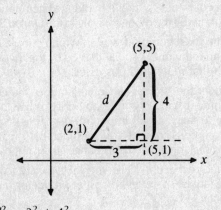

$$d^2 = 3^2 + 4^2$$
$$d^2 = 25$$
$$d = 5$$

## Social Studies Reading

1. (D) Choice D best reflects the main idea of the article. Answer A is wrong because juvenile crime is not specifically discussed in the passage. Choices (B) and (C) are also wrong because there is no information to support these answers.

2. (J) Of all the answer choices only response J — individual intelligence — is not mentioned as a reason for high crime rates in the cities.

3. (B) Paragraph three explains the answer to this item. Scholars and public administrators assume that the most predictable cause of crime in the city is the city's physical conditions, which result in its social aspects, which in turn become traditional. Answer B is the right choice, as it lists these causes in the proper order.

4. (G) The final sentence of the article summarizes that at present, a tradition of lawlessness as a result of environment is justified. Answer G is correct. Choice F is wrong because the final sentence says that this assumption *is* logical. Choices H and J are both wrong responses according to the article.

5. (B) The first paragraph states that city life and its conditions are impersonal. On this basis, answer A is wrong. Answers C and D are not suggested in the passage as related to police. B, then, is the correct answer and is suggested strongly in paragraph one.

6. (H) The first paragraph states that offenses in towns and villages "are often handled without resort to police action." One can therefore assume that these actions are dealt with by people who are close to the offender. Choices F and J are not explicitly stated in the passage; choice G does not make sense in light of the question.

7. (B) The author ends the passage stating that the findings are "adequate . . . until successfully refuted." Hence, he *tentatively* accepts the information cited. Choices A and D are incorrect because they would indicate an element of hostility; choice C is incorrect because if the author were complacent about the issue, he would express no opinion whatsoever.

8. (J) A *demographic* reason is one that is related to statistics in population distribution and settlement patterns. All of the other choices are psychosocial factors and are incorrect.

9. (A) The first paragraph of this passage elaborates upon, and provides *reasons* for, high crime rates in urban areas. Before a reason for or an elaboration on a problem is stated, the problem itself must be defined. None of the other choices satisfies this necessary condition.

10. (G) While the subject matter of this passage touches on subject matter that could be related to all four occupations, it is first and foremost a study of criminal behavior, which is criminology.

11. (D) The two views called into question share no similarities with regard to any of the first three choices. Therefore the best answer is D, "none of the above."

**12.** (J) The author is not *biased* since he does not profess to personally prefer one view over another; he is not *incensed* since he is not angry; and he is not *cavalier* since he does not seem totally indifferent to the issue. The best answer, therefore, is *detached*, choice J.

**13.** (C) The original liberal view, described in the second paragraph, emphasizes the dichotomy between members of a community and their government, with the citizens desiring to lead their own lives. This makes C the best choice.

**14.** (H) The third paragraph mentions an increasing number of society members able to participate as citizens; the paragraph also says the concept of citizenship came to "enhance social and economic well-being." Therefore, H is the best choice.

**15.** (C) The fourth paragraph says the libertarian view advocates placing restraints on government, which is clearly aligned with the original liberal view. The majoritarian view seeks to "aid the common man" and is most similar to the more developed liberal view, which "seeks to redress imbalances in social and economic life." Therefore, the best answer is C.

**16.** (F) Looking at the passage as a whole, one most conspicuously notes the evolving trends from the classical view, which emphasized deliberation on *public* issues, to the various liberal views, all of which to a degree emphasize citizens' rights as *individuals*. This makes F the best answer choice.

**17.** (C) The correct answer is implied in the first paragraph.

**18.** (G) The first passage of the sentence says, "The concept of democratic citizenship can be traced back to the classical Greeks." This indicates that the author is about to embark on a historical account of the concept of democratic citizenship.

**19.** (B) One must use the process of elimination to weed out the incorrect choices. Choice A is incorrect because the *polis*, or political community, has remained intact; choices C and D are nowhere stated nor implied in the passage. Choice B is the one most closely in accord with the main idea of the passage.

**20.** (H) Both views address concerns regarding what the role of government should be and how wealth should be distributed within the society. Therefore, H is the best choice.

**21.** (C) The first paragraph explicitly states that "the United States has remained, militarily, the most powerful state in the world." None of the other choices is mentioned.

**22.** (G) The passage focuses primarily on the international economy, and the discussion is supported by theories on how military factors might influence it. Choices F, H, and J are all incorrect because no references, either explicit or oblique, are made to these factors.

**23.** (D) The final paragraph introduced two new concepts; it would be logical to assume that the discussion will continue with the first of these two items, which is D.

**24.** (J) The correct answer is stated in the first sentence of the passage.

**25.** (D) While the first three choices could indeed be valid reasons why the United States has remained strong militarily, none are explicitly mentioned in the first paragraph. Particular attention must be paid to the question.

**26.** (G) The correct answer is revealed in the first sentence of the second paragraph, which states that military power provides only a "partial" answer to what propels the international economy.

**27.** (C) Particular attention must be paid to the gist of the paragraph. While reference is made to a decline in U.S. economic power, the paragraph ends on the point that the United States remains an important driving force in the international economy.

**28.** (F) The best answer is *didactic*, meaning "intended to instruct." There is nothing condescending or maudlin (sentimental) about the passage's tone, and if the passage were esoteric, it would contain language not understandable to the casual reader.

**29.** (C) Both a currency exchange rate agreement and a tariff and trade agreement would be a likely result of an international conference on the economy.

**30.** (H) According to the generally recognized principles of psychological development, maturation takes place at all stages of the life cycle.

**31.** (A) Martin Luther, a German scholar, challenged basic teachings of the Roman Catholic Church in a series of 95 theses (arguments) that he nailed to a church door in Wittenburg.

**32.** (G) In international trade, a quota is an example of protectionism, a policy whereby a country attempts to restrict the free flow of trade between itself and other countries.

**33.** (B) A candidate for state governor may be elected by winning only a plurality of the total votes cast.

**34.** (J) Although economists disagree on the specific causes of the 1929 stock market crash, several factors are believed to have contributed. They include low farm prices that brought ruin to farmers, overproduction of manufactured goods, an excess of credit, high tariffs, heavy war reparations burdening European economies, a fragile banking system, and failure to increase the money supply in the United States.

**35.** (A) The most common way in which people determine an individual's social class is by the amount of wealth that individual possesses.

**36.** (J) Under the Articles of Confederation, the central government had very little authority, it had no authority to tax, and all important decisions required the unanimous consent of all members of Congress—thereby making meaningful change all but impossible.

**37.** (C) Labor, either physical or mental, typically accounts for the largest share of the cost of producing a given product.

**38.** (H) On June 28, 1914, a Serbian nationalist assassinated the heir to the Austrian throne, the Archduke Francis Ferdinand. On July 28, Austria declared war on Serbia, marking the beginning of World War I.

**39.** (C) The Neanderthals, a group of early humans who flourished in Europe and Asia from about 100,000 to 40,000 B.C., are not believed to have been ancestors of today's human race. However, they coexisted for at least several thousand years with the Cro-Magnon people, the group now thought to have been our ancestors. The Neanderthals, who never practiced agriculture, subsisted by hunting and gathering.

**40.** (F) In a craft union, skilled workers doing the same kind of work are organized into their own union regardless of where they work. The American Federation of Labor (AFL) was organized in 1886 as a federation of several craft unions.

**41.** (C) The Constitution provides for the President to make treaties with foreign nations, but such treaties are effective only upon two-thirds approval by the Senate.

**42.** (J) Civilizations first emerged in approximately 3000 B.C. in four areas in Asia and Africa. Sumerian civilization arose in the Mesopotamia region of the Middle East, between the Tigris and Euphrates rivers. Egyptian civilization arose along the banks of the Nile River in Africa. An early Indian civilization emerged in the valley of the Indus River, now in Pakistan. Early Chinese civilization took shape on the banks of the Yellow River in central China.

**43.** (B) The correct answer is revealed in the last sentence of the passage, which tells of Vice-President Jefferson's need to "wrest control of the government" from the Federalist President.

**44.** (J) The passage clearly could not be characterized by choices G or H; choice F is not the correct answer because a character portrait is more descriptive than chronological. J is therefore the best answer.

**45.** (B) Given that the passage ends with the point that Jefferson was dissatisfied with the laws being passed under President Adams and wanted to assume control of the government, it is logical to assume that any further discussion would focus on Jefferson's effort to win the presidency.

**46.** (J) Reference to the "nearly mythical" Washington makes J the best choice.

**47.** (C) The author writes of Jefferson in a positive light, yet does not admire Jefferson so much as worship him. The author shows neither cynicism (skepticism) nor equivocation (lack of a clear opinion) in his writing; therefore, *admiration* makes the best choice.

**48.** (H) The passage does not indicate that it was Jefferson's lifelong ambition to become President, nor does it refer to any personal animosity between Jefferson and Adams. H is therefore the best choice.

**49.** (A) Jefferson's willingness to accept the Vice Presidency even before the presidential election was decided indicates he was a person who was amenable to compromise. Therefore, *accommodating* is the best choice.

**50.** (J) Toward the end of the passage it is said that Jefferson "genuinely respected" Adams when the latter assumed the presidency. However, after two years Jefferson's view of him became "drastically altered," and conflict emerged between the two.

**51.** (D) It is stated in the first paragraph that "The candidate who received the greatest number of votes became President; the second highest became Vice-President." Therefore, only choice D can be correct.

**52.** (H) Reference in the middle of the passage to the "deep and bitter divisions facing the nation" makes H the best choice.

## Natural Sciences Reading

**1.** (C) Equilibrium can only occur when a chemical action is reversible, that is, when both a forward and a reverse reaction can occur. Furthermore, these two reactions must be able to occur simultaneously.

**2.** (J) By Le Chatelier's Principle, when a stress such as pressure or a higher temperature is placed on an equilibrium system, that system will shift in a way that relieves the stress.

**3.** (B) When a change occurs in pressure or temperature, the various substances involved in an equilibrium system will shift from one set of concentration levels to another, stabilizing when chemical equilibrium is established.

**4.** (G) In this system the forward reaction produces heat, so the reverse reaction must absorb heat. When temperature is increased, the system will compensate by favoring the heat-absorbing reaction, and the concentrations of $H_2$ and $I_2$ will increase.

**5.** (C) When pressure is increased, this system will compensate by increasing the concentration of the reaction product that takes up less space. In this case, this is the product of the forward reaction, which is only two molecules as opposed to the three molecules making up the original materials.

**6.** (H) In this system the reverse reaction produces heat, so the forward reaction must absorb heat. Consequently, if the temperature is increased, the system will compensate by favoring the heat-absorbing reaction, and the concentrations of $PCl_3$ and $Cl_2$ will increase.

**7.** (A) In this system the reverse reaction generates heat, so the forward reaction must absorb heat. The concentration of HI will increase if the system shifts to favor the forward (heat-absorbing) reaction, which would happen if there were an increase in temperature.

**8.** (H) In this system the forward reaction produces heat and the reverse reaction absorbs heat. If the temperature is increased, the system will compensate by favoring the reverse reaction, increasing the concentrations of $N_2$ and $O_2$.

**9.** (C) An increase in pressure will cause an equilibrium system to shift in favor of the products that occupy less space. In this case, however, both the forward and the reverse reactions produce the same number of molecules. Neither takes up more space than the other, so the concentration of each substance would remain the same.

10. (G) An increase in pressure will cause the system to shift in favor of the products that occupy less space. In this case, the forward reaction produces one molecule, which occupies less space than the two molecules produced by the reverse reaction. Consequently, the relative concentration of $C_2H_6$ will increase, so the relative concentrations of $C_2H_4$ and $H_2$ will decrease.

11. (B) During the first billion years of the solar system, Earth was still sweeping up the cloud of small objects left in its orbit when the solar system was formed. Consequently, Earth was bombarded by meteoroids much more frequently at that time than it is today, when far fewer objects lie in its path.

12. (H) Most of the Moon's craters date from the first billion years of the solar system, when Earth and the Moon were still sweeping up the cloud of small objects left in Earth's orbit when the solar system was formed.

13. (D) The meteorites that fall to Earth's surface date from the formation of the solar system 4.6 billion years ago. Earth's surface rocks, by contrast, are all much younger, since the planet's surface is constantly being remade by the forces of erosion and plate tectonics.

14. (J) The Moon and Earth have probably been struck by meteoroids with about the same frequency, but because the Moon has no wind or rain to cause erosion, its craters have endured while Earth's have mostly worn away.

15. (A) The asteroid belt lies beyond the orbit of Mars. To cross Earth's orbit, a meteoroid from that region would first have to cross the orbit of Mars.

16. (H) A meteoroid that crosses Earth's orbit spends part of its time closer to the sun than Earth is and the rest of its time farther away.

17. (C) Meteorites most likely strike all parts of Earth's surface with about the same frequency. Since about three-fifths of that surface is ocean, the number that land in water is most likely greater than the number striking land.

18. (J) No flash of light would be visible; the meteoroid would not be striking any atmosphere, so it would neither heat nor melt.

19. (D) According to the passage, impact craters are formed when meteorites plunge straight through the atmosphere to the ground. Since the Hoba meteorite did not form an impact crater, most likely it entered the atmosphere at a low angle, and the friction of the air slowed its descent.

20. (G) The chemical properties of an atom are determined by the status of the electrons in the outer orbit. Atoms with electrically stable outer orbits do not usually react with other atoms. Atoms with electrical instability in the outer orbit react with other unstable atoms.

21. (C) The sequence of the nine planets around the sun is: Mercury, Venus, Earth, Mars, Jupiter, Saturn, Uranus, Neptune, and Pluto.

22. (H) Resistance is the term for opposition to the flow of electric current through a conductor and is measured in ohms.

23. (D) The planaria do not have complete digestive systems—that is, a separate mouth and anal opening. However, the digestive system does secrete enzymes. It has no specialized digestive organs, but rather a diverse, branching intestine.

24. (F) Anions are negatively charged atoms, while cations are positively charged atoms. During ionization, it is usually electrons that are gained or lost.

25. (A) During photosynthesis, glucose sugar is produced from carbon dioxide and water. Some of the sugar may be stored as starch, the presence of which can be tested. This experiment tests the effects of both the presence and absence of light and the presence and absence of chlorophyll. Only choice A relates all of these factors.

26. (J) Since the plates are moved apart by the use of insulated handles, the charge on the capacitor must remain constant. For a parallel plate, capacitor $C$ is proportional to $\frac{A}{l}$, where $A$ is the area of the plate and $l$ is the distance between the plates. Therefore, $C$ must decrease. By definition, $C = \frac{Q}{V}$. Therefore, the voltage must increase.

27. (C) Litmus paper turns red with acids ($pH < 7$) and blue with bases ($pH > 7$). The three solutions that turned litmus paper red were acids and thereby had a $pH < 7$.

28. (J) These two postulates were important in proving that no object can move faster than the speed of light. Repeated tests of Einstein's theory have yielded results that confirm the theory.

29. (C) Earthquakes do not occur randomly, but only where the lithospheric plates that cover the earth meet. This can occur on land or under water.

30. (F) Skeletal muscles that are attached to bones are muscles that are under voluntary control. Cardiac muscle is found only in the heart. Smooth muscle lines the organs and is involuntary.

31. (D) As the wavelength of a light wave increases, the amount of energy it has decreases. This shows an inversely proportional relationship as shown on the graph.

32. (J) An electrolyte is a substance that, when added to water, will conduct an electric current. In order to conduct the current it must dissolve in water and carry an electrical charge (i.e., be ionic). Therefore, an electrolyte must be ionic in solution.

33. (C) Only answers C and D are directly related to cues that are given by the photoperiod. However, D is too limited while C encompasses all activities in all plants.

34. (F) All the formulae show four other atoms bound to the carbon atom. One can deduce from this information that carbon has four bonding sites.

**35.** (B) The net forces acting on the bicycle do not equal zero; friction and air resistance produce vector forces in the opposite direction of the motion.

**36.** (J) Using $F = ma$ to solve for $a$, $a = \frac{F}{m}$. In this relationship, $a$ will increase when $F$ increases but will decrease if $m$ increases. Therefore, J is the only correct answer.

**37.** (B) Using $F = ma$, $F = 1 \text{ kg} \times 1 \frac{m}{sec^2}$. This, by definition, is the force of 1 newton.

**38.** (F) Using $F = ma$, to solve for $m$, $m = \frac{F}{a}$. $m = \frac{2.7 \text{ newtons}}{9 \text{ meters per second}^2}$, or 0.3 kg.

**39.** (C) In the absence of air, there is no air resistance or appreciable friction to reduce motion as there is under normal, everyday conditions on the earth's surface.

**40.** (H) Since the force of your foot is a downward force, the equal and opposite force of the platform is an upward force of the same magnitude.

**41.** (B) In every example of an action/reaction pair, the forces must act on two different objects. In the example of two people tugging on opposite ends of the same rope there are opposing forces, but that does not constitute an action/reaction pair. The other examples, even the static situation of the books on a table (A), are examples of Newton's third law.

**42.** (J) The science of rocketry involves determining the force necessary to overcome inertia, determining the acceleration necessary to overcome Earth's gravity, and calculating the amount of thrust caused by launching the engines enabling the payload to lift off the ground.

**43.** (B) The mass of an object (under most circumstances) is a constant. However, forces and motion are usually reduced because of the presence of friction between surfaces and the factor of air resistance.

**44.** (G) To test his hypothesis that "worms found in the meat were derived from the eggs of flies, and not from the decaying meat," Redi had to leave some jars open so that the flies would have access to the meat and others covered so that their meat could decay without visits from flies.

**45.** (A) Redi's experiments clearly refuted the seventeenth-century belief that living things could arise spontaneously from nonliving substances.

**46.** (J) Redi's belief was a guess, a working hypothesis, and the basis for the construction of his experiments. The passage does not say it was "not his own idea."

**47.** (D) The cheesecloth was not "airtight" (A); it was not described as "sterile" (B); and it was not "repulsive to flies" (D) since the passage says, "Flies also flew to the jar covered with cheesecloth." By elimination, C is correct. Presumably Redi used cheesecloth because it was available to serve as the cover that could permit flies to scent the meat yet prevent them from getting "into the jar to lay their eggs on the meat."

**48.** (G) Although the flies were stopped by the cheesecloth, airborne microscopic organisms, such as bacteria and fungi, were not; these caused the rotting of the meat.

**49.** (C) The life cycle of an insect that undergoes complete metamorphosis consists of the egg, larva (maggot), pupa, and adult. Eggs, maggots, and adult flies are mentioned or implied; the pupa stage is not mentioned at all.

**50.** (F) Redi's experiments confirmed his original hypothesis that the maggots in the meat were derived from the eggs of flies.

**51.** (B) Redi attempted to keep flies out of the cheesecloth-covered jars; Spallanzani attempted to keep microscopic organisms out of the sealed flasks of nutrient broth.

**52.** (G) A control gives an experiment a means of comparison; Redi's experiment was rather primitive, so it left room for error (F). Redi was basically trying to prove only one hypothesis, that maggots on meat came from flies, eliminating choice H. According to the passage, Redi's numerous attempts were his attempt to eliminate chance results (J).

# Practice Test 3

# ANSWER SHEET. PRACTICE TEST 3

## English Usage

| | | | | | | |
|---|---|---|---|---|---|---|
| 1 Ⓐ Ⓑ Ⓒ Ⓓ | 12 Ⓕ Ⓖ Ⓗ Ⓙ | 23 Ⓐ Ⓑ Ⓒ Ⓓ | 34 Ⓕ Ⓖ Ⓗ Ⓙ | 45 Ⓐ Ⓑ Ⓒ Ⓓ | 56 Ⓕ Ⓖ Ⓗ Ⓙ | 67 Ⓐ Ⓑ Ⓒ Ⓓ |
| 2 Ⓕ Ⓖ Ⓗ Ⓙ | 13 Ⓐ Ⓑ Ⓒ Ⓓ | 24 Ⓕ Ⓖ Ⓗ Ⓙ | 35 Ⓐ Ⓑ Ⓒ Ⓓ | 46 Ⓕ Ⓖ Ⓗ Ⓙ | 57 Ⓐ Ⓑ Ⓒ Ⓓ | 68 Ⓕ Ⓖ Ⓗ Ⓙ |
| 3 Ⓐ Ⓑ Ⓒ Ⓓ | 14 Ⓕ Ⓖ Ⓗ Ⓙ | 25 Ⓐ Ⓑ Ⓒ Ⓓ | 36 Ⓕ Ⓖ Ⓗ Ⓙ | 47 Ⓐ Ⓑ Ⓒ Ⓓ | 58 Ⓕ Ⓖ Ⓗ Ⓙ | 69 Ⓐ Ⓑ Ⓒ Ⓓ |
| 4 Ⓕ Ⓖ Ⓗ Ⓙ | 15 Ⓐ Ⓑ Ⓒ Ⓓ | 26 Ⓕ Ⓖ Ⓗ Ⓙ | 37 Ⓐ Ⓑ Ⓒ Ⓓ | 48 Ⓕ Ⓖ Ⓗ Ⓙ | 59 Ⓐ Ⓑ Ⓒ Ⓓ | 70 Ⓕ Ⓖ Ⓗ Ⓙ |
| 5 Ⓐ Ⓑ Ⓒ Ⓓ | 16 Ⓕ Ⓖ Ⓗ Ⓙ | 27 Ⓐ Ⓑ Ⓒ Ⓓ | 38 Ⓕ Ⓖ Ⓗ Ⓙ | 49 Ⓐ Ⓑ Ⓒ Ⓓ | 60 Ⓕ Ⓖ Ⓗ Ⓙ | 71 Ⓐ Ⓑ Ⓒ Ⓓ |
| 6 Ⓕ Ⓖ Ⓗ Ⓙ | 17 Ⓐ Ⓑ Ⓒ Ⓓ | 28 Ⓕ Ⓖ Ⓗ Ⓙ | 39 Ⓐ Ⓑ Ⓒ Ⓓ | 50 Ⓕ Ⓖ Ⓗ Ⓙ | 61 Ⓐ Ⓑ Ⓒ Ⓓ | 72 Ⓕ Ⓖ Ⓗ Ⓙ |
| 7 Ⓐ Ⓑ Ⓒ Ⓓ | 18 Ⓕ Ⓖ Ⓗ Ⓙ | 29 Ⓐ Ⓑ Ⓒ Ⓓ | 40 Ⓕ Ⓖ Ⓗ Ⓙ | 51 Ⓐ Ⓑ Ⓒ Ⓓ | 62 Ⓕ Ⓖ Ⓗ Ⓙ | 73 Ⓐ Ⓑ Ⓒ Ⓓ |
| 8 Ⓕ Ⓖ Ⓗ Ⓙ | 19 Ⓐ Ⓑ Ⓒ Ⓓ | 30 Ⓕ Ⓖ Ⓗ Ⓙ | 41 Ⓐ Ⓑ Ⓒ Ⓓ | 52 Ⓕ Ⓖ Ⓗ Ⓙ | 63 Ⓐ Ⓑ Ⓒ Ⓓ | 74 Ⓕ Ⓖ Ⓗ Ⓙ |
| 9 Ⓐ Ⓑ Ⓒ Ⓓ | 20 Ⓕ Ⓖ Ⓗ Ⓙ | 31 Ⓐ Ⓑ Ⓒ Ⓓ | 42 Ⓕ Ⓖ Ⓗ Ⓙ | 53 Ⓐ Ⓑ Ⓒ Ⓓ | 64 Ⓕ Ⓖ Ⓗ Ⓙ | 75 Ⓐ Ⓑ Ⓒ Ⓓ |
| 10 Ⓕ Ⓖ Ⓗ Ⓙ | 21 Ⓐ Ⓑ Ⓒ Ⓓ | 32 Ⓕ Ⓖ Ⓗ Ⓙ | 43 Ⓐ Ⓑ Ⓒ Ⓓ | 54 Ⓕ Ⓖ Ⓗ Ⓙ | 65 Ⓐ Ⓑ Ⓒ Ⓓ | |
| 11 Ⓐ Ⓑ Ⓒ Ⓓ | 22 Ⓕ Ⓖ Ⓗ Ⓙ | 33 Ⓐ Ⓑ Ⓒ Ⓓ | 44 Ⓕ Ⓖ Ⓗ Ⓙ | 55 Ⓐ Ⓑ Ⓒ Ⓓ | 66 Ⓕ Ⓖ Ⓗ Ⓙ | |

## Mathematics Usage

| | | | | | | |
|---|---|---|---|---|---|---|
| 1 Ⓐ Ⓑ Ⓒ Ⓓ Ⓔ | 7 Ⓐ Ⓑ Ⓒ Ⓓ Ⓔ | 13 Ⓐ Ⓑ Ⓒ Ⓓ Ⓔ | 19 Ⓐ Ⓑ Ⓒ Ⓓ Ⓔ | 25 Ⓐ Ⓑ Ⓒ Ⓓ Ⓔ | 31 Ⓐ Ⓑ Ⓒ Ⓓ Ⓔ | 37 Ⓐ Ⓑ Ⓒ Ⓓ Ⓔ |
| 2 Ⓕ Ⓖ Ⓗ Ⓙ Ⓚ | 8 Ⓕ Ⓖ Ⓗ Ⓙ Ⓚ | 14 Ⓕ Ⓖ Ⓗ Ⓙ Ⓚ | 20 Ⓕ Ⓖ Ⓗ Ⓙ Ⓚ | 26 Ⓕ Ⓖ Ⓗ Ⓙ Ⓚ | 32 Ⓕ Ⓖ Ⓗ Ⓙ Ⓚ | 38 Ⓕ Ⓖ Ⓗ Ⓙ Ⓚ |
| 3 Ⓐ Ⓑ Ⓒ Ⓓ Ⓔ | 9 Ⓐ Ⓑ Ⓒ Ⓓ Ⓔ | 15 Ⓐ Ⓑ Ⓒ Ⓓ Ⓔ | 21 Ⓐ Ⓑ Ⓒ Ⓓ Ⓔ | 27 Ⓐ Ⓑ Ⓒ Ⓓ Ⓔ | 33 Ⓐ Ⓑ Ⓒ Ⓓ Ⓔ | 39 Ⓐ Ⓑ Ⓒ Ⓓ Ⓔ |
| 4 Ⓕ Ⓖ Ⓗ Ⓙ Ⓚ | 10 Ⓕ Ⓖ Ⓗ Ⓙ Ⓚ | 16 Ⓕ Ⓖ Ⓗ Ⓙ Ⓚ | 22 Ⓕ Ⓖ Ⓗ Ⓙ Ⓚ | 28 Ⓕ Ⓖ Ⓗ Ⓙ Ⓚ | 34 Ⓕ Ⓖ Ⓗ Ⓙ Ⓚ | 40 Ⓕ Ⓖ Ⓗ Ⓙ Ⓚ |
| 5 Ⓐ Ⓑ Ⓒ Ⓓ Ⓔ | 11 Ⓐ Ⓑ Ⓒ Ⓓ Ⓔ | 17 Ⓐ Ⓑ Ⓒ Ⓓ Ⓔ | 23 Ⓐ Ⓑ Ⓒ Ⓓ Ⓔ | 29 Ⓐ Ⓑ Ⓒ Ⓓ Ⓔ | 35 Ⓐ Ⓑ Ⓒ Ⓓ Ⓔ | |
| 6 Ⓕ Ⓖ Ⓗ Ⓙ Ⓚ | 12 Ⓕ Ⓖ Ⓗ Ⓙ Ⓚ | 18 Ⓕ Ⓖ Ⓗ Ⓙ Ⓚ | 24 Ⓕ Ⓖ Ⓗ Ⓙ Ⓚ | 30 Ⓕ Ⓖ Ⓗ Ⓙ Ⓚ | 36 Ⓕ Ⓖ Ⓗ Ⓙ Ⓚ | |

## Social Studies Reading

| | | | | | | | |
|---|---|---|---|---|---|---|---|
| 1 Ⓐ Ⓑ Ⓒ Ⓓ | 8 Ⓕ Ⓖ Ⓗ Ⓙ | 15 Ⓐ Ⓑ Ⓒ Ⓓ | 22 Ⓕ Ⓖ Ⓗ Ⓙ | 29 Ⓐ Ⓑ Ⓒ Ⓓ | 36 Ⓕ Ⓖ Ⓗ Ⓙ | 43 Ⓐ Ⓑ Ⓒ Ⓓ | 50 Ⓕ Ⓖ Ⓗ Ⓙ |
| 2 Ⓕ Ⓖ Ⓗ Ⓙ | 9 Ⓐ Ⓑ Ⓒ Ⓓ | 16 Ⓕ Ⓖ Ⓗ Ⓙ | 23 Ⓐ Ⓑ Ⓒ Ⓓ | 30 Ⓕ Ⓖ Ⓗ Ⓙ | 37 Ⓐ Ⓑ Ⓒ Ⓓ | 44 Ⓕ Ⓖ Ⓗ Ⓙ | 51 Ⓐ Ⓑ Ⓒ Ⓓ |
| 3 Ⓐ Ⓑ Ⓒ Ⓓ | 10 Ⓕ Ⓖ Ⓗ Ⓙ | 17 Ⓐ Ⓑ Ⓒ Ⓓ | 24 Ⓕ Ⓖ Ⓗ Ⓙ | 31 Ⓐ Ⓑ Ⓒ Ⓓ | 38 Ⓕ Ⓖ Ⓗ Ⓙ | 45 Ⓐ Ⓑ Ⓒ Ⓓ | 52 Ⓕ Ⓖ Ⓗ Ⓙ |
| 4 Ⓕ Ⓖ Ⓗ Ⓙ | 11 Ⓐ Ⓑ Ⓒ Ⓓ | 18 Ⓕ Ⓖ Ⓗ Ⓙ | 25 Ⓐ Ⓑ Ⓒ Ⓓ | 32 Ⓕ Ⓖ Ⓗ Ⓙ | 39 Ⓐ Ⓑ Ⓒ Ⓓ | 46 Ⓕ Ⓖ Ⓗ Ⓙ | |
| 5 Ⓐ Ⓑ Ⓒ Ⓓ | 12 Ⓕ Ⓖ Ⓗ Ⓙ | 19 Ⓐ Ⓑ Ⓒ Ⓓ | 26 Ⓕ Ⓖ Ⓗ Ⓙ | 33 Ⓐ Ⓑ Ⓒ Ⓓ | 40 Ⓕ Ⓖ Ⓗ Ⓙ | 47 Ⓐ Ⓑ Ⓒ Ⓓ | |
| 6 Ⓕ Ⓖ Ⓗ Ⓙ | 13 Ⓐ Ⓑ Ⓒ Ⓓ | 20 Ⓕ Ⓖ Ⓗ Ⓙ | 27 Ⓐ Ⓑ Ⓒ Ⓓ | 34 Ⓕ Ⓖ Ⓗ Ⓙ | 41 Ⓐ Ⓑ Ⓒ Ⓓ | 48 Ⓕ Ⓖ Ⓗ Ⓙ | |
| 7 Ⓐ Ⓑ Ⓒ Ⓓ | 14 Ⓕ Ⓖ Ⓗ Ⓙ | 21 Ⓐ Ⓑ Ⓒ Ⓓ | 28 Ⓕ Ⓖ Ⓗ Ⓙ | 35 Ⓐ Ⓑ Ⓒ Ⓓ | 42 Ⓕ Ⓖ Ⓗ Ⓙ | 49 Ⓐ Ⓑ Ⓒ Ⓓ | |

## Natural Sciences Reading

| | | | | | | | |
|---|---|---|---|---|---|---|---|
| 1 Ⓐ Ⓑ Ⓒ Ⓓ | 8 Ⓕ Ⓖ Ⓗ Ⓙ | 15 Ⓐ Ⓑ Ⓒ Ⓓ | 22 Ⓕ Ⓖ Ⓗ Ⓙ | 29 Ⓐ Ⓑ Ⓒ Ⓓ | 36 Ⓕ Ⓖ Ⓗ Ⓙ | 43 Ⓐ Ⓑ Ⓒ Ⓓ | 50 Ⓕ Ⓖ Ⓗ Ⓙ |
| 2 Ⓕ Ⓖ Ⓗ Ⓙ | 9 Ⓐ Ⓑ Ⓒ Ⓓ | 16 Ⓕ Ⓖ Ⓗ Ⓙ | 23 Ⓐ Ⓑ Ⓒ Ⓓ | 30 Ⓕ Ⓖ Ⓗ Ⓙ | 37 Ⓐ Ⓑ Ⓒ Ⓓ | 44 Ⓕ Ⓖ Ⓗ Ⓙ | 51 Ⓐ Ⓑ Ⓒ Ⓓ |
| 3 Ⓐ Ⓑ Ⓒ Ⓓ | 10 Ⓕ Ⓖ Ⓗ Ⓙ | 17 Ⓐ Ⓑ Ⓒ Ⓓ | 24 Ⓕ Ⓖ Ⓗ Ⓙ | 31 Ⓐ Ⓑ Ⓒ Ⓓ | 38 Ⓕ Ⓖ Ⓗ Ⓙ | 45 Ⓐ Ⓑ Ⓒ Ⓓ | 52 Ⓕ Ⓖ Ⓗ Ⓙ |
| 4 Ⓕ Ⓖ Ⓗ Ⓙ | 11 Ⓐ Ⓑ Ⓒ Ⓓ | 18 Ⓕ Ⓖ Ⓗ Ⓙ | 25 Ⓐ Ⓑ Ⓒ Ⓓ | 32 Ⓕ Ⓖ Ⓗ Ⓙ | 39 Ⓐ Ⓑ Ⓒ Ⓓ | 46 Ⓕ Ⓖ Ⓗ Ⓙ | |
| 5 Ⓐ Ⓑ Ⓒ Ⓓ | 12 Ⓕ Ⓖ Ⓗ Ⓙ | 19 Ⓐ Ⓑ Ⓒ Ⓓ | 26 Ⓕ Ⓖ Ⓗ Ⓙ | 33 Ⓐ Ⓑ Ⓒ Ⓓ | 40 Ⓕ Ⓖ Ⓗ Ⓙ | 47 Ⓐ Ⓑ Ⓒ Ⓓ | |
| 6 Ⓕ Ⓖ Ⓗ Ⓙ | 13 Ⓐ Ⓑ Ⓒ Ⓓ | 20 Ⓕ Ⓖ Ⓗ Ⓙ | 27 Ⓐ Ⓑ Ⓒ Ⓓ | 34 Ⓕ Ⓖ Ⓗ Ⓙ | 41 Ⓐ Ⓑ Ⓒ Ⓓ | 48 Ⓕ Ⓖ Ⓗ Ⓙ | |
| 7 Ⓐ Ⓑ Ⓒ Ⓓ | 14 Ⓕ Ⓖ Ⓗ Ⓙ | 21 Ⓐ Ⓑ Ⓒ Ⓓ | 28 Ⓕ Ⓖ Ⓗ Ⓙ | 35 Ⓐ Ⓑ Ⓒ Ⓓ | 42 Ⓕ Ⓖ Ⓗ Ⓙ | 49 Ⓐ Ⓑ Ⓒ Ⓓ | |

# TEST 1.  ENGLISH USAGE

*40 Minutes—75 Questions*

**DIRECTIONS:** In the reading selections below, certain parts of the sentences have been underlined and numbered. In the right-hand column, you will find different ways of writing each underlined part. Choose the one that best expresses the idea and uses standard written English. If you think the original version is the best, choose "NO CHANGE." The answers to many questions depend upon material that follows the underlined part. So be sure that you have read far enough ahead before you select your answer choice.

___

### Passage 1

The outer solar system begins somewhere in the asteroid belt, beyond Mars. The first major outpost of this vast realm <u>was</u> Jupiter, the giant planet. Orbiting at
<sub>1</sub>
a mean distance of 778 million kilometers from the

<u>Sun; Jupiter being</u> the largest of the Sun's family of
<sub>2</sub>

planetary <u>companions, in that it has</u> a volume approxi-
<sub>3</sub>
mately 1,000 times that of Earth. Jupiter is not merely a

single large <u>planet, yet since</u> it is the central object and
<sub>4</sub>
master of a complex system consisting of four large

moons, at least twelve smaller satellites, a ring system,

and a powerful magnetic field that <u>influence</u> an immense
<sub>5</sub>
region of space filled with charged particles of all varie-

ties. It is the archetype of the "miniature solar systems"

common to the outer parts of our planetary system.

Exploration of the outer reaches of our solar system

began when the Pioneer 10 spacecraft, launched in 1972,

flew past Jupiter in 1973. The Pioneer program was

followed in 1979 by the spectacular reconnaissance mis-

sions of the two Voyager spacecraft. Through the eyes of

1. A. NO CHANGE
   B. had been
   C. being
   D. is

2. F. NO CHANGE
   G. Sun, with Jupiter being
   H. Sun, Jupiter is
   J. Sun: Jupiter is

3. A. NO CHANGE
   B. companion, having
   C. companions and has
   D. companions to have

4. F. NO CHANGE
   G. planet, however,
   H. planet, however;
   J. planet;

5. A. NO CHANGE
   B. are influencing
   C. influences
   D. have influenced

GO ON TO THE NEXT PAGE

Voyager, astronomers saw strange planetary surfaces

unlike anything that had previously been envisioned by
6

them, except perhaps in speculative fiction.  Compli-
7

cated electromagnetic phenomena were encountered in ·

the vast natural laboratory of plasmas and interacting

forces that surrounds the giant planet and encompasses
8

many of its large satellites.  The jovian system that has
9

come to be revealed by these preliminary explorations

suggested new dimensions of fundamental studies about

planets, satellites, the interplanetary medium, and the

formation of systems around stars.


## Passage 2

Botany is surely the more gentler of sciences.
10

The careful observation of a flower is a calm, unobtrusive

action—the peaceful contemplation of a beautiful ob-

ject.  Reduced to its essentials, it requires no laboratory
11

but the natural world and few tools and the naked eye.

Botany in its most scientific or purest form consists about
12

seeking to know more about the plant simply for the sake

of that knowledge.  Plants have not always been re-

garded as worthy of knowing or studying in themselves,
13

not on their merits as sources of food or drugs but as life

forms.  In fact, the history of botany can be viewed in

terms of repeated rediscoveries of this one theme—that

plants are worthy of study in and of themselves, quite

apart from any use they might have for mankind.

6.  F.  NO CHANGE
    G.  not like anything else one had envisioned
    H.  not like anything else one could envision
    J.  unlike anything previously envisioned

7.  A.  NO CHANGE
    B.  fiction complicated
    C.  fiction, complicated
    D.  fiction, but

8.  F.  NO CHANGE
    G.  that surround
    H.  that will surround
    J.  to surround

9.  A.  NO CHANGE
    B.  reveals
    C.  revealed
    D.  which came to be revealed

10.  F.  NO CHANGE
     G.  the most gentle of
     H.  the gentler of
     J.  the gentlest in the

11.  A.  NO CHANGE
     B.  essentials; it
     C.  essentials; botany
     D.  essentials, botany

12.  F.  NO CHANGE
     G.  consists in
     H.  consists of
     J.  consist of

13.  A.  NO CHANGE
     B.  for knowledge
     C.  of knowledge
     D.  to know

GO ON TO THE NEXT PAGE

The practical motives behind plant study should not be disparaging—the bulk of our medical history, for
14
instance, is made up of accounts of herbal remedies. But the study of the medicinal properties of plants contained a self-limiting mechanism: if a plant seemed to have no utilitarian value, it was disregarded, and no further study of it is made. The Renaissance attitude to Nature
15
changed this overly practical bent and initiated the scientific study of plants.

Botany as a pure science has certain characteristics and makes certain assumptions that prove thought-provoking and interesting. One of it's unspoken and also
16
basic assumptions is an implicit respect and regard for all living things. The botanist who studies a plant's structure or tries to have understood their functions confronts
17
nature on its own terms. Investigations of how a plant thrives or reproduces, or studies of the purposefulness of a flower's coloration and structure, are almost implicitly egalitarian and tautological. The botanist studies the flower because they exist, but because it exists, it is
18
worthy of study.

### Passage 3

The main characteristic of poverty is, of course, lack of money. A family is defined poor when its annual
19
income falls below a certain dollar amount, calculated by the Federal Government to be the minimum a family of their size would need to maintain a minimally decent
20
standard of living. In certain areas of rural America,

14. **F.** NO CHANGE
    **G.** disparaged—the bulk
    **H.** disparaging, the bulk
    **J.** disparaged; the bulk

15. **A.** NO CHANGE
    **B.** had been made
    **C.** were made
    **D.** was made

16. **F.** NO CHANGE
    **G.** it's unspoken, but basic,
    **H.** their unspoken but basic
    **J.** its unspoken but basic

17. **A.** NO CHANGE
    **B.** to understand its
    **C.** understanding it's
    **D.** having understood their

18. **F.** NO CHANGE
    **G.** it exists, but
    **H.** it exists, and
    **J.** it exists. And

19. **A.** NO CHANGE
    **B.** named
    **C.** considered
    **D.** determined

20. **F.** NO CHANGE
    **G.** there
    **H.** its
    **J.** it's

GO ON TO THE NEXT PAGE

consequently, poverty is the rule rather than the excep-
21

tion.  As many as 50 percent of the families may earn

less than the poverty level, and some may manage to
22

subsist somehow on amounts even less than half the

official poverty-level income.

    Although lack of money is the defining characteristic
23

of poverty, poverty is more than simply lack of money.

It is an entire complex of symptoms.  Low levels of

formal schooling among adults parallels low income
24

levels.  Additionally, in families below the poverty level,

the number of children and aged who depend on those

who work is in general higher than the national average

for all families.  As a consequence, fewer workers sup-

port a greater number of nonworkers than in other,

more prosperous families.

    Often, the schooling provided in low-income areas

are as inadequate like incomes.  In particular, rural
25

children get poorer schooling than city children, and

many rural poor are severely handicapped with lack of
26

education.  The general rural average is only 8.8 years of

school completed.  Moreover, low educational levels

seem to be self-perpetuating.  If the head of a rural poor

family have little schooling, the children are often handi-
27

capped in their efforts to get an education.

    It is especially difficult for people who are handi-

capped educationally to acquire new skills, get new jobs,

or otherwise adjust to an increasingly urbanized society.

21. **A.** NO CHANGE
    **B.** as a consequence
    **C.** consequent
    **D.** OMIT

22. **F.** NO CHANGE
    **G.** lower than
    **H.** less as
    **J.** lower as

23. **A.** NO CHANGE
    **B.** (Do NOT begin a new paragraph.) Although
    **C.** (Begin a new paragraph.) Since
    **D.** (Do NOT begin a new paragraph.) Since

24. **F.** NO CHANGE
    **G.** parallel
    **H.** are parallel as
    **J.** is parallel with

25. **A.** NO CHANGE
    **B.** is—like family income, inadequate
    **C.** is so inadequate as family income
    **D.** is, like family income, inadequate

26. **F.** NO CHANGE
    **G.** by the fact of their
    **H.** by
    **J.** in that they have a

27. **A.** NO CHANGE
    **B.** have had
    **C.** has had
    **D.** was to have

GO ON TO THE NEXT PAGE

This is as true on the farm rather than in urban
                                    _____
                                        28

industry since modern farming requires skills that
_____
      29

poor educated people lack.  Lacking in education, the
_____
      30
rural poor either take low-paying jobs on the farm or

elsewhere in rural areas or swell the ranks of the

unemployed or underemployed.

*Passage 4*

Traditionally, China has been called a "country of

the art of writing."  The cultural literacy of old China

was centered in the imperial dynasties; at a later date, it
                          _____
                             31
became the property of all the nobility.  By the Middle

Ages, intellectuals from among the "populace"

began involving itself with art, but the art of calligraphy
_____
      32
(unlike painting or crafts) was separated from the

illiterate people, unlike painting or craft work.

It should be noted, however, that even at this later

date, the word *populace* referred to the "shen-shih,"

or "gentlemen," that segment of the larger population

that had taken and passed the classical examinations for

senior governmental posts.  It is important to note that

these classical examinations heavily stress the importance
                            _____
                                 33
of literary knowledge.  The ones that passed the exami-
                        _____
                             34

28.  F.  NO CHANGE
     G.  rather as in
     H.  as they are in
     J.  as it is in

29.  A.  NO CHANGE
     B.  industry.  Since
     C.  industry.  On the contrary,
     D.  industry.  Nevertheless

30.  F.  NO CHANGE
     G.  poorly educated
     H.  educated poor
     J.  poor education

31.  A.  NO CHANGE
     B.  dynasties, at
     C.  dynasties at
     D.  dynasties, consequently at

32.  F.  NO CHANGE
     G.  have begun to be involved
     H.  began being involved
     J.  began to be involved

33.  A.  NO CHANGE
     B.  are stressing heavily.
     C.  heavily stressed
     D.  stressing heavily

34.  F.  NO CHANGE
     G.  Those who
     H.  The ones that had
     J.  Those that had

GO ON TO THE NEXT PAGE

nations were not only <u>bureaucrats; and</u> accomplished
<sup>35</sup>

literati.  This is the reason that <u>led to China being</u>
<sup>36</sup>
referred to as the land of the art of writing.

Japan, <u>which imported it's culture of</u> China, did not
<sup>37</sup>
have classical examinations, in the strict sense of the

word.  However, starting in the Heian era, it was consid-

ered important <u>that persons who served</u> in the Imperial
<sup>38</sup>
Court to be able to compose "waka," the thirty-one-

syllable classical Japanese form of poetry.  It is safe to

assume that China influenced this attitude.  The art of

calligraphy was part and parcel of the intellectual life at

Court.  As calligraphy came to be enjoyed and respected,

its importance became more widespread.

### Passage 5

One out of every four children who entered the fifth

grade in the fall of 1966 <u>fail to graduate</u> with his or her
<sup>39</sup>

class.  The total number <u>that should of graduated</u> was 4.1
<sup>40</sup>
million, but approximately 900,000 fell by the wayside.

Those who do not make it are called school drop-

outs.  The official definition of the term *school dropout*

<u>being a person</u> who has not yet attained age 16 who
<sup>41</sup>
leaves school before graduation for any reason except for

transfer.  School officials who work with dropouts say a

**35.** A. NO CHANGE
B. bureaucrats; but
C. bureaucrats, and
D. bureaucrats, but

**36.** F. NO CHANGE
G. led to Chinas being
H. led up to Chinas'
J. China is

**37.** A. NO CHANGE
B. which imported its culture from
C. importing it's culture from
D. with the importing of its culture from

**38.** F. NO CHANGE
G. that persons serving
H. for persons who served
J. for persons that serve

**39.** A. NO CHANGE
B. failed to graduate
C. failed graduation
D. fails to graduate

**40.** F. NO CHANGE
G. that should of been graduated
H. who should of
J. who should have

**41.** A. NO CHANGE
B. is any person
C. is that of any person
D. has been a person

GO ON TO THE NEXT PAGE

student will usually starting thinking about dropping out
42

about two years before he or she ceases to attend

school: roughly at age 14.  Absenteeism, class cutting,
43

lack of motivation, and lack of interest in school is often
44

early signs of the potential dropout.  Also, many students
45

drop out mentally very early in their school career,

despite their physical presence until graduation.

　　The dropout is most often a boy who mostly, fre-
46

quently leaves school at the age of 16 while in the tenth

grade.  He is most likely than those who stay in school to
47

score low on an intelligence test and is likely to be failing

in school at the time of him dropping out.  Yet most
48

dropouts are really no less bright than students who

remain in school until graduation.  The dropout typically

comes from the lower-income class and most often leaves

school for financial reasons.  His absences from school

increasing noticeably during the eighth grade and he
49

participates little or none in extracurricular activities.
50

The reasons a student drops out of school goes deeper as
51

a mere desire to be rid of school.  Dropping out is a

symptom; the roots of the problem are usually below the

surface.

---

42. **F.** NO CHANGE
　　**G.** usually will be starting thinking
　　**H.** starts usually thinking
　　**J.** usually starts to think

43. **A.** NO CHANGE
　　**B.** school but roughly
　　**C.** school and roughly
　　**D.** school, roughly

44. **F.** NO CHANGE
　　**G.** is oftentimes
　　**H.** are often
　　**J.** were often

45. **A.** NO CHANGE
　　**B.** dropout also
　　**C.** dropout many
　　**D.** dropout but also

46. **F.** NO CHANGE
　　**G.** most frequently,
　　**H.** most frequently
　　**J.** OMIT

47. **A.** NO CHANGE
　　**B.** more likely than those
　　**C.** most likely as one
　　**D.** more likely than one

48. **F.** NO CHANGE
　　**G.** he drops out
　　**H.** of his having dropped out
　　**J.** he dropped out

49. **A.** NO CHANGE
　　**B.** increase so that
　　**C.** increase noticeably
　　**D.** increased to the point where it was noticed

50. **F.** NO CHANGE
　　**G.** and not at all
　　**H.** or not much
　　**J.** or not at all

51. **A.** NO CHANGE
　　**B.** go more deeply than
　　**C.** go deeper as
　　**D.** go deeper than

GO ON TO THE NEXT PAGE

*Passage 6*

The idea of generating electricity with wind power is not new. But the kind of attention that idea is getting today, in terms of research and <u>development, are both</u> [52] new and encouraging to planners looking for renewable energy sources <u>satisfying</u> growing national demands. An [53] effort is being made in the United States to use one of humankind's oldest energy sources to solve one of <u>its</u> [54] most modern <u>problems, to find</u> reliable and cost-effec- [55] tive ways to harness the wind to produce electricity.

Wind machines are not the simple devices <u>that they may be appearing to be</u> and the lessons they [56] teach seldom come easy. But the potential reward to a nation that needs more energy from a renewable source is beyond calculation. Rewards for using wind power <u>have been gathered</u> by civilizations and cultures since [57] early in recorded history.

No record survives of the earliest wind machine. It may <u>have been built</u> in China more than three thousand [58] years ago. It may have been on the windy plains of Afghanistan. History hints at some sort of wind power used in the Pharaohs' Egypt <u>for the drawing of water</u> for [59] agriculture long before the birth of Christ. Hammurabi may have taken time out from developing a legal code about 2000 BC to sponsor development of some sort of

52. F. NO CHANGE
G. development, is
H. developing, is
J. development, are

53. A. NO CHANGE
B. that would have satisfied
C. to satisfy
D. with the satisfaction of

54. F. NO CHANGE
G. their
H. it's
J. your

55. A. NO CHANGE
B. problems; to find
C. problems, finding
D. problems. To find

56. F. NO CHANGE
G. they may be
H. it may seem to be
J. they may appear to be

57. A. NO CHANGE
B. has been gathering
C. is gathering
D. will have been gathered

58. F. NO CHANGE
G. have been
H. was being built
J. have been building

59. A. NO CHANGE
B. to draw water
C. in order that water be drawn
D. in order to draw water

GO ON TO THE NEXT PAGE →

wind machine. The earliest confirmed wind machines are in that same region, however. Persian writers described gardens irrigated through the means of wind-
driven water lifts several centuries before the birth of
Christ. Ultimately, we can only guess at the origin of the windmill.

Persian machines were horizontal devices, carousel-like contraptions that revolved around a center pole and that caught the wind with bundles of reeds. The carousel is perhaps the more simple design for capturing the wind; it cares nothing for the direction of the breeze, but revolves no matter where on the compass the wind may originate.

From the Middle East, wind-machine technology may have been carried to Europe by returning Crusaders. Accurate records do not exist, but soon after the Crusades windmills appeared in northern Europe and soon were found on the British Isles.

Windmills flourished, foundered, and come close to extinction, for the wind is capricious. It can fail to blow just when it is needed the most or rage into a gale when it isn't. It can blow efficiently one hour, and then the next hour it won't blow at all.

60. **F.** NO CHANGE
**G.** irrigates through
**H.** irrigates by means of
**J.** irrigated by

61. **A.** NO CHANGE
**B.** lifts several,
**C.** lifts but several
**D.** lifts and several

62. **F.** NO CHANGE
**G.** the origin of the windmill can only be guessed at
**H.** the origin of the windmill can only be guessed at by us
**J.** the origin of the windmill could only be guessed at

63. **A.** NO CHANGE
**B.** most simplest design for capturing
**C.** simpler design to capture
**D.** simplest design for capturing

64. **F.** NO CHANGE
**G.** came close to
**H.** are coming closer to
**J.** come close upon

65. **A.** NO CHANGE
**B.** hour, and then it didn't blow at all the next
**C.** hour, then not at all the next
**D.** hour, meanwhile not blowing the next

GO ON TO THE NEXT PAGE

*Passage 7*

Television and its programs do not just happen. It is
⎯⎯
66

planned products of a huge, wealthy, and highly competi-

tive commercial enterprise. The television industry,

which includes stations, networks, production compa-

nies, actors, and writers, are responsible for selecting,
⎯⎯⎯⎯⎯⎯⎯⎯⎯
67

creating and distributing programs. The three most

popular programs are the episodic series, the made-for-
⎯⎯⎯⎯⎯⎯⎯⎯⎯⎯
68

television movies, and the mini-series.

In the 1970s, the episodic series, both dramatic

and comic, was the most popular of these.
⎯⎯⎯⎯⎯⎯
69

With the advent of cable and pay television and of video
⎯⎯⎯⎯⎯⎯⎯⎯
70

disks and tapes, the television movie is rapid gaining in
⎯⎯⎯⎯⎯⎯⎯⎯
71

popularity. The past ten years have seen several changes
⎯⎯⎯⎯⎯⎯
72

in television drama. The action-adventure police drama

has lost and the situation comedy has grew in popularity.
⎯⎯⎯⎯⎯
73

Topics previously considered taboo emerged. Unmarried
⎯⎯⎯⎯⎯⎯⎯⎯⎯
74

couples living together, divorces, and single parents.

Even topics that are politically controversy can now be
⎯⎯⎯⎯⎯⎯⎯⎯⎯⎯⎯
75

the focus of programs.

---

66. **F.** NO CHANGE
    **G.** They are
    **H.** They would be
    **J.** It was

67. **A.** NO CHANGE
    **B.** writers, is
    **C.** writers are
    **D.** writers—is

68. **F.** NO CHANGE
    **G.** episodic series the
    **H.** episodic, series the
    **J.** episodic series the,

69. **A.** NO CHANGE
    **B.** was the more
    **C.** were the most
    **D.** were the more

70. **F.** NO CHANGE
    **G.** With the adventing of
    **H.** With advent
    **J.** With the beginning of the advent

71. **A.** NO CHANGE
    **B.** has rapidly gained in
    **C.** is rapidly gaining in
    **D.** will rapidly gain in

72. **F.** NO CHANGE
    **G.** see
    **H.** will see
    **J.** would be seeing

73. **A.** NO CHANGE
    **B.** has grown
    **C.** grew
    **D.** grow

74. **F.** NO CHANGE
    **G.** emerged, unmarried
    **H.** emerged unmarried
    **J.** emerged: unmarried

75. **A.** NO CHANGE
    **B.** politically controversial
    **C.** politics controversy
    **D.** political controversy

**END OF TEST**

If you complete this test before the time is up, check
back over the questions on this test only. Do not go back
to the previous test. Do not proceed to the next test until
you are told to do so.

# TEST 2.  MATHEMATICS USAGE

*50 Minutes—40 Questions*

**DIRECTIONS:** Solve each of the following problems. Choose the correct answer.

Solve as many problems as you can. Do not spend too much time on any one problem. You may return to problems so long as you have time left in this section.

Note: The figures that accompany the problems are not necessarily drawn to scale. Figures are assumed to lie in a plane unless a note states otherwise.

---

1.  A barrel contained 5.75 liters of water and 4.5 liters evaporated. How many liters of water remain in the barrel?

    A.  0.75
    B.  1.25
    C.  1.75
    D.  2.25
    E.  13.25

2.  Which of the following expressions correctly describes the mathematical relationship below?
    3 less than the product of 4 times $x$

    F.  $4x - 3$
    G.  $3x - 4$
    H.  $4(x - 3)$
    J.  $3(4x)$
    K.  $\dfrac{4x}{3}$

3.  If $\dfrac{3}{4}$ of $x$ is 36, then $\dfrac{1}{3}$ of $x = $ ?

    A.  9
    B.  12
    C.  16
    D.  24
    E.  42

4.  In the figure below, what is the value of $x + y$?

    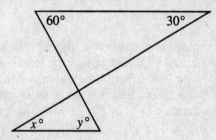

    F.  45
    G.  60
    H.  75
    J.  90
    K.  120

5.  If $n$ is a multiple of 3, which of the following is also a multiple of 3?

    A.  $2 + n$
    B.  $2 - n$
    C.  $2n - 1$
    D.  $2n + 1$
    E.  $2n + 3$

6.  Which of the following is NOT equal to the ratio of two whole numbers?

    F.  $\left(\dfrac{1}{5}\right)^2$
    G.  $\dfrac{1}{5}$
    H.  0.20
    J.  5%
    K.  $\dfrac{\sqrt{5}}{1}$

GO ON TO THE NEXT PAGE

7. If the area of a square is 16, what is the perimeter?

    A. 2
    B. 4
    C. 8
    D. 16
    E. 32

8. If $12 + x = 36 - y$, then $x + y = ?$

    F. $-48$
    G. $-24$
    H. 3
    J. 24
    K. 48

9. What is the greatest factor of the following expression?

    $3x^2 y^3 z + 6x^3 y z^3 + 2 x y^2 z^2$

    A. $3x^2 y^2 z^2$
    B. $2x^2 y^2 z^2$
    C. $x^3 y^3 z^3$
    D. $xyz$
    E. $xz$

10. Depending on the value of $k$, the expression $3k + 4k + 5k + 6k + 7k$ may or may not be divisible by 7. Which of the terms, when eliminated from the expression, guarantees that the resulting expression is divisible by 7 for every positive integer $k$?

    F. $3k$
    G. $4k$
    H. $5k$
    J. $6k$
    K. $7k$

11. If $\frac{1}{3} < x < \frac{3}{8}$, which of the following is a possible value of $x$?

    A. $\frac{1}{2}$

    B. $\frac{3}{16}$

    C. $\frac{17}{48}$

    D. $\frac{9}{24}$

    E. $\frac{5}{12}$

12. If $x^2 - y^2 = 3$ and $x - y = 3$, then $x + y = ?$

    F. 0
    G. 1
    H. 2
    J. 3
    K. 9

13. If $n$ is a positive integer, which of the following must be an even integer?

    A. $n + 1$
    B. $3n + 1$
    C. $3n + 2$
    D. $n^2 + 1$
    E. $n^2 + n$

14. If the area of a square inscribed in a circle is 16, what is the area of the circle?

    F. $2\pi$
    G. $4\pi$
    H. $8\pi$
    J. $16\pi$
    K. $32\pi$

15. Ellen bought a tape recorder that usually sells for $120 on sale for 25 percent off the usual price. If the store also collected an 8-percent sales tax on the sale price of the tape recorder, how much did Ellen pay for the tape recorder including sales tax?

    A. $106.30
    B. $101.40
    C. $97.20
    D. $95.10
    E. $88.44

16. A certain mixture of gravel and sand consists of 2.5 kilograms of gravel and 12.5 kilograms of sand. What percent of the mixture, by weight, is gravel?

    F. 10%
    G. $16\frac{2}{3}\%$
    H. 20%
    J. 25%
    K. $33\frac{1}{3}\%$

GO ON TO THE NEXT PAGE

662

**17.** The figure below is the top-view of a folding room divider, hinged at $P$ and $Q$. If sections $PR$ and $QS$ are moved as shown until $R$ and $S$ meet, what will be the area, in square feet, enclosed? (Ignore the thickness of the hinges and the screen's sections.)

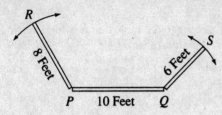

A. 6
B. 12
C. $6\pi$
D. 24
E. $12\pi$

**18.** Motorcycle X averages 40 kilometers per liter of gasoline while Motorcycle Y averages 50 kilometers per liter. If the cost of gasoline is $2 per liter, what will be the difference in the cost of operating the two motorcycles for 300 kilometers?

F. $3
G. $6
H. $12
J. $15
K. $20

**19.** If $f(x) = x^2 - 2x + 1$, then what is $f(f(3))$?

A. 3
B. 9
C. 14
D. 27
E. 39

**20.** For a positive integer $k$, which of the following equals $6k + 3$?

F. $\frac{1}{2}(k + 1)$

G. $\frac{1}{k} + 4$

H. $2k + 1$
J. $3(k + 1)$
K. $3(2k + 1)$

**21.** To mail a letter costs $x$ cents for the first ounce and $y$ cents for every additional ounce or fraction of an ounce. What is the cost, *in cents*, to mail a letter weighing a whole number of ounces, $w$ ?

A. $w(x + y)$
B. $x(w - y)$
C. $x(w - 1) + y(w - 1)$
D. $x + wy$
E. $x + y(w - 1)$

**22.** $|-3| \times |2| \times |-\frac{1}{2}| + (-4) = ?$

F. $-1$
G. 0
H. 1
J. $\frac{3}{2}$
K. 4

**23.** In the figure below, if the area of the square $OPQR$ is 2, what is the area of the circle with center $O$?

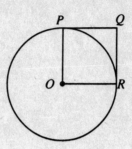

A. $\frac{\pi}{4}$

B. $\pi\sqrt{2}$
C. $2\pi$
D. $2\sqrt{2}\pi$
E. $4\pi$

**24.** Which of the following is (are) always an odd number?

I. The product of a prime number and a prime number
II. The sum of a prime number and a prime number
III. The product of an odd number and another odd number

F. I only
G. III only
H. I and II only
J. II and III only
K. I, II, and III

GO ON TO THE NEXT PAGE

25. What is the area of the shaded portion of the figure below, expressed in terms of $a$ and $b$?

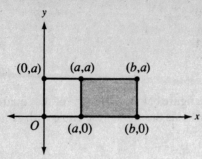

A. $a(b - a)$
B. $a(a - b)$
C. $b(a - b)$
D. $b(b - a)$
E. $ab$

26. $\sqrt{(43 - 7)(29 + 7)} = ?$

F. $3\sqrt{3}$
G. 6
H. 36
J. 42
K. 1,296

27. A certain concrete mixture uses 4 cubic yards of cement for every 20 cubic yards of grit. If a contractor orders 50 cubic yards of cement, how much grit (in cubic yards) should he order if he plans to use all of the cement?

A. 250
B. 200
C. 100
D. 80
E. 10

28. In the figure below, $QT = QR$. If $x = 120°$, then $y = ?$

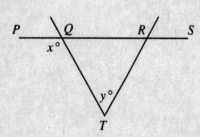

F. 30
G. 60
H. 75
J. 90
K. 120

29. If $\dfrac{x}{y} = -1$, then $x + y = ?$

A. 2
B. 1
C. 0
D. $-1$
E. $-2$

30. According to the table below, which fabric costs the *least* per square yard?

| Fabric | Cost |
| --- | --- |
| F | 3 yards for $8 |
| G | 2 yards for $6 |
| H | 4 yards for $9 |
| J | 5 yards for $7 |
| K | 6 yards for $5 |

F. F
G. G
H. H
J. J
K. K

31. In triangle $PQR$ below, if $PQ \parallel$ to $ST$, then $y = ?$

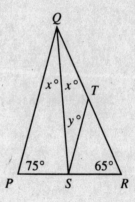

A. 20
B. 40
C. 45
D. 50
E. 55

32. $\dfrac{10^3(10^5 + 10^5)}{10^4} = ?$

F. $10^4$
G. $10^6$
H. $2(10^2)$
J. $2(10^4)$
K. $2(10^9)$

GO ON TO THE NEXT PAGE

**33.** What is the solution set for the following equation?
$x^2 - 5x + 4 = 0$

    **A.** $\{-4, -1\}$
    **B.** $\{-3, -1\}$
    **C.** $\{-1, 3\}$
    **D.** $\{1, 4\}$
    **E.** $\{2, 3\}$

**34.** The average of seven different positive integers is 12. What is the greatest that any one of the integers could be?

    **F.** 19
    **G.** 31
    **H.** 47
    **J.** 54
    **K.** 63

**35.** If $x = b + 4$ and $y = b - 3$, then in terms of $x$ and $y$, $b = ?$

    **A.** $x + y - 1$
    **B.** $x + y + 1$
    **C.** $x - y - 1$
    **D.** $\dfrac{x + y + 1}{2}$
    **E.** $\dfrac{x + y - 1}{2}$

**36.** If $5x = 3y = z$, and $x$, $y$, and $z$ are positive integers, all of the following must be an integer EXCEPT:

    **F.** $\dfrac{z}{xy}$.
    **G.** $\dfrac{z}{5}$.
    **H.** $\dfrac{z}{3}$.
    **J.** $\dfrac{z}{15}$.
    **K.** $\dfrac{x}{3}$.

**37.** What is the width of a rectangle with area $48x^2$ and a length of $24x$?

    **A.** 2
    **B.** $2x$
    **C.** $24x$
    **D.** $2x^2$
    **E.** $3x^2$

**38.** In the figure below, if the area of the triangle is 54, then $x = ?$

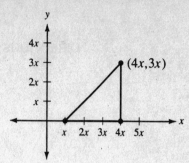

    **F.** $3\sqrt{3}$
    **G.** 3
    **H.** $2\sqrt{3}$
    **J.** 2
    **K.** $\sqrt{2}$

**39.** If $x = \dfrac{1}{y + 1}$ and $y \neq 1$, then $y = ?$

    **A.** $x + 1$
    **B.** $x$
    **C.** $\dfrac{x + 1}{x}$
    **D.** $\dfrac{x - 1}{x}$
    **E.** $\dfrac{1 - x}{x}$

**40.** A drawer contains four green socks, six blue socks, and ten white socks. If socks are pulled out of the drawer at random and not replaced, what is the minimum number of socks that must be pulled out of the drawer to *guarantee* that two of every color have been pulled out of the drawer?

    **F.** 6
    **G.** 7
    **H.** 11
    **J.** 12
    **K.** 18

## END OF TEST

If you complete this test before the time is up, check
back over the questions on this test only. Do not go back
to the previous test. Do not proceed to the next test until
you are told to do so.

# TEST 3. SOCIAL STUDIES READING

*35 minutes—52 questions*

**DIRECTIONS:** Below each of the following reading passages is a series of questions. Choose the *best* answer to each question, interpreting what is stated or implied by the passage in the light of your own background in the subject. You may refer back to the passage as often as necessary, though the answers to some questions may not be found expressly in the passage.

---

This American government, — what is it but a tradition, though a recent one, endeavoring to transmit itself unimpaired to posterity, but each instant losing some of its integrity? It has not the vitality and force of a single living man; for a single man can bend it to his will. It is a sort of wooden gun to the people themselves. But it is not the less necessary for this; for the people

(5) must have some complicated machinery or other, and hear its din, to satisfy that idea of government which they have. Governments show thus how successfully men can be imposed on, even impose on themselves, for their own advantage. It is excellent, we must allow. Yet this government never of itself furthered any enterprise, but by the alacrity with which it got out of its way. *It* does not keep the country free. *It* does not settle the West. *It* does not educate. The character

(10) inherent in the American people has done all that has been accomplished; and it would have done somewhat more, if the government had not sometimes got in its way. For government is an expedient by which men said, when it is most expedient, the governed are most let alone by it. Trade and commerce, if they were not made of India-rubber, would never manage to bounce over the obstacles which legislators are continually putting in their way; and, if one were to judge these

(15) men wholly by the effects of their actions and not partly by their intentions, they would deserve to be classed and punished with those mischievous persons who put obstructions on the railroads.

But, to speak practically and as a citizen, unlike those who call themselves no-government men, I ask for not at once no government, but *at once* a better government. Let every man make known what kind of government would command his respect, and that will be one step toward

(20) obtaining it.

Is a democracy, such as we know it, the last improvement possible in government? Is it not possible to take a step further towards recognizing and organizing the rights of man? There will never be a really free and enlightened State until the State comes to recognize the individual as a higher and independent power, from which all its own power and authority are derived, and treats

(25) him accordingly. I please myself with imagining a State at last which can afford to be just to all men, and to treat the individual with respect as a neighbor; which even would not think it inconsistent with its own repose if a few were to live aloof from it, not meddling with it, nor embraced by it, who fulfilled all the duties of neighbors and fellow-men. A State which bore this kind of fruit, and suffered it to drop off as fast as it ripened, would prepare the way for a still more perfect

(30) and glorious State, which also I have imagined, but not yet anywhere seen.

**1.** In this passage, the author's tone is:

  **A.** angry.
  **B.** mournful.
  **C.** rational.
  **D.** detached.

**2.** The main theme of the passage is:

  **F.** the ideal role of U.S. government.
  **G.** government control of trade and commerce.
  **H.** the American character.
  **J.** state-run railroads.

GO ON TO THE NEXT PAGE ➡

3. According to the author, the greatest responsibility for the freedom of the country belongs to:

A. the State.
B. the individual American.
C. the railroads.
D. trade.

4. The author calls for:

F. government-controlled trade.
G. the abolition of government.
H. democracy.
J. better government.

5. As used in this passage, the word *expedient* (line 12) means:

A. a means to an end.
B. interference.
C. adaptation.
D. occurrence.

6. According to the author, the State should treat the individual like:

F. a child.
G. a neighbor.
H. a meddler.
J. a machine.

7. According to the author, people need governments:

A. to control trade.
B. to regulate the railroads.
C. to punish mischievous persons.
D. for the sake of tradition.

8. The author views the U.S. government as:

F. a necessary evil.
G. a father figure.
H. a body opposed to change.
J. a powerful authority.

9. The author suggests that an individual can achieve better government by:

A. interfering with trade.
B. boycotting the railroads.
C. making known his desires.
D. appealing to the courts.

10. In the author's view, the State is:

F. enlightened.
G. full of vitality.
H. an independent power.
J. in need of improvement.

Although slaves were treated as objects, bountiful evidence suggests that they did not view themselves similarly. There are many published autobiographies of slaves; the Federal Writers Project left us with a voluminous record of interviews with ex-slaves. Several scholars have analyzed these records from a variety of perspectives. The humanity of these first-hand informants about slavery is obvious and abundant. Afro-American scholars are beginning to know enough about West African culture to appreciate the existential climate in which the early captives were raised and which therefore could not be totally destroyed by the enslavement experience. This is a climate that defined individuality in collective terms. Individuals were members of a tribe, within which they had prescribed roles determined by the history of their family within that tribe. Individuals were inherently a part of the natural elements on which they depended, and they were actively related to those tribal members who once lived and to those who were yet to be born. An individual African's conception of his or her humanity was thus deep and far-reaching. For example, Nobles (1972) excellently analyzes the adaptation of the West African world view to the conditions of enslavement in America. He relates how West African concepts of existence included notions very different from the usually accepted Euro-American ideas about the nature of interpersonal relationships, death, the elements, and spirituality.

The West African sense of tribal identity also accounted for intertribal rivalries, wars, and the participation of some tribal chieftains in the Atlantic slave trade. The contrasting attitudinal stance of American slavetraders and slaveholders, heavily influenced by the European superiority concept, emphasized African sameness and devalued tribal distinctions for the most part. This became especially true in North (as opposed to South) America, because of the economy of the trade and the culture of the traders.

GO ON TO THE NEXT PAGE

The colonial plantation system that was established and into which Africans were thrust did virtually eliminate tribal affiliations. Individuals were separated from kin; interrelationships among kin kept together were often transient because of sales. A new identification with those slaves working and living together in a given place could satisfy what was undoubtedly a natural tendency to be a member of a group. New family units became the most important attachments of individual slaves. Thus, as the system of slavery was gradually institutionalized, West African affiliation tendencies adapted to it.

11. The main theme of this passage is:

    A. the slave's sense of tribal identity.
    B. warfare between West African tribal chieftains.
    C. punishment of slaves on colonial plantations.
    D. slave autobiographies.

12. According to the passage, the "existential climate" in which the early slaves were raised consisted of:

    F. a sense of inferiority to Europeans.
    G. individuality defined in collective terms.
    H. quarrels among West African tribes.
    J. the colonial plantation system.

13. American slavetraders and slaveholders:

    A. encouraged intertribal rivalries.
    B. studied the existing culture of the West African tribes.
    C. emphasized African sameness and devalued tribal distinctions.
    D. published autobiographies of slaves.

14. The individual African's conception of his humanity was based primarily on:

    F. his prescribed role within the tribe.
    G. his connection with the natural elements.
    H. his relation to past and future members of the tribe.
    J. All of the above.

15. Individual West Africans adapted to the colonial plantation system by:

    A. forming new family units.
    B. maintaining interrelationships among kin.
    C. striving to maintain intertribal rivalries.
    D. eliminating tribal affiliations.

16. The author's attitude toward his subject could best be described as:

    F. laudatory.
    G. detached.
    H. biased.
    J. malevolent.

17. The sources of information scholars use to study the slaves' sense of identity include:

    A. tribal records.
    B. autobiographies and interviews.
    C. plantation reports.
    D. newspaper articles.

18. North Americans especially "emphasized African sameness" because:

    F. they feared the retaliation of tribal chieftains.
    G. they treated slaves as objects.
    H. they believed in the European concept of superiority.
    J. they separated individual Africans from their kin.

19. The best title for this passage would be:

    A. "West African Tribal Rivalries."
    B. "European Superiority and the Slave Trade."
    C. "Early Slave Records."
    D. "The Slave's Sense of Tribal Identity."

The National Security Act of 1947 created a national military establishment headed by a single secretary of defense. The legislation had been a year and a half in the making since President Truman first recommended that the armed services be reorganized into a single department. During that period the President's concept of a unified armed service was torn apart and
(5) put back together several times, the final measure to emerge from Congress being a compromise. Most of the opposition to the bill came from the Navy and its numerous civilian spokesmen, including Secretary of the Navy James Forrestal. In support of unification (and a separate air force that was part of the unification package) were the Army air forces, the Army, and, most importantly, the President of the United States.

GO ON TO THE NEXT PAGE

(10)     Passage of the bill did not bring an end to the bitter interservice disputes. Not even the appointment of Forrestal as first secretary of defense allayed the suspicions of naval officers and their supporters that the role of the U.S. Navy was threatened with permanent eclipse. Before the war of words died down, Forrestal himself was driven to resignation and then suicide.

By 1948 the U.S. military establishment was forced to make do with a budget approximately
(15)     10 percent of what it had been at its wartime peak. Meanwhile the cost of weapons procurement was rising geometrically as the nation came to put more and more reliance on the atomic bomb and its delivery systems. These two factors inevitably made adversaries of the Navy and the Air Force as the battle between advocates of the B-36 and the supercarrier so amply demonstrates. Given severe fiscal restraints on the one hand, and on the other the nation's increasing reliance on
(20)     strategic nuclear deterrence, the conflict between these two services over roles and missions was essentially a contest over slices of an ever-diminishing pie.

Yet if in the end neither service was the obvious victor, the principle of civilian dominance over the military clearly was. If there had ever been any danger that the U.S. military establishment might exploit, to the detriment of civilian control, the good will it enjoyed as a result of its
(25)     victories in World War II, that danger disappeared in the interservice animosities engendered by the battle over unification. With two of the armed services at each other's throats and the other two in opposite corners, there could be little likelihood of the emergence in the United States of a monolithic military establishment or a single-purpose military mind.

The Navy lost the interservice battle during the years under review to the extent that its plans
(30)     for a supercarrier were scrapped and it suffered drastic cuts in Naval Air and in the Marine Corps. When both Naval Air and the Marines proved their worth in Korea, Congress authorized the building of supercarriers and in 1952 strengthened the Marine Corps. Secretary of the Navy Sullivan had wanted to keep the National Security Act unchanged and to let the service secretaries and chiefs of staff work out their problems in a cooperative manner. Here he lost, for cooper-
(35)     ation could be enforced only by a secretary of defense empowered to direct and control the military services. The price of unity was thus the burgeoning of the Office of the Secretary of Defense at the expense of the services themselves.

20. According to the passage, the interservice strife that followed unification occurred primarily between:

F.   the Army and the Army air forces.
G.   the Army and the Navy.
H.   the Army air forces and the Navy.
J.   the Air Force and the Navy.

21. It can be inferred from the passage that Forrestal's appointment as Secretary of Defense was expected to:

A.   placate members of the Navy.
B.   result in decreased levels of defense spending.
C.   outrage advocates of the Army air forces.
D.   win Congressional approval of the unification plan.

22. According to the passage, President Truman supported which of the following?

I.   Elimination of the Navy
II.  A unified military service
III. Establishment of a separate air force

F.   I only
G.   II only
H.   I and II only
J.   I, II, and III

23. With which of the following statements about defense unification would the author most likely agree?

A.   Unification ultimately undermined United States military capability by inciting interservice rivalry.
B.   The unification legislation was necessitated by the drastic decline in appropriations for the military services.
C.   Although the unification was not entirely successful, it had the unexpected result of ensuring civilian control of the military.
D.   In spite of the attempted unification, each service was still able to pursue its own objectives without interference from the other branches.

24. The author is primarily concerned with:

F.   discussing the influence of personalities on political events.
G.   describing the administration of a powerful leader.
H.   criticizing a piece of legislation.
J.   analyzing a political development.

GO ON TO THE NEXT PAGE

25. The phrase "monolithic military establishment" (line 28) refers to:

   A. unity within individual services.
   B. the yielding qualities of the Navy and the Air Force.
   C. unity throughout the entire defense structure.
   D. civilian dominance over the military.

26. Congress authorized the building of supercarriers because of:

   F. Secretary Sullivan's views on the National Security Act.
   G. the proven worth of Naval Air and the Marine Corps.
   H. interservice cooperation.
   J. previous drastic budget cuts.

27. In this passage, the word *burgeoning* (line 36) means:

   A. rapid expansion.
   B. closure.
   C. reduction.
   D. impotence.

28. The chief reason for the conflict between the Navy and the Air Force was:

   F. the appointment of Forrestal as Secretary of Defense.
   G. civilian control of the military.
   H. fiscal restraints.
   J. special favors bestowed on the Air Force by President Truman.

29. According to the passage, "the cost of weapons procurement was rising geometrically." An example of a geometric progression is:

   A. 1, 2, 4, 8, 16, 32.
   B. 1, 3, 7, 9, 15, 17.
   C. 5, 8, 9, 11, 12, 15.
   D. 25, 28, 25, 31, 24.

**DIRECTIONS:** Questions 30–42 are not based on a reading passage. Choose the *best* answer to each question in accordance with your background and understanding in social studies.

30. Longitudinal studies are a primary research method used in the field of developmental psychology. In longitudinal studies:

   F. children of different ages are studied at the same time.
   G. the same children are observed over a long period of time.
   H. data are collected on children from similar geographic areas.
   J. only children of one age range are studied.

31. The Treaty of Versailles, which ended World War I, is now viewed as:

   A. having created the conditions for the political turmoil that led to World War II.
   B. a brilliant attempt to create a model for world peace.
   C. fair to both the Allies and the Germans.
   D. having divided Germany into separate East German and West German states.

32. The term for the man-made physical improvements that serve to increase the productivity of labor is:

   F. natural resources.
   G. capital.
   H. income.
   J. entrepreneurship.

33. Under the Articles of Confederation adopted by the original 13 states in 1781, all of the functions of a national government were performed by:

   A. the several states.
   B. the national executive.
   C. the national legislature.
   D. individuals appointed in Great Britain.

GO ON TO THE NEXT PAGE

**34.** The Emancipation Proclamation of 1863 granted freedom to:

- **F.** any southern state that would abandon the Confederacy.
- **G.** any captured Confederate soldier who would join the Union forces.
- **H.** the slaves in the states of the Confederacy.
- **J.** None of the above.

**35.** The looking-glass theory of socialization suggests that people develop a self-image largely as a result of:

- **A.** the reinforcers and punishers to which they are exposed.
- **B.** the conflicts between the parts of their personality.
- **C.** a reflection of the ways others see them.
- **D.** None of the above.

**36.** Changes to the Constitution can be made upon the agreement of:

- **F.** two-thirds of the states.
- **G.** three-fourths of the states.
- **H.** a majority of the states.
- **J.** all of the states.

**37.** The primary function of the Federal Reserve Board is to:

- **A.** regulate savings accounts.
- **B.** regulate mortgage practices.
- **C.** regulate the nation's money supply.
- **D.** None of the above.

**38.** The League of Nations never became a decisive power in world affairs because:

- **F.** the United States never became a member.
- **G.** Great Britain refused to join.
- **H.** no agreement could be reached on the location of its headquarters.
- **J.** All of the above.

**39.** All the available evidence indicates that the human race most likely first evolved in:

- **A.** Asia.
- **B.** North America.
- **C.** Africa.
- **D.** Europe.

**40.** A surplus is said to exist when:

- **F.** demand is greater than supply.
- **G.** supply is greater than demand.
- **H.** there is an equilibrium between supply and demand.
- **J.** None of the above.

**41.** *Marbury vs. Madison* was an early Supreme Court case in which the court asserted its right of:

- **A.** judicial restraint.
- **B.** separate but equal legislation.
- **C.** judicial review.
- **D.** chartering corporations.

**42.** Which of the following is a true statement about the medieval Crusades to the Holy Land?

- **F.** The Crusades led to the introduction of many Asian products into Europe, stimulating trade.
- **G.** The European Christians, with their superior forces, won easy victories in the Crusades.
- **H.** The Crusades resulted in the permanent expulsion of the Turks from Jerusalem.
- **J.** The Crusades lasted for a total of only five years.

With increasing prosperity, West European youth is having a fling that is creating distinctive consumer and cultural patterns.

The result has been the increasing emergence in Europe of that phenomenon well known in America as the "youth market." This is a market in which enterprising businesses cater to the (5) demands of teenagers and older youths in all their rock mania and pop-art forms.

In Western Europe, the youth market may appropriately be said to be in its infancy. In some countries such as Britain, West Germany, and France, it is more advanced than in others. Some manifestations of the market, chiefly sociological, have been recorded, but it is only just beginning to be the subject of organized consumer research and promotion.

GO ON TO THE NEXT PAGE

(10)     Characteristics of the evolving European youth market indicate dissimilarities as well as similarities to the American youth market.

The similarities:

The market's basis is essentially the same—more spending power and freedom to use it in the hands of teenagers and older youth.  Young consumers also make up an increasingly high (15) proportion of the population.

As in the United States, youthful tastes in Europe extend over a similar range of products —records and record players, transistor radios, leather jackets, and "wayout," extravagantly styled clothing, cosmetics, and soft drinks.  Generally it now is difficult to tell in which direction trans-Atlantic teenage influences are flowing.

(20)     Also, a pattern of conformity dominates European youth as in this country, though in Britain the object is to wear clothes that "make the wearer stand out" but also make him "in," such as tight trousers and precisely tailored jackets.

Both European and American youth worship and emulate "idols" in the entertainment field, especially the "pop" singers and other performers.  There is also the same exuberance and un-(25) predictability in sudden fad switches.  In Paris, buyers for stores catering to the youth market carefully watch what dress is being worn by a popular television teenage singer to be ready for a sudden demand for copies. In Stockholm, other followers of teenage fads call the youth market "attractive but irrational."

The most obvious differences between the youth market in Europe and that in the United (30) States is in size.  In terms of volume and variety of sales, the market in Europe is only a shadow of its American counterpart, though it is a growing shadow.

But there are also these important dissimilarities generally with the American youth market:

In the European youth market, unlike that of the United States, it is the working youth who provide the bulk of purchasing power.

(35)     On the average, the school-finishing age still tends to be 14 years.  This is the maximum age to which compulsory education extends, and with Europe's industrial manpower shortage, thousands of teenage youths may soon attain incomes equal in many cases to that of their fathers.

Although, because of general prosperity, European youths are beginning to continue school studies beyond the compulsory maximum age, they do not receive anything like the pocket money (40) or "allowances" of American teenagers.  The European average is about $5 to $10 a month.

Working youth, consequently, are the big spenders in the European youth market, but they also have less leisure time than those staying on at school, who in turn have less buying power.

43.  The main purpose of the passage is to:

A.  discuss new trends in the consumer patterns of European youth.
B.  analyze several advertising techniques used in gaining the youth market.
C.  compare the youth in the United States with the youth of Europe.
D.  show how economic conditions in Europe affect sales of goods to American youth.

44.  The passage states or implies that the youth market is more established in:

F.  France than it is in West Germany.
G.  Italy than it is in France.
H.  England than it is in our country.
J.  America than it is in England.

45.  According to the passage, the youth market in Europe is one that:

A.  is exceptionally easy to predict.
B.  is responsible for a larger percentage of consumption than was true a few years ago.
C.  is likely to taper off in the next decade.
D.  has never been clearly distinguished from the adult market.

46.  All of the following statements about the consumer habits of youth are true EXCEPT:

F.  European teenagers continually mimic their American peers.
G.  Flavored carbonated beverages are popular among teenagers.
H.  Teenagers in the United States as well as in Europe are "consumer conformists."
J.  English youths prefer close-fitting garments.

GO ON TO THE NEXT PAGE

47. The American and European youth markets are alike in regard to:

   A. appreciation of the same individual entertainers.
   B. amount of money per (teenager) capita spent on clothing.
   C. occurrence of frequent changes in buying habits.
   D. purchase of luxuries.

48. According to the passage, the chief reason for European youths' new affluence is that:

   F. they continue their studies past the maximum compulsory age.
   G. they receive a greater amount of pocket money than young people did ten years ago.
   H. due to the industrial manpower shortage, more youths are entering the work force.
   J. working youths have greater leisure.

49. One of the chief sources of European youth "fads" is:

   A. American T.V.
   B. "idols" in the entertainment field.
   C. store buyers in Stockholm.
   D. Western European consumer research.

50. In this passage, the author's attitude toward the subject is:

   F. scornful.
   G. amused.
   H. detached.
   J. intolerant.

51. European teenagers who continue their school studies:

   A. are less influenced by "fads."
   B. have less buying power than their working counterparts.
   C. have incomes equal to their fathers'.
   D. receive more pocket money than American teenagers.

52. In line 23, the word *emulate* means:

   F. imitate.
   G. promote.
   H. evolve.
   J. conform.

**END OF TEST**

If you complete this test before the time is up, check back over the questions on this test only. Do not go back to the previous test. Do not proceed to the next test until you are told to do so.

# TEST 4.  NATURAL SCIENCES READING

*35 Minutes—52 Questions*

**DIRECTIONS:** Each passage in this test is followed by several questions.  After reading a passage, choose the best answer to each question and blacken the corresponding space on your answer sheet.  You may refer to the passage as often as necessary.

---

Sand on a beach is not simply a haphazard collection of rock grains randomly accumulated by the sea.  On the contrary, it is part of an intricate, dynamic natural system in which landforms, waves, currents, and weather also play an important role.

For example, south of Los Angeles County, the Pacific Ocean beaches stretch southward in a long, gentle curve all the way to the rocky peninsula at La Jolla.  High bluffs line most of the beaches like a rampart; here and there seasonal rivers flow down from the interior mountains, cutting valleys through the bluffs to reach the sea.  On these beaches, a small portion of the sand is produced by the slow crumbling of the bluffs; most, however, is brought down the valleys in the northern part of the region by the rivers during spring floods.  Once on the beach, the sand acts less like a landform than like a great, slow-moving river.  During the long, mild summer, gentle onshore waves pile the sand in high mounds all along the foot of the bluffs.  Slowly the sand spreads southward, propelled by the gentle waves and currents, making a wide beach all the way to La Jolla.  Then, however, the weather changes.  Winter storms lash the beach, and the sand's southward flow speeds up.  Soon the beaches at the north end of the region lie exposed down to the bedrock, while at the south end, the sand, blocked by the La Jolla peninsula, turns seaward and plunges into a deep underwater canyon.

By midwinter, the entire stretch of beach is bare of sand.  The bluffs, which in summer were protected by the sand, now stand exposed to the full force of the sea.  Storm waves batter the bluffs at their base, and in a few places exposed headlands may crumble.

When spring comes, however, the cycle begins again.  The sea grows calmer, and spring rains in the mountains wash a new supply of sand down to the coast, where it slowly spreads southward to replenish the beach.

1. Under normal conditions in the location described, the ongoing loss of beach sand every winter:

    A.  will soon destroy the bluffs along the beach.
    B.  causes grave damage to the shoreline.
    C.  is made up by new sand accumulated every summer.
    D.  makes blufftop construction impossible.

2. The beach sand is like a river because:

    F.  it lies over a reservoir of underground water.
    G.  it flows always in one direction along the same narrow route.
    H.  it lies next to the ocean.
    J.  it is not solid like the bedrock.

3. A storm in the summer is less likely to damage the bluffs than a storm in winter because:

    A.  in summer the bluffs are protected by sand.
    B.  summer storms are always less intense than winter storms.
    C.  summer storms always approach the bluffs from the landward side.
    D.  summer storms do not create storm waves on the ocean.

GO ON TO THE NEXT PAGE →

4. An engineer proposes to stop the loss of sand in winter by building groins, long rock barricades extending across the beach and into the sea. If these were built, the result would most likely be:

   F. sand covering the entire beach all year long.
   G. no sand anywhere on the beach all year long.
   H. bluff damage north of the groins, where the beach would be exposed to the bedrock.
   J. bluff damage south of the groins, where the beach would be exposed to the bedrock.

5. At the mouth of one of the river valleys, engineers build a harbor by channeling a simple passage across the beach. In time, this harbor will most likely:

   A. increase in size through tidal action.
   B. increase in size as the surrounding bluffs crumble.
   C. become useless as sand drifts across its mouth.
   D. increase in depth through the action of winter storms.

6. At the mouth of another river valley, engineers build a second harbor. A deep channel is dredged and made secure with long jetties built across the beach and into the sea. One possible result of this construction might be:

   F. sand covering the entire beach all year long.
   G. sand entering the channel and blocking the harbor.
   H. bluff damage north of the harbor, where the beach would be exposed to the bedrock.
   J. bluff damage south of the harbor, where the beach would be exposed to the bedrock.

7. Of the following construction projects, the one most likely to result in widespread and severe damage to the coastal bluffs is:

   A. a condominium complex on top of the bluffs.
   B. a road running along the top of the bluffs.
   C. a public park at the mouth of one of the river valleys.
   D. a series of dams on the rivers to block their flow.

8. A strong winter storm causes a section of bluff to collapse. The shattered rock, gravel, and sand will most likely:

   F. be carried directly out to sea.
   G. eventually be carried southward along the beach by the sea.
   H. resolidify under the pressure of the waves.
   J. shore up the bluff against further collapse.

9. Engineers have determined that the supply of new beach sand from the rivers is going to be permanently reduced. Schemes are proposed to provide the bluffs with alternative long-term protection. Of the following, the scheme most likely to succeed is to:

   A. build jetties extending into the ocean.
   B. pour concrete across the tops of the bluffs.
   C. pour concrete around the bases of the bluffs.
   D. cover the sides of the bluffs with netting.

   Ants have not been incriminated as vectors of pathogenic bacteria affecting humans, though medical entomology abounds with citations of flies as carriers of many species of bacteria. Even cockroaches have been suspected, but ants have not been mentioned. No reference is found in the available literature as to their role in this respect. Theoretically, if flies can convey pathogens mechanically from infected to non-infected materials, other insects should be able to do likewise.

   Recently, experiments were performed using commonly prepared foods as a growth medium for *Shigella*, a bacterium that causes dysentery in humans. Quite accidentally, ants were found to be carrying the bacteria. Portions of the food—rice and beans cooked together with onions and tomato sauce—were inoculated with various strains of *Shigella* to determine whether this food was a favorable medium for the growth of the pathogens and thus a source of the dysentery so common in the tropics. Following a 24-hour incubation of the plates streaked from this food, which had been inoculated with Flexner strains of *Shigella*, they were read, covered, and left inverted on the laboratory table until the next morning. At that time unusual growths of non-lactose-fermenting colonies, later identified as *Shigella*, were observed in a pattern similar to miniature rabbit tracks. Examination revealed a few ants on the table, leaving the plates. These

GO ON TO THE NEXT PAGE

675

were caught and allowed to walk on sterile agar plates which, on incubation, produced a growth pattern similar to the original. Some ants, demonstrated to be sterile, were obtained. Food inoculated with *Shigella* was placed in one container. These ants fed readily during a period of four hours, then the food was removed and sterile plates were introduced long enough to allow ants to walk over the surfaces. These plates produced *Shigella*. Twenty-four hours after the ants fed on the infected material, sterile plates were again introduced. These, too, produced the typical growth of *Shigella* marking the footprints of the ants. The process was repeated in 48 hours, but on these last plates no colonies appeared.

10. The role of ants as carriers of pathogens, according to literature available at the time of the writing of this passage, has:

   F. changed over the past ten years.
   G. not been noted.
   H. been recorded over hundreds of independent experiments.
   J. been measured, using other insects as controls.

11. According to what this passage says, *Shigella* can be best cultured in a medium that is likely to be rich in:

   A. protein.
   B. fats.
   C. minerals.
   D. carbohydrates.

12. If *Shigella* is to be cultured in a sugar, the least successful medium is likely to be:

   F. sucrose.
   G. galactose.
   H. lactose.
   J. dextrose.

13. If ants are fed on food inoculated with *Shigella* and are allowed to leave tracks on sterile agar 36 hours later, how long will it be before *Shigella* colonies will be visible to the naked eye?

   A. 24 hours
   B. Never
   C. It is impossible to tell from the information given.
   D. More than 3 hours but less than 12 hours, because the passage establishes that *Shigella* is completely destroyed after 48 hours in the stomach of an ant.

14. This passage indicates that the pathogenic effect of *Shigella* on humans centers on the:

   F. digestive system.
   G. circulatory system.
   H. respiratory system.
   J. all of the above.

15. According to the passage, there is substantial proof in the literature to show that vectors of human pathogens include:

   A. ants.
   B. flies.
   C. cockroaches.
   D. all of the above insects.

16. According to the passage, which of the following characterize *Shigella* bacteria?
   I. There are several strains.
   II. They are colonial.
   III. They are cocci.
   IV. They are bacilli.

   F. I and II.
   G. II and III.
   H. I, II and III.
   J. I, II, and IV.

17. The original experiment was designed to:

   A. prove that ants are vectors of disease organisms.
   B. show that bacteria grow on common foods.
   C. show that *Shigella* would grow on a rice-and-bean medium.
   D. show that only a Flexner strain would grow on a food medium.

18. The study of insects that are vectors of human disease is called:

   F. insect bacteriology.
   G. parasitology.
   H. human pathology.
   J. medical entomology.

GO ON TO THE NEXT PAGE

19. If the atomic numbers of five different elements total 163, we can assume that:

    A. all of these elements will react with one another.
    B. two of these elements contain 69 and 14 protons each.
    C. there are a total of 163 electrons.
    D. three of the elements are members of the heavy metals family.

20. A star that is so dense that its gravitational field traps almost all of the electromagnetic radiation it gives off is called a:

    F. quasar.
    G. nebula.
    H. black hole.
    J. nova.

21. The image formed by a convex mirror compared to the object is usually:

    A. inverted and imaginary.
    B. erect and smaller.
    C. real and inverted.
    D. erect and imaginary.

22. The "organic soup" thought to have given rise to the first cells probably contained:

    F. glucose and amino acids.
    G. water and bubbling hot gases only.
    H. numerous green plants that supported the first cells.
    J. both F and G.

23. In order to predict the path of an electron, we must know both its position and velocity at the same time. One factor that influences this prediction is:

    A. the Heisenberg Uncertainty Principle.
    B. Trouton's Rule.
    C. Avogadro's Principle.
    D. the First Law of Thermodynamics.

24. A structure that does not include nucleic acid is the:

    F. gene.
    G. chromosome.
    H. centriole.
    J. ribosome.

25. A correct expression for the conversion of mass into energy is:

    A. $E = mc$.
    B. $m = \dfrac{c^2}{E}$.
    C. $c = \sqrt{\dfrac{E}{m}}$.
    D. $E = \dfrac{m}{c^2}$.

26. An example of a double covalent bond is:

    F. $Na^+ : \overset{..}{\underset{..}{Cl}}{}^- :$ .
    G. $H : \overset{\textstyle H}{\underset{\textstyle H}{C}} : H$ .
    H. $H : N ::: N : H$ .
    J. $: \overset{..}{O} :: \overset{..}{O} :$ .

27. The apparent pitch of a stationary sound source heard by a moving observer depends only on the:

    A. velocity of sound in air.
    B. direction of motion of the observer.
    C. speed of the observer.
    D. direction of the observer's motion relative to the source and the observer's speed.

28. Two major forms of igneous rock are:

    F. granite and sandstone.
    G. basalt and shale.
    H. shale and sandstone.
    J. granite and basalt.

29. During inspiration, the ribs:

    A. do not move.
    B. move downward.
    C. move inward.
    D. move outward.

30. Two skaters, A and B, of equal mass go around a circular rink in the same time. Skater A is twice as far from the center of the rink as skater B. Which one of the following is true?

    F. The velocities of both A and B are the same.
    G. The centripetal force on A is greater than that on B.
    H. The centripetal force on B is greater than that on A.
    J. The centripetal force on both is the same.

GO ON TO THE NEXT PAGE

31. The only common metal that is a liquid at room temperature is:

    A.  aluminum.
    B.  iron.
    C.  platinum.
    D.  mercury.

32. Species that practice internal fertilization are characterized by a:

    F.  fetus that develops entirely in the oceans.
    G.  wide range in the amount of care given to the young.
    H.  parental non-interest once the eggs have been laid.
    J.  diminished potency as they reach maturity.

33. The present picture of the atomic structure is the:

    A.  Rutherford model.
    B.  Bohr model.
    C.  Thomson model.
    D.  quantum mechanical model.

One of the most important experiments in photosynthesis was performed by an English scientist, Joseph Priestley. Priestley believed that mint could restore oxygen to an atmosphere from which this gas had been removed. To test this he placed a burning candle in a closed jar. Quickly the flame went out. A mouse was then placed in the jar; it, too, quickly died. From this Priestley concluded that a burning candle and a living mouse both extracted the same substance from the air. Priestley observed by chance that a sprig of mint had the effect of restoring the injured air to a normal state. A mouse now placed in the jar thrived as though it were breathing atmospheric air.

The experiment made by Priestley was soon followed by others. Other plants besides mint were tested and were found to have the same effect on the atmosphere as mint. It was later found that it was only the green parts of plants that possessed the ability to produce oxygen. Moreover, it was found that the formation of oxygen occurred only in the presence of sunlight. It was further shown that in the process of adding oxygen to the air, plants simultaneously extracted another gaseous material, a substance we now know as carbon dioxide. In addition to the exchange of gases with the surrounding air, there was the growth of the plant itself. From the above it was confirmed that plants consumed carbon dioxide in the production of organic material and oxygen. The plant gained considerable weight during the process. It was later established that the overall gain in weight, together with the weight of oxygen given off, equaled the weight of all the raw materials consumed by the plant. These raw materials consisted partly of the carbon dioxide removed from the air but largely of water, incorporated by the plant through a number of complex chemical processes.

34. If in Priestley's experiment the sprig of mint had been replaced by blades of grass, the results would most likely have been:

    F.  inconclusive.
    G.  reversible.
    H.  changed.
    J.  unchanged.

35. "Priestly believed that mint could restore oxygen to an atmosphere from which this gas had been removed," can best be described as a statement of:

    A.  observation.
    B.  conclusion.
    C.  hypothesis.
    D.  analysis.

36. According to this passage, oxygen concentration would be greatest in:

    F.  a cave.
    G.  a wheat field.
    H.  a frozen lake.
    J.  an animal cage.

37. We may conclude from reading this passage that oxygen is produced:

    A.  independently of sunlight.
    B.  only in the presence of sunlight.
    C.  at any time of day.
    D.  All of the above.

GO ON TO THE NEXT PAGE

38. Which of the following statements is most essential for the conclusion that "plants consume carbon dioxide in photosynthesis"?
   F. Plants extracted another gaseous material.
   G. Only the green parts of plants produce oxygen.
   H. Mint restored the injured air.
   J. The plant gained considerable weight.

39. Which of the following formulae represent two of the raw materials used by plants for photosynthesis?
   A. HO and $CO_2$
   B. $H_2O$ and CO
   C. $H_2O$ and $CO_2$
   D. $O_2$ and $CO_2$

40. If the root of a mint plant and a mouse were placed in a jar from which oxygen had been removed, the result would be:
   F. the same as with a mint leaf.
   G. the production of oxygen.
   H. a dead mouse.
   J. a decrease in the amount of carbon dioxide.

41. A mouse could survive sharing the atmosphere with a burning candle if:
   A. there was enough carbon dioxide.
   B. there was enough oxygen.
   C. there were no plants.
   D. they were placed in the sunlight.

42. Which statement correctly compares the raw materials and end products of photosynthesis with those of the combustion taking place in a burning candle flame?
   F. They are similar, but not the same.
   G. They are exactly the same.
   H. They are roughly opposite.
   J. They cannot be compared.

43. All of the following are necessary for the chemical process of photosynthesis EXCEPT:
   A. water.
   B. carbon dioxide.
   C. oxygen.
   D. sunlight.

Radioactivity means the breakdown or decay of unstable atomic nuclei into simpler nuclei along with the emission of energy in the form of particles and rays. In nature, some atoms are naturally unstable, such as those of radioactive uranium. It is not possible to predict when an unstable atom will decay. The amount of time during which half of the atoms in a sample will decay is known as a half-life. The table shows the half-life of some radioactive isotopes.

| ISOTOPE | RADIATION EMITTED | HALF-LIFE |
| --- | --- | --- |
| Nitrogen-16 | beta and gamma | 7.4 seconds |
| Sulfur-37 | beta and gamma | 5 minutes |
| Sodium-24 | beta and gamma | 15 hours |
| Gold-108 | beta and gamma | 2.7 days |
| Iodine-131 | beta and gamma | 8 days |
| Iron-59 | beta and gamma | 45 days |
| Cobalt-60 | beta and gamma | 5.2 years |
| Strontium-90 | beta | 28 years |
| Radium-226 | alpha and gamma | 1,620 years |
| Carbon-14 | beta | 5,600 years |
| Chlorine-36 | beta | 310,005 years |
| Uranium-235 | alpha, beta, gamma | 710 million years |

GO ON TO THE NEXT PAGE

Radioactive emissions were discovered accidentally. In 1896 a French scientist, Henri Becquerel, was experimenting by exposing fluorescent minerals to strong sunlight and then recording their glow on photographic plates. One cloudy day he kept the minerals and plates stored in a drawer; when he later looked at the plates, he found that they had become fogged. Becquerel figured that the uranium in the minerals emitted some kind of energy that was recorded on the plate. Becquerel had discovered beta particles, one of three types of radioactive emission. Alpha particles, the largest, are like helium nuclei; they cannot go through film or paper. Beta particles are fast-moving electrons. Gamma rays are high-energy photons and are the most penetrating kind of radiation.

44. If you were to select one atom in a sample of radioactive cobalt, how long would you have to wait until it decayed, releasing beta particles and gamma rays?

    F. 5.2 years
    G. 10.4 years
    H. 20.8 years
    J. It is not possible to make a prediction of this kind.

45. Becquerel placed the minerals and photographic plates in a drawer on a cloudy day to:

    A. store them.
    B. test for beta particles.
    C. test for radioactivity.
    D. test for fluorescence.

46. From Becquerel's work we can conclude that:

    F. all fluorescent minerals contain uranium.
    G. fluorescent minerals release energy only after exposure to light.
    H. fluorescence and radioactivity are the same thing.
    J. fluorescent minerals can release some energy whether or not they are exposed to strong sunlight.

47. When Becquerel's uranium-containing minerals were in a drawer, the emissions that could have theoretically escaped into the room are:

    A. alpha particles.
    B. beta particles.
    C. gamma rays.
    D. All of the above.

48. The radioactive emission with a mass of 4 atomic mass units is:

    F. a gamma ray.
    G. a beta particle.
    H. an alpha particle.
    J. None of the above.

49. Which isotopes produce radioactive emissions only in the form of fast-moving electrons?

    A. Radium-226 and uranium-235
    B. Nitrogen-16, radium-226, and strontium-90
    C. Carbon-14, chlorine-36, and uranium-235
    D. Strontium-90, carbon-14, and chlorine-36

50. Which one of the following statements is most nearly correct?

    F. The greater the number of kinds of radiation emitted, the longer the half-life of the isotope.
    G. Filtering out the beta radiation and leaving the gamma rays will decrease the half-life of sulfur-37.
    H. Carbon-14 cannot be used for dating archeological artifacts more than 5,600 years old.
    J. There appears to be some relationship between kind of radiation emitted and length of half-life.

51. A radioactive isotope will lose at least 99 percent of its radioactivity in:

    A. two half-lives.
    B. four half-lives.
    C. seven half-lives.
    D. fifteen half-lives.

52. Which one of the isotopes listed below has a half-life nearest the time required for iodine-131 to have expended 63/64 of its radiation?

    F. Sodium-24
    G. Gold-108
    H. Iron-59
    J. Cobalt-60

## END OF TEST

If you complete this test before the time is up, check back over the questions on this test only. Do not go back to the previous test.

# Answer Key

## English Usage

| | | | | |
|---|---|---|---|---|
| 1. D | 16. J | 31. A | 46. J | 61. A |
| 2. H | 17. B | 32. J | 47. B | 62. F |
| 3. C | 18. J | 33. C | 48. G | 63. D |
| 4. J | 19. C | 34. G | 49. C | 64. G |
| 5. C | 20. H | 35. D | 50. J | 65. C |
| 6. J | 21. D | 36. J | 51. D | 66. G |
| 7. A | 22. F | 37. B | 52. G | 67. B |
| 8. F | 23. A | 38. H | 53. C | 68. F |
| 9. C | 24. G | 39. B | 54. F | 69. A |
| 10. G | 25. D | 40. J | 55. C | 70. F |
| 11. D | 26. H | 41. B | 56. J | 71. B |
| 12. G | 27. C | 42. J | 57. A | 72. F |
| 13. A | 28. J | 43. D | 58. F | 73. B |
| 14. J | 29. A | 44. H | 59. B | 74. J |
| 15. D | 30. G | 45. A | 60. J | 75. B |

## Mathematics Usage

| | | | | |
|---|---|---|---|---|
| 1. B | 9. D | 17. D | 25. A | 33. D |
| 2. F | 10. G | 18. F | 26. H | 34. K |
| 3. C | 11. C | 19. B | 27. A | 35. E |
| 4. K | 12. G | 20. K | 28. G | 36. F |
| 5. E | 13. E | 21. E | 29. C | 37. B |
| 6. K | 14. H | 22. F | 30. K | 38. G |
| 7. D | 15. C | 23. C | 31. A | 39. E |
| 8. J | 16. G | 24. G | 32. J | 40. K |

## Social Studies Reading

| | | | | | | |
|---|---|---|---|---|---|---|
| 1. C | 9. C | 17. B | 25. C | 33. C | 41. C | 49. B |
| 2. F | 10. J | 18. H | 26. G | 34. H | 42. F | 50. H |
| 3. B | 11. A | 19. D | 27. A | 35. C | 43. A | 51. B |
| 4. J | 12. G | 20. J | 28. H | 36. G | 44. H | 52. F |
| 5. A | 13. C | 21. A | 29. A | 37. C | 45. B | |
| 6. G | 14. J | 22. G | 30. G | 38. F | 46. F | |
| 7. D | 15. A | 23. C | 31. A | 39. C | 47. C | |
| 8. H | 16. G | 24. J | 32. G | 40. G | 48. H | |

## Natural Sciences Reading

| | | | | | | |
|---|---|---|---|---|---|---|
| 1. C | 9. C | 17. C | 25. C | 33. D | 41. B | 49. D |
| 2. G | 10. G | 18. J | 26. J | 34. J | 42. H | 50. J |
| 3. A | 11. D | 19. C | 27. D | 35. C | 43. C | 51. C |
| 4. J | 12. H | 20. H | 28. J | 36. G | 44. J | 52. H |
| 5. C | 13. C | 21. B | 29. D | 37. B | 45. A | |
| 6. J | 14. F | 22. F | 30. G | 38. F | 46. J | |
| 7. D | 15. B | 23. A | 31. D | 39. C | 47. C | |
| 8. G | 16. F | 24. H | 32. G | 40. H | 48. H | |

# Explanatory Answers

## English Usage

1. (D) The past tense *was* is inconsistent with the other verbs in the paragraph. The author uses the present tense (e.g., *is* and *has*) to describe the solar system as it now is. So *was* should be *is*. B is wrong because *had been* is the past perfect tense and also refers to past conditions. Finally, C is wrong because *being* is the participle of *to be,* and a participle cannot function as the main verb of a sentence. Thus the construction that results from using C is a fragment rather than a complete sentence.

2. (H) The original contains two errors. First, *being* is a participle and (as was just noted) cannot function as the main verb of a clause. Therefore, you need a conjugated form of *to be.* Since the paragraph is otherwise written in the present tense, you should use *is.* Second, the original is incorrectly punctuated. *Orbiting* is a participle that is used as an adjective to modify *Jupiter,* and introductory participial phrases should be set off from the main part of the sentence using a comma. You can't use a colon because a colon has too much power. It fragments the sentence so that the introductory participial phrase doesn't have an obvious connection to the rest of the sentence. Only H provides the correct verb form and tense with the proper punctuation.

3. (C) The original is incorrect because the phrase *in that* is used nonidiomatically. *In that* means *because,* or *for the reason that,* or *in view of.* But Jupiter is the largest planet not because it has a volume 1,000 times that of the Earth, but simply because it is the biggest planet. C solves this problem by setting up a compound verb that describes two characteristics of Jupiter. B is incorrect because *having* is intended to modify *Jupiter,* but it is too far removed. Consequently, there is the potential for ambiguity. D is wrong because the resulting structure asserts, in essence, that Jupiter is the largest planet to have a value 1,000 times that of the Earth. But that is not the intended meaning of the original.

4. (J) The way in which the original joins the two clauses of this sentence is all mixed up. You can't use both *yet* and *since* because one signals an independent clause and the other a dependent clause. Additionally, your choice of punctuation will depend on which conjunction (if any) you finally use. J solves this problem by eliminating both conjunctions and using a semicolon to join the two independent clauses. G and H are both suspect because you really don't really need the *however.* The *not merely* already sets up a contrast with the previous sentence. G is wrong for the additional reason that a comma is not sufficient to separate the two clauses, so you get a run-on sentence. And H is wrong for the further reason that *however* belongs to the second clause, not the first.

5. (C) *That* is a relative pronoun that functions as the subject of a relative clause. Since *that* refers to *field,* it is singular, but *influence* is a plural verb. C correctly changes the verb to the singular *influences.* B and D also use incorrect plural verb forms. Additionally, D is wrong because the present perfect tense conflicts with the other verbs in the paragraph (which are in the present tense). The present perfect *have influenced* suggests an action or condition that began in the past and continues into the present. While the author certainly means to say that the conditions described exist today, he or she says nothing about when these conditions began.

6. (J) The original is needlessly wordy. First, you don't need the *by them,* since the sentence makes it clear that it is the scientists who were getting a first look at something new. Second, the adverb *previously* can do the job of the *had been,* so you don't need them both. J simplifies the sentence considerably and is the best choice available. G is wrong for at least two reasons. First, *not like* is not idiomatic. Better is *unlike.* Second, the sentence shifts from the plural *astronomers* to the singular *one.* H commits both of these errors as well.

7. (A) The original is correct as written. This point is an appropriate one at which to begin a new sentence. B and C are both incorrect because they result in run-on sentences. D does not exactly result in a run-on sentence, but it results in a sentence that is extremely complicated. As a consequence, you would need a semicolon in front of the conjunction *but* rather than a comma. (Try reading the sentence aloud using D instead of the original. When you get to the *but,* you'll want to take a deep breath. That kind of pause has to be signaled by a semicolon and not just a comma.)

8. (F) The original is correct as written. *That* is a relative pronoun that is here correctly used to introduce restrictive or essential information. Since the antecedent of *that* is *laboratory,* a singular noun, *surrounds,* is the correct form of the verb. H is wrong because the future tense is inconsistent with the other tenses in the paragraph. And J is wrong because the relative pronoun *that* functions as a subject of a clause and requires a conjugated verb.

9. (C) The original is needlessly wordy. The proof of this is that the correct choice, C, says the same thing in fewer words. The original uses an entire relative clause. C does the same job with a single word, a participle that introduces a phrase to modify *system.* B destroys the logical structure of the sentence: "system reveals by these preliminary explorations suggested. . . ." D, like the original, is needlessly wordy.

**10.** (G) The original is incorrect for two reasons. First, just as a matter of grammar, the phrase *more gentler* is wrong. The *more* is redundant of the *-er* suffix. Second, the rest of the passage makes it clear that the author means to say that botany is the most gentle of sciences. H is wrong because the rest of the passage makes it clear that the author intends the superlative *most,* and J is wrong because it is not idiomatic.

**11.** (D) The original is incorrect because the pronoun *it* doesn't have a clear and unambiguous referent. Although you can see that it must refer to *botany,* on first reading it seems that it might refer to *flower.* D eliminates the potential for misreading. B fails to make the needed correction. C, like D, makes the needed correction, but C is incorrectly punctuated. The introductory phrase is a participial phrase introduced by *reduced,* and it modifies the first noun in the main clause, *botany.* The correct punctuation is a comma to show that that is where the introductory phrase stops and the main clause begins. The problem with a semicolon is that it is too powerful.

**12.** (G) The original is not idiomatic. The correct idiom is *consists in,* not *consists about.* H and J are wrong because they, too, are not idiomatic. And J is wrong for the additional reason that it uses a plural verb with a singular subject.

**13.** (A) The original is correct as written. The other choices are not idiomatic and destroy the parallelism between *knowing* and *studying.*

**14.** (J) The original contains two errors. First, you need the past participle rather than the present participle following *should* (*disparaged,* not *disparaging*). Second, the dash disrupts the logical flow of the sentence. It seems to signal an aside or a clarifying remark, but what follows is actually another clause. J is the best choice. It uses the correct verb form, and the semicolon is a correct choice of punctuation to separate two clauses when no coordinate conjunction is used. G corrects the verb but not the punctuation error. H suffers from both errors.

**15.** (D) The present tense *is* conflicts with the other verbs in the sentence. They are all in the simple past tense. Only D makes the required change. B is wrong because there is no reason to use the past perfect. (*Had been made* suggests that one past event occurred and was completed before another past event, but that is not the intended meaning of the original.) C is wrong because the subject is *study,* a singular noun.

**16.** (J) *It's* is supposed to be a pronoun modifying *assumptions,* but *it's* is not a pronoun at all. *It's* is the contraction for *it is.* G fails to correct this problem. H is wrong because *their* is a plural pronoun and cannot substitute for the singular noun *botany.*

**17.** (B) The original contains two mistakes. First, the *to have understood* is inconsistent with the other verb forms in the paragraph, for it suggests something that will occur at a future time before some other action. (For example, John hopes to have finished his homework before his mother comes home.) Additionally, *their* is a plural pronoun and cannot substitute for the

singular *plant.* B makes both of the needed corrections. C is wrong for two reasons. First, *it's* is not a pronoun. Second, the use of the gerund *understanding* instead of the infinitive is not idiomatic. Finally, D makes the same errors.

**18.** (J) The original contains two errors. First, *they* is a plural pronoun and cannot substitute for the singular noun *flower.* Second, the *but* illogically suggests a contrast where none is intended. Only J corrects both of these problems. G fails to correct the second problem. H corrects both problems but is incorrectly punctuated. The result is a run-on sentence, because two independent clauses are spliced together by a comma.

**19.** (C) The original is not idiomatic. Although a family may be "defined as poor" when it meets certain criteria, it is not "defined poor." C corrects the problem of expression, because a family can be considered poor when it meets those criteria. B and D are wrong because those words just don't have meanings that are appropriate in this context.

**20.** (H) The original contains an error of pronoun usage. *Their* is intended to refer to *family,* which might be either plural or singular. But there is already another pronoun in the sentence that refers to *family,* and it is singular. So the first *its* determines that the author will treat *family* as a singular noun. G is wrong because *there* is not a pronoun. Finally, D is the contraction for *it is* and not a pronoun at all.

**21.** (D) The logic of the sentence does not support the use of the transitional word *consequently.* *Consequently* is used to show that one idea follows logically from another idea or that one event follows from another event as a matter of causality. Neither of these notions is implied by the sentence. The author has not yet explained why one would find more poverty in rural America than in other regions. The best course is simply to drop the word entirely.

**22.** (F) The original is correct as written. G is wrong because *lower* cannot be substituted for *less.* The phrase "earn lower than" is not idiomatic. H is wrong because the correct idiom for making a comparison like this is *less than,* not *less as.* And finally, J combines the errors of both G and H.

**23.** (A) The original is correct as written. You do need a new paragraph here because the author is taking up a new topic. Thus, B and D are wrong. As for C, *since,* which means "because of," destroys the logic of the sentence.

**24.** (G) The original is incorrect because *parallels* is a singular verb and does not agree with its plural subject, *levels.* G makes the needed change. H does solve the problem of the original, but the phrase "parallel as" is not idiomatic. Finally, J fails to solve the problem of subject–verb agreement.

**25.** (D) The original contains two errors. First, the plural verb *are* does not agree with its subject, *schooling.* Second, the phrase "as inadequate like" is not idiomatic. B corrects both errors but is punctuated incorrectly. You can treat the phrase "like family incomes" as an aside, but you cannot mark the limits of the aside with one dash and one comma. You must use either two dashes or two commas. C is guilty of illogical expression, for C seems to imply that schooling is supposed to function "as" family income. D is correct because it corrects the problems of the original and is correctly punctuated.

26. (H) The original is not idiomatic. The correct expression is "handicapped by," not "handicapped with." G and J avoid the error of the original but are needlessly wordy compared to the correct choice.

27. (C) The original is incorrect because the plural verb *have* does not agree with its singular subject, *head*. B fails to correct this problem. C and D are both singular verbs, but the *was to have* in D implies a condition that was never fulfilled (such as, "He was to have received an award but did not"). This suggestion of an unfulfilled condition is out of place here. C is the correct choice. The past perfect is acceptable because it indicates a past action (the head of the family finished school) that occurred before some other action (the children begin their education.) It would also be acceptable to use the present tense: "If the head ... has little schooling, the children are...."

28. (J) The original is incorrect because the expression "as . . . rather than in" is not idiomatic. An idiomatically correct alternative is supplied by J: "is as true . . . as." G fails to correct the problem of the original. As for H, though this is idiomatic, *they* does not agree with the demonstrative pronoun, *this,* to which it refers.

29. (A) The original is correct as written. (Although you must mark the end of an introductory dependent clause with a comma, when the dependent clause follows the main clause, a comma is optional.) B is wrong because *since* is used to introduce a dependent clause. Consequently, the resulting construction would be a dependent clause with no supporting independent clause. C and D avoid this error. What would follow the transitional words would be complete sentences, but the transitional words themselves express ideas that are not consistent with the content of the sentence. Both are used to signal contrasts, but the author does not contrast ideas at this point.

30. (G) The original is incorrect because the adjective *poor* cannot be used to modify another adjective (*educated*). You need the adverb *poorly* for that. G makes the correction. H is wrong because it changes the intended meaning of the sentence. The author is talking about poor people who are not educated, not "educated poor people." Finally, J is grammatically incorrect. The noun *education* cannot modify a noun.

31. (A) The original is correct as written. You can join two independent clauses with a semicolon. B is incorrect because it would result in a comma splice. You cannot join two independent clauses with a comma unless you also use a coordinate conjunction such as *and* or *but*. C makes no attempt to mark the separation of the two clauses, so it results in one long run-on sentence. Finally, D is wrong because *consequently* is an adverb and not a conjunction. Thus, you have the same problem in D that you have in B, a comma splice with no conjunction.

32. (J) The original is wrong on two counts. First, *itself* is a singular pronoun and cannot be used to refer to *intellectuals,* a plural noun. Second, the phrasing of the original is awkward and not idiomatic. J corrects both of the problems. G, too, corrects both problems, but the verb tense of G is incorrect. *Have begun* is in the present perfect. The present perfect is used to describe actions that were begun in the past but continue into the present, but that is a meaning that is inconsistent with the content of the sentence. Finally, H is not idiomatic.

33. (C) The original uses the present tense *stress,* but the author is at this point describing events that occurred in the past. The correct choice of tenses is given by C, the simple past tense. B is in the present progressive tense. Because it is a form of the present tense, B, like the original, is wrong. Finally, D eliminates the problem of tense since the participle *stressing* does not exhibit tense. The problem with D is that it eliminates the only main verb from the relative clause introduced by *that*.

34. (G) The original is wrong because it uses *that* to refer to people. You should use the relative pronoun *who* when referring to people. G is the only choice that makes the needed correction. H and J are wrong for the additional reason that the past perfect tense (*had passed*) is not consistent with the other verb tenses in the sentence.

35. (D) The original contains two errors. First, the semicolon is incorrect. The semicolon would be used to signal a new independent clause, but what follows is not a clause at all. Second, the *and* does not correctly signal the contrast between the two ideas in this sentence. B makes the second correction but not the first. C makes the first correction but not the second. Only D makes both corrections.

36. (J) The original is wrong on two counts. First, anytime you have a noun or pronoun that modifies a gerund, you must use the possessive case, e.g., *China's being,* not *China being*. Second, the original is very awkward and wordy, as you can see if you compare the original to the correct choice. G attempts to correct the first problem but fails. *Chinas* is not the possessive form. H does correct the problem of case but is still wordy and awkward. J is the most direct and concise rendering and is preferable.

37. (B) The original contains two errors. First, *it's* is the contraction of *it is* and is not a pronoun. Second, the *of* is not idiomatic. The correct preposition is *from*. C makes the second correction but not the first. D corrects the problems of the original, but the resulting sentence is very awkward.

38. (H) The original is grammatically incorrect. *That* is used to introduce a relative clause the subject of which seems to be *persons*. But there is no conjugated verb

for this subject. The sentence reads: "that persons . . . to be able." H solves the problem by eliminating the *that*. *Here* for is a preposition, the object of which is *persons*. Now you don't need a conjugated verb: "for persons . . . to be able." G does not eliminate the error of the original. Although J does correct the original, J is wrong because it uses *that* rather than *who* to refer to people.

39. (B) The original is wrong because the present tense *fail* is not consistent with the other verb in the sentence. The other verb describes a past action. Additionally, *fail* is a plural verb, but the subject of the sentence is *one*, a singular noun. B corrects the problem of tense (and the problem of agreement since there is only one form in the simple past). C makes the needed corrections, but the resulting phrase is not idiomatic. Finally, D does address the problem of agreement, but you still have the problem of tense.

40. (J) The original contains two errors. First, it uses *that* rather than *who* to refer to people. Second, it is not idiomatic. The correct idiom is *should have*, not *should of*. (*Of* is not a verb at all.) G corrects neither of these errors. H corrects the first but not the second. Only J corrects both errors.

41. (B) The original is incorrect because the sentence lacks a main or conjugated verb. *Being* is the participle of *to be* and cannot function as a main verb. Each of the other choices avoids this error. C, however, is wrong because the *that* has no logical function in the sentence. It's just there, not connected grammatically to anything else. D is wrong because the author means to provide a current definition, not a definition that was used in the past.

42. (J) The original is both grammatically incorrect and not idiomatic. First, *will starting* is not an English verb form at all. Second, in English, we use an infinitive (the *to* form) after a verb ending in *-ing* rather than the gerund (the *-ing* form). So *starting to think* is more idiomatic than *starting thinking*. J corrects both the problems of the original. G does not solve the problem of idiom, and H is ambiguous. The placement of *usually* suggests that it is intended to modify *thinking* rather than *starts*.

43. (D) The original is incorrectly punctuated. If, for clarity, you set the final prepositional phrase apart, you must use a comma. The semicolon is too powerful and isolates the prepositional phrase from the rest of the sentence. B and C are wrong because connecting the prepositional phrase to the rest of the sentence with a coordinate conjunction gives it an importance equal to that of the verb: "he or she ceases . . . and roughly at the age of 14."

44. (H) The original is incorrect because the singular verb *is* does not agree with its subject. The subject is a compound subject (a series of elements joined by *and*), which is plural. G fails to correct this mistake. H and J correct the error, but the use of the past tense in J is incorrect. The author is describing a current problem using the present tense.

45. (A) The original is correct. Each of the wrong answer choices creates a run-on sentence. In general, when you have two independent clauses, you can do one of three things: one, join them using a comma and a coordinate conjunction such as *and* or *but*; two, join them using a semicolon; or three, put them in separate sentences.

46. (J) The underlined part of the sentence is redundant of the *most often* earlier in the sentence. The best course of action is just to eliminate it altogether.

47. (B) The original contains a grammatical mistake. It uses *most* rather than *more* to compare two things. (The sentence compares a boy with a group. So *more* is the correct form, e.g., "John is taller than his classmates.") Both B and D make the needed correction. D is wrong, however, because the singular *one* will not agree with its verb, *stay*.

48. (G) The original is wrong for two reasons. First, it uses the objective case pronoun *him* to modify the gerund *dropping*. (You must use the possessive case *his*.) Second, the use of the gerund is in any case awkward. It is much more direct simply to say "at the time he drops out." G corrects the original and is more direct and concise as well. J would be correct except that it uses the past tense. The author uses present tense verbs to describe an ongoing problem, so you should also use the present here.

49. (C) The original is incorrect because the sentence lacks a conjugated or main verb. *Increasing* is a participle and cannot function as a main verb. Each of the other choices uses a conjugated form of *to increase* and so avoids this error. B, however, is incorrect because *so that* seems to introduce a clause, but what follows is not a clause: "so that during the eighth grade . . . ." D is wrong because it is needlessly wordy and indirect. Additionally, the past tense in D is inconsistent with the other verbs in this paragraph.

50. (J) The original is incorrect because *none* is a pronoun. What is required, however, is an adverb to explain how the dropout participates in activities: not at all. G uses the correct idiom, but the *and* results in a contradictory statement. How could one participate a little and not at all? H is incorrect because *not much* is equivalent to *little*, so the resulting statement doesn't create the "either/or" situation intended by the original.

51. (D) The original contains two errors. First, *goes* is a singular verb and does not agree with the subject of the sentence, *reasons*. Second, the phrase "goes deeper as" is not idiomatic. D corrects both of these problems. B and C do correct the problem of subject–verb agreement, but B and C are not idiomatic.

52. (G) The original is incorrect because the verb *are* does not agree with its subject, *kind*. Both G and H make the needed correction, but H makes a change that disrupts the parallelism of the sentence: research and developing. Since *research* and *development* have similar functions in the sentence (they are both objects of the preposition *of*), you should use the noun *development*.

53. (C) The original is not idiomatic. The correct idiom is "look for something to do something," not "look for something doing something." B is incorrect because the subjunctive *would have* suggests that an anticipated past event did not occur because of some other event. (John would have come to the party, but he was taken ill.) Finally, D is ambiguous. "With the satisfaction" is a prepositional phrase but it is not clear what the phrase is supposed to modify.

54. (F) The original is correct as written. *Its* refers to *humankind*. G is incorrect because *humankind* is singular. H is wrong because *it's* is the contraction of *it is* and not a pronoun at all. Finally, *your* cannot substitute for *humankind*. (This is the problem of shifting point of view.)

55. (C) The problem with the original is that the infinitive *to find* does not have a clear logical relationship to any other part of the sentence. Thus, it is just sitting there on its own. C solves this problem by turning *to find* into *finding*, which can then function as an appositive for *one* ("one of the problems"). B doesn't solve the problem of the orphaned phrase and, if anything, just makes matters worse because a semicolon is more powerful than a comma. Finally, D just creates a sentence fragment of everything that follows the period.

56. (J) The original is needlessly wordy, as you can see by comparing it to the correct choice, J. J is more concise and more direct. G is very concise, but G destroys the sense of the sentence: that they may be (what?). H is wrong because *it* is a singular pronoun and cannot refer to *machines*.

57. (A) The original is correct as written. B is wrong because the singular *has* would not agree with the subject *rewards*. C is wrong for this reason and for the further reason that the author clearly intends to make a statement about the past, not the present. Finally, D, which uses the future tense, must be wrong as well.

58. (F) The original is correct as written. Notice how the next sentence parallels the structure of this sentence. G is wrong because it eliminates this stylistic feature. (G is also wrong because the resulting sentence is ambiguous. Does the author mean to say the machine was located in China, was built in China, or was simply in China one day passing through?) H is wrong for the same reasons that G is wrong and for the additional reason that the verb tense is illogical. Finally, J is wrong because it switches to the active voice and implies that the machine was building something.

59. (B) The original doesn't contain a grammatical mistake, but it is somewhat awkward. By comparison, B is more concise and more direct than any of the other choices.

60. (J) Here, too, we have an original that doesn't contain an error but is needlessly wordy. You can render the thought more concisely and more directly by substituting *by* for *through the means of*. G is not idiomatic. The correct preposition is *by*, not *through*, and

the verb tense in G is inconsistent with the past tense point of view of the paragraph. H is like the original. It doesn't contain an egregious error, but J renders the thought more concisely.

61. (A) The original is correct as written. B is wrong because the comma separates the adjective *several* from the noun it modifies, *centuries*. C is wrong because the *but* suggests a contrast that is not intended by the author. Finally, D is wrong because the use of *and* suggests that what follows is similar to what comes before. But *water lifts* is not like *centuries*.

62. (F) The original is correct as written. It uses the active voice and is therefore more direct than any of the alternatives.

63. (D) The original is incorrect because it implies a comparison of two machines. In fact, the author means to compare one machine with all other such machines, and for that you need the superlative: *most*. B does use the superlative, but *most simplest* is redundant. Use one or the other, but not both. C fails to correct the problem of the original.

64. (G) The original suffers from a lack of parallelism. The third in the series of three verbs should have the same form as the first two: *flourished, foundered,* and *came*. Only G makes the needed correction.

65. (C) The original doesn't contain any grievous grammatical errors, but on balance C is stylistically better because C is more concise. B is incorrect because the use of *didn't* is inconsistent with the other verb in the sentence, *can*. (One is past and the other present.) D is incorrect because *meanwhile* suggests simultaneous events, but the sentence clearly talks about events at different times.

66. (G) The original contains an error of pronoun usage. *It* refers to both *television* and *products*, so a plural pronoun is required. J fails to make the needed correction. Both G and H make the correction, but H introduces a new error. The use of the subjunctive *would be* implies that an event is contingent upon the occurrence of some other event. But there is no such other event mentioned in the selection.

67. (B) The original contains an error of subject–verb agreement. The subject of the sentence is *industry*, so the verb should be singular: *industry is*. The relative clause introduced by *which* is not part of the simple subject. C fails to make the needed correction. D corrects the original but is incorrectly punctuated. The relative clause should be marked with two commas, not one comma and a dash.

68. (F) The original is correctly punctuated. G is incorrect because you must use a comma to separate the first two elements in a series of three or more elements. H is wrong because the comma separates an adjective from the noun it modifies. Finally, J is wrong because it separates the definite article *the* from the noun it modifies.

69. (A) The original is correct as written. The subject of the verb is *the episodic series*, a singular noun. And since three items are being compared, *most* is the correct choice of words.

**70.** (F) The original is correct as written. "With the advent of" is an idiom that identifies a certain point in time. The remaining choices are simply not idiomatic.

**71.** (B) The original uses the wrong verb tense and the adjective *rapid* instead of the adverb *rapidly* to modify *gaining*. The phrase "with the advent of" pegs the time as belonging to the past. So you need some form of the past tense. Only B supplies a verb that refers to a past event.

**72.** (F) The original is correct as written. The verb *have* correctly agrees with its plural subject. Also, some form of the past tense is required here since the sentence obviously refers to events that belong to the past. Thus, the other choices are incorrect.

**73.** (B) The past participle of *to grow* is *grown*. B makes the needed change. C and D are incorrect because their forms are not parallel to the other verb form in the sentence, *has lost*.

**74.** (J) In the original, everything following the period is a sentence fragment. The list contains no main verb. One use of a colon is to introduce a list, and that is what J does. G is wrong because the comma incorrectly suggests that the elements of the list will be verbs. H is wrong because it fails to mark the transition from the main part of the sentence to the list.

**75.** (B) The original is incorrect because *controversy* is intended to be an adjective modifying *topics*. But *controversy* is a noun—not an adjective. Only B makes the needed correction.

## Mathematics Usage

**1.** (B) Perform the indicated operation: $5.75 - 4.5 = 1.25$.

**2.** (F) Translate the expression into "algebrese." The product of 4 times $x$ is written as $4x$. And 3 less than that would be $4x - 3$.

**3.** (C) This question really just tests fractions. If $\frac{3}{4}$ of $x$ is 36, then

$$(\tfrac{3}{4})(x) = 36$$

$$x = 36(\tfrac{4}{3}) = 48$$

and $\frac{1}{3}$ of 48 is 16.

**4.** (K) The measure of the unlabeled angle in the triangle on the right is 90°. The angle vertically opposite it in the triangle on the left is also equal to 90°. Therefore,

$$x + y + 90 = 180$$

$$x + y = 90$$

**5.** (E) There are two ways to attack this question. One is to reason that

    **A.** $2 + n$ cannot be a multiple of 3. Since $n$ is a multiple of 3, when $2 + n$ is divided by 3 there will be a remainder of 2.

    **B.** $2 - n$ cannot be a multiple of 3 for the same reason that $2 + n$ cannot be a multiple of 3.

    **C.** $2n - 1$ cannot be a multiple of 3. Since $n$ is a multiple of 3, $2n$ will also be a multiple of 3, and $2n - 1$ cannot be a multiple of 3.

    **D.** $2n + 1$ cannot be a multiple for the same reason that $2n - 1$ cannot be a multiple of 3.

    **E.** $2n + 3$ is a multiple of 3. $2n$ is a multiple of 3; 3 is a multiple of 3; so $2n + 3$ is a multiple of 3.

You can reach the same conclusion just by substituting an assumed value into the choices. Assuming that $n = 3$,

    **A.** $2 + n = 2 + 3 = 5$   (Not a multiple of 3.)

    **B.** $2 - n = 2 - 3 = -1$   (Not a multiple of 3.)

    **C.** $2n - 1 = 2(3) - 1 = 6 - 1 = 5$   (Not a multiple of 3.)

    **D.** $2n + 1 = 2(3) + 1 = 6 + 1 = 7$   (Not a multiple of 3.)

    **E.** $2n + 3 = 2(3) + 3 = 6 + 3 = 9$   (A multiple of 3.)

**6.** (K) Remember that a ratio is just another way of writing a fraction. So just inspect each of the answer choices. As for F, $(\frac{1}{5})^2$ is equal to $\frac{1}{25}$, and both 1 and 25 are whole numbers. As for G, $\frac{1}{5}$ is the ratio of 1 to 5, so G is not the correct choice. As for H, 0.20 is equal to $\frac{1}{5}$, the ratio of two whole numbers. And 5 percent can be written as $\frac{5}{100}$, or $\frac{1}{20}$. Finally, $\sqrt{5}$ is not a whole number, so the expression in K is not the ratio of two whole numbers.

**7.** (D) If you know the area of a square, you can find its perimeter, and vice versa.

Area = side × side

side × side = 16

$$s^2 = 16$$

$s = 4$   (Remember: distances are always positive.)
Then the perimeter is equal to $4s$, or $4 \times 4 = 16$.

**8.** (J) Here you have one equation with two variables. It's not possible to solve for $x$ or $y$ individually, but you don't need to. Just rewrite the equation so that you have it in the form $x + y$.

$$12 + x = 36 - y$$

$$x + y = 36 - 12 = 24$$

**9.** (D) The coefficients are 3, 6, and 2, and 1 is the only common factor of those numbers. The smallest term containing the variable $x$ is simply $x$. So the greatest factor of those terms is just $x$. The same is true for the terms containing $y$ and $z$. So the greatest common factor is $xyz$.

**10.** (G) Again, here is problem for which there is a standard math approach and a Holmesian approach. You can analyze the problem as follows: the sum of $3k$, $4k$, $5k$, $6k$, and $7k$ is $25k$, a number that will be divisible by 7 only if $k$ is divisible by 7. If, however, the coefficient of $k$ were divisible by 7, then that number would be divisible by 7 regardless of the value of $k$. If we drop the term $4k$ from the group, the sum of the remaining terms is $21k$. Since 21 is divisible by 7, $21k$ will be divisible by 7 regardless of the value of $k$.

What would Holmes do? Assume a value for $k$, say $k = 1$. Then the total of the five terms is $3 + 4 + 5 + 6 + 7 = 25$. Getting rid of which one will yield a number divisible by 7? The answer is to get rid of the 4, because 21 is divisible by 7.

11. (C) It would be a mistake to try to convert each of these fractions to decimals to find the value that lies between $\frac{1}{3}$ and $\frac{3}{8}$. Instead, find an escape route. Use a benchmark, approximate, or use whatever else is available.

First, eliminate A, because $\frac{1}{2}$ is more than $\frac{3}{8}$. Next eliminate B. $\frac{3}{15}$ is equal to $\frac{1}{3}$, so $\frac{3}{16}$ is smaller than $\frac{1}{3}$ (a larger denominator makes for a smaller fraction given the same numerator). C is close to and slightly less than $\frac{18}{48}$, which is $\frac{3}{8}$. So C is the correct choice. But let's finish the line of reasoning. As for D, $\frac{9}{24}$ is equal to $\frac{3}{8}$, not less than $\frac{3}{8}$. Finally, $\frac{5}{12}$ is equal to $\frac{10}{24}$, and $\frac{3}{8}$ is equal to $\frac{9}{24}$.

12. (G) By this point in your study you should almost automatically factor the expression $x^2 - y^2$ into $(x + y)(x - y)$. Since $(x - y) = 3$, $(x + y)3 = 3$, so $x + y = 1$.

13. (E) You can reason this out mathematically. As for A, whether $n + 1$ is odd or even will depend on whether $n$ is odd or even. The same is true for B and C, because whether $3n$ is odd or even will depend on whether $n$ is odd or even. As for D, $n^2$ will be odd or even depending on whether $n$ is odd or even. But E is even regardless of whether $n$ is odd or even. If $n$ is even, then the expression $n^2 + n$ is equal to an even number times itself plus itself, which is an even number. And if $n$ is odd, the expression is equal to an odd number times an odd number, which is an odd number, plus an odd number, and the sum of two odd numbers is even. Or, you can just assume some numbers.

14. (H) Since the square has an area of 16, it has a side of 4 and a diagonal of $4\sqrt{2}$. The diagonal of the square is also the diameter of the circle. So the circle has a diameter of $4\sqrt{2}$ and a radius of $2\sqrt{2}$. Finally, a circle with a radius of length $2\sqrt{2}$ has an area of $\pi r^2 = \pi(2\sqrt{2})^2 = 8\pi$.

15. (C) First, calculate the sale price:

$120 - (25\% \text{ of } \$120) = \$120 - (0.25 \times \$120) =$

$120 - \$30 = \$90$

Next, calculate the sales tax:

Tax $= 8\% \text{ of } \$90 = 0.08 \times \$90 = \$7.20$

So the total price was $90 + \$7.20 = \$97.20$.

16. (G) Use the "this-of-that" formula. The "of that," which forms the denominator of the fraction, is *mixture*. How much of the mixture is there? $2.5 + 12.5 = 15$. So 15 is the denominator of the fraction, and the other number in the problem (the "this"), is the numerator:

$$\frac{2.5}{15} = \frac{1}{6}$$

And $\frac{1}{6}$ is one of the common fraction/decimal equivalents you were encouraged to memorize. Don't divide; just convert by memory:

$$\frac{1}{6} = 0.16\frac{2}{3} = 16\frac{2}{3}\%$$

17. (D) The triangle has sides of 6, 8, and 10, which you should recognize as multiples of 3, 4, and 5. So the triangle is a right triangle. The sides of 6 and 8 form the right angle, so they can be used as altitude and base for finding the area:

$$\text{Area} = \frac{1}{2} \times \text{altitude} \times \text{base} = \frac{1}{2} \times 6 \times 8 = 24$$

18. (F) Proportions make this calculation easy. First do the calculation for Motorcycle X:

$$\frac{\text{Fuel Used X}}{\text{Fuel Used Y}} = \frac{\text{Miles Driven X}}{\text{Miles Driven Y}}$$

(The X and Y here refer to the two different situations, not the motorcycles.)

$$\frac{1}{x} = \frac{40}{300}$$

Cross-multiply and solve for $x$:

$$300 = 40x$$

$$40x = 300$$

$$x = 7.5$$

So Motorcycle X uses 7.5 liters of fuel for the 300-mile trip. Now do the same for Motorcycle Y:

$$\frac{1}{x} = \frac{50}{300}$$

$$300 = 50x$$

$$50x = 300$$

$$x = 6$$

So Motorcycle Y uses 6 liters of fuel for the trip. Since Motorcycle X uses $7.5 - 6 = 1.5$ liters more than Motorcycle Y, the fuel for Motorcycle X costs $1.5 \times \$2 = \$3$ more.

**19.** (B) First, substitute 3 for $x$:

$$f(3) = 3^2 - 2(3) + 1 = 9 - 6 + 1 = 4$$

Now substitute 4 for $x$:

$$f(4) = 4^2 - 2(4) + 1 = 16 - 8 + 1 = 9$$

So $f(f(3)) = 9$.

**20.** (K) You can factor $6k + 3$: $6k + 3 = 3(2k + 1)$, which is choice K. If you miss that insight, you can assume some numbers to substitute into the choices. Assume $k = 1$. Then $6k + 3 = 6(1) + 3 = 6 + 3 = 9$. Now substitute 1 for $k$ into the choices. The correct one will yield the value 9.

**21.** (E) You can devise the formula as follows. The formula will be $x$, the cost for the first ounce, plus some expression to represent the additional postage for weight over $x$ ounces. The postage for the additional weight is $y$ cents per ounce, and the additional weight is $w$ minus the first ounce, or $w - 1$. So the additional postage is $y(w - 1)$, and the total postage is $x + y(w - 1)$.

You can reach the same conclusion by assuming some numbers to be substituted into the answer choices. Make the ridiculous assumption that the first ounce costs 1 cent and every additional ounce is free. If $x = 1$ and $y = 0$, then a letter of, say, 10 ounces ($w = 10$) will cost 1 cent. Substitute 1 for $x$, zero for $y$, and 10 for $w$ into the choices. The correct formula will generate the value 1. Even on these silly assumptions, you can eliminate every choice but D and E. Make another set of assumptions, and you'll have the correct answer.

**22.** (F) Just do the calculation. Since $|-3| = 3$ and $|-\frac{1}{2}| = \frac{1}{2}$: $|-3| \times |2| \times |-\frac{1}{2}| + |-4| = 3 \times 2 \times \frac{1}{2} - 4 = 3 - 4 = -1$.

**23.** (C) Here we have another composite figure. The side of the square is also the radius of the circle. Since the square has an area of 2, its side is:

$$s \times s = 2$$
$$s^2 = 2$$
$$s = \sqrt{2}$$

And $\sqrt{2}$ is the radius of the circle. So the area of the circle is $\pi r^2 = \pi(\sqrt{2})^2 = 2\pi$.

**24.** (G) Test each statement. As for statement I, 2 is the first prime number, and the product of 2 and any other number must be even. So I is not part of the correct answer. As for II, the sum of two prime numbers might be odd, e.g., $2 + 3 = 5$, but the sum of two prime numbers might also be even, e.g., $3 + 5 = 8$. As for III, however, the product of two odd numbers is necessarily odd.

**25.** (A) The coordinates establish that this figure is a rectangle. The width of the rectangle is $a$, and the length is $b - a$. So the area is $a(b - a)$. You can also assume values and get the same result. Assume that $a = 2$ and $b = 4$. The rectangle has a width of 2; a length of $4 - 2 = 2$; and an area of $2 \times 2 = 4$. Substitute 2 for $a$ and 4 for $b$ into the formulas in the answer choices and the correct formula will yield 4.

**26.** (H) Do the operations:

$$\sqrt{(43 - 7)(29 + 7)} = \sqrt{48(36)(36)} = 36$$

**27.** (A) Set up a direct proportion:

$$\frac{\text{Cement X}}{\text{Cement Y}} = \frac{\text{Grit X}}{\text{Grit Y}}$$

$$\frac{4}{50} = \frac{20}{x}$$

Cross-multiply:

$$4x = (20)(50)$$

$$x = \frac{(20)(50)}{4} = 250$$

**28.** (G) Let's label the other two angles in the triangle:

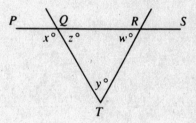

$$x + z = 180$$
$$120 + z = 180$$
$$z = 60$$

Next: $z + w + y = 180$

And since QT = QR, $y = w$. So

$$60 + y + y = 180$$
$$2y = 120$$
$$y = 60$$

**29.** (C) You have only one equation but two variables, so you cannot solve for $x$ and $y$ individually. Instead, look for a way to rewrite the first equation to give you the information you need:

$$\frac{x}{y} = -1$$

$$x = -y$$

$$x + y = 0$$

**30.** (K) Don't do lengthy calculations. Set up the cost of each fabric as a fraction and compare the fractions directly using a benchmark:

$$F = \frac{8}{3}$$

$$G = \frac{6}{2} = 2$$

$$H = \frac{9}{4}$$

$$J = \frac{7}{5}$$

$$K = \frac{5}{6}$$

K, $\frac{5}{6}$, is less than 1. The other fractions are greater than 1. So K is the smallest.

**31.** (A) Since PQ ∥ ST, the "big angle/little angle" theorem establishes that $x = y$. So if we find the value of $x$, we have found the value of $y$.

$$75 + 65 + x + x = 180$$

$$2x + 140 = 180$$

$$2x = 40$$

$$x = 20$$

So $y = 20$.

**32.** (J)

$$\frac{10^3(10^5 + 10^5)}{10^4} = \frac{(10^5 + 10^5)}{10} = \frac{10(10^4 + 10^4)}{10} = 2(10^4)$$

**33.** (D) Factor and solve for $x$:

$$x^2 - 5x + 4 = 0$$

$$(x - 4)(x - 1) = 0$$

So either $x - 4 = 0$ and $x = 4$, or $x - 1 = 0$ and $x = 1$.

Alternatively, you could substitute the values in the choices back into the equation until you found the set that works.

**34.** (K) Use the method for finding the missing element of an average. The smallest possible sum for six different positive integers is $1 + 2 + 3 + 4 + 5 + 6 = 21$. The sum of all 7 integers is $7 \times 12 = 84$. So the largest the seventh number could be (and the average of the seven numbers still be 12) is $84 - 21 = 63$.

**35.** (E) To find $b$ in terms of $x$ and $y$, you will first need to set $b$ equal to $x$ and equal to $y$:

$$x = b + 4 \qquad y = b - 3$$

$$x - 4 = b \qquad y + 3 = b$$

Now combine the two equations by adding:

$$b = x - 4$$
$$+(b = y + 3)$$
$$\overline{2b = x + y - 1}$$

So $b = \dfrac{(x + y - 1)}{2}$.

You can arrive at the same conclusion by substituting some numbers. Let $b = 1$. Then $x = 1 + 4 = 5$, and $y = 1 - 3 = -2$. Substitute 5 for $x$ and $-2$ for $y$ into the answer choices. The correct choice will yield the value 1.

**36.** (F) Since $z = 5x = 3y$, and $x$, $y$, and $z$ are integers, $z$ is a multiple of both 3 and 5, so $z$ is evenly divisible by 5, 3, and 15. And $z$ is divisible by both $x$ and $y$ individually, but $z$ is not necessarily divisible by the product of $x$ and $y$. Finally, since $5x = 3y$, and $x$ and $y$ are integers, $x$ is a multiple of 3 (and evenly divisible by 3).

You can reach the same conclusion by substituting some numbers. The most natural assumption is to let $z = 15$, so $x = 3$ and $y = 5$. But on that assumption, every answer choice is an integer. So try the next multiple of 15. Let $z = 30$, so $x = 6$ and $y = 10$. Now F is no longer an integer: $30 \div (6 \times 10) = \frac{1}{2}$.

**37.** (B) You can solve the problem by using the formula for finding the area of a rectangle:

Area of rectangle = width × length

$$48x^2 = w(24x)$$

$$w = \frac{48x^2}{24x} = 2x$$

You can reach the same conclusion by substituting numbers. Assume that $x = 2$. Then the area of the rectangle is $48(2^2) = 48(4) = 192$, and the length is 48. So 48 times the width is equal to 192, and the width is $192 \div 48 = 4$. So if $x = 2$, the correct choice will yield the value 4. Only choice B works.

**38.** (G) You can deduce the value for $x$ in the following way. The length of the base of the triangle is $4x - x = 3x$, and the length of the altitude is $3x - 0 = 3x$ (the difference in the $y$ coordinates). Now use the formula for finding the area of a triangle:

$$\frac{1}{2}(3x)(3x) = 54$$

$$(3x)(3x) = 108$$

$$9x^2 = 108$$

$$x^2 = 12$$

$$x = \sqrt{12} = 2\sqrt{3} \qquad (x \text{ is a distance, so } x \text{ must be positive.})$$

**39.** (E) Rewrite the equation:

$$x = \frac{1}{y + 1}$$

$$x(y + 1) = 1$$

$$y + 1 = \frac{1}{x}$$

$$y = \frac{1}{x} - 1$$

$$y = \frac{1 - x}{x}$$

You can arrive at the same conclusion by assuming some numbers. Assume that $y = 1$. On that assumption, $x = \frac{1}{2}$. Then substitute $\frac{1}{2}$ for $x$ in the formulas in the answer choices; the correct choice will yield the value 1.

**40.** (K) This question is a little tricky, but it doesn't require any advanced mathematics. If the room were completely dark and you were in a hurry to make sure you got at least one pair of each color, how many socks would you need to pull from the drawer? Well, what's the worst thing that might happen? You might pull all ten white socks on the first ten tries, then all six blue socks on the next six tries. So far you have only white socks and blue socks, and you have pulled 16 socks. Now there is nothing left in the drawer but green socks. Two more picks and you'd have two green socks. So on the worst assumption, 18 picks will guarantee you a pair of each color.

### Social Studies Reading

**1.** (C) The author's matter-of-fact arguments give this passage a rational tone.

**2.** (F) The passage discusses the role of government in the United States and the citizen's relation to the state.

**3.** (B) The author states that "the character inherent in the American people has done all that has been accomplished," and he offers protecting freedom, settling the West, and educating citizens as his examples.

**4.** (J) In the second paragraph, the author asks for "*at once* a better government."

**5.** (A) An *expedient* is "a means to an end" in this context.

**6.** (G) In the final paragraph, the author imagines "a State at last which can afford to be just to all men, and to treat the individual with respect as a neighbor."

**7.** (D) According to the author, "the people must have some complicated machinery or other and hear its din, to satisfy that idea of government which they have."

**8.** (H) The author sees the government as "a tradition . . . endeavoring to transmit itself unimpaired to posterity."

**9.** (C) The author suggests that "every man make known what kind of government would command his respect."

**10.** (J) The author believes that it is possible and desirable to improve on democracy.

**11.** (A) The entire passage concentrates on the slave's sense of identity within the tribe and how he or she adapted this sense to the structure of slavery.

**12.** (G) Prior to their enslavement, individual West Africans were part of a collective tribal community with each member a part of the greater whole.

**13.** (C) As stated in the second paragraph, American slavetraders and slaveholders, influenced by Europeans, did not perceive the differences between the various West African tribes.

**14.** (J) All of the listed elements were part of the individual African's conception of his or her humanity.

**15.** (A) As stated in paragraph 3, "new family units became the most important attachments of individual slaves."

**16.** (G) The clear, journalistic style of this passage gives it an unemotional, detached tone.

**17.** (B) It is stated in the first paragraph that scholars used autobiographies and interviews with ex-slaves.

**18.** (H) As previously stated, North Americans did not view the West Africans as individuals.

**19.** (D) Only this title clearly describes the main theme of the passage.

**20.** (J) In the third paragraph, it is specifically stated that the Navy and the Air Force become adversaries.

**21.** (A) The author states that not even the appointment of Forrestal allayed the suspicions of Navy officers and their allies. The "not even" allows us to infer that the appointment of Forrestal was intended to have a placating effect on those people.

**22.** (G) It is stated in the first paragraph that Truman recommended the unification of the military services. After that, according to the passage, the matter became a political issue.

**23.** (C) In the closing paragraph the author states that an unexpected result of the unification battle was that the military would never be able to establish itself as a power independent of and outside of civilian control.

**24.** (J) The author views the events discussed primarily in political terms.

**25.** (C) It is clear from the passage that "monolithic" refers to unity among all branches of the defense structure.

**26.** (G) It is stated in the final paragraph that in Korea "both Naval Air and the Marines proved their worth," resulting in Congress's approval of the supercarriers.

**27.** (A) In this context, *burgeoning* means "rapid expansion."

**28.** (H) The chief source of conflict from among the items listed was budgetary cuts in each of the branches of defense.

29. (A) A geometric progression is a sequence of terms in which the ratio of each term to the preceding one is the same throughout the sequence.

30. (G) In longitudinal studies, a specific group of children are observed over a long period of time.

31. (A) Under the Treaty of Versailles, Germany had to give up some of its territory, greatly reduce its armed forces, and pay reparations to the Allied countries for factories, farms, and other property destroyed in the war. The reparations totaled approximately $33 billion, placing an unbearable load on the German economy. The eventual result was political turmoil in Germany, setting the stage for the rise of the Nazis and, ultimately, World War II.

32. (G) *Capital* is the term used to denote the man-made physical improvements that serve to increase the productivity of labor.

33. (C) The Articles of Confederation vested all power in the national legislature, although the legislature delegated some powers to the states.

34. (H) In 1863, President Abraham Lincoln issued the Emancipation Proclamation, which granted freedom to the slaves in the states then controlled by the Confederacy. The Union armies put the Proclamation into effect as they took control of Confederate territories.

35. (C) The looking-glass theory suggests that children develop images of themselves that are largely a reflection of the ways in which others see them.

36. (G) Three-fourths of the states must agree to any Constitutional amendment.

37. (C) Functioning as the central bank of the United States, the Federal Reserve Board regulates the size of the nation's money supply. Its actions influence the rise and fall of interest rates and thus, indirectly, all the rest of the nation's economy.

38. (F) The League of Nations was first proposed during World War I by U.S. President Woodrow Wilson, who believed that such an organization could help guarantee world peace. After the war, however, the U.S. Senate refused to ratify the treaty establishing the League, and the United States never became a member.

39. (C) All the available fossil evidence indicates that the human race first evolved on the plains of eastern Africa and spread from there throughout the rest of the world.

40. (G) A surplus is said to exist when supply is greater than demand; demand greater than supply is called a shortage.

41. (C) In *Marbury vs. Madison* (1803), the Supreme Court asserted a right of "judicial review" whereby any act of the executive or the legislature that the Court determined to be unconstitutional would be rendered null and void.

42. (F) In the Holy Land, many Crusaders acquired a taste for Asian products. When these Crusaders returned to Europe, their demand for Asian goods stimulated overseas trade.

43. (A) The passage is most concerned with new trends in the consumer patterns of youth in Western Europe.

44. (H) The passage states that the U.S. youth market is well established, whereas the youth market in Britain, although more advanced than that in other European countries, is still in its infancy.

45. (B) The youth market is described throughout the passage as being a new concept in Europe and a growing phenomenon.

46. (F) Although the phenomenon of a youth market is common to America and Europe, the passage states that it is difficult to tell in which direction the influences are flowing.

47. (C) Answer C is correct and supported by the author's statement regarding the "same exuberance and unpredictability in sudden fad switches."

48. (H) It is stated that because European youths are entering the work force after completing their compulsory schooling, they reach affluency at an earlier age.

49. (B) Only this choice is listed as a source for European youth "fads."

50. (H) The journalistic form of this passage reveals the author's detached attitude.

51. (B) This answer is stated in the final sentence of the passage.

52. (F) *Emulation* is defined as "imitation."

## Natural Sciences Reading

1. (C) Under normal conditions, the loss of beach sand each winter does not pose a threat to the bluffs or the shoreline since new sand accumulates each summer.

2. (G) The beach sand is like a great, slow-moving river moving down the coastline until it finally disappears out to sea off La Jolla.

3. (A) According to the passage, the beach sand is the chief protection of the bluffs against erosion by the ocean. In summer the sand level is highest, so a storm's effects would be reduced.

4. (J) The groins would block the southward flow of new sand, leaving beaches farther south exposed to the bedrock once their sand moves away. Without protective sand, the bluffs along those beaches would be threatened by erosion from the ocean.

5. (C) A simple channel across the beach, unprotected by any other construction, will likely soon become blocked by the southward-moving sand.

6. (J) Like the groins in question 4, the jetties will block the southward flow of new sand, leaving beaches farther south exposed to the bedrock once their sand moves away. Without protective sand, the bluffs along those beaches will be threatened by erosion from the ocean.

**7.** (D) Construction of dams blocking the rivers will prevent new sand from reaching the beach. Without new sand, the bluffs along the whole stretch of shoreline will be threatened by erosion from the ocean.

**8.** (G) The remnants of the collapsed bluff will take the same southward path as the sand, propelled by the same waves and currents.

**9.** (C) According to the passage, the waves break down the bluffs by battering their bases, undercutting them and causing them to collapse. Consequently, this damage can be prevented, or at least controlled, only by protecting the bases of the bluffs. In the absence of natural sand, pouring concrete around the bases will likely offer effective alternative long-term protection.

**10.** (G) The author says categorically: "No reference is found in the available literature." This invalidates F, H, and J.

**11.** (D) The food described is rich in starch (rice) and sugar (onions), both carbohydrates.

**12.** (H) The author says *Shigella* is "non-lactose-fermenting."

**13.** (C) First of all, we do not know whether the ants would be tracking *Shigella* after 24 hours. Second, we do not know exactly how much time elapsed, in the original experiments, between exposure of the plates to the ants and the appearance of tracks thereon. All we know is that in the first stage, the period of time was overnight ("until the next morning"); in the second, long enough to achieve "incubation" (24 hours?). The best answer, then, is C. The other answers are wild guesses.
B is based on the assumption that after 24 hours results would be the same as after 48 hours (no tracks), but we do not know at what in-between point the track-making really does stop. D guesses and makes the additional mistake of assuming that all of the *Shigella* goes through the ant's stomach before being deposited at its feet. On the basis of the passage itself, which talks of conveying pathogens mechanically, we can assume that the ants walk in the food and convey it on their feet.

**14.** (F) This seems to be the basic assumption of the experimenters, who hypothesized that *Shigella*, which causes an infection of the lower intestine, gets there through certain foods introduced through the stomach. G and H are not mentioned; J is thus untrue.

**15.** (B) The passage mentions that citations of flies as vectors abound, while cockroaches have merely been "suspected" and ants have not been mentioned at all.

**16.** (F) The passage specifically mentions that various strains were used and that there was colonial growth. No mention was made of whether the bacteria are cocci or bacilli.

**17.** (C) The original experiment was to culture various strains on a food medium. The observations about the ants (A) were accidental. Choice B is not specific enough and D is too specific; the passage states that various strains were used.

**18.** (J) This term is used in the first paragraph and its definition can be inferred by its use in context.

**19.** (C) The atomic number of an element represents the number of protons in the atomic nucleus. Since atoms are electrically balanced, this number also represents the number of electrons in the atom. The proton number of the five atoms in the problem is 163, and therefore there are 163 electrons in total.

**20.** (H) The term "black hole" is given to a body that is so dense that it traps most of the radiation that passes nearby.

**21.** (B) Convex lenses are shaped like the lens of the eye. They are prescribed in eyeglasses for the treatment of farsightedness, where they shorten the focal length, creating an erect and much smaller image.

**22.** (F) Experiments by Stanley Miller and later by Sidney Fox support the hypothesis that life on Earth began with the formation of protein in the primitive oceans. Sugars like glucose supplied energy requirements for the earliest cells. Answers G and H do not relate in any way to the question.

**23.** (A) The Heisenberg Uncertainty Principle states that it is impossible to determine simultaneously the exact position and exact momentum of a body as small as an electron. The more precisely one tries to determine one of these values, the more uncertain one is of the other value.

**24.** (H) Genes are believed to be long chains of DNA. Chromosomes are coiled chromatin threads composed of genes and associated proteins. Ribosomes are composed of protein, structural RNA, and, during protein synthesis, messenger RNA. Of the cell organelles listed, only centrioles appear to lack any form of nucleic acid.

**25.** (C) The familiar form of the expression is $E = mc^2$, which is equivalent to $c = \sqrt{\dfrac{E}{m}}$.

**26.** (J) When two or three pairs of electrons are shared between two atoms in a molecule, the resulting bonds are called multiple bonds. A double covalent bond involves two pairs of shared electrons.

**27.** (D) Sound waves travel at a speed of 34,000 cm per second at normal conditions of temperature and pressure. An observer moving faster than this speed will not hear the sound, proving that the listener's rate of speed is critical to the proper perception of sound waves. Also, the direction (toward or away from) of movement is equally important in ascertaining the pitch of a sound.

**28.** (J) There are over 600 kinds of igneous rock. Of these, 95 percent are granite and basalt. The continents are granite masses floating in a sea of basalt.

**29.** (D) Inspiration is the act of inhaling. When air is taken into the lungs, the chest expands and the ribs move upward and outward.

**30.** (G) Centripetal force $F^A = \dfrac{mv^2}{r}$ where $r$ is the radius of the object's path and $v$ is its linear velocity. If $r^A = 2r^B$, $V^A$ must be 4 times $V^B$. Thus, $F^A$ must be greater than $F^B$.

31. (D) Metals are elements that conduct heat and electricity and generally melt at very high temperatures.

32. (G) Internal fertilization is important in terrestrial forms, many of which provide no care for their young, while others provide extensive care for their young.

33. (D) Erwin Schrodinger, Louis de Broglie, P.A.M. Dirac, and Werner Heisenberg contributed to the modern quantum mechanical model of the atom, which presents a view of energy levels as groupings of sublevels with different quantum numbers.

34. (J) As stated in the passage, "Other plants besides mint were tested and were found to have the same effect on the atmosphere as mint."

35. (C) A hypothesis is a tentative assumption to be tested.

36. (G) A wheat field provides ideal conditions for the production of oxygen—green plants in the sunlight.

37. (B) According to the passage, "it was found that the formation of oxygen occurred only in the presence of sunlight."

38. (F) Carbon dioxide is a gas. Therefore "to consume carbon dioxide" is synonymous with "to extract a gaseous material."

39. (C) Only C correctly represents the compounds water and carbon dioxide.

40. (H) According to the passage, the root of the plant, unlike the leaf, would not produce oxygen nor use carbon dioxide. Thus the mouse would die.

41. (B) Both the mouse and the burning candle require oxygen. With enough of this gas, the mouse would survive.

42. (H) Photosynthesis, a process in which water and carbon dioxide combine to form carbohydrates and oxygen, is often compared with respiration, a life process that is similar to combustion in that organic compounds are combined with oxygen to produce water and carbon dioxide. The reactions for photosynthesis and combustion are roughly the reverse of each other.

43. (C) Oxygen is not necessary for photosynthesis; it is formed during the process.

44. (J) According to the passage, it is impossible to predict when any one atom will decay; it is for this reason that the concept of half-life is used.

45. (A) Becquerel was unable to perform his experiment on a cloudy day—a day without strong sunshine. He stored the plates away and realized by accident that emissions occurred without exposure to sunlight. He did not know about radioactivity or beta particles.

46. (J) From Becquerel's discovery, we can only conclude that the minerals he used released some energy while they were in the dark drawer. There is nothing in the passage that suggests that all fluorescent minerals contain uranium (F); fluorescent minerals may contain other radioactive elements such as radium. Fluorescence and radioactivity are related but are not the same (G).

47. (C) Gamma rays have the greatest degree of penetration and therefore could go through the drawer into the room. Alpha particles (A) are stopped by paper and the beta particles (B) were stopped by the plate.

48. (H) The passage states that an alpha particle is a helium nucleus; such a nucleus consists of 2 protons and 2 neutrons for a total mass of 4 atomic mass units. Beta particles and gamma rays have negligible masses.

49. (D) According to the table, these three isotopes produced only beta particles, which are fast-moving electrons.

50. (J) The chart shows an array of different radiations that are emitted from radioactive elements. Some half-lives are very short; others are very long. There seems to be some correlation between the kind of radiation emitted and the duration of half-life.

51. (C) If we start with a 100-gram sample of uranium, at the end of the first half-life, 50 grams will be left; at the end of the second half-life, 25 grams will remain; third, 12.5; fourth, 6; fifth, 3; sixth, 1.5; and finally, seventh, 0.75 (less than 1 percent will remain).

52. (H) It is an established fact that seven half-lives are necessary for a radioactive element to lose approximately 99 percent of its total radioactivity. The fraction $\frac{63}{64}$ is 95 percent of an atom's total emissions. If, at the end of seven half-lives, 56 days have elapsed ($8 \times 7 = 56$), we can easily calculate that 95 percent of this is 53.2 days. Iron-59 on the chart is the closest isotope to this figure, having a half-life of 45 days.

# Practice Test 4

# ANSWER SHEET.  PRACTICE TEST 4

## English Usage

| | | | | | | |
|---|---|---|---|---|---|---|
| 1 Ⓐ Ⓑ Ⓒ Ⓓ | 12 Ⓕ Ⓖ Ⓗ Ⓙ | 23 Ⓐ Ⓑ Ⓒ Ⓓ | 34 Ⓕ Ⓖ Ⓗ Ⓙ | 45 Ⓐ Ⓑ Ⓒ Ⓓ | 56 Ⓕ Ⓖ Ⓗ Ⓙ | 67 Ⓐ Ⓑ Ⓒ Ⓓ |
| 2 Ⓕ Ⓖ Ⓗ Ⓙ | 13 Ⓐ Ⓑ Ⓒ Ⓓ | 24 Ⓕ Ⓖ Ⓗ Ⓙ | 35 Ⓐ Ⓑ Ⓒ Ⓓ | 46 Ⓕ Ⓖ Ⓗ Ⓙ | 57 Ⓐ Ⓑ Ⓒ Ⓓ | 68 Ⓕ Ⓖ Ⓗ Ⓙ |
| 3 Ⓐ Ⓑ Ⓒ Ⓓ | 14 Ⓕ Ⓖ Ⓗ Ⓙ | 25 Ⓐ Ⓑ Ⓒ Ⓓ | 36 Ⓕ Ⓖ Ⓗ Ⓙ | 47 Ⓐ Ⓑ Ⓒ Ⓓ | 58 Ⓕ Ⓖ Ⓗ Ⓙ | 69 Ⓐ Ⓑ Ⓒ Ⓓ |
| 4 Ⓕ Ⓖ Ⓗ Ⓙ | 15 Ⓐ Ⓑ Ⓒ Ⓓ | 26 Ⓕ Ⓖ Ⓗ Ⓙ | 37 Ⓐ Ⓑ Ⓒ Ⓓ | 48 Ⓕ Ⓖ Ⓗ Ⓙ | 59 Ⓐ Ⓑ Ⓒ Ⓓ | 70 Ⓕ Ⓖ Ⓗ Ⓙ |
| 5 Ⓐ Ⓑ Ⓒ Ⓓ | 16 Ⓕ Ⓖ Ⓗ Ⓙ | 27 Ⓐ Ⓑ Ⓒ Ⓓ | 38 Ⓕ Ⓖ Ⓗ Ⓙ | 49 Ⓐ Ⓑ Ⓒ Ⓓ | 60 Ⓕ Ⓖ Ⓗ Ⓙ | 71 Ⓐ Ⓑ Ⓒ Ⓓ |
| 6 Ⓕ Ⓖ Ⓗ Ⓙ | 17 Ⓐ Ⓑ Ⓒ Ⓓ | 28 Ⓕ Ⓖ Ⓗ Ⓙ | 39 Ⓐ Ⓑ Ⓒ Ⓓ | 50 Ⓕ Ⓖ Ⓗ Ⓙ | 61 Ⓐ Ⓑ Ⓒ Ⓓ | 72 Ⓕ Ⓖ Ⓗ Ⓙ |
| 7 Ⓐ Ⓑ Ⓒ Ⓓ | 18 Ⓕ Ⓖ Ⓗ Ⓙ | 29 Ⓐ Ⓑ Ⓒ Ⓓ | 40 Ⓕ Ⓖ Ⓗ Ⓙ | 51 Ⓐ Ⓑ Ⓒ Ⓓ | 62 Ⓕ Ⓖ Ⓗ Ⓙ | 73 Ⓐ Ⓑ Ⓒ Ⓓ |
| 8 Ⓕ Ⓖ Ⓗ Ⓙ | 19 Ⓐ Ⓑ Ⓒ Ⓓ | 30 Ⓕ Ⓖ Ⓗ Ⓙ | 41 Ⓐ Ⓑ Ⓒ Ⓓ | 52 Ⓕ Ⓖ Ⓗ Ⓙ | 63 Ⓐ Ⓑ Ⓒ Ⓓ | 74 Ⓕ Ⓖ Ⓗ Ⓙ |
| 9 Ⓐ Ⓑ Ⓒ Ⓓ | 20 Ⓕ Ⓖ Ⓗ Ⓙ | 31 Ⓐ Ⓑ Ⓒ Ⓓ | 42 Ⓕ Ⓖ Ⓗ Ⓙ | 53 Ⓐ Ⓑ Ⓒ Ⓓ | 64 Ⓕ Ⓖ Ⓗ Ⓙ | 75 Ⓐ Ⓑ Ⓒ Ⓓ |
| 10 Ⓕ Ⓖ Ⓗ Ⓙ | 21 Ⓐ Ⓑ Ⓒ Ⓓ | 32 Ⓕ Ⓖ Ⓗ Ⓙ | 43 Ⓐ Ⓑ Ⓒ Ⓓ | 54 Ⓕ Ⓖ Ⓗ Ⓙ | 65 Ⓐ Ⓑ Ⓒ Ⓓ | |
| 11 Ⓐ Ⓑ Ⓒ Ⓓ | 22 Ⓕ Ⓖ Ⓗ Ⓙ | 33 Ⓐ Ⓑ Ⓒ Ⓓ | 44 Ⓕ Ⓖ Ⓗ Ⓙ | 55 Ⓐ Ⓑ Ⓒ Ⓓ | 66 Ⓕ Ⓖ Ⓗ Ⓙ | |

## Mathematics Usage

| | | | | | | |
|---|---|---|---|---|---|---|
| 1 Ⓐ Ⓑ Ⓒ Ⓓ Ⓔ | 7 Ⓐ Ⓑ Ⓒ Ⓓ Ⓔ | 13 Ⓐ Ⓑ Ⓒ Ⓓ Ⓔ | 19 Ⓐ Ⓑ Ⓒ Ⓓ Ⓔ | 25 Ⓐ Ⓑ Ⓒ Ⓓ Ⓔ | 31 Ⓐ Ⓑ Ⓒ Ⓓ Ⓔ | 37 Ⓐ Ⓑ Ⓒ Ⓓ Ⓔ |
| 2 Ⓕ Ⓖ Ⓗ Ⓙ Ⓚ | 8 Ⓕ Ⓖ Ⓗ Ⓙ Ⓚ | 14 Ⓕ Ⓖ Ⓗ Ⓙ Ⓚ | 20 Ⓕ Ⓖ Ⓗ Ⓙ Ⓚ | 26 Ⓕ Ⓖ Ⓗ Ⓙ Ⓚ | 32 Ⓕ Ⓖ Ⓗ Ⓙ Ⓚ | 38 Ⓕ Ⓖ Ⓗ Ⓙ Ⓚ |
| 3 Ⓐ Ⓑ Ⓒ Ⓓ Ⓔ | 9 Ⓐ Ⓑ Ⓒ Ⓓ Ⓔ | 15 Ⓐ Ⓑ Ⓒ Ⓓ Ⓔ | 21 Ⓐ Ⓑ Ⓒ Ⓓ Ⓔ | 27 Ⓐ Ⓑ Ⓒ Ⓓ Ⓔ | 33 Ⓐ Ⓑ Ⓒ Ⓓ Ⓔ | 39 Ⓐ Ⓑ Ⓒ Ⓓ Ⓔ |
| 4 Ⓕ Ⓖ Ⓗ Ⓙ Ⓚ | 10 Ⓕ Ⓖ Ⓗ Ⓙ Ⓚ | 16 Ⓕ Ⓖ Ⓗ Ⓙ Ⓚ | 22 Ⓕ Ⓖ Ⓗ Ⓙ Ⓚ | 28 Ⓕ Ⓖ Ⓗ Ⓙ Ⓚ | 34 Ⓕ Ⓖ Ⓗ Ⓙ Ⓚ | 40 Ⓕ Ⓖ Ⓗ Ⓙ Ⓚ |
| 5 Ⓐ Ⓑ Ⓒ Ⓓ Ⓔ | 11 Ⓐ Ⓑ Ⓒ Ⓓ Ⓔ | 17 Ⓐ Ⓑ Ⓒ Ⓓ Ⓔ | 23 Ⓐ Ⓑ Ⓒ Ⓓ Ⓔ | 29 Ⓐ Ⓑ Ⓒ Ⓓ Ⓔ | 35 Ⓐ Ⓑ Ⓒ Ⓓ Ⓔ | |
| 6 Ⓕ Ⓖ Ⓗ Ⓙ Ⓚ | 12 Ⓕ Ⓖ Ⓗ Ⓙ Ⓚ | 18 Ⓕ Ⓖ Ⓗ Ⓙ Ⓚ | 24 Ⓕ Ⓖ Ⓗ Ⓙ Ⓚ | 30 Ⓕ Ⓖ Ⓗ Ⓙ Ⓚ | 36 Ⓕ Ⓖ Ⓗ Ⓙ Ⓚ | |

## Social Studies Reading

| | | | | | | | |
|---|---|---|---|---|---|---|---|
| 1 Ⓐ Ⓑ Ⓒ Ⓓ | 8 Ⓕ Ⓖ Ⓗ Ⓙ | 15 Ⓐ Ⓑ Ⓒ Ⓓ | 22 Ⓕ Ⓖ Ⓗ Ⓙ | 29 Ⓐ Ⓑ Ⓒ Ⓓ | 36 Ⓕ Ⓖ Ⓗ Ⓙ | 43 Ⓐ Ⓑ Ⓒ Ⓓ | 50 Ⓕ Ⓖ Ⓗ Ⓙ |
| 2 Ⓕ Ⓖ Ⓗ Ⓙ | 9 Ⓐ Ⓑ Ⓒ Ⓓ | 16 Ⓕ Ⓖ Ⓗ Ⓙ | 23 Ⓐ Ⓑ Ⓒ Ⓓ | 30 Ⓕ Ⓖ Ⓗ Ⓙ | 37 Ⓐ Ⓑ Ⓒ Ⓓ | 44 Ⓕ Ⓖ Ⓗ Ⓙ | 51 Ⓐ Ⓑ Ⓒ Ⓓ |
| 3 Ⓐ Ⓑ Ⓒ Ⓓ | 10 Ⓕ Ⓖ Ⓗ Ⓙ | 17 Ⓐ Ⓑ Ⓒ Ⓓ | 24 Ⓕ Ⓖ Ⓗ Ⓙ | 31 Ⓐ Ⓑ Ⓒ Ⓓ | 38 Ⓕ Ⓖ Ⓗ Ⓙ | 45 Ⓐ Ⓑ Ⓒ Ⓓ | 52 Ⓕ Ⓖ Ⓗ Ⓙ |
| 4 Ⓕ Ⓖ Ⓗ Ⓙ | 11 Ⓐ Ⓑ Ⓒ Ⓓ | 18 Ⓕ Ⓖ Ⓗ Ⓙ | 25 Ⓐ Ⓑ Ⓒ Ⓓ | 32 Ⓕ Ⓖ Ⓗ Ⓙ | 39 Ⓐ Ⓑ Ⓒ Ⓓ | 46 Ⓕ Ⓖ Ⓗ Ⓙ | |
| 5 Ⓐ Ⓑ Ⓒ Ⓓ | 12 Ⓕ Ⓖ Ⓗ Ⓙ | 19 Ⓐ Ⓑ Ⓒ Ⓓ | 26 Ⓕ Ⓖ Ⓗ Ⓙ | 33 Ⓐ Ⓑ Ⓒ Ⓓ | 40 Ⓕ Ⓖ Ⓗ Ⓙ | 47 Ⓐ Ⓑ Ⓒ Ⓓ | |
| 6 Ⓕ Ⓖ Ⓗ Ⓙ | 13 Ⓐ Ⓑ Ⓒ Ⓓ | 20 Ⓕ Ⓖ Ⓗ Ⓙ | 27 Ⓐ Ⓑ Ⓒ Ⓓ | 34 Ⓕ Ⓖ Ⓗ Ⓙ | 41 Ⓐ Ⓑ Ⓒ Ⓓ | 48 Ⓕ Ⓖ Ⓗ Ⓙ | |
| 7 Ⓐ Ⓑ Ⓒ Ⓓ | 14 Ⓕ Ⓖ Ⓗ Ⓙ | 21 Ⓐ Ⓑ Ⓒ Ⓓ | 28 Ⓕ Ⓖ Ⓗ Ⓙ | 35 Ⓐ Ⓑ Ⓒ Ⓓ | 42 Ⓕ Ⓖ Ⓗ Ⓙ | 49 Ⓐ Ⓑ Ⓒ Ⓓ | |

## Natural Sciences Reading

| | | | | | | | |
|---|---|---|---|---|---|---|---|
| 1 Ⓐ Ⓑ Ⓒ Ⓓ | 8 Ⓕ Ⓖ Ⓗ Ⓙ | 15 Ⓐ Ⓑ Ⓒ Ⓓ | 22 Ⓕ Ⓖ Ⓗ Ⓙ | 29 Ⓐ Ⓑ Ⓒ Ⓓ | 36 Ⓕ Ⓖ Ⓗ Ⓙ | 43 Ⓐ Ⓑ Ⓒ Ⓓ | 50 Ⓕ Ⓖ Ⓗ Ⓙ |
| 2 Ⓕ Ⓖ Ⓗ Ⓙ | 9 Ⓐ Ⓑ Ⓒ Ⓓ | 16 Ⓕ Ⓖ Ⓗ Ⓙ | 23 Ⓐ Ⓑ Ⓒ Ⓓ | 30 Ⓕ Ⓖ Ⓗ Ⓙ | 37 Ⓐ Ⓑ Ⓒ Ⓓ | 44 Ⓕ Ⓖ Ⓗ Ⓙ | 51 Ⓐ Ⓑ Ⓒ Ⓓ |
| 3 Ⓐ Ⓑ Ⓒ Ⓓ | 10 Ⓕ Ⓖ Ⓗ Ⓙ | 17 Ⓐ Ⓑ Ⓒ Ⓓ | 24 Ⓕ Ⓖ Ⓗ Ⓙ | 31 Ⓐ Ⓑ Ⓒ Ⓓ | 38 Ⓕ Ⓖ Ⓗ Ⓙ | 45 Ⓐ Ⓑ Ⓒ Ⓓ | 52 Ⓕ Ⓖ Ⓗ Ⓙ |
| 4 Ⓕ Ⓖ Ⓗ Ⓙ | 11 Ⓐ Ⓑ Ⓒ Ⓓ | 18 Ⓕ Ⓖ Ⓗ Ⓙ | 25 Ⓐ Ⓑ Ⓒ Ⓓ | 32 Ⓕ Ⓖ Ⓗ Ⓙ | 39 Ⓐ Ⓑ Ⓒ Ⓓ | 46 Ⓕ Ⓖ Ⓗ Ⓙ | |
| 5 Ⓐ Ⓑ Ⓒ Ⓓ | 12 Ⓕ Ⓖ Ⓗ Ⓙ | 19 Ⓐ Ⓑ Ⓒ Ⓓ | 26 Ⓕ Ⓖ Ⓗ Ⓙ | 33 Ⓐ Ⓑ Ⓒ Ⓓ | 40 Ⓕ Ⓖ Ⓗ Ⓙ | 47 Ⓐ Ⓑ Ⓒ Ⓓ | |
| 6 Ⓕ Ⓖ Ⓗ Ⓙ | 13 Ⓐ Ⓑ Ⓒ Ⓓ | 20 Ⓕ Ⓖ Ⓗ Ⓙ | 27 Ⓐ Ⓑ Ⓒ Ⓓ | 34 Ⓕ Ⓖ Ⓗ Ⓙ | 41 Ⓐ Ⓑ Ⓒ Ⓓ | 48 Ⓕ Ⓖ Ⓗ Ⓙ | |
| 7 Ⓐ Ⓑ Ⓒ Ⓓ | 14 Ⓕ Ⓖ Ⓗ Ⓙ | 21 Ⓐ Ⓑ Ⓒ Ⓓ | 28 Ⓕ Ⓖ Ⓗ Ⓙ | 35 Ⓐ Ⓑ Ⓒ Ⓓ | 42 Ⓕ Ⓖ Ⓗ Ⓙ | 49 Ⓐ Ⓑ Ⓒ Ⓓ | |

# TEST 1.  ENGLISH USAGE

*40 Minutes—75 Questions*

**DIRECTIONS:** In the reading selections below, certain parts of the sentences have been underlined and numbered. In the right-hand column, you will find different ways of writing each underlined part. Choose the one that best expresses the idea and uses standard written English. If you think the original version is the best, choose "NO CHANGE." The answers to many questions depend upon material that follows the underlined part. So be sure that you have read far enough ahead before you select your answer choice.

---

## Passage 1

### (1)

In 1849, San Francisco became the first official port of entry on the Pacific coast. In 1851, on account of the
1
rapid growth of lumbering activity and a corresponding expansion of population in the Northwest Territory, the government established the Puget Sound District of the Bureau of Customs. Nonetheless, smuggling grew rap-
2
idly, fostered by the tempting proximity of British havens and the natural cover afforded by vast forested areas and by the coves and inlets of countless heavy timbered
3
islands.

### (2)

Such fears were well foundationed. In 1851, United
4
States customs officers seize the Hudson's Bay Company
5
steamer "Beaver" for a technical violation of the revenue laws. This incident signaled an end to the era of unrestricted trade in the Pacific Northwest and drove some traders on both sides of the international border into illicit commercial arrangements. British wool, blankets,

1. **A.** NO CHANGE
   **B.** since
   **C.** because of
   **D.** for

2. **F.** NO CHANGE
   **G.** Therefore,
   **H.** Consequently,
   **J.** On the contrary,

3. **A.** NO CHANGE
   **B.** countless heavy
   **C.** countless heavily
   **D.** countless heavy

4. **F.** NO CHANGE
   **G.** well founded
   **H.** founded well
   **J.** well found

5. **A.** NO CHANGE
   **B.** seized
   **C.** were seizing
   **D.** have seized

GO ON TO THE NEXT PAGE

and liquor were the principle articles of this trade.
6

6. F. NO CHANGE
   G. were the principal articles
   H. was the principle article
   J. was the principal article

In fact, so much British wool was smuggled into the
7

7. A. NO CHANGE
   B. Furthermore,
   C. Moreover,
   D. On the contrary,

San Juan Islands selling as domestic wool by American
8

8. F. NO CHANGE
   G. and sold
   H. and would be sold
   J. to sell

sheepmen one naive textbook writer credited San Juan
9

sheep with a world's record annual production of 150

pounds of wool per animal.

9. A. NO CHANGE
   B. sheepmen, one
   C. sheepmen that one
   D. sheepmen, and a

(3)

Although American settlers in the Northwest Terri-

tory welcomed the assertion of national control to the
10

forty-ninth parallel, they were less amenable to restric-

tions on the trade with Vancouver Island.  They wanted

the duty-free rum and woolens offered by the British

10. F. NO CHANGE
    G. welcoming
    H. would welcome
    J. were welcomed by

but were fearing that the imposition and enforcement of
11

permanent tariffs on goods from British North America

11. A. NO CHANGE
    B. and were fearing
    C. and was fearful
    D. but feared

might be resulting in the losing of British markets for
12

American products.

12. F. NO CHANGE
    G. might result in the losing
    H. might result in the loss
    J. results in the loss

*Passage 2*

One of the beauties of astronomy is that one does

not have to be an expert to enjoy it.  Anyone can step

outside on a clear, moonless night, gaze at thousands

of stars shining across the vast interstellar spaces,
14

and then one can become intoxicated by a heady mix of
14

grandeur and existential chill.  The same questions come

13. Which of the following represents the most logical
    sequence of the paragraphs?
    A. 1, 2, 3
    B. 1, 3, 2
    C. 2, 3, 1
    D. 3, 1, 2

14. F. NO CHANGE
    G. spaces—and became
    H. spaces, and become
    J. spaces and becomes

GO ON TO THE NEXT PAGE

to mind time and <u>again, how</u> far away are the stars?
15

How many are there?  Are they strewn endlessly through

space, or are we a part of an island universe of suns

<u>ending</u> abruptly somewhere out there in the black ocean
16

of space?

It has been the sometimes heroic and often frustrat-

ing task of astronomers since the dawn of science <u>to chart</u>
17

our position in the cosmic ocean.  In the twentieth

century, significant progress <u>had been made</u> in construct-
18

ing an accurate map of the cosmos.  We know, for

example, that our solar system is part of a much larger

system of hundreds of billions of <u>stars this</u> system is the
19

Milky Way Galaxy, a huge disk of stars and gas.  We also

know that ours is not the only galaxy in the universe.  As

far as the largest telescopes in the world can see, there

are galaxies in every direction.  <u>The nearest galaxies to</u>
20

our own are the Magellanic <u>Clouds; the "crown</u> jewels of
21

the southern skies."

Since they are so near, they offer a laboratory in

which astronomers can study the evolution of stars and

galaxies.  The nearest large galaxy to the Milky Way is

the Andromeda Galaxy, which is about two million light

years away.  It is a giant spiral galaxy, <u>much like</u> our own
22

in size, shape, and nums-1ber and type of stars.  This

nearby sister galaxy <u>provides to us</u> an opportunity to get a
23

get a bird's-eye view of a galaxy much like our own—in

effect, to see ourselves as others do.

15. A. NO CHANGE
    B. again and how
    C. again how
    D. again.  How

16. F. NO CHANGE
    G. that ends
    H. that end
    J. ended

17. A. NO CHANGE
    B. charting
    C. having charted
    D. who charted

18. F. NO CHANGE
    G. has been made
    H. is made
    J. will be made

19. A. NO CHANGE
    B. stars, but
    C. stars.  This
    D. stars, however

20. F. NO CHANGE
    G. (Do NOT begin a new paragraph.) These
    H. (Begin a new paragraph here but not after "skies.") The
    J. (Begin a new paragraph here but not after "skies.") As the

21. A. NO CHANGE
    B. Clouds, the crown
    C. Clouds which is the "crown
    D. Clouds, the "crown

22. F. NO CHANGE
    G. much as
    H. like much
    J. much the same like

23. A. NO CHANGE
    B. provides us
    C. provide us
    D. providing to us

GO ON TO THE NEXT PAGE

## Passage 3

What we expect of a translation is a reasonable facsimile of something that might have been said in our own language.  But there implies in this notion of a

reasonable facsimile a debate between critics over to what constitutes a "reasonable" facsimile.

Most of us at heart belongs to the "soft line"

part: a given translation may not exactly be perfect

English, or the facsimile is generally reasonable.  At least nonreaders of the original language have something,

even if it is awkward, that would otherwise be unavailable.  And, of course, an author may even be well

served.  With a good translation, we have the possibility

of a true amazing event: a group of Swedish readers may award the Nobel Prize in Literature to an author

which writes in a language none of them

read.

The "hard line" party aims only for the good translation.  In this view, whether a translation does not read as

well as the original, then strangers are better off not

knowing about it, rather than wasting their time and

24. **F.** NO CHANGE
    **G.** are implied
    **H.** is implied
    **J.** is implying

25. **A.** NO CHANGE
    **B.** over
    **C.** to
    **D.** as

26. **F.** NO CHANGE
    **G.** belong
    **H.** belonging
    **J.** to belong

27. **A.** NO CHANGE
    **B.** Place before "may."
    **C.** Place before "not."
    **D.** Place after "be."

28. **F.** NO CHANGE
    **G.** English, and
    **H.** English, but
    **J.** English, the

29. **A.** NO CHANGE
    **B.** awkward that
    **C.** awkward and that
    **D.** awkward, so it

30. **F.** NO CHANGE
    **G.** A good translation,
    **H.** For a good translation,
    **J.** With a well translation

31. **A.** NO CHANGE
    **B.** truly amazing event: a group
    **C.** true, amazing event; a group
    **D.** truly amazing event, a grouping

32. **F.** NO CHANGE
    **G.** which wrote
    **H.** who writes
    **J.** written

33. **A.** NO CHANGE
    **B.** reads
    **C.** could read
    **D.** had read

34. **F.** NO CHANGE
    **G.** if
    **H.** for
    **J.** OMIT

GO ON TO THE NEXT PAGE

maybe getting the mistaken impression, the work is
35

trivial and inferior.

## Passage 4

The first astronauts entered the Mercury program in

April 1959. They were volunteer military pilots, graduated
36

of test pilot schools.  Each were required having a
37

bachelor's degree in engineering (or its equivalent) and

at least 1,500 hours of jet time.  Of the first group of 60

candidates called to Washington to hear about the pro-

gram, more than 80 percent volunteered.  Only seven

got chosen.  (Officials assumed that no more than seven
38

men would have the opportunity to fly.) These men were

true pioneers, they volunteered at a time when the plans
39

for space travel were only on paper and no one knew

what the chance of success was.

There were failures as well as spectacular successes

in the Mercury program, but scientists were able to learn

from each failure.  Fortunately they had these failures
40

early in the program.  The astronauts and the animal

passengers as well were flown without mishap when

their time came for them.
41

The most spectacular failure in the Mercury program

came to be known as the "tower flight."  The escape

tower, the parachutes, and the peroxide fuel were all

deployed on the launching pad in front of the domestic

and international press.  A relatively simple ground-circuit

defect in the Redstone launch vehicle caused the main

35.  **A.**  NO CHANGE
     **B.**  impression being that
     **C.**  impression of
     **D.**  impression that

36.  **F.**  NO CHANGE
     **G.**  pilots graduates
     **H.**  pilots; graduates
     **J.**  pilots, graduates

37.  **A.**  NO CHANGE
     **B.**  was required to have
     **C.**  required having
     **D.**  had been required to have

38.  **F.**  NO CHANGE
     **G.**  were chosen
     **H.**  had been chosen
     **J.**  has been chosen

39.  **A.**  NO CHANGE
     **B.**  pioneers but
     **C.**  pioneers yet
     **D.**  pioneers.  They

40.  **F.**  NO CHANGE
     **G.**  Fortunately, they had these failures
     **H.**  These failures occurred fortunately
     **J.**  Fortunately, these failures occurred

41.  **A.**  NO CHANGE
     **B.**  the time comes
     **C.**  their time comes
     **D.**  their time came

GO ON TO THE NEXT PAGE

rocket engine to ignite and then shutting down immediately after liftoff from the launching pad.  The "flight"
lasted only a second and covered a distance of only two
inches.

   One of the requirements of the Mercury program
was that an animal had to precede man into space.  The
flight of Ham, the chimpanzee, was a major milestone in
the program.  Again, there were some problems.  The
pickup of the spacecraft was delayed, and water leaked
into the capsule.  Ham, however, was eventually rescued
unharmed.
   Sending a man into zero gravity was among the
greatest medical experiments of all time.  Fortunately, all
astronauts found the weightlessness no problem.  All
returning to earth with no medical difficulties whatever.
In this area, the only question left unanswered by the
Mercury program was how long man could tolerate
weightlessness.  It seemed like, however, that longer

flights would require only that astronauts to have suitable
methods of exercise and nutrition.

   The Mercury program taught scientists a great deal,
and by 1962 they were working on a program to go to the
Moon.

### Passage 5

   It was not until the nineteenth century that medicine
was able, in any broad and real way, to help the suffering
individual.  During this century, technical advances aided

---

42.  F.   NO CHANGE
     G.   and then will shut
     H.   and then they shut
     J.   and then shut

43.  A.   NO CHANGE
     B.   (Do NOT begin a new paragraph.) One of the
          requirements
     C.   (Do NOT begin a new paragraph.) One
          requirement
     D.   (Do NOT begin a new paragraph.)
          A requirement

44.  F.   NO CHANGE
     G.   Place before "was."
     H.   Place before "eventually."
     J.   Place before "rescued."

45.  A.   NO CHANGE
     B.   return
     C.   returned
     D.   will return

46.  F.   NO CHANGE
     G.   seemed
     H.   seemed as
     J.   seemed to be

47.  A.   NO CHANGE
     B.   have
     C.   had had
     D.   are sure to have

48.  F.   NO CHANGE
     G.   way of help
     H.   way to help
     J.   way, of helping

GO ON TO THE NEXT PAGE

the diagnostician and also the surgeon, and the begin-
49

nings of an understanding of the fundamental mecha-

nisms of disease had been emerging.  All aspects of
50

medicine—from the research laboratory to the operating

table—was enjoying the benefits of the rigorous applica-
51

tion of the scientific method.

By the end of the nineteenth century, a person's

chances were fairly good that his doctor could not only

give a name to his medical complaint yet probably had an
52

elementary understanding of what it was and how it

progressed.  With somewhat more luck, the doctor could

select the proper treatment and he could also mitigate
53

the symptoms if not cure the disease altogether.

This transition to modern medicine depended on

three important advances.  First, it required an under-

standing of the true nature and origin of disease.

Second, it required that an organized body of standard

medical practice be available to guide physicians in diag-
54

nosis and treatment of disease.  Third, it presupposes
55

a degree of medical technology never before available.

Among the more dramatic nineteenth-century
56

medical advances were those in the field of human

physiology.  In 1822, an obscure American army camp

surgeon practicing medicine near the Canadian frontier

is transformed almost overnight into a specialist on the
57

mechanism of human digestion.  The physician, William

Beaumont, was called to treat a young trapper, acciden-

**49.**
  **A.** NO CHANGE
  **B.** as well as
  **C.** with
  **D.** as opposed to

**50.**
  **F.** NO CHANGE
  **G.** was emerging
  **H.** were emerging
  **J.** emerged

**51.**
  **A.** NO CHANGE
  **B.** were enjoying
  **C.** is enjoying
  **D.** enjoys

**52.**
  **F.** NO CHANGE
  **G.** but also probably had
  **H.** consequently probably has
  **J.** but also, probably would have

**53.**
  **A.** NO CHANGE
  **B.** but could mitigate
  **C.** and mitigate
  **D.** and can mitigate

**54.**
  **F.** NO CHANGE
  **G.** was available to
  **H.** is available for
  **J.** be available as

**55.**
  **A.** NO CHANGE
  **B.** it is presupposed
  **C.** it presupposed
  **D.** they presuppose

**56.**
  **F.** NO CHANGE
  **G.** (Do NOT begin a new paragraph.) Among
     the more dramatic
  **H.** (Begin a new paragraph.) Since
  **J.** (Do NOT begin a new paragraph.) Since

**57.**
  **A.** NO CHANGE
  **B.** gets transformed
  **C.** transforms
  **D.** was transformed

GO ON TO THE NEXT PAGE

tally shot in the stomach. <u>Beaumont's operating skill</u>
<sub>58</sub>
saved the boy's life, but the patient was left with an

abnormal opening leading to the stomach. To Beau-

mont's credit, he recognized this unique opportunity to

study the human digestive <u>process, but</u> for the next ten
<sub>59</sub>
years he conducted hundreds of experiments with the

reluctant cooperation of his not-so-willing patient.

From his experiments, Beaumont was able to de-

scribe the physiology of digestion, demonstrating the

characteristics of gastric motility <u>and describe</u> the proper-
<sub>60</sub>
ties of gastric juice. He determined that the stomach

contained hydrochloric acid and that it broke down food

by a chemical process and not by maceration or putrefac-

tion. Beaumont's pioneering work made him a famous

man. As for the young trapper, he did not fare as well.

He was forced to tour medical schools as "the man with

the window in his stomach."

### Passage 6

Newborn babies are the not passive creatures most

people assume <u>him to be.</u> Recent research shows that
<sub>61</sub>

the newborn comes well endowed <u>of</u> charm and full
<sub>62</sub>
potential for social graces. His eyes are equipped with

surprisingly good vision. Shortly after birth he begins to

watch his mother's face, which he soon comes to recog-

nize. He also learns to know her voice and will turn

---

58. **F.** NO CHANGE
 **G.** (Begin a new paragraph.) Beaumont's operat-
 ing skill
 **H.** (Begin a new paragraph.) The skill of Beau-
 mont at operating
 **J.** (Do NOT begin a new paragraph.) The skill of
 Beaumont at operating

59. **A.** NO CHANGE
 **B.** process, and
 **C.** process,
 **D.** process. But

60. **F.** NO CHANGE
 **G.** to describe
 **H.** that describe
 **J.** and describing

61. **A.** NO CHANGE
 **B.** he was
 **C.** them to be
 **D.** it is

62. **F.** NO CHANGE
 **G.** for
 **H.** with
 **J.** by

GO ON TO THE NEXT PAGE

toward her when he hears it.  This is about the time
63

when affection begins.  The infant's cry alerts the mother

and causes a biological including an emotional reaction.
64

The infant's ability to cling and cuddle communicates a

pleasurable warmth to the mother, and the infant's odor,

too, is pleasant and uniquely their own.  The newborn
65

also smiles.  The human infant, in fact, is in possession of
66

attributes that are guaranteeing his attractiveness.
67

Although there is some argument about whether the

child sparks the development of love or whether or not a
68

special physiological state of the mother prompts her to

interact with the new infant.  But most researchers agree
69

that the newborn does mold or trigger adult behavior.

The neonate organizes the mother's behavior by crying,

and by eye-to-eye contact.  The newborn is not a passive

creature at all.

### Passage 7

The "disposal problem" was the term coined by CIA

head Allen Dulles to refer to the question of what will be
70

done with 1,500 armed men who had been trained and
71

equipped by the CIA for the express purpose of invading

**63.** A. NO CHANGE
B. it, this
C. it this
D. it

**64.** F. NO CHANGE
G. and
H. with
J. but

**65.** A. NO CHANGE
B. his own
C. belongs to him only
D. belonging to him

**66.** F. NO CHANGE
G. possessed
H. possesses
J. are in possession of

**67.** A. NO CHANGE
B. guaranteed
C. guarantees
D. guarantee

**68.** F. NO CHANGE
G. or whether
H. and whether if
J. or whether if

**69.** A. NO CHANGE
B. infant,
C. infant.  On the contrary
D. infant.  Most

**70.** F. NO CHANGE
G. is being done
H. is to be done
J. to do

**71.** A. NO CHANGE
B. that have been trained
C. who being trained
D. who are training

GO ON TO THE NEXT PAGE

Cuba <u>and to remove</u> Fidel Castro from power. Although
<sub>72</sub>
Kennedy may have received prior information of the

planned invasion in campaign briefings, the information

he received on the details of the operation must have had

a disconcerting effect on the new President.

Kennedy received his initial briefing as President

from the authors of the plan in the CIA . Because of the

vested interest of the CIA in the invasion plan, the

Dulles briefing turned out to be more a persuasive

speech in favor of the invasion <u>instead of an</u> objective
<sub>73</sub>
presentation of facts. In effect, Dulles told Kennedy

that the decision to proceed with the plan would be a test

of the new administration's will to <u>allow and assisted</u> the
<sub>74</sub>
Cuban exiles to free their homeland from the domination

of a communist dictator and, as had been the policy of

the previous administration, to prevent Cuba from sub-

verting the rest of the hemisphere. Viewed in this way,

through CIA spectacles, it is not surprising that President

Kennedy gave the go-ahead for the operation . It would

be a gross oversimplification to suggest that Kennedy

made <u>a decision so momentously</u> solely on the basis of
<sub>75</sub>
his first interview with Dulles, but the first interview did

set the tone for the entire decision-making process.

72. **F.** NO CHANGE
    **G.** and removing
    **H.** and removed
    **J.** with the purpose of removing

73. **A.** NO CHANGE
    **B.** but
    **C.** than
    **D.** with

74. **F.** NO CHANGE
    **G.** allow and assist
    **H.** allowing and assisting
    **J.** allow for the assistance of

75. **A.** NO CHANGE
    **B.** a decision as momentously
    **C.** a decision as momentous
    **D.** so momentous a decision

## END OF TEST

If you complete this test before the time is up, check
back over the questions on this test only.  Do not go back
to the previous test.  Do not proceed to the next test until
you are told to do so.

# TEST 2. MATHEMATICS USAGE

*50 Minutes—40 Questions*

**DIRECTIONS:** Solve each of the following problems. Choose the correct answer.

Solve as many problems as you can. Do not spend too much time on any one problem. You may return to problems so long as you have time left in this section.

Note: The figures that accompany the problems are not necessarily drawn to scale. Figures are assumed to lie in a plane unless a note states otherwise.

**1.** If $x + 2 = 7$ and $x + y = 11$, then $y = ?$
 A. 2
 B. 4
 C. 6
 D. 7
 E. 9

**2.** In the figure below, if $y + z = 150$, then $x = ?$

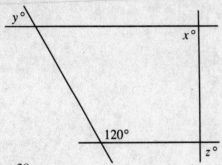

 F. 30
 G. 45
 H. 75
 J. 90
 K. 120

**3.** Which of the following equations correctly expresses the relationship described below?
The product of $x$ and 5 is equal to one-half the sum of $3x$ and 3.

 A. $5x = \dfrac{9x}{2}$
 B. $5x = 2(3x + 3)$
 C. $5x = \dfrac{(3x + 3)}{2}$
 D. $\dfrac{x}{5} = 2(3x + 3)$
 E. $\dfrac{x}{5} = \dfrac{(3x + 3)}{2}$

**4.** If $x > -5$, then $(x + 7)$ could be:
 F. $-1$.
 G. 0.
 H. 1.
 J. 2.
 K. 3.

**5.** During a sale, three of a certain item can be purchased for the usual cost of two of the items. If John buys 36 of the items at the sale price, how many of the items could he have bought at the regular price?
 A. 18
 B. 24
 C. 30
 D. 48
 E. 72

**6.** In $PQR$ below, if $PQ = QR$, then $x = ?$

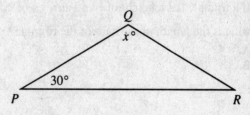

 F. 30
 G. 60
 H. 90
 J. 120
 K. 150

GO ON TO THE NEXT PAGE

7. If $px + 2 = 8$ and $qx + 3 = 10$, what is the value of $\dfrac{p}{q}$?

A. $\dfrac{3}{5}$

B. $\dfrac{8}{15}$

C. $\dfrac{10}{13}$

D. $\dfrac{6}{7}$

E. $\dfrac{16}{13}$

8. If $2^x = 16$ and $x = \dfrac{y}{2}$, then $y = ?$

F. 2
G. 3
H. 4
J. 6
K. 8

9. A sales representative is paid $500 per week plus 3 percent of the amount of her sales, $s$. Which of the following equations could be used to determine her weekly pay, $p$, in dollars?

A. $p = 500(0.03)(s)$
B. $p = 500s^{0.03}$
C. $p = 500 + s + 0.03$
D. $p = 500(0.03) + s$
E. $p = 500 + 0.03s$

10. Which of the following is the largest number?

F. $6.0 \times 10^{-8}$
G. $5.3 \times 10^{-8}$
H. $2.6 \times 10^{-7}$
J. $6.3 \times 10^{-9}$
K. $1.4 \times 10^{-6}$

11. If a triangle has a height of $\dfrac{1}{x}$ and an area of 2, what is the length of the base of the triangle?

A. $4x$
B. $x$
C. $\dfrac{1}{2x}$
D. $\dfrac{1}{4x}$
E. $x^2$

12. If the sum of three numbers is $4x$ and the sum of four other numbers is $3x$, then the average (arithmetic mean) of all seven numbers is:

F. $7x$.
G. $x$.
H. $\dfrac{x}{7}$.
J. 7.
K. 1.

13. In the figure below, if $x = y$, then $z = ?$

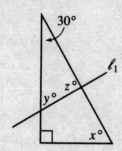

A. 30
B. 45
C. 60
D. 75
E. 90

14. If $6 \leqq x \leqq 30$, $3 \leqq y \leqq 12$, and $2 \leqq z \leqq 10$, then what is the least possible value of $\dfrac{(x + y)}{z}$?

F. $\dfrac{9}{10}$

G. $\dfrac{9}{5}$

H. $\dfrac{21}{5}$

J. $\dfrac{9}{2}$

K. 21

15. If $x \neq 0$, then $\dfrac{(-3x)^3}{-3x^3} = ?$

A. $-9$
B. $-3$
C. $-1$
D. 3
E. 9

GO ON TO THE NEXT PAGE

**16.** $|x - 2| < 6$ if and only if which of the following is true?

F. $x < 4$
G. $x > 4$
H. $x < 8$
J. $x < 8$ and $x > -8$
K. $x < 8$ and $x > -4$

**17.** If the area of the triangle in the figure below is 12, then $k = ?$

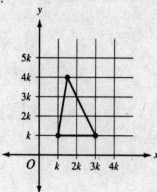

A. 1
B. 2
C. 3
D. 4
E. 6

**18.** A machine produces 18 widgets every 5 seconds. How many widgets does it produce in an hour?

F. 720
G. 1,000
H. 1,296
J. 10,000
K. 12,960

**19.** John spent $4,928 for a used car. If the price John paid was 12 percent less than the price of the car when it was new, what was the price of the car when it was new?

A. $5,600
B. $5,520
C. $5,490
D. $5,400
E. $5,136

**20.** After trimming, a sapling has $\frac{9}{10}$ of its original height. If it must grow $\frac{9}{10}$ foot to regain its original height, what was its original height, in feet?

F. 8
G. 9
H. 10
J. 16
K. 18

**21.** A tank contains $g$ gallons of water. Water flows into the tank by one pipe at the rate of $m$ gallons per minute, and water flows out by another pipe at the rate of $n$ gallons per minute. If $n > m$, which of the following equations can be used to determine $t$, the length of time, in minutes, it will take for the tank to become empty?

A. $t = \dfrac{(g - m)}{n}$

B. $t = \dfrac{g}{(m - n)}$

C. $t = \dfrac{(n - g)}{m}$

D. $t = \dfrac{(n - m)}{g}$

E. $t = \dfrac{g}{(n - m)}$

**22.** If $\dfrac{13t}{7}$ is an integer, then $t$ could be any of the following EXCEPT:

F. $-91$.
G. $-7$.
H. 3.
J. 70.
K. 91.

**23.** If $\dfrac{(x + y)}{x} = 4$ and $\dfrac{(y + z)}{z} = 5$, what is the value of $\dfrac{x}{z}$?

A. $\dfrac{1}{4}$

B. $\dfrac{1}{3}$

C. $\dfrac{3}{4}$

D. $\dfrac{4}{3}$

E. $\dfrac{3}{1}$

**24.** On Monday, Juan withdraws $\frac{1}{2}$ of the money in his savings account. On Tuesday, he withdraws another $60, leaving $\frac{1}{5}$ of the original amount in the account. How much money was originally in Juan's savings account?

F. $600
G. $300
H. $200
J. $150
K. $120

GO ON TO THE NEXT PAGE

25. A painter is planning to paint a row of three houses, using the colors red, gray, and white. If each house is to be painted a single color, and if the painter must use each of the three colors, how many different ways are there of painting the three houses?

A. 1
B. 2
C. 3
D. 6
E. 9

26. If $x = 2$, then $x^2 - 2x = ?$

F. $-4$
G. 0
H. 2
J. 4
K. 8

27. If 2 pounds of coffee makes exactly 7 pots of coffee, how many pots of coffee can be made from a 10-pound bag of coffee?

A. 3
B. 4
C. 6
D. 35
E. 50

28. If roses cost $1.00 apiece and carnations cost $0.50 apiece, how many more carnations than roses can be purchased for $10.00?

F. 20
G. 10
H. 5
J. 2
K. 1

29. If the sides of each box described below are perpendicular to each other, which box has the greatest volume?

| Dimensions of 5 different boxes | |
| --- | --- |
| Box A: | $2 \times 3 \times 4$ |
| Box B: | $2 \times 3 \times 3$ |
| Box C: | $3 \times 4 \times 5$ |
| Box D: | $5 \times 4 \times 2$ |
| Box E: | $4 \times 4 \times 2$ |

A. A
B. B
C. C
D. D
E. E

30. What is the distance between $a$ and $b$ in the Cartesian coordinate system below?

F. $\dfrac{\sqrt{2}}{2}$
G. $\sqrt{2}$
H. 2
J. $2\sqrt{2}$
K. 4

31. If $(x + y)^2 = (x - y)^2 + 4$, then $xy = ?$

A. 8
B. 4
C. 3
D. 2
E. 1

32. If $\dfrac{2}{3}$ of a number is 5 more than $\dfrac{1}{4}$ of the number, what is the number?

F. 12
G. 15
H. 18
J. 24
K. 36

33. The product of an even, positive number and an odd, negative number is:

A. negative and even.
B. negative and odd.
C. negative and either even or odd.
D. positive and odd.
E. positive and even.

34. If $w, x, y$, and $z$ are positive numbers, each of the following expressions equals $w(x + y + z)$ EXCEPT:

F. $wx + wy + wz$.
G. $wx + w(y + z)$.
H. $w(x + y) + wz$.
J. $w(x + z) + wy$.
K. $w(xy) + w(yz)$.

35. If a square has the same area as a rectangle with sides of 9 and 4, a length of a side of the square is:

A. 3.
B. 4.
C. 5.
D. 6.
E. 7.

GO ON TO THE NEXT PAGE

**36.** Originally, a group of 11 students were supposed to share equally a cash prize. If one more student is added to the group and the 12 students share the prize equally, then each new share is worth what fraction of each original share?

F. $\dfrac{1}{12}$

G. $\dfrac{1}{11}$

H. $\dfrac{1}{10}$

J. $\dfrac{10}{11}$

K. $\dfrac{11}{12}$

**37.** In the figure below, the center of the circle has coordinates (2,2). What is the area of the shaded portion of the figure?

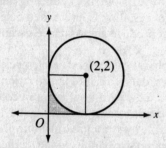

A. $2 - \pi$

B. $4 - \pi$

C. $8 - 2\pi$

D. $8 - \pi$

E. $16 - 4\pi$

**38.** The table below gives the distribution of two genetic characteristics X and Y, in a population of 100 subjects. What is the ratio of the number of people having characteristic X to the number of people having the characteristic Y?

| Having X and Y | 10 |
|---|---|
| Having X but not Y | 30 |
| Having Y but not X | 20 |
| Having neither X nor Y | 40 |

F. 1:3

G. 1:2

H. 2:3

J. 4:3

K. 3:2

**39.** If $x \neq 0$ and $y \neq 0$, what is the coefficient of the $xy$ term when $4x - 2y$ and $3x + 4y$ are multiplied?

A. 10

B. 8

C. 7

D. 6

E. 1

**40.** If $i = \sqrt{-1}$, then $(2 + 3i)(4 - i) = ?$

F. 10

G. $10i$

H. $9 + 10i$

J. $11 + 10i$

K. $12 + i$

## END OF TEST

If you complete this test before the time is up, check
back over the questions on this test only. Do not go back
to the previous test. Do not proceed to the next test until
you are told to do so.

**DIRECTIONS:** Below each of the following reading passages is a series of questions. Choose the *best* answer to each question, interpreting what is stated or implied by the passage in the light of your own background in the subject. You may refer back to the passage as often as necessary, though the answers to some questions may not be found expressly in the passage.

---

Helplessness and passivity are central themes in describing human depression. Laboratory experiments with animals have uncovered a phenomenon designated "learned helplessness." Dogs given inescapable shock initially show intense emotionality but later become passive in the same situation. When the situation is changed from inescapable to escapable shock, the dogs fail

(5) to escape even though escape is possible. Neurochemical changes resulting from learned helplessness are similar to those found in separation loss, changes that produce an avoidance-escape deficit in laboratory animals.

Is the avoidance deficit caused by prior exposure to inescapable shock, learned helplessness, or simply a stress-induced noradrenergic deficiency leading to a deficit in motor activation?

(10) Avoidance-escape deficit can be produced in rats by stress alone, i.e., by a brief swim in cold water. But a deficit produced by exposure to extremely traumatic events must be produced by a very different mechanism than the deficit produced by exposure to the less traumatic uncontrollable aversive events in the learned-helplessness experiments. A nonaversive parallel to the learned helplessness induced by uncontrollable shock, e.g., induced by uncontrollable food delivery, pro-

(15) duces similar results. Moreover, studies have shown the importance of prior experience in learned helplessness. Dogs can be "immunized" against learned helplessness by prior experience with controllable shock. Rats also show a "mastery effect" after extended experience with escapable shock. They work far longer trying to escape from inescapable shock than do rats lacking this prior mastery experience. Conversely, weanling rats given inescapable shock fail to escape shock

(20) as adults. These adult rats are also poor at nonaversive discrimination learning.

Certain similarities have been noted between conditions produced in animals by the learned-helplessness procedure and by the experimental neurosis paradigm. In the latter, animals are first trained on a discrimination task and are then tested with discriminative stimuli of increasing similarity. Eventually, as the discrimination becomes very difficult, animals fail to respond and

(25) begin displaying abnormal behaviors, first agitation, then lethargy.

It has been suggested that both learned helplessness and experimental neurosis involve inhibition of motivation centers and pathways by limbic forebrain inhibitory centers, especially in the septal area. The main function of this inhibition is compensatory, providing relief from anxiety or distress. In rats subjected to the learned-helplessness and experimental-neurosis paradigms, stim-

(30) ulation of the septum produces behavioral arrest, lack of behavioral initiation, and lethargy, while rats with septal lesions do not show learned helplessness. How analogous the model of learned helplessness and the paradigm of stress-induced neurosis are to human depression is not entirely clear. Inescapable noise or unsolvable problems have been shown to result in conditions in humans similar to those induced in laboratory animals, but an adequate model of human depression

(35) must also be able to account for the cognitive complexity of human depression.

GO ON TO THE NEXT PAGE

1. The primary purpose of the passage is to:

   A. propose a cure for depression in human beings.
   B. discuss research possibly relevant to depression in human beings.
   C. criticize the result of experiments that induce depression in laboratory animals.
   D. raise some questions about the propriety of using laboratory animals for research.

2. The author raises the question at the beginning of the second paragraph in order to:

   F. prove that learned helplessness is caused by neurochemical changes.
   G. demonstrate that learned helplessness is also caused by nonaversive discrimination learning.
   H. suggest that further research is needed to determine the exact causes of learned helplessness.
   J. refute a possible objection based on an alternative explanation of the cause of learned helplessness.

3. It can be inferred from the passage that rats with septal lesions (line 31) do not show learned helplessness because:

   A. such rats were immunized against learned helplessness by prior training.
   B. the lesions blocked communication between the limbic forebrain inhibitory centers and motivation centers.
   C. the lesions prevented the rats from understanding the inescapability of the helplessness situation.
   D. a lack of stimulation of the septal area does not necessarily result in excited behavior.

4. It can be inferred that the most important difference between experiments inducing learned helplessness by inescapable shock and the nonaversive parallel mentioned at line 13 is that the nonaversive parallel:

   F. did not use pain as a stimulus to be avoided.
   G. failed to induce learned helplessness in subject animals.
   H. reduced the extent of learned helplessness.
   J. caused a more traumatic reaction in the animals.

5. The author cites the "mastery effect" (line 17) primarily in order to:

   A. prove that the avoidance deficit caused by exposure to inescapable shock is not caused by shock per se but by the inescapability of the shock.
   B. cast doubt on the validity of models of animal depression when applied to depression in human beings.

C. explain the neurochemical changes in the brain that cause learned helplessness.
D. suggest that the experimental neurosis paradigm and learned-helplessness procedure produce similar behavior in animals.

6. The most logical continuation of the passage would be:

   F. an explanation of the connection between the septum and the motivation centers of the brains of rats.
   G. an examination of techniques used to cure animals of learned helplessness.
   H. a review of experiments designed to create stress-induced noradrenergic deficiencies in humans.
   J. an elaboration of the differences between human depression and similar animal behavior.

7. In developing her argument, the author relies on conclusions based on all of the following EXCEPT:

   A. studies of humans exposed to inescapable noise.
   B. experiments exposing animals to inescapable shock.
   C. experiments exposing animals to escapable shock.
   D. programs to cure human beings of learned helplessness.

8. As used in this passage, *paradigm* means:

   F. shock.
   G. model.
   H. anxiety.
   J. behavior.

9. In this passage, the author's tone can best be described as:

   A. outraged.
   B. guilty.
   C. detached.
   D. mournful.

10. The passage implies that inhibition of motivation centers:

    F. causes septal lesions in humans.
    G. induces stress.
    H. provides relief from anxiety and stress.
    J. enables animals to discriminate.

GO ON TO THE NEXT PAGE

The existence of both racial and sexual discrimination in employment is well documented, and policy-makers and responsible employers are particularly sensitive to the plight of the black female employee on the theory that she is doubly the victim of discrimination. That there exist differences in income between whites and blacks is clear, but it is not so clear that these differ-

(5)    ences are solely the result of racial discrimination in employment. The two groups differ in productivity, so basic economics dictates that their incomes will differ.

To obtain a true measure of the effect of racial discrimination in employment it is necessary to adjust the gross black/white income ratio for these productivity factors. White women in urban areas have a higher educational level than black women and can be expected to receive

(10)   larger incomes. Moreover, state distribution of residence is important because blacks are overrepresented in the South, where wage rates are typically lower than elsewhere and where racial differentials in income are greater. Also, blacks are overrepresented in large cities, and incomes of blacks would be greater if blacks were distributed among cities of different sizes in the same manner as whites.

(15)   After standardization for the productivity factors, the income of black urban women is estimated to be between 108 and 125 percent of the income of white women. This indicates that productivity factors more than account for the actual white/black income differential for women. Despite their greater education, white women's *actual* mean income is only 2 to 5 percent higher than that of black women in the North. Unlike the situation of men, the evidence indicates that

(20)   the money income of black urban women was as great as, or greater than, that of whites of similar productivity in the North, and probably in the United States as a whole. For men, however, the adjusted black/white income ratio is approximately 80 percent.

At least two possible hypotheses may explain why the adjustment for productivity more than accounts for the observed income differential for women, whereas a differential persists for men.

(25)   First, there may be more discrimination against black men than against black women. The different occupational structures for men and women give some indication why this could be the case, and institutionalized consideration—for competition—may also contribute. Second, the data are consistent with the hypothesis that the intensity of discrimination against women differs little between whites and blacks. Therefore, racial discrimination adds little to effects of existing

(30)   sex discrimination.

These findings suggest that a black woman does not necessarily suffer relatively more discrimination in the labor market than does a white woman. Rather, for women, the effects of sexual discrimination are so pervasive that the effects of racial discrimination are negligible. Of course, this is not to say that the more generalized racial discrimination of which black women,

(35)   like men, are victims does not disadvantage black women in their search for work. After all, one important productivity factor is level of education, and the difference between white and black women on this scale is largely the result of racial discrimination.

11.  The primary purpose of the passage is to:

A.  explain the reasons for the existence of income differentials between men and women.

B.  show that racial discrimination against black women in employment is less important than sexual discrimination.

C.  explore the ways in which productivity factors such as level of education influence the earning power of black workers.

D.  sketch a history of racial and sexual discrimination against black and female workers in the labor market.

12.  According to the passage, the gross black/white income ratio is not an accurate measure of discrimination in employment because the gross ratio:

F.  fails to include large numbers of black workers who live in the large cities and in the South.

G.  must be adjusted to reflect the longer number of hours and greater number of days worked by black employees.

H.  represents a subjective interpretation by the statistician of the importance of factors such as educational achievement.

J.  includes income differences attributable to real economic factors and not to discrimination.

GO ON TO THE NEXT PAGE

13. Which of the following best describes the relationship between the income level for black women and that for black men?

   A. In general, black men earn less money than black women.

   B. On the average, black women in the South earn less money than black men in large Northern cities.

   C. Productivity factors have a greater dollar value in the case of black women.

   D. The difference between income levels for black and white women is less than that for black and white men.

14. Which of the following best describes the logical relationship between the two hypotheses presented in lines 25-30?

   F. The two hypotheses may both be true, since each phenomenon could contribute to the observed differential.

   G. The two hypotheses are contradictory, and if one is proved to be correct, the other is proved incorrect.

   H. The two hypotheses are dependent on each other, and empirical disconfirmation of the one is disconfirmation of the other.

   J. The two hypotheses are logically connected so that proof of the first entails the truth of the second.

15. The tone of the passage is:

   A. confident and overbearing.
   B. ill-tempered and brash.
   C. objective and critical.
   D. tentative and inconclusive.

16. If the second hypothesis mentioned by the author (lines 27-30) is correct, a general lessening of discrimination against women should lead to a(n):

   F. higher white/black income ratio for women.
   G. lower white/black income ratio for women.
   H. lower female/male income ratio.
   J. increase in the productivity of women.

17. The author's attitude toward racial and sexual discrimination in employment can best be described as one of:

   A. apology.
   B. concern.
   C. indifference.
   D. indignation.

18. As used in this passage, the word *pervasive* (line 33) means:

   F. contained.
   G. spread throughout.
   H. understandable.
   J. not apparent.

19. According to the passage, black women in the work force primarily feel the effects of racial discrimination in:

   A. income levels.
   B. occupational opportunities.
   C. educational levels.
   D. sexual harassment.

20. *Mean income* (line 18) is:

   F. middle-class income.
   G. average income.
   H. lowest possible income.
   J. greatest possible income.

     War has escaped the battlefield and now can, with modern guidance systems on missiles, touch virtually every square yard of the earth's surface. It no longer involves only the military profession, but engulfs also entire civilian populations. Nuclear weapons have made major war unthinkable. We are forced, however, to think about the unthinkable because a thermonuclear
(5)  war could come by accident or miscalculation. We must accept the paradox of maintaining a capacity to fight such a war so that we will never have to do so.

     War has also lost most of its utility in achieving the traditional goals of conflict. Control of territory carries with it the obligation to provide subject peoples certain administrative, health, education, and other social services; such obligations far outweigh the benefits of control. If the
(10)  ruled population is ethnically or racially different from the rulers, tensions and chronic unrest often exist which further reduce the benefits and increase the costs of domination. Large populations no longer necessarily enhance state power and, in the absence of high levels of economic development, can impose severe burdens on food supply, jobs, and the broad range of services expected of modern governments. The noneconomic security reasons for the control of territory
(15)  have been progressively undermined by the advances of modern technology. The benefits of forcing another nation to surrender its wealth are vastly outweighed by the benefits of persuading that nation to produce and exchange goods and services. In brief, imperialism no longer pays.

GO ON TO THE NEXT PAGE →

Making war has been one of the most persistent of human activities in the 80 centuries since men and women settled in cities and became thereby "civilized," but the modernization of the
(20)　past 80 years has fundamentally changed the role and function of war. In pre-modernized societies, successful warfare brought significant material rewards, the most obvious of which were the stored wealth of the defeated. Equally important was human labor—control over people as slaves or levies for the victor's army, and there was the productive capacity—agricultural lands, and mines. Successful warfare also produced psychic benefits. The removal or destruction of a
(25)　threat brought a sense of security, and power gained over others created pride and national self-esteem.

Warfare was also the most complex, broad-scale, and demanding activity of pre-modernized people. The challenges of leading men into battle, organizing, moving, and supporting armies, attracted the talents of the most vigorous, enterprising, intelligent, and imaginative men in the
(30)　society. "Warrior" and "statesman" were usually synonymous, and the military was one of the few professions in which an able, ambitious boy of humble origin could rise to the top. In the broader cultural context, war was accepted in the pre-modernized society as a part of the human condition, a mechanism of change, and an unavoidable, even noble, aspect of life. The excitement and drama of war made it a vital part of literature and legends.

**21.** The primary purpose of the passage is to:

   **A.** theorize about the role of the warrior-statesman in pre-modernized society.

   **B.** explain the effects of war on both modernized and pre-modernized societies.

   **C.** contrast the value of war in a modernized society with its value in pre-modernized society.

   **D.** discuss the political and economic circumstances that lead to war in pre-modernized societies.

**22.** According to the passage, leaders of pre-modernized society considered war to be:

   **F.** a valid tool of national policy.

   **G.** an immoral act of aggression.

   **H.** economically wasteful and socially unfeasible.

   **J.** restricted in scope to military participants.

**23.** The author most likely places the word *civilized* in quotation marks (line 19) in order to:

   **A.** show dissatisfaction at not having found a better word.

   **B.** acknowledge that the word was borrowed from another source.

   **C.** express irony that war should be a part of civilization.

   **D.** impress upon the reader the tragedy of war.

**24.** The author mentions all of the following as possible reasons for going to war in a pre-modernized society EXCEPT:

   **F.** possibility of material gain.

   **G.** promoting deserving young men to higher positions.

   **H.** potential for increasing the security of the nation.

   **J.** desire to capture productive farming lands.

**25.** The author is primarily concerned with discussing how:

   **A.** political decisions are reached.

   **B.** economic and social conditions have changed.

   **C.** technology for making war has improved.

   **D.** war lost its value as a policy tool.

**26.** The tone of the passage is:

   **F.** outraged and indignant.

   **G.** scientific and detached.

   **H.** humorous and wry.

   **J.** fearful and alarmed.

**27.** With which of the following statements about a successfully completed program of nuclear disarmament would the author most likely agree?

   **A.** Without nuclear weapons, war in modernized society would have the same value it had in pre-modernized society.

   **B.** In the absence of the danger of nuclear war, national leaders could use powerful conventional weapons to make great gains from war.

   **C.** Eliminating nuclear weapons is likely to increase the danger of an all-out, world-wide military engagement.

   **D.** Even without the danger of a nuclear disaster, the costs of winning a war have made armed conflict on a large scale virtually obsolete.

**28.** All of the following points are mentioned as difficulties in the control of conquered territories EXCEPT:

   **F.** obligation to provide various social services.

   **G.** tensions and unrest between racially different peoples.

   **H.** fear of nuclear war.

   **J.** food shortages among large populations.

GO ON TO THE NEXT PAGE ⟩

**29.** Persuading a nation to produce and exchange goods:

    **A.** is a primary goal of armed conflict.

    **B.** is preferable to forcing that nation to surrender its wealth.

    **C.** causes tensions and unrest among the populace.

    **D.** is not possible with a racially or ethnically different nation.

**DIRECTIONS:** Questions 30–42 are not based on a reading passage. Choose the *best* answer to each question in accordance with your background and understanding in social studies.

**30.** One of Jean Piaget's main contributions to the field of developmental psychology is:

    **F.** a theory of the specific stages of cognitive development in children.

    **G.** a theory of the effect of positive reinforcement on behavior.

    **H.** actualization theory for use with children.

    **J.** a method to understand the interaction of the id, ego, and superego.

**31.** The Church of England, headed by the English king instead of by the Pope, was created because:

    **A.** the English people did not believe all the teachings of the Roman Catholic Church.

    **B.** the Roman Catholic Church denied King Henry VIII of England the divorce he requested.

    **C.** the Roman Catholic Church had lost all of its power in Europe.

    **D.** None of the above.

**32.** In the United States, workers have a legally guaranteed right to:

    **F.** receive a fixed annual wage.

    **G.** bargain collectively with employers.

    **H.** receive a yearly wage increase.

    **J.** take four weeks' annual vacation.

**33.** The Bill of Rights guarantees that certain rights shall not be infringed by the:

    **A.** federal government only.

    **B.** various state governments only.

    **C.** federal and state governments.

    **D.** President only.

**34.** Of the great European powers of the early 1800s, the only one not to be invaded by Napoleon's armies was:

    **F.** Russia.

    **G.** Prussia.

    **H.** Austria.

    **J.** Great Britain.

**35.** Today the largest component, in terms of numbers, of the American class structure is the:

    **A.** upper class.

    **B.** poor.

    **C.** working class.

    **D.** lower middle class.

**36.** In the case of *Miranda v. Arizona*, the Supreme Court held that an individual accused of a crime must be set free if upon arrest that individual is not advised of his or her:

    **F.** right to legal counsel.

    **G.** right to a trial by jury.

    **H.** right to be set free on bail.

    **J.** right to a speedy trial.

**37.** In the long run, if the market price of a product is high relative to the costs of efficient production, under the theory of competition:

    **A.** new suppliers will enter the market.

    **B.** there will be an increase in the total supply of the product.

    **C.** there will be a reduction in the market price of the product.

    **D.** All of the above.

**38.** The main reason that the United States did not enter World War II until 1941 was that:

    **F.** the U.S. government was pursuing a policy of isolationism.

    **G.** U.S. leaders did not realize that Europe was on the brink of war.

    **H.** the German leader Adolf Hitler warned the United States not to interfere in Europe.

    **J.** the European countries asked the United States not to interfere in their internal matters.

GO ON TO THE NEXT PAGE

**39.** Of the various distinct periods of prehistoric culture, the earliest is called the:

A. Paleolithic Era.
B. Neolithic Era.
C. Bronze Age.
D. Iron Age.

**40.** Most national economies in the world today can be classified as:

F. free-enterprise.
G. government-controlled.
H. a mixture of free enterprise and government controls.
J. communist.

**41.** The primary executive duty assigned to the President by the Constitution is:

A. assuring that the laws are faithfully executed.
B. acting as commander-in-chief of the armed forces.
C. making treaties with foreign nations.
D. calling Congress into special session when necessary.

**42.** Under the "Great Compromise" adopted by the Constitutional Convention of 1787:

F. slavery would be outlawed in the new territories west of the Mississippi.
G. the President would be elected by popular vote rather than by the Senate.
H. the government would be divided into executive, legislative, and judicial branches.
J. states would be represented in the lower legislative house in proportion to their population, but each state would have equal representation in the upper house.

Many critics of the current welfare system argue that existing welfare regulations foster family instability. They maintain that those regulations, which exclude most poor husband-and-wife families from Aid to Families with Dependent Children assistance grants, contribute to the problem of family dissolution. Thus, they conclude that expanding the set of families eligible for family assistance plans or guaranteed income measures would result in a marked strengthening of the low-income family structure.

If all poor families could receive welfare, would the incidence of instability change markedly? The answer to this question depends on the relative importance of three categories of potential welfare recipients. The first is the "cheater"—the husband who is reported to have abandoned his family, but in fact disappears only when the social caseworker is in the neighborhood. The second consists of a loving husband and devoted father who, sensing his own inadequacy as a provider, leaves so that his wife and children may enjoy the relative benefit provided by public assistance. There is very little evidence that these categories are significant.

The third category is the unhappily married couple who remain together out of a sense of economic responsibility for their children, because of the high costs of separation or because of the consumption benefits of marriage. This group is large. The formation, maintenance, and dissolution of the family is in large part a function of the relative balance between the benefits and costs of marriage as seen by the individual members of the marriage. The major benefit generated by the creation of a family is the expansion of the set of consumption possibilities. The benefits from such a partnership depend largely on the relative dissimilarity of the resources or basic endowments each partner brings to the marriage. Persons with similar productive capacities have less economic "cement" holding their marriage together. Since the family performs certain functions society regards as vital, a complex network of social and legal buttresses has evolved to reinforce marriage. Much of the variation in marital stability across income classes can be explained by the variation in costs of dissolution imposed by society, e.g., division of property, alimony, child support, and the social stigma attached to divorce.

Marital stability is related to the costs of achieving an acceptable agreement on family consumption and production and to the prevailing social price of instability in the marriage partners' social-economic group. Expected AFDC income exerts pressures on family instability by reducing the cost of dissolution. To the extent that welfare is a form of government-subsidized alimony

GO ON TO THE NEXT PAGE

payments, it reduces the institutional costs of separation and guarantees a minimal standard of living for wife and children. So welfare opportunities are a significant determinant of family instability in poor neighborhoods, but this is not the result of AFDC regulations that exclude most intact families from coverage. Rather, welfare-related instability occurs because public assistance lowers both the benefits of marriage and the costs of its disruption by providing a system of government-subsidized alimony payments.

43. The author is primarily concerned with:

A. interpreting the results of a survey.
B. discussing the role of the father in low-income families.
C. analyzing the causes of a phenomenon.
D. recommending reforms to the welfare system.

44. Which of the following would provide the most logical continuation of the final paragraph?

F. Paradoxically, any liberalization of AFDC eligibility restrictions is likely to intensify rather than mitigate pressures on family stability.
G. Actually, concern for the individual recipients should not be allowed to override considerations of sound fiscal policy.
H. In reality, there is virtually no evidence that AFDC payments have any relationship at all to problems of family instability in low-income marriages.
J. In the final analysis, it appears that government welfare payments, to the extent that the cost of marriage is lowered, encourage the formation of low-income families.

45. All of the following are mentioned by the author as factors tending to perpetuate a marriage EXCEPT:

A. the stigma attached to divorce.
B. the social class of the partners.
C. the cost of alimony and child support.
D. the loss of property upon divorce.

46. Which of the following best summarizes the main idea of the passage?

F. Welfare restrictions limiting the eligibility of families for benefits do not contribute to low-income family instability.
G. Contrary to popular opinion, the most significant category of welfare recipients is not the "cheating" father.
H. The incidence of family dissolution among low-income families is directly related to the inability of families with fathers to get welfare benefits.
J. Very little of the divorce rate among low-income families can be attributed to fathers deserting their families so that they can qualify for welfare.

47. The tone of the passage can best be described as:

A. confident and optimistic.
B. scientific and detached.
C. discouraged and alarmed.
D. polite and sensitive.

48. With which of the following statements about marriage would the author most likely agree?

F. Marriage is an institution that is largely shaped by powerful but impersonal economic and social forces.
G. Marriage has a greater value to persons in higher income brackets than to persons in lower income brackets.
H. Society has no legitimate interest in encouraging people to remain married to one another.
J. Marriage as an institution is no longer economically viable and will gradually give way to other forms of social organization.

49. The passage would most likely be found in a:

A. pamphlet on civil rights.
B. basic economics text.
C. book on the history of welfare.
D. scholarly journal devoted to public policy questions.

50. In the author's view, the chief economic benefit that an individual partner may derive from marriage is:

F. a widening of consumption possibilities.
G. removal of the need for welfare payments.
H. a long-term rise in socioeconomic status.
J. a guaranteed minimal standard of living.

51. According to the passage, public assistance:

A. encourages unhappily married couples to stay together.
B. decreases the benefits of marriage and the costs of separation.
C. increases the productive capacities of married couples.
D. has a social stigma attached to it.

GO ON TO THE NEXT PAGE

**52.** According to the passage, the variation in marital stability among income classes can be attributed to differences in:

- **F.** alimony.
- **G.** property division.
- **H.** stigma attached to divorce.
- **J.** All of the above.

## END OF TEST

If you complete this test before the time is up, check
back over the questions on this test only. Do not go back
to the previous test. Do not proceed to the next test until
you are told to do so.

# TEST 4.  NATURAL SCIENCES READING

*35 Minutes—52 Questions*

**DIRECTIONS:** Each passage in this test is followed by several questions.  After reading a passage, choose the best answer to each question and blacken the corresponding space on your answer sheet. You may refer to the passage as often as necessary.

---

A glacier is a huge, slow-moving river of ice.  It flows from high mountain ranges down through valleys, sometimes reaching the sea coast.  Glaciers begin forming when snow in the mountains compacts into a thick layer of ice.  As the ice grows heavier, it starts slowly sliding downhill.  Behind it, new ice forms as more snow keeps falling.  As ice keeps forming, the glacier grows larger and larger.

Within a glacier, not all of the ice moves at the same rate.  The heavy top portions tend to move forward and downward more rapidly than the bottom portions, causing deformations in the glacier's internal structure.  The movement of the ice is also aided by meltwater, which trickles down through the glacier to the bedrock and lubricates the glacier's underside.  This water later drains through channels in the ice and eventually pours from the glacier's front face.

As the glacier moves, it grinds up the rocks beneath it into gravel.  This gravel is pushed ahead of the glacier, forming a ridge called a terminal moraine.  This moraine moves steadily forward as the glacier descends the mountain slope.

When a glacier reaches lower, warmer elevations, melting speeds up.  Eventually, the ice at the glacier's face melts as fast as it is replaced, and the glacier's forward progress comes to a halt.  If the glacier reaches the sea, it may extend some distance out beyond the shoreline, pushing its terminal moraine ahead of it underwater.  The face of this so-called "tidewater" glacier thus remains "anchored" on the moraine rather than lying in deep water, where it would rapidly break up.  Even so, pieces of the glacier's face constantly break off and tumble into the sea, forming icebergs in a process called "calving."  As ice is lost in this way at the face of the glacier, its place is taken by new ice moving down the glacier's path from behind.

1. If the rate of ice accumulation at the head of a glacier is faster than the rate of melting and/or calving at the glacier's face, then:

   A. the face of the glacier will advance.
   B. the ice in the glacier will cease flowing.
   C. the face of the glacier will retreat.
   D. the face of the glacier will stop moving.

2. If the rate of ice accumulation at the head of a glacier is slower than the rate of melting and/or calving at the glacier's face, then:

   F. the face of the glacier will advance.
   G. the ice in the glacier will cease flowing.
   H. the face of the glacier will retreat.
   J. the face of the glacier will stop moving.

3. A scientist bores a hole from the surface of a glacier straight down to the bedrock.  Over time, the shape of this hole will probably:

   A. bend diagonally, with the upper portion positioned farther down the mountain slope than the lower portion.
   B. stay the same.
   C. bend diagonally, with the upper portion positioned farther up the mountain slope than the lower portion.
   D. develop into a wide pit.

GO ON TO THE NEXT PAGE

4. Sometimes the meltwater that trickles down through the glacier to the bedrock is prevented from draining out. Instead, it accumulates beneath the glacier under high pressure. When this happens, the glacier will most likely:

F. come to a stop.
G. reverse course due to the increased pressure.
H. begin melting rapidly.
J. slide rapidly forward due to increased lubrication.

5. A glacier that has extended some distance offshore begins melting rapidly. It soon retreats from its "anchor" moraine, allowing deep seawater to rush into the gap thus created. The face of the glacier will most likely:

A. soon freeze again when the deep water surrounds it.
B. resume advancing across the top of the water.
C. break up when the deep water surrounds it.
D. cause the seawater to freeze on contact with it.

6. The effects produced when a tidewater glacier retreats from its terminal moraine and becomes surrounded by deep seawater will probably continue until:

F. the glacier face starts calving.
G. the glacier face retreats back to shallow water.
H. the seawater freezes.
J. the waves break up the leftover moraine.

7. Which of the following most likely contribute(s) to the calving process?

  I. Battering of the glacier face by the sea
 II. Melting as the glacier reaches sea level
III. Snow accumulation on the glacier's surface

A. I only
B. II only
C. I and II
D. I, II, and III

8. When a glacier that is descending through a narrow valley reaches a broad coastal plain, its surface will most likely:

F. stretch and break into deep ravines.
G. refreeze solid.
H. contract under its own weight.
J. cease moving.

9. A rapidly advancing tidewater glacier completely blocks the mouth of an ocean inlet, separating it from the sea and turning it into a lake. Which of the following will most likely occur?

  I. The water level in the new lake will rise.
 II. The water in the new lake will turn from salt to fresh.
III. The water in the new lake will quickly freeze.

A. I only
B. II only
C. I and II
D. I, II, and III

The traditional scientific division of living organisms into the two basic types of "higher" and "lower" forms has been based largely on the hypothesis that all life on Earth evolved from a common ancestor—most likely a simple cell. This cell branched into the two lines of descent some four billion years ago. Now, based on finding an extraordinary organism, a research team suggests that a third evolutionary line exists that may be possibly older than the other two. This organism, which produces the combustible gas methane as its main waste produce, derives its energy and food from simple compounds such as carbon dioxide and hydrogen—the main gases that existed in the Earth's primitive atmosphere three to four billion years ago. The organism does not use oxygen, which was nonexistent on primitive Earth, and it does not use any of the complex chemicals such as sugars and amino acids which most other organisms require as food.

The methane-producing bacteria, called *Methanobacteria thermoautotrophica*, have been found only in niches swept clean of oxygen, such as in the deep hot springs of Yellowstone Park. Some of them seem to thrive best at high temperatures in the range of 65 to 70 degrees Celsius. It is felt that these bacteria are relics that have survived the passage of time since their primeval origin. Even though the primitive branchings of life left no fossil record, scientists can trace the evolutionary lines in other ways. In a sense, the living cell carries some record of its past in its genes. During the past two decades, scientists have developed ways of partially deciphering these ancient genetic texts.

In tracking the genetic record, the research team analyzed the composition of the organism's ribosomal ribonucleic acid (RNA), a constituent of all free-living and self-replicating systems. Ribosomal RNA is a major component of ribosomes—the functional units within cells where the

GO ON TO THE NEXT PAGE

messages from the genes are received and read in order to manufacture the appropriate proteins. Ribosomal RNAs are thought to be very old and represent conserved portions of the ancient replicating systems. This makes them suitable for comparative studies. When ribosomal RNA from the methane bacteria was digested with enzymes into small pieces and their molecular sequences compared, it was found that these pieces for the most part were distinctly different from the RNAs of other bacteria and of "higher" cells.

10. The atmosphere of primitive Earth, according to this passage, was:

   F. rich in methane.
   G. aerobic.
   H. anaerobic.
   J. devoid of hydrogen.

11. According to this passage, the methane-producing organism:

   A. was a type of ordinary bacteria.
   B. is a type of ordinary bacteria.
   C. existing today is unchanged from its prototype.
   D. used to coexist with ordinary bacteria in primeval times.

12. The key evidence that the methane-producing bacteria represent a unique evolutionary line is stated:

   F. in the first sentence of the passage.
   G. nowhere in this passage.
   H. in the second paragraph of this passage.
   J. in the third sentence of the first paragraph of this passage.

13. The assertion that *Methanobacteria thermoautotrophica* creates new hope that science will ultimately find out a great deal about how life came about on this planet:

   A. is an assumption of the researchers.
   B. is a conclusion confirmed by research.
   C. is not a conclusion suggested by research.
   D. does not appear in this passage.

14. *Methanobacteria thermoautotrophica*, according to this passage, have been found to exist:

   F. unchanged since their primeval origin.
   G. in a completely anaerobic environment.
   H. in fossilized remains.
   J. in numbers comparable to the RNA constituents.

15. Ribosomes' function in a cell is controlled by the

   A. endoplasmic reticulum.
   B. mitochondria.
   C. golgi bodies.
   D. ribosomal RNA.

16. The species name *Methanobacteria thermoautotrophica* most closely means:

   F. methane-producing bacteria that are self-regulating.
   G. methane-using bacteria that have a constant high temperature.
   H. methane-producing bacteria that meet their energy needs in a warm environment.
   J. methane-producing bacteria that are self-replicating in a warm environment.

17. Without any further information, which of the following could represent a general metabolic reaction for *Methanobacteria thermoautotrophica*?

   A. $2H_2O + CO_2 \rightarrow CH_4 + 2O_2 + energy$
   B. $O_2 + CO_2 + 3H_2 \rightarrow CH_4 + H_2O + energy$
   C. $CO_2 + 4H_2 \rightarrow CH_4 + 2H_2O + energy$
   D. $CO + 4H \rightarrow CH_4 + O + energy$

18. The ribosomal RNAs represent conserved portions of ancient replicating systems because:

   F. RNA is identical to the ancient DNA in the nucleus.
   G. RNA replicates by forming a mirror image of DNA.
   H. Daughter cells may receive some actual molecules of the nucleic acids from a replicating cell.
   J. Ribosomes conserved their RNA to be used at a later time.

GO ON TO THE NEXT PAGE

19. The rate of decay of a radioactive material is known as its:
    A. half-life.
    B. isotope.
    C. radioactivity.
    D. disintegration constant.

20. Sedimentary rock forms as a result of:
    F. mechanical and chemical weathering.
    G. melting of bedrock.
    H. rock being exposed to heat and pressure.
    J. volcanic activity.

21. The work required to transfer a charge of 6 coulombs against a difference of potential of 110 volts is, in joules:
    A. 18.2.
    B. $6.6 \times 10^2$.
    C. $6.6 \times 10^4$.
    D. $6.6 \times 10^6$.

22. Which is most closely associated with the process of transpiration?
    F. Root of a geranium
    G. Leaf of a geranium
    H. Gills of a fish
    J. Spiracles of a grasshopper

23. Given the following thermochemical equations:
    $$Zn + \frac{1}{2}(O_2) = ZnO + 84,000 \text{ cals}$$
    $$Hg + \frac{1}{2}(O_2) = HgO + 21,700 \text{ cals}$$
    Accordingly, the heat of reaction for the reaction
    $$Zn + HgO = ZnO + Hg + \text{heat}$$
    is:
    A. 105,700 cals.
    B. 61,000 cals.
    C. 105,000 cals.
    D. 62,300 cals.

24. A cell concerned with synthesizing and secreting large quantities of protein hormone would be expected to have:
    F. very few mitochondria, ribosomes, and a poorly developed golgi apparatus.
    G. many more chromosomes than the average human cell.
    H. large numbers of mitochondria and ribosomes and a well-developed golgi apparatus.
    J. only an endoplasmic reticulum in the cytoplasm.

25. In order for a 30-volt, 90-watt lamp to work properly when inserted in a 120-volt dc line, it should have in series with it a resistor whose resistance, in ohms, is:
    A. 10.
    B. 20.
    C. 30.
    D. 40.

26. The Heisenberg principle postulates that:
    F. the momentum and position of an electron cannot be known simultaneously.
    G. two electrons may not occupy the same orbit.
    H. for every proton there must exist an anti-proton.
    J. every radioactive decay results in the production of isotopic lead.

27. The phenomenon of interference is accepted as evidence to show that light is:
    A. a wave.
    B. transverse.
    C. longitudinal.
    D. a photoelectric discharge.

28.

| | Apparent Magnitude | Absolute Magnitude | (Sun = 1) Luminosity |
|---|---|---|---|
| 1. Sirius | −1.58 | +1.3 | 30 |
| 2. Canopus | −0.86 | −3.2 | 1,900 |
| 3. Alpha Centauri | +0.06 | +4.7 | 1.3 |
| 4. Vega | +0.41 | +0.5 | 60 |
| 5. Capella | +0.21 | +0.4 | 150 |

According to these values, the brightest star of the group is:
    F. Capella.
    G. Alpha Centauri.
    H. Canopus.
    J. Sirius.

29. A white-cell count is helpful in determining whether a patient has:
    A. an infection.
    B. antitoxins.
    C. heart disease.
    D. the Rh factor.

GO ON TO THE NEXT PAGE

726

30. Planck's constant may be expressed in which one of the following units?

F. Watt-seconds
G. Joules per cycle
H. Joule seconds
J. Ergs per second

31. The periodic table depicts the law that states:

A. the properties of the elements are periodic functions of their atomic numbers.
B. fifteen family groupings are periodically divided into elementary particles.
C. neutrons follow a periodicity in the first 92 elements.
D. no two electrons in the same atom may have the same four quantum numbers.

32. Grizzly bears, moose, wolves, squirrels, and spruce, hemlock, fir, and pine trees are characteristic of:

F. tropical rainforests.
G. grasslands.
H. deserts.
J. taigas.

33. Which one of the following is an illustration of a reversible reaction?

A. $Pb(NO_3)^2 + 2NaCl \rightarrow PbI_2 + 2NaNO_3$
B. $KNO_3 + NaCl \rightarrow KCl + NaNo_3$
C. $2Na + 2HOH \rightarrow 2NaOH + H_2$
D. $AgNO_3 + HBr \rightarrow AgBr + HNO_3$

Everyday experiences are filled with sounds that are received by our ears and interpreted by our brains. Normally we perceive sounds at various frequencies or pitches as they are generated at their sources. However, when we move or the source of a sound moves, the pitch of a sound seems to change. The change in pitch caused by the relative motion of the listener or the source is known as the Doppler effect. For example, if you are at a railroad crossing waiting for a train to pass, you may hear the train approaching by the sound of the high-pitched whistle. As the train passes, the pitch of the whistle drops. Thus, as the train approaches and the distance between the source and the listener decreases, the pitch that is heard increases. As the train moves past and the distance between the source and the listener increases at a constant rate, the pitch decreases. Examining the formula for the frequency of a sound:

$$(Eq. 1) \quad frequency = \frac{velocity}{wavelength}$$

it becomes apparent that the velocity of a sound wave has an effect on the frequency.

The frequency of the sound reaching the stationary listener in front of the moving source is higher than the actual frequency of the source. This can be expressed as:

$$(Eq. 2) \quad frequency_{(LF)} = f_{(S)}\left(\frac{v}{v - v_{(S)}}\right)$$

In this equation, $f_{(LF)}$ represents the frequency heard by the listener in front of the moving source, $f(S)$ represents the frequency at the source, $v$ is the velocity of the sound in air, and $v_{(S)}$ is the velocity of the moving source.

Similarly, the frequency of the sound reaching the stationary listener behind the moving source is lower than the frequency at the source. This can be expressed as:

$$(Eq. 3) \quad frequency_{(LB)} = f_{(S)}\left(\frac{v}{v + v_{(S)}}\right)$$

For example, a high-speed train with a whistle that has a frequency of 288 hertz (vibrations per second) may approach a crossing at a velocity of 180 km/hour. A guard stationed at the crossing hears the approaching train's whistle at a significantly higher pitch. Another factor to consider is the temperature of the air. At 25°C, the velocity of sound in air is 346 meters per second, faster than it is at colder temperatures.

34. The example in the passage describes a crossing guard who hears the whistle frequency $f_{(LF)}$ of an approaching train. To find the frequency, you would solve for $f_{(LF)}$ in equation 2. To complete the calculation, what value must you use for $v_{(S)}$ if $v = 346$ m/s?

F. 180 km/h
G. 296 m/s
H. 166 m/s
J. 50 m/s

35. In the same example, at what frequency would the guard hear the approaching train?

A. 251.6 hertz
B. 312.3 hertz
C. 336.6 hertz
D. 600 hertz

GO ON TO THE NEXT PAGE

**36.** Another train, also traveling at 180 km/h with a whistle at a frequency of 256 hertz at the source, passes through a train crossing. At what frequency does a person at the crossing hear the whistle after the train passes (provided that the air temperature is 25°C)?

   **F.**  168.4 hertz
   **G.**  223.7 hertz
   **H.**  292.9 hertz
   **J.**  299.3 hertz

**37.** In the situation described in question 36, what would be the velocity of the sound if the temperature dropped to 15°C provided that the velocity diminishes 0.6 m/s for every degree C drop in the temperature?

   **A.**  90 m/s
   **B.**  340 m/s
   **C.**  352 m/s
   **D.**  It is impossible to tell from the information given.

**38.** What effect, if any, does lowering the air temperature have on the frequency of a moving sound heard by a stationary listener?

   **F.**  It has no effect, because the same factor affects the velocity of sound in the air as well as the $v_{(S)}$.
   **G.**  It causes $f_{(LF)}$ to be slightly lower and $f_{(LB)}$ to be slightly higher.
   **H.**  It causes $f_{(LF)}$ to be slightly higher and $f_{(LB)}$ to be slightly lower.
   **J.**  It causes $f_{(S)}$ to be slightly lower.

**39.** Using equation 1, if the velocity of sound in air is held constant and the frequency is increased, what happens to the wavelength of the sound wave?

   **A.**  It gets longer.
   **B.**  It gets shorter.
   **C.**  It stays the same.
   **D.**  It doubles.

**40.** Using equation 1 as a guide, what is the formula for wavelength, known as lambda ($\lambda$)?

   **F.**  $\lambda = \dfrac{v}{f}$
   **G.**  $\lambda = vf$
   **H.**  $\lambda = v^2 f$
   **J.**  $\lambda = \dfrac{f}{v}$

**41.** In air at a temperature 0°C, a sound with a pitch of 512 hertz is generated by a stationary source. What is the frequency heard by a stationary listener?

   **A.**  489 hertz
   **B.**  512 hertz
   **C.**  535 hertz
   **D.**  The listener would not hear anything; this frequency is inaudible to the human ear.

**42.** In the example in Question 41, what would be the wavelength of the generated sound wave?

   **F.**  0.6465 m
   **G.**  0.6758 m
   **H.**  1.479 m
   **J.**  1.547 m

    In the latter part of the twentieth century, one group of useful compounds has been of great value to modern technology while at the same time sparking environmental debate. These compounds are the halogenated hydrocarbons. Organic chemicals known as hydrocarbons are chains of carbon atoms of various lengths with hydrogen atoms bonded to the carbon. It is relatively simple to attach atoms of the halogen elements—chlorine, bromine, fluorine, or iodine—to the carbon chain to form long molecules, or polymers.

    The resulting organic halogen compounds have a variety of useful properties. For example, ethene ($H_2C=CH_2$) reacts with chlorine to form 1,2-dichloroethane, in which the double bond between the two carbons is replaced by a single bond; this frees two bonding sites for two chlorine atoms, which attach to either end of the carbon chain. When heat and pressure are added, chloroethane molecules form and in the next reaction, long chains of polyvinyl chloride, or PVC, form. PVC is commonly used in plastic pipes, floor tile, clothing, and even records. Highly chlorinated hydrocarbons are chemicals which are very effective insecticides. Among them is DDT, now banned from use in the U.S. because of its deadly effects on the reproductive cycle of some living things. Another halogenated hydrocarbon is polytetrafluoroethylene, or PTFE. This is more commonly known as Teflon; its very low coefficient of friction is what gives Teflon its nonstick property. Other polymers contain both chlorine and fluorine; they are known as chlorofluorocarbons (CFCs) and have been used as refrigerants and as aerosol spray propellants until they were banned for that use. There is reason to suspect that the discharge of CFCs into the atmosphere contributes to the depletion of the ozone layer, which protects the earth from harmful amounts of ultraviolet radiation from space.

GO ON TO THE NEXT PAGE

43. The best title for this passage is:

 A. Hydrocarbons: 1001 Uses.
 B. The Making of a Polymer.
 C. Are We Destroying the Ozone?
 D. Halogenated Hydrocarbons: Helpful or Harmful?

44. All of the following are halogens EXCEPT:

 F. carbon.
 G. chlorine.
 H. bromine.
 J. fluorine.

45. The halogens can bind to the carbon chain because:

 A. they have many extra electrons to donate to the carbons.
 B. they can find covalent bonding sites near the carbons.
 C. the chain is highly ionized.
 D. they can form double bonds with the hydrogen atoms.

46. Hydrocarbons contain:

 F. carbon, hydrogen, and oxygen.
 G. carbon and hydrogen.
 H. carbon, hydrogen, and chlorine.
 J. carbon, hydrogen, and fluorine.

47. A polymer is best described as:

 A. a hydrocarbon.
 B. a long-chain molecule containing chlorine.
 C. a long-chain organic molecule.
 D. All of the above.

48. When ethene is used in the first step in making PVC, the double bond between the carbons is broken and chlorine molecules bond to either end of the two-carbon chain. Which of the following correctly identifies the number of each type of atom in a molecule of 1,2-dichloroethane?

 F. 1 atom C, 1 atom H, 1 atom Cl
 G. 2 atoms C, 2 atoms H, 2 atoms Cl
 H. 2 atoms C, 1 atom H, 2 atoms Cl
 J. 2 atoms C, 2 atoms Cl

49. The property of halogenated hydrocarbons NOT mentioned in the passage is their:

 A. low coefficient of friction.
 B. ability to repel insects.
 C. use as a coolant.
 D. use as a solvent.

50. Polymers known as PVCs are commonly used as:

 F. insecticides.
 G. nonstick coatings for pots and pans.
 H. aerosols.
 J. None of the above.

51. The use of which of the following have been banned or limited in the U.S.?

 A. PVCs and DDT
 B. PVCs and PTFE
 C. PTFE and DDT
 D. DDT and CFCs

52. Which polymers may threaten the protective layer of the earth's atmosphere?

 F. Polyvinyl chlorides
 G. Polytetrafluoroethylene polymers
 H. Highly chlorinated hydrocarbons
 J. Chlorofluorocarbons

**END OF TEST**

If you complete this test before the time is up, check
back over the questions on this test only. Do not go back
to the previous test.

# Answer Key

## English Usage

| | | | | |
|---|---|---|---|---|
| 1. C | 16. G | 31. B | 46. G | 61. C |
| 2. F | 17. A | 32. H | 47. B | 62. H |
| 3. C | 18. G | 33. B | 48. F | 63. A |
| 4. G | 19. C | 34. G | 49. B | 64. G |
| 5. B | 20. H | 35. D | 50. J | 65. B |
| 6. G | 21. D | 36. J | 51. B | 66. H |
| 7. A | 22. F | 37. B | 52. G | 67. D |
| 8. G | 23. B | 38. G | 53. C | 68. G |
| 9. C | 24. H | 39. D | 54. F | 69. B |
| 10. F | 25. B | 40. J | 55. C | 70. J |
| 11. D | 26. G | 41. D | 56. F | 71. A |
| 12. H | 27. A | 42. J | 57. D | 72. G |
| 13. B | 28. H | 43. A | 58. F | 73. C |
| 14. H | 29. A | 44. F | 59. B | 74. G |
| 15. D | 30. F | 45. C | 60. J | 75. D |

## Mathematics Usage

| | | | | |
|---|---|---|---|---|
| 1. C | 9. E | 17. B | 25. D | 33. A |
| 2. J | 10. K | 18. K | 26. G | 34. K |
| 3. C | 11. A | 19. A | 27. D | 35. D |
| 4. K | 12. G | 20. G | 28. G | 36. K |
| 5. B | 13. E | 21. E | 29. C | 37. B |
| 6. J | 14. F | 22. H | 30. G | 38. J |
| 7. D | 15. E | 23. D | 31. E | 39. A |
| 8. K | 16. K | 24. H | 32. F | 40. J |

## Social Studies Reading

| | | | | | | |
|---|---|---|---|---|---|---|
| 1. B | 9. C | 17. B | 25. D | 33. A | 41. A | 49. D |
| 2. J | 10. H | 18. G | 26. G | 34. J | 42. J | 50. F |
| 3. B | 11. B | 19. A | 27. D | 35. C | 43. C | 51. B |
| 4. F | 12. J | 20. G | 28. H | 36. F | 44. F | 52. J |
| 5. A | 13. D | 21. C | 29. B | 37. D | 45. B | |
| 6. J | 14. F | 22. F | 30. F | 38. F | 46. F | |
| 7. D | 15. C | 23. C | 31. B | 39. A | 47. B | |
| 8. G | 16. F | 24. G | 32. G | 40. H | 48. F | |

## Natural Sciences Reading

| | | | | | | |
|---|---|---|---|---|---|---|
| 1. A | 9. C | 17. C | 25. C | 33. B | 41. B | 49. D |
| 2. H | 10. H | 18. H | 26. F | 34. J | 42. F | 50. J |
| 3. A | 11. D | 19. A | 27. A | 35. C | 43. D | 51. D |
| 4. J | 12. H | 20. F | 28. J | 36. G | 44. F | 52. J |
| 5. C | 13. D | 21. B | 29. A | 37. B | 45. B | |
| 6. G | 14. G | 22. G | 30. H | 38. H | 46. G | |
| 7. C | 15. D | 23. D | 31. A | 39. B | 47. C | |
| 8. F | 16. H | 24. H | 32. J | 40. F | 48. G | |

# Explanatory Answers

### English Usage

**1.** (C) The original contains low-level usage. You should not use *on account of* as a substitute for *because of*. C makes the needed correction. B is wrong because *since* is a conjunction that introduces a dependent clause, but the material that follows is not a clause. (It contains no verb.) As for D, although *for* can be a preposition, its meaning is not appropriate in this context.

**2.** (F) The sentence is correct as written. *Nonetheless* has the meaning of "in spite of this." G and H are both wrong because the author means to say that smuggling grew in spite of government efforts—not because of government efforts. Finally, as for J, although *on the contrary* does signal an opposition, it does not have the "in spite of" meaning needed here.

**3.** (C) The original contains two errors. First, *timbered* is an adjective, and it takes an adverb to modify an adjective. So *heavy* should be *heavily*. Second, since *countless* is intended to modify *islands* and not "heavily timbered," you must place a comma after *countless*. Only C makes both of these corrections.

**4.** (G) The original and H and J are not idiomatic. The correct idiom is *well founded*.

**5.** (B) The tense of the verb in the original is not consistent with the other verbs in the paragraph. The author is describing past events, so you should use the past tense *seized*. Although C and D can be used to refer to past actions, they have meanings that are inappropriate in this context. First, *were seizing* (the progressive form of the past tense) implies an action that continued for some time in the past, e.g., during this period, customs officials were seizing tons of wool each month. Second, *have seized* (the present perfect) implies an action that began in the past but continues into the present, e.g., "the British have repeatedly seized our ships."

**6.** (G) The original contains an error of diction. *Principle* means "rule"; *principal* means "main or important." H fails to correct this problem. J makes the needed correction, but the verb *was* will not agree with the subject of the sentence. (The subject of the sentence is a compound subject—a series of elements joined by *and*—so you have to use a plural verb.)

**7.** (A) *In fact* signals an idea that will provide an illustration of or give special emphasis to a point that came just before. This is exactly what the author does. As for B and C, these words are used to alert the reader that what follows is a continuation of an idea and that the following idea has the same status as the first idea. Thus, B and C are not suited to this sentence. Finally, as for D, "on the contrary" signals a contrast of ideas, but the author does not intend to present contrasting ideas.

**8.** (G) The only conceivable role for *selling* in the original would be that of an adjective, but there is nothing for *selling* to modify. G corrects this problem by converting *selling* to a conjugated form. Now the sentence reads: "was smuggled . . . and sold." H is wrong because *would be sold* is not parallel to *smuggled*. Finally, J suffers from the same problem as the original. There is no logical role for the infinitive *to sell* in the sentence.

**9.** (C) The original begins the idiom "so much . . . that" but never completes it. C completes the idiom: "so much was smuggled and sold . . . that one . . . ." B and D fail to complete the expression.

**10.** (F) The original is correct as written. The simple past tense is consistent with the other verbs in the passage. G is wrong because it eliminates the only conjugated verb in the clause introduced by *although*. H is wrong because the tense is inconsistent with the other tenses in the paragraph. Finally, J destroys the logic of the sentence.

**11.** (D) The original is not idiomatic. The correct idiom is *were fearful*, not *were fearing*. D avoids the problem by using the verb *feared*, and the past tense is parallel to the other verb in the sentence, *wanted*. B fails to correct the problem of the original. Although C uses the correct idiom, the verb *was* does not agree with the subject of the sentence, *they*.

**12.** (H) The original contains two errors. First, the underlined verb is in the present tense and is therefore inconsistent with the use of the past tense in the rest of the paragraph. Second, "in the losing of" is not idiomatic. More idiomatic is the phrase "in the loss of." H makes both the needed corrections. G makes one correction but not the other. Finally, J uses the indicative *results*. But the indicative lacks the element of contingency: "they feared that this results." You need a verb that suggests something might or might not occur: "they feared that this would result or might result."

**13.** (B) The passage should be arranged in chronological order. (1) should come first because it describes the first event (the opening of the customs office). (3) should come next because it describes the events that come next in time (Americans were leery of the new office). (2) should be last because it is the final development (the fears turned out to be true).

**14.** (H) The original suffers from a lack of parallelism. You have a series of verbs: *can step outside*, *gaze*, and *can become*. All three verbs are governed by the *can*, so the additional *can* in the original creates a series in which the elements do not have the same form. H brings the third verb into line with the other two verbs. G fails to provide the needed parallelism, and J is wrong because *becomes* does not agree in number with the subject, *anyone*.

15. **(D)** The original is incorrectly punctuated. The comma creates a run-on sentence. D solves this problem by starting a new sentence. B and C fail to solve the problem of the run-on sentence.

16. **(G)** The original is ambiguous. *Ending* seems to be an adjective modifying *suns*, but the author intends for *ending* to modify *island universe*. G corrects this problem by creating a relative clause that modifies *island universe*. H, too, creates a new clause, but *ends* does not agree with the antecedent of *that*, which is *universe*. Finally, J suffers from the same defect as the original, because *ended* seems to modify *suns*.

17. **(A)** The original is correct as written. B is not idiomatic. Correct English requires the use of the infinitive *to chart* in this situation, not the gerund *charting*. C is wrong because there is nothing for a participle like *having charted* to modify. Finally, D destroys the logic of the sentence.

18. **(G)** The verb tense of the original is wrong. The past perfect *had been made* implies that the progress was made at a time in the past completely separated from our own time. But the phrase "in the twentieth century" indicates that the author is describing an action that is still going on. The correct verb tense to show this is the present perfect. *Has been made* correctly implies that the progress began in the past and is still going on. H is wrong because the present tense *is made* lacks the implication of a past action. And J, which uses the future tense, indicates that the progress has not yet been made.

19. **(C)** The original is a run-on sentence. At the underlined part, two independent clauses are run together. You can solve the problem by using a comma and a conjunction, by using a semicolon, or, as C does, by starting a completely new sentence. B is grammatically correct, but *but* incorrectly signals a contrast where none is intended by the author. D suffers from a similar problem (*however* also signals a contrast), and D fails to solve the problem of the run-on sentence.

20. **(H)** The material in this sentence belongs with the material in the next paragraph. So this is the point at which a new paragraph should be started, and no new paragraph should be started at the end of the sentence. Only G and J make the required change. J is wrong because *as* is used to introduce a dependent clause. The result would be a dependent clause with no supporting independent clause.

21. **(D)** The original is incorrect because a comma and not a semicolon must be used to separate an appositive phrase from the main part of the sentence. The semicolon is too powerful and makes a fragment out of everything that follows it here. B is wrong because you must mark the beginning of the phrase

placed in quotation marks. C is wrong because *is* does not agree with *Clouds*, which is the antecedent of *which*.

22. **(F)** The original is correct as written. The other choices simply are not idiomatic.

23. **(B)** The *to* is superfluous and makes the phrasing stilted. Eliminate it. B and C both make the needed correction, but C is wrong because *provide* does not agree with the subject of the sentence, *galaxy*.

24. **(H)** This is an inverted sentence, the subject of which is *debate*. (An inverted sentence is one in which the verb precedes the subject.) So the sentence asserts "a debate implies in this notion." That is obviously wrong. H solves the problem by using the passive voice: "a debate is implied." G is wrong because the subject *debate* is singular. And J is wrong because *is implying* is, like the original, in the active voice. (The *is* in J indicates the present progressive tense, not the passive voice.)

25. **(B)** The original is not idiomatic. You could say "a debate as to" or "a debate over." The other choices are just not idiomatic.

26. **(G)** The original contains an error of subject–verb agreement. The subject of the sentence is *most*, a plural noun, not *heart*. G supplies the correct verb form. H and J are wrong because they eliminate the only conjugated verb in the clause. Thus, everything down to the semicolon becomes a fragment.

27. **(A)** The original is correct as written. The various placements of *exactly* suggested by the other choices would result in phrasing that would not be idiomatic.

28. **(H)** *Or* creates an illogical connection between the two ideas it joins. The author intends to create a contrast: "not perfect but acceptable." Therefore, the best choice is H. J not only fails to signal a contrast; it results in a comma splice in which two independent clauses are joined by a comma without the needed conjunction.

29. **(A)** The original is correct as written. B is wrong because you must use a comma to mark the end of the parenthetical phrase started with *even*. C is wrong because the conjunction *and* creates an ambiguous sentence. Now *that* doesn't have a referent. Finally, D is wrong for the same reason. The resulting sentence is ambiguous because *it* doesn't have a clear referent.

30. **(F)** The original is correct as written. G is wrong because there is no grammatical role for a noun to play there. The comma seems to suggest that *translation* will be followed by an appositive, but what follows is not an appositive of *translation*. G is grammatically correct, but the *for* is not idiomatic. Finally, J is wrong because *well* is an adverb, and adverbs do not modify nouns.

31. **(B)** In the original, *true* is intended to modify *amazing*. But *amazing* is an adjective, which can be modified only by an adverb. B makes the needed correction. C solves the problem of the original but makes another error. The comma following *true*

means that *true* is modifying *event* rather than *amazing*, but what is a *true event*? Additionally, C is incorrectly punctuated. The semicolon seems to signal an independent clause, but what follows is not an independent clause. Finally, D, too, is incorrectly punctuated. The comma suggests that what follows will be an appositive, but *grouping* is not an appositive for *event*. Additionally, the use of *grouping* rather than *group* is not idiomatic.

2. (H) The original uses the wrong relative pronoun. To refer to people, you should use some form of *who*, not *which*. G fails to correct the error of the original. As for J, the use of the participle suggests that *written* is an adjective modifying *author*: "a written author."

3. (B) The subject of *read* is *none*. Since *none* is singular, you must use the singular form of the verb: *reads*. As for C and D, these verb tenses are inconsistent with the other verbs in the sentence.

4. (G) The original contains an error of diction. *Whether* and *if* have different meanings. The author intends to use the idiom "if ..., then." H is incorrect because "for ..., then" is not idiomatic. As for J, the first clause is intended to be a dependent clause, so you must use a subordinate conjunction to introduce it.

5. (D) The original is a run-on sentence. The material that follows the comma is a clause with its own subject and verb that has been spliced onto the main body of the sentence. D solves the problem by turning that material into a relative clause. (*That* refers to *impression*. The relative clause describes the "impression.") B and C are not idiomatic.

6. (J) At first, you might think that *graduated* is intended to be a verb in a phrase such as "graduated from test pilot schools." Unfortunately, the structure of the sentence doesn't permit that reading. J clarifies the issue by making *graduated* a noun. Now *graduates* can function as an appositive for *pilots*. G and H is wrong because the appositive must be set off by a comma and nothing else.

7. (B) The original contains two errors. First, *were* fails to agree in number with its subject, *each*. Second, the use of the gerund *having* is not idiomatic. B corrects both of these errors. C fails to correct the second error. D corrects both errors, but the past perfect *had been required* is inconsistent with the other verbs in the paragraph.

8. (G) The original contains low-level usage. Do not use *got* to suggest the passive voice. Use some form of the verb *to be*. G makes the needed correction. H is a form of the passive voice, but the use of the past perfect is not consistent with the other verbs in the paragraph. J is wrong for two reasons. First, the present perfect *has been* is not consistent with the other verbs in the paragraph. Second, *has* is a singular verb, but the subject of the sentence is *seven*, a plural noun.

9. (D) The original contains a comma splice. D corrects the problem of the run-on sentence by starting a new sentence. Neither B nor C addresses the problem.

40. (J) The original uses the "ubiquitous they." *They* has no referent. H and J, but not G, correct the error. But the placement of *fortunately* is not idiomatic.

41. (D) The original is needlessly wordy, as you can see by comparing it to D. B is wrong for two reasons. First, you need the possessive pronoun *their* to demonstrate to whom the opportunity belongs. Second, the present tense *comes* is inconsistent with the other verbs in the sentence. And C is wrong for this second reason.

42. (J) The underlined verb is not parallel to the other verb to which it is joined: "to ignite and then shutting down." J corrects the problem: "to ignite and then shut down." Neither G ("to ignite and then will shut down") nor H ("to ignite and then they shut down") solves the problem. And H suffers from the further defect that *they* doesn't have a referent.

43. (A) The original is correct as written. You should begin a new paragraph here because the author is taking up a new topic. (The passage switches from a discussion of failures in the program to a discussion of animals in flight.) Because you need a new paragraph, C and D are wrong.

44. (F) The original is correct. None of the other suggested positions for *unharmed* is idiomatic.

45. (C) *Returning* is not a conjugated verb and therefore cannot be the main verb in a sentence. All three choices supply conjugated verbs, but C is the only tense that is consistent with the other verbs in the paragraph.

46. (G) The *like* in the original is both superfluous and not idiomatic. G corrects the error by eliminating the extra word. H and J are not idiomatic.

47. (B) The original contains an error of grammar. It reads: "longer flights would require that astronauts to have." The infinitive, however, cannot be the verb for the subject *astronauts*. Instead, you need a conjugated verb. Each of the alternatives supplies a conjugated verb form, but only B is consistent with the rest of the sentence. C is wrong because the past perfect *had had* suggests a sequence of events that is not supported by the meaning of the sentence. And D is wrong because the sentence now reads: "would require that the astronauts are sure to have."

48. (F) The original is correct as written. G makes two mistakes. First, it leaves out an essential comma. You must mark the end of the aside begun with *in*. Second, the *of* introduces a prepositional phrase that has nothing to modify. H is wrong because it fails to mark the close of the aside. And J is wrong because *of helping* is not idiomatic.

49. (B) The original is needlessly wordy. *And* and *also* mean the same thing, so you should not use them both. B solves this problem by substituting *as well as*, a phrase that also means "and." C is wrong because *with* does not have a meaning that is appropriate in this context. And D is wrong because *as*

*opposed to* signals a contrast between two ideas that is not suggested by the content of the sentence.

50. (J) The verb tense of the original is inconsistent with that of the other verb in the sentence: *aided and had been emerging*. You should use the simple past: *aid and emerged*. Only J makes the needed correction.

51. (B) The original is incorrect because the *was enjoying* does not agree with the subject of the sentence, which is *aspects*. B makes the needed correction. C and D are wrong because they are singular, not plural.

52. (G) The original is not idiomatic. The correct idiom is "not only this but also that." G supplies the correct idiom. H is wrong because "not only this consequently that" is not idiomatic. As for J, although it supplies the correct idiom, it contains two errors. First, the comma following *also* illogically disrupts the idiom. Second, the verb *would have* is inconsistent with the other verb in the sentence.

53. (C) The original doesn't contain any grievous errors. You probably should have a comma following *treatment* because the two clauses joined there are fairly long. Additionally, the *also* is redundant of the *and*. But the main thing that is wrong with the original is excessive wordiness. C expresses the thought more concisely, so C is a better choice. B is wrong because the *but* illogically signals a contrast where none is intended. And D destroys the parallelism of the sentence: "the doctor could select and can mitigate."

54. (F) The original is correct as written. G and H use inappropriate verb forms: *require that something was available* and *require that something is available*. (The technical explanation for this is that it is one of the last vestiges in English of the subjunctive.) J is wrong because *as* does not have the meaning of "to."

55. (C) The original is wrong because the present tense *presupposes* conflicts with the other verbs in the paragraph, which are in the past tense. Although B also makes the correction, the passive voice is needlessly indirect. C makes the same correction and is more concise.

56. (F) The original is correct as written. A new paragraph is required here because the author is taking up a new topic (discussion of a particular doctor). Therefore, G and J are wrong. As for H, *since* is a subordinate conjunction and is used to introduce a dependent clause. The resulting construction would be a dependent clause with no supporting independent clause.

57. (D) The present tense *is transformed* in the original conflicts with the other verbs in the paragraph. The others are in the past tense. B is wrong because it contains low-level usage. (Do not use *get* to suggest the passive voice.) C is wrong for two reasons. First, it uses the present tense rather than the past. Second, it destroys the logic of the sentence. The active voice suggests that Dr. Beaumont transformed something.

58. (F) The original is correct as written. A new paragraph should not be started here because the following material continues the discussion about Dr. Beaumont. Therefore, G and H are wrong. J is wrong because it is awkward. (Compare the wording of J with the more direct wording of the original.)

59. (B) The original is grammatically correct, but the *but* signals a contrast that is inappropriate. The second clause explains the outcome of the first clause. B solves this problem. C is wrong because the resulting construction would be a comma splice. Finally, D is not grammatically incorrect (you could begin a new sentence), but the *but* is out of place.

60. (J) The original suffers from faulty parallelism. The verb *describe* has the same function in the sentence as the verb *demonstrating*, so they should have parallel forms. Only J makes the needed correction. The verb forms of G and H would not create the needed parallelism.

61. (C) The original contains an error of pronoun usage. *Him* refers to *babies*. C makes the needed correction by using the plural *them*. B and D are wrong because, among other things, they use singular pronouns.

62. (H) The original is not idiomatic. The correct idiom is *endowed with* and not *endowed of* or *endowed for*. As for J, although *endowed by* might appear in an English sentence, it is not appropriate here. It would be used in a different way:" . . . endowed by their Creator with certain inalienable rights."

63. (A) The original is correct as written. Although it is not necessary to start a new sentence here, it is acceptable to do so. The other choices, however, are not acceptable. B and C both create run-on sentences. And D destroys the logical structure of the sentence. You need two occurrences of *it*, one to be the object of *hears* and the other to function as the subject of the second clause.

64. (G) In the original, *including* illogically implies that an emotional reaction is a kind of biological reaction. The original intends to state, however, that an infant's cry causes two parallel reactions, one biological and the other emotional. Only a word like *and* will do the trick.

65. (B) The original contains an error of pronoun usage. *Their* refers to *infant*, but *their* is plural while *infant* is singular. B solves this problem. C and D also correct the error of the original, but those two choices are needlessly wordy and awkward, as you can see by comparing them to B.

66. (H) The original is needlessly indirect and wordy. H comes directly to the point and is more concise. G, too, is concise, but G uses a verb tense that is inconsistent with the other verbs in the paragraph. Finally, J, like the original, is too wordy. Further, the verb *are* would not agree with the singular subject of the sentence.

**67.** (D) In English, we sometimes use the present progressive to give special emphasis to an idea: "But Mom, I am doing my homework!" But nothing suggests that the author would want special emphasis here. D corrects the problem by using the simple present tense, which is the same tense used for the other verbs. B is wrong because the past tense is out of place in this selection. And C is wrong because the subject of *guarantees* is *that,* which in turn refers to the plural *attributes*.

**68.** (G) Although "whether or not" is a perfectly good English idiom, its use here is not idiomatic. The first *whether* in the sentence has set up the comparison: "whether this or whether that." G makes the needed correction. H and J are wrong because "whether if" is not idiomatic.

**69.** (B) *Although* introduces a long and complex dependent clause that ends with the period. Thus, the original is wrong because the dependent clause isn't attached to an independent clause. Only B makes the needed correction.

**70.** (J) The original is incorrect because the future tense "will be done" is inconsistent with the other verbs in the selection (such as *was* and *coined*). G and H fail to solve this problem because they use present tense rather than past tense verbs. J solves the problem by using the infinitive, which doesn't show time itself. So the infinitive does not conflict with the other verbs.

**71.** (A) The original is correct as written. *Who* is the correct pronoun since it is used to refer to people. And the past perfect is the right tense to show that the training occurred at a time prior to the time during which the government leaders discussed the "disposal problem." B is wrong because it uses *that* instead of *who* and because the present perfect *have been trained* does not correctly show the sequence of events. C is wrong because *being* is not a conjugated verb (and so *who* is a subject without a verb). And D is wrong because the present tense *are* distorts the temporal sequence of the events.

**72.** (G) The sentence suffers from faulty parallelism: *the purposes of invading and to remove*. The infinitive should be changed to the gerund. Only G makes a correction that achieves the required parallelism.

**73.** (C) The original is not idiomatic. The correct idiom is "more this than that." Only C supplies the correct idiom.

**74.** (G) The original suffers from a lack of parallelism: *to allow and assisted*. The second verb should also have the infinitive form: *to allow and assist*. As for H, although this structure would exhibit parallelism, the use of the gerunds rather than the infinitives is not idiomatic. Finally, J is wrong because it changes the intended meaning of the original.

**75.** (D) The original is not idiomatic. Only D creates an idiomatic sentence.

## Mathematics Usage

**1.** (C) First, solve for $x$:

$$x + 2 = 7$$
$$x = 5$$

Therefore:

$$5 + y = 11$$
$$y = 6$$

**2.** (J) $x + y + z + 120 = 360$
$$x + y + z = 240$$

Since $y + z = 150$:

$$x + 150 = 240$$
$$x = 90$$

**3.** (C) The product of $x$ and 5 is $5x$. And the sum of $3x$ and 3 is $3x + 3$. Since the first expression is equal to $\frac{1}{2}$ of the second expression, the entire statement can be written in "algebrese" as $5x = \frac{1}{2}(3x + 3)$, or $5x = \frac{(3x + 3)}{2}$.

**4.** (K) If $x$ is more than $-5$, then $x + 7$ must be more than 2. The only answer choice greater than 2 is K, 3.

**5.** (B) One way to solve this question is with a proportion:

$$\frac{3}{2} = \frac{36}{x}$$

$$3x = 72$$

$$x = 24$$

Or, you can assume some concrete values. For example, assume that the item usually costs $3. So two such items usually cost $6. And John can buy three on sale for $6, which is $2 apiece. If he buys 36 items at $2 apiece, he pays $72. For $72, at the regular price, he could have purchased $72 \div 3 = 24$ items.

**6.** (J) Since $PQ = PR$, angle $PRQ = 30°$, and
$$30 + 30 + x = 180$$
$$60 + x = 180$$
$$x = 120$$

**7.** (D) Here you have simultaneous equations. Look for a way to make a direct substitution of one quantity for another or for a way to compare two quantities directly. In this case, $px = 6$ and $qx = 7$. So $\frac{px}{qx} = \frac{6}{7}$, and $\frac{p}{q} = \frac{6}{7}$.

You can also solve the problem by assuming a value for $x$, say 1. On that assumption $p = 6$, $q = 7$, and $\frac{p}{q} = \frac{6}{7}$, which is choice D.

8. (K) You can arrive at the correct answer by reasoning that since $2^x = 16$, $x = 4$. Therefore, $4 = \frac{y}{2}$ and $y = 8$. Or, you can work backwards by substituting answers. If $y = 8$, then $x = 4$, and it is true that $2^4 = 16$.

9. (E) You can create the equation you need by "translating" the English into "algebrese":

   pay = \$500 plus 3% of sales

   $p = 500 + 0.03 \times s$

   Thus:

   $p = 500 + 0.03s$

   You can arrive at the same conclusion just by assuming some values for the variables. Assume, for example, that in a certain week, the sales representative had no sales. On that assumption, she would earn only the \$500 with no commissions. Subsitute 500 for $p$ and zero for $s$ into the equations in the answer choices. Only E makes a true statement.

10. (K) One way of attacking this problem would be to rewrite each answer choice in decimal form—but that's extremely cumbersome. Instead, you should reason that the negative exponent here signals a decimal fraction and the larger the absolute value of the exponent, the smaller the resulting number. Thus, since $-6$ has the smallest absolute value of all the powers of 10 shown, K will be the largest number.

11. (A) Use the formula for finding the area of a triangle:

   Area = $\frac{1}{2} \times$ altitude (or height) $\times$ base

   $2 = \frac{1}{2}\left(\frac{1}{x}\right)$(base)

   $4 = \left(\frac{1}{x}\right)$(base)

   $4x =$ base

   So the base of the triangle is equal to $4x$.

12. (G) Use the formula for finding an average:

   $\dfrac{4x + 3x}{7} =$ Average

   $\dfrac{7x}{7} =$ Average

   $x =$ Average

   Of course, you can also substitute numbers. Assume that $x = 10$. The average of seven numbers would be $[4(10) + 3(10)] \div 7 = \frac{70}{7} = 10$. When you substitute 10 for $x$ into the choices, only G yields the value 10.

13. (E) $x + 30 + 90 = 180$

   $x = 60$

   Since $x = y$, $y = 60$:

   $60 + 30 + z = 180$

   $z = 90$

14. (F) The least possible value for the expression $\frac{(x + y)}{z}$ will occur when $x$ and $y$ are the least and $z$ is greatest:

   $\dfrac{(6 + 3)}{10} = \dfrac{9}{10}$

15. (E) Just use the rules for manipulating exponents to do the indicated operations:

   $\dfrac{(-3x)^3}{-3x^3} = \dfrac{-27x^3}{-3x^3} = 9$

16. (K) If $x < 8$, then $x - 2 < 6$, so $x$ must be less than 8. Also, if $x > -4$, then $x - 2 > 6$ and so $|x - 2| < 6$. So $x$ must also be greater than $-4$.

17. (B) The base of the triangle is $3k - k = 2k$, and the altitude of the triangle is $4k - k = 3k$:

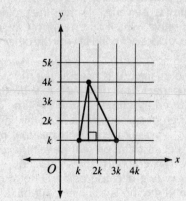

   $\frac{1}{2} \times$ altitude $\times$ base = area.

   So the area is:

   $\frac{1}{2}(2k)(3k) = 12$

   $3k^2 = 12$

   $k^2 = 4$

   $k = 2$

18. (K) Do the calculation:

   $\dfrac{18 \text{ wid.}}{5 \text{ sec.}} \times \dfrac{60 \text{ sec.}}{\text{min.}} \times \dfrac{60 \text{ min.}}{\text{hr.}} = \dfrac{12,960 \text{ wid.}}{\text{hr.}}$

**9.** (A) You can solve the problem by setting up an equation. Let $P$ be the original price of the car: John's price is equal to the original price less 12 percent of the original price

$$\$4,928 = P - 0.12P$$

$$\$4,928 = 0.88P$$

$$P = \$5600$$

Alternatively, you could test the answer choices. Start with C. If the original price was $5,490, then John's price would have been:

$$\$5,490 - (0.12 \times \$5,490) =$$

$$\$5,490 - \$658.80 = \$4,831.20$$

But John paid $4,928, so C must be wrong. Next, since $4,831.20 is less than $4,928, the original price must have been greater than $5,490. So next we test B:

$$\$5,520 - (0.12 \times \$5,520) =$$

$$\$5,520 - \$662.40 = \$4,857.60$$

Again a wrong choice. So the correct answer must be A, and you can prove that if you choose by doing the calculation.

**0.** (G) You can set up an equation. Let $h$ be the original height of the sapling:

$$\frac{9h}{10} + \frac{9}{10} = h$$

And solve for $h$:

$$\frac{h}{10} = \frac{9}{10}$$

$$h = 9$$

You can also test the choices.

**1.** (E) Since $n > m$, the net drain from the tank per minute will be $n - m$. So the time required to empty the tank is $\frac{g}{(n-m)}$. You can arrive at the same conclusion by substituting numbers.

**2.** (H) The easiest way to attack this problem is to test the test. Each of the numbers given in the choices will produce an integer except for the value given in H: $\frac{13(3)}{7} = \frac{39}{7}$, which is not an integer.

**23.** (D) Rewrite the equations:

$$\frac{(x + y)}{x} = 4$$

$$4x = x + y$$

$$3x = y$$

$$\frac{(y + z)}{z} = 5$$

$$y + z = 5z$$

$$4z = y$$

Since $3x$ and $4z$ are both equal to $y$,

$$3x = 4z$$

$$\frac{x}{z} = \frac{4}{3}$$

**24.** (H) Set up an equation, using $x$ for the original amount:

$$\frac{1}{2}(x) - \$60 = \frac{1}{5}(x)$$

$$\frac{1}{2}x - \frac{1}{5}x = \$60$$

$$\frac{3}{10}x = 60$$

$$x = 200$$

You can also test choices.

**25.** (D) If you know the method for calculating the number of permutations, you can solve this problem in 5 seconds:

$$3! = 3 \times 2 \times 1 = 6$$

If you don't know the formula, does that mean you can't answer the question? Absolutely not! Just use your common sense: count the possibilities:

Red, Gray, White

Red, White, Gray

Gray, Red, White

Gray, White, Red

White, Red, Gray

White, Gray, Red

**26.** (G) Just evaluate the expression by substituting 2 for $x$:

$$x^2 - 2x = (2)^2 - 2(2) = 4 - 4 = 0$$

**27.** (D) You can reason that a 10-pound bag will make five times as much coffee as a 2-pound bag. And $7 \times 5 = 35$. Or if need be, you can set up a direct proportion:

$$\frac{2}{10} = \frac{7}{x}$$

Cross-multiply:

$$2x = 70$$

Solve for $x$:

$$x = 35$$

**28.** (G) $10.00 buys $10.00 ÷ $1.00 = 10 roses and $10.00 ÷ $0.50 = 20 carnations. And $20 - 10 = 10$.

**29.** (C) You can solve the problem just by multiplying the numbers shown to find the volume of each box.

Box A: $2 \times 3 \times 4 = 24$

Box B: $2 \times 3 \times 3 = 18$

Box C: $3 \times 4 \times 5 = 60$

Box D: $5 \times 4 \times 2 = 40$

Box E: $4 \times 4 \times 2 = 32$

Or you can use a benchmark. For example, Box A, which is $2 \times 3 \times 4$, must be larger than Box B, which is $2 \times 3 \times 3$.

**30.** (G) If you know the distance formula, you can use it to find the distance from $a$ to $b$. But you can also use the Pythagorean Theorem:

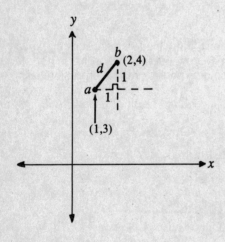

$$d^2 = (1)^2 + (1)^2$$

$$d^2 = 2$$

$$d = \sqrt{2} \quad \text{(Remember, distances are always positive.)}$$

**31.** (E) Do the indicated operations:

$$(x + y)^2 = (x - y)^2 + 4$$

$$x^2 + 2xy + y^2 = x^2 - 2xy + y^2 + 4$$

$$2xy = -2xy + 4$$

$$4xy = 4$$

$$xy = 1$$

**32.** (F) You can set up an equation:

$$\frac{2}{3}(x) = 5 + \frac{1}{4}(x)$$

Or you can just test the test. $\frac{2}{3}$ of 12 is 8; $\frac{1}{4}$ of 12 is 3; and 8 is 5 more than 3.

**33.** (A) An even number times an odd number yields an even number, and a positive number times a negative number yields a negative number. So the multiplication described in the question stem results in a number that is both negative and even. Or, you can just try numbers to test the choices.

**34.** (K) If you can't do the algebra, assume some values. Let $w$, $x$, $y$, and $z$ all be 1. On that assumption, $w(x + y + z) = 1(1 + 1 + 1) = 1(3) = 3$. Then substitute 1 for $w$, $x$, $y$, and $z$ into the answer choices. Every choice yields the value 1 except for K.

**35.** (D) The rectangle has an area of $9 \times 4 = 36$. And a square with an area of 36 has a side of:

$$s \times s = 36$$

$$s^2 = 36$$

$$s = \sqrt{36} = 6$$

**36.** (K) You can reason to a conclusion as follows. If the prize is $x$, originally each student would receive $\frac{x}{11}$. When another student is added, each student will receive only $\frac{x}{12}$. So each student will finally receive $\frac{\left(\frac{x}{12}\right)}{\left(\frac{x}{11}\right)} = \frac{11}{12}$ of what he would have originally received.

You can also solve the problem by assuming some values. For example, assume the prize is worth $132 (a convenient assumption, since $11 \times 12 = 121$). Originally a student would have received $12. After the addition of another student to the group, the prize is worth only $11. So the second prize is worth only $\frac{11}{12}$ of the first.

**37.** (B) This is a shaded area problem. The shaded area is the square minus $\frac{1}{4}$ of the circle. The square has a side of 2 and an area of $2 \times 2 = 4$. The circle has a radius of 2 and an area of $\pi r^2 = \pi(2^2) = 4\pi$. $\frac{1}{4}$ of the circle is simply $\pi$, so the shaded area is $4 - \pi$.

**38.** (J) The number of people having $x$ is $10 + 30 = 40$ and the number of people having $y$ is $10 + 20 = 30$. So the ratio is 4:3.

**9.** (A)  Just do the indicated multiplication (using the FOIL) method:

$(4x - 2y)(3x + 4y) =$

First: $(4x)(3x) = 12x^2$

Outer: $(4x)(4y) = 16xy$

Inner: $(-2y)(3x) = -6xy$

Last: $(-2y)(4y) = -8y^2$

So the $xy$ term is $16xy + (-6xy) = 10xy$. Thus, the coefficient of the $xy$ term is 10.

**10.** (J)  Multiply:

$(2 + 3i)(4 - i) = 8 - 2i + 12i - 3i^2 =$

$8 + 10i - 3i^2$

Since $i^2 = \sqrt{-1} \times \sqrt{-1} = -1$:

$8 + 10i - 3(-1) = 11 + 10i$

## Social Studies Reading

**1.** (B)  The main purpose of the passage is to review the findings of some research on animal behavior and to suggest that this may have implications for the study of depression in humans.

**2.** (J)  The author introduces the question in the second paragraph to anticipate a possible objection: Maybe the animal's inability to act was caused by the trauma of shock rather than the fact that it could not escape the shock.

**3.** (B)  The stimulation of the septal region inhibits behavior while "rats with septal lesions do not show learned helplessness." We infer that the septum somehow sends "messages" that tell the action centers not to act.

**4.** (F)  The critical difference must be the trauma — it is present in the shock experiments and not in the nonaversive parallels.

**5.** (A)  The author raises the question in paragraph 2 in order to anticipate a possible objection: The shock, not the unavoidability, caused inaction. The author then offers a refutation of this position by arguing that we get the same results using similar experiments with nonaversive stimuli.

**6.** (J)  The author closes with a disclaimer that the human cognitive makeup is more complex than that of laboratory animals and that for this reason, the findings regarding learned helplessness and induced neurosis may or may not be applicable to humans. He does not, however, explain what the differences are between the experimental subjects and the humans. A logical continuation would be to supply the reader with this elaboration.

**7.** (D)  Nowhere does the author mention programs to cure humans of helplessness.

**8.** (G)  A paradigm is a model or example.

**9.** (C)  The author uses a detached tone appropriate to this scientific passage.

**10.** (H)  The author states in line 28 that "the main function of this inhibition is compensatory, providing relief from anxiety or distress."

**11.** (B)  The conclusion of the argument is that there is little difference in the adjusted earnings of black and white women and the reason for this is the overpowering influence of *sexual* discrimination.

**12.** (J)  The author states that the actual ratio is not an accurate measure of discrimination *in employment* because it fails to take account of productivity factors.

**13.** (D)  The third paragraph gives us comparisons of ratios of earnings by black men to earnings by white men and of earnings by black women to earnings of white women. The only conclusion that can be drawn on this basis is that the differential between black and white women is less than the differential between black and white men.

**14.** (F)  Both of the hypotheses stated could contribute to the phenomenon being studied.

**15.** (C)  The passage's tone is clearly objective.

**16.** (F)  The author acknowledges the existence of racial discrimination, so elimination of sexual discrimination should result in the manifestation of increased racial discrimination against black women. The result would be a greater disparity between white and black female workers, with the white female workers enjoying the higher end of the ratio.

**17.** (B)  We must take our cue from the first paragraph, where the author refers to the efforts of "responsible employers." This indicates that the author is sympathetic to the situation of workers who are victims of discrimination.

**18.** (G)  *Pervasive* means "prevalent or spread throughout."

**19.** (A)  In the final paragraph, the author states that the education level differential between black women and white women is the result of racial discrimination.

**20.** (G)  A mean is the average number in a series.

**21.** (C)  The author's goal is to show that because of changing circumstances, the value of war has changed.

**22.** (F)  The second paragraph describes the attitude of pre-modernized society towards war: accepted, even noble, necessary.

**23.** (C)  The author's use of the term *civilized* is ironic.

**24.** (G)  This choice is mentioned as a feature of the military establishment in pre-modernized society — not as a reason for going to war.

**25.** (D)  The author's point is that because of social, economic, and technological changes, the values of war have changed.

26. (G) The tone of the passage is neutral — scientific and detached.

27. (D) We can conclude that even in the absence of nuclear weapons, war will still lack its traditional value, as argued by the author in the fourth paragraph.

28. (H) Fear of nuclear war is the only choice not mentioned in the author's second paragraph on imperialism.

29. (B) Only this choice is stated (in the second paragraph) as being the weaker alternative in this modernist age.

30. (F) Jean Piaget's main contribution to developmental psychology was his theory of the specific stages of cognitive development in children.

31. (B) When the Roman Catholic Church denied King Henry VIII of England the divorce he sought, the English Parliament created the Church of England, headed by the king rather than by the Pope.

32. (G) Under the Wagner Act, enacted in 1935, U.S. workers have the right to elect union representatives to bargain collectively with employers. None of the other choices is guaranteed by law.

33. (A) The Bill of Rights protects certain individual rights from infringement by the federal government only; the 14th Amendment extends the protection to include infringement by the various state governments.

34. (J) Between 1805 and 1807, Napoleon's armies won victories over Austria, Prussia, and Russia and extended the reforms of the French Revolution to the newly conquered territories. Of the European powers of the time, only Great Britain, defended by its powerful navy, was able to escape invasion.

35. (C) The working class consists of skilled and semi-skilled laborers and service workers. In the 1980s it represented approximately 34 percent of the U.S. population, the country's largest social class in terms of numbers.

36. (F) In *Miranda vs. Arizona* (1966), the Supreme Court held that arrests and convictions were unconstitutional under both federal and state law if the defendant was not first advised of his or her right to legal counsel and right to remain silent until that counsel arrived.

37. (D) Under the theory of competition, as long as demand remains constant, new suppliers will enter the market in search of profits, total supply of the product will increase, and the market price of the product will then fall as a result.

38. (F) Although it became clear in the late 1930s that Europe was on the brink of war, the U.S. government, supported by a very large share of the public, pursued a policy of isolationism from European affairs. Even when Germany's armies conquered Poland and France, President Franklin D. Roosevelt did not call for a declaration of war.

39. (A) The earliest period of prehistoric culture, called the Paleolithic Era or Old Stone Age, was characterized by a hunting-and-gathering method of food supply, stone tools, and the first evidence of religious beliefs.

40. (H) Most national economies today are to some extent "mixed," including both private free enterprise and government controls.

41. (A) The President's primary executive duty under the Constitution is to assure that the laws are faithfully executed.

42. (J) Under the "Great Compromise," proposed by Connecticut and later incorporated into the Constitution, states are represented in the House of Representatives in proportion to their population, but each state has the same number of Senators (two).

43. (C) The main point of the passage is that those who believe AFDC restrictions contribute to family dissolution are in error. It is not the restrictions on aid but the aid itself, according to the author, which contributes to low-income family dissolution. So the primary purpose of the passage is to analyze the cause of a phenomenon.

44. (F) The analysis in the text can be used to predict that an increase in the availability of aid would tend to increase pressures on the family unit. Reducing restrictions would actually tend to create more pressure for divorce. This would have the exact opposite effect predicted by those who call for welfare reforms such as eliminating restrictions.

45. (B) Although the author is primarily interested in low-income family stability, he never states that social or economic class is a factor in perpetuating a marriage.

46. (F) As previously stated, AFDC restrictions are not responsible for family instability.

47. (B) The scholarly treatment of the passage is best described as scientific and detached.

48. (F) Without overstating the strength of the author's case, this choice seems the closest to the actual text.

49. (D) It seems most likely, from the tone of the passage, that the selection is from a scholarly journal.

50. (F) In paragraph 3 the author states that the "major benefit generated by the creation of a family is the expansion of the set of consumption possibilities."

51. (B) The author states in the final sentence that "welfare-related instability occurs because public assistance lowers both the benefits of marriage and the costs of its disruption."

52. (J) Differences in all of these elements contribute to variations in marital stability among income classes.

1. (A) As long as the situation described continues, the face of the glacier will continue advancing.

2. (H) As soon as the situation described begins occurring, the glacier face will start to retreat.

3. (A) Since the upper portions of a glacier flow downhill more rapidly than the lower portions, a straight hole will, over time, start to bend diagonally, with the upper portion positioned farther down the mountain slope than the lower portion.

4. (J) Meltwater beneath the glacier plays an important role in lubricating the ice and allowing it to slide downhill. The more meltwater accumulates beneath the glacier, the more lubrication and the more rapidly the glacier will slide.

5. (C) According to the passage, if the face of a tidewater glacier were to lie in deep water, it would quickly break up. Consequently, when a glacier face retreats away from its moraine and allows deep seawater to rush into the gap, most likely the face will begin breaking up as the water surrounds it.

6. (G) When a tidewater glacier face retreats from its moraine and allows deep seawater into the gap, the face will continue breaking up for as long as the deep water surrounds it. Usually this means that the process will go on until the glacier face retreats back to shallow water. None of the other choices involve the effect of deep water on the glacier face.

7. (C) Calving takes place at the tidewater glacier face, where melting is occurring and the face is being battered by the sea. Both processes help break off the huge pieces of the glacier face that fall into the sea during calving.

8. (F) When a glacier leaves a narrow valley and enters a broad coastal plain, it will naturally tend to spread itself wider and thinner as it crosses the sloping ground. This process is certain to cause the surface of the glacier to stretch and crack.

9. (C) When the glacier blocks off the inlet from the sea, the new lake will have no outlet. Rain and meltwater will cause its level to rise and will turn its waters from salt to fresh. Located close to sea level, the new lake is unlikely to freeze just because the glacier is now separating it from the sea.

10. (H) According to the passage, the atmosphere of Earth three to four billion years ago consisted mainly of carbon dioxide and hydrogen, while oxygen was virtually nonexistent. This information causes G to be incorrect (*aerobic* means "having oxygen") as well as J. Although these organisms produced methane, nowhere in the passage does it suggest that the atmosphere was rich in it, making F incorrect.

11. (D) Choices A and B are wrong because the methane-producing organism is revealed in the last sentence as "distinctly different from . . . other bacteria," by no means "ordinary." Nothing in this passage supports C. Indeed, there is "no fossil record" to compare specimens with, only "some record . . . in its genes,"

and "evolutionary lines can be traced." But by definition, evolution is change. By elimination, D survives. However, it is also reasonable to assume that if this organism represents a "third evolutionary line . . . possibly older than the other two," then it did "co-exist with ordinary bacteria" in their early days (D).

12. (H) Choices F and J are ruled out because the first and third sentences, far from producing any key evidence for, only introduce the question of "a unique evolutionary line." G is patently incorrect because after the introduction, the entire passage is devoted to assembling evidence. By a process of elimination, then, this leaves only H and the question: Which part of the second paragraph would be considered "key evidence"? The only hard "fact" here that relates to all these bacteria is that they exist "only in niches swept clean of oxygen."

13. (D) While such "hope" would be a natural consequence of the suggestions made by the research team, it is nowhere asserted in this passage.

14. (G) Nowhere is there mention of any relationship between the number of such bacteria and their RNA constituents (J). H is exactly opposite what the passage states: these bacteria have "left no fossil record." Therefore no definitive statement such as F can be made about how these bacteria have changed or not changed "since their primeval origin." G is correct because the second paragraph says they are "found only in niches swept clean of oxygen," that is, in an anaerobic environment.

15. (D) Choices A, B, and C are not mentioned in the passage. The last paragraph states that the RNA is the immediate determinant of the characteristic function of an organism (D).

16. (H) Autotrophs are organisms that make their own food molecules from inorganic materials; the prefix *thermo-* refers to heat. Therefore, choice H is the only answer that correctly interprets these terms. The passage states that the organisms produce rather than use methane gas.

17. (C) Although there is no proof given in the passage that such a reaction might have existed, the only one that contains the probable compounds in a likely sequence is C. It shows carbon dioxide and hydrogen, two gases that were prevalent in the atmosphere, producing methane gas, water, and energy for the organism's metabolic needs. The other choices do not show the starting compounds that are stated in the passage.

18. (H) RNA is not identical to DNA, nor does it replicate by forming its mirror image. In fact, the most primitive organisms may not have DNA or a nucleus. Therefore, F and G are incorrect. Choice J is also incorrect; the term *conserve* in this sense means that parts of the RNA molecule stay intact during the replication process and implies that daughter cells will receive part of the original RNA molecule from a parent cell, thus carrying part of the ancient replicating system into the next generation.

19. (A) Half-life is the rate of decay of a radioactive element.

20. (F) The weathering process produces the particles that made the sediments necessary in the formation of sedimentary rocks.

21. (B) $W = qV$
    $V = 110$ volts $= 100 \dfrac{\text{joules}}{\text{coulomb}}$
    $q = 6$ coulombs
    $W = 660$ joules

22. (G) Transpiration is the evaporation of water from the leaf of a plant.

23. (D) (1) $Zn + \frac{1}{2}(O_2) = ZnO + 84,000$ cal

    (2) $HgO = Hg + \frac{1}{2}(O_2) - 21,700$ cal

    Adding (1) and (2) and dropping the term $\frac{1}{2}(O_2)$, which appears on both sides of the chemical equation, results in $Zn + HgO = ZnO + Hg + 62,300$ cal.

24. (H) Cells involved with synthesizing and secreting large quantities of protein hormone would be expected to have all of the machinery necessary to accomplish these jobs. Mitochondria supply energy for work, ribosomes are the sites for protein synthesis, and the golgi apparatus packages cell materials to be secreted.

25. (C)  $I^2R_1 = 90$ watts; $R_1 =$ resistance of lamp
    $IR_1 = 30$ volts
    $I = 3$ amps
    $120$ volts $= (R + R_1)I$
    Thus, $IR = 90$ volts
    $R = 30$

26. (F) The Heisenberg principle states quantitatively that, for any object, the product of the uncertainties in position (along a path) and velocity of the object must be unpredictable since it is not possible to measure both simultaneously.

27. (A) The concept of light as a particle cannot explain interference; only the wave concept can.

28. (J) The brightness of a star refers to its apparent magnitude. In actuality the star may be brighter or dimmer, in relation to other stars, than it appears to us on earth. The brightest stars have apparent magnitudes under 1.0 continuing into the negative numbers. The higher a positive number, the dimmer the star. Sirius appears brightest, although Canopus is actually much brighter, because of their relative distances from the Earth.

29. (A) The function of white cells is to remove unwanted organisms from the bloodstream and surrounding tissue. Of the choices given, only an infection indicates the presence of unwanted organisms. The white cell count in this case would go up.

30. (H) We may arrive at the units of Planck's constant by considering that $hv$ is equal to the energy of a photon. This gives it the units of joule-seconds.

31. (A) When the relatively stable elements are written out in order of their atomic numbers, there are properties that repeat in regular intervals, forming a periodic table of elements. Elements are arranged in rows and columns by increasing atomic number in such a way as to form families of elements.

32. (J) Taiga is a region dotted by countless lakes, ponds, and bogs. Both conifers and deciduous trees are present. Many large and small mammals are permanent residents, while many birds are present only in the summer.

33. (B) In an aqueous solution, the two products remain in solution in ionized form and the reaction is reversible. In A and D, precipitates are formed and the reactions proceed to completion. Reaction C proceeds to completion as $H_2$ gas is given off.

34. (J) 180 km/h must be converted to m/s to use in equation 2. 180 km/h $= 180,000$ m/h, and 180,000 m/h $\div 3600$ s/h $= 50$ m/s.

35. (C) Eq. 2:
    $$f_{(LF)} = f_{(S)}\left(\frac{v}{v - v_{(S)}}\right)$$
    $$f_{(LF)} = 288\left(\frac{346}{346 - 50}\right)$$
    $$f_{(LF)} \doteq 288\left(\frac{346}{296}\right)$$
    $$f_{(LF)} = 336.6 \text{ hertz}$$

36. (G) Eq. 3:
    $$f_{(LB)} = f_{(S)}\left(\frac{v}{v + v_{(S)}}\right)$$
    $$f_{(LB)} = 256\left(\frac{346}{346 + 50}\right)$$
    $$f_{(LB)} = 256\left(\frac{346}{396}\right)$$
    $$f_{(LB)} \doteq 223.7 \text{ hertz}$$

37. (B)

    $25°C - 15°C = 10°C$

    $10°C \times 0.6$ m/degree $= 6$ meters/second
    $346$ m/s $- 6$ m/s $= 340$ m/s at $15°C$

38. (H) According to equation 2, when calculating $f_{(LF)}$, $\frac{v - v_{(S)}}{v}$ will be a higher number at a cooler temperature than a warmer temperature, thus increasing $f_{(LF)}$ slightly. Conversely, when calculating $f_{(LB)}$, $\frac{v + v_{(S)}}{v}$ will be a lower number, thus decreasing $f_{(LB)}$ slightly.

39. (B) Because frequency and wavelength are inversely proportional, wavelength must shorten if frequency is increased.

40. (F) If equation 1 shows frequency $= \frac{\text{wavelength}}{\text{velocity}}$, then solving for wavelength: wavelength $= \frac{\text{velocity}}{\text{frequency}}$.

41. (B) If the source and the listener are stationary, then the frequency heard by the listener is the same. No calculations need to be done. The frequency of 512 is well within the range of human hearing, which ranges from approximately 20 to 20,000 hertz.

**2.** (F) To calculate the velocity of sound in air at 0°C:

25 degrees × 0.6 m/s degree = a reduction of 15 m/s

346 m/s − 15 m/s = 331 m/s

$$wavelength = \frac{velocity}{frequency}$$

$$wavelength = \frac{(331 \text{ m/s})}{512 \text{ hertz}}$$

wavelength = 0.6465 m

**3.** (D) This title is the most specific about the compounds discussed, the halogenated hydrocarbons; also it suggests that there are pros and cons to their use.

**4.** (F) Carbon is the only one not a halogen. All the others belong to this group in which all but one of their outer orbitals are filled with electrons.

**5.** (B) Carbons share electrons, that is, form covalent bonds and have a potential of four bonding sites per carbon atom. The halogens bond to the carbons at one of these sites. A is incorrect because halogen atoms are not electron donors. C is incorrect because carbon atoms bond covalently, not by forming ions. D is incorrect because carbon atoms and not hydrogen atoms form double bonds in hydrocarbons.

(G) By definition, carbon and hydrogen form hydrocarbons. With oxygen (F), these three elements form carbohydrates. Halogenated hydrocarbons would best describe H and J.

Although polymers are often hydrocarbons, not hydrocarbons are polymers (A). Some hydrocarbons such as methane, have only one carbon and hardly be called a long chain. Not all polymers contain chlorine, thereby making B and thus correct.

the double bond between the carbons is two chlorine atoms attach at the bonding the hydrogen atoms already bonded to the carbons do not break their bonds. Hence G shows the number of atoms.

All the other uses are mentioned or implied.

(J) PVCs are used in plastic pipes, tiles, records, and so forth. These uses are not among the choices. Highly chlorinated hydrocarbons such as DDT are insecticides (F); PTFE is used as a nonstick coating (G) and CFGs were used in aerosols (H).

(D) As stated in the passage, DDT was banned and the use of CFCs limited in the U.S. because of harm to the environment.

(J) The passage states that chlorofluorocarbons, or CFCs, remain suspect in causing damage to the Earth's ozone layer, which protects it from high amounts of ultraviolet radiation.